Another Universalism

NEW DIRECTIONS IN CRITICAL THEORY

NEW DIRECTIONS IN CRITICAL THEORY

Amy Allen, General Editor

New Directions in Critical Theory presents outstanding classic and contemporary texts in the tradition of critical social theory, broadly construed. The series aims to renew and advance the program of critical social theory, with a particular focus on theorizing contemporary struggles around gender, race, sexuality, class, and globalization and their complex interconnections.

Fascist Mythologies: The History and Politics of Unreason in Borges, Freud, and Schmitt, Federico Finchelstein

Crisis Under Critique: How People Assess, Transform, and Respond to Critical Situations, edited by Didier Fassin and Axel Honneth

Selected Writings on Media, Propaganda, and Political Communication, Siegfried Kracauer, edited by Jaeho Kang, Graeme Gilloch, and John Abromeit

Praxis and Revolution: A Theory of Social Transformation, Eva von Redecker

Recognition and Ambivalence, edited by Heikki Ikäheimo, Kristina Lepold, and Titus Stahl

Critique on the Couch: Why Critical Theory Needs Psychoanalysis, Amy Allen

Hermeneutics as Critique: Science, Politics, Race and Culture, Lorenzo C. Simpson

Capitalism on Edge: How Fighting Precarity Can Achieve Radical Change Without Crisis or Utopia, Albena Azmanova

Transitional Subjects: Critical Theory and Object Relations, edited by Amy Allen and Brian O'Connor

Fear of Breakdown: Politics and the Work of Psychoanalysis, Noëlle McAfee

The Experience of Injustice: A Theory of Recognition, Emmanuel Renault

Avicenna and the Aristotelian Left, Ernst Bloch

Naming Violence: A Critical Theory of Genocide, Torture, and Terrorism, Mathias Thaler

Queer Terror: Life, Death, and Desire in the Settler Colony, C. Heike Schotten

The Practice of Political Theory: Rorty and Continental Thought, Clayton Chin

For a complete list of books in the series, please see the Columbia University Press website.

Another Universalism

Seyla Benhabib and the Future of Critical Theory

Edited by Stefan Eich, Anna Jurkevics,
Nishin Nathwani, and Nica Siegel

Columbia University Press

New York

Columbia University Press
Publishers Since 1893
New York   Chichester, West Sussex
cup.columbia.edu

Publication of this book was made possible in part by funding from the Whitney and Betty MacMillan Center at Yale University, the Center for Contemporary Critical Thought at Columbia University (CCCCT), Columbia Law School, and the research center "Normative Orders" at Goethe University, Frankfurt.

Copyright © 2024 Columbia University Press
All rights reserved

Library of Congress Cataloging-in-Publication Data
Names: Eich, Stefan, 1983– editor. | Jurkevics, Anna, editor. | Nathwani, Nishin, editor. | Siegel, Nica, editor.
Title: Another universalism : Seyla Benhabib and the future of critical theory / edited by Stefan Eich, Anna Jurkevics, Nishin Nathwani, and Nica Siegel.
Description: New York : Columbia University Press, [2023] | Series: New directions in critical theory | Includes bibliographical references and index.
Identifiers: LCCN 2023021799 (print) | LCCN 2023021800 (ebook) | ISBN 9780231212786 (hardback) | ISBN 9780231212793 (trade paperback) | ISBN 9780231559560 (ebook)
Subjects: LCSH: Benhabib, Seyla. | Critical theory.
Classification: LCC HM480 .A47 2023 (print) | LCC HM480 (ebook) | DDC 301.01—dc23/eng/20230518
LC record available at https://lccn.loc.gov/2023021799
LC ebook record available at https://lccn.loc.gov/2023021800

Printed in the United States of America
Cover image: Seyla Benhabib, Columbia Law School website and courtesy of Bettina Strauss

In Memoriam

Drucilla Cornell (1950–2022)

Contents

Preface xi

Introduction: In Search of Another Universalism 1
Anna Jurkevics

PART I
Critique, Norm, and Utopia

1. Benhabib and Habermas on Discourse and Development 19
Thomas McCarthy

2. Normativity and Reality: Toward a Critical and Realistic Theory of Politics 36
Rainer Forst

3. Loss of World, Not Certainty: "Amor Mundi" and the Moral Psychology of Seyla Benhabib 51
Carmen Lea Dege

4. Nature as a Concrete Other: An Alternative Voice in Kant's Conception of Beauty and Dignity 67
Umur Basdas

5. "To Burst Open the Possibilities of the Present": Seyla Benhabib and Utopia 81
Bernard E. Harcourt

PART II
Thinking With and Against Arendt

6. "Thinking With and Against" as Feminist Political Theory 97
Patchen Markell

7. Arendt and Truth 108
Gaye İlhan Demiryol

8. Understanding Eichmann and Anwar: Reenactment and the Psychic Lives of Perpetrators 128
Sonali Chakravarti

PART III
Democratic Iterations and Cosmopolitanism

9. Democracy Without Shortcuts: An Institutional Approach to Democratic Legitimacy 151
Cristina Lafont

10. Another Republicanism: Dissent, Institutions, and Renewal   166
Christian Volk

11. Three Models of Communicative Cosmopolitanism   193
Peter J. Verovšek

12. At the Borders of the Self: Democratic Iterations as a Theory of Postnational Sovereignty   214
Paul Linden-Retek

PART IV

Jurisgenerativity

13. Back to the Future? Critical Theory and the Law   241
William E. Scheuerman

14. The Unfinished Revolution: The Right to Have Rights and Birthright Citizenship   254
Eduardo Mendieta

15. Genocide and Jurisgenesis   277
Max Pensky

16. Jurisgenerativity in the Age of Big Data   294
Matthew Longo

PART V
Deprovincializing Critical Theory

17. *Pachamama*'s Rights, Climate Crisis, and the Decolonial Cosmos   309
Angélica María Bernal

18. What Is the Other in Seyla Benhabib's *Another Cosmopolitanism*?   328
Drucilla Cornell

19. Border Deaths as Forced Disappearances: Frantz Fanon and the Outlines of a Critical Phenomenology   335
Ayten Gündoğdu

20. Gender Trouble: Manhood, Inclusion, and Justice in the Political Philosophy of Martin Luther King, Jr.   366
Shatema Threadcraft and Brandon M. Terry

PART VI
Philosophy and Friendship

21. Fragments of an Intellectual Autobiography   405
Seyla Benhabib

22. Swimming   417
Carolin Emcke

....

Contributors   427

Index   429

Preface

This volume emerged from a conference—"In Search of the Concrete Universal: A Conference in Honor of Seyla Benhabib"—originally scheduled to take place in New Haven in March 2020. After many twists and turns due to the global pandemic, we were ultimately able to hold the conference online in December 2020. While we missed out on serendipitous conversations over Turkish food, the new format allowed several hundred scholars from all over the world to gather remotely to celebrate the work and legacy of Seyla Benhabib, one of the foremost critical theorists in the third generation of the Frankfurt School. We are deeply grateful to the many helpers, often behind the scenes, who made this transition possible and organized not just one but two conferences. We would also like to thank the presenters, chairs, and commentators who participated in the conference but are not represented in the volume: Kenneth Baynes, Aysen Candas, Blake Emerson, Adom Getachew, Robert Gooding-Williams, Peter E. Gordon, Turkuler Isiksel, Rahel Jaeggi, Karuna Mantena, Judith Resnik, and Lorenzo Simpson. The conference and this volume were made possible through the generous support of Yale University's MacMillan Center, the Columbia Center for Contemporary Critical Thought (CCCCT), Columbia Law School, and the research center "Normative Orders" at Goethe University, Frankfurt.

What we found when we brought these essays together was a body of work that does not merely celebrate Benhabib but that comprises a rich debate about the future of the Frankfurt School. These essays thus engage with Benhabib's numerous contributions and interventions but also extend them in her spirit. Benhabib's students, interlocutors, and readers are at the same time continuing to build on her legacy in bringing questions of race, empire, and migration to the center of debates in contemporary critical theory. Above all, the pieces presented here reflect an abiding commitment to work through the intimate relationship between critique and universality within critical theory today. Just as debates in critical theory were transformed a generation ago by engagements with Jürgen Habermas, so this generation of debates is transformed by engagement with Benhabib.

For seeing the project through to publication, we would in particular like to thank Wendy Lochner, Lowell Frye, and the rest of the editorial team at Columbia University Press who took on the project and supported it throughout. We would also like to thank Amy Allen who welcomed the book to her series on "New Directions in Critical Theory." Finally, we thank Robert Demke for his excellent copyediting. A version of Ayten's Gündoğdu's chapter appeared as "Border Deaths as Forced Disappearances: Frantz Fanon and the Outlines of a Critical Phenomenology," *Puncta: Journal of Critical Phenomenology* 5, no. 3 (2022); Brandon M. Terry and Shatema Threadcraft's chapter appeared previously as "Gender Trouble: Manhood, Inclusion, Justice in the Political Philosophy of Martin Luther King Jr," in *To Shape a New World: Essays on the Political Philosophy of Martin Luther King, Jr.*, ed. Tommie Shelby and Brandon M. Terry (Harvard University Press, 2018). We are grateful to the respective editors for permission to use the material.

During the time it took us to complete this volume, a global pandemic upended all our routines and cost several million lives worldwide. Many of us lost loved ones during this time, not only related to the pandemic, and we grieve them here. But we also mourn two colleagues and friends who were directly involved with the conference and this volume. While we were compiling the book, Richard Bernstein passed away in July 2022. As we put the finishing touches on the manuscript, Drucilla Cornell—whose chapter is included in this volume—passed away in December 2022. Both were cherished colleagues, interlocutors, mentors, and friends to many contributors of this volume. We dedicate this volume to the memory of Drucilla Cornell.

Another Universalism

Introduction

In Search of Another Universalism

ANNA JURKEVICS

While this volume emerged from a conference in honor of Seyla Benhabib, these essays amount to much more than an assessment of Benhabib's work, offering instead a brimming debate over the past and future of Frankfurt School critical theory. The diverse themes and problems investigated in these essays gather around a question that critical theorists today must answer: In our age of democratic backsliding, climate crisis, and global instability, an age in which the racist and violent legacies of empire have come home to roost, is it still possible to formulate universal norms to guide emancipatory political action? This search for the universal, despite the fragmentation and contradictions of modern society, has ever been at the heart of the Frankfurt School critical theory project.

For Benhabib, any universalism today must emerge from the concrete struggles of individuals navigating the fractured lifeworlds of our global society. Embracing that idea, the essays in this volume cover a broad terrain of debates that are at the forefront of critical theory today: the relationship between democracy and cosmopolitanism, the role of law in emancipatory struggles, the task of deprovincializing the European approach to critical theory, man's domination of nature, and the ever-elusive relationship between Hannah Arendt and the Frankfurt School. It is a testament to the range of Benhabib's oeuvre that all of these themes should emerge from engagements with her work.

SEYLA BENHABIB'S SEARCH FOR THE CONCRETE UNIVERSAL

While the range of themes presented in this volume is broad, there is an underlying question that emerges in every essay, and it is a question at the heart of Benhabib's approach to critical theory: How can we mediate universal norms of human freedom, equality, and dignity with the particular contexts in which those norms are negotiated and manifested, especially contexts of exclusion, difference, and adversity? Or put it this way: Within a world of difference, disagreement, and exclusion, is universality within the realm of philosophical possibility? Each piece presented in this volume reflects the abiding commitment to the intimate relationship between critique and universality, and each is engaged in a concerted effort to search for what Benhabib, following Hegel, identifies as the *concrete universal*: the universal norm that takes the form of a concrete world, or put otherwise, the universal norms that emerge from the concrete struggles within and across diverse lifeworlds. This search for *another* universalism—one that does not fall prey to the problems of abstraction, Eurocentrism, and domination; one that takes up the perspective of society's excluded others—is the critical task that unifies the contributions of this volume.

In "Fragments of an Intellectual Biography," Benhabib paints a vivid picture of her career in impressions, moments, and philosophical commitments. She begins with her early commitment to Hegel, in whose philosophy she found the guiding principle that still informs her work today: "Be a person and respect others as persons" (*Philosophy of Right*, §36). Hegel, who "was really the first philosopher to see modernity as a normative dilemma," understood that norms of freedom and justice can only be universal if they attain actuality through concrete, intersubjective struggles in what we now call the "lifeworld." What is unique about Benhabib's approach to Hegel is that instead of looking to dominant Western institutions to find examples of the concrete universal, as Hegel himself did when he held up the achievements of the Prussian state and as others do today with the achievements of still-exclusionary Western democracies, she has sought out voices and actions that challenge these institutions, make demands from positions of exclusion, and reveal false universals. Here I am speaking of the struggles of those fighting for what Benhabib calls "dignity in adversity": migrants and refugees, women and LGBTQ2+ individuals in sexist-patriarchal societies, and, as she has increasingly acknowledged lately, those fighting for international equality in postcolonial states.

To make space for the voices of society's "others," Benhabib has fiercely guarded her theory of rational agency against what Jean-François Lyotard called "the death of the subject." The complicated quest for modern personhood—whether moral, political, or legal—brings us back to Hegel's postulate. How can we "be a person" in differentiated, fractured, and exclusionary modern societies? How can we formulate a theory of agency and rationality without suppressing those nonrational parts of us that also make us full and human? In Benhabib's own words, "how do we reconstruct a conception of agency capable of principled action, a subjectivity that is deep in dreams as well as emotions, an autonomy that is situated and embedded?" With this question, and the capacious notion of self that it implies, I am reminded of one of Benhabib's favored lines from Walt Whitman's "Song of Myself": "Do I contradict myself? Very well then I contradict myself, (I am large, I contain multitudes.).".

As Benhabib describes in her contribution to this volume, Hannah Arendt provided her a way forward. She writes, "Arendt's doctrine of judgment provided me with the key to the 'concrete universal.' This term does not signify an identity of the universal and the particular; quite to the contrary, it refers to a process of judging, acting, dialoging and negotiating that is always also full of tension. It is an iterative process through which those who have never been given a voice or those whose voice has never been heard could now speak in the name of the universal itself." The agents that emerge from this iterative process come into clear view in Benhabib's feminist opus *Situating the Self* (1992), where she presents a theory of the self that is negotiating its needs and principles in the intersubjective struggles of the lifeworld. It is in this work, as well as her first book, *Critique, Norm, and Utopia* (1986), that Benhabib engages most thoroughly with her mentor and teacher, Jürgen Habermas. For Kantians like Habermas and Rawls, we universalize our maxims in reference to an abstract, generalized other that we construct using our reason. However, because the "generalized other" lacks a contextualized perspective and concrete needs, Benhabib argues that it is an incomplete basis for universalizability. Only through negotiation and discourse with the "concrete other" can truly universal principles emerge from ethical encounters. Benhabib's early interventions in Frankfurt School critical theory thus challenged the excessive rationalism of Habermas's critical theory, opening his communicative ethics to situated perspectives. Accordingly, Benhabib argues that voices that often go unheard in the public sphere—women, migrants, minorities—must be brought into the fold *for the sake of* universality and generality.

In the last two decades, Benhabib and other notable critical theorists including Habermas himself have shifted focus to the international realm. Beginning with *The Rights of Others* (2004), Benhabib has been at work reviving and elaborating Arendt's notion of "the right to have rights" to respond to ongoing crises of statelessness. With that work and others—*Another Cosmopolitanism* (2006) and *Dignity in Adversity* (2011)—Benhabib has established herself as a leading defender of human rights and a democratic approach to cosmopolitanism. Once again, the concrete actualization of universal principles in diverse contexts is the hallmark of Benhabib's approach. With her theories of "democratic iteration" and "jurisgenerativity," which figure so prominently in selections from this volume, Benhabib has charted a theoretical path to manifest universal norms from the ground up, through the agency of the world's others. Her approach transcends the nation-state while guarding democratic sovereignty, and seeks the contours of global justice from the voices of the marginalized, the exiled, the stateless.[1]

Ultimately, we—Benhabib's students, colleagues, friends, and readers—are indebted to her unwavering guidance in what it means to theorize politically in dark times. The essays in this volume attest to that and are examples of the work that can be done when we center the search for the concrete universal in the task of critical theory. Benhabib has shown us that, through the complex mediation of otherness and difference in our societies, it is possible to reconcile the seemingly irreconcilable: agency and contingency, cosmopolitanism and democratic sovereignty, and the universal and particular. Her own words that close her "Fragments of an Intellectual Biography" are the most apt: "The task of philosophy remains what it was since Socrates: to reveal that reason and the search for justice and freedom are intrinsically linked. The task of political thinking which we exercise as citizens, residents and others is judging how to mediate principle and action."

CRITIQUE, NORM, AND UTOPIA

Benhabib's first book, *Critique, Norm, and Utopia: A Study of the Foundations of Critical Theory* (1986), remains a crucial touchstone for debates in critical theory today. In it, Benhabib joined Habermas's attempt to overcome the impasses of instrumental rationality and recover the project of critique. She defended his theory of communicative reason, but inflected it with insights from Hannah Arendt, extending his framework in the direction of situated reasoning. Against Habermas's early reliance on consensus, Benhabib drew on Arendt to emphasize action's contingency and radical indeterminacy, pushing the theory of communicative action to accommodate a greater degree of diversity. The essays in part 1 of this volume, titled "Critique, Norm, and Utopia," all push the various boundaries that Benhabib sought to expand in her early interventions in critical theory by expanding on her concept of the "concrete other," pressing her mediation of contingency and rationality, and reconsidering the relationship between empirics and normativity. The essays here go to the heart of the foundational and methodological questions that have driven Frankfurt School critical theory since its genesis: Is universality viable in our fractured modern world? Who (or what) is the subject? How ought we respond to crises of meaninglessness in a secular age? And finally, what is the relationship between philosophy and science?

In "Benhabib and Habermas on Discourse and Development," Thomas McCarthy takes a closer look at Benhabib's intellectual relationship with Habermas and draws out the implications of her account of the contingency of reason. Beginning with *Critique, Norm, and Utopia*, Benhabib has pushed Habermasian communicative ethics toward greater contextualization, taking a detranscendentalized approach to the pragmatic presuppositions of discourse in order to make more room for excluded voices. She has also avoided relying on developmental historical reconstructions to establish the binding power of universal norms, and has insisted instead on the contingency of the rationalization and learning processes that have culminated in global modernity. McCarthy probes Benhabib's commitment to "concrete universals" and asks whether her move toward contextualization and concretization of norms erodes the status of those universal principles, e.g., human dignity, reciprocity, and equality, she holds dear. Can a contextualist, Benhabibian communicative ethics withstand the challenge of relativism? Will the search for another universalism necessarily undo the central threads of the Enlightenment project?

In "Normativity and Reality: Toward a Critical and Realistic Theory of Politics," Rainer Forst addresses the need for political science to reestablish a mediated relationship between empirical and normative scholarship, between the concrete and the universal, as was outlined in the original program of Frankfurt School critical theory. Forst's chapter produces a stark, realist appraisal of the power relations that underlie politics, and shows how complex webs of justification are entangled in all claims to power. Forst writes, "Politics is a power struggle—as a struggle for justification: a struggle for the dominance of some justifications, and a struggle against them becoming dominant." In an age of rapidly shifting claims to power in fragile democracies, the task of critical theory, and political science more generally, Forst argues, must be to understand how justifications deliver and reproduce power, and then to critically reappraise the moral validity of those justifications. For him, the tools for critical appraisal of justifications are to be found in the structure of justification itself, which presumes norms of equality, reciprocity, and dignity, among others.

In "Loss of World, Not Certainty: *Amor Mundi* and the Moral Psychology of Seyla Benhabib," Carmen Lea Dege retrieves the lessons that *Situating the Self*

(1992) brings to bear on renewed debates about fragmentation and uncertainty in modern liberal societies. Habermas's recent publication of *This Too a Philosophy of History* (2019) attests to the persistent specter of meaninglessness in modernity, raising once again the question of what role religion should (or must) play in providing moral-psychological support for citizens of liberal democracies. Dege shows that Benhabib formulated a sophisticated moral psychology in *Situating the Self* that demotes the need for certainty (and with it the return to religion) by rooting the modern self in *amor mundi*, or love of the world. In drawing attention to figures whose claim to home is most unstable—exiles, refugees and the stateless, excluded groups and women—Benhabib's "world-loving self" takes the position of a social critic who attaches her agency to projects that tend to, sustain, and transform the world that we hold in common, despite and because of the contingencies of the modern world. Importantly, as Benhabib also attests to in her "Fragments of an Intellectual Biography," Dege explores Benhabib's commitment to subjective agency in the face of postmodern critiques that have proclaimed the "death of the subject." Benhabib's subject, call her the social critic or the world-loving self, is a self "capable of principled action, a [self] that is deep in dreams as well as emotions, [with] an autonomy that is situated and embedded." Ultimately, Dege shows that Benhabib's critical dialogue with Habermas, which began in *Critique, Norm, and Utopia* and intensified in *Situating the Self*, continues to be of central importance to debates in critical theory today.

In "Nature as Concrete Other: An Alternative Voice in Kant's Conception of Beauty and Dignity," Umur Basdas pushes the boundaries of Frankfurt School critical theory into the future. How universal are universal norms if they exclude nonhumans? Is it possible to expand the concept of the "concrete other" to include nonhumans? In his forward-looking essay, Basdas argues that in the context of today's climate crisis, critical theory must return to debates over the domination of nature that animated early Frankfurt School works such as Adorno and Horkheimer's *Dialectic of Enlightenment* (1944). Basdas turns to Kant's aesthetics and his treatment of nature to draw out a line of reasoning that would allow us to assign dignity to nature and approach nonhumans as concrete others. Only by responding to the challenge of nature as a concrete other can we truly test the limits of the universal and the boundaries of agency.

In the final contribution to this section, "To Burst Open the Possibilities of the Present: Seyla Benhabib and Utopia," Bernard E. Harcourt explores Benhabib's career-long effort to revive the utopian impulse in contemporary critical theory. Habermas and other members of the second and third generations of Frankfurt School critical theory deflated the critical utopianism that had once centered on the "universal class," i.e., Marx's proletariat, and had later found a home in Adorno and Horkheimer's turn to the aesthetic reconciliation. As Harcourt points out, the works of Marcuse, Habermas, Honneth, and others eschew all reference to utopia. It was Benhabib who, in *Critique, Norm, and Utopia*, returned utopia to its rightful place alongside the other constitutive features of critical theory: crisis, critique, norm, and praxis. Where did Benhabib rediscover the utopian impulse and the promise of a better world? In concrete social movements and solidarities that have, for her, manifested their calls for freedom, equality, and dignity as concrete universals in particular social contexts. In a vivid phrase that Harcourt cannily brings forth from *Critique, Norm, and Utopia*, Benhabib writes, "Such utopia is no longer utopian, for it is not a mere beyond. It is the negation of the existent in the name of a future that bursts open the possibilities of the present."[2] Benhabib, a self-described optimist, is constitutionally incapable of abandoning hope. Whether it be in the cosmopolitan politics of human rights, in the communicative acts that reveal to us the equality and dignity of the strangers with whom we constitute modern societies, or in the promise of new social struggles for freedom, Benhabib has never been at a loss in locating the wells of human agency and desire for freedom that stand ever ready to "burst open the possibilities of the present."

THINKING WITH AND AGAINST HANNAH ARENDT

One of Benhabib's central and lasting contributions has been her introduction of the major contours of Hannah Arendt's thought into the canon of Frankfurt School critical theory. Hannah Arendt herself was not a critical theorist. She was avowedly anti-Marxist and looked down on attempts to incorporate Freudian psychology into social theory. Nevertheless, Arendt's insights into political action, worldliness, and judgment provide valuable tools for critique today. It is to Benhabib that we owe the synthesis of these two styles of theory. The essays in part 2 continue in this spirit and attest to the breadth of debates that can be addressed when we theorize at the intersection of Arendtian and critical theory. Themes addressed in this section include feminism and methodology, the nature of evil, and the role of truth in politics.

Patchen Markell's "Thinking With and Against as Feminist Theory" is a contribution at once personal and methodological. Recalling his experience with Benhabib's unique approach to teaching the canon of political theory, Markell argues that our attitude to canonical works should be one neither of uncritical reverence, nor of facile debunking. Markell untangles Benhabib's method of "thinking with and against" Arendt, which draws on Arendt's practice of reading the tradition diagnostically, and which insists that we take texts seriously in their contradictory entirety. Benhabib's approach, which emerged from her feminist approach to Arendt—a nonfeminist thinker—directs us to understand how contradictions in canonical texts are not simply mistakes but remain with us today and are borne out in the crises of modern politics. Markell urges us to continue this task, which he ties back to both Arendt and Benhabib, of reconsidering the Western political tradition as a contradictory and yet unavoidable legacy.

In "Arendt and Truth," Gaye Demiryol offers an essay that is also an exhortation to citizens living in the age of "post-truth" politics: truth cannot save us, but without it there is no possibility of democracy and common world-building, and therefore we must safeguard it. Demiryol reads Arendt's "Truth and Politics" (1967) and "Lying in Politics" (1971) and argues that truth has a world-constitutive quality, and that any attack on truth as such is also an attack on our common reality. The problem with liars such as Donald Trump is not, therefore, the immorality of any single lie, but the way that lying as a mode of politics makes it impossible for citizens to invest themselves in the fabric of a common reality and engage in shared projects. Demiryol convinces us that any critique of ideology today must also contend with the foundational question of truth.

It is impossible to debate Hannah Arendt's legacy without considering the perennial controversy that has endured since the publication of *Eichmann in Jerusalem: A Report on the Banality of Evil* (1963). Benhabib has been steadfast in her defense of Arendt's "banality of evil" thesis while admitting the shortcomings of the work, including Arendt's narrow view of Eichmann's character.[3] Sonali Chakravarti's "Understanding Eichmann and Anwar: Reenactment and the Psychic Lives of Perpetrators" revisits the idea of the banality of evil and finds that, with some adjustments and updates, it is still a fruitful framework for understanding the nature of modern evil. Chakravarti poses an interesting test for Arendt's banality thesis: Can it help us understand other modern perpetrators of mass killing? And can an aesthetic account of a mass killer help us understand what perplexed Arendt about Eichmann? To answer these questions, Chakravarti turns to the documentary *The Act of Killing* (2012, dir. Joshua Oppenheimer), which chronicles Anwar Congo, a perpetrator who participated in the 1965–66 mass killings of communists in Indonesia, as he grapples with his past. Controversially, Oppenheimer helps Anwar reenact his own killings in order to gain new perspective on his role as a perpetrator. The result, Chakravarti finds, is a bold investigation that, through its use of mimesis, gives the audience a rare view of a perpetrator's self-understanding and desire for fame and power. While starkly different from Arendt's equally controversial *Eichmann in Jerusalem*,

Chakravarti sees *The Act of Killing* as a complementary project that draws on the aesthetic to bring us closer to understanding modern evil.

DEMOCRATIC ITERATIONS AND COSMOPOLITANISM

Benhabib's volume *Democracy and Difference* (1996) established her as a leading figure in democratic theory, both within and beyond critical theory.[4] Since that time, Benhabib has offered major theoretical innovations such as the concept of "democratic iterations," which refers to "complex processes of public argument, deliberation and exchange through which universalist rights claims are contested and contextualized, invoked and revoked, posited and positioned throughout legal and political institutions as well as in the associations of civil society."[5] Her approach to democratic theory champions diversity and inclusion, and lately, she has focused on the compatibility of democratic sovereignty and cosmopolitan norms. The essays in part 3 build on Benhabib's democratic innovations and consider the future of self-rule in the global era.

For example, Cristina Lafont's "Democracy Without Shortcuts: An Institutional Approach to Democratic Legitimacy" proposes a cosmopolitan democratic theory in which legitimacy is determined not only by majoritarian procedures, but also by the existence of institutional opportunities to contest laws and policies that affect the fundamental rights of all citizens. Lafont explains how this approach is commensurate with Benhabib's notion of "democratic iteration" because institutional opportunities for contest often emerge from the availability of international human rights norms that can be negotiated and implemented in domestic democratic contexts. The institutional approach justifies the creation of additional venues—international courts, ballot initiatives, and the like—for citizens to contest, contextualize, and negotiate universal norms.

Christian Volk's chapter illustrates the type of democratic theory that can emerge through encounters with Arendt and democratic critical theory. "Another Republicanism: Dissent, Institutions, and Renewal" argues that Arendt's theories of freedom, power, law, and institutions can provide the basis for a new theory of *republicanism as dissent*. Republicanism as dissent thinks through the contours of a democratic political order that can accommodate disagreement and dissent. Volk argues that the stability of such an order is not imperiled by dissent, but rather, following Arendt, is strengthened by the diverse forms of political participation that are made possible when dissent and disagreement are institutionalized.

To theorize democracy with Benhabib is to theorize *cosmopolitan* democracy. Benhabib's conception of democracy is embedded in the logics of globalization and diversity, where the boundaries of the people are always contentious and universality must emerge through diverse encounters. Indeed, with the publication of *The Rights of Others* and *Another Cosmopolitanism*, Benhabib established herself as one of the leading cosmopolitan voices in the field of political theory. Her approach to cosmopolitanism is not, like many others, preoccupied with global governance, but instead emerges from her commitment to the figures of the migrant and the refugee. As Carolin Emcke expresses in her contribution to this volume, "Benhabib's empathy with the suffering of refugees is like a watermark shining through every text." The commitment to equal moral personhood that animates Benhabib's work also underlies her cosmopolitanism. For her, the fate of global modernity is entangled in society's marginal figures and "eternal half-others."[6] Benhabibian cosmopolitanism, as the essays in this section attest to, emerges from below and responds to the experience of the mobile, the excluded, and the other.

Peter Verovšek's "Three Models of Communicative Cosmopolitanism" presents an overview of the three central theorists of what he calls "communicative cosmopolitanism." Arendt, Habermas, and Benhabib alike advocate for a transition away from the nation-state that is based on communicative freedom and discourse in an increasingly interconnected world. Verovšek argues that Benhabib's version of communicative cosmopolitanism is the strongest of the three because it is based on her notion of "democratic iteration," the process through which universal human rights are negotiated, contextualized, and implemented democratically in domestic contexts. Benhabib's suggestion for the bottom-up, democratic negotiation and contextualization of cosmopolitan norms effectively mediates Arendt's localism and Habermas's more institutional, but insufficiently contextualized, postnational constellation.

In "At the Borders of the Self: Democratic Iterations as a Theory of Postnational Sovereignty," Paul Linden-Retek uses Benhabib's notion of "democratic iterations" to lay the philosophical foundations for a theory of postnational sovereignty. Linden-Retek argues that theories of postnational sovereignty to this point have failed to shed the residue of mastery, closure, and nationalism that threaten to retrench insidious forms of sovereign domination beyond the nation-state. Linden-Retek suggests that we turn from the typical foundations of reason and will (or norm and decision) to the faculty of judgment in order to harness the power of those societal others who must judge and iterate universal norms from the view "just outside the walls of the city." It is from this position, the position of the refugee, the stateless, and the dominated, that democratic iterations offer their emancipatory potential to open diverse societies in the global age.

JURISGENERATIVITY

What role ought law to play in contemporary critical theories of democracy? Given the Marxist roots of Frankfurt School critical theory, this question has been thorny and controversial. Is law a source of emancipation or simply another oppressive institution of society's superstructure? Furthermore, even if we believe that law has an important role to play in democracies, can it also be a source of societal transformation, or should that be left to social movements? Benhabib's approach to these questions focuses on mediation: law itself is not a source of emancipation, but it can be drawn on by agents who struggle to bring new meaning and context to those laws. To think through the democratic mediation and instantiation of universal human rights norms, Benhabib has drawn on the legal scholar Robert Cover to craft a theory of *jurisgenerativity*, which describes the processes through which self-governing peoples contextualize, interpret, and vernacularize universal legal norms. The essays in this section inspect the thorny issue of law in critical theory in conversation with Benhabib and with special attention to the possibility of jurisgenesis.

In his contribution, "Back to the Future? Critical Theory and the Law," William E. Scheuerman brings us back to Benhabib's early work in *Critique, Norm, and Utopia* in order to untangle long-standing debates in Frankfurt School critical theory over the role that law should play in emancipatory struggles. This question is more urgent now than ever given the rise of authoritarian populism around the globe, which has produced attacks on the rule of law, constitutionalism, and the separation of powers. By retrieving Benhabib's revisionist Hegelian approach from *Critique, Norm, and Utopia*, Scheuerman shows the advantages of her position, which situates the law and connects it to the social struggles of the lifeworld without giving up on the emancipatory potential of the rule of law. Against doctrinaire Marxists and law-wary left-Hegelians, Scheuerman argues that critical theory must renew its commitment, best found in the works of Benhabib and Habermas, to theorize the productive tension between Kantian legalism and Hegelian ethical life.

One touchstone of Benhabib's theorizing of jurisgenesis can be found in Hannah Arendt's statement that, given the spectacular failures of sovereign states to guarantee the rights of "others," we must articulate a fundamental right that expresses the human need to belong and to be regarded as a person worthy of rights. Arendt captured this need with the idea of *a right to have rights*. These issues of belonging and rights, to which Benhabib has contributed significantly, figure prominently in Eduardo Mendieta's "The Unfinished Revolution: The Right to Have Rights and Birthright Citizenship." In this essay, Mendieta builds an argument for birthright citizenship by tracing the theme of terrestriality, earthliness, and worldliness in the philosophies of Immanuel Kant, Hannah Arendt, and Seyla Benhabib. Mendieta argues that these threads culminate in a theory of "the right to have rights" that can be interpreted as a right to have a place in the world, and thus a right to birthright citizenship. Mendieta's essay thus reflects the recent turn in philosophy and political theory to theorize the role of place and resources in human rights and human flourishing.

The great interest that both Arendt and Benhabib have in the urgency and necessity of a right to have rights is driven, in part, by concerns about genocide. But what, exactly, is genocide? This debate has only gathered momentum since Arendt's time. Max Pensky's contribution to this volume, "Genocide and Jurisgenesis," dives into the philosophical perplexities underlying historical attempts to define a crime based on group identity. Drawing on Benhabib's comparison of Arendt and Raphael Lemkin, one of the innovators of the 1948 Genocide Convention, Pensky uses new evidence about Lemkin to propose a new way of thinking about social groups. Pensky contends with Arendt's and Benhabib's respective suspicions of Lemkin's reliance on "Herderian" social ontology, which essentializes and depoliticizes group boundaries. Using a method of tracing the jurisgenesis of genocide law, Pensky rehabilitates Lemkin and shows that his real concern was not to protect "inherently valuable" group identities, but to articulate a category of crimes that are directed at the distinctive *vulnerability* of certain social groups. In this analysis, Lemkin emerges as a "'communitarian cosmopolitan,' whose ambition was to criminalize state-sponsored attacks on social groups that, for any number of reasons, were designated as group targets of exterminating state violence." Ultimately, the definition of genocide, Pensky and Benhabib both well know, will transform according to the jurisgenerative (or possibly even jurispathic) politics of international law. This type of deliberative normative reconstruction of international norms is sure to remain at the forefront of critical theory in the future.

In the final essay of this section, we move into the murky, increasingly alarming terrain of "big data." Matthew Longo's "Jurisgenerativity in the Age of Big Data" argues that the state's collection and use of big data are a classic example of what Foucault calls "disciplinarity," and moreover, it is a direct threat to the democratic negotiation and elaboration of jurisgenerative legal norms. Data surveillance stunts social movements and democratic actors from articulating rights and contesting or transforming legal interpretations. Longo argues, "the state use of data analytics has increasingly sacrificed the *rights* logic of innocent until proven guilty for the *data* logic of risky until proven safe, a trade-off that makes citizens increasingly unable or unwilling to participate in the public sphere." Using Benhabib's framework alongside a classic approach to Frankfurt-style critical theory, Longo articulates why developments in data surveillance must be addressed by those concerned with the future of democracy and human rights. Longo's contribution is an excellent example of how the fundamental tools of critical theory, as refined by Benhabib, come to our aid as we theorize the ever-changing complexities of the global age.

DEPROVINCIALIZING CRITICAL THEORY

The first and second generations of the Frankfurt School (Adorno, Horkheimer, Habermas, and so on) held their gaze fast on Europe, on its disasters and potential. Subsequent generations, including Benhabib herself, have pushed the boundaries of critique by including feminist, migrant, and other previously marginalized perspectives. This work of pushing the boundaries of critique and questioning the developmentalist and parochially European assumptions of critical theory is ongoing. The "deprovincialization" of critical theory is absolutely necessary to the project of critique if it is to grasp the contours and contradictions of global politics as they have evolved today.[7] The search for another universalism, then, must decenter hegemonic narratives that limit the project of critique from within.

The essays in this section were written by colleagues and students of Benhabib who work in the spirit of theorizing the perspectives of those concrete others who have had to establish dignity in conditions of incredible adversity. The themes that emerge are ones that will occupy the future of critical theory for years to come: postcoloniality, race and politics, the indigenization of cosmopolitanism, and the decentering of the West as the arbiter of universal norms.

In "*Pachamama*'s Rights, Climate Crisis, and the Decolonial Cosmos," Angélica María Bernal brings all of these questions together by focusing on indigenous struggles for the Rights of Nature in Latin America. She asks whether Benhabib's cosmopolitanism, which draws on European sources for inspiration, can provide a framework for engaging with decolonial movements. Bernal finds that it is possible to apply the notion of "democratic iterations" to struggles against neocolonial extractivism on traditionally indigenous lands. In these contexts, democratic iterations give traction to decolonial projects of indigenous resistance and can foster epistemological and legal shifts that help dominated peoples fight for the rights of nature, or *Pachamama*, as well as their own self-determination over and against the claims of the sovereign nation-state.

While we were preparing this volume for publication, Drucilla Cornell passed away in December 2022. We are honored to be able to include her piece "What Is the Other in Seyla Benhabib's *Another Cosmopolitanism*," which grapples with Benhabib's approach to cosmopolitanism, pushing it further toward a project Cornell calls "transnational decolonization." Cornell finds great potential in Benhabib's insistence that any viable cosmopolitanism must mediate moral universalism with ethical particularism, that is, with the concrete and particular circumstances of emancipatory struggle in all societies, especially formerly colonized ones. Cornell sees room in Benhabib's approach to give greater priority of place to non-European norms, e.g. uBuntu norms in South Africa, as examples of cosmopolitan (and yet anticolonial) concrete universals. Benhabib's cosmopolitanism, which emphasizes otherness and the mediation of universal and particular, is specially situated to support emancipatory struggles in postcolonial societies.

In the spirit of theorizing from the space outside the city walls, Ayten Gündoğdu's "Border Deaths as Forced Disappearances: Frantz Fanon and the Outlines of a Critical Phenomenology" inhabits the perspective of dehumanized and racialized migrants who perish—both in the sense of biological death, but also in the sense of political death—in the pursuit of mobility. Gündoğdu's analysis of border violence as a form of "forced disappearance" builds on Benhabib's long-standing efforts to examine the contemporary crises that emerge from the tension between territorial sovereignty and human rights. The chapter examines how these tensions have come to be exploited by states in increasingly violent, even lethal ways to deny the right to movement especially to racialized migrants, a problem that urges us to rethink the contemporary transformations of territorial sovereignty by taking into account the histories of colonialism and racism. Like Benhabib, Gündoğdu draws on Hannah Arendt in her assessment of migrant plight, but she broadens her analysis with the use of Frantz Fanon to explore more concretely how the dynamics of border violence are caught up in the legacies of colonialism and racism. Gündoğdu's sober analysis ends with a call for worldbuilding at the margins and interstices at state power, where migrants might grapple the ever-present possibility of state violence as political agents. Migrants fighting to change the system through their encounters thus exemplify the "dignity in adversity" exhibited by those "concrete others" who expose the contradictions and crises of the sovereign territorial system.

While Benhabib's work, as well as the work of many of her students, has focused on the figure of the refugee, it is possible to apply her methods and approaches to questions of race and politics in the United States. In "Gender Trouble: Manhood, Inclusion, Justice in the Political Philosophy of Martin Luther King, Jr.," Shatema Threadcraft and Brandon M. Terry employ Benhabib's method of "thinking with Arendt against Arendt" and apply it to Martin Luther King, Jr. In thinking with King against King, and by bringing questions of gender to the center of the conversation, Threadcraft and Terry show that it is possible to shed new light on King's radically egalitarian political commitments. To do so, they bring two moments of King's oeuvre into focus: first, King's deflationary critique of Black Power's masculinist politics and defense of egalitarian and inclusive political action, and, second, his defense of a basic minimum income, concern with coerced intimate labor, and antihumiliation ethics in welfare politics. To show the power of this approach, Threadcraft and Terry juxtapose it with two competing schools of interpretation in Black feminist thought: qualified acceptance, as exemplified by bell hooks and Septima Clark, and respectful rejection, as exemplified in Barbara Ransby's biography of Ella Baker and Erica Edwards's work on charisma.

PHILOSOPHY AND FRIENDSHIP

It is fitting that this volume closes with an essay from Carolin Emcke, "Swimming," which weaves together the personal, political, and philosophical in a narration of her friendship with Seyla Benhabib. By exploring themes of learning, suffering, and sharing, Emcke highlights how Benhabib's philosophical commitments emerge in both her work and her personal relationships. Just as Benhabib "sees the refugee and the migrant as an agent, someone who desires freedom and equality, someone who dares, someone who moves, who swims out into the open," so too she has prioritized the moral personhood and critical agency of her students. To study with Benhabib is to know that there is "no precondition of thinking together, no precondition of being seen or heard, no precondition of being included."

For intellectuals like Emcke, Benhabib opened the field of critical theory to new perspectives, embodied experiences of gender and marginality, and the emotions and suffering that underlie the moral self. Thus Emcke illuminates how Benhabib's contributions to contemporary critical theory have enriched the field with "reiteration, a different line of thinking or writing, one that was not blind to who one is (female, queer, multilingual), one that would be able to think with and for marginalized and excluded histories, experiences bodies, desires, and voices." Because Benhabib's project has always been aimed at the boundaries, at pushing them open and rearranging our norms through the inclusion of the concrete other, her work is a springboard for her students and colleagues to move into the future. Our goal with this volume has been not only to discuss Benhabib's legacy in Frankfurt School critical theory, but to provide a set of dialogues that look to the questions of the future: the future of liberal democracy in the global age, climate crisis in the Anthropocene, decolonization, racial justice, and the future of critical theory itself.

The central philosophical concern in this volume has been the search for another, more concrete universalism. Emcke's piece reminds us that beneath each individual search for the concrete universal here also stands a foundation of friendship. Friendship is the hidden thread that weaves this volume together. The friendships among the contributors and their friendships with Benhabib remind me of a phrase that Arendt borrowed from Karl Jaspers: *Treue ist das Zeichen der Wahrheit* (loyalty is the sign of truth).[8] Of all the philosophical lessons I gleaned from my time as Benhabib's student, it is her loyalty and friendship that have made the deepest impression. As this maxim from Arendt and Jaspers attests, those qualities cannot be divorced from our philosophical pursuits, whether we are after concrete universals, truths, justice, or the rest.

NOTES

1. See also Seyla Benhabib, *Exile, Statelessness, and Migration: Playing Chess with History from Hannah Arendt to Isaiah Berlin* (Princeton, NJ: Princeton University Press, 2018).
2. Seyla Benhabib, *Critique, Norm, and Utopia* (New York: Columbia University Press, 1986), 353.
3. Seyla Benhabib, "Whose Trial? Adolf Eichmann's or Hannah Arendt's?: The Eichmann Controversy Revisited," in *Exile, Statelessness, and Modernity*, 61–79.
4. Seyla Benhabib, ed., *Democracy and Difference: Contesting the Boundaries of the Political* (Princeton, NJ: Princeton University Press, 1996).
5. Seyla Benhabib, *The Rights of Others: Aliens, Residents, and Citizens* (Cambridge: Cambridge University Press, 2000).
6. Seyla Benhabib, "Equality and Difference: Human Dignity and Popular Sovereignty in the Mirror of Political Modernity," in *Exile, Statelessness, and Migration*, 9–33.
7. Dipesh Chakrabarty, *Provincializing Europe: Postcolonial Thought and Historical Difference* (Princeton, NJ: Princeton University Press, 2000).
8. Elisabeth Young-Bruehl, *Hannah Arendt: For Love of the World* (New Haven, CT: Yale University Press, 1982), 200.

PART I

Critique, Norm, and Utopia

I

Benhabib and Habermas on Discourse and Development

THOMAS McCARTHY

Seyla Benhabib and I were colleagues in the Boston University Department of Philosophy early in her career (1981–85), after she had taught for several years at Yale and spent time in Germany as a Humboldt Research Fellow. Those were very intense and productive years in Philosophy at BU, which, under the leadership of Bob Cohen and Marx Wartofsky, had since the 1970s become an attractive center of critical social theory for students on the left wishing to do graduate work in philosophy. Benhabib was already well versed in the tradition ranging from Kant through Hegel and Marx to the Frankfurt School and Habermas.

During those early years she published a number of articles and her first book, *Critique, Norm, and Utopia* (1986), dealing with the thought of most of the figures just mentioned, as well as with some of the contemporary debates on the same and cognate themes. We both left BU at that point, she for Harvard and I for Northwestern, but we continued to exchange and comment upon each other's current work. Thus I read many of the articles she published later in the 1980s, a number of which were revised and collected in her second book, *Situating the Self* (1992). During that same period she edited and contributed to the book *Feminism as Critique* (1987), and edited and introduced another, *The Communicative Ethics Controversy* (1990), on the debates surrounding Habermas's idea of discourse ethics, the idea that served as a starting point for her own sustained reconstruction of the normative foundations of critical social theory.

In this paper I want to examine several of her exchanges with Habermas in their ongoing conversation about these foundations and argue that their differences on certain key issues are not as deep as they are generally taken to be. I will pay particular attention to Habermas's notion of "development" as a "learning process," which Benhabib criticized as too Hegelian in her first book (1986) and does so again in a recent article (2021).[1]

INTRODUCTORY REMARKS

I recall our years together at BU not only because I have fond memories of that time, but also to set the stage for my reading of her work. Benhabib's extensive publications since then have repeatedly thematized, in a variety of contexts, the interplay between universal principles and ideals, on the one hand, and the manifold particularities of the concrete individuals and groups, situations, and contexts to which they are applied, on the other. In fact, as the title of the conference which inspired this volume—*In Search of the Concrete Universal*—suggests, that is perhaps her signature motif and no one has been better at developing it than she.

Benhabib's theoretical work in the 1980s already laid the philosophical foundations for her subsequent work on the inclusion of a vast array of excluded others—from migrants, refugees, and stateless persons to women, minorities, and sociocultural "others"—which not only built upon those foundations but repeatedly refined and reformulated them as the task at hand demanded. More specifically, she critically appropriated Habermas's discourse ethics in the 1980s and continued to reinterpret and revise it in later works so as to accommodate her strong convictions about how questions of difference ought to be dealt with in an ethics and politics based on universal respect for all human beings and a commitment to egalitarian reciprocity.

To firm up this sense of the theoretical continuity of Benhabib's work over the past four decades, I recently reread her first two books and was immensely impressed—for a second time—by the great mass of highly theoretical and extremely difficult philosophical texts she had mastered so early in her career. In *Critique, Norm, and Utopia* she adeptly reconstructed Hegel's critique of Kant's universalist ethics and then, while distancing herself from Hegel's metaphysics, inventively applied key elements of the reformulated critique to Habermas's neo-Kantian version of a universalist ethics. To be sure, a number of other thinkers were discussed in some detail—Marx, Max Weber, Horkheimer, and the Frankfurt School, among them—but the discussion of Habermas in chapters 7 and 8 is undoubtedly the theoretical highlight. In my estimation, owing to her close reading, sharp analysis, and incisive critique, it is the best discussion of his work from that period.

Over the next few years, particularly in the essays collected in *Situating the Self*, she engaged with a number of contemporary critiques of liberalism by communitarian, feminist, and postmodern theorists, in each case deftly applying the same sort of dialectical "sublation" to their opposition to Kantian-style universalism. That is to say, the general concerns behind their main points were typically acknowledged, reformulated to apply more directly to Habermas's discourse ethics, and finally incorporated into her revised program of communicative ethics. She proceeded in this way because she felt strongly that abandoning the universalist thrust of discourse ethics to such criticisms would be a serious moral-political mistake. She believed, too, that many of the deepest problems with normative theories inspired by Kant stemmed from the individualist cast of their operative notions of the subject. Habermas had already made the key move of theorizing individuation as emerging from socialization within a community of language users. Consequently, in his ethical and political writings human speech and action were conceptualized as inherently interactive, human subjectivity as inherently intersubjectivity. This rendered the crucial connection between "the universal" and "what all could agree to in discourse" much easier to theorize.

Leaving transcendental arguments behind, Benhabib focused on the process of reaching an understanding with others in and through dialogue as the linchpin of her version of communicative ethics. And, as in Habermas's original version, in hers too genuine dialogue or discourse about moral and political issues required reciprocal perspective taking, i.e., participants had to attempt to see things from one another's perspectives so as to understand better what each intended by their proposals and objections; it further required an effort by each to avoid insincerity and duplicity, as well as a chance for all to contribute to the discussion. In short, it required that participants treat one another with respect, fairness, honesty, and equal consideration. Unlike Habermas, she did not view such preconditions of genuine dialogue or discourse as "quasi-transcendental" in any sense, but she did accept his characterization of them as pragmatic presuppositions of genuine discourse aimed at consensually resolving issues of cognitive and moral validity, e.g., ascertaining the truth of a claim, the rightness of an action, or the justness of a law. As such, they were, in her view, historically emergent but deep-seated sociocultural expectations connected with certain types of interaction. This detranscendentalized approach certainly allowed for a more flexible treatment of issues concerning the moral or political status of various groups of excluded others, as Benhabib amply demonstrated in her many explorations of democratic iteration and jurisgenerativity. But in the final chapter of a recent book, *Exile, Statelessness, and Migration* (2018), she seems to wonder aloud whether the flexibility may be too great.

Having in earlier works criticized John Rawls's brand of Kantian constructivism, she there praises certain features of his later political liberalism. She notes that he finally viewed his reconstruction of fair terms of social cooperation, which ensure a just society over time, more hermeneutically and contextually, as a reflective interpretation of basic values and principles immanent in liberal constitutional democracies. But as Rawls became more contextual, she suggests, his distinction between forms of pluralism that are reasonable and rational and those that are not became increasingly contested.[2] Reflecting on his influential discussion of the "burdens of judgment," which helped account for the persistence in liberal societies of normative and evaluative disagreement, she wonders whether his basic framework of fair terms of social cooperation might itself be put in question by such burdens, and expresses concern that the indeterminacy that stems from the latter could be extended to fundamental values and principles themselves, such that a common conversation ceases to be possible.

> For Rawls, constitutional democracies have to accept the reasonable pluralism of values and the inevitable burdens of judgment. Nevertheless, such reasonable pluralism can be practiced only as long as we recognize each other as free and equal citizens to which we can attribute both rationality and reasonableness.... The question that haunts him is whether the burdens of judgment that even these principles have to bear can ensure that a common civic point of view will endure over time. How far can the divergence in burdens of judgment go without diremptive forces pushing us so far afield that a common conversation is no longer possible?

She refers to this quandary as the "Weimar Syndrome."[3]

Benhabib's discussion of the dilemma lurking within Rawls's construction of political liberalism, owing to the absence therein of a defensible philosophical border between shared "constitutional essentials" and reasonable disagreements subject to "the burdens of judgment," is persuasive; but it inevitably prompts the question of whether a similar problem besets her own account of the foundations of communicative ethics. If one closely examines her treatment of Habermas's original version in chapters 7 and 8 of *Critique, Norm, and Utopia*, an affirmative answer seems to be called for. One might even say that this is unavoidable in light of her deconstruction of the demarcation line Habermas drew between the "quasi-transcendental"—"always already [*immer schon*] presupposed"—universal normative principles underlying rational discourse, on the one hand, and, on the other hand, the particular norms and expectations that vary with communicative contexts, to which Benhabib gives ever-increasing weight across the broad expanse of her subsequent work. In short, do the intensifying effects of concretization and contextualization gradually erode the privileged status of her universal principles, as those of value pluralism seem to have done with Rawls's constitutional essentials? And if that is the case, would she be in a stronger theoretical position had she hewn a path closer to Habermas's?

BENHABIB'S "WEAK" VERSION OF UNIVERSALISM

In evaluating Habermas's accounts of epistemic and normative universalism it is misleading, in my view, to place too great an emphasis on the term *quasi-transcendental*. I take the *quasi-* here to mean "as though they were," or "in a certain sense," rather than "to a certain degree." More specifically, this characterization of certain interaction norms pertaining to discourse derives from their putative status as "universal pragmatic presuppositions" of rational discourse. To my mind, there is nothing suspect about studying pragmatic rules of language in use, any more than there is about studying syntactical and semantical rules, which are also "always already presupposed," usually without our being conscious of them. But the claim to strict universality Habermas raises for certain rules of rational discourse about truth and rightness claims is, I agree with Benhabib, open to question, since the types of communicative activity he is analyzing—rational justifications of epistemic and normative claims—have changed considerably over the course of recorded human history. And I share her view that the dissemination and institutionalization of the specific types of rational discourse he analyzes belong to what she calls "the hermeneutic horizon of modernity"—which is not to say they never appeared before that, as Socratic dialogues and Thomistic *quaestiones disputatae* suggest. If, then, these pragmatic presuppositions are not strictly universal but are endemic to modern cultures, we seem to be caught in the kind of circular argumentation that Benhabib already identified and criticized in her early work.[4] More specifically, she found this kind of circularity in Habermas's developmental arguments for the special status of modern structures of rationality, which he viewed as resulting from sociocultural learning processes underway since the axial period; and she saw in this a neo-Hegelian attempt to view the history of reason as moving toward, and culminating in, *our* (modern Western) way of doing things.[5] Having thus, in her first systematic work, challenged the validity of these (and other) arguments for the *necessity* of the universalistic principles of communicative ethics, Benhabib nevertheless continued in her subsequent work to regard them as *essential but contingent* elements of modern culture and, as such, to deploy them in her own version of communicative ethics.

If my reading of Benhabib's line of argument in her earlier work is accurate, it is not surprising that she should be concerned with the "Weimar syndrome" in her recent work on mid-twentieth century Jewish émigré intellectuals. The normative foundations of modern sociocultural and legal-political practices and institutions seem once again to be trembling beneath us. Habermas has argued, in his recent opus on philosophy and religion, *Auch eine Geschichte der Philosophie* (2019), and in many publications preceding it, that upholding the theoretically and practically privileged status of such basic normative principles as universal respect for human dignity, equal rights and consideration, equal freedom and legal-political autonomy, and the like has a critical role to play in this transitional moment. Rationally reconstructing them as the hard-won fruit of learning processes stretching across centuries could reinforce the hopes and encourage the participation of members of political societies struggling to reinterpret and maintain them in the face of widespread "regression." The theoretical price for using this last term includes, to be sure, a convincing account of the developmental processes that issued in such principles and practices.

I mention this to signal, somewhat obliquely, my motivation for emphasizing the issues of learning and development in this paper. In *Critique, Norm, and Utopia*, Benhabib repeatedly inquired of Habermas's candidates for universally valid principles of rational discourse: What "binding power" do they possess? That is, why should we feel bound by them in the absence of metaphysical or transcendental arguments for their privileged status in practical discourse? One—"weak"—response might be that their binding power derives from the fact that certain ways of doing things have proved over time to be superior to previous ways in respects in which we have a deep interest—e.g., in regard to the fairness, impartiality, context sensitivity, and openness to warranted modification of core practices and institutions. As Benhabib points out, however, this familiar sort of "development" cannot claim the necessity that Hegel claims for the development of reason. While it is undeniable that cognitive-developmental approaches have lent increasing support to the idea that some cultural changes are *cumulative and directional*, and thus can be reconstructed as learning processes, that does not mean that they are necessary and not contingent. Such processes occur only under certain sociocultural conditions and gain institutional embodiment only in particular historical circumstances; and their consequences for human welfare, however defined, vary with the contexts in which they take place and are put to use. As a result, there is an inherent ambivalence in many cognitive advances, costs as well as benefits. And the same is true, perhaps even more so, of developments in structural-functional differentiation, such as the rise and spread of market economies and state bureaucracies—as the many ills of the intensifying commodification and bureaucratization of modern life testify.

To fully comprehend Benhabib's reluctance to rely on developmental reconstructions to explicate the binding power of universal norms, however, we have to examine more closely the senses in which she characterizes justifications as "weak" or "strong," "contingent" or "necessary." In her repeated discussion of the issue in *Critique, Norm, and Utopia*, she argues that Habermas fails to attain the "necessity" of "strong" transcendental arguments with his rational reconstructions of developmental processes in individuals and societies.[6] Calling the latter "quasi-transcendental" cannot conceal the fact that they are, in the final analysis, "weak," empirically based arguments concerning "contingent" processes. While this characterization is literally correct, in my view it obscures some crucial distinctions among the meanings of "contingent." One familiar everyday meaning is "unforeseen" or "unpredictable." Her more technical usage of it to characterize *the absence of metaphysical or transcendental necessity* is, however, familiar to philosophers from discussions of the transitions to early modern philosophy in the English-speaking world and to post-Idealist philosophy on the Continent. But if we keep in mind that *all* the empirical sciences produce "contingent" knowledge in this sense, and thus that their laws and theories offer only "weak" explanations and justifications in Benhabib's usage, these characterizations lose much of their sting. In the world of our experience, contingency is all we moderns have. So the issue here is, more precisely, how strong or weak reconstructions of ontogenetic and phylogenetic developments are *in comparison to* other modes of empirical inquiry in the human sciences.

We might note, for instance, that the likelihood of human infants following a "normal" course of development to adulthood under "normal" conditions is quite high, though not as high, say, as that of the planets following their accustomed paths. In a more probative vein, we might point to the enormous and ever-expanding body of empirical studies on child development that identify and reconstruct ontogenetically emergent stages of cognition and sociality, or to studies in the history of science and technology, law and constitutional democracy.[7] On the other hand, as Benhabib points out, *theorizing* about social and cultural development is still fraught with methodological disagreements. Habermas set out his approach in considerable detail in the two volumes of *The Theory of Communicative Action* (1981). That work is the culmination of a research program he pursued during the 1970s, the main lines of which were already sketched in *Toward a Reconstruction of Historical Materialism* (1976). As this title indicates, it was Marx who served as the main point of reference for his theorizing of social development; and the empirical, social-theoretical orientation of *The Theory of Communicative Action* is signaled by the subtitle of the second volume: *A Critique of Functionalist Reason*. At the same time, Habermas was critical of Marx for treating sociocultural development as driven largely by functional development in the economic sphere, and thus he offered his own, very different account of the internal logic of sociocultural development in terms of "the rationalization of the lifeworld," which translated a number of Kantian and Hegelian motifs into empirical, historical, and social-theoretical forms.

In *Critique, Norm, and Utopia*, Benhabib provided the following overview of Habermas's developmental approach:

> Reconstructive theories analyze the *deep structures* of cognition and action.... Habermas views such deep structures as patterns of rule competencies that evolve in the history of the individual and of the species.... [Individuals] are the agents of such evolution, for it is through learning processes that they acquire the competencies.... The account of modernization as rationalization in *The Theory of Communicative Action* relies on this concept of reconstruction. To combine the "internalist" and the "externalist" perspectives in social theory, Habermas uses the concepts of *developmental logic* and *learning processes*. Social change, he maintains, cannot be viewed from the standpoint of the observer alone. There are aspects of social evolution ... that can be reconstructed internally, that is, "insightfully recapitulated from the perspective of the participants." ... Social development occurs through answers that social agents give to the ever-new problems of their lifeworld. Through institutionalization ... [they] become part of the material and cultural history of society.... [Social agents] reproduce their lifeworld by recapitulating these already available answers while creating and seeking new ones.[8]

As this summation indicates, it is not merely discrete bodies of empirical knowledge that account for the binding power of learning processes, but also—and especially—their concatenation in chains of *good reasoning* that can be "insightfully recapitulated" by others, so as to reproduce the well-grounded conviction of advances in problem-solving. As such, they can be disseminated, taught and learned, passed on and expanded, institutionalized and applied—in short, become taken-for-granted elements of culture and society. And those who simply reject their results as "unbinding" and turn instead, say, to politics, popular culture, religion, or what have you for solutions to the same types of problems will generally be regarded as unable or unwilling to appreciate the rationally binding power they do in fact possess.

PRACTICAL DISCOURSE IN THEORY AND PRACTICE

In Habermas's view, the "forceless force" of good reasons is operative not only in the development of natural-scientific and technological discourses, and of social-scientific and applied discourses, but also in the development of moral, legal, and political normative discourses; and there, too, it rationally binds participants. As noted earlier, while Benhabib accepts the universalistic principles informing rational discourse about truth claims and rightness claims, she rejects Habermas's "quasi-transcendental" characterization of them—as unavoidable pragmatic presuppositions of rational discourse as such—in favor of an understanding that "recognizes the historical and sociological 'contingency' of communicative ethics."[9] And there is, in her view, no escaping the hermeneutic dimension of such an undertaking. I want to suggest, however, that she and Habermas are *methodologically* not very far apart in these respects. *Both* acknowledge the empirical contingency of structures and processes of communicative interaction; and *both* insist on the hermeneutic dimension of our understanding of the human world. The methodological differences between them may sometimes seem larger than they actually are owing in part to terminological differences. For instance, when Habermas refers to the detranscendentalization of structures of communication as their "naturalization," he is not using the latter term in its "hard" sense of scientifically reducing knowledge of the human world to the objectifying approaches of the sciences of nature—which is the common meaning of the term in Anglo-American philosophy. He uses it rather in the "soft" sense of abandoning metaphysical and transcendental approaches for empirical approaches, *both* objectifying and interpretive, to the human world.[10] Benhabib, by contrast, uses "naturalization" in the more usual "hard" sense of objectivistic reductionism and, accordingly, uses "hermeneutic" as a contrast term. Despite these terminological differences, however, *both* she and Habermas understand the sociocultural formations of modernity as historically emergent and subject to change, and our knowledge of them as having an ineliminable hermeneutic dimension.

There are, to be sure, divergences between them on the *consequences* of the hermeneutic dimension of the human sciences. Benhabib holds that the unavoidable interpretive moment in our understanding of human affairs subverts Habermas's insistence that the aim of practical discourse in morality, law, and constitutional democracy is to arrive at agreement on the *one right answer* to the problem at hand. Habermas does allow that when we are dealing discursively with matters of individual and collective identities, of highest goods and basic values, *as variously conceived by different individuals and groups*—that is, when we are engaged in what he calls "ethical-existential" and "ethical-political" discussion—there is no one right answer. And he agrees that one aim of basic moral, legal, and democratic principles and procedures is to protect this freedom of individuals and collectives to define and pursue their own goods within the bounds of such fundamental universalistic constraints. But he also maintains that reasoned agreement on one right answer is the defining aim of moral, legal, and political practical discourse as well as of theoretical discourse. I shall not attempt to recapitulate the details of that discussion here but simply note that my own position is closer to Benhabib's in one crucial respect: the inseparability of the right and the good, in the final analysis, means that there will typically be room for *reasonable disagreement* among well-intentioned and well-informed participants in practical discourse about what is morally right, legally just, in the general interest, or for the common good.[11] And that provides ample opportunity for Benhabib to identify the structures and processes of practical judgment, jurisgenerativity, democratic iteration, and the like, which inform her extended and many-sided account of the concrete universal. It seems clear, moreover, that reasonable disagreements grounded in such structures and processes will often be deep-seated and long-lasting, and will sometimes have to be dealt with through forms of legal and political accommodation rather than through up-or-down procedures of judicial or electoral decision-making.

More broadly, the ineliminable hermeneutic moment in the comprehension, explication, and application of fundamental values and principles opens political deliberation to unavoidable differences in their interpretation, weighting, contextualization, implementation, and the like—that is to say, to the many sorts of difference that Benhabib analyzes from the perspective of concretizing and specifying abstract universals. She has convincingly argued, for instance, that differences in collective identities formed around deep social, cultural, and gender differences regularly give rise to ongoing "reasonable disagreements" concerning the interpretation and concretization of such fundamental democratic norms as equal respect, standing, consideration, and freedom, among many others. One might add that persistent differences in pervasive conditions of life such as socioeconomic class, religious community, educational level, and the like could also amount to differences in participants' "hermeneutic situations" and thus make a difference in their understandings and applications of constitutional essentials. Habermas discusses such problems in terms of the critical importance for constitutional democracy of "cohesive social solidarity," which is required to stabilize a modern polity and provide citizens with sufficient motivation to promote the common good over their own self-interest.[12] And like Benhabib, he worries that deep pluralism could destabilize actually existing constitutional democracies by dis-integrating that solidarity.[13]

But even such highly qualified versions as these of the consensual outcome of practical discourse *in its idealized form*—i.e., when it is governed by the basic normative presuppositions that Habermas and Benhabib spell out, including the possibility of reasonable disagreement—are rarely fully realized *in practice*. I am referring here to the obvious fact that the conditions of actually existing constitutional democracies fall well short even of the modulated ideality of reasonable disagreement. In short, the general state of socialization processes, of public cultures generally and of political cultures particularly, of gross inequalities in the socioeconomic conditions of life, of persistent inequities in the respect, standing, consideration, treatment, and so on afforded members of diverse groups, and the like gives rise not only to reasonable disagreement but also—and today, perhaps, increasingly—to unreasonable disagreement, fragmentation, and polarization. Broad and deep changes in the functioning of capitalist economies have served to widen and deepen such divides—think, for instance, of the impact of neoliberal globalization on socioeconomic stratification and democratic self-determination since the 1970s, or of the rapid transformation of culture, society, polity, and economy by the digitization of virtually all spheres of life since the 1990s.

My general point here is simply that the sorts of problems focused on in ideal theory, which are real enough, are often overshadowed and exacerbated by other, empirically driven problems confronting constitutional democracies. Habermas's sociohistorical heuristic of developmental learning processes in *Auch eine Geschichte der Philosophie* attempts to address such problems.[14] Accordingly, I will close with a few brief thoughts on what the idea of development*s* tied to learning process*es* adds to this discussion. I highlight the plural endings as a reminder that I am decidedly *not* considering any totalizing idea of "progress" here, but rather the idea of manifold epistemic and normative advances, achieved in dealing with multifarious types of problems, and passed on through socialization, habituation, education, celebration, institutionalization, and the like to future generations.

In "Habermas's New *Phenomenology of Spirit*," Benhabib reads *Auch eine Geschichte der Philosophie* as a reprise of Hegel's "grand narrative" of human progress.[15] In his "Reply," he rejects this reading, saying he has no place for the "bird's-eye perspective of Hegel's Owl of Minerva. Rather, learning processes are attributed to the persons who participate, in their own names, and to the formative historical backgrounds from which they draw their competences and insights."[16] And toward the end of her critique of grand narratives of progress, Benhabib expressly accepts a more modest notion of "progress" in particular domains, both epistemic and normative, which strikes me as very close to the idea of development based on learning that Habermas espouses.[17] In the coda that follows, I briefly sketch a few of the central features of development that I believe both do or could accept.

CODA: CONCLUDING THOUGHTS ON "DEVELOPMENT"

As Benhabib has often remarked, we are now living in an age of global modernity. Consider the following indicators of the rationally "binding" quality of some key cultural developments.[18] Participants in the global discourse of modernity often find themselves in similar positions with regard to the cultural resources at their disposal. Indeed, the representatives of historically excluded and marginalized groups are quite often more adept with the weapons of critique than their opponents. This capacity for critical reflection is not merely a matter of individual virtuosity; it is bound up with social and cultural conditions that are undergoing historical change. In modern societies—and in this sense "we are all moderns"—conditions are such as to provide increased cultural and institutional incentives for reflective modes of argumentation and critique. And it is important for our purposes to recognize that this heightening of reflexivity informs and structures the contemporary discourse of global modernity itself. All the various participants in this discourse take for granted the possibility of questioning received beliefs and values, of gaining critical distance from inherited norms and roles, of challenging ascribed individual and group identities. Even arguments for the value of preserving certain premodern traditions are typically not themselves traditional arguments but the traditionalistic arguments of hyperreflexive moderns. That is to say, one can argue against certain features of modern culture only by drawing upon them, which is a strong indication that they are unavoidable presuppositions of contemporary discourse, that they belong to the pragmatics of our discursive situation. For one thing, it is precisely our historically, sociologically, and culturally schooled understanding of the diversity of worldviews and forms of life, among other things, that fuels the discourse of alternative modernities. Hence we are bound, on pain of incoherence, to regard any worldview that does not reflectively comprehend itself as one possible interpretation among many others as having something to learn in that regard.

There are other general presuppositions of global discourse with which one might, perhaps, coherently take issue, but with respect to which the burdens of proof on critics are so large as to be prohibitive. For instance, it would be difficult, bordering on impossible, to produce a warranted denial that there has been a significant learning process long underway in regard to our scientific understanding of nature and our technical capacity to manipulate it. Practically living out that denial would be even more difficult. It is also important to note that our assessment of norms and values cannot remain unaffected by learning in more narrowly epistemic domains. Traditional value systems are intimately interwoven with beliefs about how the world is, such that learning processes associated with the names Galileo, Darwin, and Freud, for instance, could have profound and enduring impacts on normative and evaluative elements of modern culture. Since the reasons we regard as warranting normative judgments have to be compatible with what we have learned in other domains, whole *kinds of reasons* for acting in particular ways have lost, and are still losing, discursive weight—for instance, the justifications of unequal treatment by appeal to the "natural" inferiority and unfitness for self-rule of women and non-Europeans in general. And it is no easy matter to find substitute justifications capable of withstanding discursive scrutiny. As Benhabib argues, the global discourse of modernity is increasingly structured by a pragmatic presupposition of normative symmetry, which requires treating all participants with equal respect. The tension between that presupposition—with its attendant ideals of fairness, impartiality, toleration of difference, and so forth—and ethical views based on beliefs in fundamental inequalities is evident. The scope of *reasonable* disagreement gets considerably narrowed; but it is also not uniquely determined. One of the things inhabitants of global modernity have learned about values, for instance, is that reasonable people can reasonably hold different conceptions of the good life, that there is no one way of life that is "the" best for all individuals and groups.

As to the often-claimed unavoidability of functional developments, there are some important differences in their "binding" power worth mentioning. All contemporary societies are faced with basic problems they have to solve to survive—for instance, how to relate to a global market economy; how to organize and administer a functionally differentiated society; how to accommodate ethnic, cultural, and religious diversity in a coherent set of institutions; how to maintain political solidarity and legitimacy in the face of deep sociocultural pluralism; and so forth. From this perspective, many modern institutions appear to be not merely products of the particularities of colonial and postcolonial histories, but responses to macrohistorical challenges of a general nature, which include those arising from the ever-deeper immersion of all societies in transnational flows of capital, commodities, technology, information, communication, and culture. For instance, modern positive law must have many of the general features it has—positivity, formality, reflexivity, actionability, and the like—if it is to fulfill the functions it fulfills. Thus the fact that positive law issues from the changeable decisions of authorized legislators makes it *more* suitable as a means of ordering complex and changing modern and modernizing societies, but *less* amenable to legitimation through appeal to inherited beliefs and practices. In short, *the functions and forms* of modern law are generally tailored to one another, and something similar can be said for most other modern, functionally differentiated institutions.

We might add to this a host of other changes that seem to be irresistible in modernizing societies: a decline in the traditional agricultural modes of life that served most of humanity for most of our recorded history; growing specialization of occupational and professional roles; diversification of life styles, belief systems, value commitments, and forms of individual and group identity; institutionalized growth and dissemination of fallible, secular knowledge; the spread of mass media and mass-mediated popular culture; an exponential expansion of digital information and communication systems; and so on and so forth. How much room do such modernizing tendencies leave for deep cultural and social differences? There is obviously no generally accepted answer to this question, or to the question of just which kinds of diversity will perdure and which new kinds arise as global modernization continues apace. Here, too, the ongoing global discourse of modernity, carried on at a critical-reflective level, opens up an inexhaustible, ever-shifting horizon of possibilities for reasonable disagreement. Not only claims to universal validity have to stand up to transcultural scrutiny, but claims to advancement and improvement as well. Representing a given sociocultural change as the result of a learning process, for instance, raises the debatable claim that it offers a superior way of cognizing and dealing with a certain domain of experience. Moreover, even if that claim is justified as such, there still remains the rather different question of what place a given innovation should have in the life of a society, whether and how it should be institutionalized. Developments of our rational capacities to cope with certain kinds of problems—e.g., instrumentally effective modes of organization—leave room for disagreement about whether, how, when, and where these capacities should be institutionalized. As issues of this kind are debated in a diversity of societies and a diversity of circumstances, it is reasonable to expect a diversity of views, for they centrally involve matters of well-being, variously understood.

Benhabib has convincingly analyzed other widespread and deep-seated sources of indeterminacy. Whatever universals we consider basic to morality, law, and constitutional democracy can become actual only as concrete. Since there exists a plurality of forms of socioculturally embedded reason and the differences among them can be bridged only hermeneutically, we have continually to rethink the idea of development from the perspective of historical and cultural polyphony and continually to forge what Habermas has called "a unity of reason in the diversity of its voices." To be sure, recognition and accommodation of such indeterminacies in the idea of development do not eliminate all tensions from it, in particular, those arising from the strongly modernist assumptions underlying influential normative conceptions of human rights, constitutional democracy, the rule of law, and the like, which often clash with traditional worldviews and forms of life. That is to say, some sociocultural preconditions of the modern legal and political forms that underwrite equal standing and equal voice are in tension with some elements of the forms of life and social orders lacking such guarantees. There is no easy exit from this predicament. We may at least hope for a multiplicity of "creative adaptations" to these conditions, as Charles Taylor has put it, resulting in a degree of overlapping consensus and functional equivalence sufficient to enable global peace and promote global justice.[19]

The claimed universality of the discourse of modernity leaves it pragmatically open to dissent, criticism, and revision from historically excluded, subordinated, and marginalized others. While global modernity can't be simply avoided, the ideas and ideals informing it can be continually transformed from within, especially as postcolonial thinkers play an increasingly significant critical and transformative role. It has become more and more evident that there is not only the possibility but the reality of "multiple" or "alternative" modernities. As Benhabib has convincingly argued, convergence at an abstract, formal, or structural level is quite consistent with, and indeed necessarily accompanied by, diversity at more concrete levels. By their very nature, the universal cannot be actual without the particular, the formal without the substantive, the abstract without the concrete, or structure without content. The "dialectic" between these apparent opposites would lead us to expect, rather, that different cultures, different circumstances, and different histories—including colonial domination and liberation, for instance—normally issue in significant sociocultural differences, in plurality and hybridity, the coalescence of diverse patterns and forms. The idea that all societies are converging on the same model is based on a fundamental misunderstanding of universality as uniformity—the kind of misunderstanding that occurs when a culture is talking to itself about the shape of human history.

Notwithstanding such fundamental confusions and ideological usages, however, the idea of development cannot simply be abandoned in favor of some form of postdevelopmental thinking of difference. Not only do the roots and realities of cultural and societal modernity weigh theoretically against that, but the pressing need for collective action on a global scale to address the needs and interests of the poorest and most vulnerable communities makes it practically objectionable as well. Rather, we have to fashion a critical theory of global development that acknowledges the evident fact that European-American modernization involved a massive, pervasive, and continuous use of power and domination, force and violence—from dispossession and expropriation to slavery and exploitation—which were not merely by-products of a transformative process driven by the necessities of capital accumulation, but were among its central mechanisms. The deeply unjust patterns of economic growth they resulted in are not only morally and politically objectionable but also systemically unsustainable. "Our" way of life is not universalizable. "Leveling up" all national economies to the production and consumption patterns of the economically most developed societies would make the planet uninhabitable. Thus "development" has to be critically reconceptualized as a global problem of achieving fair and sustainable development on a planetary scale. And it is obvious that this problem cannot be solved with free-market nostrums; it has an ineluctably political core. How, for instance, can we provide for the welfare of future generations without shortchanging those presently living in conditions of extreme deprivation? Are economically more developed nations likely to relinquish their advantageous positions voluntarily? Systemically embedded conflicts of interest such as these open up the prospect of intense and protracted global struggles. Macrosociological theories of historical change are notoriously weak in predicting the future; and the contingency of history makes dystopian fears as well as utopian hopes possible in principle. But a critical theory of development is concerned with what it is reasonable to hope for and work toward, in light of what we know about past history and present conditions. It is not a predictive science but a theory of practice, constructed *in praktischer Absicht*, as Kant said of his universal history: that is, "with a practical end in view," the achievement of global justice.

NOTES

1. Seyla Benhabib, *Critique, Norm, and Utopia* (New York: Columbia University Press, 1986); Seyla Benhabib, "Habermas's New *Phenomenology of Spirit*: Two Centuries After Hegel," *Constellations* 28, no. 1 (March 2021): 33–44.
2. Seyla Benhabib, *Exile, Statelessness, and Migration* (Princeton, NJ: Princeton University Press, 2018), 181–85.
3. Benhabib, *Exile, Statelessness, and Migration*, 183–84.
4. Cf. Benhabib, *Critique, Norm, and Utopia*, 272ff.
5. Cf. Benhabib, 330–31.
6. Cf. Benhabib, 274–79.
7. For an overview of some interesting recent work in this area, cf. Michael Tomasello, *Becoming Human: A Theory of Ontogeny* (Cambridge, MA: Harvard University Press, 2019).
8. Benhabib, *Critique, Norm, and Utopia*, 264–65.

9. Seyla Benhabib, *Situating the Self* (New York: Routledge, 1992), 61–62.
10. Cf., for instance, Jürgen Habermas, *Between Naturalism and Religion*, trans. C. Cronin (Cambridge: Polity, 2008), "introduction."
11. Cf. James Bohman, *Public Deliberation: Pluralism, Complexity, and Democracy* (Cambridge, MA: MIT Press, 1996).
12. Cf., for instance, Habermas, *Between Naturalism and Religion*, chaps. 4 and 10.
13. Habermas, chaps. 4 and 10.
14. Jürgen Habermas, *Auch eine Geschichte der Philosophie*, vols. 1 and 2 (Berlin: Suhrkamp, 2019). Cf. Thomas McCarthy, "On the Interest of Practical Reason in Hope," *Constellations* 28, no. 1 (March 2021): 11–16.
15. Benhabib, "Habermas's New *Phenomenology of Spirit*," 33–44.
16. Jürgen Habermas, "Reply," *Constellations* 28, no. 1 (March 2021): 67–78, at 74.
17. Benhabib, "Habermas's New *Phenomenology of Spirit*," 42n26.
18. Cf. Thomas McCarthy, *Race, Empire, and the Idea of Human Development* (Cambridge: Cambridge University Press, 2009), pt. 2.
19. Charles Taylor, "Two Theories of Modernity," in *Alternative Modernities*, ed. Dilip Parameshwar Gaonkar (Durham, NC: Duke University Press, 2004), 172–96.

2

Normativity and Reality

Toward a Critical and Realistic Theory of Politics

RAINER FORST

PLATO'S PARADOX

The science of politics is an unusual kind of science. It has one of the longest traditions of all sciences, but it constantly struggles with that tradition. One of the reasons for this is that we have become suspicious of the ethnocentrism of that tradition. But another reason is that the oldest and still most important work in Western political thought, Plato's *Republic*, contains a paradox that still haunts us. Plato argues that the central question of those who seek the truth about politics is the nature of the just political order, and he believes that there is only one right answer to that question, an answer based on a metaphysical idea of the good. However, that idea of the good, although it is generally valid, is not accessible to everyone.

As Plato explains in the parable of the cave, those who have left the realm of the shadows that are falsely regarded as reality—fake reality, we might say—and have ascended the path leading to the recognition of the true reality of the good will never be able to return to the cave to explain what they saw, since no one would be able to believe them. Instead, those who had grasped the reality of the good would be killed by those who remain in the cave, ideologically deluded as they are. Thus the paradox is that the *real* truth about political order is politically uncommunicable, given the *realities* of social life.

So Plato—and the tradition of political thought founded by him—leaves us with a complicated heritage, a confusion as to what kind of reality political science is going to explore: the reality of the cave and its infinite power struggles or the real truth of the ideal political order that we should strive for. This tradition leads to a lot of conceptual problems and rifts, if one thinks, for example, of the ways in which the term "realism" is understood.[1] While for some (social scientists especially), it refers to the cave reality of self-interested rivalry and the normative arbitrariness of social life, for others (philosophers mainly) it refers to the view that certain values, including those guiding political life, are true and real.[2]

THE LOSS OF A SHARED LANGUAGE IN POLITICAL SCIENCE

In my view, the Platonic paradox of the political incommunicability of political truth—or, in other words, the incompatibility of two kinds of reality as the object of political science—creates a severe methodological problem within that discipline. The problem goes very deep and ultimately it raises the question of whether political science is a normative or an empirical enterprise. What is the main question of that kind of science—to understand and analyze the political orders we live in or to search for the good or just political order? You may of course say that it is both and try to muddle through somehow. Many say that the scientific part is the domain of social and political analysis—of political behavior and institutional mechanisms—and claim, following Weber and others, that the normative part is not really a scientific one.[3] Others call that position "positivism" and emphasize the importance and independence of normative political philosophy, trying to stay away from the cave.[4]

As a result, political science is a discipline that allows itself the luxury of a subdiscipline called political theory (or political philosophy) that used to define the enterprise of political science but in the meantime has given way to a new understanding of what science is. The question of the right or just political order is translated into an empirical program of what certain collectives actually recognize as a legitimate order (following Weber), while the original question is seen as being only of historical interest and a matter of (possibly postcolonial-genealogical) critique[5] or one for Platonic idealists. As a consequence, political theory and the other areas of political science have lost touch with one another and developed languages of their own.

This is regrettable, especially at a time of normative crisis when we are concerned about the future of democracy, the rule of law, and multilateral systems of international cooperation, not to speak of social justice—and when we are in need of appropriate conceptual and normative tools to determine, for example, at which point populism transforms democracy into its opposite, into authoritarianism.[6] Can the voices of political scientists or of philosophers still carry weight in the upheavals of our time if empirical analysis and normative analysis rarely meet? Isn't this a time when there is an urgent need to combine the two perspectives and when we have to resist the arbitrariness of definitions of democracy, justice, and the rule of law that use the term "democracy" for exclusionary and oppressive forms of politics?

JUSTIFICATION AS A MEDIATING TERM

The challenge I am formulating here has not gone unnoticed, of course, and I take Seyla Benhabib's work to be exemplary for developing advanced methods of political theory that bridge abstract principles and the realities of social and political life—the apt term "concrete universal" signifies this kind of thinking, as do other terms she uses such as the combination of the "concrete" and the "generalized" other[7] or the powerful concept of "democratic iterations" which she coined. The latter refers to "complex processes of public argument, deliberation, and learning through which universalist right claims are contested and contextualized, invoked and revoked, throughout legal and political institutions as well as in the public sphere of liberal democracies."[8] In her approach, a particular notion of discourse as containing certain normative principles and as a practice of what Arendt (following Kant) called "enlarged thought"[9] mediates between the ideal and the real, and in this way, she develops Habermas's discourse theory further in important and innovative ways.[10] Still, the notion of discourse used remains primarily a normative one, albeit one that connects practices of morality, law, and politics.

In the following remarks, I want to make a different (though not completely unrelated) suggestion as to how to bridge the seeming abyss between the language of normative political theory and the language of empirical analysis—one that I have developed (in dialogue with others) in the interdisciplinary research context of the Normative Orders Centre in Frankfurt.[11] What is essential indeed, in my view, are *mediating terms* that enable us both to analyze political orders and their dynamics descriptively and to develop normative reflections along the very *same* conceptual lines of analysis as in the descriptive work. The mediating term I have in mind is the concept of *justification*.

One might think that this is a typical move by a political philosopher bewitched by Plato, because the realm of justification is basically the realm of values, norms, and principles that might be required for normative reflection but is of little use when it comes to understanding real cave life political dynamics of interests, power struggles, institutional mechanisms, path-dependencies, and so on.[12] But this fear is unfounded, for I want to argue for a particular way of understanding the reality of interests, of power, and of historical situatedness. In my view, the *real reality* of politics, of the cave as well as of a perspective free (or, better, partially free) from the cave, is the *reality of justifications*. We learn to think politically and socially by understanding and using justifications about the foundations and the frameworks of our common life, accepting (often unreflexively), criticizing, and occasionally rejecting them, including some rather large and comprehensive narratives. There is no politics outside the realm of justifications. Every single political thought rests on assumptions about how our collective life is and ought to be ordered, and when we think about the "is"—as democratic, productive, one-sided, dysfunctional, or what have you—we use and reproduce justifications.

But note that to speak in this way does not mean that I am speaking of *good* justifications from a reflexive or even a Platonic viewpoint; rather, by justifications in an empirical and descriptive sense I refer to what makes people *effectively* think in certain ways and view reality in a certain light. My thesis, in short, is that we do not understand political reality if we do not have the conceptual tools to analyze the multiple—and often contradictory—justifications that constitute political reality as a reality of thought and action. We also do not understand how power works. Let me explain.

THE POWER OF JUSTIFICATIONS

I begin with a brief reflection on the concept of power, truly an essential concept for political science, for without power there is no collective normative order.[13]

Let us start with a sober definition of power, close to that of Robert Dahl, who suggested that "*A* has power over *B* to the extent that he can get *B* to do something that *B* would not otherwise do."[14] Note that B here is an agent who "does" something that A wants him or her to do—B is not a mere object, like a stone I kick away, but is still an agent with some freedom of action. So the exercise of power over B requires A to steer B's actions in such a way that they are still the actions of B, but that they now follow the lines intended by A. If B is an agent, the secret of power is to affect his or her agency internally. In other words, A has to "give" B a motivating reason to act in a particular way.

We can express this by reformulating Dahl's definition of power to say that *power is the capacity of A to motivate B to think or do something that B would otherwise not have thought or done*. Power on this definition is normatively neutral, for we need not take a stance (as many do) at this definitional level on whether what A motivates B to think or do is in B's interest or not—or whether it is justified or not. This is why (contrary to Lukes, for example) I do not think that the concept of power is "essentially contested."[15]

Note that our definition points to the fact that the real site of the resources for and the exercise of power is the cognitive realm, that is, the realm of justifications, since A needs to be able to affect and change the realm of motivational reasons for B. Thus we define power such that to have and exercise power means being able to influence, use, determine, occupy, or even seal off the space of reasons for others. Power in this sense comes in degrees and can be analyzed along a spectrum of intensities.

Our analysis is still normatively neutral, because the means that A uses to influence or colonize the realm of reasons or justifications for B can be a good speech, a sermon, an ideological world description, a lie, a threat, an order, or an act of seduction. Those who convince us as teachers or experts exercise power over us, and those who deceive us or who threaten us (credibly) do so, too. But all power is, as I put it, *noumenal* in nature—that is, it takes place in the realm of reasons and justifications. A credible threat (say, with a gun) "gives" you a reason to act in a certain way, as does an ideology. To be the subject of power means that the justifications that make you think or act in a certain way are determined in relevant ways by others: if the determining in question is unintentional, I call that an *effect* of power; if it is intentional, then it is an *exercise* of power.[16]

In this context, I use the terms "reason" or "justification" in a purely *descriptive* sense. Later, I will say something about good justifications and how they can be produced; but here it is important that we remain at a descriptive level. We fail to understand how power is exercised, either individually, collectively, or within structures, if we do not understand the justifications that guide people's actions, as those who have and those who are subject to power. We also do not understand power shifts, or what it means to lose or acquire more power, if we do not understand the justificatory dynamics in the noumenal realm of reasons. To (once again) prevent misunderstanding:[17] these reasons are for the most part not reflected upon or critically tested, but they are nevertheless effective reasons, reasons that "work." The notion of "noumenal" I am using here is an "impure" one, so to speak: it refers to the reasons that motivate us internally, but it does not imply that these are justified reasons based on some standard of reasonableness.

Based on such an analysis, we can distinguish more concrete forms of power:

Rule (*Herrschaft*) is a form of the exercise of power within structured relations based on certain understandings of legitimacy that support such structures—whatever they may rest on.

Domination (*Beherrschung*) exists where asymmetrical social and political relations backed by hegemonic justifications prevail that limit the space of justification either through ideological force or threats of violence (or both). Political domination exists in two dimensions: that of being ruled by unjustifiable norms and (as a higher-order form of domination) that of the lack of spheres and institutions of justification to discursively question dominant norms and construct alternative ones.

Violence (*Gewalt*) is an extreme form of the denial of justificatory standing to others, who are thereby reduced to mere physical objects to be moved or destroyed. Such acts often are meant to have noumenal effects of intimidation or deterrence. But with respect to those who are its direct objects, the use of violence may be a reflection of A having lost social power over them, because A no longer tries to move them internally as agents. Think of the kidnapper who kills his or her victim because the latter is not willing to comply or those who were supposed to pay the ransom refused to do so—which means that the kidnapper's power, as originally intended, fades away, and violence is a reflection of that loss of power. In more political terms, think of the moments at which the tanks in the street lose their power because people overcome their fear or are willing to take the risk of opposing them. Their physical power of destruction is the same as before, but because of a shift in the realm of justifications, their social power has been reduced.[18]

NARRATIVES, STRUCTURES, AND REALITY

Thinking realistically about politics requires that political scientists find ways to analyze and understand the justificatory dynamics that give rise to normative orders and that stabilize or destabilize them. I speak of normative orders as *orders of justification*, since they are based on, produce, and reproduce justifications for social and political structures and relations.[19] Normative orders in modern societies rest on complex narratives of justification that support existing power structures and enable individuals or groups to exercise power within such structures, that is, to use their noumenal capital as a power resource.[20] My analysis of power does not suggest that those who hold power can autonomously create a comprehensive social space of reasons for others; rather, they are able to use it in a particular way. Narratives of justification develop historically over long periods of time and form a space of social reasons that provides the justificatory resources for sustaining, changing, or rejecting particular normative orders.

Power struggles are struggles to position oneself and one's group within such a social realm in a particular way—and to influence the space of reasons for others. This is true for the nationalist who constructs a xenophobic narrative and for the revolutionary who rejects a dominant ideology. If we want to understand the power dynamics within certain normative orders, we need to understand the narratives of justification that dominant groups use and weave together—think of the many strands of discourse within a Trumpian universe, ranging from a Protestant work ethic to racial and racist discourses about who rightly owns a country, giving the term "democracy" an exclusionary meaning. Populists can only be successful if they manage to craft such narratives, combining different normative and historically situated sources and stories into a powerful way of looking at the world, what is wrong with it, and how to fix it.[21]

Such narratives of justification, combining national history, religious ideas, economic reflections, social structure, and so on, create social and political reality.[22] Occasionally, this looks like a dark cave reality, as when a certain ideology restricts the realm of justifications; but such realities can also be opened up, as occurs in a liberation struggle. Understanding political reality requires us to find ways to reconstruct dominant social narratives and their rivals. Only then can we understand why, for example, the concept of democracy, when placed in the justificatory realm of different societies, sometimes has the ring of liberation and sometimes that of colonization. As Seyla Benhabib argues in her interventions into debates about social criticism, it is necessary to locate such critique in the narratives that constitute "the horizon of our social lifeworld" and to show how "conflictual and irreconcilable" such narratives are, if we consider past struggles and their success or defeat.[23]

Can such narratives be reduced to social interests? I do not think so, for if we look at how interests get formed and defined, we eventually find: justifications. We can understand neither individual nor collective interests if we do not understand the "strong evaluations"[24] that lie at their basis—some possibly of religious origin, some guided by beliefs in security, material welfare, success, and so on. There is no basic raw empirical fact that determines what interests people have and pursue. We are justificatory beings all the way down and our interests depend on what we consider important and justified. True, we often "rationalize" and fabricate such justifications; but this is not because we do not see a justification for what we want but because we see that it is weak from a public perspective and try to bolster it. If we stick to narrow definitions of self-interest as determining people's behavior, we will never understand, for example, religious motives or the reasons why certain people support certain parties even to the detriment of their "self-interest." They may be victim to ideological justifications (justifying the unjustifiable), but still guided by (bad) reasons.

A REALISTIC NORMATIVE VIEW

If a realistic conception of political life needs to be sensitive to and analyze the justificatory resources that ground political reality, we can also develop a realistic *normative* perspective from within the cave—and go beyond it.

As I said, no normative order could exist if it was not supported by certain justifications. These have to be structurally reflected and reproduced, regardless of whether the order is a theocracy or a democracy. Following Bernard Williams, we can say that the first political question, that of securing a political order of security, stability, and cooperation, is a question of justification, such that there is a "basic legitimation demand" that requires the political order to "offer a justification of its power *to each subject*."[25] Williams draws some weak normative conclusions from this, namely, that basic political justification entails that those who are subject to rule must be offered good reasons why that is not a form of pure domination. But he also draws stronger conclusions when he argues that a purely self-serving justification cannot count as a justification: "power itself does not justify."[26] That is a normative, not a descriptive, statement, since power, of course, does justify itself (all the time) and produces justifications, though often in ideological ways. What Williams does is turn the notion of justification into a *normative* notion, adding criteria for a *good* political justification. And that leads him to a version of what he calls "the critical theory principle," modeled after Habermas's discourse theory, which states that "the acceptance of a justification does not count if the acceptance itself is produced by the coercive power which is supposedly being justified."[27]

Like Williams, I believe that this is a sound principle, but would add that it is a principle of reason. Reason is the faculty of justification, and normative criteria of good justifications—whether in science, politics, or art—are rational criteria.[28] We find such criteria not in a Platonic superworld of "real" values, but by reconstructing the criteria of validity immanent in the validity claims we make—and since the validity claim of a political norm is that it is generally and reciprocally valid, such norms must be justifiable in reciprocal and general terms.[29]

A STRONG NORMATIVE PROGRAM

This brief reflection on criteria of justification opens up the possibility of a strong normative program. I call this a strong program because it operates with heavy normative vocabulary, which, however, is grounded not in a Platonic higher reality but—along Kantian lines—in a constructivist reflection on what it means to understand ourselves as normative justificatory beings.[30] As such beings who use our faculty of reason to produce, test, and accept or reject justifications, we face the task of constructing a common world of norms that are binding on and justifiable to all who are subjected to them. As agents of construction, we ought to regard ourselves as equal authorities of the norms that bind us all equally and, as such authorities, we respect one another's *right to justification*.[31] The criteria of justification that hold between us as reasonable and responsible beings do not predetermine the content of our normative constructions, but they do determine the procedure of construction and thus also some content, given the respect we owe one another as constructive normative authorities. As such authorities, we are law-makers and law-takers at the same time, and thus the Kantian notion of *dignity* applies to us as subjects with rights and duties of justification.

Wait a minute, you might now object—how exactly did we get from the descriptive justificatory program to the strong normative one? For surely we never "are" equal normative authorities in the normative orders to which we are subject, and we probably never will be. That may hold true, I would reply, but if you agree with me that it is a serious deficiency of a political order that it does not respect its members as normative authorities who codetermine that order, you will also agree with me that we have to regard ourselves as beings owed recognition of our status as normative agents and equals, thus affirming that, in a normative sense, this is what we *are*—and, I add, what we *really* are.[32] So the thought of two realities comes back, but not, I think, in a paradoxical way—rather, in a dialectical fashion. Political science is a methodologically grounded reflection on who and what we are as political, justificatory beings, and it reveals to us that we are always members of different worlds—the world of real and effective justifications, and the world of the possibility of better justifications produced by us. This is not the true world of the ideal good, but a world of a better social and political practice than the one we live in. No actuality can eliminate that noumenal possibility completely for us.

Based on the notions of normative authority and the right to justification, which says that no one must be subject to norms, whether of a moral or a political-legal kind, that cannot be properly justified to him or her, other normative notions fall into place. Those *liberties* are justified that reflect the kind of freedom we have as equal normative authorities in the political and legal realm, that is, those liberties that cannot be reciprocally and generally rejected among normative equals. *Equality* means that from a moral point of view we are equals and that we have a basic claim to a secure and equal standing as non-dominated legal, political, and social subjects. *Domination* means being subject to a normative order without proper justification and without procedures and institutions of justification being in place; thus, non-domination in a legal, political, and social sense means having the *rights* that are required to be secure from such forms of domination and having opportunities to change the normative order one is subject to within adequate structures of collective justification.[33]

Democracy thus does not simply represent one "value" among others. Rather, it appears as the political practice of *justice*, as the institutionalization of a form of non-arbitrary political rule that reflects our standing as equal normative authorities, both in our roles as law-makers and as subjects of the law. Such a normative notion of democracy is surely a regulative notion that can only be attained in piecemeal fashion, but it is not based on an ideal form of the perfect democracy; rather, democracy progresses practically by transforming relations of rule and/or domination into relations of justification, aiming to establish a basic structure of justification that secures our standing as non-dominated, politically autonomous equals. That is how I interpret Benhabib's notion of "democratic iterations." The relevant structure of justification can be a national or a transnational structure, depending on the type of relations that need to be justified; the most important point is that those subject to this order should become its normative authority by way of proper institutions of collective justification.[34]

Such a notion of democracy as the practice of justice as justification enables us to avoid confusing democracy with the domination of minorities by majorities.[35] There is no such thing as illiberal or authoritarian democracy, just as there is no such thing as a democracy that produces structural social injustice; for all of these defects point to and create structures of exclusion that are unjustifiable among normative equals. Such deficiencies transform rule into domination.

CRITICAL THEORY

I apologize for the brevity of this introduction of the strong normative program. Here I could only outline the conceptual map of normative terms and how they fall into place. I have developed the corresponding program elsewhere and will not dwell on it further here. What I hope to have shown is how the choice of a mediating term like *justification* might help to overcome the alienation between the empirical and the normative aspects of our discipline. For if we find ways to analyze the political world of justifications—and especially of rivaling justifications—then we will also find ways to understand the power struggles that mark our present.

At the same time, we ought to shift our self-understanding in such a way that we recognize that we cannot simply observe the justificatory games we (or others) are part of from a view from nowhere.[36] We cannot describe them without some participation, as description requires understanding; we are always socially situated beings, as Benhabib argues. In addition, again following her and Habermas's critical hermeneutics, we have to take a reflexive stance, and that stance is one of evaluation and critical distance. Then we not only ask what the dominant narratives of justification are to which we are subject and how they are reproduced; we also ask whether they are *really* justified, knowing that in any enterprise of justification we are finite, fallible beings who can go wrong, both factually and normatively. But the faculty we call reason is the (finite) faculty to always ask for better justifications. Science is based on us using that faculty in the right way.

The synthesis of an empirical and a normative perspective on ourselves as justificatory beings and as members of normative orders that I have in mind is a program of critical theory. Such a theory I call a *critique of relations of justification*, and it involves five cardinal aspects.[37]

First, it calls for a scientific analysis of social and political relations of rule and/or domination that inquires into the structures of justification that reproduce such normative orders. How are justifications produced in such an order, and what are the main sources of justificatory power, ranging from institutions of the public sphere (media, churches, and the like), to economic and cultural power complexes, to institutionalized forms of decision-making and agenda-setting?

Second, it calls for a discourse-theoretical and genealogical reconstruction of the justification narratives that dominate a given space of reasons.[38] How did these narratives come about and what are their—possibly ideological—functions?

Third, we need methodological tools to criticize existing justifications of social and political relations. Are they based on proper empirical grounds and what are their normative premises, implications, and potential exclusions?

Fourth, given that a basic structure of justification is a demand of fundamental justice, such a theory must inquire into the possibilities and forces of establishing such a structure, given certain path-dependencies and the reality of rule and/or domination exercised, both within and beyond states.

Fifth, such a theory must be able to account for its own normativity in a self-reflexive, critical way. Ideally, it uses the principle of rational critique as the basis for its own constructive arguments. Thus, for example, it does not use a reified or ethnocentric notion of "false consciousness" or "true interests" when it comes to defining ideology; rather, it calls those justifications ideological that lend reciprocally and generally unjustifiable social relations the appearance of being justified.

WITHIN AND BEYOND THE CAVE

I do not want to imply that every serious social science should aim at such a synthesis of empirical and normative research in a critical spirit—an endeavor that also calls for a great deal of combined expertise. I propose it as an example for the productive work that a mediating term like justification can perform in combining the two perspectives. Then they no longer look like the antagonistic views of the cave versus that of the moral good; rather, using that mediating term enables us to see how the empirical and the normative are conceptually connected. By using the principle and the right of justification as normative foundations that are both *immanent* to practices and *transcend* them, we can avoid stale distinctions between ideal and realistic theory, while nevertheless gaining the critical distance toward social and political reality that every scientific enterprise requires. Science enables us to model reality in such a way that we can rationally understand it and orient ourselves within it. That is as true of social science (and philosophy) as it is of natural science; all that we need are the right methodological tools. Understanding and evaluating our political world as one of justifications is a way to make good on that promise.

Politics is a power struggle—as a struggle for justification: a struggle for the dominance of some justifications, and a struggle against them becoming dominant. In these power dynamics, the question of justification is often used strategically and ideologically to construct a false reality, a reality of caves. In such a rage against reality, correct news gets called fake news, indigent migrants become enemies of the people, economic exploitation becomes invisible, and so on. This leads to what I call *crises of justification*, meaning not only that we are in danger of losing sight of the criteria for proper justifications, but also that institutions for reflecting on and producing legitimate collective justifications are in danger of becoming eroded and disappearing once people forget what their purpose and ground was.

In such times of crisis, we do not need Platonic sages. But we do need critical theories that uphold the one quest that in social and political life must never rest: the quest for better, real, reciprocal, and general justifications. That we have the right to demand such justifications is as important an insight as are the many ways of uncovering how that right is constantly denied through the fabrication of false realities. The critique of such false realities is as much a task of philosophy and social science today as it was in Socrates's time—perhaps even more so. So Plato was right: Do not cling to your caves.

NOTES

I presented earlier versions of this text as a keynote at the general conference of the European Consortium for Political Research in Hamburg (August 2018) and at the annual conference of the network Economic Research on Identity, Norms and Narratives in London (June 2019). I thank Peter Niesen and George Akerlof for the respective invitations. Thanks also to Ciaran Cronin for correcting my English. These thoughts were developed in the course of our collective work in Frankfurt on Normative Orders, and I thank Klaus Günther especially for the longtime collaboration. The dialogue with Seyla Benhabib has been an inspiration from early on, when I started to form my thoughts. I dedicate this text to her.

1. This paradoxical problem has led to a number of reactions in the history of political theory, for example, to Hannah Arendt's distinction between philosophical truth and political opinion or to the distinction between a secret doctrine of political philosophy and one that can be communicated publicly by Leo Strauss. See Hannah Arendt, "Philosophy and Politics," *Social Research* 71, no. 3 (2004): 427–54; and Leo Strauss, *Persecution or the Art of Writing* (Chicago: University of Chicago Press, 1988). See also Michael Walzer, "Philosophy and Democracy," *Political Theory* 9, no. 3 (1981): 379–99; and Sheldon S. Wolin, *Politics and Vision: Continuity and Innovation in Western Political Thought* (Boston: Little, Brown, 1960). For a more recent discussion of realism, see Matt Sleat, ed., *Politics Recovered: Realist Thought in Theory and Practice* (New York: Columbia University Press, 2018); and Charles Larmore, *What Is Political Philosophy?* (Princeton, NJ: Princeton University Press, 2020).
2. See Thomas Nagel, *The View from Nowhere* (Oxford: Oxford University Press, 1986).
3. See Max Weber, *The Vocation Lectures* (Indianapolis: Hackett, 2004).
4. For example, David Estlund, *Utopophobia: On the Limits (If Any) of Political Philosophy* (Princeton, NJ: Princeton University Press, 2020).
5. See Amy Allen, *The End of Progress: Decolonizing the Normative Foundations of Critical Theory* (New York: Columbia University Press, 2016). See also the debate between Amy Allen and me in *Justification and Emancipation: The Critical Theory of Rainer Forst*, ed. Amy Allen and Eduardo Mendieta (University Park: Pennsylvania State University Press, 2019), chaps. 9 and 10.
6. See Rainer Forst, "Two Bad Halves Don't Make a Whole: On the Crisis of Democracy," *Constellations* 26, no. 3 (2019): 378–83.
7. Seyla Benhabib, *Situating the Self: Gender, Community and Postmodernism in Contemporary Ethics* (New York: Routledge, 1992), chap. 5.
8. Seyla Benhabib, *The Rights of Others: Aliens, Residents and Citizens* (Cambridge: Cambridge University Press, 2004), 19.
9. Benhabib, *Situating the Self*, 139.
10. For some discussions between us, from which I benefited enormously, see Forst, "Situations of the Self: Reflections on Seyla Benhabib's Version of Critical Theory," *Philosophy and Social Criticism* 23 (1997): 79–96; with a reply by Seyla Benhabib in the same issue: "On Reconciliation and Respect, Justice and the Good Life: Response to Herta Nagl-Docekal and Rainer Forst," *Philosophy and Social Criticism* 23 (1997): 97–114; and Seyla Benhabib, "The Uses and Abuses of Kantian Rigorism: On Rainer

11. Forst's Moral and Political Philosophy," *Political Theory* 43, no. 6 (2015): 777–92; and Forst, "The Right to Justification: Moral and Political, Transcendental and Historical: Reply to Seyla Benhabib, Jeff Flynn and Matthias Fritsch," *Political Theory* 43, no. 6 (2015): 822–37.
11. See Rainer Forst and Klaus Günther, eds., *Die Herausbildung normativer Ordnungen* (Frankfurt: Campus, 2011); and Rainer Forst and Klaus Günther, eds., *Normative Ordnungen* (Berlin: Suhrkamp, 2021).
12. See Raymond Geuss, *Philosophy and Real Politics* (Princeton: Princeton University Press, 2008).
13. See on the following my article on "noumenal power," originally in the *Journal of Political Philosophy* 23, no. 2 (June 2015): 111–27; also in my *Normativity and Power: Analyzing Social Orders of Justification* (Oxford: Oxford University Press, 2017), chap. 2.
14. Robert A. Dahl, "The Concept of Power," *Behavioral Science* 2, no. 3 (1957): 202–3.
15. Compare the countercriticism of Steven Lukes, "Noumenal Power: Concept and Explanation," *Journal of Political Power* 11, no. 1 (2018): 46–55; and my reply in Rainer Forst, "Noumenal Power Revisited: Reply to Critics," *Journal of Political Power* 11, no. 3 (2018): 294–321. The debate (together with other critical exchanges) can also be found in Mark Haugaard and Matthias Kettner, ed., *Theorising Noumenal Power: Rainer Forst and His Critics* (London: Routledge, 2020).
16. On this difficulty, see the critiques by Lukes, "Noumenal Power: Concept and Explanation"; Clarissa R. Hayward, "On Structural Power," *Journal of Political Power* 11, no. 1 (2018): 1–12; and John P. McCormick, "'A Certain Relation in the Space of Justifications': Intentions, Lateral Effects and Rainer Forst's Concept of Noumenal Power," in Allen and Mendieta, *Justification and Emancipation*, chap. 6, as well as my replies in Forst, "Noumenal Power Revisited," and Rainer Forst, "Navigating a World of Conflict and Power: Reply to Critics," in Allen and Mendieta, *Justification and Emancipation*, chap. 10.
17. Examples are Lois McNay, "The Limits of Justification: Critique, Disclosure, and Reflexivity," and Sameer Bajaj and Enzo Rossi, "Noumenal Power, Reasons, and Justification: A Critique of Forst," both in *Constitutionalism Justified: Rainer Forst in Dialogue*, ed. Ester Herlin-Karnell and Matthias Klatt (Oxford: Oxford University Press, 2019), chaps. 6 and 7. See my replies in Rainer Forst, "The Constitution of Justification: Replies and Comments," in the same volume, chap. 13. See also David Owen, "Power, Justification and Vindication," in Rainer Forst, *Toleration, Power and the Right to Justification: Rainer Forst in Dialogue* (Manchester: Manchester University Press, 2020), chap. 8; and my reply, "The Dialectics of Toleration and the Power of Reason(s): Reply to My Critics," in the same volume, chap. 9.
18. This has been an important insight by Hannah Arendt, though she uses the term "violence" in a broader way. See especially her "On Violence" in Hannah Arendt, *Crisis of the Republic* (San Diego: Harvest, 1972), 103–84; and the illuminating discussions in Seyla Benhabib, *The Reluctant Modernism of Hannah Arendt* (London: Sage, 1996), chaps. 3–6.
19. On this see Rainer Forst, *Justification and Critique: Towards a Critical Theory of Politics* (Cambridge: Polity, 2014); and Forst, *Normativity and Power*.

20. See Rainer Forst, "On the Concept of a Justification Narrative," in *Normativity and Power*, chap. 3.
21. See Jan-Werner Müller, *What Is Populism?* (Philadelphia: University of Pennsylvania Press, 2016); and Yascha Mounk, *The People Versus Democracy: Why Our Freedom Is in Danger and How to Save It* (Cambridge, MA: Harvard University Press, 2018).
22. See Charles Tilly, *Why? What Happens When People Give Reasons . . . and Why* (Princeton, NJ: Princeton University Press, 2006).
23. Benhabib, *Situating the Self*, 226.
24. Charles Taylor, *Human Agency and Language* (Cambridge: Cambridge University Press, 1985).
25. Bernard Williams, *In the Beginning Was the Deed* (Princeton: Princeton University Press, 2005), 4.
26. Williams, 5.
27. Williams, 6.
28. See Forst, *Normativity and Power*, chap. 1.
29. On the notion of validity claims, see Jürgen Habermas, *Moral Consciousness and Communicative Action* (Cambridge: Polity, 1990), as well as my analysis in Rainer Forst, *The Right to Justification: Elements of a Constructivist Theory of Justice* (New York: Columbia University Press, 2012), pt. 1.
30. See Rainer Forst, *Die noumenale Republik: Kritischer Konstruktivismus nach Kant* (Berlin: Suhrkamp, 2021).
31. Forst, *The Right to Justification*.
32. See Rainer Forst, "Noumenal Alienation: Rousseau, Kant and Marx on the Dialectics of Self-Determination," *Kantian Review* 22, no. 4 (2017): 523–51.
33. See Rainer Forst, "The Justification of Basic Rights: A Discourse-Theoretical Approach," *Netherlands Journal of Legal Philosophy* 45, no. 3 (2016): 7–28.
34. See Rainer Forst, "A Critical Theory of Transnational (In-)Justice: Realistic in the Right Way," in *The Oxford Handbook of Global Justice*, ed. Thom Brooks (Oxford: Oxford University Press, 2020), chap. 22.
35. See Forst, "Two Bad Halves Don't Make a Whole"; and Rainer Forst, "The Neglect of Democracy," *Los Angeles Review of Books Blog*, December 1, 2020.
36. See Theodor W. Adorno et al., *The Positivist Dispute in German Sociology* (London: Heinemann, 1976).
37. See Forst, *Justification and Critique*.
38. An example for this is the analysis conducted by Luc Boltanski and Laurent Thévenot, *On Justification: Economies of Worth* (Princeton, NJ: Princeton University Press, 2006), in which the term "Poleis" is used.

3
Loss of World, Not Certainty

"Amor Mundi" and the Moral Psychology of Seyla Benhabib

CARMEN LEA DEGE

Seyla Benhabib's 1992 book *Situating the Self* has been discussed by a broad range of scholars who rightly read it as an account that stakes out a middle ground between liberal, communitarian, and postmodern theories of gender and social criticism.[1] Benhabib's self is not as disembodied and abstracted from the concrete lifeworld as the subjects in Rawls's original position; she also resists the essentializing effects of group identities that communitarians struggle to curb; and she retains a sense of autonomy, judgment, and agency against and beyond the pervasive dynamics of power—something Benhabib has always found lacking in Foucauldian approaches. What the literature has discussed less, however, is the insightful anthropology of moral experience that undergirds Benhabib's idea of selfhood.

This essay returns to *Situating the Self* against the backdrop of a debate rekindled by Jürgen Habermas's most recent intervention. In *This Too a History of Philosophy*, Habermas charts a course for how we can (still) have faith in reason if modernity produces the technological, economic, and political conditions that debilitate and destroy the normative resources necessary to sustain it. What are the motivational and normative conditions of possibility, he asks, that could nevertheless encourage the modern self to take up a life of autonomous reason in a postmetaphysical world?

In *Situating the Self* and writings that followed, Benhabib offers a perceptive answer to Habermas's question that has remained neglected so far. By emphasizing the role of the concrete other in relation to the more abstract and formal universalism of postmetaphysical reason, Benhabib presents an immanent critique of Habermas's response to his own question. In particular, two aspects of her concept of the self stand out: First, Benhabib shifts the focus of motivation from the certainty of essences to a communicative practice of being-in-the-world. While her approach remains clearly Hegelian in the sense that self-transformation is motivated by an initial loss of certainty, moments of disenchantment or epistemological crisis are less of a concern or problem for her than for Habermas. I argue that this is the case because, in line with the political existentialism of Hannah Arendt, Benhabib values uncertainty as a fundamental part of the human condition. The loss of certainty does not need to provoke a longing for its return; it can also enable the self to become aware of the complex web of relations that sustains the world. In this sense, the collapse of certainty is the precondition for the self to love the world despite everything and act in it. Benhabib's self is a "world-loving self." Second, while existence might precede essence in terms of motivation, Benhabib criticizes some implications of Arendt's existentialist concept of *amor mundi*, particularly its lack of morality. In a second step, therefore, she explores the conditions of possibility for a moral commitment to the world. How is motivation structured to give rise to moral action and political agency? The rationality of science and law as well as the utopian dimension of politics and ethics becomes indispensable for Benhabib's idea of selfhood. Embedded in the mediations of the concrete and the universal, she calls herself the "social critic."

In this chapter, I shall first illustrate how in *Situating the Self* the social critic emerges from a dialogic struggle with three personas: the liberal, the romantic, and the postmodern self. The social critic emancipates herself from these three ideas of selfhood by calling into question their fundamental desire for certainty. This demand for certainty in modern conceptions of self is so pervasive that even the postmodern self's eschewal of truth and subjectivity can morph into a certitude of uncertainty itself. In a second step I follow the social critic and investigate what she calls her home, namely, the "space outside the city walls." I want to explore how the mediation of diverse perspectives—the active commitment to "in-betweenness"—can form and sustain the self's moral motivation. I finally return to Habermas and offer an immanent critique of his thesis of a normative deficit in modernity that demotes certainty in favor of worldliness.

THREE STORIES OF THE LOSS OF CERTAINTY

An underexplored dimension of *Situating the Self* consists in the book's subtle, persistent, and yet balanced critique of moral and epistemic certainty and the role it plays for human motivation. Benhabib forcefully comments on the role of certainty in political philosophy and criticizes what she considers the dominant response to the loss of certainty: gaining a new form of certitude, on a different, possibly higher level of development until the self is confronted with yet another challenge, picks up the broken pieces, and asserts herself anew. Benhabib argues that an alternative response to the loss of certainty is possible that is grounded in the in-betweenness of worldly spaces. The book therefore traces how the social critic emerges from a dynamic interaction with three types of self who constitute important perspectives of the modern world to which the social critic remains indebted.

Benhabib's self assumes a standpoint of critique that is based on what these three personas and their traditions have in common: all three place the loss of control and certainty at the core of their ethics, morality, and politics. As a result, they mutually reinforce the thesis that modernity is constituted by a normative deficit. (1) The liberal or Promethean self is primarily driven by a loss of mastery: both its embeddedness in the larger divine cosmos and its trust in the other are broken. In response, it turns to rationality, science, and the law to protect itself, reestablish control, and place a limit on moral arbitrariness. (2) The communitarian or romantic self accuses the Promethean self of exacerbating the disembedding effects from nature and tradition. It is motivated by the loss of wholeness, alienation, and a sense of anomie to which it seeks to respond through networks of compassion, care, and community. (3) In postmodern and poststructural theories, finally, we find a more affirmative or even jubilant story of the loss of absolutism, be it in the form of the death of God, knowledge, or the subject who is no longer master in her own house. The conceptions of selfhood are shaped by relations of power that are historically situated at all times. Uncertainty is not to be tamed or escaped from, but is the only condition we can be certain about. In this sense, the postmodern self turns contingency itself into a new form of certitude. These fundamentally different stories all regard the desire for certainty as an expression of moral experience. What motivates the modern self is the desire to become whole again and own itself based on an essentialized understanding of either being or nothingness.

Benhabib identifies the anthropological bedrock of the Promethean self with the medieval nominalism, modern science, and emergence of capitalist exchange relations that shook the Aristotelian-Christian worldview out of its slumber. However, the self's emancipation from cosmology and scholasticism also confronted it with fear and uncertainty. According to Benhabib, the distinction between justice and the good life, as formulated by early contract theorists, seeks to respond to this sense of loss by institutionalizing the ambivalence of scientific mastery at the heart of the modern self. Hence, the private sphere protects the embedded sense of self while justice becomes the center of moral and political theory where "bourgeois individuals in a disenchanted universe face the task of creating the legitimate basis of the social order for themselves."[2] As a result, the state of nature metaphor turns into the looking glass in which early bourgeois thinkers captured the ambivalent loss of certainty. "The state of nature is both nightmare (Hobbes) and utopia (Rousseau). In it the bourgeois male recognizes his flaws, fears and anxieties, as well as dreams."[3] Hobbes profoundly captured the anthropology of this modern self: "Let us ... consider men as if but even now sprung out of the earth, and suddenly, like mushrooms, come to full maturity, without all kind of engagement to each other."[4] This vision of men as mushrooms and the image of mushrooms as self-contained rather than highly interdependent is symptomatic of a narcissist who sees the world in his own image. Eventually, Benhabib points out, the experience of loss was turned into a "saga of loss" and narcissism became the mental structure of liberalism's response.

Benhabib compares this state of mind to the learning process that Hegel's *Phenomenology of Spirit* traces for the development of self-consciousness. The traumatic moment happens when self-consciousness is faced by another self-consciousness and can no longer be certain of its truth. It loses itself and finds itself again as another being that "has superseded the other, for it does not see the other as an essential being, but in the other sees its own self."[5] Loss becomes the spur to a new level of mastery. Even if the self changes, the logic of the Promethean self persists. "The story of the autonomous male ego is the saga of this initial sense of loss in confrontation with the other, and the gradual recovery from this original narcissistic wound through the sobering experience of war, fear, domination, anxiety and death. The last installment in this drama is the social contract: the establishment of the law to govern all."[6] Showing clear reminiscences of Theodor Adorno and Max Horkheimer's *Dialectic of Enlightenment*, Benhabib indicates that this bourgeois learning process does not cure narcissism.[7] It rather establishes legally defined ego boundaries that shift people's attention "from war to property, from vanity to science, from conquest to luxury." The liberal response to uncertainty does not transform but instead tames and disciplines the originally wounded narcissist. "The law reduces insecurity, the fear of being engulfed by the other, by defining mine and thine. . . . The law teaches how to repress anxiety and to sober narcissism, but the constitution of the self is not altered. The establishment of private rights and duties does not overcome the inner wounds of the self; it only forces them to become less destructive."[8] In this world, the experience of the concrete other has no place. Even if she is endowed with universal rights in principle, she first has to realize a certain level of self-consciousness in order to be recognized and let into the public sphere. Until then, she is kept waiting in the "ante-chamber of history." She cares, struggles, and fails "in a timeless universe, condemned to repeat the cycles of life."[9]

The romantic self attempts to fill this vacuum by shifting our focus to the meaningfulness and coherence of life forms. In doing so, it intends to resist the generalized view of justice and its alleged distortions of the nature of our moral experiences. Within the chest of the Promethean ego "clash the law of reason and the inclination of nature, the brilliance of cognition and the obscurity of emotion. Caught between the moral law and the starry heaven above and the earthly body below, the autonomous self strives for unity."[10] Driven by the same quest for unity, yet armed with the force of authenticity and passion, the romantic concept of selfhood marks the flip side of liberal individualism and moves into the homes of concrete selves. It carves out a vision of solidarity based on a sense of "value homogeneity among individuals" and, in doing so, risks drowning the other in a sea of sameness.[11] Moreover, posing the homogenous community as a source of meaning for individuals brings with it the violence of exclusion and policing of the boundaries of identity. As an alternative, Benhabib suggests a *participatory* communitarian self who can complement liberal and romantic strands and "see the problems of modernity less in the loss of a sense of belonging, oneness and solidarity but more in the sense of a loss of political agency and efficacy."[12]

Intervening in this back and forth between the liberal and romantic self, the postmodern self provides a third response to the loss of unity. It shares with the romantic self a deep sense of disenchantment with the project of modernity and considers progress an illusion. It rejects metanarratives of human emancipation and considers the modern ideal of reason complicit in and inseparable from the destruction of plurality and freedom. But unlike the romantic self, the postmodern self does not lament the loss of belonging but turns it into the opportunity of liberation. In embracing the impossibility of mastery, it removes the sting of loss and grounds human life firmly in uncertainty. Similar to the existentialism of Nietzsche and Heidegger, the self discovers itself resolutely by staring into the abyss and confronting its own nothingness. The postmodern translation of the existential lack results in replacing the subject in its entirety with "a system of structures, oppositions and différances which, to be intelligible, need not be viewed as products of a living subjectivity at all."[13]

As she discusses in her "Fragments of an Intellectual Biography" in this volume, Benhabib was never willing to give up this living subjectivity, which, for her, constitutes human agency. She writes in *Situating the Self*, "Surely, a subjectivity that would not be structured by language, by narrative and by the symbolic codes of narrative available in a culture is unthinkable." The postmodern self, she continues, can "teach us the theoretical and political traps of why utopias and foundational thinking can go wrong," but without acknowledging the existence of the subject, "not only morality but also radical transformation is [equally] unthinkable."[14] There is no question for Benhabib that the goals of emancipatory struggles like feminism are incompatible with "the Death of the Subject thesis."[15] It is important to note that this position does not simply reflect a normative preference on Benhabib's side; it rather results from a deep contradiction that she finds embedded in postmodern conceptions of selfhood: the nonexisting subject remains bound to the logic of certainty it seeks to overcome. The denial of subjectivity advances an epistemic standpoint that, with almost positivistic scrutiny, exposes the myth of an autonomous doer behind the deed. The knowledge of power that it produces does not envision social change. Yet, Benhabib counters, "we are not merely extensions of our histories, ... vis-à-vis our own stories we are in the position of author and character at once." The postmodern self cannot be author and character at once; it cannot grasp how "the situated and gendered subject is heteronomously determined but still strives toward autonomy."[16] The motivational and normative resources of critique remain unclear. What is more, its epistemological bent might even turn the postmodern self into a cynical spectator who disavows political or ethical commitments for fear of ideological complicity. This kind of pessimism, Benhabib worries, "retreat[s] from utopia." It ironically withdraws to a standpoint of unmediated certainty that is removed from the radical critique that difference can forcefully inspire.

Unlike the postmodern self, Benhabib's social critic comes to identify her sense of agency with the moral view of the world. Looking at her action from the perspective of the world, she comes to love its plurality, diversity, and contingency as the precondition of her own appearance. The loss of certainty opens her eyes to the multilayered web of human relations for which the world provides a home. The fragility of this world, which is made and not found, encourages her to become creative, to use her own agency and help to build and cultivate the web of entangled realities. In other words, the source of moral motivation is no longer the desire for certainty but the love of the world.

In engaging with the three contesting stories of selfhood, Benhabib carves out a space of communicative reflexivity that integrates parts of each story. The social critic embraces the standpoint of the concrete other in order to mediate it with the moral universalism of the generalized other and retrieve an emancipatory-utopian potential from this dialectic, which Benhabib also terms the perspective of the wholly other.

OCCUPYING A SPACE OUTSIDE THE CITY WALLS

The social critic that emerges in the space among the three other personas finds herself returning to an idea of moral motivation that is invested in the concrete interactions of subject and object and their distinct sense of agency. Without denying the importance of harmony and stability, Benhabib cautions that the normative problems of modernity might not chiefly be caused by the loss of belonging, consistency, and oneness, but by the loss of an agentive relation to the world. The social critic can be characterized as a world-loving self that places being-in-the-world prior to the essences of identity, class, and knowledge. It demotes the significance of certainty in favor of a living subjectivity. Importantly, however, this existentialist self remains indebted to the moral and political values of freedom and equality. As a result, the social critic inhabits the places between home and exile and settles in "a space outside the walls of the city,"[17] which allows her to form part of a dialectical learning process between perspectives that transform in light of the larger horizon of the world.

As one possible illustration, this movement could be described in the following way: The social critic questions the tendency in liberalism that identifies justice alone as the center of moral theory. She does so from the standpoint of the concrete other who calls our attention to the mental economy of loss. With the onset of liberalism, *political* patriarchy might have been destroyed, but it has returned in the form of *legal* patriarchy in property laws and market rules. In other words, the initial loss of control is not eliminated but tamed. The social critic might argue that the law can contain anxiety by defining rigidly the boundaries between self and other, but the law does not cure anxiety. On the other hand, she values the standpoint of the generalized other without whom we might overrate concerns of love, care, and unity. The generalized other helps to defend the universalism of the law against both an exclusionary ethics and a politics of purity. This perspective can further teach us that enlarged thought is not based on empathy alone. In fact, it might give rise to an emancipatory-utopian horizon and an insistence that no idea of concrete subjectivity can *assume* the standpoint of what remains irreducibly other. Yet again, the social critic remains committed and distanced at once. She also discerns a risk in the liberating effects of the utopian dimension, once it returns us back to an allegedly natural background of givenness and thrownness or an infinite diffusion of data points and signifiers. Against both the postmodern prioritization of difference and the romantic insistence on authenticity and reconciliation, Benhabib has never tired of emphasizing that *zoe* does not dissolve back into *bios* but emerges out of it, which requires democratic action, political institutions, and normative principles.[18]

This dialectical learning process of the social critic is demanding. As Benhabib stresses, it involves not simply a cognitive capacity but also complex psychological and motivational dimensions.[19] Tolerance of diversity, ambiguity, and contradiction plays an especially important role. Benhabib argues that the frequently expressed desire of "being at home with myself" is overrated, and it is no mistake that the figures whose agencies emerge in her works are ones whose claim to home is most unstable: exiles, refugees and the stateless, excluded groups, and women. She thus claims that Walt Whitman's lines are of central importance to moral psychology: "Do I contradict myself? Very well then I contradict myself, I am large, I contain multitudes."[20] In this spirit, and against those who follow the modern saga of loss, Benhabib unabashedly embraces the Benjaminian pearl diver:

> I regard neither the plurality and variety of goodnesses with which we have to live in a disenchanted universe nor the loss of certainty in moral theory to be a cause of distress. Under conditions of value differentiation, we have to conceive of the unity of reason not in the image of a homogeneous, transparent glass sphere into which we can fit all our cognitive and value commitments, but more as bits and pieces of dispersed crystals whose contours shine out from under the rubble.[21]

Dispersion, plurality, and multiplicity are invaluable for the social critic and her love of the world. Benhabib noticed that Arendt's concept of *amor mundi* and worldliness curiously mirrors Arendt's own ambivalent entanglements. In proceeding from the failure of philosophy to restore a sense of being-at-home-in-the-world, she worked herself out of and yet remained indebted to the Heideggerian search for authenticity (*Eigentlichkeit*). But unlike Heidegger's concept of dwelling, worldliness does not require a sense of rooted belonging. In these moments, Benhabib argues, Arendt sympathized more with Benjamin's fragmentary methodology according to which the sense of home can only be preserved if it reflects the failed hopes and efforts of world-building.[22] In her most recent book, *Exile, Statelessness, and Migration*, Benhabib further explores this world-loving ability to connect fragmentariness and imaginative normativity and envision a culture in which "those who are not at home can nonetheless find a home": "The much-maligned term 'multiculturalism' cannot capture the complexities of creating a culture in which those who are not at home can nonetheless find a home; a culture in which those who feel their otherness can nonetheless create a new vocabulary such as to extend the limits of our imagination by making us aware of the multiplicity within each of us."[23] Culture, vocabulary, and imagination mark the conditions of possibility that enable us to expose the multiplicity that is already within us. These conditions enable us to take the standpoint of the other while keeping the distance between us. We are thus able to "create that negotiable in-betweenness, through which I come to respect you as my equal, as the bearer of shared universal human dignity."[24] Taking all three perspectives together, that negotiable in-betweenness is a world-loving space: the other is concrete and therefore both irreducibly different and equal to oneself. Once these perspectives are connected and this culture of in-betweenness weaves a "web of narratives" that knits the multiplicity of human affairs together, the world comes into being.[25] In the constant and inevitable tension between the standpoint of the I and the other, "the perspectivality of the world [is] lodged."[26]

In his most recent book, *Migrants in the Profane: Critical Theory and the Question of Secularization*, Peter Gordon beautifully expands on Benhabib's perspectival notion of home reflected by the world-loving self. Along the lines of Adorno's witty remark that "it is part of morality not to be at home in one's home," he proposes the view that we are all migrants.[27] As Benhabib before, he cautions against taking this anthropological statement to imply a romantic idealization of homelessness. "The suffering of those who find themselves forced—whether by war, violence, or poverty—to flee the places where they have lived is a genuine affliction, and it is one that must be remedied through practical action, not inflated into a mere signature of the human condition." While resisting such romanticization, Gordon argues that the migrant mirrors an ambiguous and normatively significant problem-space in which the impossibility and necessity of home overlap and animate social critique. "The thought that we are all in a very deep sense homeless should inform how we conceive of home, and it should help us sustain a posture of openness and welcome toward all those who come from elsewhere."[28] This sense of homelessness acknowledges the historical, political, and psychological presence of Promethean ideas but questions their dominance. The fact that no identity can claim for itself an authentic existence that is free of contradiction is the essential background against which being-at-home-in-the-world can become possible.

(RE)TURNING TO HABERMAS: ON THE NORMATIVE AND MOTIVATIONAL SOURCES OF MODERNITY

As I have shown, in contrast to the three traditions discussed in *Situating the Self*, the social critic does not tame, escape, or romanticize the loss of certainty because it is against the background of this loss that the speech and action of a world-loving self can emerge. It therefore comes as no surprise that Benhabib, despite and because of her great indebtedness to Habermas's project, has consistently demanded a more plural and discordant view of modern life. This view concedes to Habermas that postmetaphysical reason requires sources of meaning and normativity including religion, but it raises questions about a privileged role of religion and the idea that religious sources can teach us, by way of translation, how to overcome motivational problems in postmetaphysical societies. According to Habermas, the continuous existence of religion indexes both the normative deficit of modernity and the experience of cognitive dissonance. Habermas therefore describes religion as "a thorn in the flesh of modernity" or "an alter ego that has become an old stranger in the modern house."[29] In an attempt to resolve this dissonance, he suggests that postmetaphysical thinking is able to redeem the normative potentials of religious traditions while situating its rationalizing translation squarely within mundane life. On this view, Habermas's postmetaphysical self can strengthen the autonomy and binding force of postmetaphysical reason and attenuate the pain of loss.

While in *Situating the Self* Benhabib still criticizes Habermas for relying too heavily on the Promethean self and its generalized other, she now criticizes his integration of liberal and romantic conceptions of selfhood in ways that remain bound to the saga of loss and its exclusion of the concrete other.[30] I argue that a powerful critique emerges that traces the suspicious absence of the concrete other in Habermas's account not to a missing idea of inclusion on the part of his postmetaphysical self but to a confusion of normativity with certainty. If societies based on religious agnosticism and tolerance are not less stable or expressive of meaning than premodern societies full of interfaith disputes and theological war, Benhabib asks, why then primarily turn to religion, and to Western European Protestantism in particular? From the perspective of the social critic, both Habermas's diagnosis and his cure of a normative deficit in modernity are predicated on a flawed moral anthropology that does not engage with experiences of embodiment, agency, and imagination in between (post)modern certainties and beyond European history.

In her recent commentary on Habermas's latest opus, Benhabib alerts us to the problem that the book's conversation about modern normativity takes place without women's voices and without cross-cultural engagement. There is a strong affinity between his concept of learning process, the Hegelian idea of self-development, and the extent to which it is placed within the problem zone of certainty. Self-consciousness emerges, flounders, and reemerges in a dialogic learning process that shows clear similarities to the dialectical mediation of the social critic. But Habermas's interpretation shares more with the Promethean tradition in which the experience of articulating a certainty that fails to be generalizable propels consciousness onward to ever-new truth claims. Although Habermas distances himself from Hegel's absolutism, he restricts the intersubjectively integrated community of learners to white, male thinkers in the public sphere of occidental reason. According to Benhabib, they constitute "a hypostatized collective subject in a homogeneous time that is viewed as a 'container' of development rather than as experiencing temporality as lived, discontinuous and contradictory experience." In other words, Habermas's history of philosophy tends toward historicism—it ignores and brackets "the voices of those others who are left out of the 'learning process' as it inexorably carries on forwards."[31]

Reentering the dynamic field of the concrete, generalized, and wholly other, and inhabiting the space outside the city walls, Benhabib alternatively points to Kant's attempt at writing a universal history. While "Habermas's *history of philosophy*, despite its intentions, becomes a *philosophy of history*," Kant held on to a normative perspective in light of what "he and his contemporaries did *not* know." With a *cosmopolitan intent*, he addressed humanity as a *conjectural* subject of history. "The subject of such history was a mankind-to-be—'une humanité à venir.'"[32] Since "neither genealogy nor phenomenology suffice to establish the *normativity of modernity*," this uncertainty is foundational. It shows that any narrative of the normativity of modernity needs to be global and include "the *plurality of voices* that are usually not heard."[33]

This does not imply that the notion of progress is abandoned. Invoking the perspective of the generalized other from the angle of concrete otherness, Benhabib argues "that the spread of universal human rights, despite their use and abuse by many to serve their own imperialist and neo-colonial aims, represents progress in human affairs." But the question of progress in history remains a speculative one; we cannot determine it with certainty. Navigating this ambiguity of the concrete, universal, and utopian means that we "*defend partial domains* in which progress has occurred, and recall that it was never without loss, tragedy and conflict."[34] In Habermas, conflict is not tragic. On the contrary, it indicates forms of cognitive dissonance that are resolved in learning processes.

Hence, when Habermas expresses concern about artificial intelligence, robotics, and genetic manipulation, a humanity that manufactures life, he proposes to defend universal human rights from the standpoint of a fallibilistic consciousness that learns from religious normativity without depending on its metaphysical authority. Unsurprisingly, Benhabib chooses a different response to the challenge of genetic manipulation. The problem for her is less that we lack an authority that speaks to people's hearts in ways religion has done and still does. The problem is that we lack a relationship to the world that is not primarily structured along the lines of mastery and control:

> No parent ought to have the means to *design* into existence a child with blue eyes and the IQ of a genius, for example. The element of genetic unpredictability that accompanies every act of birth is a pre-condition for human freedom. We are reminded here of Hannah Arendt's concept of "natality": the birth of each child heralds a new beginning because the actions and words of each child are different from another, and unpredictably so. . . . Natality means that children are not products of their parents but are their own free beings. This ontological symmetry between parents and their offspring—that the former can never *make* the latter—is at the heart of our human condition.[35]

Benhabib's world-loving self embraces this unpredictability and gives the Hegelian model of self-development a Benjaminian twist. "The pearl diver [realizes] . . . that the *transmissibility* of the past had been replaced by its *citability* and that in place of its authority there had arisen a strange power to settle down, piecemeal, in the present, . . . and to dig under the rubble for pearls to bring to the surface."[36] While transmissibility suggests a unilinear learning process with an authoritative directionality based on historical precedence, the citability of past events reads tradition against the grain and broadens our imagination of what it means to learn. Benhabib fears that Habermas's learning process is mostly concerned with transmissibility. It therefore turns history into the "waiting room" for those concrete others who ask for permission to enter, and into an auditorium for everybody else who subsequently unlearns the ability to ask, "*who is learning differently*?"[37] The broad and multifarious perspective of the world, which constantly reminds us of the unpredictability and plurality of human existence, recedes from view.

Gordon adds a related concern that connects the normative to the motivational dimension of Habermas's intervention. The narrative framework of historical precedence attributes to religion not only a proprietary claim on truth and meaning that is handed down to secular modernity but also a unique "form of spirit" that elevates it in comparison to philosophy or any other source of value. Contrary to this assumption, Gordon contends that it is much more plausible to argue that religion represents only an early attempt to furnish answers to questions that form "a kind of anthropological constancy"—they have preoccupied the great spiritual traditions prior to religion and migrated into the secular sphere afterward.[38] Questions about the origin of the cosmos, the essence and purpose of human life, the problem of suffering, or the meaning of truth and justice have animated century-long controversies and debates that are still ongoing. Instead of privileging specific answers or judging their value on the basis of historical precedence, the irresolvability of these debates might itself suggest an independent source of normativity that deeply constitutes the world. Viewed from this perspective, the authority of historical precedence simply becomes "an initial and even provisional effort" rather than a primary and privileged one.[39]

Just as parents are not the makers of their children, the immediate past is not the maker of the present. Yet, Habermas's postmetaphysical self is reluctant to engage with alternative sources that divert from what Gordon calls "revelation-as-pedagogy," a model that "introduces a certain asymmetry into the relationship between faith and knowledge: faith is the teacher; and knowledge is the student."[40] Alternative normative experiences of worldliness do not enter the conversation. Why? From the perspective of the world-loving self, Habermas's fidelity to the Promethean self, and its deontological view "that only judgments of justice possess a clearly discernible formal structure and thus can be studied along an evolutionary model,"[41] might have ironically prompted his religious turn. "Lived, discontinuous and contradictory experience" resists the discursive translation into validity claims that his theory demands.[42]

Yet, we may ask, is this outcome inevitable? To Benhabib it is not. Habermas's view "could also lead to the conclusion that one needed to develop a less formalistic ethical theory."[43] But before a more amorphous perspectivality of the social critic can gain importance, religion as the "thorn in the flesh of modernity" needs to lose its sting.[44] This might happen if the loss of certainty is no longer experienced as traumatic and we become aware of the normative multiplicity with which the world responds to it. Then, Max Weber's concept of modernity as a process of disenchantment must not turn into a disenchantment with modernity itself.

In this essay, I have argued that *Situating the Self* introduces a powerful critique of the modern "saga of loss" that still shapes our contemporary debates. This saga is particularly determinative for three concepts of selfhood at the core of Benhabib's critique. The liberal self cures its anxieties through law and science, the romantic self reconciles itself with the complexities of the world based on communal solidarity, and the postmodern self finds truth in the denial of the subject. Viewed in this light, Habermas's postmetaphysical self can be regarded as an intricate combination of liberal and romantic threads. The social critic, by contrast, becomes increasingly animated by the loss of the world, not certainty. She fears that we will continue to lose the world, in the end irrevocably, if our relation to it remains defined by mastery and self-centeredness. Her sense of self and agency changes as she envisions "a world in which we tend rather than control, share rather than exploit, regenerate rather than exhaust, and save rather than destroy."[45]

Most interestingly, Benhabib's critique does not lead to a rejection of the liberal, romantic, and postmodern traditions. The love of the world mediates the generalized other with the concrete other and invokes utopian imaginaries. As a result, any discussion about the normativity of modernity has to be situated *and* global. It has to engage "the *plurality of voices* that are usually not heard" or pushed into "a timeless universe, condemned to repeat the cycles of life."[46] This is why the driving question of her work concerns the agency of exiles, refugees, and the stateless, excluded groups, and women. Religious insights are not kept out of this discussion, but they are not privileged either. Belonging to our ongoing, species-wide search for answers to enduring questions, they join philosophy and science in providing certainties that have to remain incomplete, provisional, and open to critical dialogue. It is therefore from the perspective of the world that Benhabib places science, the economy, and the state within a larger moral vision: "We need a science in the service of reversing the damages inflicted by the Anthropocene on the earth; we need economic production in the service of human equality and dignity, and we need a state in which the alliance between big pharma, big capital and big data is harnessed for a new green deal rather than serving corporate greed."[47]

NOTES

1. Seyla Benhabib, *Situating the Self: Gender, Community, and Postmodernism in Contemporary Ethics* (New York: Routledge, 1992); Amy Allen, *The Politics of Our Selves: Power, Autonomy, and Gender in Contemporary Critical Theory* (New York: Columbia University Press, 2008); Margot Canaday, "Promising Alliances: The Critical Feminist Theory of Nancy Fraser and Seyla Benhabib," *Feminist Review* 74 (2003); Rainer Forst, "Situations of the Self: Reflections on Seyla Benhabib's Version of Critical Theory," *Philosophy and Social Criticism* 23, no. 5 (1997); Rainer Forst, *Contexts of Justice* (Berkeley: University of California Press, 2002); Iris Marion Young, "Comments on Seyla Benhabib, Situating the Self," *New German Critique* 62 (1994): 149–64.
2. Benhabib, *Situating the Self*, 154.
3. Benhabib, 155–56.
4. Thomas Hobbes, *"De Homine" and "De Cive" ("Man" and "Citizen")* (Indianapolis: Hackett, 1991), 205.
5. Georg Wilhelm Friedrich Hegel, *The Phenomenology of Spirit*, trans. Arnold V. Miller (Oxford: Oxford University Press, 1977), 111.

6. Benhabib, *Situating the Self*, 155.
7. Max Horkheimer and Theodor W. Adorno, *Dialectic of Enlightenment: Philosophical Fragments* (Stanford, CA: Stanford University Press, 2002).
8. Benhabib, *Situating the Self*, 155–56.
9. Benhabib, 158.
10. Benhabib, 158.
11. Benhabib, 81.
12. Benhabib, 77.
13. Benhabib, 209.
14. Benhabib, 203, 229.
15. Benhabib, 214. See also Benhabib, "Fragments of an Intellectual Biography," in this volume.
16. Benhabib, *Situating the Self*, 229.
17. Benhabib, 227.
18. Seyla Benhabib, "Ethics Without Normativity and Politics Without Historicity: On Judith Butler's 'Parting Ways. Jewishness and the Critique of Zionism,'" *Constellations* 20, no. 1 (2013): 156.
19. Benhabib, *Situating the Self*, 103.
20. Benhabib, 138.
21. Benhabib, *Situating the Self*, 75–76.
22. Seyla Benhabib, *The Reluctant Modernism of Hannah Arendt* (Lanham, MD: Rowman and Littlefield, 2003), 88.
23. Seyla Benhabib, *Exile, Statelessness, and Migration: Playing Chess with History from Hannah Arendt to Isaiah Berlin* (Princeton, NJ: Princeton University Press, 2018), 32.
24. Benhabib, 32.
25. Benhabib, 92.
26. Benhabib, 60.
27. Theodor W. Adorno, *Minima Moralia: Reflections on a Damaged Life* (London: Verso, 2005), 39.
28. Peter E. Gordon, *Migrants in the Profane: Critical Theory and the Question of Secularization* (New Haven, CT: Yale University Press, 2020), 151.
29. Jürgen Habermas, *Auch eine Geschichte der Philosophie*, vol. 1, *Die okzidentale Konstellation von Glauben und Wissen* (Frankfurt: Suhrkamp, 2019), 199, my translation.
30. Benhabib, *Situating the Self*, 80; Seyla Benhabib, "Habermas's New Phenomenology of Spirit: Two Centuries After Hegel," *Constellations* 28, no. 1 (2021).
31. Benhabib, 35.
32. Benhabib, 37.
33. Benhabib, 38.
34. Benhabib, 42.
35. Benhabib, 34.
36. Hannah Arendt, *Men in Dark Times* (New York: Harcourt, Brace and World, 1968), 193. Quoted in Benhabib, *The Reluctant Modernism of Hannah Arendt*, 93, emphasis mine.

37. Benhabib, "Habermas's New Phenomenology of Spirit," 39.
38. Peter E. Gordon, "Is There an Asymmetry-Problem in the Genealogy of Post-Metaphysical Reason?," *Constellations* 28, no. 1 (2021): 48.
39. Gordon, 48.
40. Gordon, 47.
41. Benhabib, *Situating the Self*, 80.
42. Benhabib, "Habermas's New Phenomenology of Spirit," 35.
43. Benhabib, *Situating the Self*, 80.
44. Habermas, *Auch eine Geschichte der Philosophie*, 1:199, my translation.
45. Eva von Redecker, *Revolution für das Leben: Philosophie der neuen Protestformen* (Frankfurt: S. Fischer, 2020), 287, my translation.
46. Benhabib, "Habermas's New Phenomenology of Spirit," 38; Benhabib, *Situating the Self*, 158.
47. Seyla Benhabib, "Democracy, Science and the State: Reflections on the Disaster(s) of Our Times," *Philosophy and Social Criticism* 47, no. 4 (2021): 477–85, 484.

4

Nature as a Concrete Other

An Alternative Voice in Kant's Conception of Beauty and Dignity

UMUR BASDAS

How "universalist" are anthropocentric universalisms that exclude the nonhuman nature? The early Frankfurt School critique of the "domination of nature" largely fell out of favor in the later critical theory tradition, especially after Habermas's communicative turn.[1] However, both Habermas and the later generations of critical theorists kept revisiting the question of nature.[2] As part of these efforts to bring nature back into the critical theory's focus of attention, this essay takes its lead from Seyla Benhabib's notion of "concrete other" and seeks to further extend that concept toward the nonhuman nature.

The Kantian distinction between the dignity of persons and the price of things reduces nature to a mere means for human purposes. I will start by briefly mentioning how this distinction reemerges in Habermas's discourse ethics and how Benhabib employs the notion of concrete other for a critical reconsideration of some of the dichotomies underlying Habermasian discourse ethics. I continue her move by extending this discussion to the "human vs. nonhuman" dichotomy. With that objective in mind, I turn to Kant's Third Critique and uncover a line of argument in his discussion of *sensus communis* where he undermines his own distinction between the dignity of persons and the price of things by claiming that aesthetic judgments of nature are combined with a moral interest in nature for its own sake. The implication of this argument should have been the ascription of a distinctive kind of dignity to nature, but Kant leaves his line of thinking undeveloped.

Nevertheless, the reconstruction of how Kant relates nature and *sensus communis* will help us rethink the notion of concrete other and its relationship with the generalized other. Benhabib takes the perspectives of the generalized and concrete other as two different but equally necessary perspectives. This is indeed true, but there is also a closer, immanent, and dynamic connection between these two perspectives. Just how much "generalization" the generalized other entails depends on our encounters with concrete others. Encounters with new concrete others always contest the hitherto-legitimate limits of universalization involved in taking the perspective of the generalized other. An expanded notion of concrete other that includes the nonhuman nature is therefore at the same time a challenge to the fixation of these lines on the borders of human species.

RETHINKING THE DIGNITY OF PERSONS AND THE PRICE OF THINGS DICHOTOMY

Kant's universalism excludes the nonhuman nature from the community of morally relevant beings. The boundaries are drawn through the dichotomy of the price of things and the dignity of persons, which he formulates in the *Groundwork* as follows: "In the realm of ends everything has either a price or a dignity. What has a price is such that something else can be put in its place as its *equivalent*; by contrast that which is elevated above all price, and admits of no equivalent, has a dignity."[3] Only rational beings can be persons and thus have a dignity or absolute worth. In contrast, all nonhuman natural beings have a mere price or relative worth. Thus conceived as mere "natural resource," nature is a means to whatever ends human beings may have. This Kantian distinction is a reflection of the ongoing commodification ("mere price") and instrumentalization ("mere means") of nonhuman nature. In Habermas's discourse-ethical reformulation of Kant,[4] the criterion for inclusion is no longer the capacity for rational self-legislation, but rather the capacity for communicative action. Yet the boundary erected between humanity and nature remains intact.

Benhabib's distinction between the perspectives of generalized and concrete other aims to unsettle some of the dichotomies underlying Habermas's discourse ethics.[5] Unlike the perspective of the generalized other, where we abstract from our particularities and differences and view one another as rational beings as such, the perspective of the concrete other "requires us to view each and every rational being as an individual with a concrete history, identity, and affective-emotional constitution."[6] As she puts it, once we realize that both standpoints are equally essential, "a number of oppositions on which communicative ethics seemed to rest begin to lose their force: questions of justice merge with questions of the good life; practical-moral discourses flow into aesthetic-expressive ones."[7]

She notes that a rigid dichotomy between morality and good life can be sustained only at the cost of repressing the perspective of the concrete other and "robbing inner nature of its voice."[8] Her move is intended as a "belated vindication of one of the central insights of early critical theory," namely, that "the project of the future begins by revolutionizing our needs and wants."[9] Reminiscent of Marcuse's call for a "New Sensibility," she regards the thematization of "inner nature" in communicative processes as a utopian moment, which cannot be dispensed with lest critical theory is reduced to mere "joyless reformism."[10]

It is important to note that Benhabib's intention is not a return to Marcuse (or to Adorno and Horkheimer for that matter), but rather a recuperation of a lost insight of early Frankfurt School thinkers by means of its reformulation in discourse-theoretical terms. This essay aims to accomplish a similar task by turning to Kant and by asking if one could make a similar move with regard to the "external nature." I will first show how Kant unwittingly unsettles his own dichotomy of the dignity of persons and the price of things in the Third Critique, and then explain how this may help us rethink the notions of concrete and generalized other in a nonanthropocentric direction.

SENSUS COMMUNIS AND NATURE

It may look surprising to turn to Kant's aesthetics in search of an argument for challenging the commodification and instrumentalization of nature. Especially because of its characterization of aesthetic judgments as disinterested contemplation, the Kantian aesthetic theory initially seems to be completely severed from any moral and political action. However, we will see later how his attempt to explain the possibility of aesthetic judgments leads Kant to claim that we have a moral interest in nature for its own sake (rather than as a mere means). I will first explain this moral interest and then dwell on its implications for the aforementioned distinction between dignity and price.

Kant's Third Critique employs the expression "interest" as a quasi-technical term. By "disinterested," he means that aesthetic judgments are indifferent to whether their objects exist or not.[11] For instance, suppose that we are looking at an apple. Our faculty of desire may be tempted by its smell or taste. If so, we are "interested" in the sense that the existence of this object matters to us. But if we are to approach the object aesthetically, we must temporarily silence our faculty of desire and focus solely on the form of the object's representation, regardless of whether this object actually exists or not. This characterization of aesthetic judgments prompted Nietzsche to poke fun at Kantian aestheticians contemplating naked female statues without any interest.[12] Whatever the merits of Nietzsche's critique, at least the motivation behind Kant's position is clear. If the faculty of desire were involved in aesthetic judgments, it would not be possible to attribute to them any expectation of universal assent, because the content of our desires is empirical and contingent.

The characterization of aesthetic judgments as "disinterested" and therefore not grounded on any private inclinations is Kant's first step in establishing the legitimacy of their claim to universal validity. But if they are not grounded on private inclinations, what are they grounded on? The answer to this question has more than one layer, but the first answer is that they are grounded on what Kant calls "the *sensus communis*."[13] The main objective of this part of the paper is to show how his account of the notion of *sensus communis* will reconnect aesthetic judgments with a specific kind of moral interest in nature.

The notion of *sensus communis* is first introduced in the Analytic of the Beautiful when Kant explains the "modality" of aesthetic judgments, namely, their characterization as "necessary." The "necessity" of aesthetic judgments is different both from "theoretical" necessity (i.e., efficient causality in nature) and from "practical" necessity (i.e., the moral ought). Just like the practical necessity, the aesthetic necessity is an ought. In other words, aesthetic judgments claim that everyone has to agree with their conclusion not in the sense that they are causally determined to agree but in the sense that they ought to agree. However, aesthetic necessity is still different from practical necessity in terms of how its rule expresses its demand from us.[14] The moral law entails a "command" (*Gebot*), whereas the aesthetic rule only makes a "claim" (*Anspruch*).[15] Kant should have explained this distinction a bit more precisely, but in any case it is hardly a controversial point that the violation of an aesthetic rule and the violation of a moral rule do not have the same meaning. For our purposes, more interesting is his attempt to draw an analogy between the two by saying that aesthetic judgments claim universal assent "as if it were a duty."[16] On the one hand, the qualification "as if" maintains the distinction between the aesthetic ought and the moral ought, and, on the other hand, the expression "duty" ties them to each other.

This begs the question why there is such an ought attached to the *sensus communis*. Since we have internalized and normalized the Weberian "differentiation of value spheres" in modernity, in particular the separation of the good and the beautiful, Kant's position understandably sounds strange to many of us. Why should one consider it as anything remotely like a "duty" that even just two people find the same flower beautiful (let alone there being a universal agreement on this issue)? In order to start answering this question, we should first note an ambivalence in how Kant employs the term *sensus communis*, because its relationship to aesthetic necessity changes depending on which meaning is emphasized.

In the Analytic of the Beautiful, Kant says that the notion of *sensus communis* is "the condition" for the necessity of universal assent in aesthetic judgments: "Thus only under the presupposition that there is a common sense (by which, however, we do not mean any external sense but rather the effect of the free play of our cognitive powers), only under the presupposition of such common sense, I say, can the judgment of taste be made."[17] *Sensus communis* is said to be "the effect of the free play of our cognitive powers." By "our cognitive powers," Kant here means the faculties of understanding and imagination. Aesthetic judgments are based on a "free play" of our faculties of understanding and imagination. The harmony of these cognitive faculties in the disinterested contemplation of a beautiful object produces in us a feeling of pleasure. This feeling of pleasure is what is referred to as "the effect" in this definition. We base our judgments of beauty on the absence or presence of this feeling (i.e., if we feel such a pleasure, we call the object "beautiful"). According to Kant, we can rightly expect this feeling to be common to every human being because we all share the same set of cognitive faculties and they must be working the same way in each one of us.[18] The *sensus communis* is the condition of aesthetic judgments' necessity, because universal assent is possible only if there is such a feeling common to all human beings. If universal assent were not possible, then one could not demand it as an ought, either.

Much later in the text Kant opens the subject of *sensus communis* a second time (in the Deduction of Pure Aesthetic Judgments) and redefines it as follows:

> By "*sensus communis*," however, must be understood the idea of a communal sense, i.e. a faculty for judging that in its reflection takes account (*a priori*) of everyone else's way of representing in thought, in order as it were to hold its judgment up to the human reason as a whole and thereby avoid the illusion which, from subjective private conditions that could easily be held to be objective, would have a detrimental influence on the judgment.[19]

In the earlier definition, the *sensus communis* was only "the effect" of the free play understanding and imagination, i.e., the *feeling* of pleasure that should be common to all those who encounter a particular beautiful object. In contrast, now it is a *faculty* for making judgments in a way that abstracts from one's private conditions and takes the perspective of the generalized other.

Kant uses the term *sensus communis* in both of these senses without clearly distinguishing between two. When employed in the first manner (i.e., as a feeling), the *sensus communis* is merely "the condition" of aesthetic necessity. However, when employed in the second sense (i.e., as a faculty), it is more than just a prior condition or presupposition. Instead, what is demanded from everyone as necessary *is* the exercise of *sensus communis*, namely, that they elevate themselves above their private inclinations and judge from a generalizable perspective in the manner described earlier.

Now we are in a relatively better position for understanding why aesthetic judgments claim universal assent "as if it were a duty." The "duty" in question is less about everyone experiencing the same feeling of pleasure (i.e., *sensus communis* as a "feeling") in the face a particular object such as a flower, and more about everyone elevating themselves to the standpoint of the generalized other (by exercising their "faculty" of *sensus communis*). However, this does not yet fully answer our question. In Kantian morality, taking the standpoint of the generalized other is viewed simply as a commandment of the moral law. But what legitimates such a demand when the issue is a "merely" aesthetic one? Why are we justified in demanding from everyone that they exercise their *sensus communis* (as a faculty) by elevating their standpoint above their private conditions and instead grounding their judgment on *sensus communis* (as a feeling)? Why is the exercise of *sensus communis* demanded from everyone "as if it were a duty" in an otherwise amoral context?

Kant concludes his discussion of *sensus communis* in the Deduction of Pure Aesthetic Judgments with the following statement: "If one could assume that the mere universal communicability of this feeling must in itself already involve an interest for us (which, however, one is not justified in inferring from the constitution of a merely reflective power of judgment), then one would be able to explain how it is that the feeling in the judgment of taste is expected of everyone as if it were a duty."[20] This passage reiterates the idea that aesthetic judgments are "disinterested." However, Kant now also says that there must nevertheless be some kind of an "interest" involved in aesthetic judgments in order for us to be able to explain how one can demand from everyone to exercise their *sensus communis* "as if it were a duty." It is suggested that the ought embedded in the exercise of *sensus communis* can only be justified on the basis of this "interest," whatever it may be.

Kant right away goes on to distinguish between what he calls "the empirical interest" and "the intellectual interest" in beauty.[21] As we will see, the combination of these two kinds of interest with aesthetic judgments may happen mediately (empirical interest) or immediately (intellectual interest). Regardless of this distinction, neither of these combinations conflicts with the "disinterestedness" of aesthetic judgments, because these interests are attached to aesthetic judgments only *after* having already judged an object in a disinterested manner.[22] I will later criticize how Kant distinguishes between these two kinds of interest, but let us first follow the thread of his argument.

The empirical interest in beauty is connected with our "sociability," namely, our inclination to communicate and share our pleasures with others in society. Kant's discussion of these empirical interests has the Rousseauian undertones of a critique of arts as artificial luxuries. Hence, he speaks of "the interest of vanity in decorating" our rooms "for the eyes of others."[23] Here we clearly go beyond a purely disinterested contemplation of the form of a representation. Our faculty of desire is no longer silent. Consequently, we are no longer indifferent to the existence of the object and we *act* on our interest by, for instance, buying decorative objects and displaying them for our friends to see and admire. However, this is a merely "mediate interest," namely our interest is not immediately directed at these objects, but is rather aimed at the consideration and approval of society that we may gain through them.[24] These objects are mere means for ends that are beyond them. This empirical kind of interest cannot provide us with what we are looking for in our attempt to justify the ought embedded in *sensus communis*, because its empirically mediated origin makes it contingent upon our private inclinations.

The source of our empirical interest in beauty is easily explained by its being a means to our sociability. In contrast, the nature and origin of the intellectual interest in beauty, which is said to be a "moral" interest, are harder to explain.[25] Kant says that it is "immediately" attached to the beautiful objects themselves.[26] Somehow this intellectual interest is grounded on "the quality inherent in" the beautiful nature, which "pertains to it internally."[27] Let us now try to understand a bit more precisely the immediacy of this kind of interest and then account for its origins.

The immediacy of intellectual interest in a beautiful object first of all means that we do not view this object as a mere means for some end beyond itself (such as "sociability"). This should not be confused with the disinterestedness of aesthetic judgments in general. Of course, we do not view an object as a means to anything when we are engaged in its disinterested contemplation. However, that is simply because we are indifferent to the very existence of the object. In contrast, in the case of an intellectual interest (attached to an aesthetic judgment), our faculty of desire is active and thus we are interested in the existence of the object, but we are interested in it for its own sake and not as a means to a goal beyond itself. This distinction will soon prove to be very significant, because the reintroduction of the faculty of desire into aesthetic judgments with an interest in nature for its own sake ties aesthetic judgments of nature with morally and politically relevant action and implies the ascription of a distinctive kind of dignity to nature.

Kant argues that we can have such an immediate interest only in beauties of nature and not in works of art. In his words, our judgments must be accompanied by "the thought that nature has produced that beauty."[28] He notes that, even if artificial flowers, imitations of bird songs, and the like could perfectly mimic their natural counterparts, our immediate interest in these objects would disappear the moment we become aware of the deception. That is because "an art that is *obviously intentionally* directed toward our satisfaction . . . would arouse only a mediate interest in the cause on which it is grounded, namely an art that can interest only through its end and never in itself."[29] In other words, Kant thinks that we can have an immediate interest in beauty only if we take the origin of that beauty to be the nonhuman nature, devoid of any human intention in its genesis. Why does this intellectual interest presuppose the absence of any human intention in the generation of a beautiful object?

The answer starts to become clear with Kant's following comment:

> But since it also interests reason that the ideas . . . also have objective reality, i.e., that nature should at least show some trace or give a sign that it contains in itself some sort of ground for assuming a lawful correspondence of its products with our satisfaction, . . . reason must take an interest in every manifestation in nature of a correspondence similar to this; consequently the mind cannot reflect on the beauty of nature without finding itself at the same time to be interested in it.[30]

According to Kant, there is an abyss, a seemingly unsurmountable gap between our supersensible ideas and the phenomenal world, between the freedom of humanity and the determinism of nature. Yet the moral vocation of humanity presupposes that it is at least possible for our moral ideas to be realized in the objective world, because something impossible cannot be commanded as an ought. Therefore, we have a moral interest in the existence of any "sign" or "trace" that hints at the possibility of bridging this gap. The beauty of nature can be viewed as just such a trace or sign for the following reason.

In Kant's view, nature is judged as beautiful only by human beings, namely, beings that are at once noumenal and phenomenal. Neither a hypothetical rational being without an animal body nor an animal without higher cognitive faculties can experience beauty. Furthermore, that human beings find nature beautiful in their disinterested contemplation does not in any way serve nature itself. Hence, nature could just as well be a sheer mechanism completely indifferent to any human meaning. So "how is one to explain why nature has spread beauty so extravagantly everywhere, even at the bottom of the ocean, where it is only seldom that the human eye (for which alone, after all, it is purposive) penetrates?"[31] Kant thinks that such considerations lead us to interpret beauty as a free and generous gift from nature to human beings through a formal arrangement of its appearance. In this way, he sees the nonhuman nature figuratively reaching out to humanity, offering us a trace or sign that hints at the possibility of bridging the aforementioned abyss that separates humanity and nature. He takes this as "the true interpretation of the cipher by means of which nature figuratively speaks to us in its beautiful forms."[32] Hence, this is "a language that nature brings to us and that seems to have a higher meaning."[33] We thereby no longer approach natural beings as mute objects, but rather interpret their phenomenal appearance (colors, shapes, sounds, and so on) as nature's way of communicating with us.

In other words, the beautiful nature discloses an affinity between the human and the nonhuman in their nonidentity. If "the thought that nature has produced that beauty" did not accompany our aesthetic judgment, namely, if the beautiful object were produced intentionally by human beings, then we could not interpret this object as such a trace or sign. This explains why the immediate intellectual interest in beauty presupposes the absence of any human intention in the genesis of the beautiful object. According to Kant, our moral vocation's dependence on these signs or traces of nature is the reason that we can legitimately claim universal assent to judgments of beauty "as if it were a duty." Hence, the ultimate justification of the ought embedded in the exercise of *sensus communis* is grounded on our need to be at home in nature.

DIGNITY OF NATURE AS A CONCRETE OTHER

Aesthetic judgments thereby open up the possibility of a distinct kind of respect for nature. Kant describes our moral interest in beautiful nature as follows:

> Someone who alone (and without any intention of wanting to communicate his observations to others) considers the beautiful shape of a wildflower, a bird, an insect, etc., in order to marvel at it, to love it, and to be unwilling for it to be entirely absent from nature, even though some harm might come to him from it rather than there being any prospect of advantage to him from it, takes an immediate and certainly intellectual interest in the beauty of nature, i.e., not only the form of its product but also its existence pleases him, even though no sensory charm has a part in this and he does not combine any sort of end with it.[34]

Note how this passage lets the moral discourse and the aesthetic discourse flow into each other: one is willing to endure "some harm" and forgo "any prospect of advantage" and so on. Aesthetics transgresses its own boundaries and spills over into the moral realm, because our higher faculty of desire is reconnected with our faculty of aesthetic judgments and thus we are no longer merely concerned with the "form," but also with the "existence" of the object. Furthermore, we are interested in nature for its own sake and not as a mere means. Clearly, this view of nature takes it beyond the category of mere price and toward some notion of dignity. However, this nonhuman dignity would also have to be conceived differently from the human dignity grounded in rational self-legislation. Kant unfortunately does not pursue this line of thought any further. Even though this expanded, more inclusive conception of dignity remains unexplored, his argument clearly unsettles the otherwise stark dichotomy of dignity and price.

How does Kant avoid confronting the implications of his own argument? As we saw, he reestablishes the connection between the faculty of judgment and the faculty of desire, which was severed earlier during his characterization of aesthetic judgments as disinterested contemplation in the Analytic of the Beautiful. If so, why do we still not see any connection of such aesthetic judgments with any morally and politically relevant action? If aesthetic judgments are disinterested and interested at the same time, why are they only contemplative and not at the same time active?

The answer lies in the problematic way in which he distinguishes between the empirical interest and the intellectual interest in beauty. This dichotomy rests on an opposition between the solitary lover of nature and the vain lover of art and society. Because Kant assumes that the intellectual interest in beautiful nature would remain a solitary affair, he is able to hide its significance for action as a source of competing moral and political claims. He says that the "beautiful soul" of the former "gladly leaves the room," namely, leaves the society behind, and turns to nature "without any intention of wanting to communicate his observations to others."[35] This gesture of leaving the room indicates the critical moment of breaking with the nexus of means and ends in the market society. This person aims neither at merely sensuous gratification through consumption nor at gaining the approval or consideration of society by showing off his or her delicate taste in art. However, if his or her encounter with "a wildflower, a bird, an insect, etc." generates a "free interest" in their continued existence for their own sake, would this solitary lover of nature not have to return to society and attempt to communicate and justify this moral interest to others whenever nature is threatened with destruction?

The distinction between the solitary moral interest and the sociable empirical interest is not tenable. Since this problematic distinction covers up the very real implications for action in Kant's discussion of *sensus communis* and nature, its unsettling of the "price of things vs. dignity of persons" dichotomy went unnoticed in Kant scholarship and is left without further theoretical investigation. However, once we make this hidden element explicit, it becomes clear that the Third Critique leaves us with the task of exploring the aforementioned broader notion of dignity.

IMPLICATIONS FOR RETHINKING THE NOTION OF CONCRETE OTHER IN COMMUNICATIVE ETHICS

In my concluding remarks, I will only try to help prepare the ground for accomplishing this difficult task by briefly pointing at the implications of my discussion of *sensus communis* for the notion of concrete other. As I mentioned earlier, Benhabib does not intend to replace the perspective of the generalized other with that of the concrete other. Instead, these are viewed as different yet equally necessary, complementary standpoints of moral reasoning. I agree with this point, but also believe that there is in fact an even closer, immanent relationship between these two perspectives. This relationship comes to the forefront in my reconstruction of how Kant relates nature and *sensus communis*.

In the familiar, "official" Kantian morality, reasoning from the perspective of the generalized other is a commandment of the moral law. Only rational beings endowed with the capacity for moral self-legislation have an absolute worth or dignity. In turn, the nonhuman nature is reduced to the status of a mute and instrumentalized object with only a relative worth or price. But Kant's aesthetic theory contains the makings of an alternative approach. The exercise of *sensus communis* involves an elevation above the "subjective private conditions" to the standpoint of the generalized other. However, because this takes place in what initially looks like an amoral aesthetic context, Kant can no longer simply say that it is commanded by the moral law. He is thus led to develop an alternative explanation as to why this elevation can be demanded from everyone "as if it were a duty." In this alternative account, we do not start from the universal, namely, from the moral law; instead, it is the particular that discloses the universal. The ground of the ought embedded in the exercise of *sensus communis* is revealed to us only through our encounters with "a wildflower, a bird, an insect, etc." We grasp the necessity of elevating ourselves to the standpoint of the generalized other by first taking the perspective of a natural being and interpreting its concrete, phenomenal appearance as a communicative act. In short, the elevation to the standpoint of the generalized other is justified in and through our encounters with concrete others.

To be sure, Kant would not be happy with the direction that I am here taking his aesthetic theory and he in fact suppresses the possibilities of this alternative voice in his own text. We can nevertheless contemplate on this alternative voice as a source of inspiration for reconsidering the notion of concrete other and its relationship with the generalized other. Particularly, I would like to draw attention to the dynamism of the immanent relationship between the perspectives of the concrete and generalized other.

If it is encounters with concrete others that disclose the necessity of taking the perspective of the generalized other, would one not also have to grant that the very limits of generalization entailed by the latter perspective are conditioned by such encounters? What is the proper limit of universalization? Is it "all white Europeans," "all propertied men," "all men," or even "all human beings"? Encounters with new concrete others contest the hitherto-legitimate limits of universalization involved in taking the perspective of the generalized other. Since Kant avoids confronting the implications of his own account, this dynamism in the relationship between the concrete and generalized other remains hidden from view in the text. But it is nevertheless an approach that his argument that I reconstructed earlier implies and it invites theoretical elaboration.

This further leads to the question of how one can more precisely conceptualize the expansion of the notions of dignity and concrete other beyond the borders of human species. As explained earlier, Kant undermines his own "dignity of persons vs. price of things" dichotomy through a distinct, aesthetically grounded notion of dignity for the nonhuman nature. This happens on the basis of a broader notion of communication, where natural beings are interpreted as engaging in communicative acts through "the language" of their phenomenal appearances. The key to Kant's approach is the way in which he lets aesthetic and moral discourses speak to one another, which calls for a radical reconsideration of the possibilities of communicative action. Thereby, the meaning of "concrete other" is also enlarged in a way that now includes the nonhuman nature.

The challenge that nature as a concrete other poses for us is an exploration of this distinctive, aesthetically and communicatively grounded notion of dignity that is different from both the price of things and the dignity of persons. Kant's aesthetic theory thus offers many thought-provoking resources to those who are interested in the project of rethinking the universalism of communicative ethics in a nonanthropocentric direction. The Third Critique is full of unexplored possibilities that can inspire the efforts to bring nature back into critical theory's focus of attention.

NOTES

1. For Habermas's response to the critique of "domination of nature," see Jürgen Habermas, *The Theory of Communicative Action*, vol. 1 (Boston: Beacon, 1985), esp. 366–99.
2. Just to give a few examples, see Jürgen Habermas, "A Reply to My Critics," in *Habermas: Critical Debates*, trans. Thomas McCarthy, ed. John B. Thompson and David Held (London: MacMillan, 1982), 243–49; and Jürgen Habermas, "Remarks on Discourse Ethics," in *Justification and Application: Remarks on Discourse Ethics*, trans. Ciaran Cronin (Cambridge, MA: MIT Press, 2001), 106–11. For a helpful overview and critical analysis of the concept of nature in the critical theory tradition, see Steven Vogel, *Against Nature: The Concept of Nature in Critical Theory* (Albany: SUNY Press, 1996). See also Steven Vogel, "Habermas and the Ethics of Nature," in *The Ecological Community: Environmental Challenges for Philosophy, Politics, and Morality*, ed. Roger S. Gottlieb (New York: Routledge, 1997), 175–92; Steven Vogel, *Thinking Like a Mall: Environmental Philosophy After the End of Nature* (Cambridge, MA: MIT Press, 2015). On nature and communicative action, see John S. Dryzek, "Green Reason: Communicative Ethics for the Biosphere," *Environmental Ethics* 12, no. 3 (Fall 1990): 195–210. On nature and reification, see Axel Honneth, *Reification: A New Look at an Old Idea*, with commentaries by Judith Butler, Raymond Geuss, and Jonathan Lear, ed. Martin Jay (Oxford: Oxford University Press, 2008), 60–63.
3. Immanuel Kant, *Groundwork for the Metaphysics of Morals*, trans. and ed. Allen W. Wood (New Haven, CT: Yale University Press, 2002), 52.
4. Jürgen Habermas, *Moral Consciousness and Communicative Action*, trans. Christian Lenhardt and Shierry Weber Nicholsen, intro. Thomas McCarthy (Cambridge, MA: MIT Press, 1990), 67.
5. Seyla Benhabib, *Critique, Norm, and Utopia: A Study of the Foundations of Critical Theory* (New York: Columbia University Press, 1986), esp. 339–42; and Seyla Benhabib, *Situating the Self: Gender, Community, and Postmodernism in Contemporary Ethics* (Cambridge: Polity, 1992), 148–77.
6. Benhabib, *Critique, Norm, and Utopia*, 341.
7. Benhabib, 334.
8. Benhabib, 342.
9. Benhabib, 336.
10. Herbert Marcuse, *An Essay on Liberation* (Boston: Beacon, 1969), see esp. 23–48; Benhabib, *Critique, Norm, and Utopia*, 329.
11. Immanuel Kant, *Critique of the Power of Judgment*, trans. Paul Guyer and Eric Matthews (Cambridge: Cambridge University Press, 2000), 91.
12. Friedrich Nietzsche, *On the Genealogy of Morality*, trans. Carol Diethe, ed. Keith Ansell-Pearson (Cambridge: Cambridge University Press, 2007), 74.

13. Kant, *Critique of the Power of Judgment*, see esp. 122 and 173–74.
14. Another difference between the moral and aesthetic necessity concerns the characterization of what serves as a rule in morality and aesthetics. In morality, the rule that demands obedience is "determinate" in the sense that it can be expressed as a conceptual, discursive formula (i.e., the categorical imperative). In contrast, any rule that demands assent in aesthetics has to remain "indeterminate" because it is inextricably embedded in singular, concrete objects. We can contemplate a beautiful object and sense there a rule that can guide us in other aesthetic contexts. However, we cannot give that rule an adequate and determinate conceptual expression in order to abstract it from that object and express it as a self-standing formula. Thus we always have to refer to that "exemplary" object itself within which that rule inheres.
15. Kant, *Critique of the Power of Judgment*, 50.
16. Kant, 176.
17. Kant, 122.
18. For the details of this rather dubious claim, see Kant, *Critique of the Power of Judgment*, 122–23 and 170–73.
19. Kant, 173–74.
20. Kant, 176.
21. Kant, 176–82.
22. Here one should not take this "after" in a temporal sense. Kant is making only an analytic distinction.
23. Kant, *Critique of the Power of Judgment*, 179.
24. Kant, 179.
25. Kant, 180.
26. Kant, 181.
27. Kant, 181.
28. Kant, 179.
29. Kant, 181, my emphasis.
30. Kant, 180.
31. Kant, 160.
32. Kant, 180.
33. Kant, 181.
34. Kant, 178–79.
35. Kant, 179, 178.

5

"To Burst Open the Possibilities of the Present"

Seyla Benhabib and Utopia

BERNARD E. HARCOURT

Over the course of a remarkable intellectual journey, Seyla Benhabib has renewed the utopian potential of critical theory. Beginning with the publication in 1986 of her landmark contribution to critical philosophy, *Critique, Norm, and Utopia: A Study of the Foundations of Critical Theory*, Benhabib launched a decades-long project to return the concept of "utopia" to its privileged place, alongside "crisis," "critique," "norm," and "praxis," as a key concept in the critical theory tradition of the Frankfurt School. A central argument throughout Benhabib's journey has been, in her words, "the need to recover part of the utopian legacy of early critical theory."[1]

The concept of utopia had become overly associated, in earlier critical theory, with the potentiality of one particular group in society, one collective singularity, one universal concept—the proletariat for Marx, or art and philosophy for Max Horkheimer and Theodor Adorno. Jürgen Habermas's turn to communicative ethics, by contrast, gave rise to what Benhabib identified as the possibility of a new politics of empowerment and valuation of difference. New social movements formed communities of need and solidarity that fundamentally changed "the meaning of utopia in our societies."[2] In a memorable turn of phrase, Benhabib declared: "Such utopia is no longer utopian, for it is not a mere beyond. It is the negation of the existent in the name of a future that bursts open the possibilities of the present."[3] Seyla Benhabib's utopian vision has taken different shapes over the course of her intellectual arc, from an early theory of communicative ethics, respect, and dignity, which she referred to as "communicative utopia" in the late 1980s and 1990s, to a more concrete and reflective utopia grounded in international law and human rights, which she called a "utopia of cosmopolitanism" in the 2000s and 2010s, to a reconsidered "cosmopolitanism from below" embracing as well today local and global grassroots movements.[4] Consistently and throughout, Benhabib has militated for equal treatment and dignity for all humans, and respect for everyone's differences. Benhabib has put forth at every juncture, front and center, an admirable vision that incorporates a cautious embrace of utopia from the earlier Frankfurt School, chastened by the practices of new social movements.

Benhabib always placed respect for difference at the very heart of her enterprise. In fact, it was the experience of difference—associated with her own remarkable personal biography and migration, as well as those of the new social movements—that demarcated her philosophical approach from the theory of communicative action of her mentor, Jürgen Habermas. "There is no single spot in the social structure that privileges those who occupy it with a vision of the social totality," Benhabib emphasized from early on. "The experience of difference that cannot be co-opted in imposed identity is liberatory."[5]

Benhabib's writings on cosmopolitanism have garnered many admirers, as well as critics. Within critical theory circles, I would argue, the respect for difference should extend to those theoretical and philosophical differences. The same esteem for experiences of difference must be afforded philosophical disagreements about normative foundations, epistemologies, and political praxis. Seyla Benhabib and I have debated our philosophical differences vigorously since I began as a doctoral student under her supervision in 1996.[6] In the vein of Benhabib's admirable respect for difference—which is what has made her such an extraordinary teacher, mentor, and now colleague at Columbia University—I will focus this chapter on what I admire most: the remarkable aspiration for emancipation, solidarity, equality, dignity, friendship, and respect for difference that she has consistently advanced in her writings since her very first book. I will focus, in other words, on her inspiring utopian vision.

CRITICAL THEORY AND UTOPIA

Within the critical theory tradition of the Frankfurt School, the concept of utopia played a critical role among the first generation of theorists (Horkheimer, Adorno, and later Herbert Marcuse) and their adjacent thinkers (Ernst Bloch and Walter Benjamin especially, and, still further away, Karl Mannheim). Bloch, who himself was never formally a member of the Institute for Social Research but was surely a fellow traveler of the Frankfurt School, adamantly embraced the need for utopian thinking as a spur to political action. Beginning with the publication of *The Spirit of Utopia* in 1918 and then with his three-volume treatise, *The Principle of Hope*, published between 1954 and 1959, Bloch championed utopia as a necessary stimulant for normatively positive political praxis. Bloch distinguished the idea of "Utopia," which he characterized as being merely a wish or a dream, from the concept of a "concrete utopia," which he embraced and conceived of as a form of praxis, a political practice within a specific historical context. Bloch formulated this within the framework of a Marxian philosophy of history—simultaneously and paradoxically rebuffing the classical antiutopianism (at least according to the conventional reading) of Marx and Engels.[7]

By contrast to Bloch and other adjacent thinkers—such as Walter Benjamin, who embraced a messianic vision of utopia, and Karl Mannheim, who developed a neutral sociological theory of utopia as the reverse side of ideology in *Ideology and Utopia*, published in 1929—the early Frankfurt School thinkers maintained at first an ambivalent relationship to the concept of utopia.[8] Horkheimer's early critique of utopian thinking turned on his concern that the economic and political conditions within early twentieth-century capitalism (what he referred to as the "objective conditions") were insufficiently advanced in Western society for social transformation.[9] The experience of the war, the Holocaust, and Stalinism—and their disappointment with the ossification of Eastern Bloc communism—led Adorno, alongside Bloch, to advocate for the need for utopian thinking within Soviet-style socialism.[10] Herbert Marcuse joined Bloch and Adorno, going so far as to argue that the necessity of utopian thinking to reimagine "a new definition of socialism" was nothing less than a "categorical imperative": "I believe that the Utopian is today not only an historical concept, but also an historical imperative—a categorical imperative that must serve to prevent the fossilization of socialism under new forms of rule."[11]

By the early 1970s, however, the concept of utopia had fallen into desuetude within the critical theory writings of the Frankfurt School. Marcuse had pronounced the "End of Utopia" in his 1967 lecture at the Free University of West Berlin, suggesting that the concept of utopia was no longer necessary to critical theory. Marcuse argued that radical utopian transformation should no longer be considered "Utopian," and that the concept should be reserved for futures that are in fact impossible, projects that contradict the real laws of nature, like physical or biological laws.[12] Marcuse believed at the time that technological changes had made possible the social transformation of society.[13] "In this sense," Marcuse proclaimed, "I believe we can today actually speak of an end of utopia."[14]

The period also was marked by the passing of the first generation and adjacent thinkers, with the untimely death of Adorno in 1969, of Horkheimer in 1973, and of Bloch in 1977. With their passing, the concept of utopia was eclipsed, at least momentarily, within critical theory. Jürgen Habermas did not engage the concept of utopia in his theory of communicative ethics. There is practically no mention of utopia in his two-volume treatise *The Theory of Communicative Action* (1981). The term appears only once in the first volume, a sideways and critical reference to the philosopher Hans-Georg Gadamer's "hermeneutic utopia of universal and unlimited dialogue in a commonly inhabited lifeworld."[15] To the best of my recollection, Habermas does not mention or develop the concept in the second volume. As Seyla Benhabib correctly observed, "Habermas' theory marked a shift from utopian to communicative reason in critical theory."[16] Axel Honneth as well did not mention the concept of utopia, or even use the word itself, in his first book, *The Critique of Power* (1985), which placed the early Frankfurt School in conversation with Michel Foucault and Habermas.[17] The concept of utopia went dormant.

BENHABIB AND *CRITIQUE, NORM, AND UTOPIA* (1986)

It was not until the publication in 1986 of *Critique, Norm, and Utopia* that the concept of utopia resurfaced and regained footing in critical theory. The very title of Benhabib's work restituted utopia to its privileged place as a key concept of critical theory. Benhabib critiqued Habermas's theory of communicative ethics precisely for failing to incorporate a utopian dimension: "communicative reason can motivate us only if it also contains a *utopian potential*," Benhabib emphasized.[18] The goal of her book, she explained, was "the need to recover part of the utopian legacy of early critical theory."[19] Benhabib set out to establish, in her words, "an alternative normative foundation for critical theory"—alternative, that is, to Jürgen Habermas's theory of communicative action. The question of normative foundations constituted the central question presented, one that had been triggered by the antifoundational challenges to critical theory coming from pragmatists like Richard Rorty and poststructuralists like Michel Foucault, Gilles Deleuze, and Jean-François Lyotard.[20]

In her book, published by Columbia University Press, Benhabib approached the task systematically, tracing the normative foundations of critical theory in Hegel, Marx, Horkheimer and Adorno, and ultimately Habermas. She demonstrated that the original normative foundations in Hegel and Marx rested on what she called a "philosophy of the subject," a subject who achieves emancipation through work and labor. She identified this model as well in the early writings of Horkheimer, especially his 1937 article "Traditional and Critical Theory." She documented how these normative foundations began to shift in Horkheimer and Adorno's collaborative work during the war, which highlighted the dimension of man's "non-dominating relation to nature," and then, more dramatically, in Habermas's communicative ethics. Habermas effectively shifted the normative foundations from the subject's relation to an object (labor or nature) to the linguistically mediated relation of subject to subject through communicative action.

In the final chapter, Benhabib argued that the transformation of critical theory and demise of a philosophy of the subject opened up the potential for community, solidarity, and a politics of empowerment based on recognition of difference. Benhabib hailed a new "moment of communicative utopia."[21] She proposed a stitching together of universalist and solidaristic principles. Drawing both on enlightenment strands of rights and entitlements and on critical strands of emancipation, solidarity, community, collectivity, and friendship, while emphasizing the importance of valuing our experiences of difference, Benhabib uplifted the voice of collectivities in struggle and in formation.[22] Habermasian discourse norms were essential, she argued, but insufficient without a utopian dimension—alone, they could not serve as a robust critique of the present. "Utopia is not antagonistic to norm," Benhabib concluded, "it complements it."[23]

The utopian vision that Benhabib first articulated in 1986 can be encapsulated best in a passage that reflects the values at the heart of Benhabib's entire intellectual journey: "The perspective of the generalized other urges us to respect the equality, dignity and rationality of all humans qua humans, while the perspective of the concrete other enjoins us to respect differences, individual life histories and concrete needs."[24]

Seyla Benhabib closed her book threading together, in her vision of communicative utopia, the logic of the protection of rights with the logic of friendship and solidarity. And she left the reader, in the final lines, with the words of Ernst Bloch, from his 1961 book, *Natural Law and Human Dignity*, that drew family resemblances between enlightenment theories of natural rights and human dignity on the one hand, and critical theories of social solidarity and emancipation on the other. Benhabib ended her book with Bloch:

> It is just as urgent *suo modo* to raise the problem of a heritage of classical natural law as it was to speak of the heritage of social utopias. Social utopias and natural law had mutually complementary concerns within the same human space; they marched separately but, sadly, did not strike together.... Social utopian thought directed its efforts toward human happiness, natural law was directed toward human dignity. Social utopias depicted relations in which *toil* and *burden* ceased, natural law constructed relations in which *degradation* and *insult* ceased.[25]

BENHABIB AND COSMOPOLITANISM

Over the course of a rich and ongoing intellectual journey since then, Seyla Benhabib crafted her original vision of communicative utopia into a far more concrete utopia, what she called a "utopia of cosmopolitanism."[26] Drawing on Hannah Arendt's framework of the "right to have rights," Benhabib began to combine critical social theory, from a feminist communicative ethics perspective, with a transnational human rights approach, in order to argue in favor of universalistic human rights, especially in the context of migration, asylum, and gender rights.[27] Benhabib proposed that international human rights regimes, treaties, and institutions were normatively valuable, not so much because of their enforcement or effectiveness at the empirical level, but because they generated discursive possibilities and open communicative avenues that could be deployed in the public sphere by women, migrants, and marginalized persons to resist forms of domination. They created language, expressions, and arguments that could then be used toward emancipatory efforts.

In this, Benhabib opposed an array of international human rights skeptics, including those like Samuel Moyn, who argued that human rights discourse had displaced other emancipatory alternatives; Mahmood Mamdani, who claimed that human rights were merely an imperial and neocolonialist project of domination; and Thomas Nagel and Michael Walzer, who believed that they infringe on national debates over justice. Benhabib's response was not that human rights regimes were necessarily effective at protecting vulnerable individuals, but rather that they created arguments and discourse that could then be deployed by the vulnerable as tools in political debate. This was the jurisgenerative aspect of law, to borrow Robert Cover's term. And it was, Benhabib argued, internal to the democratic conversation. In that sense, it represented a form of self-governing, not an external imposition. Rather than an imperial project, Benhabib argued, it allowed new social movements to use these discourses "to empower themselves by introducing new subjectivities into the public sphere, by articulating new vocabularies of claim-making, and by anticipating new forms of togetherness."[28]

In her most recent essay from 2023, "Cosmopolitanism Reconsidered," Benhabib refashions her concept of the utopia of cosmopolitanism into a new theory of "cosmopolitanism from below": an ideal of equal human dignity and respect for all humans, conjoined with equal respect and generosity toward their cultural, religious, gender, and ethnic differences, that finds its generative source from local and transnational grassroots movements seeking to reinvent political community.[29] With "cosmopolitanism from below," Benhabib proposes, "the universalist ideals of equality and freedom, community and solidarity find new articulations through local as well as transnational iterations."[30] It represents a renewed emphasis on the conjunction of the universal with the local, the transnational with the regional, the international with grassroots. It is intended to respond to criticisms of cosmopolitanism from both liberal and postcolonial thinkers, including Martha Nussbaum and Sylvia Wynter, both of whom Benhabib directly addresses in her essay.

THE ARC OF BENHABIB'S JOURNEY

Rereading the arc of Benhabib's intellectual journey—from her first book, *Critique, Norm, and Utopia*, published in 1986 by Columbia University Press, to her turn to cosmopolitanism as a form of utopia, for instance, in her 2009 lecture "Utopia and Dystopia in Our Times," delivered as her acceptance speech for the Ernst Bloch prize, to her most recent essay, "Cosmopolitanism Reconsidered" from April 2023—one can observe on the one hand a constant thread, consisting of the emancipatory critical theory of equal dignity and autonomy, and on the other hand several important evolutions of her thought, along three principal dimensions: law, sovereignty, and Kantianism. Let me turn now to those transformations.

On the Juridical

First, regarding law, Benhabib's writings evince an evolution from an earlier greater skepticism toward the juridical, to a later, more solid embrace of the rule of law, international law, and human rights.

In *Critique, Norm, and Utopia*, Benhabib expressed greater skepticism toward the legal and juridical realm. There was a certain ambivalence, somewhat muted, but tied to the dark side of the legalistic-juridical approach. Benhabib wrote, for instance, that "One of the central problems of late-capitalist societies lies in their viewing public life from a legalistic-juridical perspective alone, while the vision of a community of needs and solidarity is ignored and rendered irrelevant."[31] The turn to legalistic and juridical praxis represented an impoverishment of the life world that only a communicative ethics could redress. It was not determinative, but prevalent and threatening. As Benhabib wrote, "the juridification of everyday life ... can foster an attitude of dependence, passivity, and clientelism."[32] It was precisely because of that negative potential that Benhabib argued that rights and entitlements had to be conjoined with a community of needs and solidarity.

Thirty years later, I sense that Seyla Benhabib has greater faith and places greater emphasis on the legal and juridical dimensions. The legal is less tied to late capitalism in her analyses now. With cosmopolitanism, and now cosmopolitanism from below, law plays a more positive and central role. In fact, in defining cosmopolitanism, Benhabib identifies the juridical as one of the three definitional dimensions: "It [cosmopolitanism] has a legal dimension in that it defends that each human being ought to be treated as a person entitled to certain universal rights."[33] Today, international law and human rights play a far greater role in the necessary protections that Benhabib advocates for. This is, in part, due to Benhabib's encounter and dialogue with Robert Cover's notion of the jurisgenerative, which Benhabib reformulated as the discursive generative power of legal norms. Cover's writings have been formative for Benhabib.[34] It is also due, in part, to the wave of migration crises that have been a central focus of Benhabib's work and that have drawn her to immigration law and human rights—now a central focus of her research and teaching at Columbia Law School.

The concepts of rights and entitlements were always present, of course, in fact well in evidence in the concluding chapter of *Critique, Norm, and Utopia*. Hannah Arendt's concept of "the right to have rights" has always been at the heart of Benhabib's philosophical ambition. But the concrete reality of international law and of human rights law gained greater prominence in the turn from communicative to cosmopolitan utopianism.

On Sovereignty

Second, Seyla Benhabib's writings also reflect an evolving relationship to sovereignty and the nation-state. This is due, in part, to the turn to nationalism that Benhabib identifies with the critics of cosmopolitanism. But I nevertheless detect, in her earlier work, a more favorable view of the nation-state as a way to protect vulnerable groups. So, for instance, in *Critique, Norm, and Utopia*, Benhabib writes, "It is more correct to speak of a 'polity' of rights and entitlements and an 'association' of needs and solidarity. By a 'polity' I understand a democratic, pluralistic unity, composed of many communities, but held together by a common legal, administrative and political organization. Polities may be nation-states, multi-national states, or a federation of distinct national and ethnic groups."[35] At the time, Benhabib expressed more of a need for the protections of the nation-state—of course, combined with the community of needs and solidarity.

But as a result of the many critiques of her writings on cosmopolitanism, which on her account retreat into a nationalist populism or a liberal nationalism, Benhabib's view of the nation-state has soured. As she writes now, "the weakness of the liberal nationalist position is that it neglects international law constraints on the sovereignty of the demos by constructing state sovereignty as if it were solely defined by the self-assertion of the demos."[36] Benhabib strenuously defends international law and human rights against the attacks of thinkers like Martha Nussbaum, now arguing that they are not weak or inefficacious but rather necessary to the Kantian ideal of cosmopolitanism. "Cosmopolitanism begins with a critique of the *polis* and the *civitas*, in the name of the *cosmos*, of an ordered reality whose rationality transcends the many and conflicting and often unjust, *nomoi* (laws and customs) of the political world."[37]

Now, to be sure, the notion of local and transnational praxis that forms the dual constituent of "cosmopolitanism from below" means that there are local anchors, and the local can include the nation-state and national civil rights law. So it is not as if Benhabib is opposed to the nation-state. But her deep opposition to national isolationism and selfishness, which she associates with critics of cosmopolitanism, suggests a greater ambivalence. In effect, the overall evolution may be one that reduces ambivalence toward international legalism, but increases ambivalence toward the state.

On Kantianism

Third, I also detect a growing attachment to Kantianism from the earlier work to the most recent—a slight drift from Hegel and Marx to Kant, which is something that has marked the work of other critical theorists of the third generation of the Frankfurt tradition, such as Rainer Forst. If anything, cosmopolitanism has brought Seyla Benhabib closer to Kant.

In part, this has been the result of her confrontation with poststructuralist critiques of her writings. Benhabib had always distanced herself from what she called, in 1986, "the currently fashionable structuralist and post-structuralist searches for a philosophy without the subject."[38] But beginning in the 1990s, in philosophical exchanges with Judith Butler, Drucilla Cornell, and Nancy Fraser, Benhabib confronted poststructuralism more directly. The encounter reinforced her commitment to normative foundations and pushed her toward Kant.[39]

Benhabib approached those exchanges from the intersectional perspective of a critical social theorist and feminist. As such, she situated herself, in part, as a feminist critic of Habermas's communicative action theory; she would do so even more forcefully in *Situating the Self* and other writings that focused on dissent and social movements.[40] In her exchanges with Butler, though, Benhabib distanced herself increasingly from poststructuralism, because, in her words, it "place[s] in question the very emancipatory ideals of the women's movements altogether."[41] Poststructuralism undermined, Benhabib argued, the possibility of validity, universalism, hope, and feminist utopia; it proposed a radical antifoundationalism that did away, on Benhabib's reading, with agency, authorship, autonomy, and selfhood. In embracing the Nietzschean idea that there is no "doer behind the deed," poststructuralism was self-defeating and led only to "self-incoherence," in Benhabib's words.[42] Benhabib criticized poststructuralism for causing "a retreat from utopia within feminism" and a loss of hope.[43]

Coming back to the debate with Butler and Cornell a few years later, Benhabib aimed her critique more directly at Butler's theory of gender performativity. The central problem with Butler's approach, Benhabib argued, was her lack of a normative conception of agency. This produced, in Benhabib's view, a void, an absence of a normative grounding for resistance. And without that normative foundation, there was no way to properly understand and evaluate women's struggles and actions.[44] Benhabib concluded the *Feminist Contentions* debate in the following terms: "By 'normative foundations' of social criticism I mean exactly the conceptual possibility of justifying the norms of universal moral respect and egalitarian reciprocity on rational grounds; no more and no less. Whereas most of my colleagues in this volume seem to think that even this is in some sense too much, I think that to want to deny this point is like wanting to jump over our own shadow."[45]

The years, even decades, of debate with poststructuralism and other nonfoundationalist critical challenges have, if anything, reinforced Benhabib's attachment to Kantian normative reasoning. By contrast to other critical theorists, such as Axel Honneth or Rahel Jaeggi, who turned back more to Hegel, Benhabib became over time more Kantian.

NAMING UTOPIA

As Benhabib recognizes in her most recent essay, theories of cosmopolitanism have been sharply criticized, and there is much philosophical disagreement today about the genealogy and implications of cosmopolitanism. "The last decades,"

Benhabib acknowledges, "have been characterized by a disillusionment with cosmopolitanism."[46]

Within critical circles, that disillusionment had to do, first and foremost, with postcolonial challenges to its Eurocentric origins and to the dark side of universalist thought—the fact that so much universalist theorizing was born in tandem with slavery, conquest, colonialism, and imperialism. It also has to do with the way in which, at the "end of history," cosmopolitanism began to feel free-market-oriented and globalist. So the problems were not just its liberalism in the universalist sense, but also its liberalism in the economic sense as well. I think this is captured well by Benhabib's acknowledgment that, with the collapse of communism, "the Kantian ideal of uniting diverse countries under the rule of law, respect for human rights and a free market economy seemed to come alive."[47] The rapprochement of cosmopolitanism with free market economics and globalization was deeply troubling for many critical theorists.

Benhabib's most recent essay and her debate with Sylvia Wynter raise the question, though, whether the dark side of universalism—its proximity to colonialism, slavery, and imperialism during past centuries—is inherent in universalist thought or a historical accident. The question presents a counterfactual that is, of course, by definition, impossible to tranche. It is, after all, a counterfactual. But it is nevertheless a pivotal question, especially when critical thinkers argue that universalism can be stripped of its history of exclusion, domination, and conquest. Is it possible that "cosmopolitanism from below" may be a way to do that if the "from below" means that it is coming from the people who have been historically brutalized, marginalized, and disadvantaged?

I am not entirely convinced, but in the end, I am even less sure that it makes sense today to retain the Kantian framework, constructs, and grounding. Benhabib recognizes the racist elements of Kant's anthropology and geography.[48] Maybe we could avoid anchoring our utopian visions of solidarity, even universality, in those tainted theories today. Perhaps we could, in a nonfoundational way, embrace the ambitions of solidarity, equality, dignity, friendship, and respect for difference without anchoring those values in limping eighteenth-century European thought. This does not mean that we would not read and study it. It does not mean that we would not be in critical conversation with it. But it might mean that we no longer construct our utopias on top of those writings or on their basis. We no longer extend those exact theoretical constructs. Perhaps we can draw today on different sources and genealogies, and use different language, expressions, and names for our critique and praxis. Nietzsche reminds us in *The Gay Science* of the importance of "naming" things.[49] It is time, I would argue, to heed Nietzsche's warning.

Ultimately, critical philosophers may disagree about this, at both the theoretical and the praxis level. But not about the need for respect of difference. As Fred Moten reminds us, it is easy in the academic context to get carried away drawing theoretical differences over philosophical foundations and antifoundationalism, over the form of argument and rhetoric—in effect, to drive wedges between us when in fact we share similar ambitions and goals, at least among critical thinkers.[50] Here too, we can return to Benhabib's core contributions and highlight instead, with her, the need to respect difference. The vision that Seyla Benhabib has consistently advanced is nothing less than admirable. And the intellectual trajectory that has led her to "cosmopolitanism from below" is remarkable.

Seyla Benhabib recentered the concept of utopia within the critical theory tradition of the Frankfurt School. From the publication of her first book and embrace of a communicative utopia to her writings on cosmopolitanism as utopia, to her most recent writings on cosmopolitanism from below, Benhabib reinfused critical thought with the ambition of utopia. Benhabib's remarkable persistence, throughout her decades-long intellectual journey, has trained our attention on the utopian potential of critical theory and, in her words, has "burst open the possibilities of the present."

NOTES

1. Seyla Benhabib, *Critique, Norm, and Utopia* (New York: Columbia University Press, 1986), 278.
2. Benhabib, 351.
3. Benhabib, 353.
4. Benhabib, 352; Seyla Benhabib, "Utopia and Dystopia in Our Times," in *Dignity and Adversity: Human Rights in Troubled Times* (Cambridge: Polity, 2011), 184–95, 193; Seyla Benhabib, "Cosmopolitanism Reconsidered," draft paper prepared for the seminar "Utopia 12/13" held on April 12, 2023, at Columbia University, at page 19, https://blogs.law.columbia.edu/utopia1313/files/2023/04/lecture-on-cosmopolitanism-CCCCT.pdf.
5. Benhabib, *Critique, Norm, and Utopia*, 352.
6. In her review of my book *Critique and Praxis*, Benhabib discusses many of our philosophical differences, especially surrounding questions of epistemology, normativity, and truth. See Seyla Benhabib, "On the Unity and Dissonance of Critique and Praxis," *British Journal of Sociology* 72, no. 3 (June 2021): 859–63. In direct conversation with Benhabib's writings, I offered there a reconstruction of critical theory and outlined a radical critical philosophy of illusions. Bernard E. Harcourt, *Critique and Praxis: A Critical Philosophy of Illusions, Values, and Action* (New York: Columbia University Press, 2020), 158–226.

7. Ernst Bloch, *The Spirit of Utopia*, trans. Anthony A. Nassar (1918; Stanford: Stanford University Press, 2000); Ernst Bloch, *The Principle of Hope*, trans. Neville Plaice, Stephen Plaice, and Paul Knight (1954–59; Cambridge, MA: MIT Press, 1995).
8. Karl Mannheim, *Ideology and Utopia* (1929; London: Routledge, 1936).
9. See, generally, Alexander Neupert-Doppler and Charles Reitz, "Critical Theory and Utopian Thought," in *The SAGE Handbook of Frankfurt School Critical Theory* (New York: Sage, 2018).
10. Theodor Adorno in conversation with Ernst Bloch, "Possibilities of Utopia Today," trans. and ed. Jonathan Roessler, Radio Debate, Südwestrundfunk, 1964, www.academia.edu/45015963/Ernst_Bloch_and_Theodor_W_Adorno_Possibilities_of_Utopia_Today_English_Translation?auto=download.
11. Herbert Marcuse, *The End of Utopia*, trans. Jeremy Shapiro and Shierry M. Weber, in *Psychoanalyse und Politik*, lecture delivered at the Free University of West Berlin in July 1967, 1; Marcuse quoted in Neupert-Doppler and Reitz, "Critical Theory and Utopian Thought," 18.
12. Marcuse, *The End of Utopia*, 2.
13. Marcuse, 2.
14. Marcuse, 2.
15. Jürgen Habermas, *The Theory of Communicative Action*, vol. 1, *Reason and the Rationalization of Society*, trans. Thomas McCarthy (Boston: Beacon, 1984), 134.
16. Benhabib, *Critique, Norm, and Utopia*, 277.
17. Axel Honneth, *The Critique of Power: Reflective Stages in a Critical Social Theory*, trans. Kenneth Baynes (Cambridge, MA: MIT Press, 1991).
18. Benhabib, *Critique, Norm, and Utopia*, 277.
19. Benhabib, 278.
20. Benhabib, ix.
21. Benhabib, 352.
22. Benhabib, 352. ("The community of needs and solidarity is created in the interstices of society by those new social movements, which on the one hand fight to extend the universalist promise of objective spirit—justice and entitlements—and on the other seek to combine the logic of justice with that of friendship.")
23. Benhabib, 353.
24. Benhabib, 351.
25. Benhabib, 353.
26. Benhabib, "Utopia and Dystopia in Our Times," 184–95, 193.
27. Seyla Benhabib, "Claiming Rights Across Borders: International Human Rights and Democratic Sovereignty," *American Political Science Review* 103, no. 4 (2009): 691–704, reproduced in Seyla Benhabib, *Dignity in Adversity: Human Rights in Turbulent Times* (New York: Polity, 2011), 117–37; Seyla Benhabib, "The Return of Political Theology: The Scarf Affair in Comparative Constitutional Perspective in France, Germany, and Turkey," in *Dignity in Adversity*, 166–83; Seyla Benhabib, "Carl Schmitt's Critique of Kant: Sovereignty and International Law," *Political Theory* 40, no. 6 (2012): 688–713.
28. Benhabib, "Claiming Rights Across Borders," 118, 119.

29. Benhabib, "Cosmopolitanism Reconsidered." At the public seminar "Utopia 12/13," Kendall Thomas productively put this term in conversation with Stuart Hall's use of the term *cosmopolitanism from below* in his discussion with Pnina Werbner in his chapter "Cosmopolitanism, Globalisation and Diaspora," in *Anthropology and the New Cosmopolitanism: Rooted, Feminist and Vernacular Perspectives*, ed. Pnina Werbner (London: Routledge, 2008).
30. Benhabib, "Cosmopolitanism Reconsidered," 19.
31. Benhabib, *Critique, Norm, and Utopia*, 350.
32. Benhabib, 350.
33. Benhabib, "Cosmopolitanism Reconsidered," 2.
34. See, e.g., Benhabib, "Carl Schmitt's Critique of Kant," 703; Benhabib, *Dignity in Adversity*, 125–26.
35. Benhabib, *Critique, Norm, and Utopia*, 351.
36. Benhabib, "Cosmopolitanism Reconsidered," 8–9.
37. Benhabib, 12.
38. Benhabib, *Critique, Norm, and Utopia*, 55.
39. Seyla Benhabib, Judith Butler, Drucilla Cornell, Nancy Fraser, and Linda Nicholson, eds., *Feminist Contentions: A Philosophical Exchange* (New York: Routledge, 1995). Benhabib had staked out some of these positions in an earlier article. Seyla Benhabib, "Epistemologies of Post-Modernism," *New German Critique*, no. 33 (1984): 103–27. In the *Feminist Contentions* debate and Benhabib's article, the contributors use the term *postmodernism*, which I find too vague in this context. Benhabib draws on the work of Jane Flax to define the term; but given the disagreements over the term, and the fact that the exchange is about French theory in the late 1980s (mostly Foucault, Derrida, and Lacan), I use the term *poststructuralism* instead.
40. Seyla Benhabib, *Situating the Self: Gender, Community, and Post-modernism* (London: Polity, 1992). See, generally, Tony Couture, "Feminist Criticisms of Habermas's Ethics and Politics," *Dialogue: Canadian Philosophical Review/Revue canadienne de philosophie* 34, no. 2 (1995): 259–80.
41. Seyla Benhabib, "Feminism and Postmodernism: An Uneasy Alliance," in Benhabib, Butler, Cornell, Fraser, and Nicholson, *Feminist Contentions*, 20.
42. Benhabib, 21.
43. Benhabib, 30 (internal quotations omitted).
44. Seyla Benhabib, "Subjectivity, Historiography, and Politics: Reflections on the 'Feminism/Postmodernism Exchange,'" in Benhabib, Butler, Cornell, Fraser, and Nicholson, *Feminist Contentions*, 115.
45. Benhabib, "Subjectivity, Historiography, and Politics," 118.
46. Benhabib, "Cosmopolitanism Reconsidered," 1.
47. Benhabib, 2–3.
48. Benhabib, 16.
49. Bernard E. Harcourt, "Nommer, « utopier » (Naming. Utopizing)," January 13, 2023, Columbia Public Law Research Paper, forthcoming, https://ssrn.com/abstract=4323925.
50. Fred Moten presentation at "Utopia 7/13." See Columbia Center for Contemporary Critical Thought, "Utopia 7/13," February 21, 2023, https://blogs.law.columbia.edu/utopia1313/7-13/.

PART II
Thinking With and Against Arendt

6

"Thinking With and Against" as Feminist Political Theory

PATCHEN MARKELL

In the spring semester of 1995, Seyla Benhabib taught a lecture course to about a hundred undergraduates as part of Harvard University's "Core Curriculum" program under the title "The Public and the Private in Politics, Morality, and Law"; I was one of her teaching assistants. Superficially speaking, the course might have looked like a standard introduction to the "canon" of Western political theory, since the syllabus included works by Plato, Aristotle, Sophocles, Aristophanes, Hobbes, Locke, Rousseau, Marx, and Mill. But the course was also tightly focused on the ways in which these authors conceived of the "public-private distinction" and its significance for social life, which was visible both in Benhabib's decisions about which selections to assign from longer texts—the weeks on Aristotle dealt only with the first three books of the *Politics*, for example—and in the supplementary readings she chose, which included feminist scholarship by Susan Moller Okin, Carole Pateman, and Mary L. Shanley, as well as selections from Hannah Arendt's *The Human Condition*. (Benhabib's book on Arendt, *The Reluctant Modernism of Hannah Arendt*, would appear the following year.) And in the last few weeks the syllabus shifted explicitly to "contemporary controversies," with a particular focus on twentieth-century American constitutional jurisprudence about privacy, reproductive rights, and sexuality, read against the background of Virginia Woolf and Michel Foucault.

During one lecture in the first third of the semester, Benhabib paused to take questions, only to be challenged by a young man who complained about her devotion of *so* much time, lecture after lecture, to the hierarchical household relationships laid out in the first book of Aristotle's *Politics*—between parents and children, masters and slaves, husbands and wives, blah, blah, blah—and asked, in effect, when she was going to get on to the *important* stuff.[1] (Those were not exactly his words, but they capture the force and tone of his comment as I remember it, with its combination of slouching boredom and entitled indignation.) It was a tense moment, or at least it felt so to me. Yet Benhabib's response—which at the time I assumed was improvised, though now I think she was probably all too familiar with challenges like this—was calm and undefensive. She explained that when *she* had been taught Aristotle's *Politics*, her teachers largely passed over these parts of the text as if they were irrelevant to its real subject matter. But that had been bad scholarship: it tacitly reproduced what those readers took to be Aristotle's own wisdom about the stark difference in importance between the affairs of the *oikos* and those of the *polis*, while conspicuously ignoring significant parts of what Aristotle himself had actually said on the subject—and said front and center in book 1, not as an aside or an afterthought.[2] So when feminist scholars insisted on bringing the constitution of the public-private distinction into the foreground of their readings of Aristotle and other canonical authors, this was, of course, a political intervention, but it was also a matter of taking the text seriously: not as an authority, or as something to be "debunked" and then discarded, but as a work that, read carefully, could show us something, including something more or other than its author intended, about the tensions and contradictions that structured the world in which it was written (and our world too).[3] It was, I thought, a magnificent answer.

As far as I can recall, Benhabib didn't refer to what she was doing in this class as "thinking with and against" Aristotle or anybody else. But I begin with this story because I think it might shed some unexpected light on that phrase—"thinking with and against"—and its significance in Benhabib's own practice of political theory, where it's most familiar from her account of herself as "thinking with Arendt against Arendt." At one level, the meaning of the phrase seems straightforward enough: to think with and against means to learn from someone while maintaining sufficient independence to disagree with them when appropriate. Thus, on the one hand, when Benhabib began to unpack the idea of "thinking with Arendt against Arendt," she did so by praising other readers who "retrieve gems of insight [from Arendt's writing] which can still illuminate our struggles as contemporaries"; on the other hand, she has long criticized Arendt both for her failures of judgment in specific political contexts and for failing to supply her political theory with proper "normative foundations."[4] Still, if that was all there was to it, then thinking with and against might turn out to be indistinguishable from what another teacher of mine, impatient with what he saw as the excessive piety of Arendt's readers toward their subject, once suggested was the proper way to approach her work, or the work of any other thinker of the past: by ransacking and pillaging it ruthlessly, hauling away whatever you can use for your own purposes, and tossing aside whatever you find wrong-headed, outdated, or irrelevant.[5]

In this brief essay, I aim to work out the meaning of "thinking with and against" a bit more carefully, especially for the sake of understanding its difference from what we might call "critical ransacking." My twofold wager is, first, that it's crucial to approach "thinking with and against" not only as a mode of interpretation but also as part of a pedagogy, and, second, that we won't fully understand this kind of thinking, in either of these aspects, unless we take seriously its status as an element of Benhabib's practice of *feminist* political theory. That is not to say that it is the only such element. Nor is it to say that feminists can't or shouldn't be ransackers of a certain sort: as Michaele Ferguson reminds us, another feminist philosopher and political theorist of Benhabib's generation, Iris Marion Young, "once described herself as a bandita: a feminist bandit who selectively steals resources from male philosophers to serve her own political purposes, while leaving behind whatever of their work is sexist or unhelpful"—though as Ferguson also shows, just being a ransacker doesn't make you a bandita, or a feminist.[6] My claim is simply that it *matters* that Benhabib first referred to herself as "thinking with Arendt against Arendt" in what was, to that point, the most explicitly feminist piece of writing she had yet published on Arendt's political theory, an article of 1993 called "Feminist Theory and Hannah Arendt's Concept of Public Space."[7] In what follows, I'll try to explain why.

An expression like "thinking with and against" needn't mean only one thing, of course; and Benhabib's use of the phrase has some resonances that are worth noticing even if they don't flow directly from or toward feminism. Perhaps the most obvious resonance is with a polemic that the young Jürgen Habermas wrote for the *Frankfurter Allgemeine Zeitung* in the summer of 1953, in response to Martin Heidegger's newly published *Einführung in die Metaphysik*. In light of Heidegger's decision to reproduce these lectures of 1935 without altering their reference to the "inner truth and greatness" of the National Socialist movement, Habermas wrote in his closing line, "it appears to be time to think with Heidegger against Heidegger."[8] Habermas's stress in this sentence, though, fell on the word "against": this article was, at bottom, a political declaration of disaffiliation from Heidegger in the context of a postwar German political culture that Habermas thought was failing (like Heidegger himself) to confront its recent past. In Benhabib's practice of "thinking with and against," by contrast, the emphasis falls on the word "with": her 1993 article, for example, was framed as an attempt to reclaim at least some aspects of Arendt's thought *for* feminist theory in a context in which the most common reactions to works like *The Human Condition* among contemporary feminist theorists included "disappointment," "anger," and "puzzlement."[9] If there is an echo of Habermas's phrase in Benhabib's, then, I suspect it lies less in any direct parallel between their stances toward these two predecessors than in the fact that, for Benhabib, thinking with Arendt would sometimes also turn out to mean thinking against Heidegger, or at least against interpretations of Arendt's work that she thought overstated her Heideggerianism.[10]

Another resonance arises less from the specific language of the expression than from the intellectual comportment it suggests. Although Benhabib's first book, *Critique, Norm, and Utopia* (1986), does not refer to the procedure of "thinking with and against," it does trace the practice of critical theory back to Hegel's development of "the method of immanent exposition and critique," whose normative force was to be anchored in its very object of evaluation rather than in criteria dogmatically imposed upon the object by the critic.[11] So perhaps "thinking with and against" does with respect to an author what immanent critique is supposed to do with respect to society: it gets its critical leverage by attending to the ways in which an author's work fails to carry out its own stated aims successfully, or to maintain the coherence and consistency of its concepts, or to live up to the self-understanding that the author projects on the page. I think this analogy does capture something central to "thinking with and against," but it is also likely to arouse an objection, at least at first. The very idea of immanent critique, as well as the seemingly endless debates about whether any version of it can be made sufficiently critical, have been energized by the experience of a double bind, by the sense that critique at once *cannot* and *must* transcend its object; yet that pathos of redoubled constraint comes more readily when the object of critique is an encompassing social order than when it is the oeuvre of a single writer. If it takes no special Archimedean ambition or achievement to disagree with one person even down to basic premises—it happens all the time!—then thinking against someone while, and by, thinking *with* them will likewise be optional: perhaps a reflection of a contingent affinity of perspective, perhaps a sign of a particular critic's generosity of spirit, but not, in any case, an unavoidable burden felt to be imposed by the enterprise of critique as such.

There's something to this: Benhabib didn't "think with and against" just anyone, but rather someone whose "legacy," as she put it in the last line of *The Reluctant Modernism of Hannah Arendt,* "continues to inspire."[12] Habermas, likewise, might well have dropped the "with" altogether had he not spent the previous few years as what he later called a "thoroughgoing Heideggerian."[13] But the disanalogy should not be overstated, as if "thinking with and against" were just one among many methods that a well-equipped theorist will have available in their toolkit, to be chosen in those more delicate situations that don't call for philosophizing with a hammer. To the contrary, there is a sense in which "thinking with and against," like immanent critique, is also animated by the experience of a double bind or an unavoidability. And this is because the objects of these two forms of criticism are not as separate as the objection I've just rehearsed might make it seem: for many political theorists, and certainly, I think, for Benhabib, critical engagement with a single writer like Arendt is not an alternative but a *means* to critical engagement with a larger social world. To elaborate this point, I want to turn now to a third resonance of the expression "thinking with and against," one that Benhabib herself has invoked: namely, its resonance with Hannah Arendt's own approach to what she called "the tradition of Western political thought"—for what is such a "tradition" if not one of those mediations by which writers come to stand for, and bear the authority of, more than themselves alone?[14] This will bring me back around to the classroom, and, despite the not-particularly-feminist character of Arendt's own writing about this tradition, to feminism.

In one of her earliest essays on Arendt's political thought, "Hannah Arendt and the Redemptive Power of Narrative," Benhabib had already vividly drawn out the double bind to which Arendt was responding when, after the war, she began to write about what she would call, variously, "the tradition," "the Western tradition," "our tradition," "the great tradition," and the "tradition of Western political thought."[15] On the one hand, Arendt wrote in a context in which, thanks to "the events of the twentieth century," inherited categories of understanding and evaluation seemed to have lost their authority *as* a tradition.[16] (Benhabib made this point by quoting a passage from the first volume of the posthumously published *The Life of the Mind* in which Arendt declared that "the thread of tradition is broken and we shall not be able to renew it," though Arendt had already begun to sound this theme by the end of the 1940s.)[17] On the other hand, Benhabib continued, this "break" was not a release or a liberation from the past: it simply meant that "even when the thread of tradition is broken, even when the past is no longer authoritative simply because it has been, it lives within us *and we cannot avoid placing ourselves in relation to it.*"[18]

Against this background, we might notice that the essay in which Benhabib introduced the idea of "thinking with Arendt against Arendt" is driven by a compounded analogue to this dilemma. I've already mentioned that Benhabib opened "Feminist Theory and Hannah Arendt's Concept of Public Space" by observing that feminists have found Arendt hard to think with; but it's important to note *why*: because Arendt's categories of understanding, including especially her distinction between the public and private spheres, so often seem to be congruent with those of a patriarchal tradition that has in various ways gendered, denigrated, and obscured the supposedly private labor of social reproduction on which public-political life nevertheless also depends.[19] At the same time, Benhabib also insisted that Arendt is a theorist whom feminists should not avoid, and again it's important to note why: because feminists *cannot* avoid *some* relation to traditional conceptual formations like the public-private distinction. Yes, one way to relate to such a distinction would be to abandon it altogether; but this, Benhabib argued, would be politically catastrophic for feminism: "any apparently simplistic subversion of [the concepts of public and private] will at the best lead us as feminists to lose political allies and at the worst land us in authoritarian utopia."[20] Thus the only thing left to do, and the imperative that drove Benhabib's article, is to look more closely at *how* this formation has been assembled, both in Arendt's work and in the tradition she encountered—in order to see, for example, how the idea of the private as a space of physical and affective shelter has been conflated with, and so made to seem impossible without, the idea of the private as a fundamentally unfree domain of dependent and embodied labor; how this conflation has helped sustain the domination of women by men; and where exploitable seams in this assemblage might be showing, both in theory and in the world.

The presence of this kind of motivating dilemma, it seems to me, marks one decisive difference between "thinking with and against" and what I earlier called "critical ransacking." In at least some versions, the notion of "critical ransacking" imagines the contemporary theorist as an individual who ventures out in search of good ideas and finds some, inconveniently heaped together with or bonded to a bunch of bad ones, and also protected by the guards and walls of established authority; heroically, using nothing but his own intellect—for this is a quest narrative, and also a gendered model of the accession to philosophical maturity—he dispatches the guards, batters down the walls, separates the treasure from the dross, and carts it away. (We've all had that kid in class; some of us might have *been* that kid in class.) "Thinking with and against," by contrast, positions the contemporary theorist as someone caught in a bind, for whom the so-called "canonical" authors of the past, including the recent past, are no longer authoritative—and maybe never were—but who nevertheless remain unavoidable.

From this perspective, notice, the violence that the ransacker has to deploy to defeat authority has already taken place. Maybe it was the shattering historical violence that Arendt, in her essay on Walter Benjamin, said had made him into a peculiarly modern kind of "collector," who no longer needed to "destroy the context in which his object once was only part of a greater, living entity" because he was faced with an already-ruined world: "History itself—that is, the break in tradition which took place at the beginning of this century—had already relieved him of this task of destruction and he only needed to bend down, as it were, to select his precious fragments from the pile of debris."[21] Or maybe it is the ubiquitous violence of the enforcement of gender subordination in the face of the resistance to it that women undertake for the sake of a differently organized world—a violence that remains invisible, and a vision that remains illegible, from within the terms of a tradition that so often simply naturalizes both gender difference and the hierarchy that is supposed to follow from it. In either case, the result is a situation in which, at least for some readers, the "tradition falls silent when *we* ask *our* questions," as Arendt once put it, while at the same time the elements that made up that tradition continue to command attention and carry weight—including, of course, in the dynamics that govern who and what gets taken seriously in the academy.[22] Arendt made the tradition's silence articulate by reading it diagnostically; "thinking with and against" does too.

And that brings me, in conclusion, to a second decisive difference between these two ways of approaching the works of the past: the image of critical ransacking suggests the priority of the part to the whole from which it is forcibly removed, while the diagnostic approach to reading involved in "thinking with and against" doesn't. Of course, it is not "holist" in the sense of trying to restore the ruined coherence and thus the lost authority even of an individual text, much less of an entire corpus or tradition: Benhabib has long emphasized, and admired, the "fragmentary" character of the model of historiography Arendt adapted from Benjamin.[23] Still, the term *fragmentary* should not obscure Arendt's or Benhabib's conviction that some of the most important things we have to learn from the works that belong to a broken tradition—about themselves and about their world and about ours—only become visible in the relations, including the tensions and contradictions, *among* their parts. The holism of "thinking with and against" is a matter of what Jill Frank has called the practice of "looking at everything everywhere" in the text, rather than selecting parts that will allow the work or its author to be reduced to an abstractable "position" in relation to some simplified set of conceptual coordinates.[24]

Indeed, one of the things that was most compelling to me about Benhabib's answer to her impatient student, back in 1995, was the way in which she simultaneously affirmed the specific, contemporary, feminist perspective from which she was conducting her diagnostic and critical reading of Aristotle, *and* defended this precisely as a matter of doing justice to the *whole* text. This productively scrambled the usual assumptions according to which an avowedly political interpretation was presumed to sacrifice faithfulness or objectivity, while careful, patient reading was presumed to go along with political neutrality (or ideological docility). It was a brilliant move—and it was also a move made under pressure, as Benhabib, along with many others, navigated the specific dilemmas of doing feminist political theory and philosophy in the midst of disciplines where their questions were often treated as illegible, as they sometimes still are. And they are not the only ones that are. There is still, there is always, more "thinking with and against" our fields and our inheritances to be done—and the doubleness of the preposition, with its implicit combination of opposition and solidarity, may be all the more important at a time when critical scholarship has to defend itself both against the force of its own disciplines' traditions, and against reactionary political campaigns to subject the very institutions of teaching and research to intensified legislative control. I am grateful to Seyla Benhabib not only for what she's shown me about how to do this kind of work, but also for having sustained an intellectual and professional space in which doing it felt possible, welcome, and necessary.

NOTES

1. On the poetics of "blah blah blah" in relation to feminist discourse, see Elizabeth Wingrove, "blah blah WOMEN blah blah EQUALITY blah blah DIFFERENCE," *Philosophy and Rhetoric* 49, no. 4 (2016): 406–19.
2. As many feminist political theorists have noted, the notion that canonical texts were "silent" about women was the misleading effect of the secondary literature in which those texts were digested and interpreted; the texts themselves often had much to say about women (though that does not necessarily mean they addressed themselves *to* them). See, e.g., Kathleen B. Jones and Anna G. Jónasdóttir, "Introduction: Gender as an Analytic Category in Political Theory," in *The Political Interests of Gender* (London: Sage, 1988), 1; Linda Zerilli, "Feminist Theory and the Canon of Political Thought," in *The Oxford Handbook of Political Theory*, ed. John Dryzek, Bonnie Honig, and Anne Phillips (New York: Oxford University Press, 2008), 108; Lori J. Marso, "Women in Western Political Thought," in *The Encyclopedia of Political Thought*, ed. Michael Gibbons et al. (Malden, MA: Wiley-Blackwell, 2014), http://dx.doi.org/10.1002/9781118474396), 1.
3. My lecture notes indicate that Benhabib repeatedly framed the course as an alternative both to the idea that there was a single canon of "great texts" and to the

dismissal of those texts as the exclusionary work of "dead white males"; thus, in the final lecture, she explained that the alternative was to "learn to read these texts as contradictory documents and ask how and why the contradictions exist in the same theorist" (Moral Reasoning 50 lecture notes, May 19, 1995). I have taken the term *debunked* here from Benhabib's discussion of what she called the "self-righteous dogmatism of the latecomers" who "approach tradition and thinkers of the past only to 'debunk' them," in a paper published in 1995 ("The Pariah and Her Shadow: Hannah Arendt's Biography of Rahel Varnhagen"), which would shortly become chapter 1 of *The Reluctant Modernism of Hannah Arendt* (first published in 1996 but which I cite in its new ed. [Lanham, MD: Rowman and Littlefield, 2000], 3–4).

4. Seyla Benhabib, "Feminist Theory and Hannah Arendt's Concept of Public Space," *History of the Human Sciences* 6, no. 2 (1993): 100; Benhabib, *Reluctant Modernism*, 193ff.

5. This is my paraphrase of a comment I heard Jeremy Waldron—himself an appreciative reader of Arendt—make from the floor at a centenary panel on Arendt's political thought held at the 2006 Annual Meeting of the American Political Science Association; the panelists included Mary Dietz, Richard Flathman, Jeffrey Isaac, Kirstie McClure, and Dana Villa. Several months later, Waldron published an essay in the *New York Review of Books* in which he warned persuasively against the dangers of turning to Arendt's writing for lessons immediately applicable to our own time, or as a source of "sibyllic inspiration," but now without setting up an exaggerated opposition between piety and pillage: "The tribute that is owed to the particularity of Arendt's work is not imitation and it is not the application of some lessons we are supposed to have learned; it is our own resolve to think things through here and now, as she thought about them there and then" ("What Would Hannah Say?," *New York Review of Books* [March 15, 2007]; this should be read alongside Waldron's earlier essay "What Plato Would Allow," *Nomos* 37 [1995], in which Arendt figures at 167–70).

6. Michaele Ferguson, "Bandita: Iris Young and the Politics of Reading, Writing, and Citation," book MS in progress, chap. 1 (quoted with permission, and with thanks to Ferguson for sharing her work). Young's own best-known description of the figure of the bandita is as "an intellectual outlaw who raids the texts of male philosophers and steals from them what she finds pretty or useful, leaving the rest behind" ("Gender as Seriality: Thinking About Women as a Social Collective," *Signs* 19, no. 3 [Spring 1994]: 723).

7. Benhabib, "Feminist Theory," 100.

8. "Es scheint an der Zeit zu sein, mit Heidegger gegen Heidegger zu denken." Jürgen Habermas, "Mit Heidegger gegen Heidegger denken: Zur Veröffentlichung von Vorlesungen aus dem Jahre 1935," *Frankfurter Allgemeine Zeitung* (July 25, 1953). This article was reprinted under the subtitle only along with two later articles on Heidegger—"Die große Wirkung" (originally also in the *FAZ*, September 26, 1959) and "Ein anderer Mythos des 20. Jahrhunderts" (from the *Frankfurter Hefte*, March 1959)—in *Philosophisch-politische Profile* (Berlin: Suhrkamp, 1971); the third piece was omitted from the 1981 German edition, and both the first and third were omitted from the English *Philosophical-Political Profiles* (Cambridge, MA: MIT

Press, 1985). All three texts were translated together under the title "Martin Heidegger: On the Publication of Lectures from the Year 1935," in *Graduate Faculty Philosophy Journal* 6, no. 2 (Fall 1977): 155–80, of which the 1953 article thus constitutes only the first section, 155–64.
9. Benhabib, "Feminist Theory," 97.
10. "Expressed in somewhat stylized form: although Hannah Arendt, the stateless and persecuted Jew, is the philosophical and political modernist, Arendt, the student of Martin Heidegger, is the antimodernist Grecophile theorist of the *polis* and its lost glory"—which is why, to present a complex view of both sides of Arendt's "reluctant modernism," Benhabib found it vital to "decenter the place of *The Human Condition* in our reading of Hannah Arendt" in order to attend to the works that more clearly manifested her "experiences as a German Jewish woman in the age of totalitarianism," including *The Origins of Totalitarianism* and *Rahel Varnhagen* (Benhabib, *Reluctant Modernism*, xxxviii–xl).
11. Seyla Benhabib, *Critique, Norm, and Utopia: A Study of the Foundations of Critical Theory* (New York: Columbia University Press, 9). Thanks to Seyla Benhabib for pointing out the relevance of immanent critique to "thinking with and against" after the conference at which I presented an earlier version of this essay.
12. Benhabib, *Reluctant Modernism*, 215.
13. Jürgen Habermas, "Life-Forms, Morality, and the Task of the Philosopher" (1984), in *Autonomy and Solidarity: Interviews with Jürgen Habermas*, rev. ed., ed. Peter Dews (London: Verso, 1992), 189.
14. See Benhabib, "Feminist Theory," where, in the same paragraph in which she introduces the phrase "thinking with Arendt against Arendt," she writes: "Much as Arendt herself appropriated the political tradition of the West, not in the spirit of a scholastic exercise, but in the spirit of questioning and dialogue such as to orient the mind in the present, we too can engage with her work today to illuminate some of the deepest political perplexities of our times" (100).
15. Texts from Arendt's most intensive period of engagement with the problem represented by this tradition and its "break" are gathered in Hannah Arendt, *The Modern Challenge to Tradition: Fragmente eines Buches*, ed. Barbara Hahn and James McFarland, vol. 6 of *Kritische Gesamtausgabe/Complete Works: Critical Edition* (Göttingen: Wallstein Verlag, 2018). This volume will appear soon on the open access digital webportal of the Arendt Edition, published by the Freie Universität Berlin, at https://hannah-arendt-edition.net.
16. Seyla Benhabib, "Hannah Arendt and the Redemptive Power of Narrative," *Social Research* 57, no. 1 (Spring 1990): 187. An earlier version of this piece had first appeared in German translation in 1988 ("Hannah Arendt und die erlösende Kraft des Erzählens," in *Zivilisationsbruch: Denken nach Auschwitz*, ed. Dan Diner [Frankfurt: Fischer Taschenbuch Verlag, 1988], 150–74). Benhabib's first essay on Arendt, "Judgment and the Moral Foundations of Politics in Hannah Arendt's Thought," had appeared the same year in *Political Theory* 16, no. 1 (February 1988): 29–51. Elsewhere, I argue that there is an important tension in Arendt's early writing about the "break in tradition" between two accounts of when and how that break took place, one of which emphasized the sudden, shattering confrontation with the unprecedented

crime represented by the concentration camps, and the other of which emphasized that the disconnect between traditional concepts and the political situation of the twentieth century had been deepening at least since the First World War; on this, see Patchen Markell, *Politics Against Rule: Hannah Arendt and* The Human Condition, in progress, chap. 3.

17. Hannah Arendt, *Thinking*, vol. 1 of *The Life of the Mind* (New York: Harcourt Brace Jovanovich, 1978), 212, quoted in Benhabib, "Hannah Arendt and the Redemptive Power of Narrative," 187; for one early example, see Arendt's "Concluding Remarks" (composed in 1949) to the first edition of *The Origins of Totalitarianism*: "the whole of nearly three thousand years of Western civilization, as we have known it in a comparatively uninterrupted stream of tradition, has broken down" (Arendt, *The Origins of Totalitarianism* [New York: Harcourt, Brace, 1951], 434; this conclusion, omitted from later editions, was reprinted as an appendix in the 2004 Schocken edition, in which the cited passage is at 625).

18. Benhabib, "Hannah Arendt and the Redemptive Power of Narrative," 188, emphasis mine.

19. Benhabib, "Feminist Theory," 97.

20. Benhabib, 100.

21. Hannah Arendt, "Walter Benjamin, 1892–1940," in *Men in Dark Times* (New York: Harcourt Brace Jovanovich, 1968), 199–200; Benhabib cites this passage in "Hannah Arendt and the Redemptive Power of Narrative," 189.

22. Hannah Arendt to Kurt Blumenfeld, October 14, 1952, in Hannah Arendt and Kurt Blumenfeld, *". . . in keinem Besitz verwurzelt": Die Korrespondenz*, ed. Ingeborg Nordmann and Iris Pilling (Hamburg: Rotbuch Verlag, 1995), 68, translation mine.

23. Benhabib, "Hannah Arendt and the Redemptive Power of Narrative," 188–91.

24. Jill Frank, *Poetic Justice: Rereading Plato's* Republic (Chicago: University of Chicago Press, 2018), 6–9.

7

Arendt and Truth

GAYE İLHAN DEMİRYOL

In 2018, Seyla Benhabib diagnosed that the American Republic is in a crisis.[1] The United States' perpetual overseas military engagements on the international front, the human rights violations against refugees and asylum seekers, and a democracy-disparaging, hate-spewing political discourse emanating from Washington on the home front were causes for alarm. The situation has not improved much in the intervening years. At the start of 2021, a mob invaded the U.S. Capitol to stop the certification of the presidential election—an ultimately unsuccessful attempt but a serious metaphorical blow to one of the fundamental tenets of democracy, the peaceful transfer of power. The former president Donald Trump is a possible Republican contender for the 2024 presidential elections.[2]

Analyzing the crisis, Benhabib explicitly refrained from defining it as a crisis of *democracy*. She argued that attributing the ills caused by the current situation to liberal democracy is not only misleading and harmful but also a tactic employed by authoritarian leaders worldwide to discredit democracy. Instead, Benhabib claimed that, exacerbated by increased neoliberal financial globalization, the crisis has multiple facets, including the weaknesses of the representative institutions, challenges to the boundaries of demos in the form of movement of peoples across borders, and fragmentation of the public sphere.

In terms of the fragmentation of the public sphere, Benhabib draws our attention to the disappearance of reasoned public conversations. The new forms of media by which a global public sphere is constructed, while on the one hand allowing more room for documentation and revealing of human rights abuses, police brutality, and political misconduct, on the other hand reduces the public debate to fleeting images and slogans. This new form of communication contributes even more to the demise of the public space than fake news. After all, "Lies and propaganda, have always been part of politics even in the Middle Ages, haven't they?" remarks Benhabib. This sentiment is similar to Hannah Arendt's, whose book of essays *The Crises of The Republic* inspired Benhabib's essay. Arendt wrote, "deception, the deliberate falsehood and outright lie used as legitimate means to achieve political ends, have been with us since the beginning of recorded history. Truthfulness has never been counted among political virtues, and lies have always been regarded as justifiable tools in political dealings."[3]

While lies and propaganda have always been a valuable tool in the arsenal of political power, in our polarized contemporary societies, truth is more contested than ever. Since the Oxford English Dictionary chose *post-truth* as the word of the year in 2016, political commentators have been analyzing the rise of post-truth politics around the world: the United States, United Kingdom, India, Brazil, Russia, and China, among others.[4] The common thread among these analyses is the relationship between the decline of truth in the public sphere and the quality of democratic governance. If post-truth politics does indeed play a role in the fragmentation of the public sphere, then attending to the controversy around truth and post-truth in modern liberal democracies is warranted. Accordingly, this essay is an attempt to examine the political relevance of truth. Why is truth important? What is the political nature of truth-telling? How can truth be protected?

To answer these questions, I turn to Hannah Arendt. Arendt is first and foremost a theorist of action. She believes in the public space, where human beings act together to transform the world. Unpredictability and change initiated by concerted political activity are, according to Arendt, a human condition. Yet, Arendt also wrote two very influential essays on the relationship between veracity, falsehood, and political power; "Truth and Politics" (1967) and "Lying in Politics" (1971).[5] Arendt penned the first article in response to the controversy caused by the publication of *Eichmann in Jerusalem*.[6] Arendt saw herself as a truth-teller reporting the facts of the Second World War in general and the Holocaust in particular. Since her reporting caused a lot of anxiety, anger, and resentment, Arendt saw it necessary to ask: Is it always legitimate to tell the truth? Did she believe without any qualification in the maxim, "let truth come out, even though the world may perish?"[7] The second article, "Lying in Politics," is Arendt's reflections on the Pentagon Papers. In June 1971, the *New York Times* published documents from a detailed and classified Pentagon study, officially titled *Report of the Office of the Secretary of Defense Vietnam Task Force*. Leaked by a military analyst, and over seven thousand pages, the document shed light on America's involvement in Southeast Asia, and the eventual Vietnam War. According to the *New York Times*, the Pentagon Papers demonstrated that the U.S. government had systematically lied to the American public and Congress.[8] Both articles deal with lying and deception, and their ramifications for the political.

Arendt's arguments spawned many journalistic and popular accounts of our post-truth societies.[9] The scholarly literature that harkens to Arendt's work falls into two camps. The first approach, while accepting the popularity of Arendt's work, argues that in articulating the threat that fake news and post-truth presents to democracy, Arendt is not very helpful. Chambers, for example, contends that Arendt leaves the question of democracy largely out of the picture, and therefore fails to see how democracy, especially deliberative democracy, can offer strategies and practices to guard against the attacks on truth.[10] Chambers also takes issue with Arendt's perception of truth as a quasi-Platonic, singular, and final concept necessarily antithetical to politics, and insists instead on the corrigible and fallible nature of all truth claims.

A second approach recognizes the turn to Arendt in a time of politics as meaningful, yet finds that this orientation is ultimately misguided.[11] Politics and truth have always been at odds, so our contemporary problem is not about safeguarding truth but our common world. The fragmentation and polarization led to the fall of the public space and the remedy lies in its rehabilitation.

This essay takes a less-traveled third road.[12] While agreeing that the loss of our common world is of great concern, I also demonstrate that the facts are the very building blocks of our common world, and hence Arendt's insistence on safeguarding them. There would be no permanence, no stability, no perseverance in human existence without people "willing to testify to what is and appears to them because it is."[13] Truth is what we cannot change, "it is the ground on which we stand and the sky that stretches above us."[14] By demonstrating that truth has a world-constitutive quality, I argue that the attack on truth is an attack on our political community, our common world. Populist and authoritarian attacks on truth cannot be ignored if we want to safeguard our political communities.

I contribute to the debate by first offering a close reading of Arendt's different kinds of truth, which are often overlooked or too easily dismissed.[15] This discussion also establishes that Arendt is attentive to the varieties of truth claims and their implications for politics. Then I turn to the potential sources to safeguard truth that Arendt identifies in our societies, albeit liberal democratic ones. In our post-truth society, Arendt's visionary political intervention guides us in our inquiry into the nature and significance of truth-telling.

THE NATURE OF TRUTH

While Arendt qualifies the concept of truth with various adjectives, she primarily distinguishes between two types of truth: rational and factual.[16] Rational truth as distinct from factual truth denotes truth "neither given to nor disclosed to but produced by the human mind."[17] She states that this distinction is mostly a product of "the modern age" and that she will accept it "without discussing its intrinsic legitimacy."[18] While the distinction seems to emerge from a historical understanding of the philosophy of science, it warrants justification. How does Arendt defend her refusal to provide this justification? She argues that "wanting to find out what injury political power is capable of inflicting on truth, we look into these matters for political rather than philosophical reasons, and hence can afford to disregard what truth is and be content to take the word in the sense in which men commonly understand it."[19] Arendt in this work is primarily interested in the relationship between truth and politics. She wants to put aside the question of what truth is to focus on factual truth and its relationship to political power.

Before buying into Arendt's premise and moving onto factual truth, however, let us first examine its counterpart. Arendt categorizes rational truth produced by the human mind into three: mathematical, scientific, and philosophical truth.[20] Mathematical truth is mathematical axioms and theorems, such as Euclidian geometry. A more concrete illustration is Hobbes's statement "the three angles of a triangle should be equal to two angles of a square."[21] Hobbes employs this statement to demonstrate that what is right and wrong is always in dispute, especially if material interests are concerned. Hobbes argues that if there were an actual conflict of interest involved, even this mathematical statement would cause controversy that would end in the burning of geometry books.

Arendt disagrees. She contends instead that "the human mind will always be able to produce such axiomatic statements," and that the " 'burning of all books of geometry' would not be radically effective" to erase this mathematical truth from the face of the Earth.[22] The implication is that mathematical truth is a function of the structure of the human mind. According to Arendt, as long as human beings continue to think, this kind of truth will continue to exist.

This brings us to the second kind of rational truth, scientific truth. These are scientific statements such as "the Earth moves around the sun," or Einstein's theory of relativity. In the case of scientific truth, Arendt seems more concerned about the possibility of truth coming to light and being passed down to future generations, given historical precedence. She ponders, "had history taken a different turn, the whole modern scientific development from Galileo to Einstein might not have come to pass."[23] One can argue that Arendt's skepticism is betrayed by her examples. After all, Galileo recanted publicly and was prohibited by the Inquisition from ever publishing his scientific research, but we do not continue to believe that the sun revolves around the Earth. On the other hand, Arendt's worry is not completely groundless, as surveys reveal that the factuality of scientific truth is not at all indisputable. Forty percent of U.S. adults continue to subscribe to the creationist view of human origins,[24] while 20 percent believe that human activity plays little to no role in climate change.[25]

Finally, the third kind of rational truth is philosophical truth, statements such as "It is better to suffer wrong than to do wrong."[26] Philosophical truth, according to Arendt, has always been in conflict with politics.[27] This conflict is best understood as a struggle between two ways of life: on the one hand, the solitary life of the philosopher spent in pursuit of the everlasting and unchanging principles; on the other hand, the citizens' ever-changing opinions about the realm of human affairs, which itself is constantly in flux. The epitome of this conflict is Plato's philosopher, who, having seen the sunlight with his very own eyes, descends back into the cave to dispose of illusion and falsehood, only to find himself to be at best ridiculed by, at worst killed at the hands of, his fellow citizens.

This ancient antagonism, though, no longer exists in our modern world, according to Arendt. In our contemporary societies, the philosopher's truth is acknowledged not as the one truth, but as an opinion among many. Once Plato's philosopher descends back among the citizens, his truth no longer enjoys a privileged position. It is subject to criticism and challenge just like any other opinion. But this is not a disconcerting situation. On the contrary, Arendt finds it a welcome development that signifies a restoration of the political's dignity: "the insight that for men, living in company, the inexhaustible richness of human discourse is infinitely more significant than any One Truth could ever be."[28]

According to Arendt, the characteristic common to all rational types of truth is that, first, it belongs in the realm of solitary reflection; it is the fruit of the efforts of the mathematician, the scientist, and the philosopher. Second, the subject matter lies outside the political. For this reason, there is a relative permanence and stability associated with rational truth. What differentiates factual truth is that it is the product of the realm of human affairs. Facts come into existence in the fluid, ever-changing field of human activity. Factual truth is the most vulnerable and at the same time the "politically most relevant" kind of truth.[29]

Arendt observes that truth is both powerful and fragile. How can truth be powerful and fragile at the same time? There is a coercive element in factual truth, which is revealed for Arendt in the following anecdote:

> During the twenties, so a story goes, Clemenceau, shortly before his death, found himself in a friendly talk with a representative of the Weimar Republic on the question of guilt for the outbreak of the First World War. "What in your opinion," Clemenceau was asked, "will the future historians think of this troublesome and controversial issue?" He replied, "This I don't know. But I know for certain that they will not say Belgium invaded Germany."[30]

This brutal and elementary indestructibility of factuality gives truth a "despotic character" that puts it beyond dispute.[31] Facts are not constituted by the political power, they arise from without; they are "independent of the wishes of and desires of the citizens."[32] Facts also "have no conclusive reason for being what they are; they could have been otherwise, and this annoying contingency is literally unlimited."[33] Facts do not fit into our greater narratives; there is no meaning in factuality.

The strength of factuality is better understood in comparison to falsehood. Lies are more tempting and more believable "since the liar has the great advantage of knowing beforehand what the audience wishes or expects to hear."[34] Lies fit better into a narrative that we already have in our minds. The lie is easy, comforting. The lie does not shock us; it does not expect us to reason or to judge. It is in line with our expectations, beliefs, and ideologies. On the contrary, factual truth is shocking, unexpected, and sometimes even offensive. Factual truth is hard to handle.[35] But to recognize things for what they are, for Arendt, is necessary to understand them, to stand up to them, and eventually to change them.

Facts are also fragile because they do not have weight in and of themselves. They need to be witnessed, seen, heard, and communicated to others. Facts, in other words, need "testimony to find a secure dwelling place in the domain of human affairs."[36] Facts need the willingness of individuals to step into the light of the public with their testimony. Facts need our courage and trustworthiness. The prospects of truth look very bleak: "The chances of factual truth surviving the onslaught of power are very slim indeed, it is always in danger of being maneuvered out of the world not only for a time but, potentially, forever."[37]

TRUTH UNDER ATTACK

While secrecy, deliberate falsehood, and lie have always been a part of the political repertoire, in the contemporary world, factual truth is under two kinds of attack.[38] First, truth is under systematic attack by political regimes that need to erase or manipulate factual truth to neutralize opposition, suppress dissent, increase their popularity among their supporters, and consolidate their power. Arendt had dealt extensively with this full-fledged attack on truth in the context of totalitarian regimes. But while totalitarian governments and dictatorships are "by far the most effective agencies in shielding ideologies and images from the impact of reality and truth," they do not have a monopoly on this political strategy.[39] Attempts to rewrite "contemporary history under the eyes of those who have witnessed it" are common, especially by populist, illiberal, and authoritarian leaders.[40] That is not to say liberal democratic governments are immune to employing mendacity as a tool. The Bush administration's declaration that Saddam Hussein had weapons of mass destruction as justification for the invasion of Iraq without a shred of credible evidence can be easily recalled.[41]

Second, truth, especially unwelcome factual truth, risks being discredited by being reduced to mere opinion.[42] This observation constitutes Arendt's foresightful diagnosis of the post-truth society, even before the term was invented. Arendt observes that in contemporary society, factual truth is countered not by outright lies or deliberate falsehood but by opinion. Truth becomes one opinion among others, an "it seems to me."[43] When facts are reduced to opinion, they are especially vulnerable to being discredited, overlooked, ignored, and forgotten. The second attack is not unrelated to the first one.

This reflection about facts being reduced to mere opinion is one of the most puzzling observations in Arendt's essay "Truth and Politics." If we recall Arendt's arguments about rational truth, the multiplicity of opinions and the deliberation that takes into account a variety of viewpoints are celebrated by Arendt as the hallmark of the political. Then can it be argued that the same applies to facts? Isn't it to be celebrated rather than condemned that the facts can be freely examined and disputed in the public realm? Arendt contends that "factual truth must inform opinions, but these truths, though they are never obscure, are not transparent either, and it is in their very nature to withstand further elucidation."[44] In other words, doesn't the free and public contestation of facts lead to a better-informed public?

On this point, Arendt is adamant that the opposite of factual truth is deliberate falsehood, i.e., lie. Facts inform opinions, that is true, but "freedom of opinion is a farce unless factual information is guaranteed and facts themselves are not in dispute."[45] In other words, the factual matter can be interpreted in the light of different interests and passions that individuals possess, but it does not mean that it can be manipulated at will; "we don't admit the right to touch the factual matter itself."[46] No historian is allowed to write that Belgium invaded Germany. As Ari-Elmeri Hyvönen puts it: "Opinions depend on a minimal ground of shared facts so that they can be opinions about *something*, that is, different perspectives on something shared and not subjective whims."[47] The challenge to factual truth in contemporary society is a material concern for Arendt.

SAFEGUARDING THE TRUTH

Can truth be covered up indefinitely? Is there a limit to how effectively facts can be manipulated, obfuscated, and eradicated?

Arendt's answer to this question oscillates between fear and hope, between pessimism and optimism. At times, she argues that it is not completely outside the realm of possibilities that a political system can be omnipotent. At other times, she claims that lying can never be total. In what follows, I demonstrate several nonsystematic arguments and elements in Arendt's writing that pertain to the safeguarding of the truth.

The first argument is expressed in the form of a mind-body problem: truth always catches up with human beings because we can remove our minds from our circumstances, but we cannot remove our bodies.[48] Arendt presents us with a sober realism about the physical reality of the factual circumstances. But Arendt is quick to present the counterpoint, and perhaps even more convincingly. The human capacity to lie, according to Arendt, is grounded in our capacity for imagination. Even when the material circumstances are less than desirable, humans can dream of a better world. Our capacity to imagine a better alternative also drives us to act upon our physical and social environment to change it. There is an undeniable connection, therefore, between imagination, action, and freedom, which is nothing short of miraculous: "This ability to say, 'the sun is shining,' when it is actually raining cats and dogs" is fundamentally about being able to "deny in thought and word," the very physical circumstances that one happens to find oneself in.[49] Yet, Arendt also thinks that if we believe in the amazing human capacity to imagine, we have to acknowledge that the same capacity is also the foundation for lying. The lie is the capacity to think about the world in a way different than it currently manifests, an attempt to change the reality at least in the audience's imagination. Lie, it follows, is the fraternal cousin to action. And if we value the capacity of action, lie is the price to pay.[50]

The second argument why truth can ultimately prevail is related to the regime capacity. Arendt argues that covering the truth completely and indefinitely necessitates a lot of effort and no government is omnipotent that way. Organized lying requires a level of power and control that no political leader possesses. That said, Arendt does not come to this conclusion immediately, and it is interesting to track the evolution of her thought.

In the 1950s, Arendt's arguments on this subject mainly derive from her observations on totalitarian regimes. Reflecting on how totalitarian regimes employ terror to realize their ideology, Arendt remarks: "If it is untrue, said *Das Schwarze Korps*, for instance, that all Jews are beggars without passports, we shall change facts in order to make this statement true."[51] The Nazis wanted to alter the existing laws to strip Jews of their property, wealth, and citizenship to make reality correspond to their white supremacist ideology, and the totalitarian control over all aspects of society made it possible.

The next sentence from the same article takes up another example: "That a man by the name of Trotsky was ever the head of the Red Army will cease to be true when the Bolsheviks have the global power to change all history texts."[52] Arendt is fond of this example, and reiterates it, albeit with different wording in "Truth and Politics": "When Trotsky learned that he had never played a role in the Russian Revolution, he must have known that his death warrant had been signed. Clearly, it is easier to eliminate a public figure from the record of history if at the same time he can be eliminated from the world of the living."[53] The totalitarian regimes' omnipotence looms over the worldly prospects of factuality.

Arendt's opinion on the matter seems unchanged as late as 1968. The Clemenceau anecdote in "Truth and Politics" leads her to observe that erasing the historical fact that Germany invaded Belgium on the night of August 4, 1914, would require "a power monopoly over the entire civilized world," pointing out the magnitude and hence the difficulty of such a task.[54] Yet, she is also quick to add that "such a power monopoly is far from being inconceivable."[55]

However, in the 1972 article, Arendt revisits this idea, i.e., whether organized lying and deliberate falsehood can be sustained for good. A change of tone is easy to detect: "no matter how large the tissue of falsehood that an experienced liar has to offer, it will never be large enough, even if he enlists the help of computers, to cover the immensity of factuality."[56] What changed? The revelation of the Pentagon Papers seems to have boosted Arendt's confidence in the power of truth to ultimately come to the surface no matter how deeply and systematically it has been buried. She even reconsiders her prior evaluation of the totalitarian system's omnipotence:

> The liar, who may get away with any number of single falsehoods, will find it impossible to get away with lying on principle. This is one of the lessons that could be learned from the totalitarian experiments and the totalitarian ruler's frightening confidence in the power of lying.... The results of such experiments when undertaken by those in possession of the means of violence are terrible enough, but *lasting deception is not among them*.[57]

With the optimism of the Pentagon incident, Arendt now comes to argue that radical, wholesale destruction of truth is never a possibility. Even the Trotsky example takes on a new and hopeful turn: "In order to eliminate Trotsky's role from the history of the Russian revolution, it is not enough to kill him and eliminate his name from all Russian records so long as one cannot kill all his contemporaries and wield power over the libraries and archives of all countries of the earth."[58] Hitler and Stalin had the political will to completely rearrange reality, but even they did not possess physical power, infrastructural capacity, and societal influence to accomplish this goal.

The third and final argument about why deliberate falsehood and organized lie cannot be sustained indefinitely goes like this: For lies to work, one needs to be clear on the facts first. The efficiency of the lie "depends entirely upon a clear notion of the truth that the liar and deceiver wishes to hide."[59] But in organized lying the liars themselves can no longer remember the facts behind their concealments. They believe their lies to such an extent that they no longer know what it was that they were trying to hide in the first place.

Arendt has an interesting observation about the lie: A lie tears "a hole in the fabric of factuality"—but an attentive eye can recognize the lies "by noticing the incongruities, holes, or the junctures of the patched-up places."[60] If the fabric of reality is intact, the lie will show. The modern lies, however, are so big that they "require a complete rearrangement of the whole factual texture."[61] This means that the perpetrators of large-scale, deliberate lying first need to convince themselves of the veracity of their lies. The line between deception and self-deception disappears. The whole fabric of our reality becomes a lie; "a whole group of people, and even whole nations, may take their bearings from a web of deception."[62] In fact, Arendt argues that in this respect cold-blooded liars are still preferable to self-deceiving modern liars because at least with the former, the truth "has not yet been maneuvered out of the world altogether, it has found its last refuge in [the liar]."[63]

Arendt contends therefore that there will always be a time when lying becomes unsustainable and counterproductive.[64] What does it mean for lies to become counterproductive? Arendt answers that lies "confuse people without convincing them."[65] But why does Arendt consider this confusion counterproductive? Liars benefit from and sometimes deliberately sow doubt and confusion, which contributes to eroding the line between truth and nontruth. Arendt herself acknowledges that this is the ultimate damage that constant lying can inflict on the fabric of society: blurring the line between truth and falsehood, such that "truth or falsehood—it does not matter which anymore."[66]

THE GUARDIANS OF TRUTH

Who are the guardians of truth? The fragility of the facts reminds us of the necessity of the right to be informed as well as of free and open discussion in the public sphere. Arendt points toward the universities and the free press as the guardians of truth: "The chances for truth to prevail in public are, of course, greatly improved by the mere existence of independent institutions" as they "find out, stand guard over, and interpret factual truth and human documents."[67] For this reason, the free press and the universities are under fiery attack in populist, illiberal, and authoritarian regimes.

What exactly does Arendt have in mind when she refers to the guardianship role of the university in the context of truth? Is she talking about academics?

In *Lying and Politics*, Arendt expresses the opinion that academics by themselves may not necessarily further the cause of truth. She points out that half of the writers of the Secretary of Defense Robert McNamara's task force that was assigned to work on the Pentagon Papers had come from think tanks, the government services, and the universities. They were intelligent operators, who took pride in their rational approach to problem-solving. These experts were at best misguided, at worst calculating, self-interested, and even deceitful. Dubbed "problem-solvers" by Arendt, they did not refrain from participating for many years in the government's deception of the public. But the academics are not a completely lost cause. It was thanks to the impartial self-examination and basic integrity of these individuals that a record of the Vietnam War was produced at all. Whether these experts were able to interpret the facts at hand objectively was a different matter. Secretary of Defense Robert McNamara, for one, declared that his purpose in creating the task force was to write the story of the Vietnam War as a cautionary tale, but only "in retrospect," which also happens to be the title of his memoir.

So, if it is not the academics, what is it about the university? What role do universities play in safeguarding truth? Elisabeth Young-Bruehl and Jerome Kohn recall a seminar Hannah Arendt taught at the New School in 1968.[68] In this seminar, titled "Political Experience in the Twentieth Century," Arendt arranged the readings such that they would reflect the lifelong public and political experiences of an imaginary person, born in 1890. There were no philosophical or theoretical texts, but instead novels, biographies, historical narratives, and poetry. Kohn remembers reading, among others, novels by Faulkner, Hemingway, Malraux, Orwell, Sartre, and Solzhenitsyn. Joseph Heller was present in person when the group discussed *Catch-22*, "but he scarcely said a word and seemed intimidated by Arendt, which frustrated and disappointed her."[69] There was poetry by

Bertolt Brecht, W. B. Yeats, biographies of Hitler and Stalin, as well as firsthand accounts of the wartime experiences by René Char, J. Glenn Gray, and T. E. Lawrence.

Arendt wanted the students to experience these events, but not immediately, only "vicariously" mediated by these literary works. The method of engagement that she promoted did not involve "being 'swept away,'" or "being 'taken out of oneself.'" Instead, the seminar specifically aimed to "re-present" the facts (and hence the point of view of a third party that is not readily available to the reader) in one's imagination. Arendt did not believe that we could feel or think what other people think or feel, but through the words of others who were present, we can imagine the experiences that are not available to us. Only through this exercise, Arendt believed, do we become capable of thinking "for ourselves in circumstances and from points of view that are not our own."[70] This, according to Arendt, is how we comprehend the meaning of, and ultimately construct, our common world. This anecdote, I contend, illustrates the significance of the university, as a guardian not simply of factual truth, but of our common world.

In modern societies, universities serve the construction of the common world in two ways. First, they bring together individuals from different walks of life, perhaps for the first time in their lives. Face-to-face communication in the public space allows the parties to interact and engage with one another. Second, in various seminars, the students find out about the facts and are encouraged to think and reflect on them, which contributes to their understanding of the common world. Kohn remembers the atmosphere in the same seminar:

> For this theorist of action, teaching itself was an unrehearsed performance, especially in the give-and-take, what she herself called the "free-for-all," of the seminar, where she asked her students real rather than rhetorical questions and responded, usually in entirely unexpected ways, to theirs.... In her seminar, every participant was a "citizen," called upon to give his or her opinion, to insert him or herself into that miniature polis in order to make it, as she said, "a little better."[71]

This is what we call civic citizenship, or in Arendt's parlance building our common world. It is not a coincidence that authoritarian regimes throughout the world launch their most vicious attack on universities.[72] It is not only the truth that they want to systematically damage, but also the plurality of viewpoints that flourishes in and from these institutions. They want to extinguish the ability for critical reflection.

What about the press? Arendt always had high regard for the role journalists played in a free, democratic society. She believed that even though it is not our sole source of factual truth, without the information provided by journalism, "we should never find our bearings in an ever-changing world, and in the most literal sense, would never know where we are."[73] The publication of the Pentagon Papers by the *New York Times* in 1971 provided a new boost to Arendt's confidence in the free press, and she did not refrain from expressing it most enthusiastically: "What has long been suggested has now been established: so long as the press is free and not corrupt, it has an enormously important function to fulfill and can rightly be called the fourth branch of government."[74] According to Arendt, the function of the free press is above all to inquire into the executive branch of government, recognizing that "the more power the executive has, the more it has to be investigated by the media."[75]

In *The Origins of Totalitarianism*, Arendt comments on the novelty of totalitarianism as a regime type. According to her, the unprecedented feature of totalitarianism was not deliberate falsehood, but the complete manipulation of the fabric of factuality. Arendt argued that to be able to recognize and hopefully stand up to the destruction caused by totalitarianism, one first had to come to see its new and unprecedented character. This is true of all judgment, according to Arendt. From the journalists and news reporters similarly, she expected that "they would be first and foremost struck by things as they are."[76] Arendt adopted the same attitude toward the government experts and academics involved in the Pentagon task force. One of their most acute failings was that instead of seeing the reality for what it was, they were trying to fit the facts into a deterministic historical and political narrative.[77] Instead, Arendt proposes the following: "The political attitude toward facts must, indeed, tread the very narrow path between the danger of taking them as the results of some necessary development which men could not prevent and about which they can therefore do nothing and the danger of denying them, of trying to manipulate them out of the world."[78] This is how we, as a society, would arrive at and safeguard the truth.

Finally, in her reflections on the Pentagon Papers, Arendt says that the whole incident happened "in a free country where all kinds of information were available," so manipulation by falsehood never really succeeded.[79] This is a very important qualification. What hope is there for countries where the foundations of democratic institutions have not been laid securely, to begin with?

In such cases, there is one final sliver of hope according to Arendt: individuals, "truth-tellers," "who have made up their minds not to be intimidated, who would rather go to jail than see their liberties nibbled away."[80] On this final point, too, Arendt seems to have switched from a more pessimistic position to a more optimistic one.

In her earlier remarks, Arendt emphasizes that it does not matter how passionately the truth-teller stands their ground. The disadvantaged position of the truth-teller in the public light can be better understood in comparison to one of Arendt's favorite examples, Socrates. Socrates had a philosophical proposition, "it is better to suffer wrong than do wrong." How did Socrates convince the public opinion of the truthfulness of his proposition? The trial of Socrates shows that things did not go very well for him on the public stage so Socrates took a different route; he staked his life on it: "not when he appeared before the Athenian tribunal, but when he refused to escape the death sentence."[81] Such exemplary truth, according to Arendt, is how philosophical truth can claim validity in the political realm. The philosopher persuades the multitude by setting an example. That said, while setting an example is a possibility for establishing the veracity of ethical principles (such as courage or goodness), what concerns us here is the factual truth, whose "very content defies this kind of verification": "A teller of factual truth, in the unlikely event that he wished to stake his life on a particular fact, would achieve a kind of miscarriage. What would become manifest in his act would be his courage or his stubbornness, but neither the truth of what he had to say or his own truthfulness."[82] It does not matter how fervently the truth-teller defends factual truth. There is a good chance that they will not come across as more truthful or more honest than the spinner of falsehoods. The authenticity of their conviction, or the passion with which they stand their ground, will not further one ounce the cause of factual truth-teller.

This brings us to the final question: Can truth-telling ever become an action? Is there ever an action-like quality to the truth?

Here again, Arendt's first answer is a no: "the mere telling of facts, leads to no action whatever; it even tends, under normal circumstances toward the acceptance of things as they are.... Truthfulness has never been counted among the political virtues because it has little indeed to contribute to that change of the world and of circumstances."[83] But this observation is then followed by an important qualification: "Only where a community has embarked upon organized lying on principle, and not only with respect to particulars, can truthfulness as such ... become a political factor of the first order. Where everybody lies about everything of importance, the truthteller, whether he knows it or not has begun to act."[84] When organized lying has become the ruling principle of a country, truth-telling becomes a political force. Where everybody lies, truth-telling turns into political action for changing the world—reminiscent of the children's story "The Emperor's New Clothes." We are indebted to these heroic individuals, who stand up for what is right, what simply "is." They risk their jobs, reputations, freedom, even their lives, and one cannot help but be grateful. But isn't this price too high to pay?

More importantly, their heroic efforts do not change the fact that lying and manipulation threaten the very nature of our political life. Facts are the building blocks of our political community. Factual truth informs opinion. Interests, passions, and even lifestyles and political leanings may affect the way individuals interpret factual truth. But the factuality of lived, common human experience should be kept intact. Arendt argues that we might see the facts in a different light, and we are even free to arrange the facts to our liking (which is why conspiracy theories are so popular after all), but we must first agree on the facticity of the facts.

Finally, even for those who do not believe in organized lies, the outcome is a peculiar kind of cynicism, disbelief toward any news or information.[85] With the destruction of the facts, we are destroying "the sense by which we take our bearings in the world,"[86] our ability and willingness to tell right from wrong. The erosion of this faculty takes place by accumulation of falsehoods and deliberate lies over time: "Consistent lying, metaphorically speaking, pulls the ground from under our feet and provides no other ground on which to stand."[87] Without the ability to tell apart fact from fiction, falsehood from reality, we are robbed of the opportunity to determine what we can change in our common world. This ability to change, to act into the future, is the ground of our freedom, our political power as a society.

The attack on reality in our contemporary world is an attack on our political community. Going back to Benhabib's diagnosis of the crisis, the attack on truth is an integral part of the fragmentation of the public space. When we lose this common world, we are fractured, divided, polarized—not a community anymore. Indeed, the truth cannot save us, but without truth, we cannot be saved.[88] The common world upon which we can rebuild our trust in our political institutions, science and experts, our democracy, and even each other depends on truth. We need to safeguard it.

NOTES

1. Seyla Benhabib, "What Is the Crisis a Crisis Of?," Public Seminar, October 25, 2018, https://publicseminar.org/2018/10/what-is-the-crisis-a-crisis-of/.
2. A Reuters/Ipsos poll in December 2021 shows that the former president Trump commands a substantial lead as the most likely Republican candidate. Trump also tops *The Washington Post*'s chart of the Top 10 GOP candidates. *Reuters/Ipsos Poll: Large Issue Poll #6* (Washington, DC: Ipsos, December 2021), www.ipsos.com/sites/default

/files/ct/news/documents/2021-12/Reuters%20Ipsos%20Large%20Issue%20 Poll%20No%206%20Topline%20-%20December%202021.pdf; Aaron Blake, "The Top 10 GOP Presidential Candidates for 2024, Ranked," *Washington Post*, February 19, 2022, www.washingtonpost.com/politics/2022/02/19/top-10-gop-presidential-candidates-2024-ranked/.

3. Hannah Arendt, "Lying in Politics," in *Crises of the Republic: Lying in Politics, Civil Disobedience on Violence, Thoughts on Politics, and Revolution* (San Diego: Harcourt Brace, 1972), 4.

4. "Oxford Word of the Year 2016," https://languages.oup.com/word-of-the-year/2016/; Jonathan Freedland, "Post-Truth Politicians Such as Donald Trump and Boris Johnson Are No Joke," *Guardian*, May 13, 2016, www.theguardian.com/commentisfree/2016/may/13/boris-johnson-donald-trump-post-truth-politician; Rana Ayyub, "Journalism Is Under Attack in India. So Is the Truth," *Washington Post*, February 21, 2020, www.washingtonpost.com/opinions/2020/02/21/journalism-is-under-attack-india-so-is-truth/; Petra Costa, "Bolsonaro's War on Truth," *New York Times*, January 24, 2020, www.nytimes.com/2020/01/24/opinion/brazil-bolsonaro-edge-of-democracy.html; Peter Pomerantsev, "How Vladimir Putin Is Revolutionizing Information Warfare," *Atlantic*, September 9, 2014, www.theatlantic.com/international/archive/2014/09/russia-putin-revolutionizing-information-warfare/379880/; Han Zhang, "The 'Post-Truth' Publication Where Chinese Students in America Get Their News," *New Yorker*, August 19, 2019, www.newyorker.com/culture/culture-desk/the-post-truth-publication-where-chinese-students-in-america-get-their-news.

5. These are the versions of the text used throughout the essay: Hannah Arendt, "Truth and Politics," in *Between Past and Future*, rev. ed. (New York: Penguin, 2006), 227–64; Arendt, "Lying in Politics."

6. In the footnotes, Arendt suggested that this essay may "serve as an example of what happens to a highly controversial topical subject when it is drawn into that gap between past and future which is perhaps the habitat of all reflections." Arendt, "Truth and Politics," 227. She believed that the reactions to her book had "absolutely nothing with criticism of polemics in the normal sense of the word. It is a political campaign, led and guided in all particulars by interest groups and governmental agencies." Hannah Arendt and Mary McCarthy, *Between Friends: The Correspondence of Hannah Arendt and Mary McCarthy, 1949–1975*, ed. Carol Brightman, 1st ed. (New York: Harcourt, Brace, 1995), 151.

7. An allusion to the Latin phrase "Fiat iustitia, et pereat mundus" (Let justice be done, though the world may perish)." Arendt, "Truth and Politics," 228. And the answer, for Arendt, is an unconditional yes. It is important to note that Arendt is also concerned with the lies circulated about what she had written and the facts she had reported.

8. R. W. Apple Jr., "25 Years Later; Lessons from the Pentagon Papers," *New York Times*, June 23, 1996, Week in Review, www.nytimes.com/1996/06/23/weekinreview/25-years-later-lessons-from-the-pentagon-papers.html.

9. Some examples are Thomas Weyn, "An Arendtian Approach to Post-Truth Politics," *OpenDemocracy* (blog), March 12, 2017, www.opendemocracy.net/wfd/can-europe

-make-it/thomas-weyn/arendtian-approach-to-post-truth-politics; Heather Roff, "Trump and Truth: Or What Arendt Can Teach Us About Truth and Politics," *Duck of Minerva* (blog), February 14, 2017, http://duckofminerva.com/2017/02/trump-and-truth-or-what-arendt-can-teach-us-about-truth-and-politics.html; Christopher Beem, "The Burden Of Truth," *The Critique* (blog), January 15, 2017, www.thecritique.com/articles/the-burden-of-truth/; Lyndsey Stonebridge, "Why Hannah Arendt Is the Philosopher for Now," *New Statesman* (blog), March 20, 2019, www.newstatesman.com/culture/2019/03/why-hannah-arendt-is-the-philosopher-for-now.

10. Simone Chambers, "Truth, Deliberative Democracy, and the Virtues of Accuracy: Is Fake News Destroying the Public Sphere?," *Political Studies* 69, no. 1 (February 2021): 147–63, https://doi.org/10.1177/0032321719890811.

11. Linda M. G. Zerilli, "Fact-Checking and Truth-Telling in an Age of Alternative Facts," *Le Foucaldien* 6, no. 1 (2020): 1–22; Linda M. G. Zerilli, "Rethinking the Politics of Post-Truth with Hannah Arendt," in *Political Phenomenology: Experience, Ontology, Episteme*, ed. Thomas Bedorf and Steffen Herrmann (New York: Routledge, 2019), 152–64; Samantha Rose Hill, "Hannah Arendt and the Politics of Truth," *openDemocracy*, October 25, 2020, www.opendemocracy.net/en/transformation/hannah-arendt-and-politics-truth/.

12. A notable exception is Ari-Elmeri Hyvönen, "Careless Speech: Conceptualizing Post-Truth Politics," *New Perspectives* 26, no. 3 (October 2018): 31–55, https://doi.org/10.1177/2336825X1802600303.

13. Arendt, "Truth and Politics," 229.

14. Arendt, 264.

15. Beiner, for one, dismisses too quickly the distinction Arendt draws between different types of truth. Beiner, "Rereading 'Truth and Politics,'" *Philosophy and Social Criticism* 34, nos. 1–2 (January 1, 2008): 124, https://doi.org/10.1177/0191453707084277. Lukes, while agreeing with Arendt on the necessity of safeguarding the truth, also does not acknowledge the different types. Lukes, "Power, Truth and Politics," *Journal of Social Philosophy* 50, no. 4 (2019): 563, https://doi.org/10.1111/josp.12320.

16. "Impotent," "indifferent," and "relevant" being only a few examples, among others. Hill, "Hannah Arendt and the Politics of Truth."

17. Arendt, "Truth and Politics," 231.

18. Arendt, 231.

19. Arendt, 231.

20. Arendt, 231.

21. Hobbes, *Leviathan*, chap. 11, quoted in Arendt, 230.

22. Arendt, "Truth and Politics," 230.

23. Arendt, 230.

24. Megan Brenan, "40% of Americans Believe in Creationism," Gallup.com, July 26, 2019, https://news.gallup.com/poll/261680/americans-believe-creationism.aspx.

25. Responses change significantly according to the respondent's political leanings. Cary Funk and Meg Hefferon, "U.S. Public Views on Climate and Energy," *Pew Research Center Science and Society* (blog), November 25, 2019, www.pewresearch.org/science

/2019/11/25/u-s-public-views-on-climate-and-energy/. For a thorough analysis and critique of Arendt's engagement with scientific truth, see Javier Burdman, "Knowledge and the Public World: Arendt on Science, Truth, and Politics," *Constellations* 25 (2018): 485–96.

26. Arendt, "Truth and Politics," 240.
27. Arendt, 232–33.
28. Arendt, 234. Arendt takes up the same argument in more detail in her address on Lessing, delivered on the occasion of her receiving the Lessing Prize of the Free City of Hamburg in 1959. Hannah Arendt, "On Humanity in Dark Times: Thoughts About Lessing," in *Men in Dark Times* (San Diego: Harcourt, Brace, 1995), 3–31.
29. Arendt, "Truth and Politics," 232.
30. Arendt, 239.
31. Arendt, 241.
32. Arendt, 240.
33. Arendt, 242; Arendt, "Lying in Politics," 12.
34. Arendt, "Lying in Politics," 6.
35. Arendt, "Truth and Politics," 251–52.
36. Arendt, "Lying in Politics," 6.
37. Arendt, "Truth and Politics," 231.
38. Arendt, "Lying in Politics," 4.
39. Arendt, "Truth and Politics," 256.
40. Arendt, 256.
41. Elisabeth Young-Bruehl and Jerome Kohn, "Truth, Lies, and Politics: A Conversation," *Social Research* (2007): 1066; Linda M. G. Zerilli, "Truth and Politics," in *Truth and Democracy*, ed. Jeremy Elkins and Andrew Norris (Philadelphia: University of Pennsylvania Press, 2012), 55.
42. Arendt's examples of unwelcome factual truth from the Second World War include Germany's support of Hitler, France's defeat before German armies, and the Vatican's policies. Arendt, "Truth and Politics," 236. In 1963 the German playwright Rolf Hochhuth published *The Deputy*. The play problematized Pope Pius XII's actions, asking—according to Arendt the legitimate—question "Why did Pope never protest publicly against the persecution and finally mass murder of Jews?" even though he was in possession of all the relevant information. The response and criticism that the play received in the public eye, according to Arendt, was similar to the controversy around her Eichmann book. Arendt and McCarthy, *Between Friends*, 151–52. She interviewed Hochhuth and wrote a review of the play. "The Deputy: Rolf Hochhuth and Hannah Arendt" (Columbia Broadcasting System, 1964), https://search.alexanderstreet.com/preview/work/bibliographic_entity%7Cvideo_work%7C657925; Hannah Arendt, "The Deputy: Guilt by Silence?," in *Amor Mundi: Explorations in the Faith and Thought of Hannah Arendt*, ed. S. J. James W. Bernauer, Boston College Studies in Philosophy 26 (Dordrecht: Springer, 1987), 51–58, https://doi.org/10.1007/978-94-009-3565-5_4.
43. Arendt, "Truth and Politics," 237. Arendt explains this idea in an earlier text on Socrates. According to Arendt, every person "has [their] own doxa, [their] own opening to the world, and Socrates must always begin with questions; he cannot know

before hand what kind of *dokei moi*, of it appears-to-me, the other possesses." Hannah Arendt, "Philosophy and Politics," *Social Research* 57, no. 1 (Spring 1990): 81.
44. Arendt, "Truth and Politics," 242.
45. Arendt, 238.
46. Arendt, 239.
47. Hyvönen, "Careless Speech," 37.
48. Arendt, "Lying in Politics," 36.
49. Arendt is fond of this idiom and does not refrain from reiterating it multiple times. Arendt, "Truth and Politics," 250; Arendt, "Lying in Politics," 5.
50. Arendt, "Truth and Politics," 243.
51. Hannah Arendt, "On the Nature of Totalitarianism: An Essay in Understanding," in *Essays in Understanding, 1930–1954: Formation, Exile, and Totalitarianism* (New York: Schocken, 2005), 350.
52. Arendt, 350.
53. Arendt, "Truth and Politics," 253.
54. Arendt, 239.
55. Arendt, 239.
56. Arendt, "Lying in Politics," 7.
57. Arendt, 7, emphasis mine.
58. Arendt, 13.
59. Arendt, 31.
60. Arendt, "Truth and Politics," 253.
61. Arendt, 253.
62. Arendt, 255.
63. Arendt, 254.
64. Arendt, "Lying in Politics," 7, 31.
65. Arendt, 31.
66. Arendt, 7. I will consider this point in detail in the final section.
67. Arendt, "Truth and Politics," 261.
68. Young-Bruehl and Kohn, "Truth, Lies, and Politics," 1047.
69. Young-Bruehl and Kohn, 1047.
70. Young-Bruehl and Kohn, 1047.
71. Elisabeth Young-Bruehl and Jerome Kohn, "What and How We Learned from Arendt: An Exchange of Letters," in *Hannah Arendt and Education. Renewing Our Common World*, ed. Mordechai Gordon (Boulder, CO: Westview Press, 2001), 254–255.
72. Franklin Foer, "Viktor Orbán's War on Intellect," *Atlantic*, May 9, 2019, www.theatlantic.com/magazine/archive/2019/06/george-soros-viktor-orban-ceu/588070/; Subin Dennis, "India's Left University Is Fighting Back," *Jacobin*, January 13, 2020, https://jacobinmag.com/2020/01/jawaharlal-nehru-university-student-attack-far-right; Carlotta Gall, "Prestigious Istanbul University Fights Erdogan's Reach," *New York Times*, February 1, 2021, www.nytimes.com/2021/02/01/world/asia/turkey-bogazici-university-protests-erdogan.html.
73. Arendt, "Truth and Politics," 261.
74. Arendt, "Lying in Politics," 45.

75. Young-Bruehl and Kohn, "Truth, Lies, and Politics," 1054.
76. Young-Bruehl and Kohn, 1051.
77. Arendt, "Lying in Politics," 11.
78. Arendt, "Truth and Politics," 259.
79. Arendt, "Lying in Politics," 35.
80. Arendt, 46.
81. Arendt, "Truth and Politics," 247.
82. Arendt, 249.
83. Arendt, 251.
84. Arendt, 251.
85. Arendt, 257.
86. Arendt, 257.
87. Arendt, 258.
88. Hill, "Hannah Arendt and the Politics of Truth."

8

Understanding Eichmann and Anwar

Reenactment and the Psychic Lives of Perpetrators

SONALI CHAKRAVARTI

Hannah Arendt did not travel to Jerusalem in 1961 because she wanted confirmation of her impressions of Nazi officers or because of the self-satisfaction she might experience through moral condemnation of Adolf Eichmann—neither held any interest for her.[1] Rather, she made the trip to witness the particularity of Eichmann's performance on the legal stage—to see him "in the flesh."[2] It was an opportunity to be face to face with an agent of genocide in a storied hall of justice and to observe how he would reconcile the criminal charges with his own account of his action. Yet, Arendt was acutely aware of the limitations of the legal trial, not only as unable to reckon with killing at such a scale, but also in the constraints it imposes on observers' understandings of the motivations and aspirations of the defendant. In this paper, I first situate the practice of reenactment within the Frankfurt School tradition of mimesis and the emancipatory potential it holds. I will then suggest that what Arendt wished she could have learned about Eichmann was, in important ways, revealed through the reenactments of Anwar Congo, the character at the center of Joshua Oppenheimer's remarkable 2012 documentary about Indonesian death-squad leaders, *The Act of Killing*.[3]

Arendt notes that during the trial Eichmann spoke in clichés, seemed to lack the enlarged mentality that would allow him to empathize with victims, and resisted any form of remorse or reckoning. Each of these observations is instantiated by Anwar's actions over the course of the documentary in ways that are revealing about the conditions necessary for ordinary people to commit acts of violence. Much of what Arendt wanted to understand about Eichmann as a man "unable to think" is revealed to the viewer through watching the reenactments and fantasy sequences Anwar stages throughout the film. Furthermore, I will argue that *The Act of Killing* allows for Arendt's and Bettina Stangneth's findings about Eichmann to coexist in a way that demonstrates Seyla Benhabib's question *"But can Eichmann not be a convinced Nazi anti-Semite and also banal?"*[4] The documentary, in an affecting way, shows how these two understandings can exist in a perpetrator who is deeply ideologically motivated to kill but also displays mundane tendencies to narcissism and self-glorification. Just as Benhabib identifies how the complexity of Eichmann's psyche is partially captured by both Arendt and Stangneth, *The Act of Killing* portrays Anwar as exceptional in his cruelty but also mundane in his self-delusion. Lastly, I will consider whether the documentary represents a type of Faustian bargain—that is, the promise of access to the psychic life of a perpetrator only if there is a friendship between the interlocutor and the perpetrator and no threat of punishment.

While I proffer that Arendt would have been intrigued by the portrayal of Anwar in *The Act of Killing*, she would have also been very aware of their differences as perpetrators. Eichmann was, in his most symbolic form, a desk murderer, a man so far removed from the crime as to be able to pretend he was not responsible for the killings, while Anwar was the opposite—a man who twisted the wire that acted as a guillotine for his victims and worried about their blood on his clothes. While Eichmann abstracted the command of genocide so dramatically that it appeared analogous to any other order a leader might give, Anwar could not abstract away his role in the murders and even intimidated others to make sure his orders were followed. Another key difference between the two men is that, in contrast to Eichmann, we are privy to Anwar's interactions with some of his closest associates, men with whom he committed the executions and who shared his elevated status in Indonesian society because of their proximity to political power. With Eichmann, as Arendt discovered in her research, "There were two things he could do well, better than others: he could organize and he could negotiate"; but we do not have recordings of the easy comradery he may have shared with his fellow SS officers or his relationships with Jewish leaders in Vienna, Prague, and Berlin.[5] With Anwar, we observe a man in an ecosystem that supports his violent acts who is thus allowed to speak freely about his crimes; but in the case of Eichmann, the Nazi era has ended (or gone underground) and must be re-created through testimony and archival material for the purpose of the trial. Moreover, *The Act of Killing* has become an important part of the historical record in Indonesia because it prompted a national conversation about the killings of 1965–66 in a way that had not previously occurred, ushering in a period of national reckoning not unlike the one that was still unfolding in Germany in 1961when Eichmann was on trial.

THE AUTHORITARIAN PERSONALITY

While Eichmann represents a distinctly modern type of perpetrator, one who sits at a desk and administers the logistics of genocidal killing and Anwar is directly involved in these acts, they share many of the characteristics described in Theodor Adorno's *The Authoritarian Personality*.[6] Based on an ambitious study combining psychoanalysis and social psychology where participants were surveyed about their attitude toward family, religion, sex, tradition, and politics, Adorno and his coauthors found that the potential for fascism is developed early in childhood and permeates almost every facet of life. Moreover, it is continuous with liberal-democratic culture, not its antithesis, and reflects some of the pathologies of a culture fixated on the individual. Those participants who scored highly on the F-scale (fascism-scale) of the survey tended toward "conventionalism, rigidity, and stereotypical thinking" while eschewing introspection and individual expression.[7] Critically, as Peter Gordon says in the introduction, the "the psyche of the fascist is 'authoritarian' in the sense that it attaches itself to figures of strength and disdains those it deems weak."[8] The profile explained in *The Authoritarian Personality* captures significant aspects of the personalities of both Eichmann and Anwar and also suggests why the mimetic approach to understanding their actions may be fruitful. The tendency to eschew introspection, distance oneself from direct expressions of prejudice, and cathect with an all-powerful source makes it difficult for perpetrators to recognize or articulate their motivations and fears when questioned in a legal setting. Reenactment provides a way to circumvent the obstacles to communication, particularly about responsibility and justice, that arise with those who exhibit the tendencies at the crux of the F-scale. It is also sometimes hard for observers to understand why other people may be inclined to follow the lead of these perpetrators: What is it about their company that inspires confidence and leadership? A mimetic approach where perpetrators are asked to re-create their actions has the capacity to shed light on these interactions. Re-creating the atmosphere that surrounded them may thus be more informative than straightforward interrogation of the perpetrator for a public that wants to understand what occurred.

While I posit a mimetic engagement with perpetrators as a way to circumvent the defensive blocks to stifle communication put up by those who tend toward the authoritarian personality, Adorno had, in fact, already considered the liberatory potential of mimesis against the horrors of war and domination in *Dialectic of Enlightenment*, coauthored with Max Horkheimer.[9] There, he considered how a mimetic relationship to the natural world, one already enchanted by magic, would avoid the pitfalls of instrumental reason that are fated to lead to the domination of the self, others, and the planet. Still, the quest to find unity and harmony with nature through mimesis could only exist as an aesthetic project in their text because the critique of the rationality of the Enlightenment was so totalizing that no political ideals remain. The turn to the aesthetic through a mimetic reconciliation with nature in the face of political nihilism parallels the question of whether a documentary that invited perpetrators to become creative collaborators also eschews the political in favor of the aesthetic. Yet just as Habermas faults the way Adorno and Horkheimer see reason as a "cul-de-sac" and instead turns to the possibilities of communicative rationality, Oppenheimer does not solely engage in an aesthetic project and he creates an opportunity for communication with Anwar through mimetic reenactment and extends this communication and self-reflexivity to the audience as well.[10] That language (and communication more broadly) might transcend its genesis in ideology offers a way out of the abyss of a world only dominated by instrumental reason. Through eenactment, Anwar is able to see himself as a moral and agential subject and begins to understand his victims' capacity to feel pain; the mimetic endeavor of the documentary does not end in a cul-de-sac.

I agree with Ernesto Verdeja's critique of the stifled possibility for true autonomy in the account of mimesis in the *Dialectic*, but suggest that Adorno and Horkheimer find another path in the text to avoid the pitfalls of instrumental rationality—this is through the their emphasis on the particular and its relationship to the universal as the defining feature of works of art.[11] They write, "It is the nature of the work of art, of aesthetic illusion, to be what was experienced as a new and terrible event in the magic of primitives: *the appearance of the whole in the particular*."[12] For them, attending to the particular in the work of art approaches the aura achieved by magic in a previous era and interrupts the false equivalences between disparate universals that facilitate domination and exploitation in modernity. A focus on understanding the particularity of a work of art pushes against the scientific and technocratic rationalism that reigns supreme and is often quick to categorize people and objects according to universal categories. Analogously, attention to the particularity of the perpetrator, in both Arendt's text and the documentary, thus has the potential to disrupt the facile equivalence of all perpetrators with evil in a simple binary of good and evil and replace such an understanding with a more informed account of the authoritarian personality in the modern world. Rather than retreating from judgment, the examination of the particular circumstances, attributes, and actions of Eichmann and Anwar, undertaken here, is in the service of a more nuanced understanding of the ways humanity and the capacity for violence and destruction coexist in the perpetrators themselves.

THE DOCUMENTARY

Nominated for an Academy Award, *The Act of Killing* follows Anwar Congo and a group of his associates who participated in the 1965–66 state-sanctioned killings of Communists and Indonesians of Chinese descent. With the knowledge and tacit support of the United States, President Suharto oversaw the campaign in which over one million Indonesians were killed.[13] In his documentary, Oppenheimer invites Anwar and his friends to make a film about their experiences as "gangsters," thugs for hire who carried out the regime's genocidal campaign while becoming notorious in their neighborhoods, actions that continue to bring them status and respect in the present. The participants scripted and produced set pieces in a variety of genres (western, noir, war film, and so on) that referred to different types of violence they committed and took turns playing the aggressor and the victim. They depicted interrogations and murders in a newspaper office, a village, and private homes, staging each scene as accurately as they could. They also directed and performed a fantasy sequence set in paradise, complete with waterfalls and a giant fish, set to "Born Free," the popular song from 1966, which was also a reference to the translation that Anwar gives of the word *gangster* as "free men."

In an early scene, Anwar, wearing a green tropical-print shirt and white slacks, together with an associate, leads the filmmaker to the roof of a residential building. Initially, Anwar recounts how victims were here beaten to death and how the task of cleaning up the murders was arduous and foul-smelling. He then displays a device made of wood attached to a piece of wire, explaining that this tool was found to work much better for killing because the wire could be used to decapitate victims without too much blood. Asking his associate to play the role of the victim, Anwar shows how the wire is attached first to a pole and then around the victim's neck. The wood handle is then used to tighten the noose. Anwar gets into a crouching position to show how the deed is done and says, "We have to re-enact this properly." The viewer is privy to seeing both the practicality and care that Anwar displays in setting up the scene and it attests to his guilt (not that Anwar ever denied it) and to how fully he inhabited the role of gangster. Revealing the importance of image to his self-conception, he was bothered by the fact that he was wearing white pants in the reenactment, a sartorial choice he would never have made at the time. While Anwar is very aware of Oppenheimer filming him, he does not seem to be concerned with how others may judge his actions. He displays an ease and a trust with the director that we rarely see between interlocutor and perpetrator.

Oppenheimer is friendly and nonconfrontational in most interactions with Anwar we see on screen, but there is the sense in the film that moral judgment cannot be suspended forever. At some point, the viewer thinks, the conviviality and backslapping will stop. The gangsters are, at times, aware that the relatives of the victims live among them, one even participates in a scene and recounts the murder of his stepfather, an issue I discuss later. Elsewhere, Anwar interprets his nightmares in part as signs that children of his victims want their revenge. We see Anwar playing out these fears and their peaceful reconciliation in a fantasy sequence amid lush vegetation, waterfalls, dancing showgirls, and a giant fish. In these scenes, Anwar is wearing a long robe and is given a medal by one of his victims as a show of gratitude for his role in allowing the victim to go to heaven. Seeing that the victim bears no ill will, Anwar is elated to be with him in paradise. After decades of nightmares, Anwar can finally rest having finally received this ablution. Anwar's fantasy of the gratitude he receives from a victim evinces his clear desire to skip over the confrontation and moral assessment that would come from an investigation into the killings. Instead, in the fantasy film where he is both the director and the star, he immediately proceeds to a reconciliation between the victim and Anwar where both feel that they have been given exactly what they needed and deserved.

Although the fantasy sequences may feel the most removed from the historical archive of the era, Oppenheimer facilitated them to great effect as a tool of psychological reckoning. In *Beyond the Pleasure Principle*, Freud suggests that traumatic memories bypass the conscious mind and reside in the subconscious, rendering them inaccessible through conscious acts of remembering.[14] In contemporary psychological discourse, the premise that memories of trauma reside in the viscera has been further explored by clinical psychologist Bessel van der Kolk, who writes that, for traumatized people, "The past is alive in the form of gnawing interior discomfort. Their bodies are constantly bombarded by visceral warning signs."[15] Even if Eichmann and Anwar had the motivation to do so, certain memories would be inaccessible to them when asked about them directly, despite the visceral warning signs they might feel. The intervention of the fantasy sequence gives Anwar an alternative path to engaging with the legacy of the violence in his life. By giving Anwar creative control of the scenes and enabling his artistic vision, Oppenheimer facilitated the inhabitation of roles other than that of the gangster, and this process, more so than dialogue or interrogation, gives the audience clues to Anwar's aspirations and regrets. Homay King sees the fantasy sequences as a working though of the traumatic pasts of violence in a way that is productive, that is to say, the fantasy sequences allow for the difficult work of shifting perspective away from the perpetrator and to the victim.[16] He writes, "Fantasy, these scenes suggest, is an incredibly malleable instrument, one that allows its subjects to imagine themselves occupying a range of mutually exclusive positions. Moreover, its aim may not be solely to master the original trauma, as simplified accounts of the repetition compulsion suggest, but to experiment with approaching it from various angles and distances: oblique or head-on, naked or heavily disguised, coldly removed or hot with fright."[17] Fantasy is the "route back to reality" so it becomes the basis of Anwar's reckoning with himself in a way that is consistent with Freud's interpretation. It was only in departing from reality that the reality of his debilitating guilt and wish for redemption became manifest.

One might argue that we, as the audience, are invited to make a similar wager; we can be friendly with Anwar and the other participants, as long as we don't spend too much time thinking about the victims or the role of legal responsibility. We must, arguably, gloss over the work of judgment. Yet, Arendt's curiosity about who Eichmann was and her desire to know him beyond a recounting of his crimes suggest that she saw a separation between the tasks of humanistic understanding and legal judgment. Being curious about the inner life of perpetrators does not mean we lose control of our critical faculties. On the contrary, for Arendt, if we ignore the complexity of perpetrators (and victims as well) and solely focus on the legal outcome or on declarations of moral depravity, this results in an inexcusable blindness to the conditions of the world—moreover, it would make the work of politics, a realm of uncertainty, mistakes, and forgiveness, impossible.

In response to the amount of criticism Arendt received for her treatment of Eichmann, Benhabib argues that Arendt's proximity to the trauma of the Holocaust is often wrongly overlooked when interpreting her writing. She writes, "Arendt's much-misunderstood sarcasm as well as her thinly veiled contempt for Eichmann himself were like layers of additional skin in which she had to clothe herself so as to permit her to provide one of the first and most dramatic accounts of the destruction of European Jewry."[18] Just as Arendt represents the survivors of the Holocaust who stand in particular relation to retribution regarding Eichmann, the gangsters worry about the need for revenge on the part of the younger generation. While they readily dismissed criticisms from contemporaries about the legitimacy of the anticommunist genocidal campaign, they realize that these justifications will be meaningless to the children of the murdered. Whatever compelled the gangsters to kill in 1965, it will not mollify the descendants of the victims in the twenty-first century. The gangsters can, surprisingly, put themselves in the shoes of these children and their feelings of revenge and injustice, even if they cannot imagine the perspective of their victims.

THE TRIAL OF ADOLF EICHMANN: ARENDT ON IDEOLOGY AND SYSTEMIC FACTORS

From the start, Arendt's observations in *Eichmann in Jerusalem* show that she is aware that many aspects of Eichmann's personality and motivation cannot be revealed in the scope of the trial because they fit neither the prosecution's motive for highlighting the suffering of Holocaust victims, nor Eichmann's strategy to make it seem he was nothing more than a good soldier for his commander. She writes, "Justice insists on the importance of Adolf Eichmann, the man in the glass booth built for his protection ... who desperately and for the most past successfully maintains his self-control despite the nervous tic to which his mouth must have become subject long before this trial started."[19] Here we see that as much as Arendt understood the demands of a legal trial, she was convinced it was not a particularly good way to understand a defendant or his alleged actions. She made the most of the internal contradictions of the trial as a topic of reflection, but there was a nagging feeling that the deeper insights about what made the personnel machinery of the Third Reich move would not be disclosed. Arendt noted the idiosyncrasies of Eichmann's language and presentation and surmised it must reflect the interplay between the different types of motivations, ideological and bureaucratic, that animated him, but the format of the trial and the press coverage of Eichmann did not aggregate into a satisfactory source of data that allowed her to understand how he moved between them.

While the term *Schreibtischtäter* (desk murderer) did not originate with Arendt, the concept is a predominant theme for her in her coverage of the Eichmann trial. Eichmann's ability to carry out the work of genocide from afar, through the logistical management of the transportation of victims to the death camps, epitomized how instrumental rationality could be weaponized in the modern era without any possibility of an individual interrogating its ends in a meaningful way. He experienced all the trappings of a modern, bureaucratic job—one with merit incentives for advancement and institutional recognition—but the telos of the job was genocide, a jarring juxtaposition with the ideals of the German Enlightenment. While Arendt was undoubtedly interested in the structure of modernity that would allow a desk worker to orchestrate a genocide in her account of Eichmann, she was also interested in ideology. As Benhabib notes, "A cursory examination shows that Arendt's own writings contain elements of both approaches, with the emphasis on ideology predominating in her early work, while the latter work focuses more on institutional and systemic factors in the functioning of national socialism. It is simplistic therefore to reduce her reflections to one or another school of interpretation."[20] In chapter 2, "The Accused,"

Arendt lays out the question that piqued her curiosity at the beginning of the trial. Given that Eichmann pleaded "Not Guilty in the sense of the indictment," Arendt wondered, "*In what sense did he think he was guilty?*" and it was this sense of psychological curiosity about his motivations and self-conception that infused her reporting.[21] While Stangneth's analysis is able to provide greater insight into the anti-Semitism that informed his action, Benhabib captures how astute Arendt's psychological profile of Eichmann was, especially in relation to Adorno's profile of the authoritarian personality:

> She saw in him an all-too familiar syndrome of rigid self-righteousness; extreme defensiveness fueled by exaggerated metaphysical and world-historical theories; fervent patriotism based on the supposed purity of one's Volk; paranoid projections about the power of Jews and envy of them for their achievements in science, literature, and philosophy; and contempt for Jews' supposed deviousness, cowardice, and pretensions to be the "chosen people."[22]

She did not need the Sassen interviews to see the many ways Eichmann was predisposed to rigid and dichotomous thinking; but Arendt was curious about how this "all-too familiar" syndrome intersected with the institutions and sensibilities of the modern state.

The film *The Act of Killing* investigates the psychological state of Anwar much more candidly than would have been allowed in a trial. It was just this type of psychological investigation that interested Arendt, who was frustrated at the way the psychiatrists who were assembled at the trial attempted to certify Eichmann as "normal."[23] When prosecutor Hausner later revealed that other psychiatrists had found him to be anti-Semitic to a fanatical degree and to be "a man obsessed with a dangerous and insatiable urge to kill," claims that Stangneth further grounded in archival research later, Arendt did not know how to reconcile the two diametrically opposed evaluations.[24] The combination of procedural restrictions on what could be shared as evidence in the courtroom and the strategic use of mental illness as a defense strategy made it impossible for her, the judges, or the spectators to get a congruent picture. Furthermore, as Arendt notes, "nobody believed him [Eichmann]" when Eichmann spoke about his culpability and reasons for compliance with orders.[25] To Arendt, he seemed so thoroughly ensconced in his own separate reality that it was difficult for her to find any dialogic moments in the legal process that could be truly illuminating. While she found his failure to think curious, she could not find a meaningful way to sort out the lies such that the breakdown in thought could be further analyzed.

EICHMANN BEFORE JERUSALEM

The Act of Killing also provides a way to connect Arendt's and Bettina Stangneth's impressions of Eichmann through a more capacious look at his ideological motivations, particularly his anti-Semitism, a topic that was highly charged in the wake of the English translation of Stangneth's book *Eichmann Before Jerusalem*.[26] Her book drew on the Argentina Papers, a collection of documents promulgating the tenets of National Socialism, and the Sassen interview with Eichmann in 1956–57 as well as other documents, in order to paint a more detailed picture of who Eichmann was apart from his persona as a defendant, especially in his fervent promotion of the Final Solution. Time and again, Eichmann went beyond his peers to assert his anti-Semitic views and further their prominence, revealing ideological commitments that Arendt had not observed.[27] Furthermore, Eichmann, using his alias Ricardo Klement, did not seem to have a hard time adjusting to the pastoral life of a rabbit farmer in Buenos Aires.[28] Accordion to Stangneth, it was not luxury that he craved, but standing and influence among his peers and he was able to achieve it in Argentina. This same quest for local influence is seen in Anwar's recollections of his life as a gangster and in how much he enjoys the status still afforded to him by neighbors and political elites in Medan.

One aspect of Eichmann's behavior that was the most baffling for Arendt is his confidence and enthusiasm for his life's achievements. She, at first, did not understand how a man of middling intelligence and talent would be so ebullient at recounting his life for the police examiner in Israel. She was perplexed at how he "had never harbored ill feelings against his victims" but reading Eichmann through the lens of *The Act of Killing* makes salient the motivation of fame.[29] Both Eichmann and Anwar shared a love of myth-making and aspired to live the outsized lives of celebrities. Long after the war ended, Eichmann recounted the pride he felt when a newspaper called him "Czar of the Jews."[30] Moreover, he was so entertained by an erroneous article suggesting that he had been born in Palestine and was fluent in Hebrew that he tried to incorporate the fabulation into his persona as a way to tease those who were not sure what parts of the biographical account were true.

The hunger for riches and the hunger for power have often been seen together; one can recall Socrates's interventions with his early interlocutors in Plato's *Republic*. But when dealing with Eichmann and Anwar, it was the appeal of fame and the appeal of power that are more intimately connected.[31] Seeing Anwar and Eichmann as connected in their motivation to be seen as heroes provides a different perspective on the utility of extreme ideological positions such as anti-Semitism and anticommunism when the ultimate goal is fame. These types of bigotry are not necessarily cognitively compelling to the perpetrators (as was noted in the F-scale participants), but espousing them provides a fast track to success within the organization (a strategy Arendt understood) and a more defined dramatic role to inhabit (a strategy she grasped only tenuously). Stangneth's research provides many of the details that scaffold an interpretation of Eichmann as both highly focused on the Final Solution and preoccupied with his performance as an exemplary Nazi. Through the conceit of inviting Anwar and his coconspirators to collaborate on a creative project, the understandable fascination the audience has with the psychic lives of perpetrators is satisfied but via a different channel than legal interrogation or scholarly research. The documentary does not present a correlation between virulent prejudice and mass killing but rather suggests a correlation between a desire for an outsized life and genocidal violence that can be effectively fueled by prejudice, which is equally applicable to Eichmann as chronicled by Stangneth.

Stangneth returns to the issue of Eichmann's deception repeatedly in her book, making headway on a topic that vexed Arendt. Here, Stangneth describes how critical lying was for Eichmann's sense of power:

> If you make someone believe a lie, you have power over him or her. Believing a lie means you lose a part of the real world, of yourself. The liar is given the power to rebuild the world around us, and we operate according to his or her rules. . . . If you read Eichmann's note written in his cell (and not available for journalists and spectators in 1961), you can find hints that Eichmann savored this special feeling of power, even as an accused.[32]

Eichmann's lying and his sense that it was the source of his power (and satisfaction) provide another interesting parallel with Oppenheimer's strategy of attempting to access Anwar's inner life through giving him creative autonomy in the reenactments and fantasy scenes. Directing and starring in his own production allowed Anwar to put forth another type of lie, that is, the lie of the cinema, and he took pleasure as Eichmann did in rebuilding a world around him according to his own wishes. Juxtaposing Anwar's directorial choices with the deception Eichmann uses as a matter of habit leads to the possibility that it is the true lie, the one that captures the motivation and self-delusions of perpetrators as they *themselves* define it, that may be most useful in assessing the contours of the psychological motivation in perpetrators. This is the type of insight that Arendt was unable to get in her coverage of Eichmann at the trial, but that she saw as critical for understanding him.

Arendt's frustration with Eichmann's clichés, the epitome of thoughtless speech, evokes another way in which she was perhaps subconsciously drawn to what reenactment might provide. She notes in *Eichmann* the "manifest shallowness in the doer (that) made it impossible to trace the incontestable evil of his deed to any deeper level."[33] Yet, if she had primarily focused on the "shallowness" of doing, that is, on the superficial actions of a perpetrator, without explicitly looking for evidence of a deeper evil, new lines of inquiry about the conditions that make violence possible might have been opened up. The clichés evoked by Eichmann on the stand provided him with a shorthand way to (1) evoke universalism for the purpose of his defense and (2) avoid the present inquiry through deflection into prepackaged thoughts about loyalty, Zionism, and command responsibility, the substance of which Arendt found thoroughly disheartening. In contrast, reenactment, with its reliance on bodily and physical memory, cannot be reduced to cliché. Seeing the swiftness and ease of Anwar's bodily movements during the reenactments, such as with the scene of the decapitation on the rooftop described earlier, provides evidence of his guilt that stands in sharp contrast to the evasions and denials of direct responsibility at the Eichmann trial. That Eichmann was a desk murderer certainly changes the types of actions that would be reenacted, but their significance would remain. It feels fitting that twenty years into this century it is not the newness of international tribunals or truth commissions that provides great insight into thinking about the patterns of mass violence, but rather strategies of reenactment, an endeavor that includes focusing on the conscious and subconscious lives of perpetrators as ways to understand the mechanisms of violence and augment the historical record.

THE RETURN OF THE MIMETIC

Nidesh Lawtoo's astute analysis of Eichmann through the lens of mimesis, which he defines not only as imitation and mimicry (as seen in theater, which imitates the real) but also as the process of "mirroring reflexes and emotional contagion," offers another reason for the turn to reenactment in the study of perpetrators.[34] Lawtoo's definition of mimesis expands on the one presented by Adorno and Horkheimer and replaces their emphasis on mimesis as reconciliation with nature with a focus on the human tendency to the subconscious mimicry of others. The language of mimesis gives Lawtoo a way to understand Eichmann as being under a hypnotic spell of the ideology of the Third Reich (causing him to imitate the behavior he believed would be rewarded), while also being able to use his powers of rationality to further his own goals. In this way, Lawtoo considers Eichmann to be *patho-logical*, drawing on the dynamic interplay between "contagious affects that generate an irrational pathos, on the one hand, a cold capacity to play a mirroring role from a rational distance, on the other."[35] Pathos and logos thus both have a role to play in the roles that Eichmann inhabits in his life and at his trial in ways that Arendt appreciates. Yet Lawtoo's attention to the mimetic provides a compelling way to understand the parts of Eichmann's actions and demeanor at the trial that perplex Arendt—the lying, the clichés, the thoughtless speech—all of which were the result of man under the spell of mimesis. She knew the trial was a spectacle for the world but she did not carry the metaphor of theater all the way through her analysis of Eichmann's actions, where, Lawtoo suggests, he was manifesting the affective spirit of the Nazi *Volk* in ways in which he may not have been fully conscious. It was the contagious quality of this spirit that interrupted his ability to think, including thinking from the standpoint of another. Arendt's misperception can thus be understood as attributing a philosophical explanation to Eichmann's persona when a mimetic one would be more apt.

In the documentary the viewer sees in an immediate way the allure of the gangster archetype in Hollywood films for Anwar. From his dress to his movements to his choice of language, much of Anwar's justification of violence comes through an imitation of Hollywood. To put it more strongly, were it not for the Hollywood ideal, Anwar's violent acts would certainly have taken on a different character and choreography. Lawtoo's analysis would suggest that this Hollywood fascination is not just a quirk of his personality or a hobby, but rather indispensable to his work as a killer for the Suharto regime. Being asked to re-create and reenact the killings of 1965–66 in the documentary, Anwar is able to again engage directly with the object of imitation in a quest to represent it in his own film. With Anwar we see much more clearly than we do with Eichmann how he understands himself to be playing a theatrical role and how much of that role is infused with a sense of world-historical importance. Anwar wants to be encompassed by the role and it is the role that guides his affective orientation. He is tethered to this spirit in conscious and unconscious ways. The fantasy sequence in the film allows him to be uninhibited about his desire to be seen as a hero by his victims and friends, and he wanted this heroism to be patriotically represented though sound and image in a way that could serve as its own fodder for imitation: the mimetic imperative looks to the future as well as the past.

Giving Anwar creative control within the documentary film also illustrates how the hypnotic spell of mimesis of which Lawtoo speaks does not necessarily preclude other types of thinking. We see Anwar as a competent producer, concerned about casting, cinematography, and set design in a way that is distinct from his mimetic engagement as a gangster. Moreover, we see him as a grandfather and friend to Oppenheimer, able to display a range of affective orientations appropriate to those interactions. Had Arendt been able to watch Anwar's actions in *The Act of Killing*, she may have been better able to sketch a profile of Eichmann's motivations and understand the "ghostlike" quality she observed in the glass case. She may, in fact, also have been able to see how his final words before execution reveal the extent of his hypnotic state: Eichmann grandly stated, "After a short while, gentlemen, we shall all meet again. Such is the fate of all men. Long live Germany, long live Argentina, long live Austria. I shall not forget them."[36] These words, in their pastiche of funeral oration and patriotic fervor, can be understood as a type of mimetic expression. As Lawtoo says, "Amplified by wine and by the imminence of death, the complexity of mimesis generates a psychosomatic automatism that had been constitutive of Eichmann's personality all along."[37]

ROLE REVERSAL AND THE CONCRETE OTHER

One of Arendt's most crucial observations is that Eichmann shows no capacity for an enlarged mentality, that is, the ability to separate from the narrowness of his own perspective and see from the standpoint of another. In contrast, in the documentary Anwar was not asked to describe how the victims must have felt; he was made to embody it, through drawing on the movements, gestures, and utterances he remembered from 1965. In doing so, he was accessing what Seyla Benhabib has called the particularized and concrete other when the language of the generalized other was not ethically available to him or he could not articulate it. Setting a standard for enlarged mentality that can now be used to think about the orientation of perpetrators, Benhabib wrote, "The standpoint of the concrete other, by contrast, requires us to view each and every rational being as an individual with a concrete history, identity, and affective emotional constitution."[38]

The priority given to abstract thinking in schemes of moral, political, and legal legitimacy, such as Rawls's veil of ignorance, can also be seen to contribute to the opaque and maddening responses from Eichmann on the stand. Realizing that the application of any universal rational or legal principle will not judge him favorably, he creates his own translation of the Kantian imperative as an extension of the will of the Fuhrer.[39] Taking the law of the land to be the universal law, Eichmann contends that his own actions are legitimate under the standard of universalizability. The distorted abstraction he creates for himself removes any consideration of victims. Clichéd speech, as discussed earlier, becomes an escape from the pressures of considering the abstract in relation to one's own actions and a technique of distancing claims of responsibility. Just as Carol Gillian contests Kohlberg's understanding of ethical development through research on the importance of interpersonal relationships on ethical obligations, the technique of reenactment changes the calculation of ethical obligation from an abstract application of law to the interpersonal dynamics at play in a particular act of violence.[40] Reenactment thus changes the trajectory of what maturity for perpetrators might look like. It might not come through understanding their failures according to a universal standard of morality, consistent with Kohlberg's understanding of moral development, but rather through engagement with the particulars of their lives and the imagined experiences of victims in moments when it is not higher-order thinking that is required, but rather empathy in relation to the bodily experiences of shame, fear, and pain.

At the start of the film, Anwar cannot think about the experiences of victims without also considering the perceived threat of communism to the state and the lies that were required to maintain complicity between state officials and the gangsters of a previous era. In one scene in the documentary, we see how direct testimony about the violence from a descendant of a victim is received by Anwar, who hears but cannot listen. In that scene a colleague of Anwar's speaks about the death of his stepfather at the hands of the gangsters. He is tentative about giving his account and uses the pretense of the reenactment to offer details about the violence he observed that might be helpful for the script. Upon hearing this, Anwar quickly brushes his emotional testimony aside through deflection, stating that the script had been finalized and could not be changed. Anwar did not want to engage with either the act of violence or the legacy of trauma right before him and his status in the group meant that he had the power to effectively curb all discussion. It is only later in the film, through role reversal and reenactment, that Anwar can appreciate the "concrete history, identity, and affective-emotional constitution" of victims even if the experiences of that victim are primarily his own projections, rather than informed by the lived experiences of the other.[41] Still, there is a way in which inhabiting the concrete other through role-play was an ingenious strategy for Oppenheimer to have cultivated with an agent who refused abstract categories of moral responsibility because reenactment appeals to the mimetic quality of the violence itself and to the perpetrator's pride at having prevailed in the original situation.

The verisimilitude that Anwar was so eager to capture as an auteur filmmaker became the path to understanding the perspectives of a victim. In a critical scene, he plays a man being interrogated by the gangsters in a newspaper office, a frequent location for violence at the time, testifying to the role of the media in furthering the genocidal campaign.[42] He protests that he does not adhere to the communist sympathies of which he is accused. He is beaten and threatened with torture. When the intimidation and threats by the aggressor become too much for Anwar to bear, he cuts the scene short, visibly shaken. We see that the others on the sound stage offer him water and try to bring his focus back to the artificial elements of the experience. Yet, he could not easily emerge from the role. When Anwar had to imitate the actions and feelings of the victim directly, he was more vulnerable to the emotional contagion of the larger event than he had ever been before. While he had previously been able to ignore accounts from victims and rationalize his action as justified by the communist threat, it was the task of imitation and its moral implications that stayed with him even after the scene had ended. Despite knowing it was a reenactment, he experienced what it felt like, in some small way, to fear for his life.

Later in the documentary, when Anwar is watching a video recording of the scene with his young grandsons, he is again emotionally affected by the violence but is now able to put into words what he is thinking: "Did the people I tortured feel the way I do here?" He speculates, "I can feel what the people I tortured felt." Oppenheimer then challenges him in a way that is unusual for the film: "Actually, the people you tortured felt far worse because you know it's only a film. They knew they were being killed." Anwar breaks down and pleads with Oppenheimer: "But I can feel it, Josh. Really. I can feel it. Or have I sinned? I did this to so many people. Josh. Is it all coming back to me? I really hope it won't. I don't want it to, Josh."

This exchange is remarkable because it seems both spontaneous and heavily dependent on the constructed encounter between perpetrator and victim on stage that Oppenheimer has facilitated. Where previously the powerful hold of the gangster ideal would have precluded attention to the experiences of victims, now Anwar's mimetic experience as a victim takes precedence in the moment and provokes a type of rational reflection. He can "feel" his wrongdoing in a way that was philosophically impossible to him. In asking about the karmic implications of the violence ("Is it all coming back to me?"), Anwar explores the possibility that retribution might come via multiple channels, including through the discomfort he felt in the scene. Just as the mimetic pull of the gangster persona carried him through the violence of the past, he seems to understand that the figure of the sadistic murderer could also inspire imitation and contagious vengeful feelings directed toward him.

Oppenheimer engaged with Anwar as a flawed human being but a human being nonetheless and saw him as worthy of attention and care. The care and friendship that developed between them led to a space where Anwar was able to grapple with conflicting feelings of guilt, fear of reprisal, and sadness. It seemed that Anwar could speak openly with "Josh" and trust that his response would be heard under the mantle of friendship, not antagonism. It was as if Oppenheimer's silence about the moral weight of the violence in so many previous moments allowed Anwar to come to an enlarged mentality independently. Oppenheimer facilitated the psychological risk this entailed for Anwar, in a way that would be impossible in a courtroom. The intimacy of the moment as Anwar is watching a video at home with his grandsons is in stark opposition to the formality of Eichmann in the glass box. While Arendt would not have wanted to give up the possibility of punishment to get the candor that Anwar displays in the film, she was attuned to her humanistic desire to hear it and to her aspiration that even a perpetrator may develop an enlarged mentality.

In an interview for *Film Quarterly*, Oppenheimer responds to the question, as I define it, of the Faustian bargain of treating Anwar as a friend when he says, "I think if we want to understand how human beings do this to each other—because every act of evil in our history has been committed by human beings—we have to look at the people who do it as human beings and understand how and why they do this. And if we don't want to understand why we do this to each other, then we are throwing away the opportunity of preventing it."[43] Arendt's instinct is much the same; there was a reason why she wanted to be in Jerusalem for the trial and wanted to understand Eichmann as best as she was able. What *The Act of Killing* shows is how much space may be necessary for perpetrators to reveal the "why" that many want to know. Anwar and his colleagues were given time, resources, and friendship over the course of making the documentary and ended up revealing much of what contributed to the violence in 1965. Yet, the irony is that the latitude and freedom from judgment that allow insight into the perpetrators in a way that is most telling for "preventing it [violence]" create the situation that also demands some type of moral reckoning. Some critics have argued that the audience of *The Act of Killing* is left unsatisfied and destabilized when they realize that the reckoning is not forthcoming. They argue that it is infuriating to watch Anwar's lack of accountability for his actions and his tentative thoughts about what the victims might have felt when so many victims have given testimony in other contexts.[44] In 2014 Oppenheimer directed a follow-up titled *The Look of Silence*, which follows an optometrist, Adi, whose family were victims of the massacres, as he speaks to the perpetrators. In this film, Adi's recollections and that of his family are at the center while the denials and evasions from those who committed the murders are replicated in a familiar way. While this second film captures important dialogic exchanges between victims and perpetrators that could never have happened in *The Act of Killing*, it also highlights what is so distinctive about the isolated self-reflection, such as it is, that Anwar engages in as part of the reenactments when the camera is able to focus entirely on him.

There may always be a danger with projects of reenactments—they will allow perpetrators to live out their fantasies in a way that precludes their own moral investigation of their crimes—but I don't think this is the case with *The Act of Killing*. I agree with film scholar Heather McIntosh when she argues that "Oppenheimer's film refuses to allow him [Anwar] the cultural catharsis and forgiveness that he seeks."[45] She suggests that giving Anwar the opportunity to attempt to revise history and grapple with his responsibility for the violence through reenactment and fantasy is itself ethically demanding and does not symbolize complicity with the violence but rather a desire to know about all the different dimensions of the crime, including the experiences of perpetrators and its impact on their lives. The audience is not forgiving Anwar by watching his film or coming to understand his motivations. Arendt, too, did not want her curiosity about Eichmann to obscure what she thought he did and deserved as punishment. Access to the psychic lives of perpetrators as evident in Arendt's reportage, Stangneth's research, and Oppenheimer's collaboration contributes to the work of judgment, but it does not displace it. While a more expansive understanding of the life conditions and motivations that lead to violence may elicit mercy in some cases, in many others it will not. It may, however, lend even greater gravitas to the act of judging, highlighting it as a distinctive form of thinking that requires the ability to move between concrete particulars and abstract categories and to see what Max Weber refers to as the differentiation of value spheres in which there cannot be a universal rationality that transcends differing spheres of meaning. As legal judgment in cases of mass violence continues to become more defined, its limits and constraints also become more evident. While reenactment is essentially a type of aesthetic endeavor, for both the actor and the audience, the work of legal judgment aims for different ends, including that of accountability, retribution, and deterrence through punishment. One can debate whether such ends of punishment are relevant for the case at hand but this is distinct from an investigation into a defendant's motivations and aspirations. Arendt's *Eichmann in Jerusalem* was a lightning rod for controversy, in part because Arendt refused to think narrowly about Eichmann or the Nazis; her argument was a larger one about bureaucracy and the use of the state apparatus for genocide. Appreciating what the reenactments of *The Act of Killing* can show us about the motivations of perpetrators complements Arendt's larger project in innovative ways.

In Jean Améry's chilling account of his experiences of torture at the hands of the Gestapo we see another reason to attend to the particularities of perpetrators as a task separate from rendering moral judgment:

> Many things do indeed happen approximately the way they were anticipated in the imagination: Gestapo men in leather coats and pistols, but also faces: not "Gestapo faces" with twisted noses, hypertrophied chins, pockmarks, and knife scares, as might appear in a book, but rather faces like anyone else's. Plain ordinary faces. And the enormous perception at a later stage that destroys all abstractive imagination, makes clear to us how the plain, ordinary faces finally become Gestapo faces after all, and how evil overlays and exceeds banality.[46]

It is the particularity of perpetrators that must be considered to understand the event. Only then can the interplay between banality and exceptionality be properly grasped. Focusing on many different aspects of Anwar's life and recollections gives us a specificity of understanding that we would not have had if there had been a shared focus with victims. It allows for a type of enlarged mentality in the other direction—that is, in the direction of perpetrators—that does not appear to have the same ethical weight as taking the standpoint of the victim; but it is necessary to further the task Arendt begins in *Eichmann in Jerusalem*.

It is Arendt's own fearless imagination that is the inspiration for this paper, her willingness in even the darkest moment to understand humanity in all its complexity. To speculate that Arendt would have embraced the creative gambit of Oppenheimer's documentary is to see her as open and curious, even about the most deplorable of moral agents. It is also to see her account of Eichmann as one that she knew would evolve with more information. Putting together Arendt's analysis with the portrait of Anwar is to also confront another harsh truth: to better understand how violence occurred and could occur again, we must be willing to see it all when it comes to perpetrators. The glass box in Jerusalem was only the beginning.

NOTES

1. Hannah Arendt, *Eichmann in Jerusalem: A Report on the Banality of Evil* (New York: Penguin, 1963).
2. Roger Berkowitz, "The Power of Non-Reconciliation—Arendt's Judgment of Adolf Eichmann," *Journal for Political Thinking (HannahArendt.net)* 6, nos. 1/2 (2011).

3. *The Act of Killing*, directed by Joshua Oppenheimer (2012; Telluride: Final Cut for Real).
4. Bettina Stangneth, *Eichmann Before Jerusalem: The Unexamined Life of a Mass Murderer* (New York: Knopf, 2014); Seyla Benhabib, *Exile, Statelessness, Migration: Playing Chess with History from Hannah Arendt to Isaiah Berlin* (Princeton, NJ: Princeton University Press, 2018), 66.
5. Arendt, *Eichmann in Jerusalem*, 45.
6. T. W. Adorno et al., *The Authoritarian Personality* (New York: Verso, 2019).
7. Adorno et al., xxiii.
8. Adorno et al., xxiii.
9. T. W. Adorno and M. Horkheimer, *Dialectic of Enlightenment* (Palo Alto, CA: Stanford University Press, 2002).
10. Jürgen Habermas and Thomas Y. Levin, "The Entwinement of Myth and Enlightenment: Re-Reading Dialectic of Enlightenment," *New German Critique*, no. 26 (1982): 13–30, https://doi.org/10.2307/488023.
11. Ernesto Verdeja, "Adorno's Mimesis and Its Limitations for Critical Social Thought," *European Journal of Political Theory* 8, no. 4 (2009): 493–511, https://doi.org/10.1177/1474885109337995.
12. Adorno and Horkheimer, *Dialectic of Enlightenment*, 14, emphasis added.
13. Geoffrey B. Robinson, *The Killing Season: A History of the Indonesian Massacres, 1965–66* (Princeton, NJ: Princeton University Press, 2018).
14. Sigmund Freud, *Beyond the Pleasure Principle* (New York: Norton, 1961).
15. Bessel van der Kolk, *The Body Keeps the Score: Brain, Mind, and Body in the Healing of Trauma* (New York: Penguin, 2014), 97.
16. Homay King, "Born Free?: Repetition and Fantasy in the Act of Killing," *Film Quarterly* 67, no. 2 (2013).
17. King, 32.
18. Benhabib, *Exile, Statelessness, Migration*, 63.
19. Arendt, *Eichmann in Jerusalem*, 5.
20. Benhabib, *Exile, Statelessness, Migration*, 64.
21. Arendt, *Eichmann in Jerusalem*, 21.
22. Benhabib, *Exile, Statelessness, and Migration*, 69.
23. Arendt, *Eichmann in Jerusalem*, 26.
24. Arendt, 26.
25. Arendt, 26.
26. Stangneth, *Eichmann Before Jerusalem*.
27. Stangneth, 4.
28. Stangneth, 125.
29. Arendt, *Eichmann in Jersusalem*, 30.
30. Stangneth, *Eichmann Before Jerusalem*, 11.
31. Plato, *The Republic* (New York: Hachette, 1968), bk. 1.
32. David Frum, "The Lies of Adolf Eichmann," *Atlantic*, October 8, 2014, www.theatlantic.com/international/archive/2014/10/the-lies-adolf-eichmann-told/381222/.

33. Hannah Arendt and Mary McCarthy, *Between Friends: The Correspondence of Hannah Arendt and Mary McCarthy, 1949–1975*, ed. Carol Brightman (San Diego: Harcourt, Brace, 1995), xxv.
34. Nidesh Lawtoo, "The Case of Eichmann Restaged: Arendt, Evil, and the Complexity of Mimesis," *Political Research Quarterly* 74, no. 2 (2020): 2–3.
35. Lawtoo, 2–3.
36. Arendt, *Eichmann in Jerusalem*, 252.
37. Lawtoo, "The Case of Eichmann Restaged," 10.
38. Seyla Benhabib, "The Generalized and Concrete Other: The Kohlberg-Gilligan Controversy and Moral Theory," in *Women and Moral Theory*, ed. Eva Feder Kittay and Diana T. Meyers (Totowa, NJ: Rowman and Littlefield, 1987), 164.
39. Arendt, *Eichmann in Jerusalem*, 136.
40. Benhabib, "The Generalized and Concrete Other," 157.
41. Benhabib, 158.
42. Robinson, *The Killing Season*.
43. Irene Lusztig, "The Fever Dream of Documentary: A Conversation with Joshua Oppenheimer " *Film Quarterly* 67, no. 2 (2013): 52.
44. Jill Godmilow, "Killing the Documentary: An Oscar-Nominated Filmmaker Takes Issue with 'the Act of Killing,' " *IndieWire*, March 5, 2014; Colin Beckett, "Finding a Liberal Form: Oppenheimer, Morris, Godmilow," *INCITE!* (blog), https://incite-online.net/beckett5.html.
45. Heather McIntosh, "Reenactments and the Denial of Catharsis in the Act of Killing," *Critical Asian Studies* 34, no. 5 (2017): 379.
46. Jean Améry, *At the Mind's Limit: Contemplations by a Survivor on Auschwitz and Its Realities* (Bloomington: Indiana University Press, 2009), 25.

PART III

Democratic Iterations and Cosmopolitanism

9

Democracy Without Shortcuts

An Institutional Approach to Democratic Legitimacy

CRISTINA LAFONT

Perhaps the most prominent philosophical concern underlying Seyla Benhabib's work is the search for "the concrete universal." This fundamental question is as old as philosophy itself. However, in her work this abstract question shows up in terms of specific political concerns—such as how to reconcile apparently oppositional phenomena: cosmopolitanism with democratic self-governance, state sovereignty with international human rights, universal justice with cultural identity, citizenship rights with the rights of others, and so on. One key factor that lets her shed new light on such fundamental problems is that she forces her readers to inhabit the different perspectives from which the affected themselves approach these questions. Many Western cosmopolitans too easily fall under the spell of "Orientalism" and, motivated by a fear that they will be perceived as "ethnocentric," accept a view of other cultures as incommensurable and opaque wholes with an entirely different set of values that remain inaccessible to outsiders. In sharp contrast, Benhabib defends "another cosmopolitanism" and "the rights of others" by forcing readers to drop their external perspective and adopt the perspective of those who are engaged in political struggles against injustices within these "other" cultures. From this perspective, readers are forced to recognize both their own universalist aspirations as well as the concrete and differentiated understanding of these aspirations as they apply to ongoing political struggles in light of their specific social and historical contexts and circumstances. Applying the fruitful concept of "democratic iterations" to the various legal and political contexts in which the tension between the universal and the particular is at play, Benhabib helps us grasp the way in which universal principles and norms can be made concrete and appropriated by diverse communities in different ways without losing their unconditional validity or forcing any alienating assimilation.

In what follows, I defend an account of the legitimacy of political decisions and institutions that nicely fits into Benhabib's way of thinking about the concrete universal. In particular, I use the concept of "democratic iterations" and its opposite (what I call "antidemocratic shortcuts") to articulate a criterion for evaluating the legitimacy of institutions and political decisions that challenges widespread assumptions about the democratic legitimacy of majoritarian and nonmajoritarian as well as national and transnational institutions.[1] In a nutshell, the idea is as follows. If the essence of the democratic ideal of self-government is the participation of all citizens in the iterative process of interpreting, challenging, and reinterpreting the political project of their community over time, then the buildup of shortcuts that impede a properly inclusive participation in that ongoing interpretative process can only generate democratic deficits. Consequently, in order to evaluate the democratic legitimacy of different institutions and procedures, what we need to assess is the specific function that these institutions and procedures play in the political system as a whole, in particular, whether they facilitate "democratic iterations" or generate "antidemocratic shortcuts."[2]

One important advantage of this way of thinking about legitimacy is that it questions the widespread assumption that there are only two methodological choices for an account of legitimacy: either endorsing a correctness view or endorsing proceduralism.[3] The institutional approach does not fit either of these boxes. Similar to proceduralism, the institutional approach rejects a correctness view, according to which substantive correctness is necessary and sufficient for legitimacy. However, the institutional approach also rejects proceduralism's contention that procedural correctness is necessary and sufficient for legitimacy. Although there are many varieties of proceduralism, all of them assume that, in the face of substantive disagreements among citizens, the legitimacy of collective decisions ultimately rests on procedural rather than substantive grounds. While citizens disagree about the substantive correctness of majoritarian decisions, they can accept them as legitimate because of the democratic features of majority rule (as a fair, inclusive, egalitarian procedure) and because of the epistemic features of the deliberation process that came before a vote. The problem with this approach is that by making legitimacy entirely dependent on procedural features, it immunizes the substantive views of the majority from legitimate scrutiny. Since substantive disagreements have no bearing on the legitimacy of enforcing majoritarian decisions, proceduralism justifies an "antidemocratic shortcut" by which consolidated majorities can impose their substantive views on others without challenge. By contrast, adopting an institutional approach to legitimacy helps provide a more convincing account of the interplay between substantive and procedural aspects of democratic legitimacy. In addition, this account allows us to see what is wrong with interpreting the legitimacy of majoritarian and nonmajoritarian institutions in terms of an alleged conflict between popular sovereignty and rights protections. In opposition to this view, I argue that the proper standard for judging the democratic legitimacy of both majoritarian and nonmajoritarian institutions is whether they enable democratic iterations or whether they generate antidemocratic shortcuts instead.

THE PROCEDURALIST SHORTCUT

According to deliberative democrats, political decisions can claim legitimacy only to the extent that they can meet with the assent of citizens in an inclusive and unconstrained process of public deliberation. However, in light of deep and ongoing disagreements among citizens, postdeliberative consensus on political decisions can hardly be expected. This is why accounts of democratic legitimacy typically focus on how to justify the legitimacy of democratic procedures of decision-making such as majority rule. The challenge is to justify the claim that, under certain conditions, majoritarian decisions are legitimate and thus dissenting minorities should accept them as binding, even if they believe that they are wrong on their substantive merits. If legitimacy depends on citizens' assent and the outvoted minority per hypothesis disagrees with respect to the substantive merits of the decisions in question, it would seem that the legitimizing effects of assent cannot flow from substantive but rather only from *procedural* reasons that all citizens can accept. This is the key assumption behind proceduralist accounts of legitimacy. There are many varieties of proceduralism (e.g., epistemic and nonepistemic, deliberative and nondeliberative, and so on). But, what they all have in common is the claim that democratic political decisions can be legitimate (and thus deserve obedience) even if they are substantively wrong. If the procedural conditions are sufficiently met, majoritarian decisions are legitimate, whatever they are. The outvoted minority does not have to surrender its judgment on the substantive wrongness of the decisions but it can nonetheless accept the legitimacy of its enforcement, since the latter only depends on the relevant virtues of the procedure and not upon the substantive correctness of its outcomes.

Varieties of proceduralism differ with respect to their identification of the procedural features that confer legitimacy to majoritarian decisions. Deep pluralist accounts of majority rule explain the legitimacy of majoritarian decisions on the basis of nonepistemic virtues of the procedure such as the fairness of giving all those who will be subject to the decisions equal chances to influence them.[4] In contrast, deliberative democrats explain the legitimacy of majoritarian decisions not only on the basis of the procedural fairness of majority rule, but also upon the basis of the epistemic virtues embodied within the pre-vote deliberative process (e.g., as inclusive, informed, noncoercive, nondeceptive), which allows citizens to mutually justify the decisions that they favor and which grants the presumption of reasonable outcomes.[5] Still, despite any epistemically valuable benchmarks that the deliberative procedure must meet, the account of legitimacy remains procedural. If the procedural conditions in question are met, then any majoritarian decisions that are produced are legitimate, whatever they are—i.e., even if, as the outvoted minority contends, these decisions are substantively wrong (e.g., unjust, inefficient, unfair). Habermas expresses the idea behind epistemic proceduralism with the help of Rawls's distinction between "imperfect" and "pure" proceduralism. Postdeliberative majority rule "is imperfect because the democratic process is established so as to justify the presumption of a rational outcome without being able to guarantee that the outcome is right. On the other hand, it is also a case of pure procedural justice, because in the democratic process no criteria of rightness independent of the procedure are available; the correctness of decisions depends solely on the fact that the procedure has actually been carried out."[6] Postdeliberative majority rule is "imperfectly" procedural because *it cannot guarantee* that its outcomes are *substantively right* (e.g., just, good, efficient, or whatever the relevant criteria may be). However, it is "purely" procedural because *it can* guarantee that its outcomes are *legitimate*. If the procedural conditions are met its outcomes are legitimate, whatever they are. There are no substantive criteria that the outcomes must met in order to be legitimate.[7] In *Between Facts and Norms* Habermas explains the legitimacy of majority rule as follows: "Because of its internal connection with a deliberative practice, majority rule justifies the presumption that the fallible majority opinion may be considered a reasonable basis for a common practice until further notice, namely, until the minority convinces the majority that their (the minority's) views are correct."[8] We can express the proceduralist view of the legitimacy of majoritarian decisions with the following principle:

Pure majoritarianism: Let the majority prevail until the minority convinces the majority that their views are correct.

The main problem with pure proceduralist views of legitimacy is that they have no resources to make the legitimacy of political decisions dependent on the specifics of their substantive wrongness. The procedural source of legitimacy is the same for all decisions regardless of their content, i.e., regardless of how reasonable or unreasonable they may be. However, most defenders of proceduralist approaches recognize that there is a limit as to how unreasonable or unjust majoritarian decisions can be, and that the legitimacy of any decision's enforcement is undermined beyond that point. Different authors offer different examples but the basic idea is that majoritarian decisions that violate citizens' fundamental rights or freedoms are illegitimate and dissenting minorities have no duty to obey them.[9] Although this view is very plausible, it is not clear how it can be justified from within the perspective of a proceduralist approach to legitimacy. For, if one accepts such a limit, this amounts to a recognition that merely being endorsed by the majority under proper (epistemic and deliberative) conditions is not, by itself, sufficient to render all political decisions legitimate. Indeed, recognizing that majoritarian decisions that threaten fundamental rights are illegitimate would require modifying the proceduralist approach accordingly. This would yield the following principle instead:

> Modified majoritarianism: Let the majority prevail except in cases where the majority decision threatens fundamental rights.[10]

Whereas pure majoritarianism affirms that settling political questions by (postdeliberative) majority rule is always legitimate (since political decisions are legitimate "until the minority convinces the majority that their views are correct"), modified majoritarianism rejects the legitimacy of majoritarian decisions that threaten fundamental rights. It amounts to claiming that decisions that touch upon fundamental rights cannot be legitimately settled by majority rule. Instead, these decisions must be settled on the basis of their substantive merits.

This view questions the key assumption behind proceduralism that I mentioned at the beginning. If legitimacy depends on citizens' assent and the outvoted minority per hypothesis disagrees on the substantive merits of the decisions in question, it seems that the legitimizing assent cannot rest on substantive but rather only upon *procedural* reasons that all citizens can accept. However, modified majoritarianism offers an interesting intermediate alternative. Dissenting minorities may accept the legitimacy of majoritarian decisions to the extent that they can agree that they are at least reasonable from a substantive point of view, even if they think that they are not the right or best decisions. However, majoritarian decisions that violate fundamental rights of citizens would not be accepted as legitimate by dissenting minorities, even if they agree that they came about through democratic procedures that tend to yield reasonable outcomes. Following this view, it is not only the case that dissenting minorities do not have to surrender their judgment to majority opinion regarding the substantive correctness of majoritarian decisions, as proceduralists plausibly contend. It is also the case that they do not have to accept majoritarian decisions as legitimate for procedural reasons alone, if those decisions threaten fundamental rights or freedoms.

Proceduralists who worry about the limits of unconstrained majoritarianism may find modified majoritarianism more plausible, but they face two challenges in accounting for it within the constraints set by proceduralism. First, endorsing this view requires recognizing, contrary to proceduralist assumptions, that evaluating political decisions on their substantive merits is necessary. Moreover, this evaluation is necessary not only to figure out whether these decisions are substantively *right*, but also to determine whether their enforcement is *legitimate*; looking at their procedural pedigree alone is never enough to make such a determination. Second, a proceduralist who would like to endorse modified majoritarianism must offer some alternative answer to the question of how political decisions can be legitimately enforced after the limits of procedural majoritarianism are reached. Merely asserting that decisions that are too unjust are illegitimate and that dissenting minorities do not have a duty to obey them does not answer the question of what the *legitimate* alternative for collective decision-making is in such cases.

Correctness theories of legitimacy do not fare much better in that respect.[11] In contrast to proceduralist approaches, they don't have a problem justifying the idea that majoritarian decisions that threaten fundamental rights are illegitimate, even if they came about through impeccable democratic procedures. For, on a correctness view of legitimacy, only substantively correct decisions are legitimate. However, in light of the ubiquity of substantive disagreements about rights, this view of legitimacy leaves us with the same practical problem as proceduralism. It does not answer the question of how collective political decisions can be legitimately made and enforced despite citizens' deep substantive disagreements about rights. Answering this question requires us to identify an alternative way of making political decisions that touch upon fundamental rights that dissenting minorities could accept as legitimate even if they disagreed with the substantive merits of those decisions. The institutional approach to legitimacy that I defend offers just such an answer to this question.

DEMOCRATIC LEGITIMACY: NEITHER SUBSTANTIVE NOR PROCEDURAL, BUT INSTITUTIONAL

If we compare the two normative principles mentioned earlier, pure and modified majoritarianism, there is a key difference between them. Whereas majoritarian procedures are necessary and sufficient for legitimacy according to the first principle, on the second principle majoritarian procedures are insufficient for legitimacy. As a consequence, modified majoritarianism can be interpreted as a *recursive* principle. The point is not to ban the use of majority rule but to take away its finality. Decisions may be temporarily settled by majority rule, but only a "settled view" on the rights in question can bring the triggering of further scrutiny to a proper end. As a recursive principle, modified majoritarianism reminds us that nothing short of a settled view on the proper answer to questions about rights can legitimately settle decisions about them.

Following this principle, the institutional account of legitimacy adds a necessary condition to the (fairness, epistemic, and discourse) conditions that are correctly identified by epistemic proceduralists as necessary for the legitimacy of majoritarian decisions. The legitimacy of majoritarian decisions *also* depends on the existence of an actual (i.e., effective) *institutional opportunity* to contest any laws and policies that citizens find unreasonable on substantive grounds by requesting that proper public reasons be offered in their support (or else the policies in question be changed), even if those citizens belong to the outvoted minority and democratic procedures were properly followed.

In contrast to correctness views of legitimacy, the institutional approach endorses the idea found in proceduralist conceptions that legitimacy accrues to political decisions *indirectly*, in virtue of the existence of an institutional opportunity for public scrutiny, and not directly (and only) in virtue of the substantive correctness of a decision. However, this account differs from proceduralist approaches in that the relevant type of institution to settle disagreements about fundamental rights *must* guide its decisions by substantive considerations and not just by aggregating the number of supporters. As a consequence, the legitimacy of such an institution's outcomes is not *purely* procedural, i.e., it is not *guaranteed* simply by having properly followed procedures, as in the case of majoritarian institutions. It is *recursively* procedural. This is why its outcomes can in turn be contested and subjected to further scrutiny on substantive and not only on procedural grounds. Citizens cannot simply rely on the fulfillment of epistemic and discursive conditions in public deliberation in general for majoritarian decisions that touch upon fundamental rights to be legitimately enforced.

The institutional approach seems in line with democratic practices. It is a core feature of constitutional democracies that majoritarian decisions can be struck down as unconstitutional if they violate the fundamental rights and freedoms of citizens.[12] This in turn suggests that, when fundamental rights and freedoms are at stake, the intrinsic value of democratic procedures such as majority rule is *insufficient* to secure the legitimacy of its outcomes. Substantive and not only procedural standards matter for the legitimacy of political decisions that touch upon fundamental rights and freedoms. In particular, they matter for determining which majoritarian decisions are reasonable and thus merit acceptance on proceduralist grounds, even by those who think that they are substantively wrong, and which are unreasonable and thus merit legal contestation, even if the majority remains unconvinced.

According to the institutional approach, when citizens disagree about the substantive correctness of a decision it is not the case that they simply accept the legitimacy of majoritarian decisions for procedural reasons. Citizens accept the legitimacy of such decisions because and only to the extent that they *agree* that majoritarian decisions are at least reasonable from a substantive point of view (they do not violate fundamental rights and freedoms), or, if they *disagree*, then they have the effective right to unilaterally contest this legitimacy *on substantive grounds*, since institutional opportunities for legal contestation are available. The need to meet this institutional condition in turn justifies the creation of additional opportunities for contestation of decisions made by majoritarian institutions (e.g., the legislature) that citizens can utilize—such as organizing ballot initiatives and referenda, or filing complaints in a transnational court (e.g., the European Court of Human Rights).

Indeed, if one looks at human rights practice from this institutional perspective, its evolution can be retrospectively interpreted as trying to provide evermore institutional venues of scrutiny and legal contestation for claims about human rights violations that stretch beyond the local and national level to the transnational and global level. This gradual expansion seems necessary in light of the possibility that national venues for legal contestation can be exhausted before a shared view on contested rights comes about. However, according to the institutional approach of legitimacy, the point of creating transnational venues of contestation that can be triggered when national venues have been exhausted is not to establish yet another final authority. To the contrary, the point of inducing an institutional dialogue between national and transnational institutions is that it keeps the possibility of ongoing contestation and debate about the substantive merits of decisions that touch upon rights open so that, over time, a settled view on the rights in question may come about. Only such a settled view can bring the process of contestation to a proper end (i.e., an end that does not contravene the principle of modified majoritarianism).

Now, it is also important to note that acknowledging that the legitimacy of decisions that touch upon fundamental rights depends on substantive considerations does not mean that the institutional approach must identify the correct substantive criteria for interpreting and specifying rights, as a correctness view of legitimacy does. This is because arriving at a settled view on rights that brings the process of contestation to a natural end is not the same as arriving at a *correct* view about rights. It is only arriving at a view that justifies the *legitimacy* of enforcing political decisions on those who are subject to them. Since the institutional approach does not embrace a correctness view of legitimacy, it can leave the elaboration of the relevant substantive criteria to the participants themselves who make use of these institutions. One essential contribution made by the right to legal contestation is that participants can articulate alternative criteria or proposals that challenge previously accepted or unquestioned ones. As a consequence of the ongoing process of contestation, substantive criteria can change over time due to the creative efforts of all those involved in public debates about the proper content, scope, and meaning of their rights. However, this ongoing, inclusive, and open-ended process of challenging and reinterpreting the proper substantive criteria for determining the scope and meaning of our rights is possible only to the extent that citizens themselves *do not accept a pure proceduralist view of the legitimacy* of majoritarian decisions that touch upon fundamental rights and freedoms. This may not be immediately obvious, so let me explain why.

Since pure proceduralist approaches to legitimacy leave aside substantive considerations, it may seem like they too leave the determination of the proper substantive criteria of evaluation to the affected themselves. However, they do not do so in a properly *inclusive* sense. By making substantive considerations *irrelevant* to the legitimacy of coercive enforcement, these approaches actually *immunize* the substantive criteria that decisional majorities happen to endorse from legitimate challenge by dissenting minorities. For dissenting minorities can have an opportunity to effectively challenge decisions touching upon fundamental rights on their substantive merits only if it is generally accepted that the *legitimacy* of their enforcement depends on the quality of the substantive reasons and not merely on the number of supporters.

The institutional approach to legitimacy offers an alternative perspective on the democratic legitimacy of majoritarian and nonmajoritarian institutions. If we look at the nonmajoritarian institutions of judicial review from the perspective of securing citizens' rights to legal contestation, we can see that they can serve the democratic goal of securing the inclusion of dissenting minorities in the collective process of determining the proper content, scope, and meaning of citizens' rights and that, to the extent that they do, they are democratically legitimate. Far from constraining popular sovereignty from the outside, judicial institutions enable it in the first place by making it truly inclusive. Another virtue of adopting the institutional approach to legitimacy is that it does not require that every single person in fact agrees on the reasonableness of each coercive law to which they are subject for their enforcement to be legitimate; defenders of proceduralist approaches are right to contend that this would be unfeasible. But what the institutional approach does require is that institutions be in place that enable any citizen to contest laws and policies that they find unreasonable on substantive grounds by requesting that proper reasons be offered in their support (or else that the policies be changed), even if those citizens happen to find themselves in the minority.

The institutional approach supports a pluralist view of legitimacy, according to which different types of political decisions require different institutional procedures for their legitimate resolution. It also recognizes that decisions that touch upon fundamental rights and freedoms require the existence of institutional procedures that are driven by substantive considerations. However, as mentioned before, this does not mean that the legitimacy of their enforcement depends on meeting some substantive criteria of correctness to be discerned by legal experts or by philosophers, as a correctness theory may maintain. To the contrary, legitimacy depends on the existence of institutions that enable substantive debates among all citizens so that current criteria can be criticized, reinterpreted, or transformed and new criteria may be accepted as a result.

On this view, legitimacy is neither purely substantive nor purely procedural. It is institutional. The legitimacy of decisions that citizens think are wrong on their substantive merits derives from the existence of proper democratic procedures and practices. However, this does not make legitimacy (and the duty to obey) purely procedural because proper democratic procedures must include institutional opportunities to contest majoritarian decisions on substantive grounds whenever citizens think they are unreasonable (violate fundamental rights or freedoms). And they must have this opportunity even if they fail to convince the majority that their views are correct. Now, since legitimacy depends on the interpretation of the proper meaning and scope of citizens' rights and freedoms and this interpretation can only take place with the help and support of proper institutions, it is true that legitimacy cannot be assessed independently of those processes. However, this does not mean that legitimacy depends on such processes because it is purely procedural, as these processes are themselves fallible and can be effectively contested by offering new reasons, evidence, and views. Indeed, the *recursivity* of legal contestation that gives rise to evermore institutional venues for scrutiny is incompatible with the pure proceduralist claim that the legitimacy of decisions "depends solely on the fact that the procedure has actually been carried out."[13] While this is true of majoritarian procedures, such procedures are *insufficient* to legitimately enforce decisions that touch upon fundamental rights.

It is also important to note that the institutional approach does not need to assume that all disagreements about rights can be reasonably overcome at any given time. It only needs to show that the goal of reaching a settled view on contested rights is not hopeless in the following sense: it is a goal that (1) is open to all to pursue, (2) the rules for doing so can be reasonably accepted independently of resolving the specific ongoing disagreements, and (3) it can succeed (and has in fact often succeeded in the past). If there are practices and institutions in place that satisfy these conditions, then citizens are able to see how the institutions of constitutional democracies are legitimate and thus can come to reflectively endorse them. Granted, the existence of such practices and institutions is not sufficient to guarantee that all citizens will at all times only be subject to laws that they find acceptable. No human institution can guarantee that. But, in contrast to nondemocratic societies, what these institutions can guarantee is that, whenever citizens cannot reasonably accept some coercive laws or policy, they can, on their own accord, trigger a process of mutual justification that is structured in such a way that a settled view on the correct or best law or policy may be reached. There are no guarantees, other than that there is an institutional avenue to trigger the process that is open to all citizens and that is not merely a farce, i.e., it is a process that can actually succeed and has done so in the past—something that is typically absent in nondemocratic societies where citizens may have merely formal but not *effective* rights to political and legal contestation.

AN ALTERNATIVE CRITERION FOR EVALUATING THE LEGITIMACY OF MAJORITARIAN AND NONMAJORITARIAN INSTITUTIONS: ENABLING DEMOCRATIC ITERATIONS OR GENERATING ANTIDEMOCRATIC SHORTCUTS?

An interesting consequence of adopting the institutional approach to legitimacy is that it questions the widespread assumption that majoritarian institutions are per default democratically legitimate whereas nonmajoritarian institutions such as judicial review are not. Even many who accept that judicial review is necessary for rights protections assume that it is in tension with democratic self-government. The lack of democratic legitimacy is alleged to be even worse regarding transnational institutions of judicial review, since they are both countermajoritarian and foreign. However, if one agrees that majoritarian decisions that violate fundamental rights and freedoms are illegitimate and do not merit the assent of outvoted minorities who will be subject to them, then it seems that majoritarian procedures are *too exclusionary to be democratically legitimate* regarding decisions about fundamental rights. For they fail to provide permanent minorities with effective opportunities to participate as equals in the process of shaping the proper meaning and scope of their rights, leaving them no alternative but to blindly obey decisions that, by their own lights, threaten their rights and freedoms or those of others.

The institutional approach defended here offers an interesting criterion for judging the democratic legitimacy of institutions. If the legitimacy of political decisions that touch upon fundamental rights and freedoms depends on their substantive merits, and citizens have substantive disagreements about the meaning and scope of their rights, then the proper criterion for determining which type of institution is appropriate to make legitimate decisions that touch upon everyone's rights is to ask: Which institutional procedures empower all citizens to *open and reopen an inclusive debate* in which different substantive views on rights can be challenged, revised, and transformed so that, over time, a shared view can arise that brings the triggering of further scrutiny to a proper end? Following this view, the democratic legitimacy of judicial review is located precisely in the important role that it plays in securing effective participation among all citizens on equal terms in shaping the meaning, content, and scope of their rights. By contrast, institutional procedures that circumvent such a needed debate by conferring full legitimacy upon majoritarian decisions without institutional opportunities for dissenting minorities to challenge them on substantive grounds are unduly exclusionary and therefore not democratically legitimate. To mark this distinction, Benhabib's notion of "democratic iteration" is fruitful. She uses the term to describe processes of political opinion and will formation that enable a "jurisgenerative politics," that is, "cases of legal and political contestation in which the meaning of rights and other fundamental principles are reposited, resignified, and reappropriated by new and excluded groups, or by the citizenry in the face of new and unprecedented hermeneutic challenges and meaning constellations."[14] To the extent that institutional arrangements enable such inclusive processes of democratic iterations they are legitimate. By contrast, inclusive democratic iterations become impossible whenever existing institutional arrangements provide antidemocratic shortcuts by which consolidated majorities can impose their substantive views on the rest of the citizenry without opportunities for legitimate challenge, resignification, and inclusive reappropriation.

Citizens cannot see themselves as participating in a project of collective self-government if they are required to *blindly* defer to majoritarian decisions that, for all they know, may violate their fundamental rights and freedoms or those of others. So long as such (national and transnational) opportunities exist, citizens do *not* have to endorse the view that decisions that threaten their fundamental rights and freedoms are legitimate simply because they have majority support, as pure proceduralism suggests. Indeed, the existence of a legitimate institutional alternative is a way of publicly recognizing the contrary view, namely, that decisions about fundamental rights and freedoms ought to be settled on substantive grounds and not simply by counting the number of supporters. To the extent that this normative view is publicly affirmed and citizens in the minority can avail themselves of institutional venues for effective contestation, they can see themselves as equal participants in a collective project of self-government. But note that this is not only true if and when citizens happen to succeed. It is equally true when their attempts to legally contest specific decisions fail and their views do not prevail. The publicly shared rejection of pure majoritarianism upon which the institutions of constitutional democracies are predicated does not change depending on which citizens happen to be successful on which occasion. In accordance with that shared rejection, citizens whose attempts fail can *legitimately* continue to exercise their rights of political and legal contestation at the national and/or transnational levels, they may exercise civil disobedience, and so forth.

Once we adopt the perspective offered by the institutional approach to legitimacy, we can also see why the cosmopolitan norms that underlie transnational human rights institutions and practices do not have to be interpreted as trying to impose a homogeneous substantive interpretation of rights upon all political communities. To the contrary, they aim at enabling the equal participation of all citizens in democratic iterations that give rise to different interpretations of the meaning and scope of their rights that are suitable to the ever-changing contexts and circumstances in which different political communities find themselves due to their different histories and path dependencies, the different standard threats they are exposed to, and so on. The other side of this coin is that transnational human rights institutions do not simply offer additional possibilities to open and reopen debate and contestation on rights just as national institutions do. Instead, they also contribute to properly enlarging the audience of those for whom rights violations are a matter of concern. The existence of such institutional mechanism enriches national political debates about rights with a plethora of challenging views, considerations, and reasons that bear on the decisions in question but are based on the life experiences of citizens from other countries who are nonetheless engaged in the same task of reaching a settled view on the proper answer to questions about fundamental rights. There are no justified exclusions from participation in this shared, open-ended task if everyone's human rights matter equally and their violations are a matter of everyone's concern. In contrast to purely substantive and purely procedural approaches, the institutional approach to democratic legitimacy can properly account for the ongoing transformation and reinterpretation of both substantive and procedural norms that is brought about by those who make use of the institutions in question over time.

As Benhabib's work vividly shows, cosmopolitan principles and norms can be made concrete and appropriated by different communities in different ways without losing their unconditional validity or forcing an alienating assimilation upon them. But this in turn requires endorsing *inclusive* transnational institutions rather than rejecting them in the name of national sovereignty. In the same vein, the institutional approach to legitimacy helps us see why processes of concretization, vernacularization, and localization of norms that touch upon fundamental rights require *transnationalization* in order to be properly inclusive.

NOTES

1. I develop the concept of antidemocratic "shortcuts" at length in Lafont, *Democracy Without Shortcuts* (Oxford: Oxford University Press, 2020).
2. In that regard, the institutional approach to legitimacy fits best with conceptions of deliberative democracy that pay attention to the deliberative system as a whole. See, e.g., John Parkinson and Jane Mansbridge, eds., *Deliberative Systems: Deliberative Democracy at the Large Scale* (Cambridge: Cambridge University Press, 2012).
3. E.g., in *Democratic Authority* (Princeton, NJ: Princeton University Press, 2008) David Estlund distinguishes several varieties of proceduralism and contrast them with correctness theories (102). In "Pure Epistemic Proceduralism," *Episteme* 5, no. 1 (2008): 33–55, Fabienne Peter distinguishes between proceduralist and instrumentalist approaches to legitimacy. The institutional approach that I defend here does not fit either of these classifications. It is neither a purely proceduralist nor a correctness/instrumentalist approach to legitimacy.
4. For different versions of this approach see, e.g., Jeremy Waldron, *Law and Disagreement* (Oxford: Oxford University Press, 1999); Nadia Urbinati, *Democracy Disfigured: Opinion, Truth, and the People* (Cambridge, MA: Harvard University Press, 2014); Richard Bellamy, *Political Constitutionalism* (Cambridge: Cambridge University Press, 2007); Thomas Christiano, *The Constitution of Equality: Democratic Authority and Its Limits* (Oxford: Oxford University Press, 2008).
5. For different versions of this approach see, e.g., Jürgen Habermas, *Between Facts and Norms* (Cambridge, MA: MIT Press, 1996); and Habermas, "Reply to Symposium Participants," *Cardozo Law Review* 17, nos. 4–5 (1996), 1477–558; Seyla Benhabib, "Toward a Deliberative Model of Democratic Legitimacy," in *Democracy and Difference*, ed. Seyla Benhabib (Princeton, NJ: Princeton University Press, 1996); Amy Gutmann and Dennis Thompson, *Why Deliberative Democracy?* (Princeton, NJ: Princeton University Press, 2004); Rainer Forst, *The Right to Justification: Elements of a Constructivist Theory of Justice* (New York: Columbia University Press, 2011). Estlund, *Democratic Authority*; Fabienne Peter, "Democratic Legitimacy and

Proceduralist Social Epistemology," *Politics, Philosophy and Economics* 6, no. 3 (2007): 329–53; and Peter, "Pure Epistemic Proceduralism."
6. Habermas, "Reply to Symposium Participants," 1495.
7. I offer a critical analysis of Habermas's use of these Rawlsian distinctions in Lafont, "Procedural Justice?: Implications of the Rawls-Habermas Debate for Discourse Ethics," *Philosophy and Social Criticism* 29, no. 2 (2003): 167–85.
8. Habermas, *Between Facts and Norms*, 306. Benhabib, "Toward a Deliberative Model of Democratic Legitimacy," defends a similar view. However, in my opinion proceduralism is actually incompatible with her conception of democratic iterations, whereas the institutional approach to legitimacy is a much better fit.
9. For a defense of this view from the perspective of fair proceduralism see, e.g., Waldron, *Law and Disagreement*, 207; for a defense of this view from the perspective of epistemic proceduralism, see, e.g., Estlund, *Democratic Authority*, 111.
10. I take this principle from Waldron, *Law and Disagreement*, 198 and 245–46. I offer a critical in-depth analysis of Waldron's defense of "pure majoritarianism" over "modified majoritarianism" in Lafont, *Democracy Without Shortcuts*, 54–60.
11. For a discussion of correctness theories of legitimacy, see Estlund, *Democratic Authority*.
12. The idea of constitutional constraints is helpful for understanding my use of the reasonable/unreasonable distinction in this context. Not every law and policy that has majority support is "constitutional" for that reason alone. On the contrary, regardless of whether a law or policy has majority support, showing that it is unconstitutional undermines its legitimacy (and its legality). On the other hand, not every law or policy that some citizens disagree about is "unconstitutional" for that reason alone. Citizens can agree on the constitutionality of some laws and policies but nonetheless disagree about whether they are the right or best ones strictly on their merits. I use the reasonable/unreasonable distinction in a similar way, although there are two important differences. First, the constitutional/unconstitutional distinction is broader than the reasonable/unreasonable distinction. The latter applies only to questions of fundamental rights and freedoms, whereas the former applies to all other types of constitutional questions. Second, and more importantly, the reasonable/unreasonable distinction is not bound to any factually existing constitution (written or unwritten) in the way the constitutional/unconstitutional distinction is.
13. Habermas, "Reply to Symposium Participants," 1495.
14. Seyla Benhabib, *Another Cosmopolitanism*, Berkeley Tanner Lectures (Oxford: Oxford University Press, 2006), 70.

10

Another Republicanism

Dissent, Institutions, and Renewal

CHRISTIAN VOLK

For the republican revival, Hannah Arendt is largely irrelevant. To many, it seems like her work does not provide any systematic impulses for the controversy about the profile of a contemporary republican political theory. The most prominent position, neo-Roman republicanism, subsumes her political thought under the premodern "populist approach" to republicanism and argues that its focus on homogenizing notions such as popular sovereignty, collective political action, or the realization of a society-wide idea of the good life are incompatible with the diversity of values and the pluralization of heterogeneous life plans that characterize modern societies.[1] However, even for those variants of republican thought—radical, socialist, labor or workplace republicanism—that position themselves critically against the hegemony of neoepublicanism, Arendt either is not mentioned at all, is denied relevance due to her supposed ignorance regarding the social dimension of politics, or is "exoticized" as a "plebian strand" of republicanism through an overly practical and concrete adaptation of her thoughts on the council system and on revolutionary new beginnings.[2]

In my contribution, I oppose this approach to or neglect of Hannah Arendt in the current debates on republican political theory and argue that her writings inspire an independent variant of republican thought. I have developed this variant in close collaboration with Thorsten Thiel over the past years, and we call it a *republicanism of dissent*. A republicanism of dissent refers back to the line of republican tradition that stresses the role of institutions and law in rendering conflict visible. It demands both a reorientation of republicanism toward conflict and action, and a decoupling from the orthodoxy of popular sovereignty. Arendt's work, I argue, is particularly relevant here because it assumes that the idea of an "order of freedom" and the self-renewal of the republican polity is spelled out in the course of political interaction.[3] Drawing upon her insights, I will present another republicanism, one that centers on the meaning of civic engagement and the generative conditions of political action, which I will then contextualize within the current republican discourse and democratic theory.

In the first section, I defend the interpretation of Arendt as a thinker operating within the republican discourse. The point is not to reduce Arendt's multilayered position, which can doubtlessly be read in a variety of ways, to a single interpretation or to construct a systematic coherency within her work. Rather, the aim is to show that a contemporary reading of Arendt's thinking will prove fruitful in light of current controversies surrounding republicanism and political theory. The second section focuses on this contemporary reading of her thoughts and fleshes out the contours of a *republicanism of dissent* as a theoretical perspective of analysis and interpretation for modern societies. I argue that (1) a critique of domination, (2) politicization, and (3) law as relationship are the central components of this analytical perspective. The article closes with a section on the relevance and independence of a *republicanism of dissent* as an analytical perspective. For this purpose, I distinguish a *republicanism of dissent* from both the neorepublican and the radical democratic conceptualization of politics and point out the analytical advantages of this perspective. In contrast to neo-Roman republicanism, a *republicanism of dissent* has a theoretical sense for the subtle forms of domination that reach beyond intersubjective status relations. It can elaborate the significance of experiencing confrontation and dissenting opinions for the durability of a political order. And in contrast to radical democratic theory, a *republicanism of dissent* engages with the legal and institutional context of modern democracies, analyzing both the structures and conditions that oppose the experience of freedom and those that foster, enable, and channel political agency.

HANNAH ARENDT AND REPUBLICANISM

To place Hannah Arendt in any great tradition of thought, be it Republicanism, Conservatism, Marxism, Liberalism, and the like, immediately provokes skepticism. One reason for this is what she referred to as a "break in tradition" that culminated in the Shoah with all its destructiveness, and which subsequently blocked any affirmative reference back to an entrenched tradition of thought, even the republican one.[4] "Break in tradition" means that the chain that connected us via values, categories, concepts, ideas, and so on with past traditions has been broken and, in turn, the explanatory, orientation-giving, and world-revealing potentials of traditions of thought have become suspect in their coherency and applicability. In view of the "break in tradition," she sees the need for a completely different treatment of history. Seyla Benhabib has pointed out how Walter Benjamin provided Arendt with the direction in this case. In line with his thoughts, Arendt's methods can be called "fragmentary historiography."[5] Instead of referring back to entire traditions of thought, Arendt is left only with the possibility, as Benhabib has shown, of salvaging isolated fragments of thought, the so-called "pearls," from under the ruins of history.[6] Benhabib helps us excavate how Arendt takes these fragments, gathers them together, analyses them, reorders them, places them in a new context of meaning, and uses them to do political theory. Arendt's intention is not to preserve or retell the past as it was, but rather as it appears from the present-day perspective.

As far as the tradition of republicanism is concerned, the situation is further complicated by the fact that Arendt quite explicitly rejects important theoretical components of classical republicanism: the idea of popular sovereignty, the concept of man as *zoon politikon*, the strong emphasis on virtues, the idea of the good life as a community-integrating ideal, the statism of the republican tradition, and so on.[7]

On the other hand, however, central authors of the republican tradition are an important source of inspiration for Arendt, with the important exception of Rousseau, whom she outright rejects. Machiavelli, Montesquieu, the Founding Fathers, but also Cicero and the Roman tradition are here to be mentioned. In their writings, they all reflect on the conditions of a durable and stable political order, which Arendt identifies as the central promise of a republican form of government.[8] The latter aspect is indeed central as Arendt shares a positive view of the Roman Republic's achievements. In particular she praises the entanglement of institutions, which open up spaces of freedom in the first place, supports the idea that the substance of the constitution lies in organizing the division of power, and is fond of the Roman concept of law, which on her reading is inspired by the idea of connecting citizens with one another. In the Roman concept of law she sees an important modification, especially of the Greek conception of law.[9] Furthermore, Arendt shares the republican conviction that political and social conflicts should not be confined by moral or ethical metarules, and she argues instead in favor of the permanent formation of understanding in a process of public debate, political struggle, and civic activism.[10] In contrast to the liberal tradition of political thought and in concurrence with the republican view, Arendt holds that the integration of modern societies cannot take place abstractly along individualistic principles but must be rooted in political acting-together.

Instead of continuing this enumeration, however, I will focus in the following on two theoretical connections that reveal and further substantiate the basic republican orientation of her thought in systematic terms: first, the connection between power and action; and second, the connection between freedom and order. In doing so, my aim is not only to demonstrate that Arendt can be called a republican thinker but also to outline the profile of this republicanism.

Power/Action

The individual and her moral rights and duties stand at the center of a liberal understanding of politics. Therefore, every political order must ask itself whether or not it protects and advances each person's freedom.[11] In contrast to liberalism, republican approaches do not base their understanding of the political on the individual. Instead, they focus on the relationships that exist between people or groups of people in a political context and the resulting dynamics for the political process.

In order to conceptually grasp the political relationships between people, Arendt makes use of two key concepts: political action and power. Political action describes the interaction between people in the public sphere and in public matters.[12] She uses the concept of power to denote the establishment of relationships between people through action and speech, as well as the social manifestations of these relationships (for example, via institutions). In regard to the former, she speaks of "living power."[13] For the latter, she refers to "institutionalized power" or materialized power.[14]

When systematically connecting Arendt's concept of action with her understanding of power, it becomes clear that, for her, only a very specific mode of action can result in a normatively substantive constellation of power: *acting-with-one-another*. *Acting-with-one-another* distinguishes itself from *acting-for-one-another* and *acting-against-one-another* in that it is committed to preserving a specific political space in which it is possible to join one's actions with those of others. Thus, already on this basic conceptual level, it becomes apparent that Arendt's thinking is rooted in the republican paradigm because it identifies the dialectic of stability and renewal, of conflict and order, and of continuity and new beginnings as the central theoretical problem to be worked out.

However, as the central *topos* of republican thinking, not every action or constellation of power is of value regarding the preservation and realization of a free political order. Here my interpretation already diverges from many common readings of Arendt. These commonly assume that the Arendtian concept of power is "emancipatory" per se, or "intrinsically normatively positive."[15] What gets overlooked here, however, is Arendt's ambivalent view of power and the critical notion of Arendt's conception of power. Power can also, according to Arendt, have a highly repressive effect: In *On Violence*, for example, she argues that "a legally unrestricted majority rule, that is, a democracy without a constitution [based only upon power], can be very formidable in the suppression of the rights of minorities and very effective in the suffocation of dissent without any use of violence. But that does not mean that violence and power are the same."[16] In *Vita Activa*, the expanded German version of *The Human Condition*, Arendt explains: "The more a system of government is merely a manifestation and expression of power—and this is especially true in the case of an unlimited democracy—the more difficult it is for the individual to express and emphasize her individuality."[17]

In order to work out the systematic content of her discourse on power for a contemporization of republican thinking, the ambivalence of power in Arendt's work needs to be taken seriously. To this end, it is necessary to determine the contexts in which power takes on a freedom-enabling or freedom-preserving quality and those in which it does not.

That people—by coming together to form a group, party, movement, or organization—create power in the sense of *power to act in a specific way* does not preclude the possibility that this power might be experienced by other members of the polity (or beyond it, of course) as coercion, repression, or oppression and that this could be the case even without the deployment of physical violence. The key to the Arendtian conceptualization lies not in the juxtaposition of "power to" and "power over," but in an analysis of the "capacity/incapacity arrangement" that is formed through action and human interaction.[18]

What consequences does this entail for the concept of action in a republican theory of the political? According to Arendt, power—understood as a capacity/incapacity arrangement—is based on consent. For Arendt, however, unlike for Habermas, consent is neither primarily and necessarily rational, fundamentally normatively positive, or something generated only through "nondistorted communication."[19] In Arendt's eyes, the word *consensus* simply reflects "the recognition that no man can act alone, that men if they wish to achieve something in the world must act in concert."[20] Given that in the realm of politics, every consensus emerges out of a combination of human speech and action, we can see that the *normative quality of power constellations* depends not so much on the facts of action and speech per se but rather *on the ways in which action and speech* are conducted. At this point, the aforementioned distinction between the three modes of action comes into play: *acting-with-one-another*, which is contrasted with both *acting-for-one-another* and *acting-against-one-another*. All three modes of action result in the formation of power, but they differ in regard to their normative content.

Political power is created in the mode of *acting-for-one-another* when the individual puts aside her personal interests and joins with the *for* of a group or community. Thus, by the principle of *for-one-another*, the space between individuals dissolves; the plurality of opinions is subsumed under one uniting principle. Through *acting-against-one-another* as a political mode of action, a *we* is constituted through antagonism, that is, by dissociating from others. These others are no longer heard; instead, the *we* prioritizes "self-disclosure at the expense of all other factors."[21] This self-revelation and self-disclosure, however, are only ever strategic and negative in the sense that it becomes a means to distinguish oneself from the political opponent. When bound by this form of action, it is too high a risk for the individual to "disclose himself in deed or word" in positive terms.[22] Hence, "this concept of action" also forgoes the actual goals of action and is "highly individualistic."[23] Consequently, Arendt decisively rejects an agonal understanding of the political, because "the commonness of the political world [is] not seen or experienced in the relationships between the citizens."[24] For these reasons, Arendt describes these two modes of action in *The Human Condition* as "perverted form(s) of 'acting together.'"[25]

For Arendt, only one mode of political action can lead to the emergence of a normatively substantive concept of power: *acting-with-one-another*. When power is created in the mode of *acting-with-one-another*, people assemble freely; they use their right to make their views public and advocate for their positions through their individual characters. At the same time, however, they are readily agitated by the views of others. They react to their opinions and engage one another in dialogic discourse. *Acting-with-one-another* refers to a process of hearing and being-heard, in which political alternatives are spelled out. Responsivity and expressivity are the results of such discourse, one in which conflicting and sometimes wholly irreconcilable opinions are addressed and worked through. When *acting-with-one-another*, those involved have their political judgment formed by the public discourse itself, and further strengthened and renewed through the experiences of being part of this discourse. While substantive consensus is a possible result, open communication about political issues in the sense of *to agree that we disagree*—in other words, an acknowledgment of the other's position that allows for a continuation of the debate—is more important to Arendt.[26] Through *acting-with-one-another*, then, the political order is experienced as one in which political action takes place, in which political freedom can be experienced as the collective shaping of our lifeworld, and allows itself to always be realized anew.

Order/Freedom

"Being free," Arendt writes in accordance with the republican tradition, "is only possible in relation to one another," and she further specifies that freedom needs the "realm of action and the political" in order to manifest itself.[27] Based on this formulation, however, Arendt's notion of freedom can be interpreted in a myriad of ways: Dana Villa, for example, who endorses an existentialist reading of her thought, sees the core of the Arendtian notion of freedom in an "initiatory, agonistic action" that allows one "to shine forth, to be glorious."[28] On the other hand, a radical democratic reading—like that of Bonnie Honig—asserts that Arendt characterizes freedom as only a fleeting, momentary event, which comes and goes through revolutionary action. On this reading, "the moment of intervention" is the "moment of politics."[29]

In thinking of freedom as separate from or even in opposition to order, these approaches overlook something crucial: When Arendt speaks of a successful political praxis, she is, as Jeremy Waldron rightly notes, primarily concerned with "structured politics."[30] Political action that coincides with an experience of freedom always takes place in at least partially institutionalized spaces, such as *societées populaires* or councils, in which political action follows "basic rules of political procedure."[31] For, according to Arendt, only such institutionalization can ensure equality. And equality is an essential component of the experience of political freedom, which makes acting meaningful. In contrast to those critics of civic engagement who fear the "anarchistic and lawless 'natural' inclinations of a people left without the constraint of its government,"[32] Arendt believes that every political action, even in the absence of established law, contains in its embodiment the horizon of a new order in the form of the various institutions that shape that space, e.g., councils during the French Revolution. What is important is that the principles and structures of political orders are not a prepolitical given for Arendt. By referring to the rules of the game, she does not imply that moral norms or basic rights can be found outside of the political process (as it is the case with Waldron). The structures, principles, and norms of discursive-democratic institutions must, on the contrary, be formed through political action. Only in this way can the actors become aware that their practiced behaviors, including the accompanying experience of freedom, result from the very norms and principles that determine these actions and render them intelligible.

The core of Arendt's notion of freedom can thus be understood as follows: Political freedom means the experience of being able to act politically. Only by acting can I experience the potential content of a basic democratic order, and political experiences shield me in turn from disappointment and the resultant renunciation of politics. Political action therefore stabilizes political order, even if it cannot offer definitive protections against the latter's demise. Thus, political action cultivates a sensibility for the legal embeddedness of the political sphere, which is a conditio sine qua non of the ongoing unfolding of political freedom in a republican sense. Rather than adhering to a purely positive understanding of freedom, as critics (like Pettit) have repeatedly accused her of, Arendt transcends the binary distinction of negative and positive freedom altogether.[33]

Congruently, Arendt sees the greatest danger to freedom not in specific restrictions of free will or of autonomy but in the demise of democratic culture and the depoliticization of public life. For her, the demise of the public sphere means that the citizens themselves negate their own political possibilities and forget their ability to take their fates into their own hands and determine them collectively. The disintegration resulting from the renunciation of politics enervates the democratic form of life all the more, even when the legal and constitutional order seems still to be (at least temporarily) intact.[34] The problem Arendt points to here is not so much that people do not live good and fully human lives. This, however, is what neorepublican thinkers like Pettit seem to suggest, and they derive from this their criticism that Arendt's political theory represents values that are inapplicable to complex modern societies. Rather, from Arendt's point of view, the danger lies in the ossification of institutions and the negation of the element of political practice within these institutions, similarly theorized in Rahel Jaeggi's work.[35] Both developments lead to estrangement from the order—along with its institutions and its relationships that have been formed by law and politics—where political action is made possible in the first place. The institutions become foreign and inaccessible to people. In contrast, experiencing the possibility of action has a stabilizing effect on democratic order, because it affirms this order and reproduces it again and again.

CONTOURS OF A REPUBLICANISM OF DISSENT

The previous section attempted to test the plausibility of the claim that Arendt's political thinking operates within the republican discourse. In this section, I will now elaborate the contours of this Arendtian version of republican thought that I call a *republicanism of dissent*. What does a systematic republican theory drawn from Arendt's work look like? How does such a *republicanism of dissent* respond to the challenges of modern societies? And how does this version of republican thought differ from other versions?

A serious exegesis of Arendt must concede that she addressed the everyday functioning of republican orders at best by anecdotal excursions but never made it the central theme of her thought. Once this fact has been admitted, the next step is to show how the aforementioned elements of Arendt's thought can inform the development of analytical foci, theoretical vocabulary, and institutional ideas that are of value along the spectrum of modern political theory.

Following from Arendt's understanding of freedom and action, the question at the core of a *republicanism of dissent* championed here concerns the qualities necessary for a political order in which political disagreement and dissent actually take place. Critically, it must be possible to experience the contentiousness and contingency of the political in a way that is neither disintegrative nor conducive to permanent asymmetries of power. In keeping with Arendt's political thought, we are searching for political forms that make *acting-with-one-another* possible: political institutions that allow their citizens to gather freely and without coercion, while ensuring that these citizens engage with other political opinions in and through these institutions, allowing themselves to be unsettled to a certain extent and to experience political action. Following Arendt, I assume that finding such forms is not only a matter of institutional design but that the institutional aspects must always be accompanied by a sensitivity toward societal means of communication and understanding. It is not enough to identify the *correct* procedures and values for a republican order and then apply them to reality (either as a blueprint or as critique). Rather, the goal must be to understand what facilitates and what hinders political actions in concrete situations.

Reaching with Arendt beyond Arendt, then, a *republicanism of dissent* must analyze the structure and perception of political institutions much more systematically. It must do so not only in the moment of their founding but especially with respect to the *ongoing everyday operation* of democratic orders and ordering.[36] Above all this approach must pay attention to the intersection of society and politics because this is where it is decided how, and to what extent, a complex and abstract order enters into dialogue with its citizens. Such an approach is therefore best explicated in the context of concrete discourses and occurrences, such as in relation to transnational governance, digitalization and democracy, or opposition and protest.[37] Nevertheless, for the purpose of these deliberations, I would like to formulate an abstract argument and demonstrate the particular focal points of a *republicanism of dissent* by working out three central components of this analytical perspective: (1) the critique of domination, (2) politicization, and (3) law as relationship. All three components, while directly related to Arendt's political thought as presented in the previous section, leave the narrow framework of an exegetical reconstruction in order to form a new theoretical perspective. The aim is to illuminate the profile of a *republicanism of dissent* as a theoretical perspective of analysis and interpretation for modern societies and then to contrast it with current political-theoretical positions (in the next section), while also elaborating its merits.

Critique of Domination

The first important feature that characterizes a *republicanism of dissent* is the critique of domination. This Arendtian critique of domination, however, starts from quite different premises than those of the old Frankfurt School, for example. An Arendtian perspective, I argue, enables a conceptualization of domination as depoliticization. This, in turn, allows for an account of domination within a democracy, integral to a republicanism of dissent.

A reconstruction of Arendt's critique of domination can draw on a central insight from Benhabib's work on Arendt, namely, that the latter's endeavor to recover "the 'public world' through authentic political action" must also be understood as a *critical* philosophical project.[38] In this vein, she underscores how Arendt's critique of existential philosophy leads Arendt to a new interpretation of Heidegger's concept of the world. It is through this critical engagement with Heidegger, she argues, that Arendt arrives at the core assumption of her philosophical and political thinking, namely, that human existence is conditioned by plurality. With a concept of plurality derived in this way, Benhabib is able to defend Arendt against the accusation that her criticism of modernity is merely the exaggerated, conservative reflex of a thinker lost in "Hellenistic nostalgia" and that she became a "victim of a concept of politics that is inapplicable to modern conditions."[39] Instead, Arendt's critique is shown to be directed against the all-encompassing character of production and consumption processes that endanger the plurality of human forms of existence and the diversity of viewpoints in the world, leading us to "world-less-ness." In this way, Benhabib reinterprets Arendt as a critical theorist of politics and society.

What I take to be central to this program of a critical theory of politics and society on the one hand, and for further clarifying the analytical perspective of a *republicanism of dissent* on the other hand, is the Arendtian critique of domination as a way of critically analyzing democratic order.

Although Arendt's thoughts on domination are scattered throughout her work, her core idea is to conceive of domination as depoliticization. Arendt stresses the interrelationship between domination and depoliticization in her deliberations on the Nazi system of total domination. In her essay "Freiheit und Politik," which only exists in its long and detailed version in the German language, Arendt argues that we completely misunderstand the phenomenon of total domination if we assume that it is concerned with the total *politicization* of life: "Quite the opposite is the case; we are dealing with phenomena of depoliticization, like in all dictatorships and despotisms, only that this depoliticization manifests itself in such a radical way that it exterminates the element of political freedom in all activities and is not satisfied just to destroy action, which is the political capacity *par excellence*."[40] Later in the essay, she speaks about depoliticization as the destruction of the "political element." This phrase seems to imply that there are forms of social intercourse in society *in and through which* people treat one another as free and equals, creatively interact with one another, learn how the world reveals itself differently for other people, and experience the potential to alter human affairs. Besides arts, theater, literature, or poetry, there are coffee houses, regulars' tables, discussions among friends and colleagues, and so on, where people can experience these "political elements" without acting politically in the strict sense of the word.

However, for a system of *total* domination, it is crucial to ban the free flourishing of such forms of interaction in society and even to eliminate them from social and private life with a mixture of terror, secret police, and networks of spies and informants, as well as with ideology by generating fear, isolation, solitude, loneliness, and indoctrination. The consequence was that central practices of reproduction of the National Socialist order remained uncontested.

This helps us get a clearer picture of what is meant by domination from an Arendtian perspective. The term *domination* describes a political order that has become alien to the people and whose practices of reproduction are simultaneously beyond contestation. Instead of enabling political action and exchange to creatively shape public affairs, domination makes people feel detached from the supposedly invariant structures they inhabit.

This theoretical motif, namely, "domination as depoliticization," is not restricted to Arendt's analysis of Nazi Germany. With respect to the escalation of the student protests in the 1960s, Arendt argues that the dissenters in Eastern Europe "demand free speech and thought as the preliminary conditions for political action." They were living under a political order that explicitly denied these political rights. In contrast, the students in the West "live under conditions where these preliminaries, (that is) rights and institutions, no longer open the channels for action."[41] This, in her eyes, explains to some extent the radicalization of the student revolt. Arendt only gives us this brief remark, but I would like to pick it up and try to sketch how domination within a democracy could be conceptualized from an Arendtian perspective.

Domination in a democracy reveals itself when rights and institutions cease to open channels for political action. The result is that the central practices of reproduction of exactly this order remain politically uncontested. The extent to which this is actually realized must be qualified for obvious reasons. Political acting does not disappear completely from public life, not totally, but for large parts of the people living in a democratic system it is not seen as an option and they refrain from acting politically. There is a gap between the enabling of political action and the exercise of political action. The consequence of this gap is that the promises of a democratic way of life, entailed in its basic principles such as freedom, equality, justice, solidarity, and so on are not fulfilled for everyone living in such an order to an equal extent but only for the few.

If we want to know how this particular type of domination, namely, democratic domination, comes into being, we need to carefully analyze how this gap between enabling and occurring—between promise and fulfillment—is produced and reproduced on a daily basis in modern democracies. For example, this gap can be reproduced by maintaining sexual and racialized discrimination combined with a socioeconomic basic structure that leads to poverty, isolation, and social alienation, with the effect of political disaffection, political disenchantment, and political disengagement: in other words: nonparticipation. Likewise, the mediatization of politics turns citizens into consumers and addresses them with political marketing campaigns, reproducing a very narrow interpretation and institutionalization of political participation.[42] This gap may also be the result of the erosion of the institutional framework of modern democracies and the transformation of parties, leading to an estrangement with the political institutions that should be enabling political action.[43]

We can certainly think of many other forms of depoliticization. All of them are inherently connected to the particular historical materialization of the idea of democracy and the ways in which we practice democracy today. Consider, for example, how the modern notion of citizenship is utilized for achieving political inclusion and integration. It is an ambivalent, if not contentious, organizational principle that often enough fails to protect people and produces exclusion. Or consider the restrictive implementation of the idea of equality in purely legal terms, the realization of solidarity via a competitive welfare state, political participation as active and passive electoral rights in a representative party system, or modern democracy's entanglement with capitalism and the social inequality and "economization of political life" that follow from it.[44]

These are very specific historical expressions of the basic tenets of democracy that produce specific ills and consequences accordingly. Some of these consequences, like an unequal distribution of social and political power or social and political exclusion, are themselves responsible for causing democratic and political alienation in citizens. But most importantly, a republicanism of dissent's critical perspective on domination argues that it is this very particular materialization of democracy as such that has brought about a political constellation in which people refrain from using the channels available to them to claim the unredeemed promises of democracy. Accordingly, even if the status quo blatantly fails to deliver on these promises for everyone, the central political practices responsible for inequality, exploitation, and exclusion remain unchallenged.

Politicization

The second characteristic feature for a *republicanism of dissent* as an analytical perspective is marked by the concept of politicization. As such, a *republicanism of dissent* connects with the debates around the crisis of contemporary democracy and its change in form, in which politicization has come to the fore as a guiding concept. The prominence of this concept stems from its potential to substantively encapsulate and theoretically grasp the increase of protest activities and the proliferation of new forms of political participation. At the same time, the concept of politicization carries with it the abstract hope of social living conditions that are shaped reflexively, while securing citizens' equal opportunities to influence the political decision-making process, even in a highly differentiated, capitalist society. Nevertheless, both contentions remain highly controversial: it is unclear where the normative content of protest and politicization is rooted, and there is no agreement on the relationship between politicization and the promise of democracy. Here, a *republicanism of dissent* presents a theoretical proposal that not only allows for a more precise conceptual-analytical grasp of the phenomenon of politicization, but also locates and grounds it in democratic theory.

To begin with, a *republicanism of dissent* understands themes or circumstances as politicized when the public discourse surrounding them is marked by substantially differing opinions and positions. The discourse must harbor real alternatives and not only continuously reformulated variations on policy proposals. Politics must be perceived as contingent and, consequently, capable of being influenced. Such an understanding of politicization emphasizes the qualitative standing of a pluralistic public and thereby sets itself apart from both a quantitative description, focused on the representation of interests, and a formalistic description that is more concerned with the *conditions* for plurality (the existence of abstract political rights) than with the factual existence of a plurality of political options and their fair democratic competition.

Moreover, a *republicanism of dissent* does not simply rely on abstract legal equality, but it is concerned with what Pierre Rosanvallon has called "relational equality."[45] Relational equality refers to a relation of social groups, which, according to Markus Linden, "is established by democratic procedures and the accompanying disputes about factual issues and values."[46] In analyzing democratic procedures and the institutional arrangements of modern democracies, a *republicanism of dissent* is interested in whether there are comparable opportunities for the political articulation of opinion as well as whether these procedures and institutions ensure that citizens perceive themselves as equal members of the political community. Despite all clashes of interests, following Linden, "democratic modes" should lead to respect for other groups and their specific perspectives.[47]

Against this backdrop, politicization then means "the constant renewal of difference, the unceasing conversation with the other—a discourse on differences and commonalities as well as their continuation."[48] An empirical indicator for this might be, for example, the initiation of public processes of communication stemming from the peripheries and a widely shared "awareness and sense of meaning" of political processes across all levels of society.[49]

A second factor that substantively shapes the understanding of politicization for a *republicanism of dissent* is the necessity at all times of recognizing the political order *also* as a system of domination (as it was spelled out earlier) and therefore for questioning and challenging it. The lack of alternatives, which may be legitimated for reasons of security, austerity, tradition, and so on, must be countered by thinking and acting in alternatives. This, however, can only come about through confrontation understood as an attitude of identifying the given as constructed without contradicting compromise and dialogue. A specific "performative dynamic" can then be generated that prevents political life from coming to a standstill.[50] But even more importantly, such an understanding of politicization always entails a critique of domination. By publicly expressing, through their protest, a dissident interpretation of the basic principles of a democratic order that deviates from the established concretion, a group of people can make clear what cannot be realized by the current order's logic of political and societal practices of reproduction and is therefore in need of reform. Politicization, then, highlights those practices of order reproduction that are impossible or very difficult to change through the institutionalized channels of the political system.

Moreover, a third element follows from this concept of politicization, namely, that both the means of contestation and those forces that drive the decline and disappearance of political viewpoints must be considered. Furthermore, the analytical perspective of a *republicanism of dissent* must always consider how politicization can prove itself against the "attention-seeking forces of the lifeworld, interest-dominated economic patterns of thinking, and consumerism as well as empty dispersal."[51] It is precisely here that the societal focus reveals itself, one that cannot be allowed to exhaust itself in a conservative critique of culture. Instead, positive opportunities for political action, especially in societies that provide individuals with decent possibilities of expression and different modes of organizing collective action, must be taken into consideration.

At this point, it is important to recognize that politicization as consisting of these three elements does not contradict a democratic-political constitutional order. Confrontation resulting from politicization does not threaten the sustained stability of a political order, so long as this stability does not simply amount to the latter's immutability. Politicization, after all, is not understood as a process that refers to something that lies beyond the existing democratic-constitutional order or is external to it (such as "society" or "the people" as symbolic entities or ethical-moral values and basic rights in liberal thinking). Rather, politicization always refers to the democratic basic order itself and the normative (legal) principles that are abstractly established in it, such as political equality and political freedom (freedom of opinion, freedom of assembly, and freedom of association).[52] Politicization sets in motion a continuous reflection on the integration of the order as a whole, albeit one that remains inspired by Arendt's understanding of power and action elaborated earlier. Here, the benchmark for judging political action remains whether or not "action, whether disruptive or not, involves attention and responsiveness to worldly events."[53] A *republicanism of dissent*, therefore, focuses less on the history of, or justification for, a concrete form of democratic order; rather it investigates how their formations of order substantiate the abstract promise of political freedom and the unfolding of political order in a societal process. Not *politicization as possibility* but rather *politicization as experience* is the yardstick to analyze politics.

Law as Relationship

The third angle from which I discuss the contours of a *republicanism of dissent* is the understanding of law and its role in society. The systematic conceptualization of law, especially the differentiation between republican and liberal understandings of constitution, remains a desideratum in the current revival of republican theory. There are of course some exceptions, but while the republican classics contemplated law a great deal and even attempted to formulate constitutions in various ways, these central questions remain largely unexplored.[54] The consequence of this neglect is somewhat paradoxical. On the one hand, it is assumed that law is met with reservation in republican thought: law, in this view, seems lifeless and is seen in opposition to political involvement and participation, promoting individualization and leveling the political. On the other hand, the republican tradition is framed as one that ascribes an essential function to law, especially to the constitution, be it by defining an enabling space for political participation, by enshrining core virtues and values of the common good, or by organizing the division of power in a state constituted by antagonistic major social groups (by means of a mixed constitution).[55] This framing also marks the starting point of the liberal concept of constitution, which stabilizes the collectivist republican understanding of constitution, and which was fixated on founding, by grounding it in the protection of individual rights.

A *republicanism of dissent* transcends these two traditional lines of republican thinking, which are often posited as irreconcilable, by charting an altered legal-philosophical course and emphasizing a different mode of influence for law on society: one mediated through and inspired by Arendt's reading of Montesquieu.[56] When translating the aforementioned traditions into their respective visions of law, the participatory-critical line reveals an understanding of *law as command*, which must compete with self-rule because law appears as a foreign authority that withdraws itself from discussion and contradicts the latter in form, while the liberal line understands *law as demarcation*. The latter understands law primarily in relation to the task of protecting the individual's scope of action from external interference (whether from the state or from the majority).

A third way to conceive of law, however, is lost in this dichotomy: law as relationship. An exemplary formulation of this understanding can be found in the work of Montesquieu, who understands laws as "relationships [*rapport*] that emerge necessarily from the nature of things."[57] This means, essentially, that the state and civil laws of a country are an expression of both the social and political basic structures, i.e., the in-one-another and with-one-another of the nature and the principle of the form of government, as Montesquieu puts it, and the general social and political state of mind (*esprit général*). At the same time, these laws must always refer back to this basic structure and state of mind in order to ensure the "duration and prosperity" of the order.[58] Translated to a *democratic* order and its defining *principle*, this means that law must be designed in a manner that enables democratic conflict, renders this conflict visible, and makes the corresponding processes of communication within the polity possible. This includes the securing of equal rights to access the political process, social rights, and rights for the protection of the private sphere, as well as prohibiting discrimination against groups in the public realm. For a *republicanism of dissent*, the justification of these laws does not operate with a postulate of individual autonomy as it does in liberal thinking or with an ethically charged imagination of the good life in a culturally defined community as it does in classical republicanism. Instead, it bases itself on the conditions for making a vital and intact political public possible.

Given this challenging commitment to enabling political participation in the democratic process, it becomes clear that the role of judges and laws requires further reflection. For the highest court's jurisdiction and judicial review, it is not enough to simply test "whether legislation and administrative action had, indeed, come about in the right manner."[59] The requirements must be more substantial. However, "strong judicial review," i.e., the courts' "authority to decline to apply a statute in a particular case ... or to modify the effect of a statute ... or to actually strike a piece of legislation out of the statute-book altogether," would lead to a situation in which crucial political problems are decided by an administrative and juridical elite rather than by an active citizenry.[60] Politics would "evaporate under a concept of law," the consequence being the depoliticization of democracy.[61]

A *republicanism of dissent*, therefore, argues for a *system of weak judicial review*, where the court's declaration of the incompatibility of a statute could "initiate a fast-track legislative procedure to remedy the incompatibility."[62] This understanding of law sees the central task of a constitutional court to be the establishment of a common reference point for parties in conflict. Said parties should not be simply overruled, outvoted, or silenced by the court's decision. Instead, the ruling should propose a possible compromise for them. The underlying reasoning here is that there are many legitimate and justifiable perspectives in a legal dispute: the decisive question for the durability of a vibrant democratic order is how to enable and mediate between these conflicting perspectives. The constitutional court, then, uses its authority to make rulings that introduce a new level of political debate where opposing camps may encounter each other anew and review the object of the political conflict.

In this case, the "rationality" of law does not emanate solely from the learned and oftentimes creatively pedantic profession of a well-educated judicial elite, but rather from the ability for a legal decision to open up a new political space in which action can be realized and the "syntax and grammar" of an active public-political sphere preserved.[63]

ON THE RELEVANCE OF A REPUBLICANISM OF DISSENT

Thus far, I have outlined some theses that provide an overview of how a *republicanism of dissent* can be drawn from a contemporization of Arendtian theory and which problems such an understanding of the political addresses. What remains to be shown is the ground for the relevance and independence of its vocabulary. To this end, I first distinguish a *republicanism of dissent* from the currently influential neorepublican tradition and then show where it deviates from radical democratic theory, which is somehow intertwined with republican thought or at least seems to ascribe a similar prominence to the political and often even refers to Arendt in an affirmative way.

Neorepublicanism

From the neorepublican standpoint, Philip Pettit has attempted to show, through many publications and over many years, why the Arendtian position does not only differ categorically from his own but is also insufficient in and of itself. While I would also like to emphasize a difference from neo-Roman republicanism, I am convinced that this difference *cannot* be found where Pettit situates it and, subsequently, that the conclusions he draws are not convincing.

For Pettit, Arendt represents a *populist* approach to republicanism, the broad range of which runs from Greece through Rousseau and Kant all the way to the communitarians. He assumes that positions in this range can only think of freedom as *positive freedom*, that is, as resulting from active participation only, in opposition to order, and primarily concerned with the question of virtue. Referring to Isaiah Berlin, he rejects this type of freedom for its generation of collective domination. Pettit counters it with his own conception of freedom as nondomination, which he seeks to derive from a distinctly Roman understanding of freedom and the latter's resurgence in modern times (from Machiavelli to the Founding Fathers of the United States).[64] His argument here is that nondomination, as a relational concept grounded in the status of relationships between citizens, enables the formulation of a structural solution for the problem of an order of freedom.[65] He locates this solution in a combination of electoral and contestatory elements that gives citizens the freedom both to collectively make decisions over their destinies and to individually avoid ending up in unjustifiable dependencies.[66]

As has already been mentioned in the reconstruction of Arendt's approach in the first part of this chapter, Pettit's limited reading leads him to overlook the extent to which institutions are entangled with the possibility of action in Arendt's thinking. Arendt's theory is specifically not fixated on sociocultural preconditions of collective action (virtues), and her conception of *acting-with-one-another* has to be clearly differentiated from *acting-for-one-another*, which leads to the leveling of difference that Pettit rightly fears. Rather, it has been shown that Arendt, too, consciously highlights the constitutive effect of institutions and intends to enable the experience of freedom in and through them. It has also been pointed out that a *republicanism of dissent* that draws from Arendt recognizes law as an effective, and even necessary, corrective against the potential for domination and therefore appreciates the value of providing diverse forums and contexts for the unfolding of political freedom.

The difference between Pettit and Arendt does not, therefore, lie in the insistence on a concept of freedom relating to order—not even in the emphasis on the importance of nondominance.[67] The difference, rather, can be seen in the way that Pettit's attempt to formulate a minimal concept of political order, which avoids overwhelming (or making any demands whatsoever of) its citizens, and results in an almost mechanical understanding of the relationship between politics and law that relies too heavily on institutional mechanisms.[68] In this way, Pettit's analysis overlooks all forms of dominance that cannot, or can only provisionally, be described in the language of intersubjective status relations, such as complex social dependencies, dominant cultural constructs, or differently formed dispositions (be them through social roles or self-perceptions), toward making use of the possibilities for political or legal influence. Most importantly, he overlooks the subtle mechanisms and tendencies of depoliticization that do not stem from the deprivation of rights or from oppression but rather that arise from social processes and discourses or the symbolic dimension of the political. From the view of a republicanism of dissent, Pettit's position does not adequately reflect or expand on the conditions for the realization of political action, and it does not recognize the value of confrontation and experiences of other unfamiliar perspectives. Even his later writings, which aim to be more political, fail to grasp the need to take into account the social bases for the development of political disputes.[69]

One might object by arguing that Pettit does not, in fact, neglect the value of dissensus. In his democratic-theoretical considerations, his argument quickly leads him to conclude that the establishment of a *contestatory democracy* is necessary so as to transcend *electoral democracy* and provide opportunities for action for individuals and groups.[70] This conclusion, however, is the result of textbook liberal thought: Pettit requires this (at least potential) moment of action to ensure that arbitrary power is exposed and that a state of benevolent hegemony can be distinguished from a state of extensive freedom. Even in those writings, which are explicitly positioned as political theory and interested in democracy, he is only interested in civil society's role as a watchdog, and he completely neglects the social processes and dynamics of protest and political action.[71]

Pettit's citizen can even be perpetually free if she is isolated, or lives a life of self-isolation, as long as she is not subjected to domination. A *republicanism of dissent* that draws from Arendt does not believe in the possibility of such a lasting withdrawal, claiming instead that democracy must be holistically conceptualized as a social form of life to be experienced and practiced. This does not result in an obligation to public participation, much less in the relinquishing of privacy or the flattening of differences of opinion. What can be shown by a *republicanism of dissent*, reaching beyond the instrumentalizing understanding of neo-Roman republicanism, is this gap between the enabling of political participation and the occurrence of vibrant political debates. Furthermore, it reveals that, in modern liberal democratic societies, the democratic-theoretical challenges lie more often in the contextual, socially defined obstacles to the generation of political action than in abstract rights to participation.

Radical Democracy

A *republicanism of dissent* must also be distinguished from the prevailing positions in the field of radical democratic theory, which often also refer affirmatively to Hannah Arendt's political thought. The first of these differences already appears in relation to theories of freedom: a *republicanism of dissent* does not (exclusively) conceptualize freedom as "*caesura*," or the momentary realization of a previously unrealized form of political equality, the "construction of a new hegemony," an institutionalization of the social, or "the extraordinary deed of collective self-institution."[72] While radical-democratic thought and republican theory of democracy coincide in diverse and productive ways, a *republicanism of dissent* does not only thematize political action in agonal moments or as a revolutionary, counterinstitutional concept. Rather, it rigorously analyzes the structures and conditions that oppose the experience of freedom as well as the way in which institutions foster, enable, and channel political action.

Radical-democratic theorists at least partially recognize this lacuna, for example, when Rancière addresses the problem of how to "transform equality in war," which arises during political riots, street fighting, or politically motivated attacks and acts of terror, "into political freedom," or when Mouffe asks "how the dimension of antagonism can be 'tamed,' thanks to the establishment of institutions and practices through which the potential antagonism can be played out in an agonistic way."[73] Their conceptualization of conflict as antagonism and the framing of this conflict as an ineradicable confrontation between those in power and those who oppose them, however, causes them to miss what the somewhat weaker understanding of *conflict as dissent* attempts to articulate: the continued existence of opposition in modern societies, which nevertheless allows for the situational and temporary possibility of mutual understanding.[74] Radical-democratic views are, in this sense, undertheorized. They lack a sensibility for *the other of order*, which gets lost when speaking of order merely as domination and expression of hegemony. They are too quick to reject the more pragmatic issues of problem-solving and the weighing of relative advantages and improvements. They create a political metaphysics that, as articulated by Lefort, lacks the sensibility required to process the "democratic experience."[75] This was already shown earlier in the claim that democratic law is always also a condition for the possibility of political action and not only reducible to its function as a command. Democracies secure the "possibility to politicize."[76] This is their central feature and makes them preferable to other political orders. Politicization is a constant possibility in a democratic order that, through law, establishes a space for such opportunity and is able to make its internal, conflictual plurality visible and renewable via fora and institutions.[77]

REPUBLICANISM OF DISSENT AS A POLITICAL THEORY

The goal of my arguments has been to introduce another republicanism: a *republicanism of dissent* as an independent and relevant variation on republican theory. Drawing from the work of Hannah Arendt by way of a systematic reconstruction of her understanding of the relationship between freedom and order, we can make unique observations and carve out novel theoretical focal points that work against the polarization of contemporary republican debates and revitalize the question of what can result from the emergence of political action.

Arendt's work should not be understood as a blueprint for concrete institutions; instead, it must be revisited with a focus on the dialectic of order and freedom and the demanding constitution of power that comes from *acting-with-one-another*. Here, there are at least three central aspects to be considered: (1) the various conditions and often subtle developments in the realm of politicization and depoliticization, where we are often empirically confronted with seemingly opposed developments and must look for the long-term consequences of the shifting communicative relation between citizens and democratic institutions; (2) the meaning of protest as an immediate form of political experience that not only must be analyzed in its effects on established politics and thus on the achievement of goals, but, more importantly, must be taken seriously in its moments of self-organization and generation of new subjectivities and social and political imaginaries; and (3) the role of law must be analyzed more closely in its constitutive and symbolic aspects, especially because it is understood as either too liberal or too repressive in both in the republican tradition in general and in the current polarized *republican revival* in particular. A *republicanism of dissent* is relevant and important precisely because it combines political-institutional and social-theoretical arguments and thereby reaches far beyond the mainstream of democratic theory.

NOTES

This is a fully revised, expanded, and translated version of "Republikanismus des Dissenses," which I wrote together with Thorsten Thiel in 2015 and published in our edited volume *Die Aktualität republikanischer Theorie*. I thank Thorsten Thiel for his permission to develop the text independently. I am particularly grateful to Teresa Otten Dionísio and Josef Mehling for their great work in translating the initial version of this essay into English and to Max Fenner and Liesbeth Schoonheim for the carefully conducted language editing. This article is part of a project that has received funding from the European Research Council (ERC) under the European Union's Horizon 2020 research and innovation program (grant agreement no. 757452) and from the Cluster of Excellence "Contestations of the Liberal Script" (EXC 2055, Project-ID: 390715649), funded by the Deutsche Forschungsgemeinschaft (DFG, German Research Foundation) under Germany's Excellence Strategy.

1. Philip Pettit, *Republicanism: A Theory of Freedom and Government* (Oxford: Oxford University Press, 1997), 8
2. Michael J. Thompson, "Two Faces of Domination in Republican Political Theory," *European Journal of Political Theory* 17, no. 1 (2018): 57, but recently also Margaret Kohn, "Radical Republicanism and Solidarity," *European Journal of Political Theory* 21, no. 1 (2022): 25–46; James Muldoon, "A Socialist Republican Theory of Freedom and Government," *European Journal of Political Theory* 21, no. 1 (2022): 47–67; Alex Gourevitch, "Labour Republicanism and the Transformation of Work," *Political Theory* 41, no. 4 (2013): 591–617; Keith Breen, "Non-Domination, Workplace Republicanism, and the Justification of Worker Voice and Control," *International Journal of Comparative Labour Law and Industrial Relations* 33, no. 3 (2017): 419–39. Camila Vergara, *Systemic Corruption: Constitutional Ideas for an Anti-Oligarchic Republic* (Princeton, NJ: Princeton University Press, 2020), 185. I

sympathize with Vergara's reading of Arendt in large part, but I am convinced that if we focus too much on ideas such as the council system or on revolution and omit to adapt her thoughts to the realities of modern capitalist democracies (in order to analyze and interpret these), Arendt's political thinking unintentionally becomes, as Albrecht Wellmer warned in a different context, "the 'other' of the political as we know it" and is reduced to its utopian appeal, losing all "recognizable connection to the political experiences and possibilities inherent in the everyday life of complex democratic societies." Albrecht Wellmer, "Arendt on Revolution," in *The Cambridge Companion to Hannah Arendt*, ed. Dana R. Villa (Cambridge: Cambridge University Press, 2000), 226–27.

3. See Christian Volk, *Arendtian Constitutionalism: Law, Politics and the Order of Freedom* (Oxford: Bloomsbury, 2015).
4. Hannah Arendt, *Denktagebuch*, vol. 1, no. 13 (Munich: Piper, 1953), 300.
5. Seyla Benhabib, *The Reluctant Modernism of Hannah Arendt* (Lanham, MD: Rowman and Littlefield, 2003), 94.
6. Benhabib, 87.
7. Hannah Arendt is a thinker of order, but a critic of the state. Her entire political work can be read and understood as searching for a new and alternative conception of order, new and alternative "manifestations and materializations of power" (Hannah Arendt, "On Violence," in *Crisis of the Republic* [New York: Harcourt Brace Jovanovich, 1969], 140) and a new and alternative organizational logic of political life.
8. Hannah Arendt, *On Revolution* (New York: Viking, 1963), 227.
9. I tried to capture this modification by the phrase "from nomos to lex." Christian Volk, "From *Nomos* to *Lex*: Hannah Arendt on Law, Politics, and Order," *Leiden Journal of International Law* 23, no. 4 (2010): 759–79.
10. See Thorsten Thiel, "Politik, Freiheit und Demokratie—Hannah Arendt und der moderne Republikanismus," in *Ambivalenzen der Ordnung: Der Staat im Denken Hannah Arendts*, ed. Julia Schulze Wessel et al. (Wiesbaden: Springer, 2013), 260.
11. A classic example in this context is John Rawls's conceptualization of the two central principles of justice, against which every political order ought to be measured—if it is to be considered just. See John Rawls, *A Theory of Justice* (Cambridge, MA: Harvard University Press, 1971), 60–65.
12. See Seyla Benhabib, "Models of Public Space," in *Situating the Self: Gender, Community and Postmodernism in Contemporary Ethics* (Cambridge: Polity, 1992), 91.
13. Arendt, "On Violence," 140.
14. Arendt, 51. See Arendt, 140. See also Christian Volk, "Towards a Critical Theory of the Political," *Philosophy and Social Criticism* 42, no. 6 (2016): 549–75.
15. Waltraud Meints-Stender, "Reflektierende Urteilskraft als Ethos der Macht—eine Annäherung an einen emanzipatorischen Begriff von Macht," in *Politische Existenz und republikanische Ordnung*, ed. Karl-Heinz Brier, and Alexander Gantschow (Baden-Baden: Nomos, 2012), 119; Amy Allen, "Power, Subjectivity, and Agency: Between Arendt and Foucault," *International Journal of Philosophical Studies* 10, no. 2 (2010): 143.
16. Arendt, "On Violence," 42.

17. Hannah Arendt, *Vita activa oder Vom tätigen Leben* (Munich: Piper, 2002), 257. This is my own translation; the passage is missing in the English version.
18. Cf. Gerhard Göhler, "'Power to' and 'Power over,'" in *The SAGE Handbook of Power*, ed. Steward R. Clegg, and Mark Haugaard (London: Sage, 2009), 32. Volk, "Critical Theory," 554.
19. Jürgen Habermas, "Hannah Arendt's Communication Concept of Power," *Social Research* 44, no. 1 (1977): 9.
20. Hannah Arendt, *The Life of the Mind/Willing* (San Diego: Harcourt, 1971), 201.
21. Hannah Arendt, *The Human Condition* (Chicago: University of Chicago Press, 1998), 194.
22. Arendt, 180.
23. Arendt, 194; for detailed examinations of these differences, see Volk, *Arendtian Constitutionalism*, 185–89.
24. Hannah Arendt, "Philosophy and Politics," *Social Research* 57, no.1 (1990): 82, emphasis added. Originally written in 1954.
25. Arendt, *The Human Condition*, 203.
26. Likewise, in her Tanner Lecture, Seyla Benhabib tells us that "we have to learn to live with the otherness of others whose ways of being may be deeply threatening to our own." Seyla Benhabib, "Reclaiming Universalism: Negotiating Republican Self-Determination and Cosmopolitan Norms," in *The Tanner Lectures on Human Values* delivered at the University of California at Berkeley, March 15–19, 2004, 150.
27. This is my own translation of Hannah Arendt, "Freiheit und Politik," in *Zwischen Vergangenheit und Zukunft* (Munich: Piper, 1994), 201.
28. Dana R. Villa, *Arendt and Heidegger: The Fate of the Political* (Princeton, NJ: Princeton University Press, 1996), 55.
29. Bonnie Honig, "Declaration of Independence: Arendt and Derrida on the Problem of Founding a Republic," *American Political Science Review* 85, no. 1 (1991): 111.
30. Jeremy Waldron, "Arendt's Constitutional Politics," in *The Cambridge Companion to Hannah Arendt*, ed. Dana R. Villa (Cambridge: Cambridge University Press, 2000), 210.
31. Waldron, 210.
32. Arendt, *On Revolution*, 275.
33. See Pettit, *Republicanism*, 8.
34. Patchen Markell, "The Rule of the People: Arendt, Archê, and Democracy," *American Political Science Review* 100, no. 1 (2006): 12.
35. See Rahel Jaeggi, "Was ist eine (gute) Institution?," in *Sozialphilosophie und Kritik*, ed. Rainer Forst et al. (Frankfurt: Suhrkamp, 2009), 542.
36. This also disarms one of the most common critiques of Arendt's work, namely, her controversial separation of the social from the political. According to this critique, Arendt reduces the political to questions of constitutionalism and thus separates it from its original, societal driving forces. Arendt is accused of sticking to a premodern understanding of politics, in which *oikos* and *polis* are strictly separated, which supposedly makes her blind to questions of domination that arise from the private. See, for example, Hanna Fenichel Pitkin, *The Attack of the Blob: Hannah Arendt's Concept of the Social* (Chicago: University of Chicago Press, 1998), 221. Indeed, I have

meticulously tried to show that this critique fails because it ignores the reasoning behind Arendt's differentiation, which is that there just cannot be a constellation for the experience of political action under conditions of social and economic exploitation. Volk, "Critical Theory," 557–60. Nonetheless, this critique cannot be said to apply to *republicanism of dissent*, despite its Arendtian inspiration, because it explicitly demands an emphasis on the societal preconditions for politics and political action instead of only relying on the possibilities for participation in political institutions.

37. Thiel, "Politik, Freiheit und Demokratie"; Christian Volk, "Enacting a Parallel World: Political Protest Against the Transnational Constellation," *Journal of International Political Theory*, online first (2018): 1–19; Thorsten Thiel, "Anonymity and Its Prospects in the Digital World," *PRIF Working Paper* 38 (2017); Christian Volk, "On a Radical Democratic Theory of Political Protest: Potentials and Shortcomings," *Critical Review of International Social and Political Philosophy*, online first (2021): 437–59.
38. Benhabib, *Reluctant Modernism*, 12.
39. Noel O'Sullivan, "Hellenic Nostalgia and Industrial Society," in *Contemporary Political Philosophers*, ed. Anthony de Crespigny and Kenneth Minogue (New York: Dodd, Mead, 1975); Habermas, "Communication," 14.
40. Arendt, "Freiheit und Politik," 204, translation mine.
41. Arendt, "On Violence," 81.
42. Russell Dalton, *Democratic Challenges, Democratic Choices: The Erosion of Political Support in Advanced Industrial Democracies* (Oxford: Oxford University Press, 2007); Colin Hay, *Why We Hate Politics* (Cambridge: Polity, 2007).
43. Matthew Flinders, *Defending Politics: Why Democracy Matters in the 21st Century* (Oxford: Oxford University Press, 2012).
44. Wendy Brown, *Undoing the Demos: Neoliberalism's Stealth Revolution* (New York: Zone, 2015), 201.
45. Pierre Rosanvallon, *The Society of Equals* (Cambridge, MA: Harvard University Press, 2013), 11.
46. Markus Linden, "Beziehungsgleichheit als Anspruch und Problem politischer Partizipation," *Zeitschrift für Politikwissenschaft* 26, no. 2 (2016): 180, translation mine.
47. Linden, 180, translation mine.
48. Thorsten Thiel, *Republikanismus und die Europäische Union—Eine Neubestimmung des Diskurses um die Legitimität europäischen Regierens* (Baden-Baden: Nomos, 2012), 204, translation mine.
49. Thiel, 204, translation mine.
50. Thiel, 179, translation mine.
51. Thiel, 204, translation mine.
52. See Christian Volk, "Hannah Arendt and the Constitutional Theorem of De-Hierarchization: Origins, Consequences, Meaning," *Constellations* 22, no. 2 (2015): 184.
53. Markell, "The Rule of the People," 2.
54. See especially Richard Bellamy, *Political Constitutionalism: A Republican Defence of the Constitutionality of Democracy* (Cambridge: Cambridge University Press,

2007); and John P. McCormick, "Republicanism and Democracy," in *Republicanism and Democracy*, ed. Andreas Niederberger and Philipp Schink (Edinburgh: Edinburgh University Press, 2013), 89–128.

55. Especially in the 1980s and early 1990s, there were intense debates about the differences between republican and liberal constitutionalism. See inter alia Ronald Dworkin, *Law's Empire* (Cambridge, MA: Harvard University Press, 1986); Frank Michelman, "Law's Republic," *Yale Law Review* 97 (1988): 1493–537; Jürgen Habermas, *Faktizität und Geltung* (Frankfurt: Suhrkamp, 1992); Bruce Ackerman, *We the People*, vol. 1, *Foundations* (Cambridge, MA: Harvard University Press, 1993).

56. Cf. Volk, "From *Nomos* to *Lex*," 774–78.

57. Charles Louis de Montesquieu, *The Spirit of the Laws*, ed. and trans. Anne M. Cohler, Basia Carolyn Miller and Harold Samuel Stone (Cambridge: Cambridge University Press, 1989), 3 (bk. 1, "On Laws in General," chap. 1).

58. Montesquieu, 12, bk. 2, "On Laws Deriving Directly from the Nature of the Government," chap. 2.

59. Jan Klabbers, "Possible Islands of Predictability: The Legal Thought of Hannah Arendt," *Leiden Journal of International Law* 20, no. 1 (2007): 21.

60. Jeremy Waldron, "The Core of the Case Against Judicial Review," *Yale Law Journal* 115 (2006): 1354.

61. Jacques Rancière, *Disagreement: Politics and Philosophy* (Minneapolis: University of Minnesota Press, 1999), 108.

62. Waldron, "The Core of the Case Against Judicial Review," 1354–55.

63. Arendt, *On Revolution*, 165.

64. Pettit, *Republicanism*, 19.

65. Philip Pettit, *On the People's Terms: A Republican Theory and Model of Democracy* (Cambridge: Cambridge University Press, 2012), 3.

66. Pettit, 4.

67. Arendt, "Freiheit und Politik," 201.

68. With this I build on an extensive critique of the sterility of Pettit's conceptualization, as it was put forward by inter alia Nadia Urbinati, "Unpolitical Democracy," *Political Theory* 38, no. 1 (2010): 65–92; Patchen Markell, "The Insufficiency of Non-Domination," *Political Theory* 36, no. 1 (2008), 9–36; and many others.

69. See Pettit, *On People's Terms*, Philip Pettit, *Just Freedom: A Moral Compass for a Complex World* (Cambridge: Cambridge University Press, 2014).

70. Pettit, *On People's Terms*, 225–26. See also Pettit, *Just Freedom*, 129ff.

71. For this criticism, see Andreas Busen and Thorsten Thiel, "Freiheit, Gerechtigkeit und Demokratie: Renovierungsarbeiten am Neo-Republikanismus," *Zeitschrift für Politikwissenschaft* 24, nos. 1–2 (2014): 185–204.

72. Miguel Abensour, "Die rebellierende Demokratie," *Blätter für deutsche und internationale Politik* 57, no. 5 (2012), 91, translation mine; cf. Rancière, *Disagreement*, 16–19; Chantal Mouffe, *On the Political: Thinking in Action* (London: Routledge, 2005), 53; Cornelius Castoriadis, *The Imaginary Institution* (Cambridge, MA: MIT Press, 1998); Andreas Kalyvas, *Democracy and the Politics of the Extraordinary: Max Weber, Carl Schmitt, and Hannah Arendt* (Cambridge: Cambridge University Press, 2008), 204.

73. Rancière, *Disagreement*, 13; Mouffe, *On the Political*, 20–21.
74. See Mouffe, 3.
75. Claude Lefort, *The Political Forms of Modern Society* (Cambridge, MA: MIT Press, 1986), 20.
76. Michael Th. Greven, "Verschwindet das Politische in der politischen Gesellschaft?: Über Strategien der Kontingenzverleugnung," in *Das Politische und die Politik*, ed. Thomas Bedorf and Kurt Röttgers (Berlin: Suhrkamp, 2010), 68, translation mine.
77. For a more detailed account of my perception of the potentials and shortcomings of radical democratic theory, see Christian Volk, "On a Radical Democratic Theory of Political Protest: Potentials and Shortcomings," *Critical Review of International Social and Political Philosophy* 24, no. 4 (2021): 437–59.

11
Three Models of Communicative Cosmopolitanism

PETER J. VEROVŠEK

World politics has undergone a series of seismic shifts since 1945. Whereas the "container [*Behälter*] of the nation-state" appeared impermeable to international pressures before 1945, the second half of the twentieth century has produced an unprecedented "hollowing out" of Westphalian sovereignty.[1] Given its long-standing sensitivity to political practice, postwar political philosophy has sought to theorize this transformation by questioning "the assumption that the nation/state/society is the natural social and political form of the modern world."[2] In contrast to the traditional methodological nationalism of modern political thought, during the postwar period cosmopolitan ideas have increasingly come to the fore.

These new approaches, which are unified by their attempt to conceptualize the normative principles of politics outside the institutional architecture of the nation-state, also differ greatly from one another, both in their internal logics and in their ultimate goals. While some cosmopolitan thinkers rely on economic incentives, others build on ethical commitments or environmental imperatives. Similarly, whereas some within this movement aim for a truly global politics contained within a world state, others are content to develop cosmopolitan principles through existing structures and institutions.[3]

A particularly powerful strain of this new cosmopolitanism builds on the "communicative turn" of postwar continental political theory.[4] The success of this approach is due to the fact that public spheres invariably cross state borders and are increasingly becoming transnational as a result of the development of new digital media.[5] However, just as in cosmopolitanism as a whole, the similarities between these communicative approaches also mask important differences.

In this chapter, I evaluate the theories of the three leading thinkers of what I refer to as "communicative cosmopolitanism": Hannah Arendt, Jürgen Habermas, and Seyla Benhabib.[6] Despite the fact that they all offer "talk-" rather than "vote-centric" conceptions of politics, as representatives of three successive generations their models also differ in important ways.[7] Most notably, while Arendt builds on ideas of the public realm as the space of communicative appearances to recover a cosmopolitanism based on broad-based cooperation between local councils, Habermas instead argues for the creation of a deliberative "postnational constellation" based on continental regimes and a transnational public sphere (*Öffentlichkeit*).[8]

Finally, as the youngest of the three, Benhabib seeks to reconcile the insights of her predecessors by offering "another cosmopolitanism" that mediates between what she calls "concrete and generalized other."[9] Her contextual universalism encourages local actors to translate international norms into discourses at the local level through what she refers to as civic activism in a process of "democratic iterations." My basic thesis is that Benhabib's approach effectively mediates between the localism emphasized by Arendt's and Habermas's push for a postnational constellation beyond the institutional architecture of the nation-state.

My argument is organized as follows. The first three sections compare and contrast the models of communicative cosmopolitanism presented by Arendt, Habermas, and Benhabib, respectively. In presenting these approaches I also consider how they apply their views and highlight how collective memory pushes all three toward solutions that decenter the state as the primary locus of politics.[10] The conclusion reflects on the relevance of communicative cosmopolitanism to problems in world affairs today.

ARENDT'S LOCALIZED COSMOPOLITANISM

Born in 1906 to a Jewish-German family, Arendt experienced the rise of Hitler and the horrors of World War II as an adult. Her memories of the Third Reich caused her to question much of the history of political thought, which she believed was tainted by the events of 1914–45. As a political theorist—not a political philosopher, a label that she rejected—she sought a new grounding for politics in the postwar world.[11]

Arendt argues that "words and deeds" are the key feature of *The Human Condition* (1958), the title of her major work of political theory. Words and deeds are crucial because they allow individuals to distinguish themselves from one another and from the rest of the living world: "In acting and speaking, men show who they are, reveal[ing] actively their unique personal identities."[12] Although everyone is forced to engage in the activities of *labor* to take care of their physical needs and *work* to produce the physical tools and other artifacts necessary sustain their life on the Earth, the separation of individuals from the anonymous masses of human beings is possible only as a result of communicatively mediated "*action* in concert." In this way, individuals cease to be defined by work or labor, and become free citizens, living and defining their unique identities through communication with others.

According to Arendt, this kind of politics requires the creation of a political arena "where all subsequent actions could take place, the space being the public realm."[13] These kinds of political communities not only provide witnesses; they also "fabricate memory" so that great "words and deeds" can outlive their authors.[14] Through the process of storytelling past actions are not only spread *horizontally* throughout the entire community; they are also passed down *vertically* to posterity. Through their laws and institutions, political communities thus make action into something concrete: "What saves the affairs of mortal men from their inherent futility is nothing but this incessant talk about them, which in its turn remains futile unless certain concepts, certain guideposts for future remembrance, and even for sheer reference, arise out of it."[15]

Despite Dolf Sternberger's classification of Arendt as the "thinker of the polis," Benhabib has pushed back on this interpretation, highlighting instead the important role that the experience of totalitarianism played in her work.[16] As Christian Volk points out, Arendt's thought draws extensively on her personal memories of "the downfall of a European order based on the nation-state, the collapse of the Weimar Republic, and the rise of National Socialism."[17] What she found most frightening about the development of totalitarianism was its understanding of society as personified within the figure of the leader (*Führer*, *duce*), who "substitutes for the boundaries and channels of communication between individual men a band of iron which holds them so tightly together that it is as though their plurality had disappeared into One man of gigantic dimensions."[18] The spontaneity of human action is replaced by mechanistic conceptions of nature and history. In this way, by destroying the necessary preconditions for freedom, totalitarianism also destroys the human capacity for action.

Her analysis of the *Origins of Totalitarianism* (1951) leads Arendt to argue that the development of the state has increasingly forced its residents to become a homogenous, undifferentiated mass because it grounds belonging in prepolitical factors like ethnicity and nationality. Her analysis of political developments in the 1920s and 1930s leads her to conclude that "the nation conquered the state," as the particularistic notions of ethnic identities, which gave explicit preference to conationals over fellow citizens of other national backgrounds, took precedence over the universalistic conception of the state as the universal guarantor of law for all individuals.[19] As a result, the events of interwar crisis emerge as a rupture that "created a 'gap' between past and future of such a magnitude that the past, while still present, is fragmented and can no longer be told as a unified narrative."[20]

In order to combat these trends, Arendt argues that individuals must find ways to reestablish bonds that cut across social and generational boundaries. By searching the past for sources of inspiration that have "'undergone a sea-change' and survive in new crystallized forms and shapes that remain immune to the elements," Arendt eventually settled on the local council system as a possible grain of sand from the past that had "waited only for the pearl diver ... [to] bring [it] up into the world of the living."[21] Arendt locates this "pearl" of insight in a number of modern examples of revolutionary "action in concert," including Thomas Jefferson's ideas for the development of local wards, the Paris Commune of 1789, the creation of the *Soviets* in the first days of the Russian Revolution in 1917, and the 1919 German Spartacist Uprising (*Spartakusaufstand*) led by Rosa Luxemburg, as well as the councils formed during the short-lived Hungarian Revolution of 1956.

In all of these cases, Arendt argues that local councils "concerned with the reorganization of the political and economic life of the country and the establishment of a new world order" were not planned, but instead "sprang from the people as spontaneous organs of action and of order."[22] Although the party system inevitably doomed these local institutions, the fact that they were best preserved in America's federal system of self-government explains why the United States remained a beacon of hope for Arendt in the postwar world.[23] In reflecting on the legacy and imperatives of totalitarianism, Arendt concludes that humanity must return to a participatory, localized politics in order to combat the threats to freedom that permeate the modern world.

Although Arendt never sets out an institutional design or structure for global federalism, she suggests that *lex*, diplomacy, and delegation might function as mechanisms for the legal combination of local councils in her *Jewish Writings*.[24] As a result, "A federated political structure more akin to Kant's 'republic of republics' is certainly compatible with her views."[25] In fact, something along these lines seems to be precisely what she had in mind when she endorsed the "framework of universal agreements" laid out in the philosophy of Karl Jaspers.[26]

Arendt's cryptic support of a loose global federalism also helps to clarify some otherwise unexpectedly positive comments she made about European integration. For example, referring to the continent's first supranational institution, the European Coal and Steel Community (ECSC) of 1951, in a letter to Jaspers in May 1958, Arendt wrote, "I can't write about Europe yet.... This is a totally god forsaken place except for the presence of the Coal and Steel Community."[27] This suggests that much like the revolutionary councils she so admired, what Arendt saw in the creation of the ECSC was a "genuinely political [act] of foundation and cooperation" based on "the idea of freedom and public deliberation."[28] Arendt's fragmentary reflections on these issues even include something similar to the European principle of subsidiarity, as she argues that political issues should "be resolved on the lowest and most promising level of proximity and neighborliness."[29]

Her endorsement of the "very healthy and necessary efforts to federate the European nations" is also consistent her skepticism regarding national sovereignty.[30] Although there is much debate about how to classify the European Union and over how much power it actually wields, it has succeeded—at least partially—in "shak[ing] the state concept and its sovereignty."[31] From this perspective, the European Union is important because it represents a "new beginning" that has given birth to a new form of politics beyond the nation-state that Arendt so feared.

Although Arendt's proposals for a communicative cosmopolitanism based on the council system is thought-provoking, it is hard to draw firm conclusions about her thought on this topic, as she "never clearly and systematically set out her thought in this area."[32] As a result, although her basic insights are pregnant with theoretical potential, her proposals as a whole remain unconvincing. To start with—as her historical examples demonstrate—a system of governance based on local councils has never endured for any extended period of time. While these revolutionary institutions can indeed be seen as proof of the enduring human capacity to act in concert, Benhabib points out that Arendt's faith in the council system "seems to fly in the face of the realities of the modern world."[33]

Furthermore, while Arendt's endorsement of subsidiarity and a form of loose, cosmopolitan interrepublican law is suggestive, the mechanisms by which such a system could lead to "the stabilization of political freedom within a lasting political regime" need to be fleshed out further.[34] Thus, while Arendt's work clears important intellectual ground for later communicative cosmopolitans, it is too fragmentary to provide a clear foundation for such a paradigm on its own. Fortunately, Habermas and Benhabib have built on Arendt's insights to further develop a form of communicative cosmopolitanism based on "action in concert."

Using Arendt's notion of a networked council system, Habermas—to whom I now turn—seeks to develop an approach based on the transnational integration of nation-states into continental regimes. He argues that the success of the European Union shows that cosmopolitan integration can succeed without destroying structures of local and state governance through the creation of an all-encompassing world state. Although Habermas's theoretical model focuses on the development of new institutions beyond the national state, his conceptualization of the "postnational constellation" not only delegates powers "up" to transnational organizations like the European Union; it also devolves many political competences "down" to the local levels, where a more direct, council-like Arendtian politics prevails.

HABERMAS'S DISCURSIVE POSTNATIONAL CONSTELLATION

Although he is twenty-three years Arendt's junior, Habermas also experienced Nazism firsthand. Surveying the physical, moral, and political ruin of Germany in its *Stunde null*—the "zero hour" of utter destruction—as a teenager, Habermas knew that his homeland would have to learn from this tragedy in order to reclaim its intellectual tradition and its place in global society. Reflecting back on this crucial moment in his development, he notes that "the rhythm of my personal development intersected with the great historical events of the time.... These experiences undoubtedly helped develop motifs which then further determined my thinking."[35]

Much like Arendt's approach, Habermas's theoretical project also starts with "words and deeds," a basic insight that he refers to as "linguistically mediated communication." In this sense, Habermas agrees with Arendt that political power is not drawn from force or violence, but is a product of our ability to speak, understand, and persuade one another. However, he rejects what he sees as her "rigid conceptual dichotomies between 'public' and 'private,' state and economy, liberty and welfare."[36] Rather than focusing on human beings as political animals, Habermas instead seeks to expand the basic insights of Arendt's "communicative turn" to epistemology, linguistics, and social theory.

Habermas's philosophical starting point is that the essential feature of language is not grammar, but communication, which raises human beings out of nature and makes them into conscious moral agents. He argues that this basic "communicative competence" is the basis of social interaction. On his understanding, "communicative action" can be used not only objectively to refer to states of the world and subjectively to reflect personal experiences, but also—and most importantly—intersubjectively to establish mutual understanding and interpersonal relationships.

For Habermas the ultimate arbiter of the validity of these claims is the ability of the participants to defend their claims with reasons, i.e., "in terms of the capacity of responsible participants in interaction to orient themselves in relation to validity claims geared to intersubjective recognition."[37] The space and reach of this communicative politics are not limited to political life as they are in Arendt's understanding, nor are they as agonistic and rhetorical. Instead, he argues for a "shifting boundary between the private and public spheres" legitimized by discourse within the political community.[38]

The capacity of participants in discourse to come to "mutual understanding" (*Verständigung*) is crucial for any political community. It is this ability—and the shared "we-perspective" that it generates—that allows individuals to form political communities bound by ties of solidarity, without which "intelligent action [remains] permanently foundationless and inconsequential."[39] Historically, such interpersonal ties dissipated fairly quickly, not extending much beyond the village, tribe, or small city-state. However, with the advent of nationalism, the new institution of the nation-state was able to extend the circle of solidarity to a much larger community of individuals.

While extending the ties of solidarity to the state has certain advantages, it is also exclusionary and dangerous. As Habermas points out, "The formation of nation-states under the banner of ethnonationalism has almost always been accompanied by bloody purification rituals."[40] Twentieth-century European history—which forms the background for much of Habermas's thought—demonstrates how the desire for ethnic purity inevitably led to forced emigration, expulsion, disenfranchisement, and extermination. He thus agrees with Arendt's devastating critique of the deadly consequences of nationalism, noting that her diagnosis has "proved frighteningly accurate."[41]

Additionally, following Arendt, Habermas sees power (*Macht*) as rooted in the human ability to use reason and arguments to create bonds of solidarity.[42] This kind of societal dialogue is especially important if we are to "learn from catastrophe" by building on shared, collective memories of the Holocaust.[43] His desire to learn from the past while avoiding the pitfalls of the organic conceptions of peoplehood is what led Habermas to follow Theodor W. Adorno in seeking an "active remembrance—working through [*aufarbeiten*] the past and hoping for a better future."[44]

Habermas also shares the wariness expressed in Arendt's analysis of the internal problems contained within the hyphenated concept of the nation-state. While the nation-state is problematic at a general level, he argues that it has lost all legitimacy, especially in the German context with which he is most concerned, in light of the shared European experience of total war. With the tragedy of Nazism and World War II, Habermas observes, "Germans have lost the possibility of grounding their political identity on anything else than the universalistic principles of state citizenship."[45] In the aftermath of such events, he argues that national identities must be reformed and rebuilt by reflecting on "the better traditions of our history, a history that is not unexamined but instead appropriated critically."[46] This kind of learning process (*Lernprozeß*) requires full engagement with the tragedies and traumas of the past, not their silencing or repression.

Building on this analysis, which is inspired in large part by Arendt's political theory as well as her historical investigations, Habermas argues that nationalism and other "pre-established identities have become obsolete."[47] It is not just Germany that needs to learn from its past; all of Europe and the rest of the world must do so as well. Since the fall of the Berlin Wall and the end of communism in Europe, Habermas has therefore sought to ground the lessons of a "bellicose past [that] entangled all European nations in bloody conflicts" in political communities beyond the nation-state, most notably the European Union, which has been at the center of Habermas's political thought since the end of the Cold War and the unification of Germany.[48]

Since its foundation in the 1950s, the European project has built on the desire to secure peace in Europe after the horrors of World War II and the divisions wrought by the Cold War. Habermas notes that it is precisely this "historical background [that] could serve to smooth the transition to a postnational democracy founded on mutual recognition of the differences between proud national cultures."[49] Instead of building on differences, he contends that a European identity can be found in the continent's shared collective memories of two world wars, which lead to an appreciation of the need to learn from a bloody history the importance of respecting human rights, abide by the rule of law, and refrain from violence in both domestic and foreign affairs. Habermas argues that this is the mechanism by which the tragedies of the past can serve as the foundation for a new, post-totalitarian politics: "The twentieth century puts at risk its future by not learning from—by badly forgetting—its own disaster."[50]

Despite the fact that Habermas focuses on the collective memories of Western Europeans in constructing this argument, its implications are not limited to this continent. He thinks that the legacy of violence and nationalism in Europe can serve as an example to the rest of the world. Following Kant, Habermas abjures the idea of a world state for fear that it would turn into "a soulless despotism, [which] after crushing the germs of goodness, will finally lapse into anarchy."[51] In response to the dilemmas posed by global equality and diversity, Habermas instead develops a flexible, multilevel, communicative cosmopolitanism.

Although Habermas contends that the nation-state's loss of "steering capacity" means that it "is less and less appropriate to the current situation," he notes that there are still insufficient sources of legitimacy for a direct form of global politics.[52] In order to establish a contextual universalism that respects the historical differences between peoples while allowing for the creation of a system powerful enough to meet international political problems—including mass violence, climate change, and the increasing power of anonymous global market forces to dictate policy to political communities—Habermas reconceptualizes world politics in terms of what he calls a "democratically constituted world society without a world government."[53]

Building on Kant's "Towards Perpetual Peace" (1795)—which is also a core touchstone for Arendt's communicative cosmopolitanism—Habermas imagines the creation of a series of "regionally comprehensive regimes like the European Community" around the world.[54] By encouraging the creation of broad, regional identities, these continental regimes could help safeguard peace and prevent atrocities within their borders and externally by cooperating in peacekeeping and protecting human rights through a reformed version of the United Nations. These "regional or continental regimes" are meant to fill the political and legal gap between the local and the global.[55]

Since regions often share historical experiences and other cultural markers, such regimes could ensure that global debates about the implementation of basic international norms were carried out in "the intermediate arena [that] is populated by a manageable number of global players." These actors would help to ensure that international norms agreed upon at the global level received historically and culturally sensitive and enforceable interpretations at the transnational level. In this system, "The practices of a decentralized, multi-level politics ... can at least in some respects close the efficiency gaps that open up as the nation-state loses its autonomy."[56] The fact that the European Union—the prototype for these new regional institutions—often acts in the name of all its members in global negotiations on issues as diverse as trade and climate change shows how such institutions can act as a stepping stone toward a Kantian "global domestic policy" (*Weltinnenpolitik*).

In contrast to more centralized cosmopolitan visions, Habermas's proposals for a "constitutionalization of international law" also retain an important role for existing communities. His system therefore depends on universal norms, which are determined at the global level through both formal international law and informal customary norms. However, enforcement continues to be carried out by legitimate systems of coercion that are "closely linked in the historical form of the constitutional state," though in many cases these mechanisms will be further devolved to local authorities.[57]

Although police and other powers of direct legal enforcement will remain at the level of the local administration or the state, Habermas argues that continental regimes like the European Union should play a crucial role in cosmopolitan politics by replacing nation-states as the primary negotiators of agreements at the global level. Nevertheless, he severely limits the law-making authority of the global system—i.e., the ability of international law to be "transformed into administratively utilizable power"—by arguing that it should promulgate only universal "legal norms with an exclusively moral content."[58] Given the weakness of the global public sphere, Habermas argues that the United Nations can do little more than "naming and shaming" violators, leaving the implementation of even the most basic moral obligations in the hands of existing political communities.[59]

In addition to taking advantage of already-existing, historically legitimate local institutions, Habermas also seeks to build on the historical reservoirs of civic solidarity contained within existing communities. He fears that scrapping local politics in favor of a globalized system will leave individuals in a state of Durkheimian anomie by robbing them of the group ties necessary for socialization and the development of meaningful identities. Without the social bonds created by politics at the community level, citizens might lose their collective ability to combat the rise of the powerful forces of the neoliberal economic system.

Habermas's communicative cosmopolitan vision based on regional or comprehensive regimes that sit between existing states and a reformed United Nations has much to recommend it. However, its reliance on global forms of regional integration is highly problematic, as these institutions do not appear to be forthcoming. Although he repeatedly points to the European Union as a model, there is little evidence for similar forms of integration in other parts of the world. Despite some promising steps, it does not appear that the nascent African Union is moving toward the kind of deeper political integration that Habermas expects. In this sense, Habermas's vision seems to depend too much on the export of a European political model in which the rest of the world appears to show little interest.

In addition to this problem at the meso-level, Habermas's conceptualization fares no better at either the upper or the lower levels. At the former, the prospects for reform of the United Nations have also faded, while ambitious hopes for the enforcement of global moral norms have also been disappointed, most notably by the failure of the so-called "responsibility to protect" (R2P) doctrine. Additionally, at the latter level states and other local political actors have also increasingly proved unwilling to cooperate with inter- or supranational institutions or to implement international law and global norms. Instead of moving toward more powerful forms of internationalism, the world has instead experienced a powerful transnational desire to "return to the nation-state," symbolized most powerfully by Brexit and other local movements to "take back control," as the Leave campaign so successfully put it during the United Kingdom's referendum to exit from the European Union.[60]

In light of these developments, Habermas's communicative cosmopolitan vision appears further from reality at the beginning of the twenty-first century than it was when he first proposed it at the end of the twentieth. From the perspective of the present his vision is too institutional and relies too heavily on the development of supranational organizations and the direct enforcement of international law. Unlike Arendt's model, which builds on the council system but does not specify how these hyperlocal institutions will coordinate with one another, Habermas's model suffers from just the opposite problem. Following on these insights, Benhabib's approach, which seeks to mediate between the universal and the particular by relying on local actors to implement global norms within local laws and institutions, strikes the proper balance between her two predecessors.

BENHABIB'S MEDIATION BETWEEN THE CONCRETE AND THE GENERALIZED OTHER

Unlike Arendt, who lived through the entirety of Europe's age of total war (1914–45), and Habermas, whose childhood growing up in the Third Reich forced him to confront the fact that he had been living in a criminal regime after the liberation of Germany in 1945, Benhabib, with her comparatively late birth in 1950, was spared the direct experience of war and suffering that defined the lives of her predecessors. Although she grew up in the Turkey that Mustafa Kemal Atatürk had steered "away from an old and multicultural Empire toward a homogenizing modern nation-state," she describes the Istanbul of her youth as "the jewel city of the new republic" and as a cosmopolitan oasis whose "historical contradictions and memories are like throbbing veins."[61] Given her family background as a Sephardic Jew whose predecessors had been forced out of Spain by the Inquisition in 1492,

Benhabib notes that "the Golden Age in Spain, during which Jewish, Christian, and Moslem communities coexisted peacefully for several centuries, was never extinguished from our collective memory."[62]

Benhabib's discursive cosmopolitanism builds on images of "this 'other Europe,' a multicultural, multilinguistic, and multifaith polity" preserved in her memories of the secular, multicultural mid-twentieth-century Republic of Turkey.[63] Philosophically, her thought is inspired by both of her predecessors, with whom she engages critically, not just hermeneutically. Thus, although she looks up to Arendt as "the political theorist of the post-totalitarian moment," she has always "exercised a method of 'thinking with Arendt, against Arendt.'"[64]

Benhabib clearly sympathizes with Arendt's redemption of politics as the universal sphere "of the common concern for the political association" from the "rise of the social" (Arendt) rooted in the Hegelian "system of needs" (*System der Bedürfnisse*), i.e., the "domain of economic activity governed by commodity exchange and the pursuit of economic self-interest." However, she is also critical of Arendt's agonistic understanding of the public space for its neglect of "women, slaves, children, laborers, [and] non-citizen residents," who "were excluded from it while they made possible through their labor for the daily necessities of life that 'leisure for politics' that the few enjoyed." She also faults Arendt for ignoring the fact that work and labor, "insofar as they are based on power relations, could become matters of public dispute."[65]

Building on Arendt's critique of the prepolitical particularism of the nation-state, Benhabib agrees with her predecessor that within a communicative cosmopolitanism "universalist norms are mediated with the self-understanding of local communities."[66] Although she rejects Arendt's focus on local councils as out of step with the developments of the modern world, as I already noted, Benhabib still argues that politics can and should be "exercised at local and regional as well as supra- and transnational levels."[67] As a result, she endorses "a more vertical dispersal of sovereignty through increased integration into multinational, transnational and global organizations and institutions."[68]

These reflections demonstrate Benhabib's closeness to Habermas. Like her mentor during her stay at the Max Planck Institute for the Study of the Scientific-Technical World (Max Planck Institut zur Erforschung der Lebensbedingungen der wissenschaftlich-technischen Welt) in Starnberg in the early 1980s, she ultimately backs a cosmopolitanism that is not only communicative in the Arendtian sense, but discursive and participatory: "it is viewed democratically as the creation of procedures whereby those affected by general social norms and collective political decisions can have a say in their formulation, stipulation, and adoption."[69] Although she also critiques Habermas for overlooking the political implications of the distinction between public and private for women, she argues that this is ultimately just "an area of conceptual unclarity and political contestation." Benhabib therefore concludes that his deliberative model can be rescued if feminists and other subaltern groups "not only criticize Habermas's social theory but also enter into a dialectical alliance with it."[70]

As a result, the starting point of Benhabib's deliberative cosmopolitanism is quite close to Habermas. Like his, her approach is multilevel and emphasizes the important role that existing polities will continue to play. Despite her calls for the creation of porous borders, Benhabib also observes, "Political actors need bounded communities—whether they be cities, regions, states or transnational institutions—within which they can establish mechanisms of representation, accountability, participation and deliberation." Such clearly defined associations are not only important for procedural reasons; they are also crucial for identity formation.

Much like both of her predecessors, Benhabib is sensitive to the link between legitimacy, identity, and collective remembrance. Reflecting on the continuing importance of existing forms of political organization, she notes that "these institutions are not only sites, in the sense of *spaces* (*des lieux*), but also *places*, that is sites of attachment and sites of memory (*lieux de mémoires*). Furthermore," she concludes, "institutions themselves are bearers of historical memory" that are necessary for identity formation at both the individual and the communal levels.[71]

Although she endorses a multilevel approach similar to Habermas's, Benhabib criticizes the rigidity of her mentor's distinctions between the levels of sovereignty within the cosmopolitan system. More specifically, Benhabib is skeptical of Habermas's conclusion that the fact that "international law must be 'transformed into administratively utilizable power'" requires existing political communities to subordinate their popular sovereignty directly to international norms.[72] The disruptive potential of this rigid, hierarchical conceptualization of cosmopolitan law leads Benhabib to modify Habermas's approach by emphasizing local agency in a quasi-Arendtian manner.

Summing up her concerns about Habermas's cosmopolitan model based on the constitutionalization of international law, she contends, "Popular sovereignty and transnational law are not antagonistic; rather, the latter can enhance the former." Instead of conceptualizing the relationship between the international and the national or subnational as opposed to each other, she seeks to blur these conceptual boundaries by calling for the international community to "formulat[e] core *concepts* of human rights" that "permit a variety of instantiations as concrete constitutional principles." The result is what Benhabib calls "a dynamic understanding of interaction between courts, civil society and social movements" fueled by what she calls "democratic iterations."[73] This process results in a dialogue between levels—facilitated by transnational social movements—instead of a tug-of-war between international tribunals and domestic courts.

Benhabib's cosmopolitanism builds on her understanding of cosmopolitanism as "a philosophical project of mediations."[74] She seeks to square abstract universalism with actual diversity by distinguishing between what she calls the "generalized" and the "concrete" other. Whereas the former recognizes the humanity of alter "as a rational being entitled to the same rights and duties we would want to ascribe to ourselves," the latter acknowledges their unique individuality as beings "with a concrete history, identity, and affective-emotional constitution."[75] Mediating these two perspectives requires working through how general moral rules can be applied in specific communities with their own traditions, histories, needs, and desires.

Although Benhabib argues that this diversity can be bridged discursively, she notes, "The line between matters of justice and those of the good life is not given by some moral dictionary, but evolves as a result of historical and cultural struggles."[76] This insight has a number of implications for her deliberative, communicative approach. To start, it highlights the fact that we should not reduce "cosmopolitanism to a bid for imperial domination" by imposing international laws and norms on existing political communities without their consent.[77] Additionally, the discursive struggle to mediate the generalized with the concrete other guards against the tendency to regard the desires of different communities as uniform. On the contrary, Benhabib emphasizes that we must keep in mind that the aspirations of alter are also "constituted through contested practices," just as our own are.[78]

The normative lesson of this insight is that discursive engagement can spur the concrete other to take up universal moral norms from within. Benhabib argues that deliberation within the domestic public sphere allows communities at the legal level to accept generalized, cosmopolitan rules without the need for external intervention. In the course of these discursively mediated "democratic iterations," Benhabib notes that "cosmopolitan norms are suffused with historically specific content."[79] This does not occur once for all time, but is repeated in multiple iterations by different individuals at different times in response to different situations. Such democratic processes not only mediate between moral universalism and democratic self-determination; they also infuse abstract ideals "with content [by] drawing on experiences that could not have guided those rights in their initial formulation, . . . open[ing] up new worlds and creat[ing] new meanings."[80]

Benhabib's discursive cosmopolitanism thus demonstrates how potentially dangerous it is to force abstract legal principles onto local communities without internal support, i.e., without allowing for translation into local idioms and traditions. Instead of leading to an internal debate and the legitimation of new rights that reaffirm the human dignity of all citizens, the direct imposition of external rules and norms is often counterproductive, as they are seen locally as products of a dictatorial nascent world state. Robert Post therefore argues, "Benhabib's profound insight is to conceptualize the emergence of cosmopolitan law as a dynamic process through which the principles of human rights are progressively incorporated into the positive law of democratic states."[81]

Building on her commitment to deliberation in the public sphere, Benhabib's approach emphasizes the importance of domestic debate about global norms. She notes that it is only by stimulating discourse at the local level that the abstract expectations of the invariably "weak" global public presupposed by Habermas's more rigid model can be filled with content. By incorporating global principles into national legislation through bottom-up processes, she argues, "the content of democratic law is progressively reconstructed along lines that reflect principles of ethical universalism."[82] Borrowing the terminology of Judith Resnik, Benhabib refers to this phenomenon as "law's migration."[83]

In addition to cosmopolitan law and norms at the local level, she argues that this flexible, context-sensitive approach also fosters the development of democratic culture at the local and national levels. By engaging with global expectations as well as the demands of human rights declarations, treaties, and other supranational agreements, local actors within nascent democracies learn "to enter the public sphere, to develop new vocabularies of public claim-making, and to anticipate new forms of justice to come in processes of cascading democratic iterations." Although these local debates about the implementation of global norms are contentious, they have the potential to "set in motion processes of mutual challenging, questioning, and learning."[84] Most importantly, because they come from the inside and are generated from the bottom up, such an approach to mediating the generalized, universal and the local, concrete other is less likely to generate resistance and hostility than outside, top-down impositions by international courts, outside interventions, and the like. In contrast to existing approaches, her discursive cosmopolitanism thus depends both "on *nonstate actors* as well as on *state actors*."[85]

Another advantage of this approach is that it gives social movements at the local level a direct role to play within the cosmopolitan system. Although

Habermas recognizes that "without social movements nothing moves" (*ohne soziale Bewegungen bewegt sich nichts*), he has generally placed little emphasis on the Arendtian need for "action in concert" within civil society at the local level.[86] Thus, although Benhabib's argument clearly works at the abstract level of political theory, it also highlights clear, realistic actions that cosmopolitans can take to bring a more just, global system into being by emphasizing the need for global social movements to work across borders by linking with and empowering local actors within existing communities to bring about change through agitation and discursive interventions. Although the extent to which her approach has the capacity to bring about true change is questionable, given that it can be seen as merely normatively describing what is already happening (i.e., local actors are already drawing vocabularies from international networks and agreements), I still argue that Benhabib's approach effectively mediates between the localism emphasized by Arendt and Habermas's argument for the need to push politics beyond the institutional architecture of the nation-state.

In this essay I have outlined the three different models of communicative cosmopolitanism presented by Arendt, Habermas, and Benhabib. Whereas Arendt's conceptualization is rooted in local councils connected by a loose federalism akin to a Kantian "republic of republics" and Habermas's is based on a functional division of sovereignty between various levels, Benhabib's approach emphasizes how abstract cosmopolitan norms and international law give concrete local activists, lawmakers, and other leaders "new vocabularies of claim-making." In presenting this material, I argued that Benhabib's approach is the most convincing because it effectively mediates between the localism emphasized by Arendt and Habermas's more institutionalized plea for the development of a new form of cosmopolitanism that pushes politics beyond the institutional infrastructure of the nation-state.

Regardless of which of these three theorists is right, they start from the "assumption that the era of nation-states is coming to an end and that the creation of institutions of a global domestic policy must be opened up for discussion."[87] In this sense, all three are searching for a form of cosmopolitan "politics that will gradually *catch up* with runaway markets."[88] Although economic integration has pushed ahead of political integration, this situation is not inevitable, nor is a return to the nation-state a solution to it. Instead, the task of communicative cosmopolitanism is to find a way to reassert the primacy of politics in the modern world.

Insofar as Benhabib's approach emphasizes the role that social movements play in translating cosmopolitan rules and norms into local political idioms, it does the best job of specifying the "catalyst and agent of social transformation" in a clear, realistic, and actionable way.[89] In this way, Benhabib's discursive cosmopolitanism not only clearly specifies the relationship between the "generalized" and "concrete other"; it also successfully mediates between the "ideal" and the "real" in a way that can lead to "concrete" political change in the present. For a scholar who started her intellectual journey with a dissertation on Hegel, I can think of no higher form of praise.[90]

NOTES

1. Ulrich Beck and Edgar Grande, *Das kosmopolitische Europa: Gesellschaft und Politik in der zweiten Moderne* (Frankfurt: Suhrkamp, 2004); Adam Tooze, *The Deluge: The Great War and the Remaking of Global Order, 1916–1931* (London: Allen Lane, 2014), 5.
2. Andreas Wimmer and Nina Glick Schiller, "Methodological Nationalism and Beyond: Nation-State Building, Migration and the Social Sciences," *Global Networks* 2, no. 4 (2002): 302.
3. See Garrett W. Brown and David Held, *The Cosmopolitanism Reader* (London: Polity, 2010).
4. See Peter J. Verovšek, "A Case of Communicative Learning?: Rereading Habermas's Philosophical Project Through an Arendtian Lens," *Polity* 51, no. 3 (July 2019); Maeve Cooke, "Realism and Idealism: Was Habermas's Communicative Turn a Move in the Wrong Direction?," *Political Theory* 40, no. 6 (2012).
5. Jürgen Habermas, *Ein neuer Strukturwandel der Öffentlichkeit und die deliberative Politik* (Frankfurt: Suhrkamp, 2022); Peter J. Verovšek, "Authorship and Individualization in the Digital Public Sphere," *Constellations* 30, no. 1 (2023): 34–41.
6. See Peter J. Verovšek, "Integration After Totalitarianism: Arendt and Habermas on the Postwar Imperatives of Memory," *Journal of International Political Theory* (2018).
7. Simone Chambers, "Deliberative Democratic Theory," *Annual Review of Political Science* 6 (2003): 308.
8. Hannah Arendt, *The Origins of Totalitarianism* (New York: Brace Harcourt, 1951); Jürgen Habermas, *The Postnational Constellation: Political Essays*, ed. Max Pensky, trans. Max Pensky (Cambridge, MA: MIT Press, 2001).
9. Seyla Benhabib, *Another Cosmopolitanism*, ed. Robert Post (Oxford: Oxford University Press, 2006); Seyla Benhabib, *Situating the Self: Gender, Community, and Postmodernism in Contemporary Ethics* (New York: Routledge, 1992).
10. See Peter J. Verovšek, *Memory and the Future of Europe: Memory and Integration in the Wake of Total War* (Manchester: Manchester University Press, 2020).
11. See Peter J. Verovšek, "Unexpected Support for European Integration: Memory, Rupture and Totalitarianism in Arendt's Political Theory," *Review of Politics* 76,

no. 3 (2014); Peter J. Verovšek, "Memory, Narrative, and Rupture: The Power of the Past as a Resource for Political Change," *Memory Studies* 13, no. 4 (2020).
12. Hannah Arendt, *The Human Condition* (Chicago: University of Chicago Press, 1998), 179.
13. Arendt, 194–95.
14. Hannah Arendt, *Between Past and Future: Eight Exercises in Political Thought* (New York: Penguin, 1977), 64.
15. Hannah Arendt, *On Revolution* (New York: Penguin, 1990), 220.
16. Dolf Sternberger, "Hannah Arendt—Denkerin der Polis," in *Pysiognomien: Philosophen des 20. Jahrhunderts in Portraits*, ed. Eckhard Nordhofen (Königstein: Athenäum-Verlag, 1980).
17. Christian Volk, *Arendtian Constitutionalism: Law, Politics and the Order of Freedom* (Oxford: Hart, 2017), 172.
18. Arendt, *Origins of Totalitarianism*, 465–66.
19. Arendt, 275; see also Peter J. Verovšek, "Caught Between 1945 and 1989: Collective Memory and the Rise of Illiberal Democracy in Postcommunist Europe," *Journal of European Public Policy* (2020); Peter J. Verovšek, "'The Nation has Conquered the State': Arendtian Insights on the Internal Contradictions of the Nation-State," *Review of International Studies*, forthcoming.
20. Seyla Benhabib, *The Reluctant Modernism of Hannah Arendt* (Lanham, MD: Rowman and Littlefield, 2003), 92.
21. Hannah Arendt, "Walter Benjamin: 1892–1940," in *Illuminations: Essays and Reflections*, ed. Walter Benjamin (New York: Schocken, 1977), 51.
22. Arendt, *On Revolution*, 263.
23. See Arendt, 156–70.
24. Hannah Arendt, *The Jewish Writings*, ed. Jerome Kohn and Ron H. Feldman (New York: Schocken, 2007), 349–50, 395, 400.
25. Patricia Owens, *Between War and Politics* (Oxford: Oxford University Press, 2007), 146.
26. Hannah Arendt, *Men in Dark Times* (New York: Harcourt, Brace and World, 1968), 93.
27. Quoted in Lotte Kohler and Hans Saner, eds., *Hannah Arendt Karl Jaspers: Correspondence, 1926–1969*, trans. Robert and Rita Kimber (New York: Harcourt Brace Jovanovich, 1993), 351.
28. Lars Rensmann, "Europeanism and Americanism in the Age of Globalization: Hannah Arendt's Reflections on Europe and America and Implications for a Post-National Identity of the EU Polity," *European Journal of Political Theory* 5, no. 2 (2006): 160, 146.
29. Arendt, *Jewish Writings*, 400.
30. Hannah Arendt, *Essays in Understanding, 1930–1954* (New York: Harcourt, Brace, 1994), 416–17.
31. Hannah Arendt, *Crises of the Republic* (New York: Harcourt Brace, 1969), 231.
32. Patricia Owens, "Walking Corpses: Arendt on the Limits and the Possibilities of Cosmopolitan Politics," in *International Relations Theory and Philosophy: Interpretive Dialogues*, ed. Cerwyn Moore and Chris Farrands (London: Routledge, 2010), 72–82, 73.

33. Benhabib, *Reluctant Modernism*, 165.
34. James Muldoon, "The Origins of Hannah Arendt's Council System," *History of Political Thought* 37, no. 4 (Winter 2016): 789.
35. Jürgen Habermas, *Autonomy and Solidarity: Interviews*, ed. Peter Dews (London: Verso, 1992), 77; see also Peter J. Verovšek, *Engaged Critical Theory: Jürgen Habermas as Public Intellectual* (New York: Columbia University Press, forthcoming).
36. Jürgen Habermas, *Philosophical-Political Profiles*, trans. Frederick G. Lawrence (Cambridge, MA: MIT Press, 1983), 178.
37. Jürgen Habermas, *The Philosophical Discourse of Modernity: Twelve Lectures*, trans. Frederick G. Lawrence (Cambridge, MA: MIT Press, 1987), 314.
38. Jürgen Habermas, "Reconciliation Through the Public Use of Reason: Remarks on John Rawls' Political Liberalism," *Journal of Philosophy* 92, no. 3 (March 1995): 129.
39. Jürgen Habermas, *The Past as Future: Vergangenheit als Zukunft*, trans. Max Pensky (Lincoln: University of Nebraska Press, 1994), 96.
40. Jürgen Habermas, *The Inclusion of the Other: Studies in Political Theory*, trans. Ciaran Cronin (Cambridge, MA: MIT Press, 1998), 142.
41. Jürgen Habermas, *Between Facts and Norms: Contributions to a Discourse Theory of Law and Democracy* (Cambridge, MA: MIT Press, 1996), 508.
42. Habermas, *Philosophical-Political Profiles*, 171–88.
43. Habermas, *Postnational Constellation*, 26–37.
44. Quoted in Martin Joseph Matuštík, *Jürgen Habermas: A Philosophical-Political Profile* (Lanham, MD: Rowman and Littlefield, 2001), 10.
45. Quoted in Matuštík, 173.
46. Jürgen Habermas, *The New Conservatism: Cultural Criticism and the Historians' Debate*, trans. Shierry Weber Nicholsen (Cambridge, MA: MIT Press, 1989), 234.
47. Jürgen Habermas, *Zur Rekonstruktion des historischen Materialismus* (Frankfurt: Suhrkamp, 1976), 115.
48. Jürgen Habermas, "February 15, Or: What Binds Europeans," in *Old Europe, New Europe, Core Europe: Transatlantic Relations After the Iraq War*, trans. Max Pensky (London: Verso, 2005), 12.
49. Jürgen Habermas, "Does Europe Need a Constitution?," in *Time of Transitions*, trans. Cronin Ciaran and Max Pensky (Cambridge: Polity, 2006), 105.
50. Quoted in Matuštík, *Habermas*, 139.
51. Immanuel Kant, *Kant Political Writings*, ed. H. S. Reiss (Cambridge: Cambridge University Press, 1991), 113.
52. Habermas, *Postnational Constellation*, 69.
53. Jürgen Habermas, "The Constitutionalization of International Law and the Legitimation Problems of a Constitution for World Society," *Constellations* 15, no. 4 (2008): 445.
54. Jürgen Habermas, "Remarks on Dieter Grimm's 'Does Europe Need a Constitution?,'" in *Constitutionalism and Democracy*, ed. Richard Bellamy (Aldershot, UK: Ashgate, 2006), 500–5, 503.
55. Jürgen Habermas, *Between Naturalism and Religion: Philosophical Essays* (Cambridge: Polity, 2008), 324–25, emphasis removed.
56. Habermas, *Postnational Constellation*, 70.

57. Habermas, "Constitutionalization," 445.
58. Habermas, *Postnational Constellation*, 108; Habermas, *Inclusion of the Other*, 249.
59. Habermas, "Constitutionalization," 451.
60. Peter J. Verovšek, "The Immanent Potential of Economic Integration: A Critical Reading of the Eurozone Crisis," *Perspectives on Politics* 15, no. 2 (2017).
61. Seyla Benhabib, "Istanbul Seminars: Toward New Democratic Imaginaries," in *Toward New Democratic Imaginaries—Istanbul Seminars on Islam, Culture and Politics*, ed. Seyla Benhabib and Volker Kaul (Switzerland: Springer, 2016), xxxiii, xxxiv.
62. Seyla Benhabib, *Transformations of Citizenship: Dilemmas of the Nation State in the Era of Globalization, Two Lectures* (Amsterdam: Koninkljke van Gorcum, 2001), 7.
63. Benhabib, 7.
64. Benhabib, 8, 11.
65. Seyla Benhabib, "Models of Public Space: Hannah Arendt, the Liberal Tradition and Jürgen Habermas," in *Habermas and the Public Sphere*, ed. Craig J. Calhoun (Cambridge, MA: MIT Press, 1992), 75, 80.
66. Benhabib, *Another Cosmopolitanism*, 71, 172.
67. Benhabib, *Reluctant Modernism*, 165.
68. Benhabib, *Transformations of Citizenship*, 63.
69. Benhabib, "Models of Public Space," 87.
70. Benhabib, 87, 93, 94.
71. Benhabib, *Another Cosmopolitanism*, 169.
72. Habermas, *Inclusion of the Other*, 249.
73. Seyla Benhabib, "The New Sovereigntism and Transnational Law: Legal Utopianism, Democratic Scepticism and Statist Realism," *Global Constitutionalism* 5, no. 1 (2016): 112, 119, 130.
74. Benhabib, *Another Cosmopolitanism*, 20.
75. Benhabib, *Situating the Self*, 158–59.
76. Benhabib, 75.
77. Seyla Benhabib, *Dignity in Adversity: Human Rights in Troubled Times* (Cambridge: Polity, 2011), 3.
78. Seyla Benhabib, *The Claims of Culture: Equality and Diversity in the Global Era* (Princeton, NJ: Princeton University Press, 2002), viii.
79. Benhabib, *Another Cosmopolitanism*, 170.
80. Benhabib, 159.
81. Robert Post, "Introduction," in *Another Cosmopolitanism*, ed. Robert Post (Oxford: Oxford University Press, 2006), 4.
82. Seyla Benhabib, "Twilight of Sovereignty or the Emergence of Cosmopolitan Norms?: Rethinking Citizenship in Volatile Times," *Citizenship Studies* 11, no. 1 (February 2007): 31.
83. Benhabib, 31; see also Judith Resnik, "Law's Migration: American Exceptionalism, Silent Dialogues, and Federalism's Multiple Ports of Entry," *Yale Law Journal* 15, no. 7 (2006).
84. Benhabib, *Dignity in Adversity*, 15; Benhabib, *Claims of Culture*, 35.
85. Benhabib, *Another Cosmopolitanism*, 24.

86. Jürgen Habermas, "Ich bin alt, aber nicht fromm geworden," in *Über Habermas: Gespräche mit Zeitgenossen*, ed. Michael Funken (Darmstadt: Wissenschaftliche Buchgesellschaft, 2009), 199.
87. Jürgen Habermas, "Reply to My Critics," in *Habermas and Religion*, ed. Craig J. Calhoun, Eduardo Mendieta, and Jonathan VanAntwerpen (Cambridge: Polity, 2013), 378.
88. Jürgen Habermas, "The European Nation-State and the Pressures of Globalization," *New Left Review*, no. 235 (1999): 52.
89. David Held, *Introduction to Critical Theory: Horkheimer to Habermas* (Berkeley: University of California Press, 1980), 395.
90. Seyla Benhabib, "Natural Right and Hegel: An Essay in Modern Political Philosophy," PhD diss., Yale University, 1977.

12

At the Borders of the Self

Democratic Iterations as a Theory of Postnational Sovereignty

PAUL LINDEN-RETEK

*The gift (*doron*) of Mnemosyne, Socrates insists, is like the wax in which all that we wish to guard in our memory is engraved in relief so that it may leave a mark, like that of rings, bands, or seals. We preserve our memory and our knowledge of them; we can then speak of them, and do them justice, as long as their image (*eidolon*) remains legible. But what happens when the lover of Mnemosyne has not received the gift of narration? When he doesn't know how to tell a story? When it is precisely because he keeps the memory that he loses the narrative?*

—Jacques Derrida, "Mnemosyne," *Mémoires for Paul de Man*

If there is a principal moment in autobiography or analysis that Seyla Benhabib's work centers, it is the cosmopolitan moment: diasporic, searching, tenuous, critical, transformative. And in that moment, the figure of the refugee, the exile. In her latest book, *Exile, Statelessness, and Migration*—as biographical and autobiographical as it is analytic—Benhabib ends with a rumination on hope and fear: hope for new beginnings and better times; fear for their fragility and for what is continually lost and must be mourned. Such words—as they resonate clearly for so many in these days of pandemic and threat—to the refugee, the exile, and the migrant have never ceased to ring true. Hope, Benhabib writes, must triumph over fear—and indeed her lifetime of contribution by argument and by example has shown how to think about and work to realize such ambitions in ethical and political practice.

Charles Baudelaire, in his famous poem "The Swan" from *Fleurs du mal* recalls successive images of dislocation and loss, beginning with the swan itself, "silly like all exiles, he says, and sublime, endlessly longing." I want to linger on this. The sublime of the exile has something to do with an endless longing. Can one live between categories—at the edge of inclusion—beyond the bounds of political community as one inherits it? How to recover agency in this in-between? How to give an account that seeks not just to correct for that in-between but to treat it as a moment of sublime inspiration for something otherwise: to find in that in-between a new way to live that might leave the injustices of old behind.

To think the political beyond nationality or any other inherited memberships and distinctions, and to think the human politically. Benhabib's work suggests enduring and vital insights into these profound questions. In this essay, I want to explore a particular context in which such questions are being asked and, in their own ways, answered—and to consider how thinking informed by Benhabib's insights might reveal a great deal more at stake in those answers.

This essay inquires into the philosophical foundations of sovereignty beyond the nation-state. Debates over the future organization of postnational politics and law (globally and in the European Union in particular) grapple with crises of globalization and international liberalism but also with the persistence of national sovereignty as a normative value citizens and public officials alike seek to retain.[1] Theorists accordingly have developed conflicting, often-confounding accounts of why sovereignty should be dispensed with in a political, sociological, and legal context for which it is no longer normatively desirable or descriptively accurate (the era of "postsovereignty"), or, to the contrary, why the unitary, hierarchical sovereignty of the national state remains essential and relevant.[2]

Further still, others have inquired whether sovereignty might be divided, parceled, and distributed in new legitimating institutions beyond the national state.[3] Conceptual amalgams like "late sovereignty," "mixed sovereignty," "pooled sovereignty," or "disaggregated sovereignty" promise to reorient the structures of sovereignty in the emerging postnational order.[4] Sovereignty has become an elastic and "essentially contestable concept," as the ends to which sovereign action is put are subject to critique.[5] This work has been complemented by revived debates in European political theory over the identity of constituent power in the European

Union, most prominently theorized as "mixed constituent power" (*pouvoir constituant mixte*), to which I will devote most of my attention in later parts.[6]

Sovereignty's ends and the manner in which sovereign power is parceled among actors within and beyond the nation-state might be in these ways transposed. But such contemporary debates continue to reflect the older conceptual models of political order they inherit from the history of political thought. These center the human faculties of reason and will: Hobbes's voluntaristic act of covenant; Kant's moral ordering of freedom as rationality; and Rousseau's institutional expression of the collective general will.[7] Self-government finds itself in either "the universalism of reason or the act of consent" or in the attempt to reconcile reason and will together through constitutional law.[8] Constitutional theory has traced precisely this same structure, as so-called decisionists, normativists, and relationalists have debated the conceptual grounds of the *pouvoir constituant* and its constitutional authority on the basis of will, reason, or rationalized will-formation, respectively.[9]

This theoretical schema has informed but also constrained thinking about sovereignty, and it now narrows the emancipatory possibilities of postnational political authority. These conceptual models of order signified by reason and will remain tied in essential respects to an understanding of sovereignty as mastery and the site of supreme authority—whether normative or material—in a manner that preserves the insular forms of "ordering" that postnational challenges to sovereignty aimed to overcome.[10] No space is left, in these accounts, for that work of longing, for the presence of an in-between. And thus the presumed conception of the self, the character of political principle, and the nature of the free act each remain confined to the modernist vision of agency that reproduces, rather than challenges, the prerogatives of national sovereignty.

This is a fundamental and persistent difficulty. Scholars have noted, for instance, that the wholly divergent accounts given by Carl Schmitt and Hans Kelsen of the locus of sovereignty nevertheless are guided by a central logical structure: the search for the supreme order that would exercise "effective control."[11] This view privileges authority's uniformity and singularity—no matter whether grounded in the self-standing autonomy of will or the superseding rule of validity freed of rational contradiction.[12] Contemporary debates over sovereignty under globalization for this reason cluster around the "decisionistic" revival of will-formation in the national state or the "normativist" creation of a federated structure in which principles of international law (universal human rights, territorial integrity, self-determination, and sovereign equality) render clear the lines of authority among national and global governing institutions.[13]

Even relationalist thinkers—for whom pluralism and the dynamic relationship of law and politics supranationally are precisely at issue—tend to reproduce this same distortion.[14] Accounts proposing open-ended, provisional forms of constitutional ordering might rearrange sovereignty into conceptual compounds like "shared sovereignty." But they do not in fact modify—and make *plural*—the nature of sovereign power itself. In the division or sharing or distribution of that power, its essence and nature are not yet themselves the subjects of modulation or critique.

Considering the reordered political space of the European Union as our foremost example, we encounter various deformations: corrosive illiberalisms, an internal fiscal hegemony of German-crafted ordoliberalism, and, externally, a violent regime of border control and migration deterrence. These are complex problems; but they together signal a distinctive concern: that we find an architecture of power but not a transformation of power itself or a transformation, more specifically, of that desire for mastery still at the root of modernist sovereign authority. If new relationships are created in this revised architecture of power, they tend to be rather thin and transactional ones: market-inflected; intergovernmental; executive-led; administrative and regulatory in character; and, not least, deeply exclusionary at Europe's external borders.

This suggests a limit to our imagination about politics and public power: either a narrow liberal nationalism, or an increasingly insulated and violently self-sufficient continental regime. These are registers of sovereign realignment. But they betray a rather fundamental misunderstanding of the problems, struggles, conflicts, and miseries of the present. They retreat from the task of more foundational democratic and critical renewal that would take seriously the position of the in-between.

The enduring investment in sovereignty as "mastery" neglects, in the first instance, the potential of sovereign authority to *relate* individuals and communities—not merely to order or to command without interference. It limits the promise of a postnational form of sovereignty that would more creatively transform a political community's claim to self-identity and would alter the terms of recognition and acknowledgment it sets for its relationship with others. This distorts, in particular, the character of free political action with others, eliding the central agonist insight that politics always retains its potential to challenge the more insular dividing lines national sovereignty demarcates.[15] It restricts how we might envision sovereign agency beyond the aspiration, as Patchen Markell puts it, "to be able to act independently, without experiencing life among others as a source of vulnerability, or as a site of possible alienation or self-loss."[16] And in this sense it ignores, symbolically and in practice, the voices and lessons of the migrant, the exile, and the refugee. In what follows, I tie each of these concerns together in a preliminary sketch of postnational sovereignty inspired by Seyla Benhabib's concept of "democratic iterations."

As its terminology suggests, "democratic iterations" is a delicate balance of thinking in modern and postmodern registers—a normative commitment to democratic agency, and an acknowledgment of the iterable and iterated character of any shared normative meaning. It is this balance that promises political agency, while rejecting the lure of mastery. How so? "Democratic iterations" reframes the work of rational opinion- and will-formation as a process of remembering, reinterpreting, and reconfiguring public norms. This is a recurring, creative, generative practice of "public argument, deliberation and exchange through which universalist rights claims are contested and contextualized, invoked and revoked, posited and repositioned, throughout legal and political institutions, as well as in the associations of civil society."[17] Its iterative character hinges on the ability of political subjects to see in the past a contingent experience that could have been otherwise—to rescue surplus meaning from the categories and events one inherits. Perhaps in the spirit of Walter Benjamin's pearl diver, who "select[s] his precious fragments from the pile of debris."[18] Iterations might appear, in their own way, as a rich and strange form of autonomy: a sublime if endless longing—in a sense always deferred but also redemptive of the norms it carries.

Iteration evolves a norm's semantic meaning; but it also suggests, further, that this political development of normativity is a condition for the norm's continued existence as such. A norm—its meaning, its authoritative presence—only functions insofar as it is iterated, as political actors set the proportion of continuity and discontinuity through time. As Benhabib writes: "Every act of iteration involves making sense of an authoritative original in a new and different context through interpretation. . . . Meaning is enhanced and transformed; conversely, when the creative appropriation of that authoritative original ceases or stops making sense, then the original loses its authority upon us as well."[19] This insight holds profound consequences for the legitimacy of the national constitutional state—and, in turn, for the character of a postnational sovereign relation.

"Democratic iterations" centers the practice of selection and description—the construction of stories—that underlies any principle or rule and imbues it with meaning and legitimacy. As long as this practice functions beneath the surface of politics and law, unreflectively, it is the source of ideological closure—as it often is for the national state. But by bringing this practice to the fore, an iterative framework of politics and law subjects itself to creative interpretation—to retelling by "outsiders," however conceived, who might always challenge and disrupt dominant renderings of law and thus challenge the cultural and moral values of a particular public order.

To see the constructive relationship between public meaning and iteration attunes us differently, therefore, to the accepted discourses that stabilize relations among us, to what public principles and legal rules *are* and what it means to apply them, and, finally, to the identity of the public "author" who writes them. Iteration thus introduces resources in public life—hermeneutic, social, relational, institutional—to resist homogenizing our legal order. Let me explore more closely why and how this might be the case, with reference to the three points of intellectual contact for Benhabib's reflections on the iterability of politics and law: the thought of Jacques Derrida, Hannah Arendt, and the constitutional theorist Robert Cover.

While complex as an account of semantic meaning and the tensions alive in the essence of sovereignty, the concept of "iterability" is perhaps most vividly captured in Derrida's retelling of the story of Echo. In Ovid's allegory, Echo can be heard by the Narcissus she loves only by appropriating his voice, by repeating what he has spoken. But with those same words Echo creates meaning that is her own. Derrida writes, "Echo thus lets be heard by whoever wants to hear it, by whoever might love hearing it, something other than what she seems to be saying. Although she repeats, without simulacrum, what she has just heard, another simulacrum slips in to make her response something more than a mere reiteration."[20] We find in Echo's story the implications of iteration for the location of the self, for how one's self-definition is preceded by the words one inherits from the other, and thus for how the dislocation of meaning in time shatters a coherent, intact, sovereign self, but thereby also frees it from isolation. One is forever speaking another's language, borrowing it in order to speak, and returning its words with new meaning. Derrida's reading of this scene captures the creative possibility of iterability and of democratic iterations—it is "at the intersection of repetition and the unforeseeable" that "one does not see *coming* what remains *to come*."[21]

The expectations of iterability as at once a structure of meaning and a presupposition for political practice signal its vital link, in Benhabib's thought, with Hannah Arendt's articulation of a narratival view of political action and political freedom. On Arendt's account, one is pressed as an actor by the immediacy of present aims, unable to understand the significance of what one does, or even one's own deeper motivations for acting. The compression of the present, where future and past are "aimed at the one who is creating his present," means the creativity of action—its ability to initiate something new in the world—is tied to its unpredictability.[22] But if agency depends on the "boundlessness" of action, from the viewpoint of the actor, agency is experienced as a confounding burden.[23] The actor, Arendt writes, "appears much more the victim and the sufferer than the author and doer of what he has done."[24] And this vulnerability means an actor is never the author who decides alone, a fact that often drives frustration and disappointment with action and thereby yields reason "to hold in contempt the human capacity for freedom."[25] Because the world is essentially perspectival, actors are always becoming "the object of the tale of others."[26]

This is why, for Arendt, action must be "completed" by the spectator's interpretation, by the storyteller who weaves the narrative of what has happened, such that spectator and actor alike might understand its significance. The spectator understands the way action is vulnerable to forgetfulness and to the passage of time, its fragility. And, thereby, the spectator invokes the salience of a broader community of memory in which action can find such a home, which can free actors of their own presentism.[27] Action is thus immersed, as Benhabib writes, in a "web of interpretations," what she calls "narrativity."[28] The narrativity of action reflects the fact that action relies on the interpretation of others for its preservation over time—for the full disclosure of the action's meaning and, with it, the identity of those who act.[29]

Arendt's phenomenological reconstruction of political action holds implications for the traditional conception of sovereignty. If understood as "the ideal of uncompromising self-sufficiency and mastership," sovereignty is "contradictory to the very condition of plurality": the recognition that "men, not Man, live on the earth and inhabit the world."[30] And insofar as it denies plurality, sovereign action also undermines the possibility that it will be comprehended and that its effects will endure in time. The temporality of the web of narratives thus creates a nuanced, paradoxical relationship in political action between dependency and the potential for creativity and freedom into the future. Arendt's rendering suggests that a proper revision of sovereignty lies with reclaiming the connections between narrative, plurality, and time.[31] This is precisely, I argue, what the concept of "democratic iterations" aims to do. Let us delve further still to understand how it might do so.

This shift in our understanding of sovereignty foregrounds the two familiar moments or modalities or potentialities of Arendtian political action: promising and forgiving. These together sustain political freedom while denying sovereignty's tendency toward closure and its conceit of self-sufficiency. The first moment is the making of a promise. "Sovereignty, which is always spurious if claimed by an isolated single entity," Arendt writes, "assumes, in the case of many men mutually bound by promises, a certain limited reality."[32] Promise-making aims to stabilize the expectations of a passing present and thereby to assuage the unpredictability of action. But the promise, because it is always expressed through the narrative fabric of the world and remembered through the interpretive stories spectators tell, must itself remain faithful to the plurality of action. It is premised on its potential to be misremembered or broken. A promise as promise affirms its vulnerability to iteration.

This breakability of the promise occasions the second moment of narrative agency: forgiveness. If the breakability of promise-making points to the ways action can always be corrupted but not "undone," forgiveness offers a "possible redemption."[33] "Without being forgiven, released from the consequences of what we have done," Arendt writes, "our capacity to act would, as it were, be confined to one single deed from which we could never recover."[34] To act without the possibility of forgiveness would undermine the very same plurality and open-ended character of action. Plurality is erased to the same extent that the sublime longing for time is given no public form. The absence of forgiveness confines an act, so to speak, to timelessness and thereby to a solitude—an alienation from others and an alienation from the narrative fabric of the world. It condemns the actor, as Arendt writes in her retelling of Kafka's parable "He," to "an extended Now on which [the actor] spends his life."[35] The act of forgiveness, however, is not a reaction that simply closes the existing circuit: "it is the only reaction which does not merely re-act but acts anew and unexpectedly, unconditioned by the act which provoked it."[36] Forgiveness recomposes the narratives that confer identity to allow for the actor to go on in a different way. Forgiveness is neither forgetting nor antipolitical. It is a public act that shifts an existing narrative's meaning, thereby resituating the identities of those it describes in a manner conducive to a shared future. This grants new possibility for both "the one who forgives and the one who is forgiven."[37]

Insofar as promising and forgiveness sustain the iterable character of political action, they also hold open the possibility of a postnational agency, a shared agency that relies on the other to endure. It reminds the polity that its actions will form part of its narrative history, interpreted by other states and other generations. The expectations of sovereign freedom are, on this account, not to act in isolation without burden or contradiction but instead to act in a manner for which one can take responsibility among others. The measure of freedom is not degree of mastery but degree of critical awareness of what is done, with what effect, to whom, and why. Narrative freedom is not merely one's own, precisely by virtue of the rhythm by which we are able to make promises and to forgive.

This revised character of agency recommends a further analytic shift. The proper domain of democratic iterations is neither the faculty of reason nor that of will, each of which admits a more limited, less dynamic notion of political time. Democratic iterations centers, instead, the faculty of judgment. Judging, Arendt writes, "removes itself only temporarily [from the world] and with the intention of a later return."[38] Unlike the withdrawal of the philosopher, which is "solitary" and "self-sufficient," the withdrawal of judgment remains dependent on "the views of others," embedded within the plurality of the world.[39] Arendt's critical reading of Kant illuminates how this element of human plurality is present in the *Critique of Judgment* but ignored in the *Critique of Pure Reason* and the *Critique of Practical Reason*: Kant's reasonable being and his moral actor are concerned more with self than with the plurality of the world.[40] The modes of evaluation differ accordingly: the "spectator" appeals in his judgment not to the "laws of practical reason" subject to a metaphysics of general validity but to the "communicability" of precisely those stories that provide "completion" to human action.[41] Human beings—"earthbound creatures, living in communities, endowed with common sense, *sensus communis*, a community sense"—are "not autonomous" as the observer seeks to be.[42] They "need each other's company even for thinking."[43] The place of judgment is this in-between: between past and future, between self and other. To judge is to be attuned to the curious passage of time outside of one's prerogative of control: that is to say, the passage of time, as "democratic iterations" suggest, between what is promised and what might yet be forgiven.

To conceive sovereignty as the authority to *judge* advises a distinctive mode of sovereign self-authorship, in which legitimation attaches no longer to the coherent unfolding of commitments on the basis of norm or decision but instead to keeping alive a shifting "web of narratives" whose meanings are fragile, complex, and interdependent. This special character of judging resignifies the universal over time and takes responsibility for the partiality of any such resignification. That is to say, at the heart of a particular claim to judgment is the admission of its constitutive limits: the dialectical movement of the "concrete universal." This is how the forces that had previously consolidated the universal—a preceding and overriding concept or rule—are revealed to be more contingent and less fully formed or comprehended in themselves. And this is how, in the course of iteration, the identity of a democratic public itself can intelligibly change. An exposure to critique and difference, without losing hold of agency altogether.

Judgment has a normativity of its own that is distinct from reasoned decision-making. It is based of the specific requirements of the "power of judgment" that must aim to situate actors in history and time within a "web" of narratives among a plurality of others.[44] To judge, as Mark Antaki writes, is "to locate oneself in and tell a story."[45] The power of judgment rests, in effect, on staging an encounter between actor and spectator—in comprehending what forgiveness means in light of the promise made and what was promised in light of what can be forgiven. The story a judgment tells asserts reasons and offers justifications; but its normative work functions only through the strands of recollection the story sustains. It tests claims to validity as much as and insofar as it engages the work of hermeneutic disclosure.

The faculty of judgment confirms the curious temporal arc at the borders of selfhood and identity: that our shared norms are in fact always a product, not just a basis, of our engagement with others. The structure of judgment cannot be confined to a logic of mastery, for its reliance on plurality calls forth as a political question the identity of the relevant community of memory that can lay claim to forgive. This is why the "memory" produced by the power of judgment can be no straightforward recollection of the past. It is an iterative understanding of recovery—an original appropriation of the past, making the past speak as one looks toward the future. One begins, as does the internal critic or the common law judge, with the language one inherits in order to move that language into a new world. There is, Arendt writes, "an element of experiment in the critical interpretation of the past."[46] A promise always addresses a community whose bounds are not fully known or certain at the moment the promise is made. And if this is the case, in turn it means that the identities of those who promise are, in the act of promising, themselves decentered, deferred over time, in expectation of what, through an act of forgiveness, they will understand themselves to have been. A sublime longing for agency becomes, in truth, the only form of agency open for us to have.

These are abstract reflections. But I suggest we see in this a structure of postnational sovereign authority. If this still appears an unusual way to conceive a sovereign relation, consider if we read the currently vogue theories of mixed constituent power in the European Union in precisely this manner. To appreciate the full implications of this reassessment, let me first outline in brief strokes the rendering given to *pouvoir constituant mixte* by Jürgen Habermas. Placing himself in the debate over European democratic authority between its dominant poles of *demoi*-cracy and regional cosmopolitanism, Habermas has adopted the concept as the most promising frame in which to apprehend European constituent power.[47] The concept names a dual constitutional subject comprising individuals acting in two distinct roles at once: as European Union citizens, on the one hand, and citizens of the national member states, on the other.[48] The status of EU citizenship provides new standing for individuals to act directly on behalf of a supranational political community with its own legislative powers. Citizens as the bearers of popular sovereignty are "split into two personae from the beginning."[49] This serves as a rational reconstruction of political authority in the European Union.

But Habermas's rendering of this dual structure of authority entails a questionable presumption: that the accepted purpose of postnational sovereignty is to carry "levels of justice and freedom" achieved by the national constitutional state through to the level of transnational democracy.[50] This creates an untenable asymmetry, at once favoring national orderings of constitutional rights and cutting short the critical evaluation of those rights as part of postnational politics.[51] A decisive feature of this asymmetry, I argue, is precisely its narrowing of political time: a form of "presentism," which foreshortens the historical and imaginative dimensions of political life to a conflict among the constellation of interests that are taken to be fully formed in the present. This obscures a central promise of postnational sovereignty: to put to scrutiny the extent to which existing national systems continue to draw upon a history of stabilized claims of identity and recognition to prejudge for others what should remain democratically contestable. It retrenches the old sovereigntist exercise of control.

But what if we placed this schema of postnational sovereignty in the frame of "democratic iterations"? Consider the national and supranational pendants of *pouvoir constituant mixte* to create a space in which the distinctive capacity for iterated judgment can arise, a space intended to disclose the iterative character of norm and decision. And consider how disclosing this iterative character entails, in part, demystifying the contingent and historical bounds of peoplehood, the complex entanglements of political economy, the cultural and ideological presuppositions that are consolidated under the heading "nation-state," or "the international system." The fault with the Habermasian rational reconstruction of *pouvoir constituant mixte* is that it neglects to secure the plurality of political action: not just in its homogenization and retrenchment of national interest, but also in the way the abstraction of supranational community encouraged a metaphysical retreat from the world. In Habermas's view, the future-oriented disposition of supranational politics is not conceived as a practice of promise-making that could form certain defined relationships of interpretation, remembrance, and forgiveness with the national constituent power. And the national constituent power is bound to its past in a way that is insufficiently reflective. It is, in Arendt's terms, reactive and defensive, caught in its own world of deeds that cannot be redeemed. What is lost is the cycle of promise-making and forgiveness that connects both pendants of mixed constituent power—where both national and supranational actors have futures and pasts that intertwine. This link would rescue both the fleetingness of future-oriented promises, and the settled histories of national traditions whose exclusionary or extractive qualities might be forgiven. It would offer supranational community a certain permanence and durability in the world, and to national polities it would recover a new beginning.

If the supranational and national powers are each to promise and to forgive, they must alternatively serve as actors and spectators, creating together the web of narratives in which such faculties can be exercised. The model of shared sovereignty as a narrative agency of democratic iterations proposes just this structure. It reflects Arendt's insight, expressed exquisitely by Margaret Canovan, that "it is the space between them that unites them, rather than some quality inside each of them."[52] Formed by the alternation of "seeing and being-seen, hearing and being-heard," narrative agency is characterized—descriptively and normatively—by (a) action in anticipation of interpretation by others and (b) interpretation of others in view of one's own renewed action to come. In the *pouvoir constituant mixte*, remember that one assumes a split posture, acting in alternation as citizen of a national and a supranational polity. When one acts in the first role, one also subsequently interprets this action as a spectator from the perspective of the second, and vice versa. One perceives one's own action only by the traces this action leaves.

The actor makes a promise that is left for the spectator to interpret. If the spectator "withdraws to return," the actor returns in anticipation of a withdrawal. The art of a faithfully postnational agency lies in sustaining this rhythm: to know that one's action must claim a response over which one cannot exercise control; and to know that one's interpretation of another's action is always a trace left for that other to judge, in turn.

This practice of narrative interpretation grounds a different kind of *polis*, where the process of remembrance and inscription is spread across political communities, and where the need for translation becomes more acute. If in Arendt's account the Greek *polis* served as the "community of memory" that would enable acts to be remembered and thereby give them both duration and meaning, the mixed constituent power pluralizes the web of narratives in which one acts and remembers.[53] In so doing, a post-national *polis* entails a kind of risk, an opening, an augmentation that is particularly demanding—precisely because it asks citizens to anticipate how they might remember others who are not immediately their fellows.[54] When the community of memory is pluralized, when there are multiple communities of memory that are tasked with remembering, the terms by which any one particular community can remember are altered. This requires that citizens enter politics with the intention more than merely to test their previously settled criteria for validity. They are asked, instead, in the words of Linda Zerilli, to "learn new meanings for words, new ways in which objects can be disclosed."[55]

To be more concrete, the notion that the constitutional orders of EU member states are "guarantors of the level of justice and freedom already achieved" would here be put to the interpretation of both national and supranational citizens alike.[56] Such achievements are not merely to be defended as they are; to be truly defended and endure, they must be given an interpretation. For otherwise one would risk misapprehending the achievements of national states as merely there, and merely one's own. This small interval of temporal deferral, when one can no longer understand these achievements as fully formed in the present, creates the space for imaginative critique and for forgiveness of past exclusion. And the same is true for the institutions created by the nascent supranational polity. They similarly do not point to a future set apart from the judgments of the past; they require the past, as much as the future, to interpret their meaning. For this reason, new supranational forms of predominantly market citizenship, for example, should rightly be judged for how they interrupt and modify the previously valued social relations within national communities and for how they might be reembedded within those relations.

The structure of mixed constituent power is better conceived, then, as a form of shared and iterated judgment. This judgment scrutinizes how the decisions and institutions of presently *constituted* powers affect communities beyond the narrow definition of distinct national or territorial groupings. Such scrutiny works through the construction of narratives. It complicates how existing problems are projected and narrated as experiences merely for existing political subjects—the "we" of a particular national community, for example. Instead, the plural web of narratives draws attention to analogous and entangled concerns, a sensitivity to those "shared predicaments" that was previously obscured by the national frame alone. Such a model of agency takes its cue from various strands of critical theory, which hold that structures of power are reproduced by the stories society tells, and thus that counternarratives can be deployed to bring such structures to the surface for scrutiny. Objective measures—metaphysical points of value—such as more abstract and formal entitlements of rights, for example, are on their own insufficient for comprehending or counteracting the lived experiences and subjectivities through which domination, discrimination, and injustice are enacted.

There is a further, vital consequence of this way of thinking about sovereignty in a globalized world. The joining of sovereignty to judgment suggests the necessary place within the postnational constellation, as Benhabib has long emphasized, of refugee and asylum law. By returning the democratic citizen to the fragile grounds of action, we also connect democratic authority to the fate of the refugee. When understood as democratic iterations, the legal claims of the refugee avail of the same form of normativity as does the political standing of the social critic or the critical hermeneutics of the common law judge. Despite a veneer of human rights *simpliciter*, they do not project a "view from nowhere"; instead, they reveal a view from just "outside the walls of the city," without which the symbolic and material repressions of the *polis*—and thus its ethical limits— would remain illegible, unamenable to judgment, and, thus, in the end, democratically illegitimate. If democratic iterations reframes the work of rational opinion- and will-formation as a process of remembering, reinterpreting, and reconfiguring public norms, it sets for jurists and for legal process a correlative task. Benhabib's engagement with the work of American constitutional theorist Robert Cover—as well as the connection between "democratic iterations" and Cover's notion of "jurisgenerativity"—is essential to understanding how the legal claims of others, argued before courts exercising judicial review, are constitutive of the legitimacy of democratic communities.[57]

Consider a case that Professor Benhabib and I have often discussed: *X and X v. Belgium* before the European Court of Justice—and, in particular, the exemplary opinion of Advocate General Mengozzi.[58] The case concerned a married couple from Aleppo and their three infant children. The father traveled at great risk to the Belgian Embassy in Beirut, Lebanon, where he submitted applications for humanitarian visas for his family. The stated purpose of his application was to bring his family from the inferno of Aleppo and to apply for asylum in Belgium directly. One immediately understands the salience of this application and the great saving power it would afford to the family—not only from war but also from a possible perilous crossing across the sea to Europe. The humanitarian visa was, admittedly, a short cut to the more dangerous and uncertain process thousands of other refugees contemplate each day.

The question posed to the European Court of Justice by the referring Belgian court was whether the EU Charter of Fundamental Rights imposes a positive obligation on Member States to grant humanitarian visas, if it is known that such protection is necessary to avoid exposing applicants to inhuman and degrading treatment or torture and to indirect *refoulement*, in violation of Articles 4 and 18 of the Charter. In a terse judgment of only fourteen substantive paragraphs, the Court concluded that the case fell outside the scope of EU law and thus the provisions of the EU Charter were inapplicable. The intended aim for which the family requested the visa—a subsequent application for asylum—was not a legitimate purpose covered by the EU Visa Code, and thus no human rights protections under the Charter could be activated. Discretion to grant or deny the humanitarian visa was left exclusively to the national law of Member States.

As a counterpoint, the advisory opinion written by Advocate General Mengozzi resisted the Court's formalism and sought more from the law and its jurisgenerative potential.[59] He concluded that the Charter does apply, and that EU states do indeed have a positive obligation to issue humanitarian visas under EU law when fundamental human rights are in question. Although Mengozzi's opinion is constructed around the human rights provisions in European law, he does not take these as simple markers of universal status, an objective kind of value to be read off as authoritative. Indeed, were he to do this, his words would perhaps be no more persuasive than the formalistic logic of the Court itself. Mengozzi does something more involved, more difficult, and more remarkable for it. His analysis illuminates a number of the dimensions of postnational thinking and its narrative form of political agency. His opinion shows that this idea is not fanciful but can, at least in part, be found in existing judicial practice of international organizations.

Let me illustrate Mengozzi's method with just a few examples. Bookending Mengozzi's opinion is the concern that EU actors—the Member States and European Commission alike in their submissions to the Court—have failed in their responsibility to interpret the values of the European Union in light of the exigencies of the present moment: to trace, in other words, the narrative possibilities of European law. Mengozzi in his opening paragraphs expresses a rare and valuable sensitivity to this narrative structure of judgment. "Need it be recalled," he writes, "that the Union 'is founded on the values of respect for human dignity... and respect for human rights' and its 'aim is to promote... its values,' including in its relations with the wider world?"[60] Here, the values noted in the European treaties are called to mind not in any simplistic sense, as though they were always available to be applied to whatever facts might come. They are instead caught in the play of time, at risk of being forgotten, displaced, or ignored. Mengozzi is prompted to refer to them in an act of judgment because of the facts of the case at hand—in light of the suffering of those in need of international protection. In so recovering these values, he subtly reframes them, rearticulating their meaning and their relevance anew. Mengozzi continues by noting with regret that none of the fourteen Member State governments who made submissions to the Court made reference to these values. What prompts this regret is not a neglect of those values generally as a matter of respect for any timeless meaning of the Treaties. Rather, it is due to their resonance, as he writes, "in relation to the situation into which the applicants in the main proceedings have been plunged."[61] Mengozzi remains guided in his judgment by the relation to the facts and to the ethical exigencies of the singular case.

Further, Mengozzi's motivating concern anticipates the peril of new situations in which European state power untethers itself from Charter protections. A narrow reading of the Charter's applicability would threaten to sever the "parallelism between EU action, whether by its institutions or through its Member States, and application of the Charter."[62] Citing the Court's decisions in *NS and others* and *Fransson*, Mengozzi argues that neither the state's discretion in applying Article 25(1)(a) of the Visa Code nor the extraterritorial deployment of such discretion negates the Charter's application.[63] To the contrary, they require it—for otherwise not only would any implementation of the Visa Code likely escape the Charter's protections but such consequences "would go beyond the field of visa policy alone."[64]

Mengozzi conceives doctrinal rules and principles as nodal points in time, corresponding to decisions with a history and a pedigree and a set of expectations that can be realized or disappointed or revised. Particular determinations of rights are singular events that establish a narrative chain but also suggest, in their singularity, how such a narrative could have developed differently and might yet do so in the future. Constitutional principles and the present patterns of fact each have past genealogies and future iterations that are relevant for the legal judgment. Mengozzi's opinion thus invokes the Court's case law here as an inheritance to the present, against which the meaning of the EU's guiding values—as he cites from Article 3 of the Treaty on European Union—might be again interpreted and "given concrete expression."[65] Mengozzi depicts in no uncertain terms the temporal dimensions of law: "It is the *credibility* of the Union and of its Member States which is at stake."[66] The European Union, in other words, had made a promise.

Mengozzi devotes much time to comparisons with the European Convention on Human Rights—most of them concerning the lack of the ECHR's "jurisdictional clause" in the Charter and the status of Convention rights as forming a floor but not a ceiling on Charter-based protections.[67] But Mengozzi's analogical comparison with the ECHR is especially remarkable in the following paragraphs, worth quoting in full:

> 166. One thing struck me whilst re-reading the case-law of the European Court of Human Rights for the purposes of dealing with the present case: the findings of that court relating to the situations—always horrible and tragic—[in which positive obligations have not been fulfilled] are findings made *ex post*, most often where the treatment in question has been fatal for the victims.

167. On the contrary, in the present case, all hope for the applicants has not, thus far, been lost. The proposal that I have just submitted to the Court demonstrates indeed that there is a humanitarian path, within the framework of EU law, which requires the Member States to prevent manifest infringements of the absolute rights of persons seeking international protection before it is too late.[68]

This comparison is grounds for a responsibility Mengozzi finds difficult to deny. He feels the law as it is structured today is always arriving "too late." His conclusion—a quite revolutionary reorientation to the human rights possibilities of EU law—is at once an appeal to and a vehicle for forgiveness.

As I have argued, in the space between a promise made and forgiveness sought, new relationships among citizens and communities and still excluded others are newly imagined to be possible. The open possibility of relatedness becomes the central characteristic of politics. Jurisgenerative interpretations of law create such relations by drafting the "materials and methods of a discourse" to which citizens are asked to respond.[69] As James Boyd White writes, the judicial opinion—just as it establishes for the court "an ethos, or character"—does the same for the "parties to a case and for the larger audience it addresses—the lawyers, the public, and the other agencies in government."[70] A jurisgenerative opinion explores the meaning of roles and perspectives; it rehearses certain understandings, voices, languages, and modes of thought. It stages encounters between differing points of view, sometimes resolving them but sometimes not. It retells histories and attempts, always, to speak for others who in that moment cannot speak directly for themselves.

Advocate General Mengozzi does this in several parts of his opinion. In the opening paragraphs, he writes that the "particularly alarmist tone" taken by the Czech Government in its submissions to the Court on the possibly "'fatal' consequences for the EU" must be more soberly assessed in comparison with both the broader situation and, in particular, the possible fate of asylum seekers themselves. "Although the European Union is going through a difficult period, I do not share that fear," Mengozzi writes. "It is, on the contrary, as in the main proceedings, the refusal to recognise a legal access route to the right to international protection on the territory of the Member States—which unfortunately often forces nationals of third countries seeking such protection to join, risking their lives in doing so, the current flow of illegal immigrants to EU's borders—which seems to me to be particularly worrying."[71] Mengozzi's tone here is firm but tolerant, attempting to persuade Member States and their citizens that the practical concerns they might have must be contextualized.

In the concluding paragraphs of the opinion, Mengozzi does something similar, this time positioning certain actors together in novel ways. He refers to the "principle of solidarity and fair sharing of responsibility . . . between the Member States,"[72] which is enshrined in Article 80 of the Treaty on the Functioning of the European Union but has hardly helped thus far to correct for the Dublin Regulation's systemic imbalances. Mengozzi then brings the point home, drawing a comparison between those EU states on its external border and the applicants themselves: "In extreme conditions such as those that the applicants have endure," he writes, "their option to choose is as limited as the option of the Member States of the Mediterranean Basin to turn themselves into landlocked countries."[73]

It is a powerful rhetorical move, illuminating relations of solidarity and mutual feeling that are not immediately self-evident. Mengozzi does not resolve the tension between core and peripheral states at the heart of Dublin's inequities. But he does connect this tension, explicitly, with the violence done to refugees. Indeed, he aligns the plight of European citizens with those who seek to find safety and shelter among them. The present inadequacies of European policy, then, imperil not only refugee lives but also Europe's own foundational authority to judge the merit of their claims. Mengozzi reveals poignantly how, to tell stories about ourselves, we depend on the narratives of others. The European Court of Justice in the end did not follow the opinion of its advocate general. The Court was, as Robert Cover would say, unprepared to see the law grow. But surely this kind of imaginative recounting—this telling of a story—belongs in a legal opinion. It concerns questions of norm and of fact—but it casts them, in the final analysis, as questions concerning our ability to judge.

Shahram Khosravi in a recent essay recounted the following story of a deportation from Europe to Afghanistan: "Early in the afternoon of May 8th, 2019, people who were in the departure area of the Budapest International Airport witnessed several police officers dragging a woman towards a gate to put her onboard an airplane for deportation to Kabul. She resisted and screamed words, which historicised a potential future for many of us: 'One day you will be refugees too, like me, and that day you will remember this day.' " "The presence of the stranger," Khosravi writes, "reminds us of a past we don't want to remember, and of a possible future we don't want to imagine."[74] What will we have remembered; what will the other have made us remember—that we otherwise have worked so hard to repress, to keep out of mind? The contingent comfort of our own security of personhood, of home, predicated on the tolerance of dislocation and despair elsewhere. What will we have remembered—and what will we have learned about ourselves? Who will we then have understood ourselves to be? It is a curious arc of memory and narrative that the judgment of others presents to us—that accepting the open iterability of our own norms and decisions reveals. As Guyora Binder once put it, "Every act of sovereignty inscribes a history upon the ruled; every history is a claim to sovereignty."[75] The contradictions of national sovereignty in a globalized world will remain until we perceive the depth of this idea, and find a way to bring these sovereignties—dueling and violent—into the frame of a common world we share, in which democratic judgment is again possible.

The great innovation in European postnationalism, I have argued, is the possibility of institutionalizing the narrative character of political action. Benhabib's vision of democratic iterations begins with a simple gesture—a taking up of meaning that appears more stable and whole than it in fact is. In this sense does mixed constituent power promise to challenge the more insular and inward-looking forms of democratic self-authorship that have hitherto shaped influential understandings—and the social imaginary—of popular sovereignty. Just as the threads between past and future enable judgment, the narrative structure of constituent power enables what can be recognized as postnational political authority and agency. The learning process of the postnational state functions in these terms: as the spaces created among peoples also create a space within one's own polity for imagination and learning. For we know—exactly as we reflect on Seyla Benhabib's work in this volume—that we cannot learn alone.

NOTES

1. Neil MacCormick, "Beyond the Sovereign State," *Modern Law Review* 56 (1993): 1; Neil MacCormick, *Questioning Sovereignty: Law, State, and Nation in the European Commonwealth* (Oxford: Oxford University Press, 1999); Jürgen Habermas, "The European Nation-State: On the Past and Future of Sovereignty and Citizenship," *Public Culture* 10, no. 2 (1998): 397–416; David Grewal, "Three Theses on the Current Crisis of International Liberalism," *Indiana Journal of Global Legal Studies* 25, no. 2 (2018): 595–621; see Robert Jackson, *Sovereignty: The Evolution of an Idea* (Cambridge: Polity, 2007), 113.

2. MacCormick, *Questioning Sovereignty*; Thomas Pogge, "Cosmopolitanism and Sovereignty," *Ethics* (1992): 103; Andreas Paulus, "The International Legal System as a Constitution," in *Ruling the World?: Constitutionalism, International Law, and Global Governance*, ed. J. Dunoff and J. Trachtman (Cambridge: Cambridge University Press, 2009), 69; Michael Fowler, *Law, Power, and the Sovereign State: The*

Evolution and Application of the Concept of Sovereignty (University Park: Penn State University Press, 1995).

3. Neil Walker, "Taking Constitutionalism Beyond the State," *Political Studies* 56 (2008): 519.
4. Neil Walker, "Late Sovereignty in the European Union," in *Sovereignty in Transition*, ed. N. Walker (Oxford: Hart, 2003), 3; Richard Bellamy, "Sovereignty, Post-Sovereignty and Pre-Sovereignty: Three Models of the State, Democracy and Rights Within the EU," in Walker, *Sovereignty in Transition*, 186; Robert Keohane and Stanley Hoffmann, *The New European Community: Decisionmaking and Institutional Change* (Boulder, CO: Westview, 1991); Pierre Pescatore, "L'apport du droit communautaire au droit international public," *Cahier de Droit Européen* 501 (1970); Anne-Marie Slaughter, "Disaggregated Sovereignty: Towards the Public Accountability of Global Government Networks," *Government and Opposition* 39, no. 2 (2004).
5. Samantha Besson, "From Integration to Integrity: Should European Law Speak with Just One Voice?," *European Law Journal* 10 (2004): 257, 271.
6. See generally the March 2017 symposium in the *Journal of Common Market Studies*, titled "The EU's Pouvoir Constituant Mixte," *Journal of Common Market Studies* 55, no. 2 (2017): 165–222. See also Claudio Franzius, *Europäisches Verfassungsrechtsdenken* (Tübingen: Mohr Siebeck 2010); Armin von Bogdandy, "The European Lesson for International Democracy: The Significance of Articles 9 to 12 EU Treaty for International Organizations," *European Journal of International Law* 23, no. 2 (2012): 315–34.
7. Thomas Hobbes, *Leviathan*, ed. C. MacPherson (1651; New York: Penguin, 1968), 228 (defining commonwealth as "One Person, of whose Acts a great Multitude, by mutuall [sic] Covenants one with another, have made themselves every one the Author, to the end he may use the strength and means of them all ... for their Peace and Common Defence"; emphasis removed); Immanuel Kant, *Toward Perpetual Peace: A Philosophical Sketch* (1795; Sonnenschein, 1903); Jean-Jacques Rousseau, *The Social Contract*, trans. M. Cranston (1742; New York: Penguin, 1968); *The Federalist*, ed. C. Rossiter (New York: Signet, 1961).
8. Paul Kahn, "Reason and Will in the American Founding," *Yale Law Journal* 98, no. 3 (1989): 449–517, 452.
9. Carl Schmitt, *Constitutional Theory*, trans. J. Seitzer (1928; Durham, NC: Duke University Press, 2008); Hans Kelsen, *Introduction to the Problems of Legal Theory [Reine Rechtslehre]*, trans. B. L. Paulson and S. L. Paulson (Oxford: Clarendon, 1992), 57; Relational theorists of constituent power respond to Rousseau's "paradox of founding" by substituting dialectical, process-oriented, or procedural approaches involving a multitude of actors joined together in political action. See Jürgen Habermas, *Between Facts and Norms: Contributions to a Discourse Theory of Law and Democracy*, trans. William Rehg (1992; Cambridge, MA: MIT Press, 1996), 136, 486; see Martin Loughlin, "The Concept of Constituent Power," *European Journal of Political Theory* 13 (2014): 218.
10. See Patchen Markell, *Bound by Recognition* (Princeton, NJ: Princeton University Press, 2003).

11. Hans Kelsen, "Sovereignty and the International Law," *Georgetown Law Journal* 47, no. 4 (1960): 631. See Jonathan Havercroft, *Captives of Sovereignty* (Cambridge: Cambridge University Press, 2011) 5; see also Jens Bartelson, *Sovereignty as Symbolic Form* (London: Routledge, 2014). This is the reason Hobbesian thinking and Kantian thinking about internationalism run rather easily together. See David Grewal, "The Domestic Analogy Revisted: Hobbes on International Order," *Yale Law Journal* 125 (2016): 618 (observing that, despite earlier interpretations to the contrary, the two traditions in fact offer a remarkably harmonious diagnosis of how international peace among commonwealths and republics should arise: through intergovernmental cooperation, not supranational political membership).
12. See Christian Volk, "The Problem of Sovereignty in Globalized Times," *Law, Culture, and the Humanities* (2019): 1–23, 8.
13. Dieter Grimm, *Sovereignty: The Origin and Future of a Political and Legal Concept* (New York: Columbia University Press, 2015); Jean Cohen, *Globalization and Sovereignty: Rethinking Legality, Legitimacy, and Constitutionalism* (Cambridge: Cambridge University Press, 2014).
14. Bellamy, "Sovereignty, Post-Sovereignty and Pre-Sovereignty," 186; Miguel Poiares Maduro, "Contrapunctual Law: Europe's Constitutional Pluralism in Action," in Walker, *Sovereignty in Transition*, 521.
15. See generally Mark Wenman, *Agonistic Democracy: Constituent Power in the Era of Globalisation* (Cambridge: Cambridge University Press, 2013).
16. Patchen Markell, *Bound by Recognition* (Princeton, NJ: Princeton University Press, 2003), 12.
17. Seyla Benhabib, *The Rights of Others: Aliens, Citizens and Residents* (Cambridge: Cambridge University Press, 2004), 179, as well as the same at 19–24; Seyla Benhabib, *Dignity in Adversity: Human Rights in Troubled Times* (Cambridge: Polity, 2011), 129; Seyla Benhabib, "Democratic Exclusions and Democratic Iterations: Dilemmas of 'Just Membership' and Prospects of Cosmopolitan Federalism," *European Journal of Political Theory* 6, no. 4 (2007): 449.
18. See Hannah Arendt, "Walter Benjamin: 1892–1940," in *Men in Dark Times* (New York: Harcourt Brace, 1968), 200.
19. Seyla Benhabib, *Another Cosmopolitanism: Hospitality, Sovereignty and Democratic Iterations*, ed. R. Post (Oxford: Oxford University Press, 2006), 48.
20. Jacques Derrida, *Rogues: Two Essays on Reason*, trans. P. A. Brault and M. Naas (Stanford: Stanford University Press, 2005), xii.
21. Derrida, xii, emphasis in original.
22. Hannah Arendt, *The Life of the Mind*, vol. 1, *Thinking* (New York: Harcourt, Brace and Jovanovich, 1977), 205.
23. See Hannah Arendt, *The Human Condition* (Chicago: University of Chicago Press, 1958), 233ff.
24. Arendt, 234.
25. Arendt, 233.
26. Seyla Benhabib, "Judgment and the Moral Foundations of Politics in Arendt's Thought," *Political Theory* 16, no. 1 (1988): 29–51, 35.

27. See Sheldon Wolin, "Hannah Arendt and the Ordinance of Time," *Social Research* 44, no. 1 (1977): 91–105, 97 ("Audience is a metaphor for the political community whose nature is to be a community of remembrance.").
28. Benhabib, "Judgment and the Moral Foundations," 32.
29. Arendt, *The Human Condition*, 184.
30. Arendt, 234, 7.
31. See Arendt, 236 ("the capacity for action [might indeed] harbor within itself certain potentialities which enable it to survive the disabilities of non-sovereignty").
32. Arendt, 245.
33. Arendt, 237.
34. Arendt, 237.
35. Arendt, *The Life of the Mind*, 1:205.
36. Arendt, *The Human Condition*, 241.
37. Arendt, 241.
38. Arendt, 92.
39. Arendt, 94.
40. Hannah Arendt, *Lectures on Kant's Political Philosophy*, ed. R. Beiner (Chicago: University of Chicago Press, 1982), 19–27.
41. Arendt, 40; Hannah Arendt, "Preface: The Gap Between Past and Future," in *Between Past and Future: Six Exercises in Political Thought* (1961; New York: Penguin, 1977), 6.
42. Arendt, *Lectures on Kant's Political Philosophy*, 27. See also p. 72.
43. Arendt, 27.
44. Hannah Arendt, *Denktagebuch*, vols. 1 and 2, ed. U. Ludz and I. Nordmann (Munich: Piper, 2003), 818.
45. Mark Antaki, "The Rationalism of Proportionality's Culture of Justification," in *Proportionality and the Rule of Law: Rights, Justification, Reasoning*, ed. G. Huscroft and others (Cambridge: Cambridge University Press, 2014), 284–308, 298.
46. Arendt, "Preface: The Gap Between Past and Future," 14.
47. Kalypso Nicolaïdis, "European Demoicracy and its Crisis," *Journal of Common Market Studies* 51, no. 2 (2013): 351–69; Erik Eriksen, "Regional Cosmopolitanism: The EU in Search of Its Legitimation" *European Journal of Futures Research* 2, no. 51 (2014): 1; Jürgen Habermas, *The Crisis of the European Union: A Response*, trans. C. Cronin (Cambridge: Polity, 2012). While Habermas's earlier engagement with European politics defended a vision of a "Federal States of Europe," his elaboration of *pouvoir constituant mixte* turns instead to a (nonstate) federation (*Bund*) as Europe's political form. Compare Jürgen Habermas, *The Postnational Constellation: Political Essays*, trans. M. Pensky (Cambridge, MA: MIT Press, 2001), 90. By contrast with Jean Cohen's federalist account structured foremost as a composite of collectivities and instead building critically on the work of Armin von Bogdandy and Claudio Franzius, Habermas pitches his reading in an "individualist idiom." Peter Niesen, "The 'Mixed' Constituent Legitimacy of the European Federation," *Journal of Common Market Studies* 55, no. 2 (2017): 183–97, 186. Compare Claudio Franzius, *Europäische Verfassungsreschtsdenken* (Tübingen: Mohr Siebeck, 2010); Armin von Bogdandy, "The European Lesson for International Democracy: The Significance

of Articles 9 to 12 EU Treaty for International Organizations," *European Journal of International Law* 23, no. 2 (2012): 315–34.
48. Habermas, *The Crisis of the European Union*, 28–37.
49. Habermas, 38.
50. Habermas, 34ff.; see generally Jürgen Habermas, "The Crisis of the European Union in the Light of a Constitutionalization of International Law," *European Journal of International Law* 23, no. 2 (2012): 344ff.
51. See Niesen, "The 'Mixed' Constituent Legitimacy of the European Federation."
52. Margaret Canovan, "Politics as Culture: Hannah Arendt and the Public Realm," *History of Political Thought* 6, no. 3 (1985): 617–42, 634.
53. See, e.g., Arendt, *The Human Condition*, 197.
54. See generally Bonnie Honig, "Declarations of Independence: Arendt and Derrida on the Problem of Founding a Republic," *American Political Science Review* 85, no. 1 (1991): 97–113; Andreas Kalyvas, *Democracy and the Politics of the Extraordinary: Max Weber, Carl Schmitt and Hannah Arendt* (Cambridge: Cambridge University Press, 2008); Wenman, *Agonistic Democracy*.
55. Linda Zerilli, *A Democratic Theory of Judgment* (Chicago: University of Chicago Press, 2016), 267.
56. Jürgen Habermas, "Democracy in Europe: Why the Development of the EU Into a Transnational Democracy Is Necessary and How It Is Possible," *European Law Journal* 21, no. 4 (2015): 546–57, 554, emphasis removed.
57. See Robert Cover, "The Supreme Court, 1982 Term—Foreword: *Nomos* and Narrative," *Harvard Law Review* 97 (1983): 4.
58. Case C-638/16 PPU, *X and X v État belge* [2017] ECLI:EU:C:2017:173.
59. Opinion of Advocate General Mengozzi, Case C-638/16 PPU, *X and X v État belge* [2017] ECLI:EU:C:2017:93. I discuss this case at length in Paul Linden-Retek, "History, System, Principle, Analogy: Four Paradigms of Legitimacy in European Law," *Columbia Journal of European Law* 26, no. 3 (2021).
60. Opinion of Advocate General Mengozzi, Case C-638/16 PPU, *X and X v État belge*, para. 6.
61. Opinion of Advocate General Mengozzi, Case C-638/16 PPU, *X and X v État belge*, para. 7.
62. Opinion of Advocate General Mengozzi, Case C-638/16 PPU, *X and X v État belge*, para. 91.
63. Opinion of Advocate General Mengozzi, Case C-638/16 PPU, *X and X v État belge*, paras. 82–88 (also citing judgment of 26 September 2013, *IBV & Cie* [C-195/12, EU:C:2013:598, paras. 48, 49, and 61]); Opinion of Advocate General Mengozzi, Case C-638/16 PPU, *X and X v État belge*, paras. 91–93 (citing judgments of 26 February 2013, *Åkerberg Fransson* [C-617/10, EU:C:2013:105, para 21], and of 30 April 2014, *Pfleger and Others* [C-390/12, EU:C:2014:281, para 34]).
64. Opinion of Advocate General Mengozzi, Case C-638/16 PPU, *X and X v État belge*, paras. 93, 92.
65. See Opinion of Advocate General Mengozzi, Case C-638/16 PPU, *X and X v État belge*, para. 165 and para. 165n82 ("I would point out that, as provided in Article 3[1] and [5] TEU 'the Union's *aim* is to promote peace [and] its *values*, . . . ' and that it

'uphold[s] and *promote[s] its values*,' 'in its relations with the wider world,' by contributing to 'the protection of human rights, in particular the rights of the child' [emphasis added]").
66. Opinion of Advocate General Mengozzi, Case C-638/16 PPU, *X and X v État belge*, para. 165, emphasis added.
67. See Opinion of Advocate General Mengozzi, Case C-638/16 PPU, *X and X v État belge*, paras. 96–99.
68. Opinion of Advocate General Mengozzi, Case C-638/16 PPU, *X and X v État belge*, paras. 166–67.
69. James Boyd White, *When Words Lose Their Meaning: Constitutions and Reconstitutions of Language, Character, and Community* (Chicago: University of Chicago Press, 1984), 266.
70. James Boyd White, *Justice as Translation: An Essay in Cultural and Legal Criticism* (Chicago: University of Chicago Press, 1990), 102.
71. Opinion of Advocate General Mengozzi, Case C-638/16 PPU, *X and X v État belge*, para. 6.
72. Opinion of Advocate General Mengozzi, Case C-638/16 PPU, *X and X v État belge*, para. 174.
73. Opinion of Advocate General Mengozzi, Case C-638/16 PPU, *X and X v État belge*, 174.
74. Shahram Khosravi, "Bordered Imagination," *Crisis Magazine* (December 9, 2020), https://crisismag.net/2020/12/09/bordered-imagination/.
75. Guyora Binder, "The Dialectic of Duplicity: Treaty Conflict and Political Contradiction," *Buffalo Law Review* 34 (1985): 329, 549.

PART IV
Jurisgenerativity

13

Back to the Future?

Critical Theory and the Law

WILLIAM E. SCHEUERMAN

I distinctly recall encountering Seyla Benhabib's first book, *Critique, Norm, and Utopia* (1986), in the context of trying to decide whether to pursue graduate studies—and, if so, in philosophy, political science, or sociology.[1] When I managed to visit the Harvard Government Department during the spring of 1987 and encountered Seyla's special combination of intellectual rigor with what I would call "good sense," any questions in my mind about my future plans were immediately answered. The fact that Seyla's office wall also displayed an old German SDS poster from the sixties ("Alle reden vom Wetter. Wir nicht.") closed the deal, at least from the perspective of this erstwhile twenty-one-year-old political activist and aspiring critical theorist.

But this is not the right moment for personal reminiscences. Too much is presently at stake, both politically and intellectually. As I hope to show, *Critique, Norm, and Utopia* remains directly pertinent to contemporary—and also future—critical theory, particularly for those of us with a sustained interest in the intersection of Frankfurt critical theory and legal scholarship. The rise of authoritarian populism means that a critical yet normatively nuanced theory of basic rights, constitutionalism, and the rule of law has to be a top priority. Seyla not only has made significant contributions to that theory but also can help us further develop it.

BACK TO THE FUTURE?

Critique, Norm, and Utopia started with an appreciative but also appropriately critical reconstruction of the young Georg Friedrich Hegel, with special attention to his critique of modern natural law—the topic, if I recall correctly, of Seyla's unpublished dissertation, and also of an insightful, previously published essay on Hegel's ideas about "abstract right." Although sympathetic to Hegel's famous criticisms of Immanuel Kant, *Critique, Norm, and Utopia* effectively documented how the young Hegel had nonetheless underestimated the "normative force of modern natural law theories."[2] As Seyla had previously argued in greater detail in "Obligation, Contract, and Exchange: On the Significance of Hegel's Abstract Right" (1984), despite his hostility to the contractarian tradition, Hegel endorsed its view of "the individual as someone entitled to rights."[3] To be sure, he repudiated the claim—commonplace in modern political thought since Thomas Hobbes—that the contract model could serve as an acceptable basis for legitimate political authority.[4] However, it would be wrong to conclude that Hegel denied *any* nexus between political legitimacy and the idea of the social contract: "Hegel transform[ed] the contractarian paradigm of legitimacy into a philosophical justification of the rule of law in the modern state."[5]

Although anticipating Weber's idea of an elective affinity between modern capitalism and "the regulation of social life through general norms issued publicly in a formally correct procedure," Hegel, unlike Karl Marx and his followers, never reduced the rule of law "to a mere ideological justification of bourgeois property relations."[6] Seyla praised Hegel, in other words, for successfully avoiding Marxism's reductionist views of law. Unfortunately, Hegel's reworking of modern natural right still decoupled the idea of the rule of law from *sovereignty*, which she defined—citing first-generation Frankfurt political and legal theorist Franz L. Neumann—as "the political identity, or the governmental form, to be assumed by ... a social unity."[7] Even more specifically, Hegel's model of a modern rule of law–based state—for him, the lasting normative legacy of modern natural right—was decidedly *un*democratic: "Hegel replaced political democracy in the modern world by participation in non-political organizations such as corporations or professional associations."[8] Hegel salvaged modern natural right but "at the price of sacrificing the concept of participatory democracy and citizenship."[9] His political model ultimately meshed with what the intellectual historian Leonard Krieger, in a classic study of German political thought, accurately diagnosed as the legalistic yet basically undemocratic "German idea of freedom."[10]

Seyla's appreciative while aptly critical view of the Hegelian legacy remained on display throughout *Critique, Norm, and Utopia*. The volume's first chapter concisely showed how Hegel's selective reading of modern natural law and the contractarian tradition generated normative oversights that later plagued left-Hegelian notions of *immanent critique*, flaws that left their marks on both Karl Marx and the early Frankfurt School. A second chapter, devoted to the strengths and weaknesses of *prefigurative critique*, similarly traced its limitations and mixed record within critical theory partly to its normatively ambivalent Hegelian genealogy. Although *Critique, Norm, and Utopia* highlighted, in a Habermasian spirit, the limitations of the *philosophy of the subject*, a central worry, as in the previous essay on Hegel and natural right, remained the deeper roots of Hegel's (and his myriad disciples') tendency to obscure modern politics' most valuable (still insufficiently tapped) normative and especially democratic possibilities.

A particularly troublesome consequence of this legacy for the main figures of the early Frankfurt School, Seyla pointed out, was their "denigration of political liberalism."[11] Only Neumann and Otto Kirchheimer, somewhat marginal members of the Institute for Social Research, successfully avoided their colleagues' political and legal-theoretical lacunae: they broke with other Frankfurt School thinkers who "by and large retained the orthodox Marxist distrust towards questions of legitimacy and the normative dimension of political institutions."[12] In particular, Neumann was credited with offering "one of the finest treatments of the history of liberal political thought."[13] In the process, Neumann and Kirchheimer tentatively foreshadowed Habermas's path-breaking communicative-theoretical turn and its enormously productive consequences for a critical theory of politics and law. (Within a few years, of course, Habermas would go on to craft his landmark *Between Facts and Norms: Contributions to a Discourse Theory of Law* [English translation published in 1996, originally published in 1992], Frankfurt critical theory's greatest single contribution to political and legal theory.)[14]

Critique, Norm, and Utopia emphatically endorsed Habermas's communicative turn, while nonetheless complaining that his version of critical theory had taken on too much neo-Kantian baggage. Consequently, his otherwise path-breaking insights were unnecessarily vulnerable to familiar Hegelian criticisms. Despite the Hegelian tradition's own flaws, there were still vital lessons; in short, it could teach critical theorists. In the book's final chapter, Seyla targeted Habermas's Kantian excesses, i.e., a certain tendency to privilege the perspective of the "generalized" and not "concrete" other. Only by retrieving left-Hegelianism's lasting contributions could critical theory *both* successfully fulfill "the legacy of bourgeois revolutions and of the liberal-democratic tradition" *and* advance a radical, transformative, and potentially utopian "democratic-participatory vision of public life [and] community of needs."[15] The latter, Seyla argued, had been pushed to the sidelines by Habermas, despite the imposing building blocks he had provided for successfully reconstructing critical theory.

I cannot sufficiently document this claim here, but there is no question that Seyla's complex relationship to left-Hegelianism has continued to shape her thinking. This is perhaps most obvious in an illuminating recent exchange with Rainer Forst, whom she faults with Kantian "rigorism" (and moralism), and whose own impressive version of critical theory she views as even more neglectful of Hegel's lasting lessons than Habermas's.[16] To be sure, her left-Hegelian instincts are less pronounced in those more recent writings on cosmopolitanism where Kant looms large. Yet Seyla has never forgotten where she, in philosophical terms, comes from. As with Habermas, there is an attempt to mediate fruitfully between Kant and Hegel, but there is no question that her Hegelian background has remained significant and sometimes decisive.

So why does this matter for present-day critical theory, and particularly for those of us—including this author—who have followed in the footsteps of Benhabib's *Critique, Norm, and Utopia*, as well as Habermas's *Between Facts and Norms*, and tried to construct an identifiably Frankfurt-inspired account of law?

Critical theory comes today in many different shapes and sizes. I cannot say much here about a growing body of Frankfurt-oriented theorizing that draws on poststructuralism and political anarchism: when it comes to developing a critical theory *of law* that takes modern law's normative resources and merits seriously, I am skeptical that it gets us anywhere, or at least anywhere we want to go.[17] Nor can I presently explore what now apparently entails, in Nancy Fraser's most recent work, a quasi-Marxist skepticism about post-Habermasian Frankfurt-oriented work on law and constitutionalism, a body of research Fraser views as clear evidence for its recent inappropriately "legalistic" preoccupations.[18]

However, I will note that in a political context in which authoritarian populism remains ascendant, such antilegal—and sometimes antiliberal—tendencies risk reproducing the highly ambivalent, in some cases: politically disastrous views of basic rights, constitutionalism, and the rule of law that plagued orthodox Marxism and the early Frankfurt theory. (I realize that many younger critical theorists have not witnessed the disasters of state socialism or recall the upheavals of 1989. But this is why we have history books.) It also potentially represents theoretical *regression* in the sense that it obscures the lasting insights of a rich tradition of Frankfurt political and legal theory extending from Neumann and Kirchheimer to Habermas, a tradition that *Critique, Norm, and Utopia* so powerfully helped revive. As Seyla correctly pointed out, "one of the irreversible gains of the paradigm shift to communicative rationality and action" was to have "refocused attention on this neglected [political and legal-theoretical] dimension" of critical theory, as previously thematized by Neumann and Kirchheimer.[19] That tradition offered decidedly critical accounts of modern law, while aptly acknowledging its normative potential. Without constructively building on that legacy, contemporary critical theorists are unlikely to construct the requisite ideas about basic rights, constitutionalism, the rule of law, or separation of powers, let alone provide a sufficiently compelling analysis of how we should view them in relation to democracy.

The most obvious reason why *Critique, Norm, and Utopia* remains relevant today is that it usefully recalls consequential theoretical moves that impeded previous critical theorists from developing properly nuanced ideas not just about democracy and political liberalism, but also about modern law, basic rights, and constitutionalism. Not surprisingly, *Critique, Norm, and Utopia* played a vital role in opening the door to the impressive revival of critical theory–based work in political and legal theory we have experienced since the early 1990s, a revival by no means uncritical of Habermas, yet appropriately appreciative of the ways in which his reconstruction of critical theory's fundaments allows us to make sense of political and legal practices. Seyla's writings since the early 1990s have produced many fresh and original insights not just for democratic theory and feminism, but also concerning major legal and legal-theoretical matters, e.g., human rights, international law, and how best to conceive of them in relation to democracy in the context of intensified globalization.[20] Her (closely related) ideas of *democratic iteration* and *jurisgenerativity* represent significant conceptual contributions to critical theory, as many colleagues have already rightly acknowledged.[21] Other authors in this volume will have more to say about these and other recent innovations; I revisit them in this essay's final section.

Hegel, Critical Theory, and the Law

But let me first note another lesson we can draw from Seyla's early writings. There is no question that, once again, we are witnessing significant neo-Hegelian revivals within Frankfurt critical theory. Most recently, Axel Honneth's *Freedom's Right: The Social Foundations of Democratic Life* represents an impressive attempt not only to reconstitute critical theory on a neo-Hegelian basis, but also to update the basic arguments of Hegel's *Philosophy of Right* (1821) in accordance with contemporary democratic and social conditions.[22] Rahel Jaeggi's similarly creative recent contributions to another possible neo-Hegelian version of critical theory should also, of course, be mentioned here.[23] Her work has already garnered a great deal of acclaim.[24]

A question I would like to pose for further discussion is whether these revivals reproduce, albeit inadvertently and in highly complex ways, some elements of the theoretical Achilles's heel so effectively identified in *Critique, Norm, and*

Utopia. Despite her own left-Hegelian proclivities, Seyla, of course, was an astute diagnostician of that tradition's normative and political flaws. One reason *Critique, Norm, and Utopia* remains pertinent today is that it anticipated key features of these more recent Hegelian revivals *while circumventing their worrisome legal-theoretical lacunae*.

Critique, Norm, and Utopia recalled, with some sympathy, that Hegel had worried about Kant's tendency to privilege "the domain of juridical and quasi-juridical relations," while remaining congenitally oblivious "to all else that escapes such classification—like friendship, professional duties, citizenship, or political partisanship."[25] Of course, any claim that we can encapsulate a complex philosophical work within a single sentence is unserious. However, if we were forced to do so for Honneth's *Freedom's Right, that* sentence from *Critique, Norm, and Utopia* might not be a bad choice.

At any rate, Honneth now believes that contemporary critical theory has succumbed to overstated neo-Kantian legalist or juridical preoccupations that betray the Frankfurt School's left-Hegelian fundaments. Not surprisingly, *Freedom's Right* proffers far-reaching criticisms of "legalism," defined as an "absolutization of legal freedom" that entails a counterproductive recourse to legal and juridical modes of regulation and thinking. In part because neo-Kantian theories of justice and such "legalism" apparently are married at the hip, those critical theorists accused of jettisoning left-Hegelianism sources for liberal (typically Anglophone) theories of justice also ignore legalism's pathologies. For Honneth, legalism constitutes a major, real-life social pathology that needs to be combated: recent critical theory's failure to do so means that it has abandoned its original aim of providing a critical theory of *society*. Although able to circumvent the more extreme antilegal views of some recent Frankfurt colleagues, Honneth apparently shares Fraser's anxieties that

> [a] great deal of the post-Habermasian currents of critical theory have entered into a kind of disciplinary specialization: people doing moral philosophy, philosophy of law, political theory disconnected from social theory.... It's a kind of politicism, or moralism or legalism—a single-minded focus on constitutional theory. I appreciate that no one can do everything, and that there is academic specialization, but I think this is a sad outcome for critical theory: it has lost the attempt to think about the social totality, which Habermas, at an early stage, did try to do, for better or for worse.[26]

Elsewhere I have argued that Honneth's critique of legalism, despite some virtues, misfires.[27] Honneth sometimes points in the direction of a nuanced assessment of modern law and its accomplishments. Yet such productive theoretical tendencies coexist uneasily alongside less fruitful moments, i.e., his reworked (and excessively communitarian) Hegelianism, in which Hegel's emphatic defense of many features of modern law fades into the background. Honneth relies on a selective reworking of Hegel that downplays some of his nuanced ideas about the rule of law, the judiciary, and legal interpretation. He also makes some overstated empirical claims, borrowed from—but since abandoned by—Habermas, about so-called "juridification" and its perils. Last but not least, he exaggerates legalism's concrete political dangers.

For her part, Jaeggi has little, if anything, to say about law or legal institutions, perhaps because she, with echoes of Honneth, implicitly associates recent critical theory's heightened interest in such matters with its purported Kantian excesses and flaws, e.g., Habermas's "ethical abstinence," which allegedly leads him mistakenly to draw clear borders for ethics and morality.[28] If so, she risks throwing the baby out with the bath water: there is no reason why a neo-Hegelian version of critical theory necessarily must neglect vital insights from a rich tradition of Frankfurt legal-theoretical reflection extending from Neumann and Kirchheimer to Habermas.

Here it seems useful to recall Seyla's thesis, stated in the closing pages of *Critique, Norm, and Utopia*, of a "necessary complementarity" between the perspective of the "generalized other," and its close ties to a "legal-juridical concept of public life" (e.g., legal equality), on the one hand, and the "concrete other," and its intimate links to participatory democracy and a "community of needs and solidarity," on the other.[29] Precisely because of this "necessary complementarity," Seyla's early left-Hegelianism never degraded so-called "liberal" legal ideas, though it did, to be sure, acknowledge their limits: basic rights, the rule of law, and constitutionalism are necessary yet, of course, insufficient conditions for a robust, more fully participatory democracy. We need to recognize what basic rights, the rule of law, and constitutionalism can—and cannot—achieve, without ignoring their indispensable contours or exaggeratedly overstating possible dangers. Whether specific types of legal regulation result "in an increased demand for participation or self-government" or instead "dependence, passivity, and clientilism" is always a complex empirical question requiring careful examination.[30]

Admittedly, this does not yet fully answer the question at hand: What exactly about Seyla's appreciative yet critical reconstruction of Hegel fruitfully opened legal-theoretical doors that seem to have been closed to others? A crude answer comes immediately to mind: hers is a significantly less communitarian and/or phenomenological (or perhaps even social psychological) reading of Hegel than found among recent critical theorists.[31] If you think, as I do, that critical theory needs to situate its normative bases somewhere between Kant and Hegel, without losing what is valuable about its left-Hegelian roots, this question clearly deserves more attention.[32]

Jurisgenerativity and Democratic Iterations

During the last two decades, Seyla has creatively redeployed the late Yale jurist Robert Cover's idea of *jurisgenerativity* as part of her quest to formulate a cosmopolitan vision of democracy and human rights. By jurisgenerativity she understands "the law's capacity to create a normative universe of meaning that can often escape the 'provenance of formal lawmaking' to expand the meaning and reach of the law itself."[33] What perhaps chiefly appeals to her is that by viewing human rights declarations and treaties jurisgeneratively we can properly appreciate how they may enable "new actors—such as women and ethnic, linguistic, and religious minorities—to enter the public sphere, to develop new vocabularies of public claim-making, and to anticipate new forms of justice."[34] Jurisgenerativity is closely related to the idea of *democratic iterations*, which refer to the myriad ways human rights (and other legal materials) are "enacted and re-enacted in strong and weak public spheres, not only in legislatures and courts, but often more effectively by social movements, civil society actors, and transnational organizations across the borders."[35] Not surprisingly, given her theory's Habermasian inflections, *communicative* freedom figures prominently in her account. "The people" here are envisioned as "not merely subject to the law but also as authors of the law," as they deliberatively interpret and reconceive human rights in potentially novel and more inclusive ways.[36] In the process of doing so, "the people" reinterpret their own boundaries and reinvent their collective identities. Both a normative and an empirical concept, democratic iteration "involves complex processes of public argument, deliberation, and exchange through which universalist rights claims are contextualized, invoked, and revoked, posited and positioned throughout legal and political institutions."[37]

If I understand the nexus between the two concepts properly, jurisgenerativity specifically underscores what Cover described as the "uncontrolled character of [legal] meaning," whose potentially "destabilizing influence on power" appealed to him (and now Seyla).[38] Without some prospect of jurisgeneratively reinterpreting law and rights such that their meanings can be enhanced and transformed so as to challenge existing power relations, fruitful processes of democratic iteration would be impossible. In order for politically dynamic democratic iterations to occur, in short, far-reaching alterations to settled interpretations of even otherwise authoritative legal materials need to occur.

By allowing Seyla to weigh in on a number of major political-theoretical questions, the conceptual twins of jurisgenerativity and democratic iteration have proved enormously fruitful. Nonetheless, I would like to conclude with some critical questions that have not yet, at least on my reading, been fully addressed. Readers will quickly note that my concerns are inspired by precisely that tradition of Frankfurt political and legal theory, extending from Neumann and Kirchheimer to Habermas, whose virtues Seyla astutely identified in *Critique, Norm, and Utopia*.

Seyla's recent writings have had a great deal to say about jurisgenerativity and democratic iteration in the context of human rights and international legal norms, matters of vital importance to her, given her cosmopolitan intentions. However, their implications for some core components of the modern political and legal landscape remain somewhat less clear. I wonder, for example, how they might help us speak to matters of democratic-institutional and constitutional design along the lines ambitiously pursued, for example, by Habermas in *Between Facts and Norms*. What view of the separation of powers, or what way of delineating ordinary from "higher" constitutional lawmaking, potentially follows from them? What of the idea of the rule of law, understood as legal regulation that is general, prospective, public, and relatively stale? Or the familiar vision of independent courts as exercising properly legal and judicial but not political or at least partisan functions?

Described in *Another Cosmopolitanism* (2004) as "linguistic, legal, cultural, and political repetitions-in-transformation, invocations that are also revocations," jurisgenerativity and its conceptual twin, democratic iteration, seem fundamentally to *challenge* the possibility of some, however porously conceived, boundaries between political action and legal hermeneutics.[39] How might we usefully differentiate between popular democratic and institutional decision-making, (sometimes creative) political action (and legislation) and legal (and sometimes judicial) interpretation, and perhaps even fundamental or "higher" lawmaking and lesser "ordinary" legislation?[40] When might we distinguish between radical and perhaps revolutionary examples of jurisgenerativity, for example, and less ambitious types, and what institutional consequences might we then draw?

Seyla may be right to follow Jacques Derrida in claiming that "we never simply produce a replica of the original usage and its meaning; rather, every repetition is a form of variation."[41] She never denies the central role of a legal (and presumably codified) "authoritative original" to which institutional players and civil society actors necessarily appeal.[42] Yet, what her sensible rejection of crudely mechanical ideas of legal interpretation precisely entails for many features of constitutional and rule of law–based democracy, as both nation-state-based and cosmopolitan projects, requires elaboration. Presumably, some institutional actors (e.g., legislators) might be given leeway to engage in more creative "reenactments" of standing law and basic rights than others (e.g., the executive). Would we not also need to delineate jurisgenerativity and democratic iteration when practiced by civil society actors, for example, from those instances where powerful institutional players *enforce* their "reenactments" on others? If the ideas of jurisgenerativity and democratic iteration are to succeed in overcoming the long-standing divide between natural law and positivist views of law, as Seyla promises, we will need answers to these and other related questions.

Such answers can probably be provided. Nonetheless, I worry that Seyla may have inadvertently smuggled in troublesome features of Cover's fascinating, yet in many ways problematic, theory of law. His was a decidedly antiformalist and antipositivist jurisprudence that highlighted legal meaning's dynamic and "destabilizing" contours at the cost of downplaying the traditional view of the rule of law as guaranteeing predictability, stability, and a basic measure of legal security. I worry that an account of law that similarly highlights its virtues as a *dynamic* source of creative "enactment and reenactment" risks sidelining indispensable *stabilizing*, protective functions.[43] Seyla notes in *Another Cosmopolitanism* that a rigid, "legalistic" view of law can be "jurispathic."[44] In some instances, however, such "legalism" can prove emancipatory, or at least indispensable: recall Neumann's observation that clear, predictable, stable legal norms and practices protected mid-century Germany's most socially vulnerable, whereas monopoly capitalists and powerful political blocs preferred open-ended, indeterminate legal practices that they were best positioned to exploit.[45] With occasional echoes of Ronald Dworkin, Seyla sometimes appears to jettison the traditional "model of [legal] rules" account of the rule of law in favor of a right-based reinterpretation.[46] Dworkin's views, of course, nonetheless raise difficult questions.[47]

Reminiscent at times of political realism, Cover's implicit theory of the state seems strikingly anti-Hegelian—and, indeed, fundamentally antinormative—in its preoccupation with state violence.[48] That rather one-sided view of the state shaped core features of his jurisprudence, e.g., Cover's view of judicial decision-making as congenitally violent. Of course, Seyla never endorses this facet of his theory. However, its strongly anti-institutionalist implications may resurface in her own theory's institutional silences.

I realize that these concluding reflections sound too much like a family quarrel. Yet it remains vital for our little "family" of critical theorists to acknowledge and then discuss such disagreements if we are to contribute to the sufficiently rich "democratic-participatory public life" and "community of needs and solidarity" we have yet to see.[49] With the rise of authoritarian populism, it is more urgent than ever that we formulate a subtle account of modern law that is both normatively appreciative of its merits and socially critical.

NOTES

1. Seyla Benhabib, *Critique, Norm, and Utopia: A Study of the Foundations of Critical Theory* (New York: Columbia University Press, 1986).
2. Benhabib, 31.
3. Seyla Benhabib, "Obligation, Contract and Exchange: On the Significance of Hegel's Abstract Right," in *The State and Civil Society: Studies in Hegel's Political Philosophy*, ed. Z. A. Pelczynski (New York: Cambridge University Press, 1984), 159.
4. Benhabib, 159.
5. Benhabib, 159–60.
6. Benhabib, 166, 176.
7. Benhabib, 300n12.
8. Benhabib, 177.
9. Benhabib, 177.
10. Leonard Krieger, *The German Idea of Freedom* (Chicago: University of Chicago Press, 1957). Krieger thanks first-generation Frankfurt School jurist and political scientist Otto Kirchheimer for his advice.
11. Benhabib, *Critique, Norm, and Utopia*, 378n14.
12. Benhabib, 348.
13. Benhabib, 378n14. The reference here is to Neumann's 1936 dissertation, published in English under the title *The Rule of Law: Political Theory and the Legal Systems in Modern Society* (Leamington Spa: Berg, 1986). Unfortunately, the obscurity of the publisher, as well as fact that the published volume could have used some additional copyediting, has impeded the work's reception. At any rate, Seyla's comments about Neumann and Kirchheimer were the launching pad for my dissertation and first book: Scheuerman, *Between the Norm and the Exception: The Frankfurt School and the Rule of Law* (Cambridge, MA: MIT Press, 1994), as well as my abiding interest in Neumann, Kirchheimer, and Habermas as sources for a critical theory of law, e.g., Scheuerman, *Frankfurt School Perspectives on Globalization, Democracy, and Law* (New York: Routledge, 2008).
14. Habermas, *Between Facts and Norms: Contributions to a Discourse Theory of Law*, trans. William Rehg (1992; Cambridge, MA: MIT Press, 1996). Habermas was indebted to scholars already long at work at the intersection of critical theory and legal scholarship, e.g., Ingeborg Maus and Ulrich Preuss.
15. Benhabib, *Critique, Norm, and Utopia*, 343.
16. Seyla Benhabib, "The Uses and Abuses of Kantian Rigorism: On Rainer Forst's Moral and Political Philosophy," *Political Theory* 43 (2015): 777–92, with Forst's response in the same issue.

17. See, e.g., Christoph Menke, *Kritik der Rechte* (Frankfurt: Suhrkamp, 2015); Daniel Loick, *Juridismus: Konturen einer Kritischen Theorie des Rechts* (Berlin: Suhrkamp, 2017).
18. William E. Scheuerman, "Recognition, Redistribution, and Participatory Parity: Where's the Law?," in *Feminism, Capitalism, and Critique: Essays in Honor of Nancy Fraser*, ed. Banu Bargu and Chirara Bottici (New York: Palgrave, 2017), 139–56.
19. Benhabib, *Critique, Norm, and Utopia*, 348.
20. Seyla Benhabib, *Dignity in Adversity: Human Rights in Troubled Times* (Cambridge: Polity, 2011), esp. chaps. 4–5, 7.
21. See, for example, the discussion of *The Rights of Others* (New York: Cambridge University Press, 2004) in *European Journal of Political Theory* 6 (2007): 406–62, with contributions from Benhabib as well as T. Alexander Aleinikoff, Rainer Bauböck, Angela Means, and Saskia Sassen. See also the remarks by Bonnie Honig, Will Kymlicka, Robert Post, and Jeremy Waldron in Seyla Benhabib, *Another Cosmopolitanism* (New York: Oxford University Press, 2006).
22. Axel Honneth, *Freedom's Right: The Social Foundations of Democratic Life* (2011; New York: Columbia University Press, 2014).
23. Rahel Jaeggi, *Alienation* (New York: Columbia University Press, 2014); Rahel Jaeggi, *Critique of Forms of Life* (Cambridge, MA: Harvard University Press, 2018).
24. Amy Allen and Eduardo Mendieta, eds., *From Alienation to Forms of Life: The Critical Theory of Rahel Jaeggi* (New York: Columbia University Press, 2018).
25. Benhabib, *Critique, Norm, and Utopia*, 78.
26. Nancy Fraser, interviewed by Jo Littler, "An Astonishing Time of Great Boldness: On the Politics of Recognition and Redistribution" (2014), downloaded from www.eurozine.com, August 5, 2020.
27. William E. Scheuerman, "Recent Critical Theory: Down on Law?," *Constellations* 24 (2017): 113–25, and Honneth's response in the same issue.
28. Jaeggi, *Critique of Forms of Life*, 12–16.
29. Benhabib, *Critique, Norm, and Utopia*, 342–43.
30. Benhabib, 350, where Benhabib speaks of "juridification," but not so as to load the deck analytically or empirically against legal regulation, and minus the troublesome tendency to romanticize "norm-free" modes of social life found in Habermas's original usage and also in Honneth's latest version.
31. See the critical remarks on Jaeggi in Christoph Henning, *Theorien der Entfremdung* (Hamburg: Junius, 2015), 170–208.
32. For some initial reflections relevant here, see Dana Schmalz, "Social Freedom in a Global World: Axel Honneth's and Seyla Benhabib's Reconsiderations of a Hegelian Perspective on Justice," *Constellations* 26, no. 2 (2020): 301–17.
33. Benhabib, *Dignity in Adversity*, 15.
34. Benhabib, 15.
35. Benhabib, 15.
36. Benhabib, 15–16.
37. Benhabib, 16.
38. Cited in Benhabib, 15. The crucial essay from Cover is his "Foreword: Nomos and Narrative," *Harvard Law Review* 97 (1983): 4–68.

39. Benhabib, *Another Cosmopolitanism*, 48. Of course, the courts and acts of legal interpretation are always "political," but they represent a very different kind of politics than what we find in civil society, legislatures, and the like.
40. Benhabib, 48.
41. Benhabib, 47.
42. Benhabib, 48.
43. Thus, I have a hard time making sense of Bonnie Honig's criticism of Seyla's ideas about law as excessively formalist: Honig, "Another Cosmopolitanism?: Law and Politics in the New Europe," in Benhabib, *Another Cosmopolitanism*, 109.
44. Benhabib, *Another Cosmopolitanism*, 50.
45. Franz L. Neumann, "The Change in Function of Law in Modern Society" (1936), in *The Rule of Law Under Siege: Selected Essays of Franz L. Neumann and Otto Kirchheimer*, ed. William E. Scheuerman (Berkeley: University of California Press, 1996), 101–41.
46. Benhabib, *Dignity in Adversity*, 74. For Dworkin's initial justification for the shift from the "model of rules" to an alternative that "takes rights seriously," see Ronald Dworkin, *Taking Rights Seriously* (Cambridge, MA: Harvard University Press, 1977).
47. See, for example, Habermas, *Between Facts and Norms*, 213–22.
48. Cover, "Nomos and Narrative," 40–53. The nexus between law and violence in Cover's work has spawned a lively debate; e.g., Austin Sarat, ed., *Law, Violence, and the Possibility of Justice* (Princeton, NJ: Princeton University Press, 2001). In Cover's view, only those judges who abandon a strict rule-based, positivist understanding of their activities can at least partly "extricate" themselves "from the violence of the state" (59). In stark contrast, Neumann and Kirchheimer worried that state action decoupled from strict legal norms invited acts of sovereign "power" that tended to favor politically and socially privileged groups.
49. Benhabib, *Critique, Norm, and Utopia*, 343.

14

The Unfinished Revolution

The Right to Have Rights and Birthright Citizenship

EDUARDO MENDIETA

In this essay I aim to develop a normative argument on behalf of birthright citizenship, i.e., that one is automatically citizen of the country, or sovereign territory, where one is born. There are two ways in which I could proceed to develop such an argument. One way would be to engage in what has been called sometimes pejoratively "ideal theory" building. Another way would be to engage in either a philosophical-anthropological or phenomenological-ontological grounding (what could also be called a "political phenomenology") of the normativity of birthright citizenship.[1] I am aware of the hazard of proceeding this way, as this would mean incurring the liabilities of the "is-ought" fallacy. I appealed to the reader to suspend judgment on whether this is possible and advisable or impossible and undesirable. Nonetheless, I will proceed to build this plausible argument by showing the terrestrial, earthly, worldly references to the "right to have rights" in the works of Kant, Arendt, and Benhabib. At the very least, the "right to have rights" is linked to a right to a place in the world. I argue, however, how certain insights into what we call the "human condition" both require and command that we develop "norms," maxims, and imperatives for regulating how we interact with one another in a world that is finite and in which we cannot but come upon one another and thus have to interact.[2] The goal, more precisely, is to develop a phenomenological-ontological argument for why "birthright" citizenship is not simply a contingent historical development but a constitutional and legal development that addresses and aims to confront a fundamental fact of human existence. The aim is to affirm that although citizenship based on *Jus Soli*, i.e., birthright citizenship, is a contingent historical development, when we sift through the ashes of burning history to retrieve the embers of the ideal, we can nonetheless rescue the normative seeds for the grounds on which we must reject citizenship based on *Jus Sanguinis* and affirm *Jus Soli*.[3] The unfinished revolution that marked the U.S. Civil War is the struggle for the unfinished institution of citizenship, which is the unfinished constitution.

The essay will precede by unearthing a "terrestrial anthropology" that links right, i.e., law, to place, a place on the Earth. Kant argued that a metaphysics of morals cannot be based on a moral anthropology. I will try to show that Kant does in fact presuppose a moral anthropology that is in fact what I call a "terrestrial anthropology." Then, I will aim to link Arendt's famous notion of the "right to have rights" to the right to place in the world that is linked to human plurality, i.e., the right to have rights as a right to inhabit and thus as the interdiction against cohabitation. This will be developed in terms of Arendt's argument against the Nazi policies of "not wanting to share the earth" with Jews and other nations, as it is laid out in the epilogue to *Eichmann in Jerusalem*. The "right to have rights" is above all a right to "a place on the earth." Then, I will turn to Seyla Benhabib, who, I will argue, will help us expand this Arendtian insights with reference to some of her most recent works, those in which she advances her own generative readings of Arendt's sometimes elusive, and not normatively grounded, "right to have rights." I will argue that Benhabib's commitment to moral universalism that is twined by justificatory universalism commits her to juridical universalism, which results from the jurisgenesis instigated by democratic iterations. My claim is that this juridical universalism also commits us to what Frank Michelman calls most felicitously "dialogical constitutionalism."[4] The aim of this investigation is to arrive at the conclusion that the "right to have rights" is the "right to citizenship," and that the most jurisgenerative instantiation of citizenship is birthright citizenship.[5]

TERRESTRIAL ANTHROPOLOGY OR THE GROUND OF *IUS*

In *The Metaphysics of Morals* Kant introduces the term "moral anthropology" (6:217) to talk about the biological conditions for the moral improvement of the human, but then insists that a doctrine of morals cannot be based on that type of anthropology.[6] This is a very strange claim, as we will see, because in the end the metaphysics of morals cannot but appeal to the fundamental earthly character of humans. Yet, for Kant, the earthly or terrestrial character of the human being is not to be treated as an empirical fact from which one can derive the universal doctrine of right; instead, it is "a postulate incapable of further proof."

Arthur Ripstein has clearly and succinctly elaborated why Kant makes this improbable claim. I quote, extensively, as it is important and enlightening:

> Kant's central claim is that we are rational beings who occupy space. This postulate is "incapable of further proof," because nothing would qualify as a successful proof of it. It cannot be given a proof from concepts, because, as Kant argues in the Transcendental Aesthetic, space is nonconceptual and cannot be reduced to any concept or relation because them. The details of that argument are complex and contested, but its basic gist is simple and familiar: space is nonconceptual because it has a different kind of generality than any concept does. A concept is general in the sense that (possible) instances fall under it. Space, in contrast, has parts rather than instances. Instances of a concept are more specific than it, and have more determinate content, so that the concept of a horse is more determinate than that of a mammal; parts of space are all the same, and differ only in their external relations, that is, their location. Moreover, Kant argues that space as a whole is prior to its parts: it is not built up of discrete parts, but rather its parts are demarcated by dividing it. The parts of space thus stand in a conceptual form of incompatibility relations. Nor could the postulate be given a proof from either experience or *a priori* intuition of space, as neither of these contains the concept of a rational being. If no proof is available, then a postulate is required to introduce the norms governing the concept of an embodied rational being, that is, one that both occupies space and falls under the laws of freedom.[7]

One may speculate whether there could be a rational being that does not require being, or that could be, disembodied, something like a God. Could a rational God dispense with all spatiality, be everywhere and nowhere, as it were?[8] Kant, however, is interested in embodied rational beings that are free. This freedom, it is to be recalled, is the will that is determined not by inclination but by reason. This will, in turn, is based on the faculty of desire, namely, the power to "be the cause of the objects" of one's representation (6:218). Then, Kant writes: "The faculty of a being to act in accordance with its representations is called *life*" (6:211). Life, then, is to be able to act on the world, to have efficacy, in the world by means of one's representations of the objects of one's wants and needs. There is no freedom without willing, and no will without the faculty of desire, which means, essentially, our biological embodiment, a body of space and in space. Ripstein, however, nicely summarizes the thrust of Kant's argument, thusly:

> If moral persons are individuated spatially, then the only way to have freedom under universal law is for each embodied rational being to have, in virtue of its

humanity, a right to its own person—that is, to its own body. Such a right must be innate, because nothing could count as an affirmative act establishing it— *the right applies to any rational being that occupies space, because its right is nothing more than the right that it has to the space that it happens to occupy.*[9]

In other words, embodied rational beings are individuated by their spatiality. By virtue of their humanity, i.e., their embodiment and rationality, they have a right to their own personhood, of which their bodies are integral, a sine qua non, i.e., no personhood without a body. By the same token, if one has a right to one's body, one has both de jure and de facto rights over the space one occupies, for one's body occupies space. But from this also follows that the right to one's body is a right not simply to this specific space, but to space, to spatiality as such: not just this space, but spatiality, for otherwise this embodied rational being would be a prisoner of the spot on which it happens to be.[10] Indeed, before there is a here, or a there, or a yonder, there is spatiality as such, and to that extent, the right of spatiality-individuated beings is a right to space, or rather spatiality, as such. It is for this reason that no one, no people, no nation, can claim exclusive primitive right over the whole of the Earth, or even a part of it. The whole Earth belongs to humanity as such, insofar as humans are spatially individuated rational and moral beings.

It is for this reason that when Kant begins to talk about the "ground" of right, he refers to the very terrestrial, i.e., spatial, nature of the human being. I thus want to argue that part of his moral anthropology is a terrestrial anthropology, i.e., the human being is first and foremost a being of the Earth. We are above all earthlings.

Let me begin with Kant's *Toward Perpetual Peace* (1795), the "Third Definitive Article for Perpetual Peace": "Cosmopolitan right shall be limited to conditions of universal *hospitality*" (8:357). There, Kant writes in the first paragraph the following:

> Here, as in the preceding articles, it is not a question of philanthropy but of *right*, so that *hospitality* (hospitableness) means the right of a foreigner not to be treated with hostility because he has arrived on the land of another. The other can turn him away, if this can be done without destroying him, but as long as he behaves peaceably where he is, he cannot be treated with hostility. What he can claim is not the *right to be a guest* (for this a special beneficent pact would be required, making him a member of the household for a certain time), but the *right to visit*; this right, to present oneself for society, *belongs to all human beings by virtue of the right of possession in common of the earth's surface on which, as a sphere, they cannot disperse infinitely but must finally put up with being near one another*; but originally no one had more right than another to be on a place on the earth. (8:357–58, italics added)[11]

In the *Cambridge Edition of the Works of Immanuel Kant* we now have access to *Lectures and Drafts on Political Philosophy*.¹² In this collection of drafts, mostly from the late 1780s and early 1790s, we find the following passages, which made their way in a different phrasing, but with the same argumentative thrust, into Kant's *The Metaphysics of Morals*.

> Originally I find myself on some land since it is inseparable from my existence (that I once as it were took it by birth is a related concept which can be set aside). Thus I am the occupant of this land; whether by right this occupancy is to continue permanently so that the occupancy is at the same time possession can here remain unspecified.—I thus have an innate but still created **right in a thing** which yet may not be regarded as acquired because it is connected with my existence, I may also have been on this land from eternity.—From this right all of my *jura in re* (*externa*) [rights in things (external)] must be derivable—Therefore everyone must allow me some land or other, hence it someone takes my occupancy, this can occur only on condition that he assigns me another on which I can live (not to leave to my fate which land one would grant me).
>
> This *detentio* (occupancy) as such is bound with the use which is required for my existence, and I do not become obligated to anyone through that occupancy when it does not depend upon my power of choice. This even holds if I voluntarily end up on some land, because I must be able to be somewhere: **even if there are also previous occupants of it specifically in relation to borders.** (23:237, bold in English translation)¹³

Then, a couple of pages later—which were made up of loose sheets—we find the following notes:

> 1. The *communio originaria* is not empirically grounded as a *factum* or event but rather a right to land without which no human being can exist, which itself follows from freedom in the use of things.
>
> One must assume that mine and yours in things can only occur within the universal possession of the earth's land, for then contemporaries and later generations are limited by the *prior occupans* [one previously took control] to the conditions of the possession actually taken by the first who master it. The limits of this prerogative, however, are determined unilaterally, yet in relation to those who in the future might their share.
>
> All synthetic rights in things (for in themselves they are analytic) have as their ground the *fundus communis* [communal land] and thus can be regarded as founded before possession is taken. (23:241)¹⁴

Now, this is how these notes were transformed, edited, and paraphrased in the text of *The Metaphysics of Morals* (1797). We have to turn to the "The Doctrine of Right," paragraph 13.

> All human beings are originally (i.e. prior to any act of choice that establishes a right) in a possession of land that is in conformity with right, that is, they have a right to be wherever nature or chance (apart from their will) has a placed them. This kind of possession (*posessio*)—which is to be distinguished from residence (*sedes*), a chosen and therefore an acquired *lasting* possession—is a possession *in common* because the spherical surface of the earth unites all the places on its surface; for if its surface were an unbounded plane, human beings could be so dispersed on it that they would not come into any community with one another, and community would not be then a necessary result of their existence on the earth—The possession by all human beings on the earth which precedes any acts of theirs that would establish rights (as constituted by nature itself) is an *original possession in common* (*communio possessionis originaria*), the concept of which is not empirical and dependent upon temporal conditions, like that of a supposed *primitive possession in common* (*communio primaeva*), which can never be proved. Original possession in common is, rather, a practical rational which contains *a priori* the principle in accordance with which alone human beings can use a place on the earth in accordance with the principles of right. (6:262)[15]

I would like to summarize Kant's claims thus far with the following aphorisms:

1. The ground of justice, of the doctrine of right, is the Earth.
2. All humans possess in common, and not individually or separately, the Earth.
3. There is no human being that can claim exclusive and original ownership of the Earth.
4. The spherical character of the Earth destines, fates, humans to enter into community.
5. This is the very same condition that is the ground for cosmopolitan right and right, or law, in general.
6. Every human being has a right to a place on the Earth. A right that is consequent to the original right of freedom.
7. In short, then, terrestrial anthropology is prior to moral anthropology, and both are prior to the metaphysics of morals.

THE ANARCHIC RIGHT OF EARTHLINGS OR THE RIGHT TO HAVE RIGHTS

Before I start this next section, let me interject some, perhaps important, notes about Arendt's relation to Kant. Kant appears in *The Origins of Totalitarianism*, but only in a couple of places (four times according to the index), and most notably only once in the section where Arendt develops her ideas about the "right to have rights." But there is no sustained engagement with Kant's political ideas, neither with "Perpetual Peace" nor with "A Universal History with a Cosmopolitan Intent," and there is no mention of *The Metaphysics of Morals*. Kant is not even in the bibliography, at least in the books that I am focusing on. Arendt's *Lectures on Kant's Political Philosophy* focuses mostly on the *Critique of Judgment* and the *Groundwork for the Metaphysics of Morals*, but again, no discussion of what is without question the key texts in Kant's corpus.[16] Furthermore, when I read through Arendt's *Kant Notebook* and her *Philosophical Notebooks*, what is notable is the absence of engagement with Kant's historical-political works of the 1780s and 1790s. Arendt does not seem to have read *The Metaphysics of Morals*, which is why the epilogue of the Eichmann book is the more striking and remarkable.[17]

Hannah Arendt's phrase "the right to have rights"—which has rightly become one of the most notable philosophemes of the twentieth century—first appeared in the article titled "'The Rights of Man': What Are They?" from the 1949.[18] It appears in this sentence: "We only became aware of the existence of a right to have rights (and that means to live in a framework where one is judged according to actions and opinions) and a right to belong to some kind of organized community, when there suddenly emerged millions of people who had lost and could not regain these rights because of the new global political situation."[19] The sentence appears verbatim in *The Origins of Totalitarianism*, from a decade later.[20] It is important to note the following: the sentence appears several pages after Arendt has offered an analysis of the "plight" of the rightless. Arendt diagnoses what it was that the stateless and the rightless lost. The first loss that the rightless, the stateless, the so-called "displaced persons" had was the loss of "their homes, which meant the loss of their entire social texture into which they were born and within which they had established for themselves a distinct *place in the world*."[21] This loss, however, was compounded, as it was not simply that the stateless lost their home, but that now they now faced the "*impossibility of finding a new one*."[22] "All of a sudden, *there was no place on earth*" where this displaced people could go, "no territory where they could found a new community of their own." This, however, was not a problem of "space but of political organization."[23]

The second calamity, or loss, was the "loss of government protection. This did not just imply the loss of legal status in their own, but in all countries."[24] Arendt then notes that nations have "woven around earth" a web of treaties and international agreements in such a way that citizens of a nation can, so to speak, carry with their person the rights that their nation grants them. The stateless, the rightless, however, have been expelled even from this web of legality. The stateless and the rightless find themselves in the calamitous situation in which they have been thrown out of the reach of any law, in which no law could claim them. To this extent, they have also been exiled from the Earth, rendered worldless. To be stateless is to be in a "condition of complete rightlessness" and worldlessness.[25] In the paragraph before the paragraph where the sentence "the right to have rights" appears, Arendt writes: "The fundamental deprivation of human rights is manifest first and above all in the *deprivation of a place in the world* which makes opinions significant and actions effective."[26]

The sections used from the *Modern Review* in *Origins* appears to stop at page 34, which ends with the sentence: "The danger is that a global, universally interrelated civilization may produce barbarians from its own midst by forcing millions of people into conditions which, despite all appearances, are the conditions of savages."[27] The essay, however, continues and makes more explicit, and unambiguous, what this "right" to have "rights" means. Arendt argues that "the concept of human rights can be meaningful again" if we redefine them in light of the tragedy of the first half of the twentieth century. What this tragedy, or these tragedies, have taught us is to understand what Edmund Burke intimated but did not yet fully understand, namely, that rights exist only because of and within political communities. They are articulated and depend for their protection on our fellow human beings, and on what Arendt calls at the end of the essay the "comity of nations."[28] And yet, there is one right that "transcends" and is antecedent to the schedule of human rights, and this is the "right of very human being to membership in a political community."[29] Arendt notes, additionally, that it would be a philosophical error to "define" this one right, which is not mentioned in the eighteenth-century enunciation of the Rights of Man, because this right does not fit in the "categorical framework of the eighteenth century. A parenthetical remark indicates that these rights are based on some no longer tenable conception of these rights being derived from the very nature of the human being, i.e., that they are inalienable, i.e., that they belong by nature to the human being, or because they have been bestowed on human beings by God, and are thus inalienable since they derived their authority from their creator."[30] Arendt closes this discussion with the following powerful, although just as cryptic, sentences: "Rights exist only because of the plurality of men, because we inhabit the earth together with other men, while divine command, derived from man's having been created in the image of God, as well as natural law, derived from man's 'nature,' remain true even if there existed only one single human being." (Again, note the bifurcation: habitation of the Earth by a plurality of humans and the view [common in the eighteenth century] of human rights as deriving from God, or some sort of "human nature.")[31] Human rights exist, first, because of the worldliness, the worldhood, having to be on the Earth along with other similar beings, and, second, because of the plurality of the human being, having to share the Earth with others.

These arguments are in accord with Arendt's claim that "We are not born equal; we become equal as members of a group on the strength of our decision to guarantee ourselves mutually equal rights."[32] Yet, and again, there is one right that transcends all other enumerated human rights, which may be said to be ground, the soil, the earth, on which all other rights rest, and this is the "right never to be excluded from the rights granted by his community . . . and never to be deprived of his citizenship."[33] The "right to have rights" is the transcendent right, the anterior right, to citizenship, which is the right to the rights of the citizen. For the moment, I want to flag an apparent paradox, a paradox that is already announced in the singular and plural grammar of the sentence: "a" right to have "rights." Human rights, claims Arendt, can have relevance and meaning in our world if we dissociate them from eighteenth-century notions of natural law, an abstract conception of the human being, and the derivation of these rights from God's alleged creation of humanity. This means we have to bring human rights from the realm of the transhistorical or the ahistorical. Rights exist because humans enter into political associations. Human rights, more emphatically, are not grounded on some transhistorical conception of the human, on what could be called a transhistorical anthropological universalism. Human rights are human artifacts, and as such they are historical products. Yet, there is a right that is prior to all rights, the right to political membership, and from this right, the rights of citizens are derived. But where does this right arise? What is its normative justification? as Seyla Benhabib asked.[34] Both the *Modern Review* essay and its version in chapter 5, or the second part of *Origins*, make it quite clear that this right is derived from the worldliness, the earthliness, and the plurality of men. I like to call this a "philosophical-anthropological" foundation, i.e., an explication of what the ontic-phenomenological condition of the human reveals about the "human condition." I understand "philosophical anthropology" in the following way: as a type of reflection, analysis, critique that (to quote J. M. Bernstein) "involves the categorical articulation of the orienting structures of human life that derive from the unique placement of humans as essentially living beings inhabiting a physical and living environment that they share with the teeming abundance of plant life and the vast animal kingdom."[35] I will return to this suggestion later on.

I want to turn to another place in Arendt's corpus where the questions of worldhood, worldliness, belonging, and human plurality appear, although stripped of the language of rights. Arendt's epilogue to her book *Eichmann in Jerusalem: A Report on the Banality of Evil* closes with what she thought the judges should have said to Eichmann as they delivered their guilty verdict. They should have addressed him with the following words:

> Let us assume, for the sake of argument, that it was nothing more than misfortune that made you a willing instrument in the organization of mass murder; there still remains the fact that you have carried out, therefore actively supported, a policy of mass murder. For politics is not like the nursery; in politics obedience and support are the same. And just as you supported and carried out a policy of not wanting to share the earth with the Jewish people and the people of a number of other nations—as though you and your superiors had any right to determine who should and should not inhabit the earth—we find that no one, that is, no member of the human race, can be expected to want to share the earth with you. This is the reason, and the only reason, you must hang.[36]

This is a fascinating argument that appears only at the end, in the epilogue, of her book, which for the most part is in fact reportage of the trial. At first reading, this conclusion seems to come out of nowhere. There are references to Kant, which one may think would have anticipated the argument, but these references have to do with Arendt's arguing against Eichmann's appeals to his having been a good Kantian, or her clarifying that they are preposterous, "outrageous," and "incomprehensible," a complete misunderstanding of the philosopher of duty (see chapter 8, "Duties of a Law-Abiding Citizen").[37]

In my analysis, the argument seems to be that genocide is the result of not wanting to share the world with a "certain" race. More specifically, genocide is the alleged master race arrogating for itself the right to determine who can inhabit the world. This alleged right is thus the right of refusal of cohabitation, the denial to others the right to a piece of the Earth. But no one has a right to say who or who can't inhabit the Earth. There is no right to genocide based on the right of refusal of cohabitation because this right would be a contradiction, a right that other races could claim, which could mean the genocide of the race claiming that right. This argument, the argument for the execution of Eichmann, is in accord with the insights gained in the *Modern Review* essay and *The Origins of Totalitarianism*, as we saw earlier.

If we put together these three texts, we have the following aphorisms:

1. No one has a right to determine who can inhabit the Earth.
2. No one has a right not to share the Earth.
3. No one has a right to refuse cohabitation.
4. No one has a right to determine with whom they share the Earth.
5. All rights derive from the right to the Earth and to inhabit it.
6. All rights are based on the right to the world.
7. There is one transcendent right, the right to have rights.
8. Genocide results from the denial of cohabitation, which is the right to have rights.

But why is there no such right, the right to refuse cohabitation, to dwell on the commonly shared Earth—why is this alleged right a null right, or no right at all?

We can appeal to Kant here, namely, that there is no right where what is claimed cannot be in accordance with the freedom of everyone else. Thus, there is no right of refusal of cohabitation because this is not something that can be claimed that could be in accordance with the claim to cohabitation of others.[38]

DEMOCRATIC ITERATIONS ARE CONSTITUTIONAL ITERATIONS, OR TRANSCENDENCE FROM WITHIN/WITH IUS

Seyla Benhabib has been writing on Hannah Arendt for the most part of her scholarly career. She is without question one of the key points of reference for any contemporary engagement with Arendt's philosophical-political-theoretical bequest. Indeed, most of our most recent engagements with Arendt have been framed by both her critiques and her generative readings of Arendt.[39] Thus, there are many loci in Benhabib's own corpus where we could engage her productive readings of Arendt. Given the circumscribed aims of this chapter, I will focus on two texts, perhaps too quickly, but I hope not superficially. I will focus on one in particular, which I think is her most original and generative reading of Arendt, which brings Arendt into the twenty-first century, as I imagine she would have wanted to be made "contemporary."

The first text is Benhabib's rich *The Right of Others: Aliens, Residents, and Citizens* from 2004, a book with a title that we can only imagine Arendt would have endorsed and loved, even if it does not say "*right* of the other" but the "rights of others"—I want to argue that Benhabib's collapse of right into rights is deliberate and significant.[40] Throughout the book Benhabib spells out and defends a distinction that is key to her interpretation of Arendt. This is the distinction between rights in a "moral" and a "juridico-civil" sense. With this distinction Benhabib think she is making sense of the disjunction, and apparent paradox, between "right" to have "rights," where the former refers to a moral claim and the later to the rights that citizens are endowed with, or granted by, the state to which they belong. The distinction is partly justified with reference to Kant's *Metaphysics of Morals*, where he argues that there is one basic right, from which all other rights derive, namely, the right by which every "action which by itself or by its maxim enables the freedom of each individual's will to co-exist with the freedom of everyone else in accordance with a universal law is *right* [*gerecht*]."[41] According to Benhabib, this formulation is not about the schedule, or list, of rights that are owed to the citizen, but about what can be called the "universal principle of right" (6:230). Thus, the "right" to have rights belongs to this metaorder, the order of the "principle of right" as such. Nonetheless, Benhabib wants to take from Kant's *begründung*, or "justification," the "principle of right." She wants to cleanse it of its metaphysical, subjectivistic, egoistic, and nonintersubjective aspects. She wants to show how the principle can be rearticulated in what she calls "discourse-theoretic" terms, i.e., in terms of postmetaphysical, intersubjective, dialogic ground. This means, at the very least, shifting not to asking what each one of us could will without self-contradiction to become a universal law, but to asking what norms, rules, laws could be considered valid by all those who would be affected were they to be implemented and who would have debated, dialogued, discoursed about them in real and practical discourses. Succinctly put, the shift is from a solipsistic *in foro interno* dialogue, to a public, practical, with others discourse. The question then becomes "If I am able to justify to you why it is right that you and I should act in a certain way, then I must respect your capacity to agree or disagree with me on the basis of reasons which equally apply to us both."[42] What in Kant was simply acknowledging my freedom, so long as it does not violate the freedom of others, becomes with discourse ethics, i.e., with Benhabib's perspective, "communicative freedom." To acknowledge freedom is to acknowledge that there is only freedom if there is freedom with and through others. Thus, the "principle of right" is grounded in the "communicative freedom" of all humans, i.e., acknowledging their autonomy.[43]

The immediate goal of developing a discourse-theoretic justification of the "principle of right" is to arrive at the argument that the "basic human right to communicative freedom enables us both to justify the *human right* to *membership* and to interdict *loss of membership* or denaturalization."[44] Translating

Arendtian into Benhabian, we could say that the "right to have rights" is the right to "communicative freedom," which is the right to membership, the right not to be denationalized, i.e., rendered stateless and rightless. It must be asked, nonetheless, if this translation has extracted us from Arendt's own seemingly paradoxical formulation. If "law's empire"—to use Ronald Dworkin's felicitous expression—is a product of history and a human artifice, how can there be something antecedent to that history, to that empire?[45] Further, one must ask, if part of linguistifying Kant's moral philosophy, which is what discourse ethics does, is to scrub it of its metaphysical trappings, then is it part and parcel of that project to historicize not just moral insight but also "freedom" itself? "Communicative freedom," the freedom of each in accordance with the embodied freedom of others, is historically indexed. Freedom has a history, and so does "communicative freedom," and part of that history is the history of the institutions, rules, norms, and so on through which we acknowledge one another's freedom, by acknowledging one another's rights, as we "discover" or "invent" them.

It may be argued that in contrast to Arendt, Benhabib does not push under the rug the seeming paradox of a right that is the ground of all other real and possible rights. In fact, Benhabib acknowledges that the right to have rights, namely, the right membership, which is the right to citizenship, straddles "two broad categories: human rights and civil and political rights."[46] In the Hohfeldian understanding of rights, we must concur that rights are relational: where there is one right (i.e., power, claim, exception, liability), there are other rights. The discourse of right already gets us going on the path of rights, and to claim rights implies that one has at least one right, the right to claim rights. Either there is right, i.e., rights, or there is no right, i.e., no rights. This is why Benhabib quotes Frank Michelman instead of Ronald Dworkin, for while the latter talks of empire, the former talks of "law's republic," which, when we read him, we find out means the republic of laws.[47] For Benhabib, that the right to membership straddles these two realms, namely, the moral and political-legal, means that "*entitlement* to all civil rights—including rights to association, property, and contract—and eventually to political rights, must itself be considered a human right."[48] If there is the "right" to "rights," it is to the whole fabric of rights. For the moment I'd like to say that to claim a right, the right to have rights, however we want to understand that "transcendent" right, put us into the "space of rights." Better, to claim any one right is to have entered into a kind of language game, a grammar in which one right entails all other rights, even if we do not know what they may be. The language of rights is like a fabric, whose threads we can't separate lest the whole cloth tear and shred. Conversely, to acknowledge the right to a "right," which again in the Hohfeldian fashion is to acknowledge a whole host of other correlative rights, means that we are tightening the weave and expanding it. I think this is at least one of the best ways to make sense of Benhabib's elaboration of the idea of "democratic iterations" that is linked to "jurisgenesis," which she elaborates in chapter 5 of *The Rights of Others*.

The other text I want to focus on is Benhabib's 2006 American Philosophical Association, Eastern Division, presidential address, titled "Another Universalism: On the Unity and Diversity of Human Rights."[49] My argument is that in this lecture Benhabib offers us sophisticated tools to make sense not only of Arendt's critique of human rights, but of her own arguments, as she had developed them up through *The Rights of Others*. In the context of a critique of Martha Nussbaum's derivation of human rights from her Aristotelian-inspired philosophical anthropological ideas about human capabilities, Benhabib notes that such an approach does not differentiate between rights as "moral principles" and rights as "entitlements," on one side, and the "principle of right" and "schedule of rights," on the other. When a human being's right to have rights is acknowledged under the Universal Declaration of Human Rights (UDHR), the "principle of right" has been acknowledged, without thereby specifying what is the schedule of rights that antecedent acknowledgment has thus invoked. In order to navigate Nussbaum's too-substantive and too-metaphysically-laden interpretation of human rights, and Arendt's too-minimalist political reading of human rights, Benhabib will turn toward a discourse-theoretic account of human rights, which is neither too prescriptive nor too minimalist. It is important to flag that with this move Benhabib is taking distance from her own earlier readings of Arendt, in which she sought to mediate the tension between the moral and the political. Now she believes that Arendt collapsed the moral into the political, paradoxically subordinating the moral claims of human rights to a "statist" interpretation of human rights. Indeed, one could argue that one possible reading of Arendt's arguments about the "right to have rights," in which it is interpreted as the right to political membership, that is, the right to citizenship, circles us back to the priority and primacy of the state, which was originally the culprit in the failure of human rights as moral claims not beholden to state power.[50]

In order to develop her discourse-theoretic approach to human rights, Benhabib distinguishes among the following: *First*, essentialist universalism, which believes that there is some essential human nature that is invariant across history. This is the type of universalism that Arendt imputed to the eighteen-century philosophers and thinkers that first formulated human rights. Among those to whom Benhabib attributes this universalism are Thomas Hobbes, David Hume, Adam Smith, Claude-Adrien Helvétius, and Paul-Henri Thiry, Baron d'Holbach. Yet, not all universalists are essentialist, as is the case with Jean-Jacques Rousseau,

Immanuel Kant, and Jean-Paul Sartre. *Second*, in more recent times in philosophy, universalism has come to mean a "justificatory strategy." Among those that embrace this approach are hermeneuticists, strong contextualists, postmodern skeptics, and genealogists of the Foucault type. They all, in one way or another, all of which attempt to justify one's arguments, are "imprisoned" within one's horizon of argumentation, what Jameson called "the prison house of language." Opposed to those that see justification as a self-referential strategy are the "justificatory universalists." While they do hold on to some essentialist conception of human nature, they are committed to defending the "normative" structure and content of human reason, namely, the norm-bounded procedures of scientific inquiry, deliberation, verification, coherence among beliefs, and above all self-reflexivity. Among these "justificatory universalists" Benhabib includes Karl-Otto Apel, Jürgen Habermas, Hilary Putnam, Robert Brandom, and John Rawls, and one would have to include Rainer Forst as well as Benhabib herself.

Third, there is the distinction of *moral universalism*, which Benhabib defines as "the principle that all human beings, regardless of race, gender, sexual background, are entitled to equal moral respect."[51] The "hard" question is whether commitment to moral universalism requires commitment to some sort of cognitive universalism, whether of the essentialist or justificatory kind. Indeed, on what grounds can we claim and affirm *moral universalism* without reference to some means of justifying or knowing whether in fact all humans are entitled to such moral consideration and respect?

Fourth, and finally, Benhabib notes that universalism can and should be understood in a *juridical* sense. While there are many who argue against some notion of human nature on which the claim to human rights could be based, there are many others who argue that "following norms and principles *ought* to be respected by all legal and political systems claiming legitimacy."[52] One way to put this distinction is that even if one is abstemious about moral and cognitive universalism, one can still be a *juridical* universalist.

All of these distinctions are extremely useful as they allow us to clarify the relationships among the moral, the legal, the political, and the cognitive. They also allow Benhabib to scaffold her argument in the following way: the political justification of human rights, which is none other than juridical universal, presupposes commitment to justificatory universalism, which in turn presupposes moral universalism. Moral universalism Benhabib now defines using the language of discourse ethics as "equal respect for the other as a being capable of communicative freedom." Deferring to this moral universalism, however, does not entail commitments to either some notion of human nature or some substantive moral, religious, or scientific worldview. Here reference to a "concrete" or "generalized" other suffices. Nonetheless, and this is key, *juridical* universalism is incoherent and untenable without a defense of *moral* universalism, at least in the minimalist sense of a reference to a generalized and concrete other.

In keeping with the rhetorical strategy of this text, I would like then summarize Benhabib's arguments thusly:

1. The discourse of human rights requires that we distinguish among the moral and juridico-political levels of justification.
2. Justification as to what norms, rules, laws could be in accord with the freedom of all requires that we acknowledge the communicative freedom of each.
3. Any justification of human rights must rest on an acknowledgment of the communicative freedom of each human being.
4. Acknowledging communicative freedom commits us to moral universalism.
5. This moral universalism commits us to justificatory universalism.
6. In fact justificatory universalism is the Janus face of moral universalism, for acknowledging the communicative freedom of each demands of us that we provide "justifications" for the norms, rules, laws that would impact each and all.
7. Moral universalism, qua justificatory universalism, commits us to juridical universalism.

Perhaps these aphorisms can be boiled down to three:

1. No juridical universalism without justificatory universalism.
2. No justificatory universalism without moral universalism.
3. No moral universalism without communicative freedom, which is the "right to justification."

This distilled list of aphoristically expressed philosophical claims, however, fails to highlight an important dimension of Benhabib's work, namely, her important contribution to democratic theory, and, in particular, her contributions to discourse-theoretical understanding of "democratic legitimacy." In *The Right of Others*, Benhabib argued that democratic legitimacy is entangled with deference and acknowledgment of human rights, or at the very least "the right to have rights," as they may be enshrined in a bill of rights within a constitution. In other words, democratic legitimacy has a catalyzing normative dimension that sets democracy on a path of "democratic iterations," by which she means "complex processes of public argument, deliberation, and exchange through which universalistic rights claims and principles are contested and contextualized, invoked and revoked, posited and positioned, throughout the legal and political institutions, as well as in the civil society."[53] Benhabib quotes an important passage from Max Pensky to build up this definition:

> All modern constitutions offer membership according to a schedule of rights, and these rights are justified in terms of universal, rather than merely local or parochial, attributes of members.... Modern constitutions therefore tend to make normative claims that they cannot possibly fulfill. This is one way of describing the problem of constitutional scope. The normative force of democratic constitutions coherently demands the extension of inclusion to all persons while simultaneously retracting that inclusion to all members of a set of arbitrarily designated persons in order to actually succeed in *constituting* a polity.[54]

This is why then, for Benhabib, democratic constitutions have a "context-transcending, cosmopolitan character."[55] Benhabib has called elsewhere this transcendence from within "interactive universalism."[56] Pensky's arguments, which help us understand Benhabib's own normativist democratic legitimacy, make explicit at the very least two distinct and essential characteristics of constitutional democracies: first, constitutionalism commits democracies to an open-ended, and one may say asymptotic, universalism, i.e., democracies are beholden to normative claims that the present democratic status quo can claim to live up to only partially; and second, the polity, the present configuration of democratic institutions themselves, is based on local, temporal, historical, and thus arbitrary acts of inclusion by exclusion and exclusion by inclusion.

What I am trying to make explicit is that Benhabib's commitment to moral universalism, justificatory universalism, and juridical universalism is linked to democratic iterative constitutionalism, i.e., constitutional jurisgenesis, or what Frank Michelman called "dialogical constitutionalism."[57]

CONCLUSION: CONSTITUTIONAL CITIZENSHIP AND BIRTHRIGHT CITIZENSHIP

Bringing together Kant, Arendt, and Benhabib, I aimed to develop a normative argument on behalf of birthright citizenship, that is to say, one is automatically a citizen of the country, or sovereign territory, where one is born. I built this argument by showing the terrestrial, earthly, worldly references to the "right to have rights" in the works of Kant, Arendt, and Benhabib. The "right to have rights," at the very least, is linked to a right to a place in the world. I have argued, however, that what we call the "human condition" both requires and commands that we develop "norms," maxims, and imperatives for regulating how we interact with one another in a world that is finite and in which we cannot but come upon one another and thus have to interact. The goal, more precisely, was to develop a phenomenological-ontological argument for why "birthright" citizenship is not simply a contingent historical development but a constitutional and legal development that addresses and aims to confront a fundamental fact of human existence. I have sought to argue from within the contingency of U.S. history. Here, I would, perhaps naively, assume that readers know, or at least are familiar with, some history of the United States, above all the Civil War, and more specifically the formulation and ratification of what have been called the Reconstruction Amendments to the U.S. Constitution (the Thirteenth, Fourteenth, and Fifteenth). As U.S. historian Eric Foner argued persuasively, the Reconstruction Amendments constituted a "Second Founding" of the United States and "remade" the constitution as a true document of freedom, equality, and inclusion.[58] The antebellum constitution was unquestionably a slavery constitution supported by proslavery constitutionalism.[59] The "remade constitution" after the Civil War became an antislavery constitution that was accompanied by antislavery constitutionalism.[60]

In my estimation the amendments to the U.S. Constitution after the bloody Civil War constitute the most illustrative exemplars of what Benhabib has called "democratic iterations" and "jurisgenesis." It is important to underscore that the Thirteenth Amendment was indispensable to the abolishment of slavery, and thus with it, the abolition, or at least the renunciation, of a racial polity or raciocracy. The Fourteenth Amendment, famously and definitively, constitutionalized, and thus federalized, citizenship, while also abolishing citizenship based on racial descent. Citizenship henceforth would not be bestowed by means of racial descent, but simply by the right of the soil, the claims of territorial legality and legitimacy. Therefore, the aim was to affirm that although citizenship based on *Jus Soli*, i.e., birthright citizenship, is a contingent historical development, when we sift through the debris of history, we can nonetheless retrieve some normative gems, such as *Jus Soli*. The unfinished revolution unleashed by the amendments to the U.S. Constitution after the Civil War is the unfinished institution of citizenship, which is the unfinished constitution. Both propel each other up the normative gradient.

NOTES

1. See Klaus Held, "Towards a Phenomenology of the Political World," in *The Oxford Handbook of Contemporary Phenomenology*, ed. Dan Zahavi (Oxford: Oxford University Press, 2012), 442–59.
2. Another source for my thinking about this project and its promise is Bernhard Waldenfels. See in particular his Tang Chun-I Lectures for 2004, printed as Waldenfels, *The Question of the Other* (Hong Kong: Chinese University Press and State University of New York, 2007); and Waldenfels, *Phenomenology and the Alien: Basic Concepts*, trans. Alexander Kozin and Tanja Stahler (Evanston, IL: Northwestern University Press, 2011).
3. For important historical and comparative work on *Jus Soli*, see Polly J. Price, "Jus Soli and Statelessnes: A Comparative Perspective from the Americas," in *Citizenship in Question: Evidentiary Birthright and Statelessness*, ed. Benjamin N. Lawrance and Jacqueline Stevens (Durham, NC: Duke University Press, 2017), 27–42. See also Noah M. J. Pickus, ed., *Immigration and Citizenship in the Twenty-First Century* (Lanham, MD: Rowman and Littlefield, 1998).
4. Frank Michelman, "Law's Republic," *Yale Law Journal* 97, no. 8, Symposium: The Republican Civic Tradition (July 1988): 1493–537, 1524.
5. See the outstanding work by Alison Kesby, *The Right to Have Rights* (Oxford: Oxford University Press, 2012).
6. On Kant's "moral anthropology," see the excellent collection by Brian Jacobs and Patrick Kain, eds., *Essays on Kant's Anthropology* (Cambridge: Cambridge University Press, 2003), especially the chapter by Robert B. Louden, Werner Stark, and Reinhart Brandt. For a discussion of Kant's *The Metaphysics of Morals*, see Lara Denis, ed., *Kant's Metaphysics of Morals: A Critical Guide* (Cambridge: Cambridge University Press, 2010), especially the chapters by Manfred Kuehn and Ottried Höffe.
7. Arthur Ripstein, *Force and Freedom: Kant's Legal and Political Philosophy* (Cambridge, MA: Harvard University Press, 2009), 370.
8. In this context we have to consider Kant's fascinating text "What Does It Mean to Orient Oneself in Thinking?" (1786), now in Immanuel Kant, *Religion and Rational Theology* (Cambridge: Cambridge University Press, 1996), 1–18, in which the very possibility of orienting oneself theoretically and in thinking presupposes something like the ability of a terrestrial being to find the sun in the sky and from there begin to determine the coordinates of space, and their location in any given place. One can speculate whether a creature not of the Earth, let us say, living on a comet or a planet so large it takes years to gravitate around the sun and its own axis, has the same sense of space as an earthling.
9. Ripstein, *Force and Freedom*, 372, italics added for emphasis.
10. This is how B. Sharon Byrd and Joachim Hruschka put it in their magnificent commentary on Kant's *Doctrine of Right*: "The right of freedom is the decisive assumption we must make in order to give our concrete actions and omissions legal relevance. Accordingly, the right to freedom is an *original* right. By taking three steps, Kant arrives at the original community of the earth and its

corresponding originally united will. The first step leads to a (my) right to a place on this earth, which we shall discuss immediately. The second step leads to the original community of the earth (section 3), and the third step to the original united will of that community (section 4). The first step is based on the original right to freedom, the scarcity of the land, and the fact that I can exercise my right to freedom only if I am in possession of a piece of land. Kant emphasizes the scarcity of the land resulting from the spherical nature of the earth. The earth is not an unlimited plane, on which there are an infinite number of pieces of land. Instead "nature has confined [us] together (by virtue of the spherical form [of our] location, as *globus terraqueus*] within specific borders" [quoting here AA VI, § 62, p. 352, II. 9–11. AA XXIII (*Preparatory DoR*), p. 322.] Under this assumption, the right to a piece of land on this Earth follows from the right to freedom each of us has. Kant states: "All human beings are originally (i.e. before any act of choice with legal effect) in rightful possession of the earth; i.e. they have a right to be where nature or fate (without their will) has placed them. [quoting AA VI, § 13, p. 262, II, 17–20.]." B. Sharon Byrd and Joachim Hruschka, *Kant's Doctrine of Right: A Commentary* (Cambridge: Cambridge University Press, 2010), 126–27.

11. Here, quoting from Immanuel Kant, *Practical Philosophy*, trans. and ed. Mary J. Gregor (Cambridge: Cambridge University Press, 1996), 328–29.
12. Immanuel Kant, *Lectures and Drafts on Political Philosophy*, ed. Frederick Rauscher, trans. Frederick Rauscher and Kenneth R. Westphal, Cambridge Edition of the Works of Immanuel Kant in Translation (Cambridge: Cambridge University Press, 2016).
13. Kant, 273.
14. Kant, 276.
15. Quoting from Immanuel Kant, *The Metaphysics of Morals*, ed. Lara Denis, trans. Mary Gregor (Cambridge: Cambridge University Press, 2017), 55–56.
16. Hannah Arendt, *Lectures on Kant's Political Philosophy*, ed. with an interpretative essay by Ronald Beiner (Chicago: University of Chicago Press, 1992).
17. Arendt's library, with four thousand volumes, is now held at Bard College's library in the "Arendt Collection." Many of Arendt's marginalia to her books have and are being digitized. As of now, I have yet to find marginalia on Kant's *The Metaphysics of Morals*.
18. See the outstanding collection by Stephanie DeGooyer, Alastair Hunt, Linda Maxwell, and Samuel Moyn, *The Right to Have Rights*, with an afterword by Astra Taylor (London: Verso, 2018); Hannah Arendt, "'The Rights of Man': What Are They?" *Modern Review* 3, no. 1 (Summer 1949): 24–37.
19. Arendt, 30.
20. Hannah Arendt, *The Origins of Totalitarianism*, introduction by Samantha Powers (New York: Schocken, 2004). I will refer to this edition, which has restored some of the text of Arendt's appendix and concluding remarks. This edition has also renumbered the chapters, so the chapter where the sentence appears, originally chapter 9, is now chapter 5 of the second part. See page 376 for the sentence in question.
21. Arendt, "'The Rights of Man,'" 26, italics added. See Arendt, *Origins*, 372.
22. Arendt, "'The Rights of Man,'" 26. See Arendt, *Origins*, 372, italics in original.

23. Arendt, "'The Rights of Man,'" 26. See Arendt, *Origins*, 372–73, italics added.
24. Arendt, "'The Rights of Man,'" 27. See Arendt, *Origins*, 373.
25. Arendt, "'The Rights of Man,'" 29. See Arendt, *Origins*, 375.
26. Arendt, *Origins*, 376. Compared with Arendt, "'The Rights of Man,'" 29, italics added.
27. Arendt, *Origins*, 378. Compared with Arendt, "'The Rights of Man,'" 34.
28. Arendt, "'Human Rights,'" 37.
29. Arendt, 34.
30. Arendt, 34.
31. Arendt, 34.
32. Arendt, 33. See Arendt, *Origins*, 382, where this amazing sentence closes a paragraph.
33. Arendt, "'Human Rights,'" 36.
34. Seyla Benhabib, *The Reluctant Modernism of Hannah Arendt* (Oxford: Rowman and Littlefield, 2000), 82.
35. J. M. Bernstein, "Foreword: Toward a Philosophical Anthropology," in *Laughing and Crying: A Study of the Limits of Human Behavior*, by Helmut Plessner, trans. James Spencer Churchill and Marjorie Green (1970; Evanston, IL: Northwestern University Press, 2020), vii. Here I can point in the direction, as partial proof of my claim, to chapter 1 of Arendt's *The Life of the Mind* (San Diego: Harvest, 1981), 19–23, where Arendt writes: "Living beings, men and animals, are not just in the world, they are *of the world*, and this precisely because they are subjects and objects—perceiving and being perceived—at the same time" (20).
36. Then, Hannah Arendt, *Eichmann in Jerusalem: A Report on the Banality of Evil* (1964; New York: Penguin, 2006), 279.
37. Arendt, 136; A fascinating counterpart to Arendt's argument that Eichmann did not understand Kant is Michel Onfray's argument that Eichmann was in fact a faithful and dutiful Kantian. See Michel Onfray, *El sueño de Eichmann,* Precedido de *Un kantiano entre los Nazis*, trans. Alcira Bixio (Barcelona: Editorial Gedisa, S.A., 2009). This is a translation of Onfray's play *Le Songe d'Eichmann*, which is accompanied with an essay about Eichmann's claims about his alleged Kantianism.
38. A very important question arises, which I had not considered until Anna Jurkevics raised it to me. How is Arendt's grounding of the right to have rights similar to or different from Carl Schmitt's own "territorial" grounding of law? I was not aware until I read Jurkevics's excellent and revealing essay on Arendt and Schmitt that Arendt had read so judiciously and critically Schmitt's *The Nomos of The Earth*. See Anna Jurkevics, "Hannah Arendt Reads Carl Schmitt's *Nomos of the Earth:* A Dialogue on Law and Geopolitics from the Margins," *European Journal of Political Theory* 16, no. 3 (2017): 345–66. As Jurkevics's argues persuasively, Arendt is closer to Kant than to Schmitt, which means that Schmitt's basic concept of appropriation (*nehmen*) is the foundation of law (*nomos*) in his etymology of law, whereas common agreement to coinhabit and coshare the Earth is the basis of right (*Recht* and *Ius*), for both Kant and Arendt. In *Nomos of the Earth*, Schmitt refers often to Heraclitus as a source for his understanding of the relationship between law and a spatial ordering. Schmitt may have had in mind Heraclitus's aphorism that has been translated as "People ought to fight to keep their law as to defend the city's walls" (Heraclitus,

Fragments, trans. Books Haxton [New York: Penguin, 2001], 67), or as "The people should fight for their law as for a wall" (see Hippocrates, Heracleitus, *Nature of Man. Regimen in Health. Humours. Aphorisms. Regimen 1–3. Dreams. Heracleitus: On the Universe*, trans. W. H. S. Jones, Loeb Classical Library 150 [Cambridge, MA: Harvard University Press, 1931], 503). Putting a stone on a field and saying beyond here is yours, from there it is mine requires, as Kant and Arendt point out, that we convene to accept the stone as a marker of thine and mine. Prior to the stone and the wall is the agreement to respect the marker as marking a law. I would summarize the difference between Arendt (and thus Kant) and Schmitt in the following way: while the former grounds law on the fundamental condition of having to share the Earth, and thus agreeing to partition it, the latter grounds law in the primacy of taking land and then partitioning. In the former case, the will to taking the law is under the normative guide of agreeing to "law"; in the later, law is a function of the will to possess and claim ownership. This fundamental difference is why I am trying to develop what I call a political phenomenological grounding of normativity that circumvents what we can call the Schmittian voluntarism of spatial division.

39. I would also recommend Peg Birmingham, *Hannah Arendt and Human Rights: The Predicament of Common Responsibility* (Bloomington: Indiana University Press, 2006); and Richard J. Bernstein, *Why Read Hannah Arendt Now* (Cambridge: Polity, 2018).
40. Seyla Benhabib, *The Rights of Others: Aliens, Residents, and Citizens* (Cambridge: Cambridge University Press, 2004).
41. Benhabib, 131. Benhabib is citing an early edition and translation, but I think she must be quoting the passage in the introduction, the section titled "The Universal Principle of Right" (6:230).
42. Benhabib, 132–33.
43. Benhabib, 133.
44. Benhabib, 136.
45. Ronald Dworkin, *Law's Empire* (Cambridge MA: Belknap Press of Harvard University Press, 1986).
46. Benhabib, *The Rights of Others*, 140.
47. Frank Michelman, "Law's Republic," *Yale Law Journal* 97, no. 8, Symposium: The Republican Civic Tradition (July 1988): 1493–537.
48. Benhabib, *The Rights of Others*, 140.
49. Seyla Benhabib, "Another Universalism: On the Unity and Diversity of Human Rights," *Proceedings and Addresses of the American Philosophical Association* 81, no. 2 (November 2007): 7–32.
50. Benhabib, 11.
51. Benhabib, 12.
52. Benhabib, 12.
53. Benhabib, *The Rights of Others*, 179.
54. Benhabib, 176, italics in original.
55. Benhabib, 175.
56. Seyla Benhabib, *Another Universalism: Sovereignty, Hospitality, and Democratic Iterations*, Berkeley Tanner Lectures, with Responses by Jeremy Waldron, Bonnie

Honig, and Will Kymlicka, ed. Robert Post (New York: Oxford University Press, 2006).
57. Michelman, "Law's Empire," 1524.
58. Eric Foner, *The Second Founding: How the Civil War and Reconstruction Remade the Constitution* (New York: Norton, 2019).
59. Martha S. Jones, *Birthright Citizens: A History of Race and Rights in Antebellum America* (Cambridge: Cambridge University Press, 2018).
60. James Oakes, *The Crooked Path to Abolition: Abraham Lincoln and the Antislavery Constitution* (New York: Norton, 2021).

15

Genocide and Jurisgenesis

MAX PENSKY

Among the distinctive features of Seyla Benhabib's normative political theory is her reconstruction of the emergence of universalist, cosmopolitan ideals in law and democracy from the very particular circumstances of men and women caught in times and circumstances that threatened to annihilate them. This narrative fusion of political theory and intellectual history reached its fullest expression in Benhabib's 2018 collection, *Exile, Statelessness and Migration: Playing Chess with History from Hannah Arendt to Isaiah Berlin*, which maps out the terrain of European Jewish identity in the face of genocide.[1] But one of this approach's most poignant and challenging exercises remains Benhabib's essay on Hannah Arendt and Raphael Lemkin, in which she confronts directly the vexing question of how, from each of their intertwined yet utterly distinct intellectual perspectives, genocide emerges as a distinctive form of human horror.

"International Law and Human Plurality in the Shadow of Totalitarianism: Hannah Arendt and Raphael Lemkin" originally appeared in 2009.[2] Like so many of Benhabib's works, the essay begins with the facts of exile, and the intellectual commitments that that experience created for a generation of European Jewish emigres living in the United States during the Second World War and its aftermath. Lemkin and Arendt came from and fled from similar worlds, and walked the same New York streets, as they struggled to make sense of the loss of those worlds. Benhabib describes the "astonishing parallels" in their biographies: growing up in proximate East Prussia and Poland, both succeeded in reaching safety in the United States only after extraordinary journeys including a number of very close calls. Both managed to find professional success, in different forms, in American academic and legal institutions; both spent much of that time in New York with overlapping professional and personal circles.

And yet these parallels, striking as they are, seem to have run their separate courses without ever having converged. No evidence exists of the two having ever met. Moreover, as Benhabib points out, Arendt shows no awareness or interest in Lemkin's life project. The effort to adapt his own conception of genocide, developed over the course of the 1930s, into a version that the newly formed United Nations would adopt as its first major instrument of international law for the postwar global order, famously consumed him.[3] Nor did Lemkin, for his part, ever exhibit any awareness of Arendt's work, in particular *The Origins of Totalitarianism*, which appeared three years after the 1948 Genocide Convention. That book expressed both Arendt's mistrust of international law as a response to the catastrophe of global war and the Holocaust, as well as her conviction that these twin disasters represented a radically novel form of the assault on human plurality, one that could not be theorized, or even registered, under existing conceptual frames.

Benhabib's essay locates the distinctiveness of the international crime of genocide as a force field between these two narratives, kept so close to each other yet never actually touching. Situating itself between Lemkin's well-known preoccupation with the special value and specific vulnerabilities of social groups, and Arendt's even better-known dislike—bordering on a kind of intellectual revulsion—of the social in favor of the world-making capacity of individuals in political action, the essay asks whether Lemkin's or Arendt's contrasting approaches to identifying the distinctiveness of genocide share some common ground. And if they do not, is there good reason to prefer one approach over the other?

She locates the heart of Lemkin's group-based position in a distinctive combination of two sources: the experience of the Minority Treaties in the interwar years, and a strongly essentialist, "culturalist," and Herderian conception of the uniqueness and holism of social groups, which Lemkin endows with both intrinsic and instrumental value, generating distinct versions of human experience that genocide targets and destroys. By contrast, Arendt's hostility to collectives urges her to reject this group-based social ontology entirely, and (by the time of *Eichmann in Jerusalem* in 1963) propose her own conception of human plurality as the specific target of genocidal violence.

As a reluctant Arendtian, who shares much of Arendt's suspicion regarding the role and normativity of ascriptive social identities, Benhabib suggests that Arendt's strategy of shifting the distinctiveness of the crime of genocide to its status as an assault on human plurality, rather than on intrinsically valuable social groups, marks a tentative advance in giving the crime of genocide the modest ontological grounding required if we are to make sense of its claim to be a distinct form of human wrongdoing. This advocacy for Arendt is hardly surprising. But is the choice as clear-cut as it may appear?

This chapter has two parts. First, a reconstruction of Benhabib's argument in "International Law and Human Plurality" will attempt to show that the essay ends up in a more aporetic conclusion than may be obvious. I diagnose this aporetic conclusion as resulting from a reading of Lemkin that overestimates his dependence on a "Herderian" conception of the ontological and normative significance of social groups. At the same time, the reading may also overestimate the potential of Arendt's concept of human plurality for providing a clear alternative to Lemkin's valorization of social groups as a way of identifying the distinctive wrong of the crime of genocide.

The chapter's second part turns to one of Benhabib's most significant theoretical resources: Robert Cover's conception of jurisgenesis, which Benhabib adopts, mutatis mutandis, as a way of clarifying how the abstract, procedural universalism of the modern, postwar international human rights regime was appropriated, transformed, and given concrete content as it structured the claims of oppressed, marginalized, and persecuted groups struggling for legal and political acknowledgment. International human rights law, on Benhabib's account, sponsored a jurisgenerative process that was driven by successive democratic iterations. This dialectic between universalism and the situated political actor is the distinctive "other" cosmopolitanism Benhabib sees as the potential of international human rights law.[4] I argue that this adaption of Cover's legal thought, from domestic to international human rights law, holds promise for international criminal law as well, in particular as a way of understanding the distinctiveness of the international crime of genocide.

Genocide, as the new international crime and the point of origin in the explosive growth of international criminal law in the post–World War II international order, is, famously, a crime of groups. The language of the Convention specifies five categories of criminal act—killing, causing serious bodily or mental harm, deliberately inflicting conditions of life calculated to bring about physical destruction, imposing measures intended to prevent births, and forcibly transferring children—that are genocidal if two further conditions are met. First, any one of these acts must be directed against members of a national, ethnic, racial, or religious group "as such." The second, "mental element" requires that these acts, against this specific set of groups, be committed with an intent to destroy one of these groups, "in whole or in part."

The precise terms of the Genocide Convention only approximate Lemkin's own vision. What emerged as the final text of the Convention reflected (as all international treaties do) the compromises and elisions that the great powers were willing to accept at the opening of a new, bipolar international order. This inevitable refraction of the normative commitments of the idea of the legal recognition and protection of social groups through the lens of Realpolitik led to some distinctive features that distinguish between the legal concept of genocide as it has developed over the past seventy years and Lemkin's conception. Among these differences, most relevant for our purposes are, first, the significant limitation in the Convention of the crime of genocide to intentional acts directed at an artificially restricted set of four groups—national, religious, ethnic, and racial. Both the United States and the Soviet Union found it disagreeable to include political groups in this list, each for reasons of its own. Lemkin himself was bitterly opposed to this omission, a fact that already complicates the view that he was operating with a problematic essentialist social ontology regarding the nature of social groups.

Second, the Convention determines the crime of genocide to consist only in a set of five narrowly specified acts. This narrow focus of coercive, usually physically violent state policies rules out much of what Lemkin understood by the earlier notion of "vandalism"—less overtly violent state policies that targeted the physical, geographical, ritual, or linguistic bases of group identity. What is often now referred to as cultural genocide, in other words, was deliberately excluded from the narrow definition of the international crime—again for reasons that both the United States and the Soviet Union found expedient. This exclusion once again draws attention to the fact that the crime Lemkin spent so much time and energy lobbying for was significantly distinct from the broader and finer-grained prohibition on state policies directed at vulnerable groups that he himself preferred.

Third, the language of the Convention included a high evidentiary bar for determination of the mental element of the crime of genocide. The notorious "special intent" (*dolus specialis*) requirement mandates that any successful prosecution for the crime of genocide requires the establishment, beyond reasonable doubt, that any one of the five predetermined acts were committed with the specific intent to destroy one of the four protected groups, in whole or in part, "as such." In practice, of course, such special intent is notoriously difficult to prove to the degree required by this evidentiary bar, a barrier to successful prosecution that, once again, was likely a desired and not just a foreseeable outcome of the negotiations among the emergent global powers in the immediate postwar era.

These distinctive features of what became the "narrow" legal definition of the crime of genocide in the Convention stand in obvious tension with the broader and subtler conception of genocidal state policies that Lemkin had intended.

Moreover, the narrow legal definition usually represents the starting point for processes of political and even moral interpretation of the meaning, scope, and implications of genocide, including the interpretive processes of international and domestic courts, political and diplomatic actors, major and smaller nongovernmental organizations, corporations, journalists, and even novelists and film makers, interpretations that have continued with few interruptions from the end of the 1940s to the present.

The interpretive history of the crime of genocide also includes the history of attempts to push back against the narrow legalism of 1948, advocating for the inclusion of groups and acts expressly or implicitly excluded, or for a less strict interpretation of the special intent requirement specified in the language of the Convention. Conversely, this seventy-year interpretive history must also include efforts by international and domestic courts, experts in international law, and many genocide and Holocaust scholars to resist attempts to broaden the narrow legal definition, whether from a concern that a larger list of relevant groups would "dilute" the specific focus of the Convention on racial, ethnic, religious, and national groups, opening the door to a conception of relevant groups so capacious as to become frivolous, or from the worry that the Convention's creation of strong legal obligations on state signatories would weaken if the narrow reading were not carefully maintained and reserved for "genuine" genocides (where the means and methods of attacks on groups consist predominantly of mass killing) and included "mere" cultural genocides (where the bases of the identity of groups are undermined and destroyed without either the lethality or the documentation of genocidal intent that the Convention demands).

Lemkin's original conception remains highly relevant in this back-and-forth interpretive struggle between narrow and broad readings of the meaning and distinctiveness of genocide. This is especially true for the fraught question of Lemkin's social ontology—his views on why social groups were so significant and valuable that they required the special protection of binding international law. Generations of interpreters of Lemkin, including Benhabib, have taken as their starting point that Lemkin's vision of the value of groups rested on an outdated and deeply problematic social ontology. In such an ontology, groups have an existence and intrinsic value independent of their members. This intrinsic value is "culturalist," as Benhabib puts it, in the sense of a social group's capacity to create unique cultural products. Intrinsic value is instrumental as well, in each social group's potential to share its unique culture with the world and thus enrich it. Finally, such an ontology sees groups as holistic, containing a more or less complete set of normative and interpretive commitments composing a distinct and irreplaceable form of life, deserving of recognition, appreciation, and protection.

Lemkin, in other words, is on Benhabib's reading a "Herderian" evaluator of social groups, guided by the Herderian belief in the group as the conditio sine qua non of all human artistic and cultural achievement. Groups in this view are virtually natural kinds, with nearly exclusively ascriptive identity conditions for members.

If this Herderian, essentialist social ontology is really the basis for Lemkin's concern about protecting social groups through international law, then it is easy to see why Benhabib and other readers of Lemkin have found it so concerning. It is sociologically naïve, indeed dangerously so, insofar as it replicates some of the most toxic views of Otherness, especially of the most marginalized and vulnerable populations, responsible for so much of the risk of genocidal state policies in the first place. This mistrust of Lemkin's social ontology is characteristic of the view that Lemkin's own view of groups and their value is too theoretically inept, antiquated, and compromised to be of use in contemporary interpretive battles over the distinctiveness of the crime of genocide.

But is this judgment of Lemkin's social ontology warranted? There is good reason to suspect it is not. Drawing extensively on archival resources that became available only after Benhabib's essay, both A. Dirk Moses's and Douglas Irvin-Erikson's painstaking reconstructions of Lemkin's shifting (and not entirely consistent) views on the social ontology and normativity of groups complicate the picture significantly. Moses—himself not an enthusiastic supporter of Lemkin's work—nevertheless disputes the standard view of Lemkin's Herderian social ontology, noting that the valorization of social groups, for instance, in the context of the national groups in Central Europe that the Minority Treaties sought to protect, was largely instrumental: Lemkin's concept of genocide was less a reflection of a normative social ontology valuing groups as such than a form of cosmopolitan legal thought focusing on groups as *particularly vulnerable* to unaccountable state violence due to political factors, not their intrinsic qualities.[5]

More recently, Irving-Erickson has argued even more forcefully against the view that Lemkin endorsed a Herderian valorization of social (national, ethnic, or religious) groups as such.[6] Notwithstanding the several passages in Lemkin's work that appear to do just that, Irvin-Erickson reconstructs the highly pragmatic (and not always consistent) arguments that Lemkin employed to generate international support for the Convention, beneath which was a core conviction of the distinctive *vulnerability* of social groups. This conviction is certainly compatible with the parallel claim of groups' intrinsic value, but is nevertheless importantly distinct from it. Here, the paradigmatic cases for Lemkin were less the imperiled national minorities in Central and Eastern Europe, left stranded in unfriendly sovereign territory as a result of redrawn national borders, but rather the Indigenous peoples of the Americas and the Global South, at the mercy of European and North America colonial settler violence. Lemkin's focus on what we now call cultural genocide—programs to eliminate social groups by deliberately and systematically destroying the religious, linguistic, and artistic foundations of a group—arises from this view of colonial settler violence, and not Central European politics.

On this revisionist reading, Lemkin emerges as a somewhat peculiar, but hardly reactionary, kind of "communitarian cosmopolitan," whose ambition was to criminalize state-sponsored attacks on social groups when, for any number of reasons, those groups were designated as targets of eliminationist state violence. What is distinctive about social groups, in other words, is the vulnerability that they bear *as groups*. Integration surely can mitigate this distinctive targeting, but (as the example of the Jews of Europe shows all too well) under the "right" conditions can have the opposite effect as well. How much or little integration will protect minority groups is the outcome of a large number of variables. As Benhabib points out, this is why (in sharp contrast to Arendt) Lemkin was not convinced that Nazism, or totalitarianism in general, constituted a radical break with the history of state-led eliminationist attacks on minority groups, whether internally or (as in Lemkin's most important examples) in the colonial possessions of the imperial European powers.

The result of this reconstruction is a social ontology of groups far less ascriptive, and with far messier, contested, politically fraught, and constructed boundaries and membership criteria, than the standard reading of Lemkin has supposed.[7]

The *distinctiveness* of the crime of genocide is thus related not only to its gravity, but to the specific form of vulnerability that social groups assume *as* groups. The question of whether the specific harm that the criminalization of genocide was meant to prevent and deter consisted in the first instance of harm to groups, and hence in a secondary and derivative sense to the individual persons who composed them, or conversely whether the primary harm was to individuals, who assumed greater vulnerability and hence need for protection due to their strong affiliations with social groups, is a disjunction that Lemkin did not seem to regard as pressing.

As both Benhabib and others have reconstructed, Hannah Arendt's dismissive attitude toward international law in general, and toward the treaty-based international prohibition against the crime of genocide in particular, changed significantly in the decade between the emergence of *The Origins of Totalitarianism* in

1951 and *Eichmann in Jerusalem* in 1963. The earlier work took a dim view of the prospects of international legal mechanisms to impose a normative order on the chaotic conditions of the immediate postwar years and the emerging bipolar world order. Arendt was as skeptical about the prospects for legal regulation of mass atrocity in the Genocide Convention as she was about the legalization of cosmopolitan norms of universal human dignity in the Universal Declaration of Human Rights, which the UN General Assembly voted to approve the day following the adoption of the Genocide Convention in December of 1948.

And yet, as Benhabib observes, little more than a decade later, *Eichmann in Jerusalem* offered a powerful defense of the moral foundations of the legal prohibition against genocide, even as Arendt, characteristically, insisted on translating the legal terminology of the Convention into her own preferred theoretical vocabulary. For Arendt in *Eichmann*, the distinctive harm of the Holocaust—and by inference of genocide in general—is the intentional assault on the very foundations of a *world*, in Arendt's distinct sense, that is, of the possibility of distinctively human life, sustained by the fact of human plurality.

Benhabib reads Arendt on genocide as a corrective to Lemkin's misplaced valuation of social groups as intrinsically valuable *as* groups. On her reading, while Lemkin saw the cultural, religious, and linguistic diversity of social groups as the very value the criminalization of genocide was intended to protect, Arendt's hostility toward social groups as such motivated her to identify the distinctive wrong of genocide by reference to her own concept of human plurality as a foundation of the possibility for individual human agents to take part in the political life of their polities.

While a full reconstruction of human pluralism is well beyond the scope of this chapter, it's worth recalling its centrality for Arendt's political philosophy. Plurality—the possibility of the *creation of meaning* through the maximally free interaction of differently situated persons in a single political space—is the very possibility for the coming-into-being of a world, in Arendt's distinct sense.

This is a powerful evocation of the world-destroying aspect of genocide as the targeting of human plurality itself, and is an example of how Arendt's distinctive concepts and terminologies can sharpen and clarify the question at stake in genocide's distinctiveness. And yet, as Benhabib herself acknowledges, shifting from Lemkin's purportedly essentialist account of the intrinsic value of social groups to Arendt's evocation of pluralism is, in effect, shifting from one social ontology to another: and the two may be far more closely related than Arendt's famous distaste for social groups and social identities would suggest.

Human plurality is a fact and norm together, attaching to the reality of our shared humanness as species of comembers while at the same time registering the irreducible differences among individual persons, on whose basis political life and a human world are possible. "Plurality," Benhabib writes, "is the condition of human action because we are all the same, that is, human, in such a way that nobody is ever the same as anyone else who ever lived, lives, or will live."[8] This is why genocide is a crime against the human condition. Arendt responds to the problematic thematization of social groups as the target of destruction in the language of the Convention by, in effect, changing the subject. She insists instead that individual human beings, and the human condition as such, are the micro- and macrosubjects of harm, regarding prioritization of the meso-level of social groups, which Lemkin and the Convention prioritize, as little more than a sort of philosophical mistake.

This move of course bears on the *distinctiveness* of the crime of genocide, which now merges back to what Arendt saw as the category of crimes against humanity. Characteristically, she redefined the legal term according to her own preferences, as a crime against the human condition. In the famous condemnation of the convicted Eichmann at the close of *Eichmann in Jerusalem*, Arendt asserts that the justice of the sentence of death for Eichmann rests in the claim that no one can be expected to share the Earth with a person who arrogated to himself the right to determine which persons could or could not share the Earth with him: in effect, Eichmann deserved to die because his arrogation to himself of the right to dispose over human plurality made a world with him in it intolerable.

For Benhabib, this use of the bespoke terminology of human plurality and the human world marks a significant step in giving the concept of genocide a needed "ontological grounding" that Lemkin's Herderian social ontology could not offer. Benhabib observes that Arendt's conception of human pluralism "enables Arendt to escape both the ascriptivism and the culturalism of Lemkin's concept of the group."

I am unconvinced that the shift to an Arendtian conception of plurality does this, however. Certainly, Arendt's deep hostility to the very idea of social groups entails the view that *all* such groups ought to be at least in principle taken as voluntary, rather than ascriptive in their self-constituting collective identity. Legal protection of groups would be aimed at the individuals comprising them, rather than the reifying claim that groups were entitled to legal protection "as such." As David Luban has noted, Arendt's lecturing the Israeli court in *Eichmann* that they did not really understand the meaning of the Genocide Convention (since they did not grasp that it was, in fact, criminalizing assault on the human condition in her preferred sense) is incoherent if, as it appears, the weight of the wrong is Eichmann's, and the Nazi state's, not wanting to share the Earth with Jews.[9] Presumably no murderer wants to share the Earth with his victims. *Pace* Benhabib,

Luban argues that Arendt's rejection of any role for the concept of the human group in the determination of the distinctiveness of genocide fails to provide genocide with a "firm ontological grounding." In fact, the argument accomplishes just the opposite, by erasing the distinction between the crime of genocide and crimes against humanity altogether.

To be sure, this blurring—or undermining—of the distinction between the crime of genocide and adjacent international atrocity crimes, such as crimes against humanity or war crimes, does have a good amount of potential legitimacy. At the time of the negotiation of the Convention, the jurist Hersch Lauterpacht developed substantive arguments for why genocide's distinctiveness did far more harm than good, effectively replicating the same group-based logics that perpetrators relied on.[10] Arendt is not alone in believing that, once the focus on social groups is found unsatisfactory, there may be no pressing need to make sharp distinctions between, say, genocide and crimes against humanity, implying that the Convention was something of a long-term detour, with not entirely helpful results.[11] We may read Arendt in this manner, but this does little to clarify the question of the distinctiveness of genocide as a normative-legal concept in its own right.

The end result of Benhabib's analysis, then, is aporetic in several dimensions. It is no longer plausible to retain a reductive, Herderian reading of Lemkin's ontology of social groups. In fact, Lemkin seems to have had few difficulties affirming the plastic, dynamic, and contested aspect of group identity, a position that is not compatible with the view that he regarded social groups as quasi-organic natural kinds. He appears entirely open to the route of justifying the legal protection of groups less on the basis of their intrinsic value than on their instrumental disvalue, that is, the specific forms of vulnerability to lethal state power that individuals assume by virtue of their ascription (whether by themselves, by the perpetrator state, by some third agent, or indeed by a combination of all three) of group belonging.

But if this is true, then it's not possible to maintain the distinction between Lemkin's and Arendt's supposedly antagonistic and incompatible accounts of genocide's distinctiveness. For Arendt, the distinctive wrong of genocide lies in its deliberate destruction of human plurality, its un-worlding of persons for whom being in a world touches on the very heart of their humanity. But even allowing for some substantive differences entailed by Arendt's conceptual shift from "belonging to a group" to "enjoying human plurality," what seemed like a stark opposition between Arendt and Lemkin appears more like a difference in nuance and emphasis, a difference perhaps misleadingly magnified by Arendt's habitual insistence on her own preferred terminology.

The remainder of this chapter develops an alternative approach to the question of the distinctiveness of the crime of genocide, and does so by shifting from one component of Benhabib's approach to normative political theory—the dialectic between universal cosmopolitan norms and the particular biographical circumstances and intellectual commitments of the small group of Jewish émigrés during the middle decades of the twentieth century—to another, equally productive component: Benhabib's appropriation of Robert Cover's conception of jurisgenesis.

I argue that a more promising and revealing answer to the question of the distinctiveness of the crime of genocide can be found less in analytical disagreements over the social ontology of social groups than in the rich, productive processes of new *legal meaning* that were touched off by the advent of the Convention in 1948. In Cover's sense, *jurisgenerative effects* have resulted as a range of "nomic groups" have appropriated, transformed, challenged, fought over, and reworked the legal meaning of genocide as parts of their own narrative processes of collective self-creation.

In Cover's deeply radical conception of jurisgenesis, it is these nomic groups, and their creative, often deeply agonistic reworkings of the legal concept of genocide, who *make the law*, no less than state parties drafting international legal instruments, legislatures debating their ratification, and courts applying them to cases. The central claim here is that the jurisgenerative *process* that created the legal meaning(s) of genocide is deeply unlike those processes that generated the meanings of other international crimes: crimes against humanity and war crimes (and, in a more indirect sense, the criminal act of ethnic cleansing). Genocide as law and concept has been the subject of a rich, unruly, creative, and distinctive jurisgenerative history, as groups narratively interpret the legal concept, deny the interpretations of other groups, contest the range and content of its core claims, and endow it with the concrete, lived specificity that makes law a social practice. This, I will argue, is where we ought to look for the distinctiveness of the crime of genocide.

Benhabib's appropriation of Robert Cover's conception of "jurisgenesis" has proven to be a useful and productive tool for the overarching goal of a normative political theory with the objective of interpreting the development of international law in the postwar world as an expression of cosmopolitan justice.

This was far from an obvious choice. Cover's original conception is notoriously elliptical and terse (and was never fully developed, given Cover's early death). It also expresses an agonistic vision of law and politics, and of the relation between the law and the violence of coercive state power, that I suspect few normatively minded legal theorists would be inclined to endorse fully. Finally, while expansive enough to address the full spectrum of contemporary forms of coercive legal regimes, Cover's conception of jurisgenesis foregrounds the role and function of constitutional jurisprudence in democratic regimes, a fact that makes the most sense out of the communitarianism that underlies Cover's theory of law, but also poses difficulties for the transposition of that theory into international law in general, and in particular into the origins of modern International Human Rights Law, the specific domain in which Benhabib is most concerned.

Jurisgenesis is, famously, "the creation of legal meaning."[12] This is the work of a "nomic community," a social group that encounters coercive legal statues issuing from the state authority and, as part of its ongoing narrative construction of a normative universe, *creates* law as a crucial resource, thus filling with narratives the space that separates the legal from the nonlegal sphere. This communitarian claim, that *social groups* are the drivers of legal meaning, is frequently overlooked in Cover's work, yet it is central.[13] Nomic communities—narratively self-creating and self-sustaining social groups—are *the primary sources of law*, rather than law's passive addressees.[14] Legislatures, courts, and state agents wielding coercive, violent power are no longer to be seen as the definitive sources of law than the "jurispathic" *killers* of law, pruning back the lush growth of legal meaning as it constantly arises from these nomic communities, using state-legitimated violence, even lethal violence, to put an authoritative stop to legal meaning-creation. As Cover famously and succinctly put it in "Violence and the Word," "legal interpretation takes place in a field of pain and death."

"Paideiac" jurisgenesis is Cover's term for the profusion of legal meanings that nomic groups *produce*; "imperial" jurisgenesis, by contrast, is the equally odd term that Cover uses for the complementary and equally important process where other groups push back against the profusion of meanings—of "too much law"—arising from paideiac jurisgenesis, using their social power to restrict, diminish, and undermine what they (from their own perspective) demand is an inappropriate, untrue, or inauthentic meaning of a legal essential. Between them, these two constitute the respiratory process of legal meaning. Jurisgenesis in this double, dialectical sense is ultimately the work of *public* communication, requiring a civil society and public sphere capable of receiving, and contesting, both the profusion of legal meaning and its agonistic responses.

Jurisgenesis is an example of what realist legal scholars refer to as "law in action": law not as a static reservoir of statutory language awaiting application, but law as it actually operates in life.[15] "Meaning in law," as Cover put it, arises from shared interpretive commitments: the way people and institutions appropriate legal concepts as a cultural practice of self-creation. For Cover, jurisgenesis is *not* a secondary or derivative phenomenon that somehow finds and distorts law that arrives, as it were, intact from the state authority. "No set of legal institutions or prescriptions exist," Cover insists, "apart from the narratives that locate it and give it meaning."[16]

Cover's preferred example of this jurisgenerative phenomenon is the appropriation of the U.S. Constitution's First Amendment Establishment and Free Exercise Clauses by a minority religious community (Mennonites), as they take on a distinct meaning beyond the putative secularist normative universe of meaning of the founders, and reemerge as part of a narrative interpretation of the religious injunction to separate *from* secular society, an injunction now rendered meaningful *through*, rather than in simple opposition to, the constitutional essential.[17]

The jurisgenerative power of domestic law naturally focuses Cover's attention on constitutional legal concepts. In a parallel manner, surely, the transfer of jurisgenerative lawmaking from the domestic, constitutional to the international sphere, and postwar International Human Rights Law in particular, also reconstructs how abstract legal concepts acquire legal meaning only through the work of nomic communities' narrative processes of self-creation. However, unlike the grounding in domestic, specifically constitutional legal history, the international legal phenomenon of jurisgenesis has far less direct connection to a concrete democratic polity, since international law has far fewer points of democratic access than domestic constitutional law. Moreover, Cover's claim regarding the jurispathic work of state power, in the figure of judges, to kill jurisgenesis, to stop the growth of legal meaning and authorize a definitive version backed by coercive state power, is missing in the largely anarchic international legal context.

This does not necessarily mean that there can be no jurispathic moments in international law, and later in this chapter I will suggest one way of thinking about one of these moments. But it is also possible, as many interpreters of Cover suggest, that the international legal arena offers possibilities for a more jurisgenerative function of international courts and tribunals, and for less of the jurispathic function that Cover sees as distinguishing courts in the domestic context, a function that he always equates with the imposition of state-sanctioned violence.[18] This possibility of a more jurisgenerative role for international courts also connects to Benhabib's views on the potentially cosmopolitan contributions that international law makes toward a project of global legal pluralism.[19]

Benhabib's version of the "democratic iterations" that structure the process of international-legal jurisgenesis shows how nomic communities appropriate and transform the abstract, procedural universalism of international human rights claims, forging these claims into narratives that "make law" by endowing those abstract concepts with concrete, living content. How this version is put into practice is significant both for its continuities and differences from Cover. His reading is profoundly communitarian, in the hermeneutic sense of collective self-identity maintained through constant self-interpretation. His examples (frequently of religious communities) illustrate how universalist legal concepts are made alive through their appropriation in particular minority groups, whose interests and values are predictably and deeply different from those of the majority culture. This dialectic of universalism and the situated particular is of course the heart of Benhabib's normative political theory as well.

Turning to the question of genocide and jurisgenesis, we can advance the following claim: beginning with the adoption of the United Nations Convention on Genocide on December 10, 1948, a new legal concept was subjected to repeated iterations of both paideiac and imperial jurisgenesis. This dialectical process has been predominantly structured by the overarching significance of the Holocaust for the history and concept of genocide. At its core, both paideiac ("creative") and imperial ("critical") meanings arose from the global discourse surrounding the meaning of the Holocaust: the implication of the event for surviving Jews, particularly in the newly founded state of Israel, in the United States, and in the global Jewish diaspora.

As a matter of international law, and as a practical matter of international law enforcement, there is no hierarchy of gravity of international crimes.[20] While often referred to as the "crime of crimes," even by its most distinguished legal interpreters, genocide is, as a matter of law at least, not graver, more serious, or more deserving of due legal and political responses than other international crimes: crimes against humanity, war crimes, and crimes of aggression. Indeed, many atrocity prevention practitioners privately (and increasingly publicly) bemoan the common perception that genocide stands at the apex of a hierarchy of gravity, with the inevitable and often horrible consequence that the political will to protect populations from mass atrocities often evaporates once a public determination is made that a crime is "only" a crime against humanity.[21]

The jurisgenerative processes attaching to the crime of genocide distinguish it from adjacent international crimes, which, notwithstanding their gravity, have never produced—and likely will never produce—any comparably rich, contested, and agonistic "normative universe of meaning." The implication—strange as it may sound—is that genocide, in relation to the other international crimes, is distinguished less by the ontology of social groups, however better or worse argued, than by the meanings that have attached to it.

The creative appropriation of the Holocaust, of the genocide against the Jewish People, has such a foundational and complex status for the "nomic community" of Israel that I will not attempt so much as a brief summary here. The point is that there is no creative jurisgenesis without its complementary, critical countermovement. The relation of the Holocaust to the legal category of genocide has embodied this double movement as any number of social groups have sought to appropriate genocide into their own narrative histories, and, in many cases, have had to contend with the critical response that doing so extended the meaning of genocide beyond its acceptable bounds.

The genocide scholar James Waller describes a range of jurisgenesis (not his term, obviously) attempting to extend the narrow legal definition of targeted groups, ranging from the powerfully persuasive, such as political groups, gender, and LGBTQIA+, to the facially ridiculous, trivializing, and offensive, such as against farmed turkeys, for instance.[22] This spectrum of meaning-creating narratives is the foreseeable and not at all undesirable reflection of the force of the original legal conception in its conjunction with the singular event of the Holocaust. Our responses to these appropriations—whether they elicit reactive attitudes of resentment or indignation, or whether we are inclined to support the extension of the concept to new circumstances, beyond the narrow language of the Convention or well beyond the ultimate paradigmatic case of the Holocaust—will depend on a myriad of factors and cannot, and should not, be predetermined. This is the messily democratic iterative process of legal meaning that the concept of genocide consists of.

Ought social, political, gender-based, or other affiliative groups that are not narrowly defined according to the terms of the Convention come under legal protection (and recognition) in the public appropriation of the concept of genocide? Ought "cultural genocide" that does not entail the physical destruction of biological persons "count" as genocide, in keeping with Lemkin's original intentions but potentially in contradiction to the paradigm case and the relevant caselaw? What authorizes any actor to make these determinations in a definitive way—ought we to take the "bottom-up" jurisgenerative transformation of the meaning and applicability of the statutory language as bearing an equal, even a greater, weight than the jurisprudence of courts?

This chapter has argued that the narrative reconstruction of Lemkin's and Arendt's differing paths toward a conception of the distinctive wrongfulness of genocide may be advanced better through a repurposed use of one of Benhabib's own most powerful theoretical tools, Cover's notion of jurisgenesis. Making this argument required both a critical reading of the outcome of Benhabib's own analysis of the normativity and ontology of social groups in both Lemkin and Arendt, and a reading of Cover that emphasizes his distinctively communitarian and agonistic view of the dynamic of jurisgenesis that I suspect goes beyond what Benhabib herself would endorse. Yet I regard the argument, truncated though it is here, as having some promise for encouraging further discussion of the jurisgenerative dimension of international criminal law, which in contrast to human rights law is frequently overlooked by those analyzing international law as a potential driver of cosmopolitan norms. If another result of the argument is to continue to read deeper into the life and thought of Raphael Lemkin, then this would be a very welcome outcome.

NOTES

1. Seyla Benhabib, *Exile, Statelessness, and Migration: Playing Chess with History from Hannah Arendt to Isaiah Berlin* (Princeton, NJ: Princeton University Press, 2018).
2. Seyla Benhabib, "International Law and Human Plurality in the Shadow of Totalitarianism: Hannah Arendt and Raphael Lemkin," *Constellations: An International Journal of Critical and Democratic Theory* 16, no. 2 (June 2009): 331–51. Reprinted in Seyla Benhabib, *Dignity in Adversity: Human Rights in Troubled Times* (Cambridge: Polity, 2011), 41–56.
3. UN General Assembly, *Universal Declaration of Human Rights*, December 10, 1948, 217 A (III).
4. See Seyla Benhabib, *Another Cosmopolitanism: Hospitality, Sovereignty, and Democratic Iterations* (Oxford: Oxford University Press, 2006).
5. A. Dirk Moses, "Genocide," *Australian Humanities Review* 55 (2013): 23–44.
6. Douglas Irvin-Erickson, *Raphael Lemkin and the Concept of Genocide* (Philadelphia: University of Pennsylvania Press, 2017).
7. See Irvin-Erickson, 67–68.
8. Benhabib, "International Law and Human Plurality," 73.
9. David Luban, "Arendt on the Crime of Crimes," *Ratio Juris* 28, no. 3 (September 2015): 307–25.
10. For a vivid reconstruction of this debate between Lemkin and Lauterpacht, see Philippe Sands, *East West Street: On the Origins of "Genocide" and "Crimes Against Humanity"* (New York: Vintage, 2017).
11. For an explicit argument on merging the crime of genocide "back" into a larger category of crimes against humanity, see Larry May, *Genocide: A Normative Approach* (Cambridge: Cambridge University Press, 2010).
12. Robert M. Cover, "The Supreme Court, 1982 Term—Foreword: *Nomos and Narrative*," *Harvard Law Review* 97, no. 4 (1983).
13. See Franklin G. Snyder, "Nomos, Narrative, and Adjudication: Toward a Jurisgenetic Theory of Law," *William and Mary Law Review* 40 (1999): 1623–729.
14. "When groups generate their own articulate normative orders concerning the world as they would transform it, as well as the mode of transformation and their own place within the world, the situation is different [than in the case of individual rights]—a new nomos, with its attendant claims to autonomy and respect, is created. Insofar as the vision and objectives of such a group are integrative, however, the structure of its nomos differs from that of the insular sectarian model." Cover, "The Supreme Court, 1982 Term," 34.
15. For a discussion, see Paul D. Carrington and Erika King, "Law and the Wisconsin Idea," *Journal of Legal Education* 47, no. 3 (September 1997): 297–340.

16. Cover, "The Supreme Court, 1982 Term," 4–5. For a discussion, see in particular Julen Etxabe, "Nomos, Conflict, and the Tragedy of Adjudication: The Jurisprudence of Robert Cover" (December 2006), https://ssrn.com/abstract=952888 or http://dx.doi.org/10.2139/ssrn.952888.
17. See Judith Resnik, "Living Their Legal Commitments: Paideic Communities, Courts, and Robert Cover," *Yale Journal of Law and the Humanities* 17, no. 7 (2005): 17–53.
18. For a discussion, see Paul Schiff Berman, "A Pluralist Approach to International Law," *Yale Journal of International Law* 32 (2007): 301–29. International criminal courts and criminal tribunals obviously do have coercive power to impose criminal sanctions on convicted defendants, and so in this sense share some, but not all, of the state-backed violence that Cover sees as the distinctive power of domestic courts. In this sense, the closest jurispathic legal actor for the jurisgenerative dimension of genocide (and other international crimes) would consist in the use of coercive power to hold and punish prisoners. However, in terms of the power to *determine where jurisgenesis ends*, in Cover's sense, the International Court of Justice, not itself a criminal court and backed by no coercive power, is arguably the most jurispathic legal actor, insofar as it has (in both its decision in *Serbia v Bosnia-Herzegovina* and its preliminary findings in *The Gambia v Myanmar*) adopted an exceptionally strict and narrow interpretation of the Convention, particularly of its *dolus specialis* requirement.
19. See Paul Schiff Berman, "Jurisgenerative Constitutionalism: Procedural Principles for Managing Global Legal Pluralism," *Indiana Journal of Global Legal Studies* 20, no. 2 (Summer 2013): 665–95; and in general Berman, *Global Legal Pluralism: A Jurisprudence of Law Beyond Borders* (Cambridge: Cambridge University Press, 2012).
20. On the denial of such a hierarchy generally, see Payam Akhavan, *Reducing Genocide to Law* (Cambridge: Cambridge University Press, 2012).
21. On the dangers of a supposed hierarchy of international crimes for prevention, see Scott Straus, *Fundamentals of Genocide and Mass Atrocity Prevention* (Washington, DC: United States Holocaust Historical Museum, 2016), chap. 2.
22. James Waller, *Confronting Evil: Engaging Our Responsibility to Prevent Genocide* (Oxford: Oxford University Press, 2016), 45–49.

16

Jurisgenerativity in the Age of Big Data

MATTHEW LONGO

States increasingly use large quantities of data—so-called Big Data—to evaluate, monitor, and control their citizens and scrutinize political activity. This is true worldwide, including within democratic polities. One need look no further than reports about the extensive digital surveillance of the Black Lives Matter movement (#BLM) in the United States during the summer of 2020. Activists were watched and photographed—including by drones and helicopters—their images fed through facial recognition software and used for predictive policing; they had their social media accounts and private online communities infiltrated by undercover police and federal agents.[1]

The moral concerns raised by the use of data analytics in statecraft are considerable, and far beyond the limitations of this short chapter.[2] Here I will focus on one particular aspect of this problem: that the state use of Big Data neuters what Seyla Benhabib, following Robert Cover, calls *jurisgenerativity*, or the law's capacity to generate norms outside of its formal expression. It does so, I argue, by placing a disciplinary mechanism (data) at the center of citizen-sovereign relations. Rather than facilitate *democratic iterations* or spaces for public claim-making, disciplinary mechanisms restrict those spaces as well as our capacity to inhabit them. Thus there is a double bind: in a data-driven world, the law increasingly can neither stimulate individual action nor keep disciplinary systems at bay.

Before proceeding, some definitions are instructive. According to Benhabib, "jurisgenerativity" refers to "the law's capacity to create a normative universe of meaning" outside the "provenance of formal lawmaking." The normativity of the law isn't limited to its "formal validity" or its legality as such. Rather, it can "structure an extra-legal normative universe by developing new vocabularies for public claim-making, by encouraging new forms of subjectivity to engage with the public sphere, and by interjecting existing relations of power with anticipations of justice to come."[3] "Democratic iterations," in turn, describes the processes of argumentation and deliberation by which "universalist rights claims are contested and contextualized, invoked and revoked, posited and positioned throughout legal and political institutions, as well as in the associations of civil society."[4]

By situating the law as the nexus by which democratic processes can be engendered, Benhabib helps articulate its value even in contexts where formal lawmaking and law enforcement fall short. This is instrumental to her defense of human rights—the subject of her book *Dignity in Adversity* (2011). Against skeptics who argue that human rights are illegitimate because they cannot be enforced—i.e., they fail their formal mandate—Benhabib defends their extralegal purchase, namely, inculcating values and inspiring social movements to embody them. The jurisgenerative potential of law is of course not limited to the international domain, as Benhabib points out regarding undocumented workers in the United States who are not legal citizens, but "have become political agents by actively engaging in the public sphere through their strikes, petitions, and demonstrations."[5]

Given the significance of the jurisgenerative capacity of law, we should be wary of anything that might delimit its efficacy and scope. This is where the problem of Big Data comes in. In what follows, I first explain what Big Data is and why it poses a challenge to the law. Second, I argue that the specific problem data presents to jurisgenerativity is best understood via the tension between law and discipline. Finally, I give substance to this tension by showing how Big Data may have a chilling effect on the public sphere, using the #BLM protests in summer 2020 as an illustration. I conclude by considering the argument going forward.

DATA AND DISCIPLINE

What Is Big Data?

Big Data is shorthand for the massive accumulation of data in recent years—including biometric, biographic, and behavioral data—which plays an increasingly central role in state decision-making, including monitoring citizens without their consent.[6] There are a number of features of this phenomenon, which will be explicated in brief. *Algorithms* are the means by which individuals are sorted, classified, and filtered.[7] Individuals can be measured and evaluated along a number of different axes. Most important for our purposes, they can be sorted according to risk. Due to the sheer quantity of data available, states can now *data mine*, uncovering things about individuals they didn't even look for.[8] State use of data to home in on specific features of individuals is called *profiling*, a

> technique [whereby] a set of characteristics of a particular class of person is inferred from past experience, and data-holdings are then searched for digital personae with a close fit to that set of characteristics.... Profiling is used by government agencies to construct models of classes of person in whom they are interested, such as terrorists, drug couriers, persons likely to commit crimes of violence, tax evaders, social welfare frauds, [etc.].[9]

Here discrimination is a feature, not a bug: the point is to discriminate based on riskiness. The state is using data to generate a complete portrait, or "360° view," of individual trustworthiness—what I have elsewhere described as the *pixelated subject*.[10]

The subject of Big Data usage in statecraft is broad; the point here is simply to flesh out how it might delimit the jurisgenerative capacity of law. With this in mind, this section will focus on one feature in particular: *predictive analytics*, or the state use of data for social forecasting—to "predict events, based on patterns of behavior," or "uncover, characterize, understand and potentially even predict threat-actors before they act."[11] Here the problem that Big Data poses to the law is laid intuitively bare—clearly challenging the vaunted notion of innocent until proven guilty. Indeed, predictive policing shares some affinity with futuristic renditions of crime-solving, as in Philip K. Dick's notion of "pre-crimes" portrayed in the film *Minority Report*.

Law enforcement in the United States increasingly uses predictive analytics to solve crime, drawing from past behavior and other aspects of a person's characteristics—via profiling and data mining—to anticipate crimes before they happen. For example, police departments routinely compile "heat lists," indexes that segment individuals according to risk ratings, which then justify surveillance.

> The Los Angeles Police Department, the Chicago Police Department, and other agencies in dozens of U.S. cities use conclusions drawn from big data [to] predict crimes and identify potential offenders.... The New York Police

Department also uses social media to monitor the activity of citizens, specifically young people of color.... These tactics raise many questions about how communication systems, from software-based social media algorithms to hardware such as drones, are being used for discriminatory profiling, surveillance, and police abuse.[12]

The use of data in this manner is widespread. The FBI's Next Generation Identification System is an example of an advanced program designed to predict where crimes are likely to occur. Recently, the American Civil Liberties Union protested against Amazon's "Rekognition" software, sold to U.S. police forces to surveil crowds, as well as social media culling platforms like Geofeedia. And of course, it's not just the police but a very wide range of public services that use Big Data, ranging from public health, to education, to city government—usually grouped under the moniker of the "smart city."[13]

Across the board, data is increasingly interwoven into the fabric of governance in ways fundamentally altering the relationship between citizen and state. I suggest this phenomenon is best conceptualized via the tension between discipline and law.

Data as Discipline: Excursus to Foucault

Disciplinary mechanisms are the means by which the state turns heterodox, ungainly subjects into uniform, measurable ones. Foucault explains this in his "Security, Territory, Population" lectures at the Collège de France: "[Discipline] breaks down individuals, places, time, movements, actions, and operations. It breaks them down into components such that they can be seen, on the one hand, and modified on the other ... and finally, on the basis of this, it establishes the division between those considered unsuitable or incapable and the others. That is to say, on this basis it divides the normal from the abnormal."[14] This is part of a broader process of state *rationalization*, or the management of a state by scientific principles. The rational state takes on the role of overseer. "Discipline regulates everything. Discipline allows nothing to escape."[15] It controls the totality of its subjects and distinguishes between them as individuals, via what Foucault calls "dividing practices." Examples in his work are familiar: madness and sanity, illness and health, and so on. To this list we can add the data dichotomy: risky and nonrisky.

The linkages between the problem of Big Data and Foucault's conceptualization of discipline are immediately evident. Data is a tool for population control and the classification of individuals. Understanding data in this way—as a mode of discipline—allows us to appreciate the tension with the law, a familiar trope in Foucault's writing. For example, in his lectures "Society Must Be Defended," he details how disciplinary mechanisms are "colonizing the procedures of the law."[16] In *Discipline and Punish*, he suggests disciplinary mechanisms act as a kind of "counter-law," which "effect a suspension of the law."[17] But why is this relationship so problematic? The answer hinges on the question of the *unknown*. According to Foucault, law leaves room for that which is unknown to be allowable, but for discipline, what is unknown is precisely the least allowable: "In the system of the law, what is undetermined is what is permitted; in the system of disciplinary regulation, what is determined is what one must do, and consequently everything else, being undetermined, is prohibited."[18] Thus while in the sphere of law, one is innocent until proven guilty; in the sphere of discipline, one is risky until proven safe. This is because the logic of disciplinary governance is *action-independent*—just as when states employ predictive analytics to anticipate future wrongdoing, making would-be criminals of individuals who have not committed wrongful acts. Returning to jurisgenerativity, the problem is now clear. In Benhabib's model, the law engenders progressive norms, which can then be enforced. But since discipline restricts all norms it cannot foresee, data counters the jurisgenerativity of the law. Rather than walk alongside the rule of law, data is parasitic on it.

The basic tension Foucault describes between discipline and law is exacerbated by the specific nature of data governance—namely, that it is an instrument of ascertaining *riskiness*. Risk is different than other means of categorizing individuals because it repositions the unknown as the central threat to the system. Riskiness is an undefined state, a state to come, and thus fundamentally vulnerable. It is this condition of not knowing—which the state seeks to overcome—that makes sense of the panopticon, Foucault's most enduring image of power: "The panopticon is the oldest dream of the oldest sovereign: none of my subjects can escape *and none of their actions is unknown to me*."[19] Seen in this light, data is not simply a kind of discipline, but the most articulate tool of its expression, lending society in the data-state certain characteristics of the penal system. To further appreciate the tension between discipline and law in terms of jurisgenerativity, it is helpful to revisit the problem of data governance on the public sphere—the site of democratic iterations—including with a careful look at the example of state use of data in the monitoring of Black Lives Matter (#BLM).

DATA, JURISGENERATIVITY, AND THE PUBLIC SPHERE

Data and Public Sphere Theory

Insofar as data is a mechanism of discipline, it presents a specific challenge to the public sphere—and the kind of democratic society that political theorists like Benhabib envision—because it circumscribes the law's ability to generate spaces for democratic iterations.[20] At its most basic, a public sphere infused with technologies of state surveillance and control will suffer restrictions on individual agency and critical thinking, and is thus less likely to be a site of deliberation—considered by many to be the sine qua non of democracy—for the obvious reason that it can make people uncomfortable and unwilling to articulate their views.[21] This fact is further exacerbated by social media, as people become locked into different information communities, often described as "filter bubbles," or instances of "algorithmic censorship."[22] And of course, there is almost no capacity for individuals to seek redress against this data collection, as it cannot be easily retraced.

Critics warn of a number of troubling consequences for publics that result from the rise and spread of data mining: less privacy, more surveillance and social discrimination, and a new means of controlling how publics come to be represented and understood. Meanwhile, the tools and systems that generate such knowledge are typically opaque and are rarely open to public scrutiny and supervision.[23] This is especially devastating for social movements, which are subject to the utmost state scrutiny, especially via social media—once considered a boon for the public sphere, but increasingly understood as a liability.[24]

This shrinking of actors away from a public sphere in which they consider themselves to be vulnerable is unlikely to abate due to the inherent inequality between states and citizens in terms of their analytic capacities. Governments, like large corporations, have access to the best tools and facilities for data collection and analysis, and thus their power to surveil populations vastly exceeds that of communities attempting to evade this surveillance.[25] A similar point obtains with regard to elections, as parties are getting evermore powerful in their ability to use data to manipulate citizens' political voices and identities. This means that representation is getting tilted away from citizens, whose only recourse is to try to avoid scrutiny—to escape digital publics rather than engage them—an attempt that is itself futile, as studies show time and again.[26]

A data-saturated public sphere also generates inequality among citizens. Now that we are increasingly measurable entities—with specific risk-ratings and data profiles—individuals within any given public are situated in conditions of wildly different standing, especially as algorithmic governance tends to home in on already vulnerable populations.[27] An example of this are what we might call "new citizens," or individuals of foreign descent who have recently acquired full membership in the polity. These communities are routinely singled out as risky and monitored—not because they don't have papers, but because legal citizenship is no longer sufficient to protect their rights. Indeed, there has been a rise in denationalization campaigns across the West.[28]

The use of data described here may be helpful for the state in distinguishing between citizens, but it is completely destructive of the normative model on which the public sphere rests—as per Joshua Cohen's claim that democracy requires "*manifest equality* among citizens," or Habermas's defense of status-free deliberation such that the "unforced force of the better argument" can prevail.[29] A hierarchical, nondeliberative public sphere simply cannot function as the autonomous space of will formation once imagined. Further, the increasing state saturation of the public sphere undermines its role as an intermediary between citizen and state, as Habermas argues in *Between Facts and Norms*.[30]

The democratic harms of data governance are manifold, seriously challenging the notions of equal citizenship and popular sovereignty that comprise its normative core. It seems fair to say that whatever promise the public sphere once had in the data age is increasingly in jeopardy.

The Chilling Effect: Data Surveillance and Black Lives Matter (#BLM)

To understand precisely how state use of data can suppress the jurisgenerative capacity of law, it is helpful to look at the example of the 2020 Black Lives Matter (#BLM) protests and how the state used data to monitor and infiltrate them. To give a sense of the sheer magnitude of data surveillance on the movement, consider this account from an op-ed in *The Conversation*: "U.S. police forces have been turning to technology to track down Black Lives Matter protestors. Content from social media platforms and affiliated sites has been instrumental in the authorities being able to identify protestors based on photos of their faces, clothes and hair, or on the fact that they posted while at the protests."[31] The list of tactics used against protestors is extensive, including collecting images from hundreds of hours of video surveillance and filtering them through facial recognition software (used for predictive identification and "after-the-fact" arrests), seizing protestors' cell phones with the aim of extracting their data, and so forth.[32] As Brandi

Collins-Dexter, an activist for the civil rights group Color of Change, puts it, "law enforcement agencies spend a breathtaking amount of money to aggressively track, target, and surveil Black communities"—disciplinary tactics par excellence.[33] The police also solicited photographs of activists from the local population, turning citizens into law enforcement agents and sowing community distrust.

One of the most active watchdogs regarding digital surveillance is the Brennan Center for Social Justice. One issue they have fixated on is the police use of fake social media accounts to infiltrate #BLM activists and communities, and the "chilling effect on free speech and communications" this engenders.[34] In one high-profile case, a Memphis, Tennessee, police officer created a fake Facebook profile in order to infiltrate activist communities and gather information on them. According to the Brennan Center, this kind of digital police infiltration is widespread and delimits the ability of social movements to organize. It is also more expansive and effective than ever would have been possible in the pre-digital age.[35]

A full account of state use of Big Data to monitor and control Black Lives Matter protestors is beyond the purview of this short chapter. But clearly a public sphere so constituted—saturated with data and disciplinary technologies—is not the open, discursive space once imagined.

Jurisgenerativity (and Jurispathy) Reconsidered

To understand why state use of data to surveil movements like Black Lives Matter is so important for the study of jurisgenerativity, it is helpful to revisit the original language of Robert Cover. For Cover, the creation of legal meaning—what he calls "jurisgenesis"—is a cultural process, rooted in narrative and the meaning-making practices of local communities, usually independent of the state. Social movements are here essential, as sites of alternative legal interpretation that can resist the hegemony of court decision-making—which is "jurispathic," or law-destroying, imposing a hierarchy on legal meaning, winnowing the field and selecting certain interpretations at the expense of others.

The fact that states might delimit the norm-generating capacity of social movements was precisely what Cover was concerned about, as while there are nominal protections of such groups, such as via freedom of association and freedom of speech, these alone are insufficient. To be effective, groups must generate and enforce boundaries to protect themselves from state interference, as it is only when social movements are freed of state pressure that they can gather strength and actually confront and change the law. "People associate not only to transform themselves, but also to change the social world in which they live. Associations, then, are a sword as well as a shield ... When groups generate their own articulate normative orders concerning the world as they would transform it ... a new *nomos*, with its attendant claims to autonomy and respect, is created."[36] With this in mind, the #BLM example is particularly potent, as it is precisely this kind of group that thinkers like Cover and Benhabib seek to protect, emblematic of the public sphere to which we normatively aspire but which data statecraft makes harder to obtain. The data-disciplinary mechanisms described in this chapter clearly run counter to these aims, reducing the field of extralegal interpretation and action for groups outside the state and undercutting their norm-generating capacity. In this way, we might say that state use of data isn't just disciplinary, but jurispathic too.

In political theory, we frequently take the importance of the law to be self-evident. It is the glue linking citizen and state, an expression of popular sovereignty, and a beacon of justice. Yet, everywhere around us, it is participant to systems of inequality and abuse. The data surveillance and infiltration of the Black Lives Matter movement (#BLM) is emblematic of this problem. While one may be hopeful about the emancipatory potential of law, it doesn't take much historical perspective to be skeptical. So how do we reconcile these facts: the beauty and power of a law well designed and the problems of its imperfect embodiment? One of Seyla Benhabib's lasting legacies is bringing to political theory a way of understanding how the law can be emancipatory, even given its imperfections—what she, following Robert Cover, calls *jurisgenerativity*, or the law's capacity to generate norms outside of its formal expression.

The point of this chapter was to express concern that the jurisgenerative capacity of the law is losing its potency due to the rise of Big Data in statecraft, and the privileging of discipline over law. The state use of data increasingly sacrifices the *rights* logic of innocent until proven guilty for the *data* logic of risky until proven safe, a trade-off that makes citizens increasingly unable to participate in a free, open public sphere. Thus, while the law may still provide a platform for public claim-making, data undercuts the value of that platform, thereby delimiting its jurisgenerative potential.

The subject of Big Data, and especially its more nefarious aspects like predictive policing, may for many of us seem far-fetched; but the problem is not going away. As political theorists, we need to dedicate time to thinking how society can be protected from such data-driven advances. Reclaiming a public sphere in which the law can be jurisgenerative is essential to this project.

NOTES

1. Zolan Kanno-Youngs, "U.S. Watched George Floyd Protests in 15 Cities Using Aerial Surveillance," *New York Times,* June 19, 2020; Molly Wood, "How Constant Surveillance Puts Protestors at Risk," *Marketplace Tech,* September 18, 2020.
2. Studies variously show that Big Data exacerbates inequality, including generating and sustaining discrimination against racial minorities, threatens civil liberties, and raises concerns about the loss of agency and the meaning of "consent" in data-driven societies; see, e.g., Helen Kennedy and Giles Moss, "Known or Knowing Publics?: Social Media Data Mining and the Question of Public Agency," *Big Data and Society,* July–December (2015): 1–11; Zeynep Tufekci, "Engineering the Public: Big Data, Surveillance and Computational Politics," *First Monday* 19, no. 7 (July 2014).
3. Seyla Benhabib, *Dignity in Adversity: Human Rights in Troubled Times* (Cambridge: Polity, 2011): 125–26.
4. Benhabib, 129–30.
5. Benhabib, 145.
6. Rafal Rohozinski, "Big Data Analysis and Intelligence," remarks at Canadian Association of Defence and Security Industries (CADSI) SecureTech Conference, Ottawa, Canada, October 30, 2012; Tufekci, "Engineering the Public"; Robin Mansell, "Surveillance, Power and Communication: Keynote Speech Delivered at the International Communication Association (ICA) Conference," *Open Democracy,* July 20, 2016. The term *dataveillance,* or mass surveillance by data, is used to refer to this problem; see, e.g., Roger Clarke, "The Digital Persona and Its Application to Data Surveillance," *Information Society* 10, no. 2 (June 1994): 77–92.
7. Samantha Shorey and Philip N. Howard, "Automation, Big Data, and Politics: A Research Review," *International Journal of Communication* 10 (2016): 5032–55.
8. Kennedy and Moss, "Known or Knowing Publics?"
9. Clarke, "The Digital Persona and Its Application to Data Surveillance."
10. This article draws on fieldwork conducted for my book: Matthew Longo, *The Politics of Borders: Sovereignty, Security, and the Citizen after 9/11* (Cambridge: Cambridge University Press, 2018). For an explication of this method of using ethnographic research to address arguments in political theory, see, e.g., Matthew Longo and Bernardo Zacka, "Political Theory in an Ethnographic Key," *American Political Science Review* 113, no. 4 (2019): 1066–70; Bernardo Zacka, Brooke Ackerly, Jacob Elster, Signy Gutnick-Allen, Humeira Iqtidar, Matthew Longo, and Paul Sagar, "Political Theory with an Ethnographic Sensibility," *Contemporary Political Theory* 20, no. 2 (2021): 385–418.
11. Rohozinski, "Big Data Analysis and Intelligence"; Christopher Munn, personal interview, Washington, DC, January 13, 2013.
12. Shorey and Howard, "Automation, Big Data, and Politics," 5039–40.

13. Shorey and Howard, 5039–40.
14. Michel Foucault, *Security, Territory, Population: Lectures at the Collège de France, 1977–1978* (New York: Vintage, 2007), 57.
15. Foucault, 44–45.
16. Michel Foucault, *"Society Must Be Defended": Lectures at the Collège de France, 1975–1976* (New York: Picador, 2003), 39.
17. Michel Foucault, *Discipline and Punish: The Birth of the Prison* (New York: Vintage, 1977), 223.
18. Foucault, *Security, Territory, Population*, 46.
19. Foucault, 66, emphasis mine.
20. For an example of the importance of the public sphere in Benhabib's thought, see, e.g., Seyla Benhabib, *The Claims of Culture: Equality and Diversity in the Global Era* (Princeton, NJ: Princeton University Press, 2002), ix.
21. See, e.g., James Bohman and William Rehg, eds., *Deliberative Democracy: Essays on Reason and Politics* (Cambridge, MA: MIT Press, 1997); Amy Gutmann and Dennis Thompson, *Why Deliberative Democracy?* (Princeton, NJ: Princeton University Press, 2004); Mansell, "Surveillance, Power and Communication."
22. For example: "News-filtering algorithms serve a gatekeeping function, editing what social media users see.... Personalization through algorithms has the potential to create 'filter bubbles' in which algorithms favor information that users find agreeable and eliminate other types of information." Shorey and Howard, "Automation, Big Data, and Politics," 5038.
23. Kennedy and Moss, "Known or Knowing Publics?," 1–2.
24. In the early days of social media there were many who believed that it might actually be propitious for the public sphere. For example, A. Michael Froomkin argued that digital technology might provide the best mechanism of achieving Habermasian discourse, envisioning a multiplicity of interactive, web-based public spheres. Froomkin, "Habermas@Discourse.Net: Toward a Critical Theory of Cyber-Space," *Harvard Law Review* 116, no. 3 (January 2003): 867. To her credit, Jodi Dean was presciently skeptical, arguing that new digital spaces were merely vehicles for capitalistic cooptation all the more nefarious as the public is blinded by its great "democratizing" potential. Jodi Dean, "Why the Net Is Not a Public Sphere," *Constellations* 10, no. 1 (2003).
25. John Naughton, "'The Goal Is to Automate Us': Welcome to the Age of Surveillance Capitalism," *Guardian*, January 20, 2019.
26. Tufekci, "Engineering the Public."
27. Virginia Eubanks, "Want to Predict the Future of Surveillance?: Ask Poor Communities," *American Prospect*, January 15, 2014.
28. Other sites of denationalization include Belgium, France, the Netherlands, and the United Kingdom. Patti T. Lenard, "Democratic Citizenship and Denationalization," *American Political Science Review* 112, no. 1 (2018): 99–111.
29. Joshua Cohen, "Deliberation and Democratic Legitimacy," in *Democracy*, ed. D. Estlund (Malden, MA: Blackwell, 2002), 89; Jürgen Habermas, *Between Facts and Norms: Contributions to a Discourse Theory of Law and Democracy* (Cambridge, MA: MIT Press, 1996), 306.

30. Habermas writes: "in complex societies, the public sphere consists of an intermediary structure between the political system, on the one hand, and the private sectors of the lifeworld and functional systems on the other." Habermas, 373.
31. Anjuli R. K. Shere and Jason Nurse, "Police Surveillance of Black Lives Matter Shows the Danger Technology Poses to Democracy," *Conversation*, July 24, 2020.
32. Kanno-Youngs, "U.S. Watched George Floyd Protests"; Wood, "How Constant Surveillance Puts Protestors at Risk."
33. Sam Biddle, "Police Surveilled George Floyd Protests with Help from Twitter Affiliated Startup Datamnr," *Intercept*, July 9, 2020.
34. Brennan Center, "Civil Rights Concerns About Social Media Monitoring by Law Enforcement," *Brennan Center for Social Justice*, 2019.
35. Brennan Center, "Civil Rights Concerns."
36. Robert M. Cover, "The Supreme Court, 1982 Term—Foreword: *Nomos and Narrative*," *Harvard Law Review* 97, no. 4 (1983): 33–34.

PART V
Deprovincializing Critical Theory

17

Pachamama's Rights, Climate Crisis, and the Decolonial Cosmos

ANGÉLICA MARÍA BERNAL

Twenty years ago, when I entered the doctoral program at Yale, one of the first things I learned in Seyla Benhabib's class was the power of narrative. In that spirit, I'd like to begin with a story. On August 20, 2019, hundreds gathered inside the courtroom of the Pastaza Judiciary in the town of Puyo, Ecuador, to listen to hours of arguments surrounding a planned hydroelectric plant on the Piatúa River. The hearing was initiated by Indigenous Kichwa people from the communities of Santa Clara who sought a protective injunction to halt plans by the GENEFRAN hydroelectric company.[1] Since the company was first granted an exploratory license in 2014, Indigenous groups have been resisting in a range of ways: from road blockades and marches, to protests on social media (through their #PiatúaResiste campaign) and most recently a lawsuit.[2] In this resistance, Indigenous peoples challenged not only the company's actions but the state's authority as well as the legitimacy of their claims to sovereign management and exploitation of natural resources. And they have done so in novel ways. Their lawsuit argued that building the dam would have deleterious environmental impacts that infringe Indigenous rights to free prior and informed consent under international human rights documents like the UNDRIP, the UN Declaration on the Rights of Indigenous Peoples, which was ratified in 2007 and incorporated into Ecuador's 2008 Constitution. They also situated their claims within the innovative rights of nature declared in that Constitution, thus asserting the rights of the Piatúa River itself as a sacred site.

While no other thinker of the past few decades is more associated with cosmopolitanism and its contemporary revival than Seyla Benhabib, Benhabib's cosmopolitanism and Indigenous politics and thought are not often considered "thought partners." Likewise, cosmopolitanism and decolonial thought are not paired as complementary thought-streams given the historical linkages between imperialism and cosmopolitan projects, and more recent anti-imperial critiques of thinkers such as Immanuel Kant and Hannah Arendt, both of which are central to Benhabib's cosmopolitanism.

The aim of this chapter is to bring these two seemingly antithetical schools of thought together. What drives this interpretive endeavor, I must confess, is not actually or initially political-theoretic concerns with cosmopolitanism or European critical theory. Rather, the "stakes" of this exercise emerge from fieldwork I have conducted with Ecuador's Indigenous movements and my commitment as an engaged scholar to these movements and to their own concerns.

These concerns and one of the questions broached in this essay center, to adopt David Scott's terminology, on the "problem-space" of how to make human rights protections and norms binding upon the state.[3] This question is not just a normative question of binding; beyond that, it is a question on which the preservation of modes of life and life itself depends.

In this chapter, I focus my reflections by situating Benhabib's cosmopolitanism in the context of Indigenous rights cases such as Ecuador's and our current planetary climate crisis to make the case for what I term the "decolonial cosmos," an alternative cosmopolitanism that is more adept as a political and ethical position for orienting our thinking and politics in addressing this question and with it addressing the urgent need to tackle the political impasse on climate crisis.

There's been no greater time when our species has been more acutely aware of the fragility of our human condition on Earth than the present. The ongoing harm inflicted by human activities—from aggressive extraction and overdependence on fossil fuels to deforestation and pollution—coupled with increasing extreme weather events such as unprecedented forest fires, hurricanes, and winter storms, to name a few, has made it painfully clear that we are facing possible irreparable damage to our planet, if not extinction.[4] In the era of the Anthropocene, we are now presented with a new political paradox. On the one hand, we have the urgent need for immediate, radical political action within and between states to address climate change and crisis. On the other hand, we have the actions by and between states that create significant political and economic obstacles to addressing this very challenge, from inaction on carbon emission reductions and climate change denial to the reduction of environmental protections and most egregiously the direct intensification of extractive industries and projects.

At the heart of Benhabib's cosmopolitanism is likewise a paradox: *the paradox of democratic legitimacy*. The paradox is that in constitutional democracies legitimacy is derived from precommitments to guarantee basic human rights and also from the will of democratic majorities, whose will might run roughshod in unjust and exclusionary ways against those very guarantees.[5] The paradox is not simply theoretically relevant, but as Benhabib has made powerfully clear in her work on the "rights of others" within states—aliens, immigrants, refugees, and asylum seekers—deeply politically relevant.

I believe there is an important link to be made between the two paradoxes, and with it an urgency for cosmopolitan projects such as Seyla Benhabib's in an age of climate crisis. The focus of my intervention here will be on addressing one aspect of this crisis, which speaks to the larger political, economic, colonial, and racial intersections underpinning climate crisis as a social justice issue, mainly *neocolonial extractivism*. By neocolonial extractivism I mean the contemporary turn toward intensified extractivism: the extraction of natural resources—such as fossil fuels (petroleum, natural gas, tar shands, and the like), water, timber—for profit and exchange in the commodity market of global capitalism. The costs of this extractivism have been squarely borne by black, brown, and Indigenous populations, ushering in new processes of colonial violence, exploitation, and dispossession.[6]

Benhabib's paradox addresses the fundamental challenge faced by cosmopolitan norms: that while the rise in international human rights has been an important development, what makes these binding on states and democratic majorities within them is problematic. To adapt Benhabib's formulation, let me phrase our central question as this: within this context of neocolonial extractivism and climate crisis, how can cosmopolitan norms such as those expressed in the UN Declaration on the Rights of Indigenous Peoples become binding on states and democratic legislatures? In what follows, I propose that Benhabib's cosmopolitan project and her theory of "democratic iterations" offer a framework for answering this question and give traction to decolonial projects and resistance by Indigenous peoples in countries like Ecuador. In this, I argue that democratic iterations reflect a shift in epistemological, cultural, legal, and political grounds toward what Walter Mignolo called a "decolonial cosmopolitanism" and I term the "decolonial cosmos."[7] To begin, I briefly discuss Indigenous internationalism and cosmopolitan norms.

INDIGENOUS INTERNATIONALISM AND COSMOPOLITAN NORMS

In *Another Cosmopolitanism*, Benhabib writes that since 1948 we have transitioned from a system of international norms to a system of *cosmopolitan* norms. Benhabib draws a distinction between the two as norms that set out binding obligations and regulations between states, and norms that "accrue to individuals as moral and legal persons in a worldwide civil society."[8] Indigenous cosmopolitan norms reflect this definition while also expanding upon it. This expansion can be understood in two ways. First, via the subject of cosmopolitan norms. Second, by recasting the notion of a *worldwide* civil society (emphasis on the "world").

In *Indigenous Peoples in International Law*, Indigenous lawyer, scholar, and former UN Special Rapporteur for Indigenous Peoples James Anaya outlines the evolution of Indigenous rights as part of a global human rights movement. For Anaya, this movement expanded the scope of international law and challenged state sovereignty, while it also "promoted the demise of international law's historical linkage to the pervasive individual/state perceptual dichotomy of human organization," to reflect cultural patterns of association that "exist independent of state structures," such as those by Indigenous peoples around the world.[9] These changes within the global movement were propelled by Indigenous peoples themselves.

Self-determination defines what has been termed "Indigenous internationalism."[10] Since the onset of European imperialism, Indigenous peoples have been the subject of international law, rights, and norms, but as the objects of imperial rule and colonization. By contrast, Indigenous internationalism pertains to the contemporary global Indigenous rights movement that emerged in the mid-1970s and that established Indigenous peoples as no longer just subjects but agents in world politics and international law. Drawing on decolonial movements, thought, and activism emerging in the 1950s and 1960s in Africa, and the Third-Worldist movement's ideas of international cooperation, national sovereignty, and self-determination, Indigenous internationalists began coordinating activist efforts in international institutions and forming transnational networks.[11] Key in this process of coordination and organization was the articulation of a shared identity, in the language of Benhabib, a new "concrete universal" to organize as *Indigenous peoples* and articulate *Indigenous rights* within international institutions as self-determined subjects in international law.

Indigenous internationalism reflected the emergence of a global Indigenous civil society shaped by networks of Indigenous activists around new transnational, Pan-Indigenous organizations, organizational efforts and activism within existing and new bodies of the formal UN system, and the support of allied NGOs. The World Council of Indigenous Peoples (WCIP), the first pan-Indigenous organization in the world cofounded by the Secwépmec activist and intellectual

George Manuel in 1975, and the internationalist wing of the American Indian Movement (AIM), the International Indian Treaty Council, played instrumental roles in developing networks between Indigenous groups around the world and advancing Indigenous representation within bodies such as the UN Economic and Social Council.[12]

Indigenous peoples' international advocacy subsequently yielded important gains in the development of new mechanisms of international representation and a new regime of international Indigenous rights. In 1977, the landmark UN-sponsored International Nongovernmental Organization Conference on the Discrimination Against Indigenous Populations provided a critical event for identity formation and agenda-setting for the following decades.[13] Two of its main resolutions would come to fruition. In 1982, the Working Group on Indigenous Populations (WGIP) was created to provide a formal mechanism for monitoring violations of Indigenous rights within nation-states, a vehicle for the representation of Indigenous peoples and for subsequently developing international standards on Indigenous rights. By 2000, this work resulted in the formation of the UN Permanent Forum on Indigenous Peoples, and by 2007, after two decades of elaboration and political advocacy, the ratification of the UN Declaration on the Rights of Indigenous Peoples (UNDRIP).

The UN Declaration on the Rights of Indigenous Peoples (UNDRIP) is the principal international instrument for contemporary Indigenous rights. It is not the first of its kind, with earlier instruments such as the International Labor Organization's (ILO) Indigenous and Tribal Peoples Convention 169 of 1989 playing a foundational role in establishing an emerging Indigenous human rights regime. The UNDRIP represents an evolution in the establishment of Indigenous rights that supersedes ILO 169. I will argue that it also marks the transition, to adapt Benhabib's insights, from a regime of international to one of Indigenous *cosmopolitan* norms of justice. By this theoretical distinction, I aim to capture the transition from a politics and international law regime that remains centered upon nation-state actors as the agents of treaty-making and sovereignty to a normative, political, and emergent legal context that extends beyond the nation-state to reflect a rising Indigenous civil society and Indigenous transnational activism that has championed rights, concepts, and norms that accrue to individuals and groups as Indigenous peoples beyond nation-state members. The limitations and conflict surrounding ILO 169 can best illustrate what I mean by this distinction.

Departing from the UN Charter and other instruments for the prevention of discrimination, ILO 169 outlines a new regime of collective human rights for groups self-identified as "tribal" and "Indigenous" that included rights to equal political participation, citizenship, economic protections, cultural and religious recognition, freedom from discrimination, vocational and labor opportunities, educational rights, and limited recognition of property rights.[14] As the first of its kind, ILO 169 was historic but its effectiveness was severely limited given its circumscription of Indigenous rights that situated them in the shadow of traditional notions of state sovereignty. While the collective rights asserted carved out a new domain for Indigenous self-determination and rights, this normative domain was tenuous, identifying the subject of rights by way of the now-obsolete, nation-state-centered understanding of "tribal populations." Although it also included the terminology of "Indigenous peoples" within the text, this usage was problematic on two counts. First, it identified Indigenous in relation to the state, as populations that inhabited the "geographical location to which the country belongs" prior to colonization or state-boundary formation, thus constituting it primarily along state territorial dimensions. Second, it severed any political, legal, or normative weight associated with the notions of *peoples*, thus excluding Indigenous peoples' assertions to sovereignty and circumscribing peoplehood once again as strictly within the domain of the state and its sovereignty.[15]

By contrast, the UNDRIP preamble corrects ILO 169's limitations. Situating itself within the principles of the UN Charter, it defines the subject of the Declaration, "Indigenous peoples," as "equal to all other peoples."[16] It also situates Indigenous rights within second-and third-generation human rights: social, economic, cultural, and solidarity or collective rights.[17] Through these novel articulations, UNDRIP establishes Indigenous rights on *cosmopolitan* terms, as rights that adhere to Indigenous peoples independent of the state and as members of a global civil society. The "global" here is inflected to reflect an alternative understanding of the context of human rights from a unified or homogenous "universe" to what decolonial theorists have termed as "pluriverse."[18] The concept of pluriverse is inspired by the Zapatista concept of *un mundo donde quepan muchos mundos* (a world in which many worlds fit), which defines the *cosmos*/world and world-making on nonhomogenizing, anticolonial, and plural terms.[19]

Where UNDRIP and ILO 169 share some similarities is in the challenges of state compliance with its norms. When it was initially ratified in 2007, the United States, Canada, New Zealand, and Australia voted against it.[20] Meanwhile, states have exercised their prerogative to challenge various articles, as the United States did in 2010 to reject Article 10, which protects Indigenous peoples from forcible removal from their lands without free prior and informed consent.[21] So we return back to Benhabib's paradox and her question of how cosmopolitan norms can become binding on states and on what authority.

THE "INTERNATIONAL TURN," NATIONAL MOBILIZATION, AND THE QUESTION OF BINDING IN ECUADOR

Before addressing this paradox and question, it's important to answer why they're important as not merely theoretical but political problems, particularly as it pertains to the case at hand, Indigenous rights in Ecuador. Let me first address the question's political importance.

To understand Indigenous internationalism, it's necessary to understand why Indigenous peoples have turned to international law and international institutions. The reasons are varied, depending on the groups, but one pattern is that Indigenous peoples have posed their claims before international institutions and have sought the recourse of international law in asserting claims against and protections from the state and its colonial violence. This turn, in fact, antedates the formation of the United Nations, with Indigenous leaders such as Deskaheh and the Iroquois Confederacy turning to the League of Nations in the 1920s in support of their struggles with the Canadian state.[22]

In *The Fourth World*, George Manuel explicates the contemporary turn. In his travels to New Zealand and Australia, he observed that the Maoris "found their voices were somewhat 'drowned out' by white representation," while Aborigines were "subject to relentless institutionalized white racism," a racism that was to "justify the infringement of their rights, the ongoing theft of and encroachment on their lands, and the undermining of their legal traditions and spheres of jurisdictional authority."[23] Indigenous peoples' frustrations with the state made it clear that an *international* politics of resurgence was necessary to wield much needed political leverage.

The Ecuadorian turn to international law and institutions mirrored other Indigenous groups' contemporary turn. In the early 1990s, transnational activist efforts with other Indigenous groups of Abya Yala (the Indigenous concept for the Americas) to contest planned continental celebrations commemorating five hundred years since Christopher Columbus's arrival proved especially important for situating long-standing claims against the Ecuadorian state, for unifying efforts of previously loosely connected groups around the banner of "500 Years of Resistance," and for the subsequent formation of a *national* Indigenous movement, which burst onto the political scene with national demonstrations in 1992.[24] This national movement brought together Indigenous groups from the Andean, coastal, and Amazonian regions through the organizing vehicle of the CONAIE, the Confederation of Indigenous Nationalities of Ecuador.[25] From the beginning, the CONAIE used a legal strategy as central to its organizing efforts. This legal strategy centered on dual efforts to both contest national laws and transform those laws, particularly through constitution-making. The movement's first success came with its successful push for writing a new constitution in 1997, and its inclusion of a new series of Indigenous collective rights in the subsequent 1998 Constitution.[26] These collective rights—which included rights to political participation, bilingual education, recognition of political and legal authorities, cultural recognitions, and other rights of self-determination—themselves drew from OIT 169, and indeed Ecuador's ratification of this document was used to further the incorporation of these new rights into Ecuador's Constitution.[27]

The incorporation of emerging, global Indigenous rights into national higher law, however, did not necessarily grant them authoritative binding upon the Ecuadorian state. For instance, Indigenous self-determination was a new cosmopolitan norm that did not exist until, as already noted, the international developments starting in the 1970s. Despite adoption of the terminology of self-determination in the constitution, Ecuador's Indigenous groups found this norm time and time again in conflict with the will of democratic majorities and the state. This issue, then, brings us back to the paradox of democratic legitimacy. The paradox speaks to a tension that for Benhabib cannot be dissolved, but rather can only be, in her terms, "mediated." I completely agree. To propose a resolution would be at best Pollyannaish, and at worst, dangerously unaware of the realities of power and inequality faced by Indigenous groups. But in light of those realities, can we even speak of mediations? What does mediation mean in practice?

PACHAMAMA'S RIGHTS, COSMOPOLITAN NORMS, AND DEMOCRATIC ITERATIONS

In *The Rights of Others*, Benhabib makes the notion of mediations fruitful with her theory of democratic iterations. Drawing on the work of Jacques Derrida, Robert Cover, and Frank Michelman, Benhabib defines *democratic iterations* as

> complex processes of public argument, deliberation, and exchange through which universal rights claims and principles are contested and contextualized, invoked and revoked, posited and positioned, through legal and political institutions, as well as in the associations of civil society. These can take place in "strong" public bodies of legislatures, the judiciary, and executive, as well as in the informal and "weak" publics of civil society association and the media.[28]

Democratic iterations provide a fruitful framework for understanding the complex processes by which mediations between new normativity surrounding

Indigenous rights and the will of democratic majorities in Ecuador have taken shape since the late 1990s. In this chapter, I want to focus on those that have taken place post the ratification of UNDRIP in 2007. My focus here stems from two reasons. First, 2007 marks an acceleration in reckoning with these tensions, given the ratification of UNDRIP as well as the emergence of a refoundational movement and process in Ecuador that same year. Second, it also accentuated these tensions in new, profound ways with another cosmopolitan norm development noted earlier: the emergence of the "rights of nature." Indeed, the story of Ecuador's contemporary democratic iterations is the story of *Pachamama's* rights.

One of the most recent developments in the international human rights regime is environmental norms. From the Rio Convention to the Kyoto Protocol and Paris Agreement, environmental norms mark a new generation of human rights—the fourth generation—that defines new cosmopolitan rights of human beings to a safe and clean environment and new duties, obligations, and international standards for and between nation-states to address climate change and the ongoing political, economic, and human costs of our climate crisis.[29]

The *rights of nature* have been a critical part of this evolution. They reflect the interpenetration between, on the one hand, transnational activism and emerging cosmopolitan norms and, on the other hand, regional and national activism and norms surrounding popular ecology, postneoliberal development, and Indigenous collective rights to self-determination. By the "rights of nature" I understand both an idea and a rising global movement centered on a biocentric understanding that Nature is an agent of moral respect, ethical treatment, and political and legal rights.[30] The idea has a long history in comparative political thought, drawing upon Buddhist philosophy, Christian theology, and Indigenous cosmologies, to name a few.[31] In the contemporary legal sphere, the idea and projected application of the rights of nature make their appearance in *Sierra Club v. Morton* (1972), a case surrounding the Sierra Club's fight to halt the building of a proposed ski resort by the Disney Corporation in the Mineral King valley of California.[32]

Now, fast forward to Ecuador in 2007–08. After decades of failed neoliberal governance, the country's Indigenous movement once again raised the prospects of constitution-making to address these failures and deal with ongoing legitimation and democratic representation crises resulting from them.[33] The idea was subsequently adopted by a rising presidential candidate, university professor and former finance minister Rafael Correa, who made it central to his campaign. Correa succeeded in bringing together a vast range of public sector organizations and social movements, among these initially the Indigenous movement (under the banner of inaugurating a "Citizens' Revolution") that would return the patria back to its people and create social and economic policies (under the banner of a "Socialism of the Twenty-First Century") to benefit the many, not the few. Correa positioned himself and the Citizens' Revolution squarely as a repudiation of all that neoliberal governments of the past had been: elite-driven, inegalitarian, capitalist, and governed more by the interests of imperialist masters in the Global North than by its own people. A critical component of instantiating it would be the convening of a constituent assembly to draft a new constitution to decolonize existing structures by refounding the state.[34]

In the Constituent Assembly charged with drafting a new constitution, the issue of the rights of nature arises as a powerful tool for dealing with long-standing violations of Indigenous rights to self-determination, particularly in relation to the natural resource extraction activities by previous governments and foreign corporations. Two factors influenced the subsequent incorporation and reiteration of rights of nature norms at the national level through the Constituent Assembly. The first, noted earlier, was the ratification of UNDRIP. For Indigenous representatives on the Constituent Assembly such as Monica Chuji, UNDRIP played a critical role as an instrument for influencing the incorporation of the rights of nature. Although this language does not appear in the UNDRIP, its normative underpinnings are established in a range of articles elaborating new norms of Indigenous self-determination with regard to resource management, principal among these the right to *free prior and informed consent* (Articles 10, 11, 19, 28, 29) and rights to land (Article 25 establishing "the right to maintain and strengthen their distinctive spiritual relationship with their traditionally owned or otherwise occupied and used lands, territories, waters ... and other resources").[35] Although these did not establish nature as an agent of rights, it established a normative understanding of human rights that reflected Indigenous conceptions of nature as kinship and spiritual relations with nonhuman others. Second was the instrumental role played by transnational networks, activism, and learning processes between Ecuadorian Indigenous and environmental activists, regional and global rights of nature movement leaders, and postdevelopment scholars and scholarship on identity-centered development.[36]

In 2008, Ecuador became the first country in the world to recognize nature with constitutional rights. According to Article 71 of Chapter 7, titled the "Rights of Nature": "Nature, or *Pacha Mama*, where life is reproduced and occurs, has the right to integral respect for its existence and for the maintenance and regeneration of its life cycles, structure, functions and evolutionary processes. All persons, communities, peoples and nations can call upon public authorities to enforce the rights of nature."[37] This incorporation represented the culmination of prior jurisgenerative processes, with the Constituent Assembly not only reappropriating preexisting international environmental and Indigenous rights norms, but moreover infusing them with new meaning as "the rights of nature" or the rights of *Pachamama* (the Kichwa Andean term for "Mother Earth" or "mother of the universe," space, and time). It also reflected the ways in which, for Indigenous activists, conceptualizing rights in biocentric terms (rights of nature) was coconstitutive of conceptualizing Indigenous rights. Such rights, while instrumental to the advancement of the self-determination of human actors, are themselves centered on the presupposition of nature as a coextensive living entity or entities to Indigenous peoples, rather than on Eurocentric terms as an externality to be mastered by human beings.[38]

The drafting of a new constitution in 2008 did not mean, of course, guaranteed binding and compliance with these new norms. Benhabib clarifies that democratic iterations are not singular processes but are better conceptualized as ongoing and cascading.[39] Democratic iterations generate new mediations between the global, national, and local that can lead to new constitutional rights and iterations of cosmopolitan norms, and that, in turn, open new spaces and create new grammars for claims-making, interpretation, and contestation. This has been the case in Ecuador as iterative processes continued that expanded the meaning of "rights of nature" from a legal discourse to a discourse of resistance by so-called "weak" publics of civil society. This resulted from activism by Indigenous and ecological movements against simultaneous "jurispathic" or "populistic jurisgenerative processes" involving contestation between social movements' and the president's conflicting interpretations of constitutional norms and claims to speak in the name of nature.[40]

This has been crucial for public opinion mobilization and formation, given two troubling developments in the aftermath of the 2008 Constitution: (a) the Correa government's pursuit of aggressive extractivism and (b) the government's attempt to co-opt these original achievements through the development regime of *Buen Vivir*. Buen Vivir, or *sumak kawsay* (which translates from Kichwa as "the good life"), was to be a new model of development for creating a biosocialist republic. In discourse after discourse, Ecuador's President Rafael Correa rightly proposed that a critical mission of the state was to alleviate poverty, but wrongly sought to do it by establishing the "good life of all" on the backs of Indigenous peoples by expanding the extractive frontier from petroleum to mining.[41] Throughout this period of neoextractivism, "rights of nature" emerged less in terms of successful cases or litigation protecting Indigenous rights and more in terms of new discourses of political resistance. Protest after protest saw Indigenous and non-Indigenous allies alike speak of "keeping it in the ground" because the land is our mother, oil is blood, and the rainforest is a living being that can't be exploited or sold.

This learning process involving the expansion of rights of nature from legal discourse to discourses of resistance has been important for dealing with one of outcomes of jurispathic processes: violence.[42] Over the past decade, the Correa's government neocolonial expansion of the extractivist frontier has been accompanied by increased militarization, repression, criminalization of dissent, and violence.[43] The rights of nature have been crucial in two dimensions to counter this violence. First, they maintained a vital civil society against government repression and the fragmentation and criminalization of the Indigenous movement. This we saw in full force in October 2019, when, after two weeks of confrontations with government forces, protests led by the Indigenous movements succeeded in forcing Correa's successor, current president Lenin Moreno, to reject Decree 883, which would have instated new structural adjustment plans in preparation for an IMF loan.[44] We also saw it in the passage of a public referendum in February 2018 prohibiting metallic mining in protected areas. Second, they helped to challenge state co-optation and bring greater unity to a fragmented Indigenous movement. Despite the state's co-optation of Buen Vivir, Indigenous activists protesting on behalf of the rights of nature have worked to continually assert themselves as equal constitutional interpreters and have managed to distinguish this concept as a state/colonial imposition from that of *sumak kawsay*, its Indigenous Kichwa version.

As Robert Cover argued in *Nomos and Narrative*, the state's monopoly on the legitimate use of violence raises the stakes of interpretative exercises, given that the state is the most powerful interpretative entity and that it can back up its interpretations with not just the law's coercive power but actual coercion and violence.[45] In a rich normative universe, "when the state and community offer conflicting interpretations, the community must elaborate the hermeneutics of resistance or of withdraw."[46] The hermeneutics of resistance in Ecuador have extended in more recent years from the streets to the courts. Between 2008 and 2016, ten out of thirteen cases successfully applied rights of rights of nature norms.[47] Yet, many of these cases were used to protect governmental or private landowner interests: for instance, to squash down on artisanal mining and clear the path to a government monopoly on mining activities, or to assert state police force and military presence in rural communities.[48] Since then, there have been a series of new cases that have applied the rights of nature to cancel the extractive activities of transnational corporations. At the onset of this chapter, I noted one, the Piatúa case. I want to highlight two other prominent cases.

In 2018, the Provincial Court of Azuay rejected the government's appeal of an earlier decision by Judge Paul Serrano, which revoked the mining license on the Rio Blanco project of the Chinese firm Ecuagoldmining.[49] In these two decisions, this became the first case to apply the rights of nature to cancel the extractive activities of a corporation on the basis of the protection of citizens and the river itself from potential pollution. During advocacy efforts organized to build coalitions between affected Indigenous and non-Indigenous residents, movement leader Yaku Pérez Guartambel and others joined arguments on "affected interests" of local populations (present and future generations) with biocentric arguments that joined Indigenous and Christian cosmologies on the sacred nature of riverways.[50] By 2019, on the heels of this successful campaign, Yaku Pérez was elected the first Indigenous governor of the Province of Azuay, and earlier in 2021 emerged as a surprising presidential candidate when he was the runner-up in the February first-round elections.[51]

The second in April 2019 was an internationally high-profile case brought by the Waorani Amazonian nation to stop the government's planned auctioning of seven million acres of their lands for oil extraction.[52] The case was an important watershed for developing greater government compliance and binding of the UNDRIP norm that was later adopted in the 2008 Constitution of free prior and informed consent (FPIC).[53] According to the Court's finding, the government had failed to engage in appropriate consultative processes. What is crucial to note here is that part of the legal strategy and demands of plaintiffs included claims that their way of life as Indigenous communities was existentially tied to their understandings of nature, and thus that assert the rights of nature. Waorani president and lead plaintiff Nemonte Nenquimo—recently named to Time's list of one hundred most influential people in the world and awarded the prestigious Goldman Environmental Prize—put it more precisely: "We will never sell our rainforest to the oil companies.... The government's interests in oil is not more valuable than our rights, our forest, our lives."[54] The Court supported two protective injunctions on this basis.[55]

As we have seen with this pandemic and the increasing manifestation of climate change devastation—from wildfires in California and the Amazon to stronger and more destructive hurricanes in the Caribbean and record floods—our contemporary condition is one that makes more visible our mutual dependency as a species with the other-than-human environment around us. In the *Rights of Others*, Benhabib offers us a definition of cosmopolitanism that speaks perfectly to our condition: "Cosmopolitanism" as "concern for the world as if it were one's polis."[56] The Ecuador case of *Pachamama's rights* reiterates this in a new direction, toward decolonial projects that affirm a care for our polis as if it were our cosmos, for building international solidarity and collective power to generate urgent action. I want to therefore end with the conjunction that I began with: between decoloniality and cosmopolitanism.

COSMOPOLITANISM WITHOUT ILLUSIONS AND DECOLONIAL COSMOPOLITANISM

In his engagement with the Frankfurt School through a series of lectures in the early 1990s, Argentine-Mexican philosopher Enrique Dussel challenged the construction of modernity advanced in the works of canonical modern and contemporary European thinkers such as G. W. F. Hegel and Jürgen Habermas. For Dussel, this "mythic" reconstruction of the constitution of subjectivity and modernity not only placed Europe at its center, but did so through the *encubrimiento* (covering over) of Europe's others. The constitution of European subjectivity, rationality, and modernity takes shape through a covering over by way of processes of erotic, political, pedagogical, economic, and cultural modernization and colonization, which viewed, represented, and subsequently dominated and invisibilized Europe's Others through self-referential categories. In Dussel's words, European colonization "subsumed (or alienated) the Other under the Same," thus denying the Other in their radical alterity to assert modern rationality and its universalism.[57]

If, for Dussel, European colonization and imperialism set into motion the mythic construction of European modernity and subjectivity, for the Peruvian sociologist Aníbal Quijano, it also established a colonial power structure predicated on the hierarchical demarcation of groups along racial, ethnic, and national configurations, which, even after the end of formal systems of European colonization, still persists as Western imperialism.[58] "Coloniality," writes Quijano, "is still the most general form of domination in the world today, once colonialism as an explicit political order was destroyed."[59] Quijano has famously encapsulated this interrelation between global power and systems of racial hierarchy in his concept of the "coloniality of power."[60] Its problematic nature extends, however, beyond the problem of racist social relations in light of its emergence with the consolidation of European capitalism and its relation to the production of knowledge.[61] The production of knowledge must thus be understood as constructed by and as part of a Western imperialist power structure that defines what counts as the rational, whose knowledge counts, and the purposes/ends of knowledge.

Building on the insights of Dussel and Quijano, Latin American scholars such as Walter Mignolo, María Lugones, Rita Segato, Catherine Walsh, Silvia Rivera Cusicanqui, and Arturo Escobar have outlined a contemporary emancipatory project predicated on the "decolonization" of contemporary systems of knowledge and power from their fundamental links to European global imperialism and colonization. Given the problematic of Eurocentric epistemology and power posed by decolonial theory, is decoloniality compatible with cosmopolitanism? Or more pointedly, can a cosmopolitan project such as Seyla Benhabib's, which draws for inspiration upon European thinkers such as Kant, provide a framework for engaging with decolonial processes and movements?

What I offer here in this chapter is, I hope, the beginnings of a conversation, or better yet an invitation to a conversation, en route to more fully answering these questions. I began with the preliminary response that the answer could be yes. I have sought to support that yes with the empirical insights and theoretical connections revealed when democratic iterations are applied to cases such as Pachamama's and Indigenous rights struggles in Ecuador. But is that enough to compel a decolonial interpretation?

Environmental norms and cosmopolitan rights applying to nonhuman entities are certainly outside the scope of Benhabib's project. The project has also not dealt directly with the legacies of colonialism or imperialism. Nevertheless, the connection to decolonial projects is warranted and indeed Benhabib's work opens that invitation. Throughout her work, Benhabib has advanced a revised understanding of universalism: one that is not monological but dialogical; that connects a Generalized to a Concrete Other; that has theorized the porosity of borders, not only physical, but also cultural, political, and intellectual; and that understands that cosmopolitanism must not harbor myths or illusions. Indeed, Benhabib defines her "cosmopolitanism without illusions" as resisting the "Pollyannaish" embrace of a "ceaseless affirmation of global oneness and unity."[62] But her theory can and must go beyond that as well. In *The Darker Side of Modernity*, Walter Mignolo writes, "To maintain cosmopolitan ideas, we (all those who engage in this project) need to decolonize cosmopolitanism which means moving toward a decolonial cosmopolitan order no longer modeled on the law of nature discovered by science but from various models of conviviality that Western cosmopolitanism suppressed."[63] For Mignolo, *decolonial cosmopolitanism* would involve rethinking cosmopolitanism from the perspective of colonial difference and from those others (such as Indigenous peoples) that have outlined equally powerful and alternative but also related models of cosmopolitan thinking.[64] Democratic iterations open this possibility by way of its iterability and its effects in dismantling, overcoming, and transforming what was once authoritative. As Benhabib writes, "Every act of iteration involves making sense of an authoritative original in a new and different context.... Iteration is the reappropriation of the 'origin'; it is at the same time its dissolution as the original."[65]

NOTES

1. "Yo Defiendo al Río Piatua," Facebook page, www.facebook.com/piatuaresiste.
2. Antonio José Paz Cardona, "Pleito: indígenas Kichwa se oponen a polémica hidroeléctrica en la Amazonía ecuatoriana," *Mongabay*, July 23, 2019. https://es.mongabay.com/2019/07/hidroelectrica-rio-piatua-amazonia-ecuador-kichwa/?fbclid=IwAR1ZHIBsneTrZBfBSHBtEKu1NWxas3LACH8pM10S_JWWBCgpoYoBF6pYSWk.
3. David Scott, *Conscripts of Modernity: The Tragedy of Colonial Enlightenment* (Durham, NC: Duke University Press, 2004).
4. "The Causes of Climate Change," in *Global Climate Change: Vital Signs of the Planet*. https://climate.nasa.gov/causes/.
5. Seyla Benhabib, *The Rights of Others: Aliens, Residents, and Citizens* (Cambridge: Cambridge University Press, 2004), 43–48; and Seyla Benhabib, *Another Cosmopolitanism* (New York: Oxford University Press, 2009), 32–36.
6. Angélica María Bernal, "Ecuador's Dual Populisms: Neocolonial Extractives, Violence, and Indigenous Resistance," *Thesis Eleven* 164, no. 1 (2021): 1–28.
7. Walter Mignolo, "Border Thinking and Decolonial Cosmopolitanism: Overcoming Imperial/Colonial Differences," in *Routledge Handbook of Cosmopolitan Studies*, ed. Gerard Delanty (New York: Routledge, 2018).
8. Benhabib, *Another Cosmopolitanism*, 16.
9. James Anaya, *Indigenous Peoples in International Law*, 2nd ed. (New York: Oxford University Press, 1996), 52.
10. Manuela Picq, *Vernacular Sovereignties: Indigenous Women Challenging World Politics* (Tucson: University of Arizona Press, 2019); Ronald Niezen, *The Origins of Indigenism: Human Rights and the Politics of Identity* (Berkeley: University of California Press, 2003); Jonathan Crossen, "Another Wave of Anti-Colonialism: The Origins of Indigenous Internationalism," *Canadian Journal of History* 52, no. 3 (2017); and Crossen, "Decolonization, Indigenous Internationalism, and the World Council of Indigenous Peoples" (PhD diss., University of Waterloo, 2014).
11. Crossen, "Another Wave of Anti-Colonialism"; David Temin, "The Fourth World— George Manuel and the Politics of Resurgence," in *Remapping Sovereignty: Decolonization and Self-Determination in North American Indian Political Thought* (Chicago: University of Chicago Press, 2023), chap. 4; and Glen Coulthard, "Introduction," in *The Fourth World* (University of Minnesota Press, 2019), xiii–ix.
12. Niezen, *Origins of Indigenism*, 45.

13. Anaya, "Developments Within the Modern Era of Human Rights," *Indigenous Peoples in International Law*, chap. 2; and Mary Lawlor "Indigenous Internationalism: Native Rights and the UN," *Comparative American Studies*," 1, no. 3:351–69.
14. "C169—Indigenous and Tribal Peoples Convention, 1989 No. 169," International Labor Organization, www.ilo.org/dyn/normlex/en/f?p=NORMLEXPUB:12100:0::NO::P12100_ILO_CO.
15. Anaya, *Indigenous Peoples in International Law*, 59–60.
16. "United National Declaration on the Rights of Indigenous Peoples," A/RES/61/295. www.un.org/development/desa/Indigenouspeoples/declaration-on-the-rights-of-Indigenous-peoples.html.
17. Council of Europe, "The Evolution of Human Rights," www.coe.int/en/web/compass/the-evolution-of-human-rights.
18. See, for instance, Arturo Escobar, *Designs for the Pluriverse: Radical Interdependence, Autonomy, and the Making of Worlds* (Durham, NC: Duke University Press, 2018); Escobar, *Pluriversal Politics: The Real and the Possible* (Durham, NC: Duke University Press, 2020); and Walter Mignolo, *The Darker Side of Modernity: Global Futures, Decolonial Options* (Durham, NC: Duke University Press, 2011).
19. Subcomandante Insurgente Marcos, *Ya Basta! Ten Years of the Zapatista Uprising* (Oakland, CA: AK Press, 2004).
20. "How the UN Declaration on the Rights of Indigenous Peoples Can Be Used to Protect Against a Trump Agenda," *Indian Law Resource Center*, https://indianlaw.org/implementing-undrip/how-un-declaration-rights-Indigenous-peoples-can-be-used-protect-against-trump-agenda.
21. www.cwis.org/2010/12/us-government-on-undrip-yes-but-no/.
22. Anaya, *Indigenous Peoples in International Law*; and Niezen, *The Origins of Indigenism*.
23. Glen Coulthard, "Introduction," in *The Fourth World* (Minneapolis: University of Minnesota Press, 2019), xiii–ix.
24. Angélica Bernal, *De la exclusión a la participación: Pueblos indígenas y sus derechos colectivos en el Ecuador* (Quito: Abya Yala, 2001).
25. Mark Becker, *Pachakutik: Indigenous Movements and Electoral Politics in Ecuador* (New York: Rowman and Littlefield, 2010). See the website of the Confederation of Indigenous Nationalities of Ecuador (CONAIE), https://conaie.org.
26. See Bernal, *De la exclusion a la participación*, chap. 2. See also Bernal, *Beyond Origins: Rethinking Founding in a Time of Constitutional Democracy* (Oxford: Oxford University Press, 2017), chap. 5.
27. Bernal, *De la exclusion a la participación*.
28. Bernal, *De la exclusion a la participación*.
29. Lindsay Maizland, "Global Climate Agreements: Successes and Failures," *Council of Foreign Relations*, October 29, 2021, www.cfr.org/backgrounder/paris-global-climate-change-agreements.
30. See the Community Environmental Legal Defense Fund's website, https://celdf.org/rights-of-nature/.
31. See Roderick Frazier Nash, *The Rights of Nature: A History of Environmental Ethics* (Madison: University of Wisconsin Press, 1989).

32. Nash, *The Rights of Nature*.
33. Bernal, *Beyond Origins*, chap. 5.
34. Bernal, chap. 5.
35. Angélica Maria Bernal, "The Promise and Perils of Presidential Refounding in Latin America," *Constellations* 21, no. 4:440–56. See also "UN Declaration on the Rights of Indigenous Peoples" (UNDRIP).
36. This included the work on postdevelopment of the anthropologist Arturo Escobar, the Uruguay sociologist Eduardo Gudynas, and the U.S.-based Community Environmental Legal Defense Fund (CELDF) and its cofounder Mari Margil, who was instrumental to the drafting of the rights of nature legislation in the 2008 Constitution. See Eduardo Gudynas, *Diez tesis urgentes sobre el nuevo extractivismo, extractivismo, politica, y sociedad* (2009), 187, www.rosalux.org.ec/pdfs/extractivismo.pdf#page=187. Jane Gleeson White, "It's Only Natural: The Push to Give Rivers, Mountains, and Forests Legal Rights," *Guardian*, March 31, 2018, www.theguardian.com/australia-news/2018/apr/01/its-only-natural-the-push-to-give-rivers-mountains-and-forests-legal-rights.
37. http://pdba.georgetown.edu/Constitutions/Ecuador/english08.html.
38. Angélica María Bernal, "Ecuador's Dual Populisms: Neocolonial Extractivism, Violence, and Indigenous Resistance," *Thesis Eleven* 164, no. 1 (2021): 9–36; and Marisol de la Cadena, *Earth Beings: Ecologies of Practice Across Andean Worlds* (Durham, NC: Duke University Press, 2015).
39. For Benhabib, this cascading is a practical outcome of democratic iterations but also democratically desirable. See especially Benhabib, *Another Cosmopolitanism*, 67–74.
40. "Jurispathic" is Robert Cover's term. The second by Benhabib more aptly characterizes the situation in Ecuador. See Benhabib, *Another Cosmopolitanism*, 49–50.
41. For another analysis of this period, see the outstanding book by Thea Riofrancos, *Resource Radicals: From Petro-Nationalism to Post-Extractivism in Ecuador* (Durham, NC: Duke University Press, 2020).
42. Robert Cover speaks of the violence of jurispathic courts in terms of their capacity for decision and adjudication. Cover writes: "Judges are people of violence. Because of the violence they command, judges do not create law, but kill it. Theirs is the jurispathic office. Confronting the luxuriant growth of a hundred legal traditions, they assert *this one* is law and destroy or try to destroy the rest" (53). See Robert Cover, "Nomos and Narrative," *Harvard Law Review* (1983–84).
43. This violence is particularly surprising given that it takes place in the context of a New Left government. For a more in-depth analysis, see Bernal, "Ecuador's Dual Populisms," 9–36.
44. Catherine Walsh, "On the October Awakening(s) and the Condor: Notes from Ecuador and the Region," *Black Issues in Philosophy* (November 12, 2019), https://blog.apaonline.org/2019/11/28/on-the-october-awakenings-and-the-condor-notes-from-ecuador-and-the-region/.
45. See Cover, "Nomos and Narrative," 51–53.
46. Cover, 53.
47. Craig M. Kauffman and Pamela Martin, "Constructing Rights of Nature Norms in the U.S., Ecuador, and New Zealand," *Global Environmental Politics* 18, no. 4 (2018): 43–62.

48. Such as the case of mining in the Esmeraldas region in 2011. Gonzalo Ortiz, "Ecuador: Government Shuts Down Illegal Mines," *Inter Press Service*, May 31, 2011, www.ipsnews.net/2011/05/ecuador-govt-shuts-down-illegal-gold-mines/.
49. "Ecuador: Court Cancels Rio Blanco Mine to Protect Waterways," *Telesur*, August 3, 2018, www.telesurenglish.net/news/Ecuadorean-Court-Cancels-Rio-Blanco-Mine-After-Resistance-20180803-0011.html.
50. "Ecuador: Court Cancels Rio Blanco Mine to Protect Waterways."
51. Roberta Rice, "Two Different Visions of the Left Divide Ecuador in the 2021 Presidential Election, *NACLA*," February 13, 2021, https://nacla.org/news/2021/02/13/two-different-visions-left-divide-ecuador-2021-presidential-election.
52. Rachel Riederer, "Fighting Covid-19 in the Amazon, with Herbs and the Internet," *New Yorker*, December 11, 2021, www.newyorker.com/news/news-desk/fighting-covid-19-in-the-amazon-with-herbs-and-the-internet.
53. Amazon Frontlines, "Waorani People Win Landmark Legal Victory Against Ecuadorian Government," April 26, 2019, www.amazonfrontlines.org/chronicles/waorani-victory/; and Reynard Loki, "How Indigenous Peoples Won a Landmark Victory Protecting the Amazon from Oil Drilling," *Open Democracy*, June 5, 2019, www.opendemocracy.net/en/democraciaabierta/los-pueblos-ind%C3%ADgenas-han-ganado-una-victoria-histórica-protegiendo-a-la-amazon%C3%ADa-del-extractivismo-en/.
54. Amazon Frontlines, "Waorani People Win Landmark Legal Victory Against Ecuadorian Government."
55. Observatorio Jurídico de Derechos de la Naturaleza, Caso Waorani, www.derechosdelanaturaleza.org.ec/caso-waorani/.
56. Benhabib, *The Rights of Others*, 172.
57. Enrique Dussel, *The Invention of the Americas: Eclipse of the "Other" and the Myth of Modernity*, trans. Michael D. Barber (New York: Continuum, 1995), 45–48.
58. See Aníbal Quijano, "Coloniality of Power, Eurocentrism, and Latin America," *Nepantla: Views from the South* 1, no. 3 (2000); and Aníbal Quijano, "Coloniality and Modernity/Rationality," *Cultural Studies* 21, nos. 2–3 (March/May 2007): 169.
59. Quijano, "Coloniality and Modernity/Rationality," 170.
60. Quijano, 171.
61. Quijano, 171–72.
62. Seyla Benhabib, *Dignity in Adversity: Human Rights in Troubled Times* (Cambridge: Polity, 2013).
63. Mignolo, *Darker Side of Modernity*, 270.
64. Mignolo, *Darker Side of Modernity*. See also Walter Mignolo, "The Many Faces of Cosmo-Polis: Border Thinking and Decolonial Cosmopolitanism," *Public Culture* (2000).
65. Benhabib, *The Rights of Others*, 180.

18
What Is the Other in Seyla Benhabib's *Another Cosmopolitanism*?

DRUCILLA CORNELL

Seyla Benhabib is unquestionably a great dialectical thinker. Of course dialectics is also a philosophy of the material world. So what do I mean by a dialectical thinker? All too often political and ethical debates freeze into static antagonisms, each side bitterly attacking the other. Dialectical thinking incorporates what is "right" in both positions by coming up with a new conceptualization that allows us to think differently about the entrenched sides and provides us with a new conceptualization that allows us to creatively move forward in politics and ethics. Let me give an example. Feminists after Carol Gilligan's pathbreaking work *In a Different Voice* seemingly fell into two camps.[1] One camp, often following their interpretation of Carol Gilligan's thinking, argued that women had a different voice that focused ethical judgments on concrete situations without appealing to abstract universals, including the abstract universal of the purportedly autonomous person. On the other side were feminists who insisted that at the very heart of feminism was the idea that women were indeed autonomous persons and that women's issues were human rights. Simply put, the ethic of care was in conflict with the ideal of justice to which feminists must appeal. Enter Benhabib.

In her important work *Situating the Self*, Benhabib argues that both sides were partially right but that we needed a new concept of how to think about the self and its relationship to ethics.[2] Benhabib argued that we needed to distinguish between the concrete and generalized other. We need both. The generalized other is precisely the abstract person and autonomous self that we need in order to develop universal norms. On the other hand, the concrete other is exactly how we relate to individuals in their situatedness. The differentiation of the concrete and generalized other has traveled well beyond the context of a feminist debate even as it played a central role there. That it has so traveled shows the power of Benhabib's dialectical thinking.

My central argument today is not about Benhabib's *Situating the Self.* It instead seeks to address her adamant defense of cosmopolitan codependence and the obligation it imposes on European states. She has suggested that there are three positions: (1) liberal nationalism, (2) international liberalism, and (3) cosmopolitan codependence, Benhabib's own position. She insists that cosmopolitanism is not a moral ideal guiding one nation, but rather opens us to grapple with the realities of global capitalism and the way in which not only economies but peoples are subjected to forces that are inseparable from the way in which we understand ourselves as a part of the global world. My challenge to her is to recognize a fourth normative position in her writings on international law and the development of universal moral norms that goes beyond those already embodied in treaties. To quote Benhabib,

> For some, cosmopolitanism signifies an attitude of enlightened morality that does not place "love of country ahead" of "love of mankind" (Martha Nussbaum); for others cosmopolitanism signifies hybridity, fluidity, and recognizing the fractured and internally riven character of human selves and citizens, whose complex aspirations cannot be circumscribed by national fantasies and primordial communities (Jeremy Waldron). For a third group of thinkers, whose lineages are those of Critical Theory, cosmopolitanism is a normative philosophy carrying the universalistic norms of discourse ethics beyond the confines of the nation-state (Jürgen Habermas, David Held, and James Bohman).[3]

Benhabib allies herself with the third group but uneasily. She worries that the scope and reach of "discursive space" has not been given serious enough consideration. I agree. She expresses her worries and anxiety and the way it pushes her beyond the definitions she describes as follows: "I will insist on the necessary disjunction as well as the necessary mediation between the moral and the ethical, the moral and the political. The task is one of mediations, not reductions. How can one mediate moral universalism with ethical particularism?"[4]

It is precisely because Benhabib asks this question that I will offer a fourth normative position of how universal global norms are generated out of ethical particularity. Benhabib has offered us a number of powerful critiques of the competitors, liberal nationalism and international liberalism. Her own original position is cosmopolitan codependence. I will offer a fourth: transnational decolonization. The idea of transnational decolonization rose out of over a century of liberation struggles that have placed on the agenda an entirely different way of thinking about justice and a fair world. The term came out of the Bandung Conference on April 18–24, 1955, which included twenty-nine states, mostly from the Global South, with the explicit program of fighting against imperial domination, and in my terms transnational decolonization. The significance of this conference went way beyond those days in 1955, leading to, for example, the creation of the Non-Aligned Movement (NAM) in 1961, and a number of other organizations in Asia, South America, and Africa who took seriously the need to realize nonalignment with Europe and the United States as well. I will discuss this more at the end of this essay and I will suggest that transnational decolonization can offer new fresh answers to the question that haunts Benhabib about how to mediate ethical particularism and moral universalism.

So how can the addition of a fourth normative position help us answer this question? First and perhaps foremost, struggles for decolonization almost always appeal to the creation of a new humanity, indeed sometimes a new beginning in which a new species of human beings would arise after the horror of colonization and imperialism. To quote Frantz Fanon:

> The Third World must start over a new history of man which takes account of not only the occasional prodigious theses maintained by Europe but also its crimes, the most heinous of which have been committed at the very heart of man, the pathological dismembering of his functions and the erosion of his unity, and in the context of the community, the fracture, the stratification and the bloody tensions fed by class, and finally, on the on the immense scale of humanity, the racial hatred, slavery, exploitation, and above all, the bloodless genocide whereby one and a half billion men have been written off.[5]

Fanon concludes *The Wretched of the Earth* with the call: "For Europe, for ourselves and for humanity, comrades, we must make a new start, develop a new way of thinking, and endeavor to create a new man."[6] Do I think that Benhabib's thinking demands of us that we make a new start and develop a new way of thinking? Indeed I do, and her *Another Cosmopolitanism*, with its emphasis on the right of hospitality and the moral obligations of European states to respect that right, as well as her insistence on the rights of migrants and refugees, is a new way of thinking in cosmopolitanism because of its insistence on our codependence.[7] Does she directly connect her arguments for the moral obligations of the European states to refugees and migrants to the bloody history of colonialism and imperialism that Fanon graphically describes? She does not do so explicitly. She can and she should, but I will suggest that her deeply moving accounts of refugees and migrants can easily be connected to such a history. But for now I want to turn to her question: How can concrete universal norms be generated out of ethical partiality? Obviously, decolonization aspires to the universal in its cry for a new humanity not rooted in the horror of imperial domination, but how does that cry get institutionalized? That is an unbelievably complicated question and much ink has been spilled addressing it, but much more important are the many experiments of decolonization after the liberation of colonized peoples who claim sovereignty for themselves.

I want to turn to two examples from the South African Constitution of how ethical partiality generates universal norms. Before doing so I need to note that South Africa explicitly integrates the norms of international law into the South African Constitution. The global law and the state law were integrated as a necessary part of what Emeritus Justice Lourens Ackermann calls the legal nature of the South African Revolution.[8] But let me now turn to the examples of how ethical partiality inherent in transnational decolonization generates universal norms. The first is Justice Ackermann's interpretation of section 10 of the South African Constitution, which reads as follows: "Everyone has inherent dignity and the right to have their dignity respected and protected."[9] Justice Ackermann, in a series of important judgments and articles, emphasized the significance of the "and." How so? For Justice Ackermann the "and" separates the moral mandate of dignity from its legal protection as a matter of right. Benhabib writes, "The law provides the framework within which the work of culture and politics go on. The laws, as the ancients knew, are the walls of the city, but the art and passion of politics unfold within these walls and very often politics leads to the breaking down of these barriers or at least to assuring their permeability."[10] For Ackermann the permeability must never again deny the moral mandate of dignity, for that is the foundational wrong of white supremacy, which insists that only whites have such dignity. We are returned to Fanon's description of what it means to throw billions of people below the bar of humanity, denying of course their inherent dignity as well as all of the basic rights of citizenship.

If there ever was a case of "dignity in adversity" it was the constitutional negotiations in South Africa.[11] The undoing of apartheid demanded that the particularities of that crime against humanity be addressed in the name of this moral mandate of dignity.[12] In that way, a "new law on earth" (to use Berkowitz's telling phrase) arises out of the ashes of apartheid and generates a moral mandate as a concrete universal. It is also an example of what Benhabib, in her original interpretation of Robert Cover, calls jurisgenerative politics.[13] The moral mandate of dignity delimits politics in the name of a moral ideal that in turn infuses the political struggle to undo apartheid in its name. Am I arguing that the South

African Constitution sought to be a document of transnational decolonization? Yes I am. The ideals of the Freedom Charter were not just for South Africans but for all oppressed peoples struggling for liberation in the name of a new humanity. I am here writing on the level of ideals that inspired the struggle of the African National Congress. What has happened in the actual transfer of power in South Africa is beyond the scope of an essay to honor Benhabib.[14]

I want to turn now to my second example of how transnational decolonization can generate new universal norms. Colonization seeks to destroy indigenous values and ways of life in the name of subjecting peoples to European imperial control. Therefore revival and respect for indigenous ways of life are crucial to decolonization. How to do this and what this means are hotly contested questions, as they should be.[15] But let me return to the question of how indigenous values can generate universal norms. In the *Khosa* case, Emeritus Justice Yvonne Mokgoro wrote for the majority of the Court using "uBuntu thinking" to conclude that the exemption of noncitizens from receiving grants was inconsistent with section 27 of the Constitution, which accords *everyone* the right of access to health care, water, shelter, and social security.[16] Justice Mokgoro strongly emphasized that the wording of section 27 grants socioeconomic rights to everyone.[17] *UBuntu* is a Xhosa/Zulu word that is not translated when it is used in the courts and on the ground, but for the purposes of this essay I will say that uBuntu is both an ontology and an ethic of how human beings can live together and flourish. We live in an affective field in which all of our actions impact others. It is not a communitarian philosophy in the Anglo-American debate, but one that insists that human beings can only individuate in conditions of support. Hence Justice Mokgoro's insistence on everyone because no one should fall below the bar of the human. In terms of Benhabib's insistence on the right of hospitality, here such a right is thought through uBuntu. Justice Mokgoro does not speak of such a right, but it is implicit in her insistence that section 27 of the South African Constitution includes everyone, not just citizens. These examples, and of course there are many others, demonstrate that South African and more broadly African philosophy can generate new concrete universals and help Benhabib to think through the question of how ethical partiality can generate universal norms.

Did I pick the fourth position of transnational decolonization out of a hat? I certainly did not. It arises from my own attempt to come to terms with the overriding significance of the Bandung Conference of 1955, which lives as a challenge to ways in which international law remains infused with imperialist practices and the racist rejection of the significance of what the liberation struggles in the Global South demand in terms of reform of international law.[18] At this conference, there were committees that discussed controversial ideas of development such as nonalignment with Europe. Some of the leaders were engaged with experiments in socialism. Its legacy is hotly contested, but one notable aspect of the conference was that it challenged international law for its racism (they used the word "racialism") and refused to come to terms with imperialist domination. To quote from the introduction to the excellent collection edited by Luis Eslava, Michael Fakhiri, and Vasuki Nesiah,

> Bandung inserted the concepts of equality and justice into international law in a way that cannot be undone. Bandung's significance for international lawyers arises from the fact that it is both an idea and a project, a collective imagination of a new world and a practical effort to make that idea a reality. It is for every generation to argue and debate over what justice and equality mean for international law, and in so doing to resist normalization and to open the possibility of an alternative, fairer, and more just world order, like a rumor without any echo of History, really beginning.[19]

I began this essay by honoring Benhabib as a great dialectic thinker. Do I think she will rise to the demand of the spirit of Bandung? Indeed I do. In a recent article on the Refugee Convention, she already expresses concern about how the struggles against imperialism must be given much greater weight in international law.[20] But the spirit of her *Another Cosmopolitanism* already opens her own understanding of the challenges in the future. I leave her with the last word: "My concern is less with the kind of ontological universe in which cosmopolitan norms can be said to exist, than with how these norms, whatever their ontological status, can shape, guide, and constrain our political life, by creating new spaces for evaluative articulation and by extending our political imagination."[21]

NOTES

1. Carol Gilligan, *In a Different Voice: Psychological Theory and Women's Development* (Cambridge, MA: Harvard University Press, 1982).
2. Seyla Benhabib, *Situating the Self: Gender, Community, and Postmodernism in Contemporary Ethics* (London: Routledge, 1992).
3. Seyla Benhabib, *Another Cosmopolitanism*, ed. Robert Post (New York: Oxford University Press, 2006), 17–18.
4. Benhabib, 19.
5. Frantz Fanon, *The Wretched of the Earth* (New York: Grove, 1963), 238.
6. Fanon, 239.
7. See generally Seyla Benhabib, *The Rights of Others: Aliens, Residents, and Citizens* (Cambridge: Cambridge University Press, 2006).

8. Drucilla Cornell, Stu Woolman, Sam Fuller, Jason Brickhill, Michael Bishop, and Diana Dunbar, eds., *The Dignity Jurisprudence of the Constitutional Court of South Africa*, vol. 2 (New York: Fordham University Press, 2013).
9. *Constitution of the Republic of South Africa*, sec. 10, 1996.
10. Benhabib, *Another Cosmopolitanism*, 60.
11. Seyla Benhabib, *Dignity in Adversity: Human Rights in Troubled Times* (Cambridge: Polity, 2013). See also Drucilla Cornell, Karin Van Marle, and Albie Sachs, *Albie Sachs and Transformation in South Africa: From Revolutionary Activist to Constitutional Court Judge* (London: Birkbeck Law Press, 2014).
12. See Roger Berkowitz, "Dignity Jurisprudence: Building a New Law on Earth," in Cornell, Woolman, Fuller, Brickhill, Bishop, and Dunbar, *The Dignity Jurisprudence of the Constitutional Court of South Africa*, vol. 1 (New York: Fordham University Press, 2013). See also Drucilla Cornell, "Law and Revolution in South Africa," in *Law and Revolution in South Africa: UBuntu, Dignity, and the Struggle for Constitutional Transformation* (New York: Fordham University Press, 2014).
13. Benhabib, *Another Cosmopolitanism*, 49–50.
14. I agree with those critics who argue that the lofty ideals of the Freedom Charter were forsaken by the capitulation of the ANC to the mandates of neoliberal capitalism. See Patrick Bond, *Elite Transition: From Apartheid to Neoliberalism in South Africa* (London: Pluto, 2000); and Sampie Terenblanche, *Lost in Transformation: South Africa's Search for a New Future Since 1986* (Johannesburg: KMM Review, 2012).
15. The uBuntu Project advocated for the reconstitutionalization of uBuntu, which played an important role in the interim Constitution. There is now an uBuntu jurisprudence, which has been challenged by those who argue that an African value cannot be imported into a constitution, particularly one influenced by European ideals. This is not my position but it is an important debate.
16. Drucilla Cornell and Nyoko Muvangua, "The *Khosa* and *Mahlaule* Cases," in *uBuntu and the Law: African Ideals and Postapartheid Jurisprudence* (New York: Fordham University Press, 2012). This is an edited version of the case. *Constitution of the Republic of South Africa*, sec. 27, 1996.
17. Justice Mokgoro noted further that the exclusion of noncitizens also violated sections 9 and 10 of the Constitution.
18. Luis Eslava, Michael Fakhri, and Vasuki Nesiah, eds., *Bandung, Global History, and International Law: Critical Pasts and Pending Futures* (Cambridge: Cambridge University Press, 2018).
19. Luis Eslava, Michael Fakhri, and Vasuki Nesiah, "Introduction: The Spirit of Bandung," in Eslava, Fakhri, and Nesiah, *Bandung, Global History, and International Law*, 32.
20. Seyla Benhabib, "The End of the 1951 Refugee Convention?: Dilemmas of Sovereignty, Territoriality, and Human Rights," *Jus Cogens* 2, no. 1 (August 2020): 75–100.
21. Benhabib, *Another Cosmopolitanism*, 26.

19
Border Deaths as Forced Disappearances

Frantz Fanon and the Outlines of a Critical Phenomenology

AYTEN GÜNDOĞDU

On February 6, 2014, around four hundred migrants from sub-Saharan Africa attempted to cross the Spanish border in Ceuta, a town near Morocco, by swimming around the Tarajal seawall. The Spanish border control officers responded to this attempt by shooting rubber bullets, smoke canisters, and detonator blanks, creating a mayhem at sea and resulting in the drowning of fifteen migrants. According to the Spanish authorities, the lethal action was justified, given the migrants' "belligerent attitude." The legal investigation of the case confirmed that conclusion, as the judge presiding in the case ruled that it was the migrants who placed themselves in harm's way by willingly "accept[ing] the risks of illegally entering Spanish territory."[1]

The Spanish case illustrates that border enforcement has become increasingly lethal with the adoption of ever more restrictive policies and technologies of immigration control. According to a conservative estimate of the International Organization of Migration (IOM), over fifty-eight thousand migrants have died or disappeared as they tried to cross borders from 2014 to 2023.[2] States that routinely adopt lethal border control policies have so far remained unaccountable for their actions. This "international regime of impunity" goes hand in hand with an institutionalized indifference to the migrants who die or disappear in transit, as can be seen in the lack of any systematic effort to locate their whereabouts, recover remains, identify the dead, inform families, and have proper burials.[3]

How do we account for the regime of impunity surrounding migrant deaths and disappearances resulting from border control practices? To answer this question, there is a need to attend to the organizing principles of the nation-state system, particularly the principle of territorial sovereignty that continues to delimit entitlement to human rights.[4] Endowing states with a prerogative to control entry into their borders, this norm renders migrants suspected of unauthorized entry ineligible for even the most fundamental rights such as the right to be free from indefinite detention and arbitrary deportation.[5] These subjects "exist at the limits of all rights regimes," as Seyla Benhabib incisively puts it, "and reveal the blind spot in the system of rights where the rule of law flows into its opposite: the state of exception and the ever-present danger of violence."[6]

But territorial sovereignty does not render every border-crosser equally vulnerable to arbitrary state violence. Terms such as *illegal* and *unauthorized*, and even *migrant*, are labels reserved for racialized subjects crossing borders.[7] There is a need to understand how violence wielded in the name of territorial sovereignty targets certain categories of migrants by considering the impact of racism and racialization, shaped by histories of slavery, colonialism, and imperialism, on contemporary migration policies.[8] We could recall the Tarajal massacre cited at the outset, particularly the Spanish authorities' remark about the "belligerent attitude" of migrants who stormed to the beach in large numbers and tried to swim around the border. The Spanish authorities argued that they had to use anti-riot gear in order to "delimitate the border line in the water" in response to the migrants' act that (in their eyes) violated the sacrosanct principle of territorial sovereignty.[9] Border-crossing in this case was deemed to be not only a breach of Spanish sovereignty, however, but also an act of "belligerence" because the subjects in question were perceived as suspicious and violent due to racialized assumptions about their identity and conduct; the fact that the act was collectively undertaken further fueled the perception. The Spanish authorities' justification of their lethal action introduces us to a perceptual field saturated by racialized images, including the colonial representations of "Africans" as "savage hordes" innately disposed to violence.

This chapter aims to examine the racialized forms of violence enacted by contemporary border regimes by rethinking border deaths as "forced disappearances." Within international human rights law, this term is used to describe state practices of arrest, detention, or abduction that make someone "disappear," followed by a refusal to acknowledge the fate of that person. Although "forced disappearance" is often associated with military dictatorships, I extend it to border control policies that push migrants beyond the pale of the law, make it difficult to find out about their fates or whereabouts, and render their lives disposable. In the case of the Tarajal massacre, while the official death toll was fifteen, an unofficial estimate suggests that it was at least twice as high.[10] The bodies that were not recovered remain uncounted and unidentified. The authorities even failed to identify all the bodies that were recovered, burying them in potter's fields without informing the families or conducting proper forensic investigation.[11] Spain denied visas to the families who wanted to identify the bodies and participate in commemorative events,[12] and the legal investigation relied primarily on the testimonies of the Spanish officers and systematically set obstacles to survivors who wanted to appear in court.[13] The posthumous condition of rightlessness in the Tarajal case underscores that contemporary border control policies give rise to forced disappearance, as they place their targets outside the protection of the law and can even make them vanish without a trace, as if they never existed.

In thinking about border deaths as "forced disappearances," I also move beyond the strictly juridical meaning of this term and foreground its *phenomenological* resonances to pay particular attention to "the way other persons become visible to us, or cease to be visible to us."[14] How does someone cease to appear as a living being with whom we inhabit the world? Through what kinds of processes do we fail to apprehend their killing as murder? Why are their bodies treated as inanimate things stripped of rights after death?[15] Such questions demand a phenomenological inquiry into the conditions of appearance and disappearance, including the social structures, normative orders, and linguistic representations that make and unmake one's relations to the world and other living beings.

To undertake such an inquiry, I engage with the works of Frantz Fanon and examine how borders establish racialized partitions among both the living and the dead. Within a perceptual field saturated by racial schemas that regulate visibility, racialized others become subject to various forms of violence that shatter their intersubjective experience of the world as embodied beings and transform them into thing-like entities deprived of agency, presence, and rights. "Forced disappearance," I argue, entails not only an obliteration of legal and political status but also the imposition of invisibility in an ontological sense. Fanon's account of colonialism highlights that, within a perceptual field permeated by anti-Black racism, Black subjects are held captive to dehumanizing representations that deprive them of any individuality, treat them as mere specimens of a race, and render their very appearance suspect on the basis of their skin color. In a world that renders Black appearance "illicit," the "only acceptable being" for Black subjects becomes "nonexistence, nonappearance, or submergence."[16] If being is identical with appearance from a phenomenological perspective, in the sense that we become who we are by appearing to others who can testify to our existence in this world, then racialized subjects experience a form of "forced disappearance" as they are denied the right to appear and relegated to "a zone of nonbeing."[17]

The chapter develops this argument as follows: First, I provide an overview of border deaths, focusing particularly on the differential allocation of rights, including the right to life, in a world of securitized borders. Second, I propose the concept of "forced disappearance" to capture state crimes that obstruct the movement of racialized others across borders, expel them from the world of the living, and justify their annihilation with impunity. Third, I examine with Fanon how certain elements of colonialism—spatial compartmentalization, immobilization, routinized violence, legalized lawlessness—reappear within border governance. These elements can help us understand how border controls render mobility an exclusive privilege of whiteness and subject racialized others to "forced disappearance." Fourth, I turn to Fanon's analysis of racism—especially his concepts of "historical-racial schema" and "epidermal racial schema"—in order to understand the differential vulnerability to death, injury, and disappearance at the border.[18] In the fifth and final section, I build on Fanon's critical insights into the functioning of law under colonial rule and examine how courts of law often endow state violence wielded in the name of border control with an aura of legitimacy. For the most part, courts of law have also become sites of "forced disappearance," testifying to the expulsion of racialized migrants from a world reserved as a privileged habitat for those eligible for rights, as evidenced by the Tarajal case.

In examining border deaths critically with the help of Fanon, I focus on the Euro-Mediterranean border regimes for two key reasons. First, the Mediterranean Sea, particularly the Central Mediterranean route, has become "the world's deadliest border."[19] Second, the Mediterranean also invites us to situate the racialized violence of contemporary borders within the *longue durée* of colonialism, imperialism, and slavery, as emphasized by the recent efforts to rethink migration to Europe through the conceptual lens of "the Black Mediterranean."[20]

Fanon provides us with critical insights into the legal, political, social, and even ontological dimensions of "forced disappearance" as a problem of "racialized rightlessness."[21] But as I underline in the conclusion of this chapter, his work also cautions us against a death-bound understanding of Blackness and invites attention to various forms of struggle that strive to "create the ideal conditions of existence for a human world."[22] What arises from an engagement with his works is a critical phenomenology that explores borders simultaneously as "death-worlds"[23] and as sites of "world-building"[24] in which the meanings of *life*, *humanity*, and *rights* are continuously and resiliently reinvented.

DIFFERENTIAL ALLOCATION OF RIGHTS IN A WORLD OF BORDERS

Since the late 1990s, states have adopted increasingly restrictive border control policies that have criminalized migration, militarized borders, and pushed migrants to make ever more perilous journeys.[25] As a result, major migration routes such as the Central Mediterranean route stretching from sub-Saharan Africa to Italy and the Sonoran Desert between Mexico and the United States have turned into zones of death and disappearance. We have become accustomed to photos of capsized boats and body bags lined up on a Mediterranean beach, or news stories of migrants who died of hyperthermia or hypothermia on their way to the United States. But border control policies are much more lethal than what the media coverage of this problem suggests, and there is a need to move beyond these more familiar visions of death in order to understand the scope of the problem.[26] In addition to the more visible deaths at key border crossing sites, there are less publicized deaths that result from the enforcement of routine border control policies—for example, deaths in immigration detention centers, deaths that result from deportation decisions, or deaths connected to the refusal of asylum claims. I use the term *border deaths* to include all these deaths that result directly or indirectly from border enforcement—and not just the deaths that occur in transit, as is often the case in official counts.[27] Additionally, there is a need to reconsider "death" beyond its physical meaning since contemporary migration controls also give rise to certain forms of "civil death," which denotes being "dead" in the eyes of the law and losing one's status as a rights-bearing subject.[28] Migrants forcefully "disappeared" by border control policies are subject to this kind of civil death, even in cases where they are not killed. We also see civil death in policies such as indefinite detention and arbitrary deportation that deny migrants even the basic protections associated with the rule of law.

Border deaths demonstrate that fundamental human rights are allocated unequally. Within a human rights framework, each human being is assumed to be entitled to a set of universal rights by the mere fact of their humanity. But territorial borders install hierarchical divisions within humanity, leaving migrants in an irregular status with a narrower set of rights that have only precarious guarantees.[29] Even the right to life is not secured equally for all. Whereas states take on far-reaching obligations to ensure the safety of those who have prior authorization to travel, they evade these obligations in the case of border-crossers cast as "illegal"—an increasingly racialized status, as I will discuss later.[30]

The differential allocation of the right to life also goes hand in hand with the differential treatment of the bodies and remains of migrants.[31] In Italy, for example, the recovered bodies and remains are often photographed and given a code; they are then buried in graves marked with these codes; in the absence of a database that connects the photos, numbers, and burial locations, it is very difficult for families to find these graves. There is also no institutionalized effort to collect DNA evidence for purposes of identification.[32] If "ours is the age of necronominalism," understood in terms of "the moral imperative to know the exact numbers and names of the dead," migrant deaths, for the most part, appear to be a remarkable exception to this rule.[33] The lack of proper burial in most cases indicates "a posthumous exclusion from the cultural and political order, an obliteration of personhood after death."[34]

The language used to describe migrant deaths often reflects the posthumous obliteration of personhood. For the most part, these deaths are treated as "accidents," as can be seen in the frequent use of the term *tragic* in news accounts: small, overcrowded, flimsy boats seem to be doomed to capsize with the gale force of winds and crashing waves. It is difficult to think of criminal liability when an action is cast as an accident, especially one that results primarily from the desperation of those who are ready to risk everything, even their lives, for refuge or opportunity. Language itself becomes a means of disavowing responsibility and accountability—a site where migrants die or disappear once again.

The regime of impunity surrounding migrant deaths and disappearances has recently been challenged, however, to address questions of state responsibility and legal accountability. For example, in a 2017 report submitted to the UN General Assembly, Agnes Callamard, the then UN Special Rapporteur on Extrajudicial, Summary or Arbitrary Executions, argued that border deaths are "extrajudicial killings."[35] Criminal liability for these deaths, according to Callamard, lies not only with individuals such as smugglers and border control agents but also with states that have adopted "policies based on deterrence, militarization and extraterritoriality."[36] Another crucial effort in this regard is the dossier submitted in 2019 by two lawyers, Omer Shatz and Juan Branco, to the International Criminal Court in order to hold the member states of the European Union accountable for border control policies in the Mediterranean and to prosecute them for "crimes against humanity."[37] Along these lines, several scholars, humanitarian practitioners, and migrant rights' activists have also adopted the legal concept of "forced disappearances" and argued that border control practices such as detention, deportation, and pushbacks are comparable to the strategies of deterrence, control, and terror that military dictatorships deployed to make dissidents "disappear" and deprive them of legal protections and rights.[38]

The aforementioned approaches have strategically mobilized the resources of international criminal and human rights law to address the problem of legal accountability in the context of migrant deaths and disappearances. In what follows, I join these efforts to rethink border deaths as "state crimes" and adopt "forced disappearance" as a conceptual lens that can help us attend to the different kinds of violence inflicted by lethal border policies.[39] Unlike in existing approaches, however, I do not use "forced disappearance" only in a juridical sense but also attend to the phenomenological resonances of this term in order to examine political, social, and ontological forms of forced invisibility and nonexistence that cannot be captured easily from a legal perspective. In fact, once reconsidered phenomenologically, "forced disappearance" urges us to think about existing legal frameworks, including human rights norms, much more critically, particularly to understand their limitations in providing migrants with robust guarantees of protection against arbitrary state violence. As the ruling of the judge in the Tarajal massacre highlights, law itself often participates in the justification of the violence that state agents use against migrants, sets obstacles to assigning responsibility for migrant deaths and disappearances, and leaves migrants in a condition of rightlessness in life and in death. Law's own complicity in the reproduction of a regime of impunity surrounding migrant deaths and disappearances urges us to critically examine law itself as a site of forced disappearance especially for racialized migrants.

FORCED DISAPPEARANCE: A LEGAL AND PHENOMENOLOGICAL ANALYSIS

The term *forced disappearance* entered the human rights vocabulary particularly in the wake of the crimes committed by the military-authoritarian regimes of Latin America in the 1970s and 1980s. It refers to "the arrest, detention, abduction or any other form of deprivation of liberty by agents of the State or by persons or groups of persons acting with the authorization, support or acquiescence of the State, followed by a refusal to acknowledge the deprivation of liberty or by concealment of the fate or whereabouts of the disappeared person, which place such a person outside the protection of the law."[40] While forced disappearance is often associated with extrajudicial killing and arbitrary detention, it cannot be reduced to either. In some cases, there might not be any killing, and the condition of rightlessness generated by forced disappearance exceeds the problem of arbitrary detention. As Andrew Clapham and Susan Marks highlight, forced disappearance exposes its victims to "*the possibility* of being seriously harmed or ultimately killed," and that possibility results from the loss of legal status, expulsion from political community, and banishment to "a limit zone between life and death."[41]

It is in this sense that we can speak of forced disappearances in the case of border control practices such as the interception of migrant boats in the Mediterranean by European states and the return of migrants to detention centers in countries such as Libya. Such practices place these migrants outside the protection of the law, make it difficult to locate their whereabouts, and put them at risk of injury and death. Given the crucial importance of language in shaping what we see and how we see, the term *forced disappearance* offers a much-needed counter to the euphemism *missing migrants*, which obfuscates the problem and displaces the question of state responsibility.[42] It also allows us to consider the crimes and harms of border control policies beyond the migrants directly affected by them. In cases of forced disappearance, *victim* is defined not only as the disappeared person but as anyone "who has suffered harm as the direct result of an enforced disappearance," which would allow migrants' families, among others, to demand investigations and seek restitution and reparations.[43]

By reframing border deaths as *forced disappearances*, my goal is not, however, to use this term only in its legal sense, as others have successfully done.[44] I suggest that we rethink the term primarily in a phenomenological sense to inquire into why forced *disappearance* amounts to *nonbeing* (in legal, political, social, and even ontological ways) and how racial schemas govern the field of perception in a world of borders. Moreover, rather than simply appealing to law for the resolution of the problem, I also argue for the need to approach existing legal frameworks critically. As Clapham and Marks underscore in their account of forced disappearance, "the reassertion of rights is insufficient unless accompanied by efforts to investigate the ways in which law may have helped to make possible the deprivation of rights in the first place."[45] In the case of migrant deaths and disappearances, it is ultimately law that has to settle whether state agents have used violence legitimately or arbitrarily, proportionately or excessively in enforcing the borders of the state. Each time courts of law declare violence wielded in the name of border control to be a legitimate enactment of sovereign power, they also become complicit in the perpetration of that violence with impunity. In thinking about law critically, I aim to draw attention to how the *force* involved in forced disappearance is often authorized by law.

To unpack these points briefly, a phenomenological perspective anchors itself in the world of appearances (*phainómena*, or "things appearing to view") and emphasizes the interchangeability of "being" and "appearance" for living, embodied, sensing beings.[46] As Hannah Arendt strikingly puts it, "just as the actor depends upon stage, fellow-actors, and spectators, every living thing depends upon a world that solidly appears as the location for its own appearance, on fellow-creatures to play with, and on spectators to acknowledge and recognize its existence."[47] Arendt's observation, which highlights how our sense of the reality of the world ultimately depends on the assurances we receive from other living things that what we perceive is also perceived by them and hence real, does not simply have epistemological consequences. It also has crucial political and normative implications in its suggestion that all living things that appear in the world depend on one another for an acknowledgment of their distinctive existence. From a phenomenological perspective, the world is an "intermundane space" (*l'intermonde*), to use Maurice Merleau-Ponty's term, "where our gazes cross and our perceptions overlap."[48] This intersubjectivity, or, more precisely, intercorporeality, is an ineliminable dimension of the constitution of the world, and it is the sine qua non of our being/appearing in this world.

In foregrounding the world of appearances as the primary site of inquiry, phenomenology also draws attention to the *conditions* of perception, including the social norms, historical contexts, and relations of power that continuously shape what we perceive and how we perceive.[49] Fanon's work deserves attention for its critical attention to the conditions under which some living beings are banished from the intercorporeal world of coappearance and coperception described earlier. For example, in his account of the racial schemas that permeate the field of perception, Fanon emphasizes how "the white gaze" unmakes the reciprocity or intersubjectivity that Arendt and Merleau-Ponty take to be implicit in the very fact of belonging to a world in which every living being is both a sentient subject and a sensed object.[50] Racialized bodies targeted by "the white gaze" are reduced to phobic objects on the basis of negative representations attached to the color of their skin. They are turned into thing-like entities bereft of any living presence, and their appearance in the world is received and judged through racial schemas that deny to them the possibilities of individuating themselves through their interactions with the world and other embodied, sentient subjects. Within a racist social order, racialized embodiment is a form of visibility (even hypervisibility) that is simultaneously an enforced invisibility to the extent that the meaning of one's appearance/being is already determined before one does or says anything. As I discuss later, border control policies that make generalizations about racialized others (e.g., "sub-Saharan Africans") and render them ineligible for freedom of movement result in forced disappearance in this more phenomenological sense: They make their targets vanish not only from a juridico-political stage but also from a world in which they can elicit from others a "tacit acknowledgment" of their distinctive existence.[51]

This kind of violence is not accidental or incidental but rather endemic to systems that hierarchically stratify the living, and it is often sanctioned by law. As Fanon's analysis of French colonialism in Algeria makes clear, within a social order in which racialized violence has become routinized, law itself is often reduced to a seal of approval.[52] This conclusion can be extended to border deaths, as courts have a tendency to uphold territorial sovereignty as a sacrosanct principle and shift culpability to migrants themselves for crossing borders without prior authorization. Rethinking border deaths as forced disappearances then also urges us to examine the ways in which law itself enables, condones, and legitimizes lethal violence enacted in the name of border control. Working with this phenomenological understanding of forced disappearances, I turn below to Fanon's analyses of colonialism, racism, and legalized violence in order to discuss the regime of impunity surrounding border deaths.

COLONIAL PARTITIONS AND THE POLITICS OF IMMOBILIZATION

Fanon's account of colonialism, particularly in *The Wretched of the Earth*, brings to view the spatial configuration of "a compartmentalized world" that colonial domination engenders. "The dividing line, the border," between the colonist sector and the colonized sector installs an "apartheid," immobilizing the colonized and making sure that they "remain in [their] place and not overstep its limits."[53] This border establishes a relationship of "mutual exclusion" between the sectors of the colonists and the colonized, as it gives rise to fundamentally different socioeconomic, juridical, and normative orders.[54] The colonist's sector is one of affluence and extravagance, parasitic on the dispossession and destitution of the colonized. Besides this socioeconomic disparity, the border introduces us to "the barracks and the police stations" that maintain colonial rule.[55] The police or the military become direct enforcers of law under colonialism, without any intermediaries between "the exploited and the authorities," and they deploy "a language of pure force" in order to keep the colonized under control.[56]

Colonialism, for Fanon, transforms the subjects over whom it rules into rightless entities who can be subject to arbitrary rule and violence with impunity. It does that by establishing "a Manichean world" in which the colonized symbolize "absolute evil" and are declared "impervious to ethics."[57] Since the colonized subjects do not belong to the same normative order with the colonizers, they "can be arrested, beaten, and starved with impunity"; moral principles such as "human dignity" are completely emptied of their meaning within this context.[58] Even the most extreme forms of violence such as torture are legalized and normalized under these conditions; torture becomes, in effect, "a fundamental necessity" and "a way of life" under colonialism.[59] The colonial juridical order does away with the fundamental rights and basic protections associated with the rule of law, and it instead elevates "lawlessness, inequality, and multiple daily murder of humanness" to the status of "legislative principles."[60] Within this normative universe, even the massacres of the colonized subjects will not arouse any moral indignation.[61]

Fanon's account of colonialism can provide crucial insights into the violent practices that contemporary border control policies entail.[62] His analysis assumes a critical force especially in the wake of recent scholarship that has challenged the tendency to trace the origins of border control to the rise of the modern nation-state and urged us instead to look into the practices of immobilization and forced displacement that accompanied histories of slavery, colonialism, and imperialism.[63] More specifically, Fanon's work can help us examine how border enforcement incorporates and refines certain elements of colonialism—i.e., spatial compartmentalization, immobilization, lawlessness, and racialized violence—as it substitutes the "migrant" for the "native."

To revisit the Spanish-Moroccan border introduced at the outset of the chapter, Ceuta and Melilla, two Spanish enclaves located in North Africa, are the only land borders between the European Union and the African continent. These borders are heavily militarized especially because of the desire to maintain a racialized partition that is quite similar to the one under colonialism. In an interview with CBS, a Spanish border control officer confirms this desire, as he explains that the border marks "the difference between the Third World and the industrialized world."[64] Characterizing "the Third World" in terms of an absolute lack (of hope, food, and future) and Europe as a space promising "future, democracy, and liberty," he reproduces the Manichean framework that Fanon criticized, overlooking that the prosperity of Europe entails the impoverishment of "the Third World" and that the border he guards can only be maintained through the day-to-day violation of democratic principles propounded by Europe.[65]

The Spanish-Moroccan border also shows how contemporary migration control interweaves colonial techniques of immobilization that Fanon examined—policing, barbed wire—with new technologies such as motion sensors, heartbeat detectors, and cameras tracking body heat.[66] But the technological sophistication should not detract us from the cruel intentions built into the border fences in Ceuta and Melilla, manifested powerfully by their design. These three six-meter-high fences, equipped with anticlimbing grids, are "topped with barbed wire or even coils of razor blades," which can cause injuries and death; in one case, a

Senegalese migrant died due to a pierced artery.[67] Spain's socialist government declared in 2018 their intention to replace the razor wire with other measures that "are less bloody and more respectful of the integrity of the people," according to a statement of the Spanish Interior Ministry.[68] But even that declaration, moved by a purportedly humanitarian concern, stands as an unwitting admission that the European borders cannot be permanently sealed without violence; "less bloody" measures, after all, are not altogether bloodless.

Just like the colony in Fanon's analysis, the Spanish-Moroccan border is placed under the lawlessness of an arbitrary military-police rule; as I discuss in the last section, to the extent that this lawlessness is legally regulated and sanctioned, it should not be understood as the absence of law altogether. The Guardia Civil, Spain's paramilitary police force, cooperates with the Moroccan border guards to block migrants particularly from "sub-Saharan Africa" from entering Europe. Routinized violence that migrants face in the hands of Spanish and Moroccan officers—e.g., beating migrants with truncheons and wooden sticks, shaking the fence to force migrants to fall down, forcefully expelling even injured migrants who need medical assistance—have been extensively documented through video footage, migrants' testimonies, and investigations by various organizations.[69] As Fanon's account of colonialism reminds us, such acts of violence should not be seen as exceptional or incidental. Just as in the colony, within the context of contemporary border control, even the most extreme forms of violence—including those that amount to torture—have been routinized as a necessary component of keeping racialized others in their place.

Fanon's work urges us to understand forced disappearance beyond its legal sense in order to attend to practices that render certain categories of living beings superfluous, justify or disavow the violence inflicted upon them, and cast their deaths as foreordained (hence unnoteworthy) incidents. I draw this conclusion from Fanon's claim that the colonized can be subject to violence with impunity because their lives are deemed to be of no substance: "You are born anywhere, anyhow. You die anywhere, from anything."[70] Because they are perceived to lead lives that seem to lack "the specifically human reality," to use a phrase from Hannah Arendt, they can be injured and killed with impunity.[71] There was no "death" to be noted, accounted, mourned, and remembered since there was no "life" worthy of living, to begin with. In the migration context, ordinary forms of violence that racialized migrants routinely face do not elicit much attention because they are perceived as destitute bodies reduced to mere existence. The lives they had in their countries of origin are deemed to lack those elements or traits characterizing a truly "human" life, according to the racialized images of "the Third World," particularly "Africa," as a place of absolute deprivation, devastation, and precariousness.[72] Their dangerous journeys to Europe are taken to be an incontrovertible attestation to their desperation, and if they happen to die on their way, their deaths do not elicit any recognition or outrage because such perils are considered to be intrinsic risks of their own wretched lives. There may be some exceptions to this general trend, as we see, for example, in the case of shipwrecks with large numbers of fatalities spectacularized by the media. But any atrocity that cannot be spectacularized remains invisible within this framework, often normalized as an inescapable, albeit tragic, consequence of an inherited and insurmountable destitution. That invisibility, even when it does not amount to extrajudicial killing or torture, also deserves to be described as a form of forced disappearance, phenomenologically speaking. If all living beings are in need of others who can testify to their appearance/being in the world, various forms of legal, political, social, and cultural nonrecognition that attend the deaths and disappearances of racialized migrants consign them to a state of oblivion, as if they have never appeared on the face of this earth.

RACIAL SCHEMAS AS CONDITIONS OF FORCED DISAPPEARANCE

How is it possible for human beings to be turned into rightless entities to be maimed and annihilated with impunity? Fanon's answer to this question can be found in his analysis of racism as an organizing principle of colonialism: "Looking at the immediacies of the colonial context, it is clear that what divides this world is first and foremost what species, what race one belongs to."[73] Racism is a ruling device that puts the humanity of colonized subjects into question, often animalizing them with "zoological" references.[74] It also suspends their status as living beings inhabiting a world characterized by interrelatedness or intersubjectivity, as it exposes them to a "suffocating reification."[75] Phenomenologically speaking, embodied beings are not only sensed objects but also sentient subjects actively interacting with and responding to the world around them and other embodied beings. Within a racist social order, however, bodies at the receiving end of the "white gaze" are reduced to mere objects to be looked at through the racialized schemas that affix negative, mythologizing, and deindividuating representations to the color of their skin.[76] Regardless of what they do or say, they are perceived as "phobogenic" objects that exist solely for the gaze of the (white) other.[77] Building on Fanon, I suggest that border control policies occasion forced disappearances also because they hold racialized migrants captive to "a *visible appearance* for which [they are] not responsible."[78] Every move of these subjects is perceived as suspicious on the basis of "solely negating" representations that predetermine the meaning of their existence and deny to them any possibility of responding to the world and individuating themselves through their actions.[79]

Fanon examines the devastating effects of racism on the subjects who experience it on a daily basis by revisiting the key assumptions that phenomenologists make about the body schema. "Body schema" denotes a prereflective sense of one's body and its capacities in relation to the world. As theorized by Merleau-Ponty, the concept foregrounds a reciprocal relationship (i.e., "co-existence" or "communion") that exists between the body and the world:[80] it is my situatedness in the world that allows me to have a sense of the powers and coordinates of my body, and it is my body that orients me to the world, allows me to perceive it, and endows me with a "habitual knowledge" of it.[81] The body that we encounter in Merleau-Ponty's account of the body schema seems to be truly at home in the world: It navigates its environment with ease, maintains its stability and unity in its dynamic interactions with the world, and summons its powers in response to the possibilities opening within its perceptual field. Only in the pathological cases that Merleau-Ponty discusses do we see a disruption of the kind of bodily awareness, coordination, and synthesis that he associates with the body schema. Fanon has this phenomenological understanding of the body schema in mind as he gives the following example illustrating the prereflective and effortless movements of a body engaging in an everyday activity: "I know that if I want to smoke, I shall have to stretch out my right arm and grab the pack of cigarettes lying at the other end of the table. As for the matches, they are in the left drawer, and I shall have to move back a little. And I make all these moves, not out of habit, but by implicit knowledge."[82] The example is followed by a brief summary of Jean Lhermitte's argument in *L'image de notre corps*, which was a crucial source for Merleau-Ponty: the body schema denotes "a slow construction of myself as a body in a spatial and temporal world," one that is "not imposed on me" from the outside but rather formed through "a genuine dialectic between my body and the world."[83]

Fanon takes issue with the generalizing assumptions that phenomenologists make about the body schema, as he examines how racism obliterates the mutually reinforcing relationship between the body and the world and points out that "in the white world, the man of color encounters difficulties in elaborating his body schema."[84] To illustrate these difficulties, he recounts an encounter he had on the train with a little white boy who pointed to him and shouted to his mother in fear—"Look, a Negro! *Maman*, a Negro!"[85] The boy's frightened call to his mother interrupts Fanon's first-person experience of the world as a living, embodied subject, as it locks him out of the world and into his body, or, more specifically, into an artificially constructed and denigrating representation of his body. As Fanon becomes aware of his own body through the third-person perspective of the white other, he finds his body torn asunder and pulled in different directions by its embodied experience of the world, the racist representation imposed on it forcefully from outside, and his own internalization of that representation.[86] If the body is supposed to be "an expressive unity"[87]—coordinating movements, synthesizing sensory perceptions, and orienting the living being in the world—racism reduces that unity to ruins: "My body was returned to me spread-eagled, disjointed, redone, draped in mourning on this white winter's day."[88] Fanon's account of the encounter with the white boy highlights how racial schemas permeate even the most mundane forms of sociability, obstruct possibilities of individuating oneself in the eyes of the others, and leave behind fragmented and undone object-like entities that are denied a share in the world of the living.

In light of this negating experience of the body within a racist social order, Fanon revises the phenomenological understanding of the "body schema" with two interrelated concepts: "historical-racial schema" and "epidermal racial schema." In the case of racialized subjects, the experience of the world via the body is significantly shaped and undermined by the mythologized narratives constructed "by the Other, the white man, who had woven me out of a thousand details, anecdotes, and stories."[89] These artificial constructs, forming the historical-racial schema, make it impossible for racialized subjects to appear as individuals with distinct trajectories and perspectives. They are instead seen as representatives of a "Blackness" that is inextricably tied to "cannibalism, backwardness, fetishism, racial stigmas, slave traders, and above all, yes, above all, the grinning *Y a bon Banania*."[90] Fanon's concept of "an epidermal racial schema" points to the ways in which these historical representations become naturalized as they are affixed to the skin color. As Jeremy Weate puts it, "the epidermal marks the stage where historical construction and contingency is effaced and replaced with the facticity of flesh."[91] "Epidermalization," for Fanon, captures "the inscription of race," understood as a biological or genetic fact, on the skin.[92]

Fanon's account of the historical and epidermal racial schemas suggests that one of the key harms of racism is "reification," or being reduced to the status of thing-like entities on the basis of enduring phantasmic images produced by the white imaginary.[93] Such objectification can also be understood as a form of forced disappearance—one that severs living beings from their embodied experiences of the world, holds their bodies captive to racist representations, and denies them any possibility of individuating themselves through a reciprocal engagement with the world and other living beings. To unpack this point, appearance and being are interchangeable from a phenomenological perspective, as discussed earlier; we become who we are as our appearance in the world is received and acknowledged by others who are also living, embodied subjects. But Fanon's account of racism highlights how appearance can also amount to a form of disappearance when its meaning is already given on the basis of racializing and racist schemas; in that context, one's "appearance undermines and invalidates all his actions."[94] George Yancy clarifies Fanon's point, as he points out how the racist gaze locks the Black body into its exterior, hypervisible surface and reduces it to "a single black thing, unindividuated, threatening, ominous, *Black*."[95] Objectification renders "the very material presence" of the Black body "superfluous," Yancy argues, assigning it a pre-determined, fixed meaning and refusing to see it in any other way.[96] Because the racist gaze stops at the very surface of a body and marks that surface with a stigma, it makes it impossible for those at its receiving end to appear in their distinctness.[97] Objectification makes the living body of the embodied subject disappear from the face of the earth, in other words, and leaves in its place a figment of the white imagination.

How do we rethink racism in relation to border controls that have given rise to increasing numbers of deaths and disappearances? The history of immigration controls is notoriously racist, as illustrated by infamous examples such as the Chinese Exclusion Act (1882) in the United States, the "White Australia" policy (1901), and the Commonwealth Immigrants Act (1962) in Britain.[98] It is tempting to think that the current system of passports and visas, working with the purportedly color-blind criterion of "nationality," is a far cry from these old policies that explicitly discriminated on the basis of "race" and "ethnicity." But as Fanon reminds us, racism continuously reinvents itself and takes "more refined" forms especially in contexts where "vulgar" forms of racism, which are "genotypically and phenotypically determined," cannot be as easily maintained.[99] Within the migration context, "nationality" continues to function in ways that are very similar to "race" and "ethnicity" in constructing "whiteness" as a privileged status granting its beneficiaries unhindered access to mobility and relegating racialized others to a status of "illegality."[100] Technologies that are used to enforce border controls are not race-neutral either. New forms of "epidermalization" are introduced with "smart" border controls that incorporate biometric databases (of fingerprints, facial traits, DNA, iris and retinal scans, and the like), algorithmic assessments of risk and threat, thermal imaging, gesture and gait recognition technologies, and drone surveillance.[101]

The racialized partition of the world, instituted by contemporary immigration policies and technologies, highlights that the historical and epidermal racial schemas that Fanon examined permeate the border as a perceptual field. Within the debates on migration in Europe, these schemas can be detected in the imagery of a "civilization" under threat by "savage" hordes on the move. Take, for example, the recent use of the term *ensauvagement*, which can be translated as "becoming savage," within the French political circles. It was Marine Le Pen, the leader of the far right National Rally (formerly known as the National Front), who popularized this term to draw an association between an alleged rise in crime and "mass migration."[102] In July 2020, the term moved to the mainstream, as the French interior minister, Gérald Darmanin, used it in the wake of a series of violent crimes that involved the youth from the *banlieues*.[103] The savage/civilized dichotomy at work in this recent political debate highlights that the mythologized narratives about "Blackness" have not ceased to exist with the formal end of colonialism. They continue to represent Black bodies as an undifferentiated mass, reduce them to phobic objects, and make it impossible for them to appear in their distinctness.

In many respects, *ensauvagement* names the racial anxieties that drive the border control policies of Europe and mark Black bodies as inherently threatening in ways reminiscent of the train scene recounted by Fanon ("Look, a Negro! Maman, a Negro!"). It captures the desire to close off the continent to migrants from African countries. This desire is manifest in the various cooperation schemes that the European Union (EU) devised in order to outsource migration control. Particularly since the 2015 Valetta Summit, which established the EU Trust Fund for Africa, the EU has been providing financial assistance to African countries in return for their cooperation in migration control.[104] The European Union and its member states have also signed bilateral agreements with countries such as Morocco, Libya, Mauritania, Nigeria, Senegal, and Ethiopia.[105] These efforts are often presented in a humanitarian light, as if the goal was to stop human trafficking and smuggling and protect human rights and lives. That framing conveniently overlooks how such cooperation schemes have criminalized most migration from Africa to Europe, created trafficking and smuggling businesses, and led to the use of more dangerous routes. These schemes, euphemistically defined as "mobility partnerships," aim to immobilize migrants from sub-Saharan Africa in particular, as can be seen in the agreement that the European Union signed with Morocco in 2013. The partnership aims, among other things, to support Morocco "in implementing the return of third-country nationals, for the most part sub-Saharan Africans."[106]

Within the European debates on migration, "sub-Saharan Africa" operates as a code phrase inextricably entangled with the colonial imagery of the "Dark Continent." Far from a race-neutral, geographical designation, the term lumps together all of the countries in the African continent despite their numerous differences and excludes only the countries in North Africa whose inhabitants are perceived to be closer to whiteness.[107] Fanon's account of racialized embodiment underscores the need to understand forced disappearance in relation to such racial schemas that immobilize migrants on the basis of reifying representations about who they are and where they come from. Turning borders into "dead spaces of non-connection" and "impassable places" for racialized migrants, these representations make it impossible for them to appear with their distinct life stories and rights claims, as I discuss further later.[108]

LAW AS A SITE OF *FORCED* DISAPPEARANCE

Phenomenology, as exemplified by Fanon's critique of colonialism and racism, can help us attend to the different kinds of injury inflicted by forced disappearances within the context of border control. Differing from the earlier sections that focused more on unpacking the meaning of "disappearance," this final section turns to the term *force* to understand how law endows racialized violence with an aura of legitimacy. To this date, domestic and international courts have reaffirmed sovereign justifications of violence wielded in the name of border control and shifted culpability from states to migrants crossing borders without prior authorization. Purportedly acting in a color-blind fashion, they have also turned a blind eye to racialized attributions of this culpability, as they have insisted on authorized border-crossing as a condition of eligibility for rights, disregarding the de facto impossibility of such authorization in the case of migrants from certain regions and countries.

Fanon's reflections on law under colonial rule offer critical insights into its complicity in the justification of racialized violence. In describing the crimes committed by colonial authorities, Fanon argues that they are "irremediably outside the law."[109] But this lawlessness should not be understood as a problem arising from the absence of law altogether. Instead, Fanon draws attention to the monstrous peculiarities of colonial law itself as a mechanism that condones routinized perpetration of atrocities such as torture: "The police agent who tortures an Algerian infringes no law. His act fits into the framework of the colonial institution."[110] Fanon draws attention to this legally tolerated regime of lawlessness also in his critique of the commissions established to investigate the crimes committed by colonial authorities: "In the eyes of the colonized, these commissions do not exist. And in fact, soon it will be seven years of crimes committed in Algeria and not a single Frenchman has been brought before a court of justice for the murder of an Algerian."[111] This statement highlights how law participates in the production of a regime of impunity in which the colonizer is in effect exculpated of any wrongdoing.

For Fanon, colonial law is "a form of violence that legalizes, a form of legality that imposes violence," as Gary Boire aptly puts it.[112] To unpack this somewhat puzzling point, we can recall that, even within a noncolonial context, it is ultimately law that delineates the line between legitimate "force" enacted by state agents and illegitimate "violence" perpetrated by nonstate actors, and it is again law that determines what would be an "excessive" or "disproportionate" use of force by state agents. Within a colonial context, law makes these determinations often without the conventional norms and principles associated with the rule of law (e.g., equality before the law, impartial application of the law). For example, in April 3, 1955, France declared in Algeria a state of emergency (renewed in 1956), justifying it as a response to the increase in bombings by the FLN (Le Front de libération nationale), the main nationalist actor in the Algerian anticolonial struggle. Law No. 55–385 allowed civil liberties to be suspended, removed restrictions on police power, and effectively sanctioned the routinized practice of torture in Algeria.[113] This historical context illuminates Fanon's distrust of legal procedures within the colony and illustrates that the regime of lawlessness within the colony is paradoxically maintained by law itself.

While colonial law exempts the colonizer from any culpability, it also presumes the colonized to be always "guilty."[114] This presumption is justified on the basis of racist narratives such as the "North African criminality" thesis that depicts "the North African" as biologically disposed to criminality, impulsiveness, and aggressiveness.[115] Within this pseudoscientific theory, these traits were characterized as congenital defects tied to the underdevelopment of the cortex—a presupposition that reduces "the normal African" to "the lobotomized European," according to Fanon.[116] Colonial law sanctions this "racial allocation of guilt," as it recognizes the colonized as legal subjects only to attribute criminal liability to them.[117] As a result, the colonized are relegated to a "negative personhood"; they are denied law's protective elements such as the presumption of innocence and stand before it as always-already suspect and ineligible for rights.[118] To the extent that colonial law works with racial schemas, it engages in the kind of reification that Fanon criticizes in *Black Skin, White Masks*: it turns racialized subjects into phobic objects to be surveilled, disciplined, and punished. Reproducing the white gaze, colonial law participates in forced disappearance in a phenomenological sense, as it makes the colonized vanish as living, embodied subjects and leaves in their place the negating, dehumanizing representations produced by the white imagination.

Law operates in a quite similar fashion within the migration context, as exemplified by the 2020 ruling of the European Court of Human Rights (ECtHR) in the case of *N.D. and N.T. v Spain*.[119] This case concerns the "pushback" of two migrants, *N.D.* from Mali and *N.T.* from Ivory Coast, by Spain to Morocco. N.D. and N.T. were part of a group of around six hundred migrants who tried to cross the Spanish-Moroccan border through the border fence in Melilla in August 2014. They succeeded in doing so, but the Spanish authorities immediately returned them to Moroccan authorities, without conducting any identification procedures or any assessment of their individual circumstances. The question before the Court was whether Spain violated the prohibition against collective expulsion and the right to effective remedy by depriving these migrants of the means to challenge their immediate return. In 2017, a Chamber of the ECtHR found violations on both counts, but then the case was referred by Spain to the Grand Chamber, which delivered a troubling ruling in February 2020. The Spanish pushback did not amount to a human rights violation, the Court concluded, because it was the applicants themselves who "placed themselves in an unlawful situation" as they "chose not to use the legal procedures . . . to enter Spanish territory lawfully."[120] With this move, the Court created a disturbing exception and declared that only those migrants who entered a territory lawfully should expect protections against collective expulsion and access to effective legal remedy. The Court's decision sanctions the rightlessness of migrants who cross borders without prior authorization, as it announces that their culpability disqualifies them from entitlement to human rights.

But the ruling is much more sinister in that it condones "racialized rightlessness" in ways that bear disturbing resemblances to the functioning of law under colonial rule, especially when it comes to assumptions about culpability.[121] In the guise of targeting conduct, the Court targets status; anyone who enters the European space without prior authorization is rendered an "unlawful" being, declared ineligible for rights.[122] Within the context of the Spanish-Moroccan border control, "unlawfulness" is a racialized status that disproportionately befalls migrants from "sub-Saharan Africa" who are systematically denied access to legal entry procedures. This problem was even acknowledged by the representative of the United Nations High Commissioner for Refugees, Grainne O'Hara, who testified during the court proceedings that access to legal avenues is in practice available to only persons from the Middle East and North Africa and "virtually impossible for sub-Saharan Africans."[123]

Paying no heed to the overwhelming evidence documenting this problem, the Court instead presented the applicants as irrational subjects who could not produce "cogent reasons based on objective facts" for not following the legal procedures for entering Spain.[124] Lurking beneath that seemingly color-blind reasoning were the racialized assumptions about disposition to law-breaking, aggressiveness, and impulsiveness—not unlike the assumptions that underlie "the North African criminality" thesis criticized by Fanon, albeit this time attributing culpability to "sub-Saharan Africans": "In the light of these observations, the Court considers that it was in fact the applicants who placed themselves in jeopardy by participating in the storming of the Melilla border fences on 13 August 2014, taking advantage of the group's large numbers and using force."[125] That conclusion, in its deceptively measured tone, calls into question the rationality of the migrants who would rather climb three fences, risk being injured by razor wire, and expose themselves to violence by border guards instead of completing the legal paperwork for asylum. Abou Baker Sidibé, a refugee from Mali and a filmmaker, questions that stupefying reasoning, as he responds to the claim that these migrants could have simply applied for asylum at a Spanish consulate such as the one in Nador: "When I hear such a claim ... I can't stand it! It is like making fun of people. *Making fun of the human beings that we are.* We are not even allowed to be in the region of Nador."[126] As this statement strikingly puts it, just as the colonized did not expect the commissions and courts established by the colonial power to deliver justice, migrants who are regularly subject to racism at the border have no such expectation.

This recent case demonstrates the ways in which law itself becomes a site of forced disappearance in the migration context, rendering racialized migrants ineligible for rights, closing off avenues of redress, restitution, and reparation, and relieving states of any legal responsibility for violent practices of border enforcement. Law is complicit in forced disappearance also in a much more phenomenological sense: reproducing the racial schemas that permeate the perceptual field, it declares nonwhite (especially Black) migrants to be inherently suspicious and culpable. The mere act of crossing a border becomes perceived as a belligerent act that can justify even the most disproportionate use of force by state agents, as illustrated by both the Tarajal case discussed at the outset and the ECtHR case examined in this section. Given this problem, we cannot simply appeal to law to remedy the problem of border deaths. Fanon's analysis highlights that lawlessness was authorized by law itself under colonial rule; similarly, the regime of impunity surrounding border deaths has been, for the most part, upheld by existing legal frameworks. Lawlessness, which exposes racialized subjects to violence with impunity, goes hand in hand with a certain form of "hyperlegality" that generates an ever-expanding repertoire of legal formulas invented to evade human rights and the rule of law—even the basic premise of the equality of all persons before the law.[127] What we need is nothing less than a radical critique that carefully examines how law itself becomes complicit in the racialized governance of borders, and Fanon's work offers crucial insights in this regard as it invites us to think about the numerous ways in which the operations of colonial law resurface within the migration context.

This chapter makes a case for rethinking Fanon's work in response to contemporary border control policies, particularly the problem of migrant deaths and disappearances. I argued that Fanon's analysis of colonialism, racism, and law provides critical insights into the legal, political, social, and ontological forms of nonexistence engendered by racialized migration controls. The term *forced disappearance* offers a critical lens for understanding this problem, especially when reinterpreted beyond its legal meaning and in the light of Fanon's critical engagements with the phenomenological tradition. Fanon's account of racialized embodiment suggests that a much more fundamental type of forced disappearance occurs when racial schemas render nonwhite, especially Black, bodies hypervisible as phobic objects, deprive them of their living presence as embodied subjects navigating and inhabiting the world with other living beings, and lock them into dehumanizing representations that undermine their efforts to individuate themselves and pursue their distinct life trajectories. Forced disappearance, understood in terms of an objectification inflicted by the white gaze, can also occur in the legal domain that is supposed to be a site of remedy and redress. As Fanon's account of colonialism highlights, the operations of law are not immune to racial schemas and can often reproduce them in its determinations of culpable conduct and entitlement to rights.

One of the most fundamental harms inflicted by the racialized partitions of the world then is the transformation of certain categories of living beings into object-like entities. But Fanon also emphasizes that the success of this operation is by no means certain to the extent it is always subject to contestation by those reduced to the status of things. As he puts it in the context of French colonialism in Algeria, "the colonist achieves only a pseudo-petrification," which is continuously threatened by the resistant acts of the colonized.[128] It is the struggles of those subjects who refuse to be reified, petrified, and eradicated that carry the fragile promise of "the birth of a human world, in other words, a world of reciprocal recognitions."[129]

One key example of such "world-building" is the numerous struggles waged by the families of migrants subjected to forced disappearance by border control policies.[130] We can think of, for example, the several organizations established by the Tunisian families of disappeared migrants (e.g., La Terre Pour Tous, Les Mères des Disparus).[131] With their sit-ins, demonstrations, and petitions, these families contest the regime of impunity surrounding migrant deaths and disappearances and draw attention to the racialized governance of borders. In a petition submitted to the European Union in 2013, for example, Tunisian families highlight the European border policies that push non-European, nonwhite migrants to ever more dangerous journeys: "Our sons and daughters . . . left crossing the Mediterranean in the only way allowed to them, namely on small boats, as European policies prevent Tunisians to take a plane or a liner boat with the same freedom allowed to European citizens when they come to our country."[132] Such efforts also challenge states' efforts to make these migrants disappear without a trace. Pushing states to recognize these migrants as "legal subject[s] with rights that include identification, return, burial, and memorialization," they question the assumption that those who have been forcefully disappeared are banished from the world of the living—stripped of their presence, agency, belongings, and rights.[133]

To conclude, rethinking border deaths as forced disappearances, with the help of Fanon, draws attention to not only the routinized efforts to immobilize, petrify, and obliterate racialized others but also the struggles that vigorously contest such projects of racialized annihilation. As Achille Mbembe puts it, we owe to Fanon "the idea that in every human subject there is something indomitable and fundamentally intangible that no domination . . . can eliminate, contain, or suppress, at least not completely."[134] The struggles arising from migrant deaths and disappearances reanimate that ineliminable element through the work of remembrance, endurance, refusal, and resistance. In doing that, they bring to view a world in which every living being can claim an equal share.

NOTES

A slightly different version of this chapter was first published in *Puncta: Journal of Critical Phenomenology* 5, no. 3 (2022): 12–41, and I would like to thank two anonymous reviewers for the journal for their constructive feedback and Kaja Jenssen Rathe for her editorial guidance. I am grateful to Bud Duvall for providing helpful feedback on an earlier version. I have also benefited significantly from feedback received at the annual meeting of the Association for Political Theory, Cornell Political Theory Workshop, and Princeton University Social Criticism and Political Thought Speaker Series. I would like to thank the organizers and participants of these events, especially Begüm Adalet, Alexia Alkadi-Barbaro, Angélica Bernal, Atticus Carnell, Shirley Le Penne, Jill Locke, Patchen Markell, Paulina Ochoa Espejo, and Tessy Schlosser. Last but not least, my thinking on migration owes an immense debt to the work of Seyla Benhabib; I extend my gratitude to her and the editors of this volume for inviting me to contribute to this volume.

1. Rocía Abad, "Investigation Into Death of 15 Migrants on Ceuta Beach Dropped," *El País* (English edition), October 16, 2015, https://english.elpais.com/elpais/2015/10/16/inenglish/1444983469_974647.html.
2. IOM, "Missing Migrants Project," https://missingmigrants.iom.int/.
3. Agnès Callamard, "Unlawful Death of Refugees and Migrants," United Nations General Assembly, Report No. A/72/335, August 15, 2017, https://digitallibrary.un.org/record/1303261?ln=en.
4. For the classic account of the tensions between sovereignty and human rights within a nation-state system, see Hannah Arendt, *The Origins of Totalitarianism* (1951; San Diego: Harcourt Brace Jovanovich, 1968), 267–302. For contemporary reconfigurations of these tensions, see in particular Seyla Benhabib, "The End of the 1951 Refugee Convention?: Dilemmas of Sovereignty, Territoriality, and Human Rights," *Jus Cogens* 2, no. 1 (2020): 75–100.
5. I provide a detailed account of this problem elsewhere; see Ayten Gündoğdu, *Rightlessness in an Age of Rights: Hannah Arendt and the Contemporary Struggles of Migrants* (Oxford: Oxford University Press, 2015).
6. Seyla Benhabib, *The Rights of Others: Aliens, Residents and Citizens* (Cambridge: Cambridge University Press, 2004), 163.
7. For an analysis of "illegal" as a racialized label in the United States, see José Jorge Mendoza, "*Illegal*: White Supremacy and Immigration Status," in *The Ethics and Politics of Immigration: Emerging Trends*, ed. Alex Sager (London: Rowman and Littlefield, 2016), 201–20. For a similar argument about the racialized functioning of binary categorizations such as refugee/migrant and regular/irregular within the European context, see Tazreena Sajjad, "What's in a Name?: 'Refugees,' 'Migrants' and the Politics of Labelling," *Race and Class* 60, no. 2 (2018): 40–62.
8. See, among others, E. Tendayi Achiume, "Migration as Decolonization," *Stanford Law Review* 71, no. 6 (2019): 1509–74; Cristina Beltrán, *Cruelty as Citizenship: How Migrant Suffering Sustains White Democracy* (Minneapolis: University of Minnesota Press, 2020); Nadine El-Enany, *Bordering Britain: Law, Race and Empire* (Manchester: Manchester University Press, 2020); Encarnación Gutiérrez Rodríguez, "The Coloniality of Migration and the 'Refugee Crisis': On the Asylum-Migration Nexus, the Transatlantic White European Settler Colonialism-Migration and Racial Capitalism," *Refuge* 34, no. 1 (2018): 16–28; Lucy Mayblin, *Asylum After Empire: Colonial Legacies in the Politics of Asylum Seeking* (Lanham, MD: Rowman and Littlefield, 2018); Lucy Mayblin and Joe B. Turner, *Migration Studies and Colonialism* (Cambridge: Polity, 2021); Radhika Mongia, *Indian Migration and Empire: A Colonial Genealogy of the Modern State* (Durham, NC: Duke University Press, 2018); Harsha Walia, *Border and Rule: Global Migration, Capitalism, and the Rise of Racist Nationalism* (Chicago: Haymarket, 2021).
9. Guardia Civil, quoted by the European Center for Constitutional and Human Rights (ECCHR), "Case Report: Justice for Survivors of Violent Push-Backs from Ceuta," April 2019, p. 2, www.ecchr.eu/fileadmin/Fallbeschreibungen/Case_Report_Ceuta_April2019.pdf.

10. Marc Herman, "To Repel Migrants, European Border Patrol Turns Bloody," *Deca*, December 11, 2015, https://decastories.com/to-repel- migrants-european-border-patrol-turns-bloody.
11. Herman, "To Repel Migrants."
12. "Spain Denied Visas to Relatives of Migrants Drowned in Tarajal Tragedy," *El País* (English edition), February 7, 2017, https://english.elpais.com/elpais/2017/02/07/inenglish/1486459922_718046.html.
13. ECCHR, "Case Report," 4.
14. Elaine Scarry, *The Body in Pain* (Oxford: Oxford University Press, 1985), 22.
15. For similar questions about the unequal distribution of vulnerability to state violence, see, in particular, Judith Butler, *Precarious Life: The Powers of Mourning and Violence* (London: Verso, 2004).
16. Lewis Gordon, "Through the Hellish Zone of Nonbeing: Thinking Through Fanon, Disaster, and the Damned of the Earth," *Human Architecture: Journal of the Sociology of Self-Knowledge* 5, special issue (Summer): 5–11, at 11.
17. Frantz Fanon, *Black Skin, White Masks*, trans. Richard Philcox (1952; New York: Grove, 2008), xii.
18. Fanon, 91–92.
19. Maurizio Albahari, *Crimes of Peace: Mediterranean Migrations at the World's Deadliest Border* (Philadelphia: University of Pennsylvania Press, 2015).
20. See, among others, Ida Danewid, "White Innocence in the Black Mediterranean: Hospitality and the Erasure of History," *Third World Quarterly* 38, no. 7 (2017): 1674–89; Alessandro Di Maio, "The Mediterranean, or Where Africa Does (Not) Meet Italy," in *The Cinemas of Italian Migration: European and Transatlantic Narratives*, ed. Sabine Schrader and Daniel Winkler (Newcastle upon Tyne: Cambridge Scholars Publishing, 2013), 41–52; Michelle Murray, "Visualizing the Black Mediterranean," in *Liquid Borders: Migration as Resistance*, ed. Mabel Moraña (Abingdon, UK: Routledge, 2021), 289–302; Gabriele Proglio, "Fanon in the Black Mediterranean," in *The Black Mediterranean: Bodies, Borders, and Citizenship*, ed. The Black Mediterranean Collective (Basingstoke, UK: Palgrave Macmillan, 2021), 57–81.
21. Lisa Marie Cacho, *Social Death: Racialized Rightlessness and the Criminalization of the Unprotected* (New York: New York University Press, 2012).
22. Fanon, *Black Skin, White Masks*, 206.
23. Achille Mbembe, *Necropolitics*, trans. Steve Corcoran (Durham, NC: Duke University Press, 2019), 92.
24. Hannah Arendt, *The Human Condition*, 2nd ed. (1958; Chicago: University of Chicago Press, 1998), 96.
25. Leanne Weber and Sharon Pickering, *Globalization and Borders: Death at the Global Frontier* (Basingstoke, UK: Palgrave Macmillan, 2011).
26. Walia, *Border and Rule*, 107–8.
27. For the latter, see the IOM's "Missing Migrants Project," which "tracks incidents involving migrants, including refugees and asylum-seekers, who have died or gone missing in the process of migration towards an international destination." "Data," Missing Migrants Project, IOM, https://missingmigrants.iom.int/data.

28. Colin Dayan, *The Law Is a White Dog: How Legal Rituals Make and Unmake Personhood* (Princeton, NJ: Princeton University Press, 2011).
29. For an analysis that shows how the stratifications that borders establish within humanity render migrants in an irregular status ineligible for human rights, see Alison Kesby, *The Right to Have Rights: Citizenship, Humanity, and International Law* (Oxford: Oxford University Press, 2012), chap. 4. For an examination of these stratifications within the context of immigration detention and deportation, see Gündoğdu, *Rightlessness in an Age of Rights*, chap. 3.
30. Thomas Spijkerboer, "Wasted Lives: Borders and the Right to Life of People Crossing Them," *Nordic Journal of International Law* 86, no. 1 (2017): 1–29.
31. Alexandra Délano Alonso and Benjamin Nienass, "Deaths, Visibility, and Responsibility: The Politics of Mourning at the U.S.-Mexico Border," *Social Research* 83, no. 2 (2016): 421–51; Jason De León, *The Land of Open Graves: Living and Dying on the Migrant Trail* (Berkeley: University of California Press, 2015); Iosif Kovras and Simon Robins, "Death as the Border: Managing Missing Migrants and Unidentified Bodies at the EU's Mediterranean Frontier," *Political Geography* 55 (2016): 40–49.
32. Barbie Latza Nadeau, "Giving Dead Migrants a Name," *Scientific American*, August 9, 2017, www.scientificamerican.com/article/giving-dead-migrants-a-name/.
33. Thomas Walter Laqueur, *The Work of the Dead: A Cultural History of Mortal Remains* (Princeton, NJ: Princeton University Press, 2015), 414.
34. Laqueur, 148.
35. Callamard, "Unlawful Death," 21.
36. Callamard, 6.
37. Omer Shatz and Juan Branco, "Communication to the Office of the Prosecutor of the International Criminal Court Pursuant to the Article 15 of the Rome Statute; EU Migration Policies in the Central Mediterranean and Libya (2014–2019)," June 2019, www.statewatch.org/media/documents/news/2019/jun/eu-icc-case-EU-Migration-Policies.pdf.
38. Valentina Azarova, Amanda Danson Brown, and Itamar Mann, "The Enforced Disappearance of Migrants," *Boston University International Law Journal* 40, no. 1 (Spring 2022): 133–204; Emilio Distretti, "Enforced Disappearances and Border Deaths Along the Migrant Trail," in *Border Deaths: Causes, Dynamics and Consequences of Migration-related Mortality*, ed. Paolo Cuttitta and Tamara Last (Amsterdam: Amsterdam University Press, 2020), 117–30; Alonso Gurmendi, "On Calling Things What They Are: Family Separation and Enforced Disappearance of Children," *Opinio Juris*, June 24, 2019, http://opiniojuris.org/2019/06/24/on-calling-things-what-they-are-family-separation-and-enforced-disappearance-of-children/; Robin Reineke, "*Los Desaparecidos de la frontera* (The Disappeared on the Border)," in *Migrant Deaths in the Arizona Desert: La vida no vale nada*, ed. Araceli Masterson-Algar, Raquel Rubio-Goldsmith, Jessie K. Finch, and Celestino Fernández (Tucson: University of Arizona Press, 2016), 132–49; Estela Schindel, "Deaths and Disappearances in Migration to Europe: Exploring the Uses of a Transnationalized Category," *American Behavioral Scientist* 64, no. 4 (2020): 389–407; John Washington, "'I Didn't Exist': A Syrian Asylum-Seeker's Case Reframes Migrant

Abuses as Enforced Disappearances," *Intercept*, February 28, 2021, https://theintercept.com/2021/02/28/enforced-disappearances-asylum-migrant-abuse/.
39. Fran Cetti, "Border Controls in Europe: Policies and Practices Outside the Law," *State Crime Journal* 3, no. 1 (2014): 4–28.
40. See Article 2 of the International Convention for the Protection of All Persons from Enforced Disappearance, United Nations Office of the High Commissioner for Human Rights, www.ohchr.org/en/hrbodies/ced/pages/conventionced.aspx.
41. Andrew Clapham and Susan Marks, *International Human Rights Lexicon* (Oxford: Oxford University Press, 2005), 131, 132.
42. "Missing migrants" is the euphemism preferred in international circles, as it is used by major organizations such as the IOM and the International Committee of the Red Cross.
43. See Article 24 of the International Convention for the Protection of All Persons from Enforced Disappearance, United Nations Office of the High Commissioner for Human Rights, www.ohchr.org/en/hrbodies/ced/pages/conventionced.aspx.
44. See the references in note 38.
45. Clapham and Marks, *International Human Rights Lexicon*, 122.
46. Tom Rockmore, "Hegel and Husserl: Two Phenomenological Reactions to Kant," *Hegel Bulletin* 38, no. 1 (2017): 67–84, at 68; Karl Schuhmann, "Phenomenology: A Reflection on the History of the Term," in *The Routledge Companion to Phenomenology*, ed. Sebastian Luft and Søren Overgaard (London: Routledge, 2012), 657–88, at 675.
47. Hannah Arendt, *The Life of the Mind*, vol. 1, *Thinking* (New York: Harcourt Brace Jovanovich 1978), 21–22.
48. Maurice Merleau-Ponty, *The Visible and the Invisible*, ed. Claude Lefort, trans. Alphonso Lingis (1964; Evanston, IL: Northwestern University Press, 1968), 48.
49. More recently, the term *critical phenomenology* has been used to describe efforts to examine "the constitutive social, political, psychological, economic, historical, and cultural dimensions of the phenomena under investigation." See Gail Weiss, "Phenomenology and Race (or Racializing Phenomenology)," in *The Routledge Companion to the Philosophy of Race*, ed. Paul C. Taylor, Linda Martín Alcoff, and Luvell Anderson (New York: Routledge, 2018), 233–44, at 233. On the convergences and tensions between phenomenology and critical theory, see especially Gayle Salamon, "What is Critical About Critical Phenomenology?," *Puncta: Journal of Critical Phenomenology* 1 (2018): 8–17.
50. Fanon, *Black Skin, White Masks*, 90.
51. Arendt, *The Life of the Mind*, 46.
52. Frantz Fanon, *The Wretched of the Earth*, trans. Richard Philcox (1961; New York: Grove Press, 2004), 50.
53. Fanon, 3, 15.
54. Fanon, 4.
55. Fanon, 3.
56. Fanon, 4.
57. Fanon, 6.
58. Fanon, 9.

59. Frantz Fanon, *Toward the African Revolution*, trans. Haakon Chevalier (1964; New York: Grove Press, 1967), 66.
60. Frantz Fanon, *Alienation and Freedom*, ed. Jean Khalfa and Robert J. C. Young, trans. Steven Corcoran (London: Bloomsbury Academic, 2018), 434.
61. Fanon, *The Wretched of the Earth*, 47.
62. Proglio, "Fanon in the Black Mediterranean."
63. See note 8 for examples of this scholarship.
64. CBS, "How a Border Wall Works in Melilla, Spain, a Gateway Between Europe and Africa," January 18, 2019, www.youtube.com/watch?v=SaILY9TG-fQ.
65. CBS, "How a Border Wall Works."
66. CBS, "How a Border Wall Works."
67. BBC, "Ceuta and Melilla: Spain Wants Rid of Anti-Migrant Razor Wire," June 14, 2018, www.bbc.com/news/world-europe-44485995.
68. Quoted in Julian Hattam, "The Razor Wire That Separates Europe from Africa Might Be Coming Down," September 10, 2018, www.pri.org/stories/2018-09-10/razor-wire-separates-europe-africa-might-be-coming-down.
69. See, for example, the European Committee for the Prevention of Torture and Inhuman or Degrading Treatment or Punishment, "Report to the Spanish Government on the Visit to Spain Carried Out by the European Committee for the Prevention of Torture and Inhuman or Degrading Treatment or Punishment, from 14 to 18 July, 2014," Strasbourg, April 9, 2015, www.refworld.org/country,COI,COECPT,,ESP,,553e4fbc4,0.html.
70. Fanon, *The Wretched of the Earth*, 4.
71. Arendt, *The Origins of Totalitarianism*, 192. For a similar point, see Judith Butler, *Frames of War: When Is Life Grievable?* (London: Verso, 2009).
72. Achille Mbembe, *Critique of Black Reason*, trans. Laurent Dubois (Durham, NC: Duke University Press, 2017), 48–53.
73. Fanon, *The Wretched of the Earth*, 5.
74. Fanon, 7.
75. Fanon, *Black Skin, White Masks*, 89.
76. Helen Ngo, *The Habits of Racism: A Phenomenology of Racism and Racialized Embodiment* (Lanham, MD: Lexington, 2017), 64–65.
77. Fanon, *Black Skin, White Masks*, 132.
78. Fanon, 18, emphasis in the original.
79. Fanon, 90.
80. Maurice Merleau-Ponty, *Phenomenology of Perception*, trans. Donald A. Landes (1945; London: Routledge, 2012), 221.
81. Merleau-Ponty, 247. For an explication of Merleau-Ponty's concept of "body schema," see Taylor Carman, *Merleau-Ponty*, 2nd ed. (Abingdon, UK: Routledge, 2020), 100–104.
82. Fanon, *Black Skin, White Masks*, 90–91. Fanon's example is very similar to the one that Merleau-Ponty gives in *Phenomenology of Perception*, as he describes the prereflective and nondiscursive awareness of his own body as he stands in front of his desk and holds his pipe; see Merleau-Ponty, *Phenomenology of Perception*, 102.

83. Fanon, *Black Skin, White Masks*, 91. For a comparative analysis of Merleau-Ponty's and Fanon's conceptions of "body schema," see Dilan Mahendran, "The Facticity of Blackness: A Non-Conceptual Approach to the Study of Race and Racism in Fanon's and Merleau-Ponty's Phenomenology," *Human Architecture: Journal of the Sociology of Self-Knowledge* 5 (Summer 2007): 191–204.
84. Fanon, *Black Skin, White Masks*, 90.
85. Fanon, 91.
86. Fanon's declaration that "I existed in triple" underscores the fragmented experience of the body schema by racialized subjects; see Fanon, 92. Lisa Guenther identifies the three subjects arising from this fragmentation as follows: "a living, embodied subject of experience; a degraded artifact of white history; and a third being whose skin is formed both in and against a white mask." See Guenther, "Seeing Like a Cop: A Critical Phenomenology of Whiteness as Property," in *Race as Phenomena: Between Phenomenology and Philosophy of Race*, ed. Emily S. Lee (Lanham, MD: Rowman and Littlefield, 2019), 200.
87. Merleau-Ponty, *Phenomenology of Perception*, 213.
88. Fanon, *Black Skin, White Masks*, 93.
89. Fanon, 91.
90. Fanon, 92.
91. Jeremy Weate, "Fanon, Merleau-Ponty and the Difference of Phenomenology," in *Race*, ed. Robert Bernasconi (Malden, MA: Blackwell, 2001), 174.
92. Stuart Hall, "Why Fanon?," in *Selected Writings on Race and Difference*, ed. Paul Gilroy and Ruth Wilson Gilmore (1996; Durham, NC: Duke University Press, 2021), 339–58, at 342. "Epidermalization" also denotes the Black subject's internalization of the racist representations of Blackness; see Fanon, *Black Skin, White Masks*, xv.
93. Fanon, *Black Skin, White Masks*, 89.
94. Fanon, 189.
95. George Yancy, "Elevators, Social Spaces and Racism: A Philosophical Analysis," *Philosophy and Social Criticism* 34, no. 8 (2008): 843–76, at 861.
96. George Yancy, "White Gazes: What It Feels Like to Be an Essence," in *Living Alterities: Phenomenology, Embodiment, and Race*, ed. Emily S. Lee (Albany: State University of New York Press, 2014), 43–64, at 57. Alia Al-Saji makes a similar argument about why hypervisibility of racialized subjects entails invisibility in her analysis of veiled Muslim women: "Racialized bodies are not only seen as naturally inferior, they *cannot be seen otherwise*." Al-Saji, "The Racialization of Muslim Veils: A Philosophical Analysis," *Philosophy and Social Criticism* 36, no. 8 (2010): 875–902, at 885, emphasis in the original.
97. Mahendran, "The Facticity of Blackness," 201; Richard Schmitt, "Racism and Objectification: Reflections on Themes from Fanon," in *Fanon: A Critical Reader*, ed. Lewis R. Gordon, T. Denean Sharpley-Whiting, and Renée T. White (Cambridge, MA: Blackwell, 1996), 35–50, at 42.
98. Sarah Fine, "Immigration and Discrimination," in *Migration in Political Theory: The Ethics of Movement and Membership*, ed. Sarah Fine and Lea Ypi (Oxford: Oxford University Press, 2016), 126–50.
99. Fanon, *Toward the African Revolution*, 32.

100. Mendoza, *"Illegal."* Radhika Mongia's history of passport controls highlights that "nationality" was introduced as "an alibi for race" within the debates on migration in the British Empire; see Mongia, *Indian Migration and Empire*, 136. For a phenomenological account of racialized experiences of motility and mobility, see Sara Ahmed, "A Phenomenology of Whiteness," *Feminist Theory* 8, no. 2 (2007): 149–68.
101. Simone Browne, "Digital Epidermalization: Race, Identity and Biometrics," *Critical Sociology* 36, no. 1 (2010): 131–50; Tamara Vukov, "Target Practice: The Algorithmics and Biopolitics of Race in Emerging Smart Border Practices and Technologies," *Transfers: Interdisciplinary Journal of Mobility Studies* 6, no. 1 (2016): 80–97.
102. John Lichfield, "The Racist Myth of France's 'Descent Into Savagery,'" *Politico*, September 7, 2020, www.politico.eu/article/marine-le-pen-racist-myth-france-descent-into-savagery/.
103. "Gérald Darmanin: 'Il faut stopper l'ensauvagement d'une partie de la société,'" *Le Figaro*, July 24, 2020, www.lefigaro.fr/politique/gerald-darmanin-il-faut-stopper-l-ensauvagement-d-une-partie-de-la-societe-20200724.
104. EU Emergency Trust Fund for Africa, https://ec.europa.eu/trustfundforafrica/content/about_en.
105. European Commission, Migration and Home Affairs, https://ec.europa.eu/home-affairs/what-we-do/policies/international-affairs/africa_en.
106. General Secretariat of the Council of the European Union, "Joint Declaration Establishing a Mobility Partnership Between the Kingdom of Morocco and the European Union and Its Member States," June 3, 2013, www.statewatch.org/media/documents/news/2013/jun/eu-council-eu-morocco-mobility-partnership-6139-add1-rev3-13.pdf.
107. Susan Ball, Sébastien Lefait, and Lori Maguire, "From Tarzan to the Black Panther: The Evolving Image of Africa," in *Modern Representations of Sub-Saharan Africa*, ed. Lori Maguire, Susan Ball, and Sébastien Lefait (Abingdon, UK: Routledge, 2021), 1–17, at 5.
108. Mbembe, *Necropolitics*, 99.
109. Fanon, *Alienation and Freedom*, 621.
110. Fanon, *Toward the African Revolution*, 71.
111. Fanon, *The Wretched of the Earth*, 50.
112. Gary Boire, "Legalizing Violence: Fanon, Romance, Colonial Law," in *Law and Literature: Current Legal Issues*, vol. 2, ed. Michael Freeman and Andrew D. E. Lewis (Oxford: Oxford University Press, 1999), 581–601, at 588.
113. Boire, 587.
114. Fanon, *The Wretched of the Earth*, 16.
115. Fanon, 223.
116. Fanon, 227.
117. Fanon, *Black Skin, White Masks*, 83. As Alia Al-Saji points out, Fanon highlights how colonialism disavows its own guilt and projects it onto the colonized; see Al-Saji, "Frantz Fanon," in *The Routledge Handbook of Phenomenology of Emotion*, ed. Thomas Szanto and Hilge Landweer (Abingdon, UK: Routledge, 2020), 207–14, at 212.

118. Colin Dayan, *The Law Is a White Dog: How Legal Rituals Make and Unmake Personhood* (Princeton, NJ: Princeton University Press, 2011), 42.
119. Grand Chamber of the European Court of Human Rights, *N.D. and N.T. v. Spain*, February 13, 2020, https://hudoc.echr.coe.int/spa#{%22itemid%22:[%22001-201353%22]}.
120. *N.D. and N.T. v. Spain*, §242.
121. Cacho, *Social Death*.
122. Cacho, 9.
123. See the video prepared by the Forensic Architecture, "Pushbacks in Melilla: *ND and NT v. Spain*," June 15, 2020, https://forensic-architecture.org/investigation/pushbacks-in-melilla-nd-and-nt-vs-spain.
124. *ND and NT v. Spain* §229; for the Court's insistence on such "cogent reasons," see also §§210, 211, 218, and 220.
125. *ND and NT v. Spain* §231.
126. See the interview excerpts in the video prepared by the Forensic Architecture, "Pushbacks in Melilla: ND and NT v. Spain," June 15, 2020, https://forensic-architecture.org/investigation/pushbacks-in-melilla-nd-and-nt-vs-spain.
127. Nassar Hussain, "Hyperlegality," *New Criminal Law Review* 10, no. 4 (2007): 514–31. See also Dayan, *The Law Is a White Dog*, 190–91.
128. Fanon, *The Wretched of the Earth*, 17.
129. Fanon, *Black Skin, White Masks*, 193.
130. Arendt, *The Human Condition*, 96.
131. Farida Souiah, "Corps absents: des fils disparus et des familles en lutte? Le cas des migrants tunisiens," *Critique Internationale* 83, no. 2 (2019): 87–100.
132. "We Demand Your Knowledges: A Petition by the Mothers and the Families of Missing Tunisian Migrants," February 2013, https://leventicinqueundici.noblogs.org/?p=1528.
133. Kim Rygiel, "Dying to Live: Migrant Deaths and Citizenship Politics Along European Borders: Transgressions, Disruptions, and Mobilizations," *Citizenship Studies* 20, no. 5 (2016): 545–60, at 549.
134. Mbembe, *Critique of Black Reason*, 170.

20

Gender Trouble

Manhood, Inclusion, and Justice in the Political Philosophy of Martin Luther King, Jr.

SHATEMA THREADCRAFT AND BRANDON M. TERRY

Feminist approaches to the interpretation and assessment of Martin Luther King, Jr.'s political philosophy have primarily been characterized by two stances: qualified acceptance and respectful rejection. The first, qualified acceptance, combines a trenchant critique of King's sexism with an attempt to extract and salvage other features of his work for feminist thought and praxis. In one sense, this tradition follows that of black women activists who were contemporaries of King and worked alongside him, despite their criticisms. Septima Clark, the heroic educator and organizer of the Citizenship School movement, for example, criticized the sexist leadership of King's Southern Christian Leadership Conference (SCLC), where she served on the board. Recalling meetings where women were routinely prevented from placing items on the agenda, or openly mocked, Clark lamented, "Those men didn't have any faith in women, none whatsoever. They just thought that women were sex symbols and had no contribution to make."[1] Despite her "great feeling that Dr. King didn't think much of women," Clark still "adored" King and "supported him in every way [she] could," although she thought that SCLC should do more to promote local leaders and rely less on King. Nonetheless, she insisted that King's political philosophy and the example of "his courage, his service to others, and his non-violence" remained worthy of devotion.[2] Further, Clark appears to suggest that the internal logic of King's thought and praxis would have soon led him toward a more consistent egalitarianism in line with the demands of gender justice.[3]

Among contemporary critics, bell hooks similarly indicts Martin Luther King and other civil rights leaders of the 1950s and 1960s for "following the example of white male patriarchs" and being "obsessively concerned with asserting their masculinity."[4] The misguided way that movement leaders and intellectuals entangled "integration" and "equality," she argues, encouraged an imitative ethos that, in positing white elites as the norm, intensified black support for patriarchy and diminished the political standing and participatory parity of black women.[5] Nevertheless, hooks insists on the profound philosophical import of King's core ideals of the "beloved community" and an ethos of love that informs contentious politics.[6] In a world ravaged by systemic oppression and brimming with value pluralism, hooks sees these ideals—and King's theorization of them—as performing a crucial role in theorizing justice, sustaining the commitment to resolve conflict, and inspiring the practical faith in transformation necessary to sustain and expand human sympathy and solidarity.[7]

In a recent interview with hooks, the philosopher George Yancy asks her, "What should we do in our daily lives to combat, in that phrase of yours, the power and influence of white supremacist capitalist patriarchy?" hooks's answer is illustrative of how, for her, King—once disentangled from his sexism—remains arguably the central touchstone of political and moral judgment: "Rather than saying, 'What would Jesus do?' I always think, 'What does Martin Luther King want me to do today?' Then I decide what Martin Luther King wants me to do today is to go out into the world and in every way that I can, small and large, build a beloved community."[8] This tradition, while inspiring in its commitment to endorsing substantive ethical ideals, tackling difficult ethical questions that emerge from political struggle, and treating King's thought with charity and sympathy, nevertheless confronts a fatal problem. This approach tends to treat the ideas to be recovered as easily disentangled from sexism and androcentrism without adequately self-reflexive inquiry.

As Thomas McCarthy has persuasively argued, "general norms are always understood and justified with an eye to some range of standard situations and typical cases assumed to be appropriate, and that if that range shifts, then so too do the understandings and justifications of those norms, the conceptual interconnections and warranting reasons considered relevant to them."[9] In other words, the imagined subjects, scenarios, and societies that circulate through King's thought may not be so easily accommodating of women, and certainly cannot be presumed to be when these background presuppositions remain buried and unthematized. Indeed, when confronted with Susan Moller Okin's enduring and effective query of whether his thought "can sustain the inclusion of women in its subject matter, and if not, why not," a range of serious dilemmas emerges.[10] In particular, the qualified acceptance approach tends to fail to adequately consider the conceptual and political implications of King's recalcitrantly gendered division of labor, his close association of masculinity with productive labor, and his beliefs regarding the importance of normative family structures for moral-psychological development (including the capacity for love) and social stability.

The respectful rejection approach, by contrast, encourages us tacitly and explicitly to turn away from King as a source of political-philosophical wisdom and from his exemplarity as a touchstone for political judgment. These feminists are part of a broader, although not solely feminist, effort to recover, reconstruct, and duly champion the work of "local people" and previously unsung women and queer people of color within the civil rights movement.[11] A distinguishing feature of the feminist strand of this historiography and criticism is that the turn away from King is not simply explanatory or descriptive, but normative. Woven throughout their historical narratives and explicit political arguments is a critique of King's thought and praxis for its acquiescence to the gender hierarchies and norms from both a socially conservative black religious tradition and the mores of the broader middlebrow public. Superadded to this is a criticism of hierarchical and antidemocratic modes of political action and charismatic leadership. These criticisms, while leavened with genuine respect for King's enormous personal sacrifices, are deemed fatal to his project and grounds for its disavowal.

Perhaps the leading exemplar of this approach is Barbara Ransby's brilliant biography of the life and work of Ella J. Baker. Baker, a legendary grassroots organizer, played a crucial role in the world-making political successes of the three most important black-led civil rights groups of the twentieth century, the National Association for the Advancement of Colored People (NAACP), the Student Nonviolent Coordinating Committee (SNCC), and SCLC.[12] Ransby recovers Baker in large part to champion her as an exemplar and proponent of a profeminist, nonhierarchical, and radically democratic form of political struggle, and to criticize, by comparison, a conception of politics she attributes to King.[13]

Building upon Baker's own critique and diagnosis of King and SCLC, Ransby argues that the organization's sexism was, in large part, influenced by patriarchal attitudes prevalent within a larger black church culture. "The role of women in the southern church," Baker argued, "was that of doing the things that the minister said he wanted to have done ... not one in which [women] were credited with having creativity and initiative and capacity to carry out things."[14] These attitudes, as Ransby points out, played a role in otherwise-inexplicable decisions such as inviting neither "Rosa Parks nor Joanne Gibson Robinson nor any of the women who had sacrificed so much to ensure the Montgomery boycott's success ... to play a leadership role" in SCLC, and even refusing to allow them to speak at events like the 1963 March on Washington for Jobs and Freedom.[15]

Ransby quotes from King's 1954 memo of recommendations to his Dexter Avenue Baptist Church congregation—"Leadership never ascends from the pew to the pulpit, but... descends from the pulpit to the pew"—to underscore this critique, but the memo's broader context is perhaps more damning. King goes on to state that, at least within the church,

> The pastor is to be respected and accepted as the central figure around which the policies and programs of the church revolve. He must never be considered a mere puppet for the whimsical and capricious mistreatment of those who wish to show their independence, and "use their liberty for a cloak of maliciousness." It is therefore indispensable to the progress of the church that the official board and membership cooperate fully with the leadership of the pastor.[16]

This dictate suggests an implicit hermeneutics of suspicion that interprets criticism, disagreement, and even independent initiative within the church as rooted in objectionable vices and as incommensurate with collective "progress."[17] Wherever such a stance rises to absolute authority within a social movement with egalitarian and democratic aims, ethical abuses are sure to arise.

Crucial to the respectful rejection analysis, however, is the contention that the depth of sexism in SCLC was intimately tied not just to the culture of black southern religion, but to an antidemocratic and authoritarian mode of political organization based on charismatic leadership. Baker, for instance, vehemently disagreed with SCLC's incessant promotion of King's celebrity, and what she saw as an overreliance on charisma and spectacular events for organizing. Erica Edwards, self-consciously building upon Baker, explains that charisma "names a phenomenon, a dynamic structure, a figural process of authoring and authorizing," that mixes "sacred and secular narrative impulses" to "situate authority or the right to rule, in one exceptional figure perceived to be gifted with a privileged connection to the divine." This phenomenon, moreover, is always dependent upon what she calls a charismatic scenario and aesthetic.[18]

In other words, the attribution and apprehension of "charisma" to someone like King rely upon certain public narratives, rituals, symbols, affective states, and bodily performances.[19] The edifice of African American political charisma, Edwards argues, entails constitutive forms of violence—the silencing of local people and mass action, antidemocratic and repressive forms of authority, and the reinforcement of patriarchal hierarchies and sexual norms by equating charisma with normative masculinity. In the name of democracy and equality, Baker wanted to tear down much of this scaffolding, depriving traditional forms of charisma of their stage, and divesting them of their political authority and aesthetic force.

"Instead of the leader as a person who was supposed to be a magic man," Baker argued, "you could develop individuals who were bound together by a concept that benefited the larger number of individuals and provided an opportunity for them to grow into being responsible for carrying out a program."[20] Behind this vision lay a set of expansive commitments to democracy as a broad ethical ideal and a set of egalitarian sociopolitical habits and practices.[21] This conception of democracy aims to attain respect for the dignity and self-interpretation of everyday people, empower citizens to defend themselves from the arbitrary domination and hegemony of elites, and facilitate the cultivation of both individual human excellence and cooperative social goods.

This conception of democracy has evaluative standards that apply both to the broader social order and within insurgent social movements. "Anytime you continue to carry on the same kind of organization that you say you are fighting against," Baker argued, "you can't prove to me that you have made any change in your thinking."[22] Black political organizing, on Baker's and Ransby's account, should focus on local groups of citizens, helping them articulate their own needs and demands, building their capacity to democratically achieve their ends against elite resistance over time, and creating forums for political speech and action that are antihierarchical, inclusive, and consensus-oriented.[23] These efforts, they argue, are incompatible with King-inspired visions of charismatic and messianic leadership, which are criticized for disparaging local knowledge, short-circuiting deliberative discussions, and, ironically, intensifying everyday folks' sense of their own inadequacy by generating messiah and inferiority complexes. Worse yet, with charismatic authority, political initiatives are subject to the caprice and veto power of one individual, whose authority, in turn, is dependent upon the whims of media and culture industries for publicity and staging.[24]

While we both have been strongly influenced by the respectful rejection approach, it is important to acknowledge that it has faults as well. Though it readily acknowledges King's sacrifice, it leads far too easily to a broad dismissal of King's thought and to thin accounts of his praxis. Often it falls into this trap by allowing King's public image, a critique of a certain kind of claim to racial representation, and the staging of his charismatic authority to overdetermine our judgments. To say nothing of other concerns with power and representation, King's judgments about how to run SCLC, for example, are inflated, as if they describe his judgments about how to run any social movement organization, when there is evidence (such as his refusal to try to exert power over SNCC, his donations of his own prize monies and SCLC funds to other organizations, his criticism of media elites for fixating on spokespersons and protest rather than community organizing) that his views are not dogmatic on these questions.[25] Even more importantly, this approach tends not to engage with, or take seriously, King's personal struggles and intellectual shifts regarding gendered questions of justice, politics, and political economy—even though his work still falls short in many respects. Finally, work within this tradition tends to miss what the first approach gets right, and therefore loses an opportunity to retrieve crucial resources for a resurgent emancipatory politics, informed by King's political thought, and oriented toward gender justice. In light of the faults of both of these stances, a better approach, and one open to political theorists, is to "think with King against King."

In her influential reconstruction of Hannah Arendt's political thought, Seyla Benhabib enjoins political theorists to think "with Arendt against Arendt." By this challenge, she means to call for not only "a reinterpretation of Hannah Arendt's thought but a revision of it as well," one where we "leave behind the pieties of textual analyses and ask ourselves Arendtian questions and be ready to provide non-Arendtian answers."[26] Specifically, Benhabib is concerned to subvert Arendt's problematic sociology, reconstruct her ontological categories, and retrieve from her political theory "those gems that can still illuminate our struggles as contemporaries."[27]

It strikes us that this is a promising interpretive approach to take toward Martin Luther King's political philosophy as well. In thinking with King against King, especially where questions of gender, identity, and justice are concerned, one must similarly challenge King's sociological premises (such as his sociology of the family), reconstruct his social ontology (his ontology of gender, for instance), and rethematize his political-philosophical arguments (for basic minimum income and so on). We hope to show that, although difficult, this project allows us to constructively revise some of King's most incisive critical insights and his most persuasive (and radically egalitarian) political commitments. In particular, two themes are of indispensable significance: (1) King's deflationary critique of Black Power's masculinist politics and the egalitarian and inclusive dimensions of his defense of nonviolent, mass civil disobedience as a preferred mode of agonistic political action; and (2) his defense of a basic minimum income and anti-humiliation ethics in welfare politics as a crucial part of a theory of justice.

REAL MEN: TOWARD A CRITIQUE OF BLACK POWER AND BLACK PROTEST MASCULINITY

Peter J. Ling takes an interesting approach to King's sexism and Ransby's implicit call to turn away from his work in favor of the work of others. Ling acknowledges the sexism and the role it played in King's dismissing the considerable expertise of seasoned activists like Baker, but he invites his readers to consider possible benefits of King's particular brand of masculinity. Ling goes so far as to suggest, contra many feminist critics, that King's need to prove and perform manhood and manliness within his philosophical commitments may have helped to advance the cause of civil rights in his most influential years. Ling argues that Baker (and Ransby by extension) "underestimated the value of the kind of formal leadership—a combination of prophetic ministry, media politics and summitry—that Dr. King exerted between 1963 and 1965," and a "mode of masculinity [that] prompted him towards a program of dramatic protest that pushed civil rights to the top of America's legislative agenda."[28] This thesis deserves more scrutiny than it has received, especially given the respectful-rejection tradition's persuasive case for the costs of SCLC gender ideology. Here, however, we want to focus on where Ling's contention seems most promising—as a reading of King as a critic of, or comparative foil to, other modes of black protest masculinity that were on offer.

One of the most pressing challenges to King's political philosophy and praxis emerged from critics who mobilized a conception of dignity that competed with and dissented from King's ethical-political commitment to nonviolence. In *Stride Toward Freedom*, King describes his speech at the mass meeting that inaugurated the boycott as seeking "to arouse the group to action by insisting that their self-respect was at stake and that if they accepted such injustices without protesting, they would betray their own sense of dignity and the eternal edicts of God Himself." Yet that evening, and throughout his career, King insisted that love and nonviolence should be the regulative ideals of such dignity-engendering protest. On his account, these ideals are not simply compatible or commensurate with carrying out the duty to defend one's dignity by refusing to acquiesce without protest to injustice, but constitute "the only morally and practically sound method open to oppressed people in their struggle for freedom."[29]

For a prominent group of militant black intellectuals and activists, however, the refusal to embrace, or even countenance, violence was itself an undignified stance. For these thinkers, this judgment stemmed partly from King's politics running afoul of the presumed ethical demands of "manhood" in his embrace of ostensibly "feminine" ideals like love, or eschewal of the presumed masculine domain of violence. That this is such a prominent feature of African American political thought should be no surprise, for, as Wendy Brown has argued, "politics has historically borne an explicitly masculine identity" and "been bound up with protean yet persistent notions and practices of manhood" that subtly manifest themselves in the vocabularies and presuppositions of political thought.[30] Indeed, with regard to "manhood" discourse, one of the most distinctive features of African American political thought compared to other traditions might be how broadly "manhood" is figured as an aspirational telos of black political strivings, and how jarringly explicit and forthright much of the tradition has been about the significance of "manhood" as an organizing thematic of black politics.

Frederick Douglass, undoubtedly the most influential African American intellectual and activist of the nineteenth century, plays a crucial role in the preeminence of this frame. "Not only our equality as a race is denied," Douglass complains, "but we are even denied our rank as men; we are enslaved, oppressed, and even those most favorably disposed towards us, are so from motives more of pity than respect." This diagnosis leads Douglass to laud the "noble work" that awaits African Americans, describing black politics in his era as an attempt to "prove our equal manhood... [and] redeem an entire race from the obloquy and scorn of the world."[31] One especially influential argument within this tradition links dignity to its purported realization through manhood, and links manhood to the will and capacity to deploy defensive violence.

Douglass, again, is illustrative here. In perhaps the most famous vignette in African American literature, Douglass narrates his life-risking fistfight with an infamously brutal "slave-breaker," William Covey, as the moment that "revived a sense of [his] own manhood": "I was a changed being after that fight. I was nothing before; I was a man now.... A man without force is without the essential dignity of humanity. Human nature is so constituted, that it cannot honor a helpless man, though it can pity him, and even this it cannot do long if signs of power do not arise."[32] Elsewhere Douglass extrapolates this contention to a broader, collective praxis of self-defense in resistance to fugitive slave catchers. Juxtaposing "submission" and violent resistance, he argues that submission can be justified only where it is recognized as virtuous and can have "some moral effect in restraining crime and shaming aggression." Where this does not hold, a failure to risk life and take life will be "quoted against them, as marking them as an inferior race." In this context, Douglass declares, "every slave-hunter who meets a bloody death in his infernal business is an argument in favor of the manhood of our race."[33]

King's political career overlapped with the most dramatic resurgence and popular promotion of these arguments since the 1850s. Robert F. Williams, the militant proponent of organized self-defense and author of the manifesto Negroes with Guns, for example, argued in response to state-abetted racial terror, "We as men should stand up as men, and protect our women and children. I am a man and I will walk upright as a man should. I WILL NOT CRAWL."[34] The black nationalist icon Malcolm X, indicting King and others for falling short of this standard, declared, "We don't deserve to be recognized and respected as men as long as our women can be brutalized... and nothing [is] done about it, but we sit around singing 'We shall overcome.'"[35] On this account, a necessary element of the right to equal respect and recognition, as well as honorable manhood, becomes the capacity and will to achieve the patriarchal role of familial protector of women and children.[36] As is often the case in nationalist discourse, however, there is an easy slippage between family and nation, and this purported duty becomes inflated from a familial one to a racial one.[37] The argument amounts to the claim that racial stigma is reproduced, in part, through the humiliating "failure" of black men to live up to this charge in the face of ritual humiliations visited upon the race, thus refracting even the unique degradations suffered by black women through a "lack" of manhood.

In light of this history and the allure of contemporaneous black nationalist militancy, King did not have an easy time persuading African Americans that his politics of nonviolence and love had much to offer those looking for a route to "manhood." This was compounded by the fact that the gender composition of southern congregations skewed away from male adolescents and adults. King was the leader of a Baptist church, and his flock, like the flock across town in America's most segregated hour, was predominantly women and children. His authority over male adolescents, who would have been trying on manhood models at the time of his greatest influence, was tenuous. Moreover, as Ling argues, African American men were not particularly disposed to nonviolence's ritual asceticism and performances of self-denial. Instead, like most American men, they delighted in "the athleticism, financial success and physical power of Joe Louis and Jackie Robinson" and tended to confuse nonviolence with a "pacifism that seemed to require an 'unmanly' repudiation of the right to self-defense."[38] Black youth culture in our own day contains elements that reject King's idolization on these very grounds. Tupac Shakur, to take one illustrative example, raps in his "Words of Wisdom" (1991): "No Malcolm X in my history text, why's that? / 'cause he tried to educate and liberate all blacks / Why is Martin Luther King in my book each week? / He told blacks if they get smacked, turn the other cheek."[39]

Thus, while King benefited from the resonance of the philosophy of nonviolence with Christian teachings to "turn the other cheek," he also confronted a long-standing black self-defense tradition that advocated the use of violence to protect family and community. Lance Hill, the leading historian of the civil rights era self-defense group the Deacons for Defense, self-consciously channels one of this tradition's central contentions: "Nonviolence required black men to passively endure humiliation and physical abuse—a bitter elixir for a group struggling to overcome the southern white stereotype of black men as servile and cowardly." Nonviolence, Hill continues, also "tested the limits of [black men's] forbearance," by demanding that they "forgo their right to defend family members who joined nonviolent protests."[40] Disturbed by these charges, and certainly aware of the cultural imprimatur of figures like Joe Louis and the countercultural allure of outlaw violence, King took considerable time contesting these challenges in ways that are worth evaluating in the present.[41] His deflating responses to the masculinist conflation of violent self-defense with manhood, and manhood with dignity, can be separated into two modes: (1) inversion and (2) dissociation.

DEFLATION AS INVERSION

King's writing reveals not only that he was under considerable pressure to demonstrate the "manliness" of nonviolence, but also that he often acquiesced to that pressure. However, it is important to acknowledge that King's concessions (or compulsions) toward inherited vocabularies and significations of manliness have, in some registers, a subversive quality—even if in other registers they reinforce objectionable forms of hierarchy.[42] King's subversion manifests itself both in his rhetorical inversions, associating masculinity with nonviolent praxis, and in his practical action, which entailed what Linda Zerilli has called a productive or creative moment of figuration, the "newly thinkable."[43]

King inverted militaristic language usually reserved for the instruments and organization of violence to redescribe nonviolence, repeatedly referring to his "nonviolent army" and to those "who enlisted in an army that marches under the banner of nonviolence."[44] Further, King tried to claim the mantle of "true" manhood from Malcolm X and defenders of violence by playing on the gendered distinctions between activity and passivity, subtly turning the tables on his antagonists who defended violence partly by availing themselves of this age-old association. Malcolm X, for example, when drawing his (in)famous distinction between the figures of the House Negro / Uncle Tom (representing the "feminine" spheres of domesticity and accommodation) and the Field Negro (representing the "masculine" domains of productivity and rebelliousness), went so far as to equate the nonviolent movement not only with the House Negro, but also with a passivity on par with anesthesia:

> Just as the slavemaster of that day used Tom, the house Negro, to keep the field Negroes in check, the same old slavemaster today has Negroes who are nothing but modern Uncle Toms, twentieth-century Uncle Toms, to keep you and me in check, to keep us under control, keep us passive and peaceful and nonviolent.... It's like when you go to the dentist.... You're going to fight him when he starts pulling. So he squirts some stuff in your jaw called novocaine, to make

you think they're not doing anything to you. So you sit there and because you've got all of that novocaine in your jaw, you suffer—peacefully.[45]

King sought to invert these associations, reframing militant bromides launched from the relative safety of northern ghettos as far more passive than the nonviolent movement's harrowing and deadly acts of protest, and again using military imagery to characterize the work of direct action:

> Many of these extremists misread the significance and the intent of nonviolence because they fail to perceive that militancy is also the father of the nonviolent army. Angry exhortation from street corners and stirring calls for the Negro to arm and go forth to do battle stimulate loud applause. But when the applause dies, the stirred and the stirring return to their homes and lie in their beds for still one more night with no progress in view. They cannot solve the problems they face because they have offered no challenge but only a call to arms, which they themselves are unwilling to lead, knowing that doom would be its reward.... The conservatives who say, "Let us not move so fast," and the extremists who say, "Let us go out and whip the world," would tell you that they are as far apart as the poles. But there is a striking parallel: They accomplish nothing.[46]

It is important to note here that while King's efforts of inversion aspired to a kind of epistemic critique of what his fellow citizens thought they "knew" about masculinity, their most compelling quality is ultimately linked to the productive novelty of his praxis.[47] By actually staging and performing an enactment of manhood commensurate with nonviolence, King and his allies helped introduce and give ethical-aesthetic force to a divergent model of the dignity-manhood-violence relation. With the subjective certainty suggested by King's willingness to risk and ultimately lose his life to adhere to principle, this mode of action—when set alongside the inaction of nonviolent rhetoricians—helped clear the ground for partially dissociating violence and masculinity.

DEFLATION AS DISSOCIATION

King was acutely aware of the difficulty of what he was advocating, and of how it flew in the face not only of prevailing dispositions of African American manhood but of American manhood writ large—which he characterized as having accepted the "eye-for-an-eye philosophy" as its "highest measure." "We are a nation that worships the frontier tradition," King diagnosed, "and our heroes are those who champion justice through violent retaliation against injustice. It is not simple to adopt the credo that moral force has as much strength and virtue as the capacity to return a physical blow; or that to refrain from hitting back requires more will and bravery than the automatic reflexes of defense."[48] Undaunted by this broader cultural challenge, King tried to deflate its pretensions by dissociating these "lower" iterations of manhood from their claims to constitutive, higher-order virtue.

Locating part of the appeal of the rhetoric of violence in its relationship with an American "frontier tradition," King sought to disentangle it from this "heroic" veneer. Rightly linking this self-conception to the genocide of indigenous peoples, King reminds us that "our children are still taught to respect the violence which reduced a red-skinned people of an earlier culture into a few fragmented groups herded into impoverished reservations."[49] Not only does this disposition toward violence, King warns, contain the horrifying possibility of genocidal atrocities as its outer limit, but it also involves the further objectionable quality of being imitative of white supremacy. "One of the greatest paradoxes of the Black Power movement is that it talks unceasingly about not imitating the values of white society," King proclaims, "but in advocating violence it is imitating the worst, the most brutal and the most uncivilizing value of American life."[50]

Elsewhere King attempts to dissociate violence, manhood, and courage, arguing that the turn to violent conflict has its roots in fear. "We say that war is a consequence of hate," King admonishes, "but close scrutiny reveals this sequence: first fear, then hate, then war, and finally deeper hatred." The turn to stockpiling armaments is an attempt to "cast out fear," but ironically it tends only to produce "greater fear."[51] Underscoring the significance of fear in his political thought, King attempts to unmask the "aura of paramilitarism among the black militant groups" as speaking "more of fear than it does of confidence." Putting pressure on the link between fear, violence, and manhood, King objected that one's need for arms reveals a lingering fear of death, and that its function was essentially a phallic totem—"one's manhood must come from within him," King insisted, not from the barrel of the gun.[52]

More subtly, King pursued the work of dissociation through his introduction of a hierarchical account of the body where, in moments of crisis, a demonstration of proper manhood entailed control and mastering of one's emotions. Not only did nonviolent protest show a true willingness to put bodies on the line that was absent in militants who advocated violence but were "all talk," but King claimed for his mode of protest an even greater degree of "sophistication": a willingness to put "properly ordered" (Platonically ordered, even) bodies in control of animalistic emotions on the line for grand social ideals. This appeal to self-mastery, more expansive notions of protection, and the disciplining of disorderly affective states associated with unbridled masculinity (such as anger, hatred) and femininity (impulsivity) was narrated and defended, in part, as a higher-order vision of manhood. King's contrast here is evident:

> It is always amusing to me when a Negro man says that he can't demonstrate with us because if someone hit him he would fight back. Here is a man whose children are being plagued by rats and roaches, whose wife is robbed daily at overpriced ghetto food stores, who himself is working for about two-thirds the pay of a white person doing a similar job . . . and in spite of all this daily suffering it takes someone spitting on him or calling him a nigger to make him want to fight. Conditions are such for Negroes in America that all Negroes ought to be fighting aggressively.[53]

King's usurpation of the mantle of the "real" fighter also takes aim at the broader cultural fascination and investment in pugilistic sport as the truest expression of manhood, and the iconography around black boxers. In an especially pernicious and politically circumscribed version of the charismatic leadership scenario theorized by Edwards, African Americans' excellence in sport often functioned through the culture industry as a cipher for black political hope, social strivings, and other, darker desires for revenge and counterhumiliation. King, in a bit of cultural psychoanalysis, recalled the story of a teenage black boy being put to death in a southern gas chamber in the 1930s. As he suffocated on poison gas, he offered a last prayer in his final minutes, repeating, "Save me, Joe Louis."

For King, this cry shows "the helplessness, the loneliness and the profound despair of Negroes in that period"—a "groping" in a barren terrain for "someone who might care for him, and [who] had power enough to rescue him." But whereas this hopeless boy put his last faith in "a Negro who was the world's most expert fighter," King argued that the civil rights movement helped blacks—of all genders, notably—discover their own fighting spirit, internally and in solidarity, replacing the "bizarre and naïve cry to Joe Louis" with "confidence" in their own nonviolent direct action. In the wake of this transformation, King reports that when the contemporaneous world heavyweight champion, Floyd Patterson, came to Birmingham—he came "not as a savoir," but to "give heart to the plain people who were engaged in another kind of bruising combat."[54]

MANY RIVERS TO CROSS: INCLUSION AND AGENCY

These appeals to constructs like "the plain people" or the "nonviolent army," particularly in the context of arguments about the paramilitary vanguard leadership of black men, contain egalitarian content that is worth teasing out and restating to draw out their power. These formulations, and King's accounts of nonviolent direct action elsewhere, suggest that courage, active resistance, an ethic of community protection, and dignity need not necessarily be gendered in exclusionary or hierarchical ways. That such a position is not inconsistent with the core of King's thought, suitably reconstructed, is borne out in his argument that "a nonviolent army has a magnificent universal quality" and can transcend many of the exclusions that violence (or even politics, in some traditions) places on participation or standing: age, physical disability, and status or rank.[55]

The egalitarian dimension of King's description is best underscored via juxtaposition with Malcolm X's mockery of the aesthetic force of sit-in demonstrations precisely for their supposed lack of masculine virility. "It's not so good," Malcolm warns, "to refer to what you're going to do as a sit-in. That right there castrates you.... An old woman can sit. An old man can sit. A chump can sit, a coward can sit.... it's time for us today to start doing some standing and some fighting to back that up."[56]

The growing empirical literature on nonviolent resistance suggests that King's vision is not simply an ideal. As Erica Chenoweth and Maria Stephan argue, violent insurgency often requires demanding physical skills, facility with weapons, and isolation from family and society, whereas nonviolent resistance generally is more open to female or elderly populations.[57] While it must be admitted that "female operatives—such as female suicide bombers and guerillas—have sometimes been active in violent campaigns in Sri Lanka, Iraq, Pakistan, Palestine, El Salvador, and East Timor, they are nevertheless exceptions in most cases."[58] Timothy Garton Ash also underscores this point, arguing, "If violent action has traditionally been a man's business, women often come to the fore in non-violent action, and in opposition to further violence," which, it bears noting, in conflict and postconflict situations often involves rampant sexual assault.[59]

Instead of forthrightly arguing in this register, or describing his insights in this fashion, however, King and his colleagues expended an unsettling amount of energy trying to demonstrate that nonviolence did not actually involve unmanly submission to white domination. They were not above invoking their own phallic imagery to frame conflicts, as did King when speaking of a confrontation during the Birmingham campaign, presenting the power of nonviolence as nonviolent adherents met a group of police. In King's account of one Sunday demonstration, Bull Connor, the notoriously racist Birmingham commissioner of public safety, screamed to his police officers, "Dammit. Turn on the hoses." The marchers "stared back, unafraid and unmoving. Slowly the Negroes stood up and began to advance. Connor's men, as though hypnotized, fell back, their hoses sagging uselessly in their hands while several hundred Negroes marched past, and without further interference, held their prayer meeting as planned."[60]

More disturbingly, despite appealing to the "magnificent universal quality" of a nonviolent army, King's characterizations of women's political agency suggests that underneath the invocation of inclusion lay objectionable patterns of interpretation and evaluation based on androcentrism and sexism. This is perhaps clearest in the case of the Montgomery bus boycott, the event that not only is credited with kicking off the "classical" phase of the civil rights movement but also rocketed the young Martin Luther King, Jr., to fame. Catalyzed by a woman, conceived by a woman, sustained by women—those among us who do not shy away from grandiose statements might claim that without women, there would be no King. But why were women so important? And how did gender structure King's recounting of the boycott? What can his recounting tell us about his understanding of women and agency and the role this plays in his broader political thought?

The reasons women were central to the protest are simple: they spent the most time on buses, they experienced far and away the worst treatment on buses, and therefore they had the most to gain from the amelioration of conditions therein. The boycott's success disproportionately improved the lives of working-class black women. Occupational segregation by sex, traditional gender roles, and cultural misogyny all structured transportation access and black women's experiences riding buses; taken together, they account for why working-class black women rode the bus more often than black working-class males, and why their experiences on buses were often much worse than black males'.

There have been a number of explanations offered for the causes of the boycott—including King's reference to "suprarational" divine force—but one must emphasize the material causes of the protest.[61] When describing the conditions, interpreters have long emphasized the insults blacks faced and among these insults the physical and verbal abuse blacks experienced at the hands of drivers, white passengers, and police; often armed drivers and passengers simply behaved as police. From this vantage point one might see the boycott as a black battle for human dignity, as devoid of any significant intersections and notable as a struggle that eventually transcended class boundaries. However, when one stops to consider how access to transportation is structured by class, and how simply purchasing a car would allow the better-off among Montgomery's blacks to avoid the insults mentioned earlier, it becomes clear that it is crucial to view the protest as, in large part, the culmination of a long struggle for human dignity waged by Montgomery's transit-dependent poor, a protest that gained much-needed support when the black (male) middle class and black spiritual elite joined the efforts. This is particularly evident if one expands one's notion of protest and resistance to include what Robin D. G. Kelley has called the "infrapolitics" of Alabama's black working class.[62]

Yet without attention to gender as well as class, the picture is still incomplete. Among the working class, as with the wider American society and in truth with most societies, men and women rarely perform the same jobs. Montgomery was no exception to this, and it had not only a racial problem, but a spatialized gendered occupational problem as well. One question contemporary spatial feminists have put to urban planners—a question worth considering in the context of the protest—is this: Are female-dominated job sites as well served by transportation routes as male-dominated job sites? As it happens, buses are often best suited to serving working-class women's employment-related transportation needs, unlike traditional hub-and-spoke transit models designed to move people from the residential margins to the industrial and financial centers.[63] This was certainly the case in Montgomery, where half of black working-class women worked as domestics in white homes and therefore had to travel from black neighborhoods across town to white ones each day.[64]

Perhaps this explains why so many of Alabama's pre-Parks bus protests involved women. Kelley writes that in Birmingham in 1941–42, "nearly twice as many black women were arrested as black men, most of them charged with either sitting in the white section or cursing."[65] Kelley also points out that "unlike the popular image of Rosa Parks's quiet resistance, black women's opposition tended to be profane and militant."[66] This resistance was often violently quelled, with women brutally assaulted and arrested. The gendered pattern Kelley observed in 1940s Birmingham would be repeated in 1950s Montgomery; Danielle McGuire reports thirty complaints in 1953 alone, noting that "most of these complaints came from working class black women who made up the bulk of Montgomery's City Lines' riders, over half of whom toiled as domestics."[67]

The historical record—including arrest records—shows that working-class black women were not immune from physical violence, or horrific sexual harassment and humiliation. McGuire argues that the gender-specific abuses black women faced were important factors in the decision of Parks and with her a predominantly black female working-class ridership to sustain the year-long boycott: "African-American women constantly complained about the atrocious treatment they received on buses.... Bus drivers, [Jo Ann] Robinson recalled, disrespected black women by hurling nasty sexualized insults their way. Ferdie

Walker, a black woman from Fort Worth, Texas, remembered bus drivers sexually harassing her as she waited on the corner. 'The bus was up high,' she recalled, 'and the street was down low. They'd drive up under there and then they'd expose themselves while I was standing there and it just scared me to death.'" In McGuire's analysis, "Verbal, physical and sexual abuse"—including epithets like "black niggers," "black bitches," "heifers," and "whores"—"maintained racial hierarchy in an enclosed space where complete separation of whites and blacks was all but impossible."[68]

And yet while this makes it clear that black women had more than adequate reason to leave the buses after the protest was called, McGuire also makes clear that they risked a great deal more than their male counterparts when they made the decision to leave the buses. They were constantly endangered on the sidewalks and roadways, threatened with what Montgomery activist E. D. Nixon called "a ritual of rape in which white men in the segregated South abducted and assaulted black women with alarming regularity and stunning uniformity."[69]

Finally, McGuire makes a particularly compelling case for the role of racialized sexual violence played in Parks's resolve to keep her seat, as her archival research uncovered Parks's hitherto-unknown anti–sexual violence work on behalf of the NAACP and strongly suggests the importance of that work in Parks's decision to keep her seat that fateful day. Ten years prior to Montgomery, Parks was part of a group that formed the Alabama Committee for Equal Justice for Mrs. Recy Taylor, and was part of a larger group that spread the story of Taylor's gang rape by white men, "from the back roads of Alabama to the street corners of Harlem." McGuire writes, "By the spring of 1945, they had recruited supporters around the country and had organized what the Chicago Defender called the 'strongest campaign for equal justice to be seen in a decade.'"[70] She later notes: "Indeed, many of the African Americans who cut their political teeth defending black women like Recy Taylor who were raped by white men in Alabama in the 1940s brought their experiences and organizational insight into other struggles for dignity and justice in the 1950s and 1960s. Like E. D. Nixon and Rosa Parks in Montgomery, they often became pillars of the modern civil rights movement."[71] Ransby, it should be noted, does not fail to point out Ella Baker's role in forging the protest. As it happens, Parks attended one of Baker's leadership conferences designed to spark action among the grassroots. The Atlanta conference was Parks's first trip outside of Montgomery, and Ransby notes that it made a lasting impression on the civil rights icon.[72]

Again, women made the boycott, and this was no accident—the conditions leading up to the boycott are impossible to understand without gender analysis; gender relations, specifically inter- and intraracial gender hierarchy, were important factors in transit use and transit experiences. Yet in the end, McGuire says, though observers noted women's importance in the boycott itself, "when the boycott took off, no one called it a women's movement."[73] How does a movement so rooted in the experiences of working-class black women come to be told as a story about blacks as such, without intersections of gender or class, and what is King's role in this process?

Was gender significant in King's understanding of the boycott? No and yes. His failure to attend to much of what we described in his analysis of the boycott makes him an unreliable witness to the event itself, yet examining his account of the boycott with particular attention to how he saw women within the protest event and how he described them—their appearance, their age, and most importantly their agency, or more often their lack thereof—is revealing. So too is attention to when and how he mobilized women to advance arguments.

Take King's description of Parks, which is particularly striking in light of McGuire's recovery of her early activism. Much has been written regarding the role of the "politics of respectability" and what it necessitated regarding skin tone and gender presentation in the figure of Parks, and how the boycott coalesced around her case and not that of the darker-skinned and eventually pregnant single teen Claudette Colvin.[74] But how did King see Parks? And how did he, as one of the first to present an account of the boycott, help to construct the Parks we had to unlearn? To King, Parks is not only "an attractive Negro seamstress," she was also "tired from long hours on her feet."[75] Although he first dispels the myth that she is an NAACP "plant" by saying "she was planted there by her personal sense of dignity and self-respect," he goes on to undermine that characterization by presenting her as he does many other women in his texts—an issue to which we turn later—as less agential, as a "victim" in fact, "of both the forces of history and the forces of destiny. She had been tracked down by the Zeitgeist—the spirit of the time."[76]

The Zeitgeist, too, seemed to have a thing for light-skinned, attractive women. King felt Parks was "ideal for the role assigned to her by history. She was a charming person with a radiant personality, soft-spoken and calm in all situations. Her character was impeccable and her dedication deep-rooted. All of these traits made her one of the most respected people in the Negro community."[77] His account is striking when contrasted with that of another of the boycott's participant-observers. Founding Women's Political Council president Mary Fair Burks describes Parks as "the catalyst"—not a victim or someone carried aloft by history, destiny, or zeitgeist, but an agent who made a decision:

> There is no doubt that Rosa Parks was the catalyst. Her quiet determination, her belief in principles, her sense of justice and injustice, her certainty of right and wrong, her never failing dignity, her courage in the face of adversity—all

these qualities made her the inevitable catalyst.... Rosa as a rule did not defy authority, but once she had determined on a course of action, she would not retreat. She might ignore you, go around you, but never retreat. I became convinced that she refused to give up her seat not only because she was tired, but because doing so would have violated her humanity and sense of dignity as well as her values regarding right and wrong, justice and injustice.[78]

Some of this divergence must be attributed to King's understanding of divine forces intervening in the boycott. However, he repeats this lack-of-agency attribution so often in his descriptions of women that it must motivate deeper concern.

Gender analysis, in addition to class analysis, is useful in evaluating King's thinking regarding how each class responded to the injustice of the bus system and racial oppression in Montgomery more broadly. King described Montgomery's uneducated—presumably the city's working class—as quiescent, its middle-class as indifferent, and the boycott as the moment the two came together, awakened and emboldened. Robin Kelley's analysis of pre-1955 dissent on buses, together with his insistence that one must attend to what the political anthropologist James Scott refers to as infrapolitics in order to get an accurate picture of the political history of the oppressed, casts doubt on the first part of King's claim. Kelley quotes Scott as saying of "infrapolitics" that "the circumspect struggle waged daily by subordinate groups is, like infrared rays, beyond the visible end of the spectrum. That it should be invisible . . . is in large part by design—a tactical choice born out of a prudent awareness of the balance of power." Kelley insists that "these daily acts"—petty theft, footdragging, and destruction of property, but also folklore, jokes, and songs—may "have a cumulative effect on power relations."[79] Indeed this is true, but it is only in attending to the work of women that we are able to dispel the second part of King's statement.

While it is true that all but a few middle-class black males and most middle-class black female organizations shied away from direct challenge to Montgomery's racial hierarchy, there is a glaring omission that would have been right in front of King. Women, specifically the middle-class women of Dexter Avenue Baptist Church's Women's Political Council, mounted the first organized resistance to blacks' treatment on the city's buses.[80] Founded in 1946, with Mary Fair Burks as its first president, the organization protested blacks' treatment on the city's buses as part of their three-tiered approach, which included political action and education aimed at increasing voter registration. When Jo Ann Robinson took over as president in 1950, she focused the group's attention on bus integration and fair treatment. Both Burks and Robinson were professors, middle-class, and not dependent on public transit. Robinson's horrific treatment on a bus on a day when she did not have access to her car saw her calling for a boycott as early as 1949. In 1955, she mimeographed and distributed an estimated 30,000 to 52,500 leaflets to drum up support for the December 5 boycott.

That King and his advisors overlooked the work of a group of women so close to him in evaluating pre-Parks Montgomery activism fits with his other failures on the question of gender equity. Like W. E. B. Du Bois before him, King tended to give names and descriptive specificity to men's activism and to generalize and caricature women and their activism, often leaving them unnamed or assessing their physical attributes. Men's ages do not factor in his descriptions but women's very often do, and he demonstrated a preference for noting the good deeds of older women alongside the attractiveness of younger women.

Three instances come to mind regarding King's assessment of women and agency during the boycott, which necessitate reading him alongside female observers of the boycott to get more perspicacious descriptions of what happened. The first, most egregious concern is that the women who conceived the boycott are unnamed in his account. In detailing the origins of the boycott King says: "Later in the evening word got around to a few influential women of the community, mostly members of the Women's Political Council. After a series of telephone calls back and forth they agreed that the Negroes should boycott the buses. They immediately suggested the idea to Nixon and he readily concurred. In his usual courageous manner he agreed to spearhead the idea."[81] It would be left to feminist historians to recover these "influential women."

King's description also provides clues to how quickly a boycott catalyzed by a woman and conceived by women became men's business, as here Nixon valiantly agrees to "lead" something women initiated. King seemed all too comfortable with this, later writing, "While our wives plied us with coffee, and joined the informal discussion, we laid plans and arrived at agreements on policy."[82] Robinson tells the story differently, reversing the pulpit-to-pew conception of leadership: "One minister read the circular, inquired about the announcements, and found that all the city's black congregations were quite intelligent on the matter and were planning to support the one-day boycott with or without their ministers' leadership. It was then that the ministers decided that it was time for them, the leaders, to catch up with the masses.... Had they not done so, they might have alienated themselves from their congregations and indeed lost members for the masses were ready and they were united!"[83]

King not only tends to leave unnamed women whose physical attributes presumably do not interest him, he also often portrays older women as helpless. King writes of a man who helped an "elderly" woman across a street: "In the course of the day police succeeded in making one arrest. A college student who was helping an elderly woman across the street was charged with 'intimidating passengers.' "[84] Jo Ann Robinson also gave an account of the event, and the differences are stark: "A 19 year old college student, Fred Daniel, full of joy, pranks and frivolity, took hold of the arm of his friend, Mrs. Percival, and playfully 'helped' her across the street. The motorcycle police were upon him in a flash. They accused him of hindering the passenger from getting on the bus and held him until a patrol car came to take him to jail, where he was booked for disorderly conduct."[85] In Robinson's account the woman appears without reference to her age, she is named, and she does not need help. King's account is also devoid of the emotional richness Robinson's provides. She presents man and woman as happy equals, finding subversive joy in protest politics.

King and Robinson also both tell the story of a black domestic who leaked news of the boycott to whites, and thus to the white press. King tells a story of an illiterate, helpless domestic: "A maid, who could not read very well came into possession of one of the unsigned appeals that had been distributed Friday afternoon. Apparently not knowing what the leaflet said, she gave it to her employer. As soon as the white employer received the notice she turned it over to the local newspaper and the Montgomery Advertiser made the contents of the leaflet a front-page story on Saturday morning."[86] Robinson, by contrast, attributed malice, literacy, and agency to the woman:

> Domestic workers who worked late into the day toyed with the slips of paper carrying the important information of the protests. Most of them destroyed the evidence, buried the information in their memories, and went merrily on their way to work. However, one lone black woman, a domestic loyal to her "white lady," in spite of her concern over the plight of her black peers and without any sense of obligation to her people, carried the hand bill to her job and did not stop until the paper was safe in her "white lady's" hands.[87]

Finally there is King's frequent willingness to explain southern black women's agency by reference to innate, organic, and untutored virtue. Despite Jo Ann Robinson being a crucial force in initiating and sustaining the boycott, King's reference to the college professor is as an "attractive, fair-skinned and still youthful" woman who "came by her goodness naturally." In sharp contrast to the veritable philosophical bibliography narrated in his own "Pilgrimage to Nonviolence," he presents Robinson as someone who "did not need to learn nonviolence from any book."[88]

These modes of rhetoric give with one hand and take away with the other. The "universal quality" of nonviolence is celebrated, on one hand, and the leadership and agency of women devalued on the other. The masculinist conflation of dignity, manhood, and violence is deflated on one hand, while "real" manhood reasserts itself in another register. The question that remains for us, as inheritors of King, is how we should respond to this ambivalent legacy.

King's work aimed to convince adherents not only that nonviolence was morally superior and strategically sound, but that the means of nonviolence have an intrinsic connection to important ends, and these features are worthy of serious consideration for feminists. King was attempting important reconstructive work, in separating manhood from violence, and attempting to provide black males an alternative path to "manhood" that did not require violence. This may be unavoidable, indeed laudable, in a nonideal context, where sexist ideology, androcentrism, and patriarchy deeply structure people's value judgments and identities, making it difficult to gain critical scaffolding without more immanent forms of criticism. What is necessary, however, is to think with King against King, and place these efforts in a continuum or process that has as its self-conscious telos a restatement of those positively egalitarian and inclusive formulations in his work that emphasize the importance, for anyone's dignity, of resisting oppression and the defensibility of nonviolent forms of resistance. This restatement, moreover, would have to restate and distill these commitments' importance for fulfilling an ideal of participatory parity and principle of antimarginalization, while also bringing under scrutiny those sexist practices that King and SCLC leaders did not see as incommensurate with their arguments for inclusivity. In particular, it would require uprooting King's ontology of gender and sociology of the family, and reconstructing arguments about equality to disavow androcentrism. In our conclusion, we will briefly sketch what this might look like in the domain of King's arguments about economic inequality.

GENDER AND ECONOMIC JUSTICE IN KING'S THOUGHT

King intervened powerfully in debates about economic inequality, poverty, and justice that are only recently starting to be appreciated by political philosophers.[89] His later work, in particular, weaves together many compelling arguments about the incompatibility of poverty with political and civic equality, the need for basic liberties to be buttressed with economic parity, and, above all, the significance of social relations for individual dignity.[90]

In addition to these concerns, moreover, King argues passionately about features of economic inequality that are neglected in mainstream political theory.

He is deeply concerned about poverty engendering inescapable feelings of humiliation in an affluent society. Further, he expresses concern about the injuries and civic responsibilities that might be said to arise when a democratic government spends national wealth extravagantly on war or luxury, while many citizens languish in severe material deprivation.[91] Of particular moral urgency for King was the dilemma of the rapidly consolidating postindustrial black ghettos within the United States, and the unique forms of marginalization, stigma, poverty, and exploitation they entail.[92]

Less noted, however, is that King often addresses questions of poverty in ways thoroughly inflected by his conception of gender. Intertwined with these arguments about poverty as corrosive of dignity, poverty as engendering of humiliation, and ghetto poverty being uniquely galling are claims about what economic inequality means for the achievement and consolidation of gender norms. The "castration" or "diminished manhood" frames for understanding injustice that King productively unsettles in the domain of violence, for instance, come roaring back in the realm of political economy.

The 1960s were a moment of intense anxiety among intellectuals and political elites about the coming socioeconomic consequences of "automation," the catch-all phrase they often invoked to explain the intensification of capital investments in robotics and machinery, the spread of early computing technology, and the concomitant increase in economic productivity.[93] Of particular interest, of course, was the effect these changes were likely to have on employment, with some pessimists predicting that automation would put the United States on a path toward full unemployment rather than the full employment then championed by left-liberals.[94] Important currents of this discourse emphasized the link between automation and disparity in black and white unemployment rates, identifying racial discrimination and the comparable lack of education and skills among blacks (especially black migrants from the South) as problems.[95] In a 1963 speech to the American Association of Advertising Agencies, NAACP president Roy Wilkins echoed these themes, expressing his worry that while "the trained and talented Negro" had an unprecedented array of occupations and opportunities, automation was "threatening the unskilled and semi-skilled Negro with economic extinction ... [and] permanent unemployment."[96]

The mid- to late 1960s also were a time of extraordinary controversy about the relationship between changes in political economy and the dynamics of black family formation. Out-of-wedlock births, promiscuity, female-headed households, and welfare dependency had long been grist for black nationalist bromides, but it is indisputable that this particular moment of discursive intensity revolved around the infamous 1965 "Moynihan Report." Drafted by Daniel Patrick

Moynihan, a sociologist serving in the Johnson administration as assistant undersecretary of labor, the report argued that the dynamics of black family life and formation, forged in racial domination and exacerbated by industrial and postindustrial black male unemployment, were an existential threat to the quest for racial and economic equality. On Moynihan's account, which drew heavily from the African American sociologist E. Franklin Frazier's *The Negro Family in the United States* (1939), "centuries of injustice"—including slavery, Jim Crow, and contemporaneous discrimination—had brought about deep-seated structural distortions in the life of the Negro American," most perniciously a "matriarchal structure which, because it is too out of line with the rest of the American society, seriously retards the progress of the group as a whole, and imposes a crushing burden on the Negro male and, in consequence, on a great many Negro women as well."[97] In order to break the "tangle of pathology" characteristic of black poverty, social policy and activism should aim at "strengthening" conventional family structure by "restoring" men to their normative place as the family's chief wage earner and head of household, and rebuilding their subjective sense of manhood.

King first responded to the leaked Moynihan Report with enthusiasm, perhaps unsurprisingly given Frazier's broader influence on his thought and his own long-standing ideas about families. "I am particularly concerned with the Negro family," King remarked in the report's wake, citing both its "alarming conclusion that the Negro family in the urban ghetto is crumbling and disintegrating" and its contention "that the progress in civil rights can be negated by the dissolving of family structure and therefore social justice and tranquility can be delayed for generations."[98] King's analysis, which declared the black family as "fragile, deprived and often psychopathic," focused especially on male joblessness and masculine authority, arguing that "the ultimate way to diminish our problems of crime, family disorganization, illegitimacy and so forth will have to be found through a government program to help the frustrated Negro male find his true masculinity by placing him on his own two economic feet."[99] In addition to the material harm of poverty and the cultural harm of "emasculation," King thought that black male unemployment corroded the sense of love and solidarity within families, fostered intimate violence, coercively pushed black women into an exploitative labor market instead of allowing them to concentrate on child rearing, and subjected blacks to the arbitrary and humiliating domination of welfare bureaucrats.[100]

At times, and especially early in his career, King's proposed solution to this problem appeared to be increasing black men's access to jobs that paid a "family wage," and the expansion of welfare programs traditionally organized in accordance with this ideal. The social ideal of the family wage, as Nancy Fraser writes, presumes that people are organized in heterosexual nuclear families with a male head-of-household who works a job earning enough to support the family while women work uncompensated domestic labor, and is commensurate with welfare policies that distribute social resources to support homemaking as well as the indigent, unemployed, disabled, and elderly.[101] In some of King's arguments, it appears that only the racial stratification of this arrangement is objectionable. A mark of racial injustice, he argued, was that the "average Negro woman"—unlike many white women—"has always had to work to help keep her family in food and clothes."[102] Elsewhere he decried, in the voice of aggrieved black manhood, "our fathers and our men not being able to be men, not being able to support their families." Black men needed to struggle for the "right for our wives and our mothers not to have to get up early in the morning, and run over to the white ladies' kitchen and clean and wash their clothes ... but to be able to stay at home and raise their children."[103] What this demonstrates is a connection between paid labor and masculinity that he did not see as essential to femininity. In fact, he implies that true femininity was connected to the performance of unpaid labor inside the home.

This view, however, relied upon a number of misguided sociological, ontological, and political claims. Operative in the background are the essentialist presuppositions that the natural and normative place of women is the "domestic" sphere of childrearing and housework, and that productive labor outside the home is the natural domain of men. Some of the most sustained (and understudied) evidence that King's conception of gender and family supports these views comes from an advice column he wrote for *Ebony* magazine in the late 1950s and two sermons he delivered on families, "The Crisis in the Modern Family" (1955) and "Secrets of Married Happiness" (1961).

By 1955 King was already decrying a crisis of "disintegration" in American family life, evidenced by escalating rates of divorce and patterns of juvenile delinquency he associated with "broken homes." The ideal family, in King's imagination, "should be an intimate group of people living together in an atmosphere of good will, where the joys and successes of one are the joys and successes of all, and where the problems and failures of one are the concern of all."[104] One of the keys for success in a marriage, King argues, is that family life is informed by an "understanding of the nature of man and the nature of a woman," as they "differ decidedly in taste, opinion and temperament." King's particular exposition of these "natures" is a textbook notion of masculinist gender stereotypes: "A man's world is largely one of action. He is never happy unless he can measure his success or failure in terms of conquest in the exterior world. On the other hand, despite all her success in the exterior world, a woman is never happy outside an emotional world. She is most at home in the world of love and maternity. Woman is subjective, realistic, concrete. Man is objective abstract and general."[105] This romantic, complementarity-based ideal of the family, King worried, was under threat from the residual social dislocations of World War II and the Korean War, shifts in political economy that required women to work outside of the home, the temptations of urbanization, and, crucially, a pernicious individualism. "Rugged individualism," he lamented, had "seeped into the family . . . so today every individual in the family asserts his or her rights with little regard for the thoughts of the family as a whole."[106]

This insistence on gender complementarity, and separation of "rights-talk" from the sphere of the family, serves as a useful backdrop for understanding the advice he parceled out to readers of *Ebony*. When responding to letters from women complaining about their husbands' "tyrannical" behavior, verbal humiliation, or alcoholism, King never counsels the involvement of law enforcement, likely reflecting his skepticism about intrafamily rights claims, as well as the undeveloped regime of domestic violence law and the prevalence of racist policing.[107] Instead, he invariably asks women to first ask whether they are doing anything that might "arouse" or "precipitate" such abusive behavior, and to pursue reconciliatory dialogue and pastoral counseling to rebuild the relationship and reform male deviance.[108] This deference to family integrity stems as much from his larger sense that "decay in the family is the first step toward the decay of the nation" as it does from his assertion that women (naturally) and children (God's will) find their greatest fulfillment in married households.[109]

We should reject nearly all of this. The family wage is the product of a historical conflict between capitalists and white male workers regarding access to (black and white) women's labor power. In her classic piece "The Unhappy Marriage of Marxism and Feminism," Heidi Hartmann argues that in the late nineteenth- and early twentieth-century disputes between capitalists and organized labor, it was evident that capitalists wanted women in the paid labor force and male workers wanted women at home, serving them. Most organized labor, instead of fighting for gendered equality in the workforce, fought for male gender privilege. The family wage was a resolution to the fight over women's labor power, where a non-wage-earning wife became part of the standard of living for a male wageworker. As men fought for and received a family wage, it meant women commanded lower wages and needed the family, complete with a male wage earner, to survive. By shutting women out of jobs and intensifying sexist occupational segregation, the wage differentials ensured that women's work—that is, female-dominated occupations—was undervalued, less paid, and less esteemed.

Where King defends a vision of economic justice based on a family wage, it falls short of gender justice. That ideal, especially when buttressed by the views on family and gender just described, leaves far too many women dependent upon men and marriage to avoid poverty, subjects them to forms of exploitation and arbitrary subjection in the home, contributes to sexist forms of income inequality and leisure time distribution, and denies women full participation and equal respect in a democratic society.[110] Worse yet, while King sees the family as the crucial space within which children are to develop a sense of justice and a capacity for love, it would appear that the acquisition of these virtues would be deformed and undermined by habits of sexism, androcentrism, and patriarchy.[111] An ideal of gender justice actually worth our assent would avoid installing new forms of dependency and domination, would disentangle gender identity from access to paid labor, government assistance, and childrearing and household duties, and would champion equal respect, dignity, and participation. Is there a King that does this work?

If we think with King against King on these questions, we can deploy other dimensions of his thought against these retrograde commitments. Crucially, by 1964 King himself begins to downplay family wage agitation in favor of a guaranteed annual income (GAI), a commitment that grows in importance toward the end of his life.[112] Having long insisted that poverty is a threat to human dignity, King came to believe that the best way to cut through the inefficiencies of welfare bureaucracy, blunt the force of labor discrimination, and avoid the negative consequences of automation would be to introduce a constitutional right of GAI to all citizens.[113] Most importantly, in perhaps King's most radical argument, he insists that the American economy had reached such a level of productivity and affluence that continuing to allow the labor market under advanced capitalism to dominate the rules by which a society distributes income was arbitrary, obscene, and unjust. Other interests in human dignity, civic equality, individual flourishing, and political participation should take precedence in an age of affluence, and it was thus incumbent upon the government (which created the possibilities for such affluence) to ensure that all citizens had a reasonable and nonhumiliating standard of living.[114] This move from wages based on market valuations and meager, stigmatized welfare support to income granted in recognition of one's dignity and capacities is central to left feminism and points toward a radical revaluation of the values that distribute wealth and income. "If the society changes its concepts by placing the responsibility on its system, not on the individual," King prophesied, "and guarantees secure employment or a minimum income, dignity will come within reach of all."[115]

In addition to these claims, King thought that a guaranteed annual income served a crucial role in preventing humiliation and arbitrary domination. A "stable," "certain," and constitutional entitlement would help avoid some of the stigmatization of more narrowly means-targeted programs and protect GAI recipients from the capricious whims and reactionary power of welfare administrations. In 1967–68, as King tried to organize for his ill-fated Poor People's Campaign, he sought out alliances with the National Welfare Rights Organization (NWRO), a prominent group made up largely of African American women that organized welfare recipients and their supporters to advocate for a family minimum, protect recipients from bureaucratic abuse, and inform eligible citizens of their entitlements.[116] Learning deeply from the struggle of the NWRO, King began to object to the "uncontrolled bureaucratic or political power" exercised by welfare officials, from arbitrary humiliation to politicians removing insurgent citizens from the welfare rolls to coerce acquiescence.[117]

Not only does this King show a deep concern with vulnerability to exploitation and humiliation by state officials commensurate with left feminism, but he also champions the development of welfare and tenants unions as a significant moment in the history of democracy. Invoking the work these unions were doing in the late 1960s to organize public housing residents and welfare recipients, King argues that they are responsible for securing not only new rights but "new methods of participation in decision-making." He claims for them significance akin to that of labor unions, and demands that similar federal protections for collective bargaining be implemented so as to secure welfare recipients from "reprisals and intimidation."[118] Indeed, his conception of the alliance that would bring about genuine social democracy in the United States prominently featured these groups.[119]

Although not articulated in an explicitly feminist register, King's celebration of this form of political agency points quietly to a growing appreciation of women's activism, and also gives further evidence that King's views on representation and charismatic leadership were more variegated than is usually claimed. It is precisely in the context of discussions about organizing the poor that King excoriated a group of journalists for focusing incessantly on "prominent personalities," militant rhetoric, and spectacle, while ignoring "very constructive but quiet programs of progress."[120] Moving from King's view of SCLC to his conception of the broader movement may clear much more egalitarian terrain for participatory parity across gender.

What still looms ominously over this discussion, however, is King's ontology of gender and his normative view of the family. Are there similarly redemptive countercurrents in King's thought? King undoubtedly is much weaker on this front, but there are glimmers of hope for a feminist reconstruction. Although King advances indefensible conceptions of femininity, he also forcefully rejects those extreme reactionary ideas that women's overriding end is childbearing, that a husband exercises rights of dominion over other members of the household, that marriage should subsume the individuality of women, and that men should not participate in childcare.[121] These moves, however, are gestural, occasional, and woefully inadequate, not part of a systematic and comprehensive vision. They point, nevertheless, to glaring contradictions within King's understandings of gender identity and ideal family structure, and show the way toward the rejection of the gendered division of labor, within the family and without, as well as a jettisoning of the ideology of complementarity, which a fully persuasive reconstruction would have to pursue.

In our contemporary moment, where King's iconography holds a peculiar place in debates about the means and ends of black activism, we hope that this effort of thinking with King against King helps clarify what is at stake within his complex legacy. In this approach, we take some measure of inspiration from the work of Martin's wife, Coretta Scott King. Self-consciously laying claims to her slain husband's legacy, she devoted a great deal of her postassassination activism to the pursuit of guaranteed basic minimum income and guaranteed employment, and organizing for the NWRO.[122] Despite her sense of philosophical continuity with her husband, however, she saw fit to break institutionally and politically from SCLC over the "disrespect" with which she was treated by the Baptist preachers who "thought that women should stay in the shadows."[123] Like Scott King, we recognize that Martin Luther King's views on gender norms, his ideal of the family, and his support of the family wage suffer from severe problems. Our hope is to have shown that many of his other commitments can be reconstructed to criticize those views and generate more emancipatory visions of society. It is crucial to subject King's gender ideology to unmasking critique, as we have tried to do, but it would be tragic to lose track of other elements of his thought, including his important deflation of Black Power and black protest masculinity, his defense of civil disobedience as an inclusive mode of politics, and his radical positions on economic justice. In a world where productivity grows increasingly unmoored from income, equality, and employment, and where conventional gender norms are undergoing profound changes, it seems especially right to turn to this epochal figure, and linger over his insights and his failures.

NOTES

1. Septima Clark, *Ready from Within: Septima Clark and the Civil Rights Movement*, ed. Cynthia Stokes Brown (Tremont, NJ: Africa World Press, 1990), 77. This does not mean that all ministers were equally abhorrent. Clark's interviews and recollection evince great esteem for King, but she is utterly disdainful of Ralph Abernathy, at one point describing him as "just a spoiled little boy" who needed to "grow up and be a real man" (Clark quoted in David J. Garrow, *Bearing the Cross: Martin Luther King, Jr. and the Southern Christian Leadership Conference* [New York: Vintage, 1988], 366).
2. Clark, *Ready from Within*, 77–78.
3. Clark, 79. See also, for example, Clark's account of political differences with Ella Baker on the question of sexism in the movement: "Ella Baker sees things and gets very angry about them, and I see things and I want to work on them, but without the hostility. I see the same things that she saw, but I'm not going to be hostile. I'm not going to get mad with a man because he said I shouldn't be on the. . . . I just sit up there and listen to what he has to say, and then when I get a chance I let him know that I have made a contribution and that I can make a contribution." Oral History Interview with Septima Poinsette Clark, July 25, 1976, Interview G-0016, Southern Oral History Program Collection no. 4007, Southern Historical Collection, Wilson Library, University of North Carolina at Chapel Hill, published by Documenting the American South, May 16, 2017, http://docsouth.unc.edu/sohp/G-0016/G-0016.html.
4. bell hooks, *Ain't I a Woman: Black Women and Feminism* (New York: Routledge, 2015), 177; also see 94–95.
5. bell hooks, *We Real Cool: Black Men and Masculinity* (New York: Routledge, 2004), 10.
6. bell hooks, *Killing Rage: Ending Racism* (New York: Routledge, 1995), 263–72.
7. bell hooks, "The Beloved Community: A Conversation with bell hooks," *Appalachian Heritage* 40, no. 4 (Fall 2012): 76–86.
8. George Yancy and bell hooks, "bell hooks: Buddhism, the Beats and Loving Blackness," *New York Times: The Stone* (December 10, 2015), https://opinionator.blogs.nytimes.com/2015/12/10/bell-hooks-buddhism-the-beats-and-loving-blackness/?_r=0.
9. Thomas McCarthy, *Race, Empire, and the Idea of Human Development* (New York: Cambridge University Press, 2009), 36.
10. Susan Moller Okin, *Women in Western Political Thought* (Princeton, NJ: Princeton University Press, 1979), 4.
11. Charles Payne, a leading historian of this "view from the trenches," aptly characterizes these historiographical and critical accounts of the civil rights struggle as shifting the analytical focus: instead of focusing on national political elites and events, they look at local conflict and community organizing; in place of unified accounts of black politics and identity, these newer accounts tend to emphasize fragmentation and difference; and they look back from the short period of intense contention in 1954–68 to a longer tradition of activism and struggle within black

communities. Charles Payne, "Debating the Civil Rights Movement: The View from the Trenches," in *Debating the Civil Rights Movement, 1945–1968*, 2nd ed., ed. Steven F. Lawson and Charles Payne (Oxford: Rowman and Littlefield, 2006), 125–26.
12. Barbara Ransby, *Ella Baker and the Black Freedom Movement: A Radical Democratic Vision* (Chapel Hill: University of North Carolina Press, 2003).
13. For Ransby, one way of describing this conflict is as a tension between the "missionary" tradition, which she associates with Baker and those women who have historically organized in more decentralized and democratic forms within the church, and the "messianic" or "ministerial" tradition, which she associates with King and other male ministers.
14. Oral History Interview with Ella Jo Baker, September 4, 1974, Interview G-0007, Southern Oral History Program Collection no. 4007, Southern Historical Collection, Wilson Library, University of North Carolina at Chapel Hill, published by Documenting the American South, May 16, 2017, http://docsouth.unc.edu/sohp/G-0007/menu.html (51 for Ella Baker interview with Walker).
15. Ransby, *Ella Baker*, 175–76.
16. Martin Luther King, Jr., "Recommendations to the Dexter Avenue Baptist Church for the Fiscal Year 1954–1955 (September 5, 1954)," in *The Papers of Martin Luther King, Jr.* (hereafter cited as *Papers*), ed. Clayborne Carson (Berkeley: University of California Press, 1994), 2:287.
17. For the classic statement on "the hermeneutics of suspicion," see Paul Ricouer, *Freud and Philosophy: An Essay on Interpretation* (New Haven, CT: Yale University Press, 1970). For a compelling, contemporary reconstruction, see Brian Leiter, "The Hermeneutics of Suspicion: Recovering Marx, Nietzsche, and Freud," in *The Future for Philosophy*, ed. Brian Leiter (New York: Oxford University Press, 2006), 74–106.
18. Erica Edwards, *Charisma and the Fictions of Black Leadership* (Minneapolis: University of Minnesota Press, 2012), 16, 13.
19. Edwards, 19.
20. Baker, quoted in Ransby, *Ella Baker*, 188.
21. In this sense Baker's conception of democracy is closer to that of someone like John Dewey rather than those who restrict the definition of democracy to decision-making procedures and political institutions. For Dewey, democracy refers to a broader cultural milieu that involves social inquiry, habits of citizenship, conceptions of the common good, and the cultivation of individuality. See, for example, John Dewey, *The Public and Its Problems*, ed. Melvin Rogers (Athens: Ohio State Press, 2016).
22. Baker, quoted in Ransby, *Ella Baker*, 369.
23. For an important attempt to restate Baker's scattered speeches and interviews, and accounts of her organizing presented in the idioms of democratic political theory, see Andrew Sabl, *Ruling Passions: Political Offices and Democratic Ethics* (Princeton, NJ: Princeton University Press, 2002), 280–88.
24. Ransby, *Ella Baker*, 191.
25. "On King's personal donations to SNCC and CORE, see Garrow, *Bearing the Cross*, 368. This is beyond the scope of this paper, but the existing civil rights literature on leadership, power, hierarchy, and representation seems to suffer from

two conceptual deficiencies. First, while the charismatic mode has been subjected, rightly, to trenchant critique on questions of marginalization, a similarly sophisticated level of analysis has not yet emerged to understand the forms of power, hierarchy, and influence that flourish in self-described "leaderless" or "leader-full" organizations in black communities. The touchstone for this sort of analysis remains Jo Freeman, "The Tyranny of Structurelessness," *Berkeley Journal of Sociology* 17 (1972–1973): 151–65. Second, this literature in African American studies has largely ignored the recent renaissance in the study of representation in political theory, which, in taking a suprainstitutional and constructivist turn, offers other important terms of description and forms of evaluation for King's practice of leadership in a Jim Crow racial order. See, for example, Jane Mansbridge, "Rethinking Representation," *American Political Science Review* 97, no. 4 (2003): 515–28; Nadia Urbinati and Mark Warren, "The Concept of Representation in Contemporary Democratic Theory," *Annual Review of Political Science* 11 (2008): 387–412; Michael Saward, *The Representative Claim* (New York: Oxford University Press, 2010); and Lisa Disch, "The Constructivist Turn in Democratic Representation: A Normative Dead-End?," *Constellations* 22, no. 4 (2015): 487–99.

26. Seyla Benhabib, *The Reluctant Modernism of Hannah Arendt*, 2nd ed. (Lanham, MD: Rowan and Littlefield, 2003), 198.
27. Seyla Benhabib, "Feminist Theory and Hannah Arendt's Concept of Public Space," *History of the Human Sciences* 6, no. 2 (May 1993): 97–114.
28. Peter J. Ling, "Gender and Generation: Manhood at the Southern Christian Leadership Conference," in *Gender and the Civil Rights Movement*, ed. Peter J. Ling and Sharon Monteith (New York: Routledge, 1999), 108.
29. Martin Luther King, Jr., *Stride Toward Freedom: The Montgomery Story* (Boston: Beacon, 2010), 48, 85, emphasis added.
30. Wendy Brown, *Manhood and Politics: A Feminist Reading in Political Theory* (Lanham, MD: Rowman and Littlefield, 1988), 4.
31. Frederick Douglass, "The Do-Nothing Policy (9 / 12 / 1856)," in *Frederick Douglass: Selected Speeches and Writings*, ed. Philip Foner (Chicago: Lawrence Hill, 1999), 343, emphasis added.
32. Frederick Douglass, *The Life and Times of Frederick Douglass* (Hartford, CT: Park, 1883), 177.
33. Frederick Douglass, "Is It Right and Wise to Kill a Kidnapper?," in Foner, *Frederick Douglass*, 279.
34. Robert F. Williams, quoted in Timothy Tyson, introduction to Robert F. Williams, *Negroes with Guns* (Detroit: Wayne State University Press, 1998), xxv.
35. Malcolm X, "With Mrs. Fannie Lou Hamer," in *Malcolm X Speaks: Selected Speeches and Statements*, ed. George Breitman (New York: Grove, 1965), 107.
36. For a similar account, see Jacquelyn Dowd Hall, "The Mind That Burns in Each Body: Women, Rape, and Racial Violence," in *Powers of Desire*, ed. Ann Snitow, Christine Stansell, and Sharon Tompson (New York: Monthly Review Press, 1983), 335.
37. Partha Chatterjee, *The Nation and Its Fragments: Colonial and Postcolonial Histories* (Princeton, NJ: Princeton University Press, 1993), chap. 7.

38. Ling, "Gender and Generation," 112.
39. 2Pac, 2Pacalypse Now, Interscope ntEastWest Records America, 1991. More recent echoes of this sentiment can be found in T. I., "Switchin' Lanes," *U.S. or Else: Letter to the System*, Grand Hustle / RocNation, 2016; and Pusha T, "Sunshine," *King Push—Darkest Before the Dawn*: The Prelude, GOOD Music / Def Jam, 2015.
40. Lance Hill, *The Deacons for Defense: Armed Resistance and the Civil Rights Movement* (Chapel Hill: University of North Carolina Press, 2004), 27. It should be noted that while Coretta Scott King participated in many marches, SCLC studiously avoided situations where she was likely to be assaulted. One can only imagine how King's critics would have used such images to challenge his "manhood."
41. Richard Bak, *Joe Louis: The Great Black Hope* (Dallas: Da Capo, 1998); William Van Deburg, *Hoodlums: Black Villains and Social Bandits in American Life* (Chicago: University of Chicago Press, 2004); Cecil Brown, *Stagolee Shot Billy* (Cambridge, MA: Harvard University Press, 2004).
42. Saba Mahmood, *The Politics of Piety: The Islamic Revival and the Feminist Subject*, 2nd ed. (Princeton, NJ: Princeton University Press, 2011), 9.
43. Linda Zerilli, *Feminism and the Abyss of Freedom* (Chicago: University of Chicago Press, 2005), 60.
44. Martin Luther King, Jr., *Why We Can't Wait* (Boston: Beacon, 2011), 32.
45. Malcolm X, "Message to the Grassroots," in *Malcolm X Speaks*, 12.
46. King, *Why We Can't Wait*, 36–37. See also Martin Luther King, Jr., *Where Do We Go from Here: Chaos or Community?* (Boston: Beacon, 2010), 19.
47. For the classic statement on how the inversion of values can weaken the certainty of associations between valuations and social kinds or groups, see Friedrich Nietzsche, *On the Genealogy of Morality*, trans. Maudemarie Clark and Alan Swensen (Indianapolis: Hackett, 1998).
48. King, *Why We Can't Wait*, 31.
49. King, 147.
50. King, *Where Do We Go from Here*, 66.
51. Martin Luther King, Jr., *Strength to Love* (Minneapolis: Fortress, 2010), 124.
52. Martin Luther King, "A Testament of Hope" (1968), in *A Testament of Hope*, ed. James Washington (New York: HarperCollins, 1991), 322–23.
53. Martin Luther King, Jr., "Nonviolence: The Only Road to Freedom," in *A Testament of Hope*, 57.
54. King, *Why We Can't Wait*, 129–30.
55. King, 36–37.
56. Malcolm X, "The Ballot or the Bullet, Delivered at King Solomon Baptist Church (April 12, 1964)," available at *Say It Plain, Say It Loud: A Century of Great African American Speeches*, http://americanradioworks.publicradio.org/features/blackspeech/mx.html.
57. Erica Chenoweth and Maria J. Stephan, *Why Civil Resistance Works: The Strategic Logic of Nonviolent Conflict* (New York: Columbia University Press, 2011), 35.
58. Chenoweth and Stephan, 35.

59. Timothy Garton Ash, "A Century of Civil Resistance: Some Lessons and Questions," in *Civil Resistance and Power Politics*, ed. Adam Roberts and Timothy Garton Ash (New York: Oxford University Press, 2009), 379.
60. King, *Why We Can't Wait*, 117–18.
61. King, *Stride Toward Freedom*, 54.
62. Robin D. G. Kelley, *Race Rebels: Culture, Politics, and the Black Working Class* (New York: Simon and Schuster, 1996), 8.
63. Edward Soja, *Seeking Spatial Justice* (Minneapolis: University of Minnesota Press, 2010).
64. Kelley, *Race Rebels*, 68. Gendered spatial occupational segregation was an important factor, but so were traditional gender relations, specifically traditional gender hierarchy. Even among working-class households with access to a car, men would be more likely to keep the car during the day and drop women off, either at work or at a nearby bus stop.
65. Kelly, 67–68.
66. Kelly, 67–68.
67. Danielle L. McGuire, *At the Dark End of the Street: Black Women, Rape, and Resistance: A New History of the Civil Rights Movement from Rosa Parks to Black Power* (New York: Vintage, 2010), 59.
68. McGuire, 59–60.
69. McGuire, 59–60. These were risks they faced simply getting to and from work, to say nothing of the workplace sexual harassment they faced in white homes.
70. McGuire, 13.
71. McGuire, 39.
72. Ranbsy, *Ella Baker*, 142.
73. McGuire, *Dark End of the Street*, 39.
74. Brooks Barnes, "From Footnote to Fame in Civil Rights History," *New York Times*, November 25, 2009.
75. King, *Stride Toward Freedom*, 30.
76. King, 31.
77. King, 31.
78. Mary Fair Burks, "Trailblazers: Women in the Montgomery Bus Boycott," in *Women in the Civil Rights Movement: Trailblazers and Torchbearers*, ed. Vicki L. Crawford, Jacqueline Anne Rouse, and Barbara Woods (Bloomington: Indiana University Press, 1990), 71–72.
79. Kelley, *Race Rebels*, 8.
80. McGuire, *Dark End of the Street*, 62.
81. King, *Stride Toward Freedom*, 31–32.
82. King, 60.
83. Jo Anne Gibson Robinson, *The Montgomery Bus Boycott and the Women Who Started It: The Memoir of Jo Anne Gibson Robinson*, ed. David J. Garrow (Knoxville: University of Tennessee Press, 1987), 53.
84. King, *Stride Toward Freedom*, 43.
85. Robinson, *Montgomery Bus Boycott*, 59.

86. King, *Stride Toward Freedom*, 37.
87. Robinson, *Montgomery Bus Boycott*, 54. For sustained interrogations of the question of racial disloyalty, see Randall Kennedy, *Sellout: The Politics of Racial Betrayal* (New York: Vintage, 2009); and Brando Simeo Starkey, *In Defense of Uncle Tom: Why Blacks Must Police Racial Loyalty* (New York: Cambridge University Press, 2015).
88. King, *Stride Toward Freedom*, 64.
89. Tommie Shelby and Brandon M. Terry, eds., *To Shape a New World: Essays on the Political Philosophy of Martin Luther King, Jr.* (Cambridge, MA: Harvard University Press, 2018).
90. King, *Where Do We Go from Here*, 91–92.
91. King, 119.
92. Tommie Shelby, "Prisons of the Forgotten: Ghettos and Economic Injustice," in *To Shape a New World: Essays on the Political Philosophy of Martin Luther King Jr.*, ed. Tommie Shelby and Brandon M. Terry (Cambridge MA: Harvard University Press, 2018).
93. Howard Brick, *Age of Contradiction: American Thought and Culture in the 1960s* (Ithaca, NY: Cornell University Press, 2000).
94. See, for example, the volume by Detroit-based Marxist intellectual and labor leader James Boggs, *The American Revolution: Pages from a Negro Worker's Notebook* (New York: Monthly Review, 1963), esp. chap. 4.
95. Indeed, by 1963, John F. Kennedy's advocacy for a civil rights bill included a sustained argument about how "unemployment falls with special cruelty on minority groups." Kennedy proposed a series of interventions meant specifically to reduce black unemployment and the negative externalities thought to accompany it ("delinquency, vandalism, gang warfare, disease, slums and the high cost of public welfare and crime"). See John F. Kennedy, "President Kennedy's Report to Congress Outlining a Civil Rights Bill," in *The Civil Rights Reader: Basic Documents of the Civil Rights Movement; Excerpts from Speeches and Reports*, ed. Leon Friedman (New York: Walker, 1967), 252–56.
96. Roy Wilkins, "At American Association of Advertising Agencies," in *Talking It Over with Roy Wilkins: Selected Speeches and Writings*, ed. Helen Soloman and Aminda Wilkins (Norwalk, CT: M & B, 1977), 23–24.
97. Daniel Patrick Moynihan, *The Negro Family: The Case for National Action* (Washington, DC: U.S. Government Printing Office, 1965), www.dol.gov/oasam/programs/history/webid-meynihan.htm.
98. Martin Luther King, quoted in Daniel Patrick Moynihan, *Family and Nation* (New York: Harcourt Brace Jovanovich, 1987), 39.
99. King, *Where Do We Go from Here*, 114, 133.
100. King, 113–14, 123, 210–12.
101. Nancy Fraser, *Fortunes of Feminism: From State-Managed Capitalism to Neoliberal Crisis* (Brooklyn: Verso, 2013), 111–12.
102. King, *Why We Can't Wait*, 16.
103. Thomas F. Jackson, *From Civil Rights to Human Rights: Martin Luther King, Jr., and the Struggle for Economic Justice* (Philadelphia: University of Pennsylvania Press, 2013), 346.

104. Martin Luther King, Jr., "The Crisis in the Modern Family, Sermon at Dexter Avenue Baptist Church (May 8, 1955)," in *Papers*, 6:211–12.
105. Martin Luther King, Jr., "What Then Are Some of the Secrets of Happy Marriage," in *Papers*, 6:432.
106. King, "Crisis," 211.
107. For the classic account of theoretical issues raised by domestic violence against women of color, see Kimberle Crenshaw, "Mapping the Margins: Intersectionality, Identity Politics, and Violence Against Women of Color," *Stanford Law Review* 43, no. 6 (July 1991): 1241–99.
108. King's "Advice for Living" columns are collected in *Papers*, vol. 2.
109. King, "Crisis," 210–12.
110. For more on these as appropriate standards for gender justice, see Nancy Fraser, *Fortunes of Feminism*, 116–21.
111. For a similar argument, see Susan Moller Okin, *Justice, Gender, and the Family* (New York: Basic, 1989).
112. Jackson, *Civil Rights to Human Rights*, 205.
113. King, *Where Do We Go from Here*, 172.
114. King, 171–75.
115. King, 92.
116. Jackson, *Civil Rights to Human Rights*, 345. The NWRO also advocated for men's employment so that men could "assume normal roles as breadwinners and heads of families.
117. King, *Where Do We Go from Here*, 210–11.
118. King, 210–12.
119. King, 150.
120. Jackson, *Civil Rights to Human Rights*, 300.
121. King, "Crisis" and "Advice for Living."
122. David P. Stein, " 'This Nation Has Never Honestly Dealt with the Question of a Peacetime Economy': Coretta Scott King and the Struggle for a Nonviolent Economy in the 1970s," *Souls* 18, no. 1 (January–March 2016): 80–105.
123. Coretta Scott King with Barbara Reynolds, *My Life, My Love, My Legacy* (New York: Holt, 2017), 189.

PART VI
Philosophy and Friendship

21

Fragments of an Intellectual Autobiography

SEYLA BENHABIB

Retirement is not a point in one's life when one stops teaching, researching, and thinking. In our days of flexible life-plans, it is yet another phase when one is as busy as ever. At such moments, though, it is irresistible to look back upon the beginnings and unfolding of one's intellectual career.

In the last few years, much to my own surprise, Hegel has been on my mind again. I completed my PhD in 1977 at Yale with a dissertation called "Natural Right and Hegel: An Essay in Modern Political Philosophy." I had been reading Leo Strauss's *Natural Right and History* and was intent on developing arguments against his critique of historicism and of Max Weber. Jürgen Habermas and his work were already present in my intellectual universe. In 1971, when I was still an undergraduate philosophy major at Brandeis University, I had participated in a study group on *Knowledge and Human Interests*, led by James Miller. Having attended a yearlong course taught by Alasdair MacIntyre at Brandeis during 1970–71 on Hegel's *Phenomenology of Spirit*, I had no background in critical theory as such. I had declared myself a Marxist during the 1968 student movement, which had also reached us in Istanbul, Turkey, and I had read Herbert Marcuse's *One Dimensional Man* with great interest and admiration. When I was awarded a scholarship to study at Brandeis in 1970, it took me some time to realize that Marcuse was no longer there but had left for the sunny shores of San Diego.

At Yale as a PhD student in Philosophy, I learned a great deal about Aristotle, Kant, Dewey, and of course Heidegger from a great teacher—Karsten Harries. As far as Hegel was concerned, I had to leave Connecticut Hall in which the Philosophy Department was housed, and hike across the campus to the now-torn-down political science building on Prospect Street, to take a course taught by

Zbigniew Pelczynski—a Polish-born Hegel scholar who was affiliated with Pembroke College at Cambridge University. Norman Birnbaum was visiting the Yale Sociology Department in those years, and he provided my first formal introduction to the critical theory of the Frankfurt School when we read Alexander Mitscherlich's *Society Without the Father: A Contribution to Social Psychology* and Horkheimer and Adorno's *Dialectic of Enlightenment* in his seminar.

I was still preoccupied with Hegel's critique and *Aufhebung* (negation and sublation) of modern natural right theories. In what ways was Hegel's theory of Abstract Right also a critique of the social contract theories of Hobbes, Locke, Rousseau, and Kant? Why did Hegel's theory of the modern state begin with such a radical abstraction called "personality," exercising free will and embodying itself in objects? What was Hegel's defense of property, including the sale of labor power as a commodity, based upon? What was the relationship between the consent-theory of political legitimacy and "civil society," *die bürgerliche Gesellschaft*? I was resisting the Marxist reduction of the freedom of the person to the liberties of commodity owners in the market place, since I believed—and still do—that any free social and political order must begin where Hegel began, i.e., with respect for individuals as persons, capable of responsible agency, accountability, a sense of the good and the right. Hence Hegel's proposition: "Be a person and respect others as persons" (PhR, §36).[1]

As is well known, Isaiah Berlin distinguished thinkers into foxes and hedgehogs. The fox knows many things and realizes that we are part of a larger scheme than we can fully understand. We ourselves live in this whole and are wise only in the measure in which we make our peace with it.[2] The hedgehog, by contrast, will not make peace with the world. She is not reconciled. She seeks to know one big thing and strives without ceasing to give reality a unifying shape. We each have the fox and the hedgehog within us. When I think over the trajectory of my intellectual career from my dissertation to my first book, *Critique, Norm and Utopia* (1986), and more than thirty years later to *Exile, Statelessness and Migration: Playing Chess with History from Hannah Arendt to Isaiah Berlin* (2018), I have been acting more like the hedgehog and asking over and over again this one question: *What is the political legacy of modernity?* What social, economic, cultural, and religious presuppositions does the phrase "Be a person, and respect others as persons" entail? How can we reconcile respect for individual personhood with a "community of needs and solidarity," as I have called this utopian moment in *Critique, Norm and Utopia*?[3] And when do societies reach such a point that relations of mutual respect among human beings are no longer possible?

These Hegelian beginnings came back to me because of two recent dialogues I was engaged in: one in response to Jürgen Habermas's *Auch eine Geschichte der*

Philosophie, and the other in a festschrift for Axel Honneth called "Hegel's Concept of the Person and International Human Rights."[4] In the latter article, I argued that Hegel makes the recognition of the individual as a person, that is, an individual entitled to the exercise of certain rights, the cornerstone of the legitimacy of the modern state as a *Rechtsstaat*. Yet he limits such rights to the private enjoyment by subjects of certain economic, moral, and personal liberties in a well-organized state, thereby blunting any critical potential that may result from the exercise of their citizenship rights. Still, the right of personality has a subversive and expansionist dynamic that even Hegel's well-known pronouncements on the inequality of the sexes and the backwardness of African peoples could not contain. Precisely because freedom must realize itself as Idea, i.e., as concept and actuality, Hegel cannot limit its manifestations to the institutions of the early nineteenth-century Prussian state alone (PhR, §4). The search to embed freedom as Idea will be expressed through multivarious social and historical struggles and at different moments in time. The Left-Hegelians were right that freedom transcends its own historical boundaries.

There is a surprising convergence between the Hegelian concept of the person and Hannah Arendt's concept of "the right to have rights," in that the recognition of the individual as a right-bearing person is also a foundation of the *constitutio libertatis* in Arendt's thought. The international human rights regime came into existence after 1948 precisely because the European nation-state system and the institutional regime of sovereignty of the interwar years had collapsed. Hegel's *Philosophy of Right* and Hannah Arendt's *The Origins of Totalitarianism* can be read as bookmarks of this epoch of European history, and more generally, they can serve as markers of the weaknesses and paradoxes of the modern nation-state.[5] Surely, Arendt's concept of freedom transcends the boundaries of the *Sittlichkeit* set by Hegel, but this elective affinity between their thought has been often overlooked.

In attempting to retrieve from Hegel's discussion of abstract right a concept of the person such as may help illuminate some of the aporias of the present, I am not denying the significance of Hegel's theory of ethical life, *Sittlichkeit*. Unlike the early communitarian interpretations of Hegel in the past decades, however, I believe that Hegel is a theorist of a differentiated modern state structure in which individual rights and modern law, morality and ethical life complement rather than exclude one another. Axel Honneth is correct that Hegel's concern is with "Das Recht der Freiheit" (Freedom's Right). Today the right of freedom has a transnational and cosmopolitan dimension in our world, which Hegel could not have anticipated and maybe even would not have endorsed but whose emancipatory as well as challenging potentials we must reflect upon.

In my response to Habermas's magnum opus, *Auch eine Geschichte der Philosophie*, "Habermas's new *Phenomenology of Spirit*: Two Centuries After Hegel," I recalled that Hegel was the first philosopher who saw in modernity a normative dilemma.[6] He viewed this "new epoch" not as a fall from the grace of antiquity as he had thought in his early writings, but as a fateful moment in human history whose losses and gains had to be reckoned with. Once the principles of subjectivity, reflexivity, and the rights of the person had emerged in historical consciousness as Idea, all attempts to escape them would carry the marks of this genesis nonetheless. There is no going back to pure tradition or a mythic past. This is Hegel's central claim.

In *Auch eine Geschichte der Philosophie* Habermas defends human dignity and rationality in an age where we are stranded between the shores of naturalism and religion. This quest(ion) takes the form of a reconstruction of the history of "occidental reason" from the Axial Age onward via the Church Fathers, Luther, the scientific revolution, and the French and Scottish Enlightenments, to Kant and the German Idealists, and on to Feuerbach, Marx, Kierkegaard, and Peirce. Habermas's claim is that the encounter between faith and knowledge in the West is a learning process (*Lernprozess*) that can be "rationally reconstructed." Philosophy sublates the truths of faith through an intellectual operation that Rainer Forst calls "redemptive translation," or *rettende Übersetzung*.[7] Forst has in mind Habermas's striking formulation that "Religion . . . remains a thorn in the consciousness of a secular society" (*Sie bleibt "ein Stachel im Bewusstsein einer säkularen Gesellschaft"*).[8] The present constellation between philosophy, science, and religion must be understood in the light of a "rational reconstruction of one's own form of thought" as it emerges at the end of this process.[9]

It is impossible to do justice to the subtleties of Habermas's narrative; its scope and erudition will escape the boundaries of any single commentary. Yet for me the nagging question remains: How might a fallibilistic consciousness of universal human rights, open to learning from other cultural traditions in a world-society, be constructed in terms of the genealogy of occidental reason alone? Why can a narrative of the encounter between faith and knowledge in the Western tradition provide a response to the puzzles confronting humanity in our times—such as the clash between global capitalism, on the one hand, and family life and religious communities, on the other; the spread of robotics and the loss of jobs and meaningful work; the appropriation of genetic technologies by the superrich (e.g., Elon Musk) who one day may very well *have* the capacity to manufacture their offspring? How can such universal questions be satisfied through such a geographically and culturally circumscribed narrative?

One key to unlocking the answer is to compare Habermas's book with Hegel's *Phenomenology of Spirit* (1807). Hegel also presented modernity's achievements and the place of his own philosophy in the modern age as a grand narrative that he reconstructed as a learning process. Yet, both Hegel's phenomenological method and Habermas's reconstructive one are vulnerable to repeat the fallacies of a certain kind of historicism. They treat developmental processes as if they were carried out by a hypostatized collective subject in a homogeneous time that is viewed as a "container" of development. But such processes are more properly assessed by looking through the prisms of individual and collective consciousnesses as they experience a discontinuous and contradictory temporality. Habermas tries to reconcile the perspective of the participants and that of the observer, but nonetheless his reconstructive history of Western reason has the consequence of ignoring and bracketing the voices of participants, the voices of those others, left out of the learning process as it inexorably carries on. Large swaths of human societies are then condemned to the "antechamber" of history, and it is forgotten that we inhabit the same and yet different historical temporalities, that the history of global modernity can no longer be told through the encounter of reason and faith in the West alone.

In Dipesh Chakrabarty's words, we cannot posit historical time as a measure of the cultural distance (at least in institutional development) that is assumed to exist between the West and the non-West.[10] We can no longer say "first in Europe, then elsewhere."[11] Historicism becomes "somebody's way of saying 'not yet' to somebody else."[12]

A major strength of Chakrabarty's analysis is to show how elites in non-Western countries as well used this antechamber view of history to say to their own people, "not-yet: you are not ready for universal suffrage, for women's rights, for democracy." The conversation of global modernity then is not between the holistic categories of Occident and the Orient but between those committed to human equality and dignity everywhere and others who use historicist logic to condemn the masses of the people to wait in the antechamber of history. Certainly, nothing can be further from Habermas's intention than disrespecting and ignoring the needs of those who are still waiting to enjoy freedom and dignity and a sense of human worth. His whole life's work has been committed to defending these ideals. My argument is only that the logic of rational reconstruction at work in *Auch eine Geschichte der Philosophie* gives rise to such deceptive assumptions.

Why then bother with Hegel? Why search for the "concrete universal" at all? Why not accept the critique of postcolonial thinkers and view the claims of modernity as a hoax perpetrated by the colonizers upon the colonized? Why not side with the Foucauldian power theorists who regard every claim to normativity as a ruse for a power grab? The fraught relation between power and normativity in different intellectual traditions was at the heart of a dispute among feminist friends in the early 1990s.

In one of the most bitter encounters of my intellectual life, those of us who were dear friends and colleagues—Judith Butler, Nancy Fraser, Drucilla Cornell, and myself—initially collaborated on a much-celebrated volume called *Feminism as Critique: Essays on the Politics of Gender in Late Capitalist Societies*.[13] A version of this volume was then translated into German in 1993 as *Der Streit um Differenz* and back into English as *Feminist Contentions* in 1996.[14] This was a historically difficult moment in the encounter between German and French intellectual traditions. A struggle that had been brewing over postmodernism burst into public view in those years. German critical theorists criticized the nonchalant appropriation of Nietzsche and Heidegger by French thinkers who refused to consider the history and political implications of these latters' philosophies. Habermas claimed that neoconservative German thinkers were reappropriating French thought to relieve themselves of the burden of guilt and responsibility toward the German past and the Holocaust. French thought had become a *fröhliche Wissenschaft* (a gay science), to use Nietzsche's brilliant terminology.

Why or how we, as feminist thinkers, had to be drawn into the quagmires of this antagonism and why I became the defender of the Enlightenment and the scourge of postmodernist frivolities against Judith Butler, who had once been my student and a friend, is a question that still puzzles me. Much more than Foucault, it was Jean-François Lyotard's essay "La condition postmoderne" that drew me into this polemic. I denounced the themes of the "death of the subject," "the death of History," the "death of Grand Narratives" in Lyotard's short and influential essay.[15]

In retrospect, Lyotard was right with regard to at least two of his three funeral orations: the myth of History with a capital H and the myth of Grand Narratives are gone. I still believe that the thesis of "the Death of the Subject" is wrongheaded. What is meant by this grandiose phrase is that a rationalistic construction of the subject as the disembodied agent of thought, as conceptualized by Descartes and Kant, is to be rejected. Who believes in that anyway? I am here leaving aside the question of whether this is a fair characterization of Descartes and Kant. Yet how do we reconstruct a conception of agency capable of principled action, a subjectivity that is deep in dreams as well as emotions, an autonomy that is situated and embedded? My early disagreement with Butler was that her performative theory could not help us in this task. It did not convince me that "there was no Doer behind the deed" (Nietzsche) and that the self was the sum total of her performances.

In the ensuing years, our positions have come much closer as the concept of "iterations," inspired by Derrida's work, has made its way into mine, and a vision of "grievable life," of an embodied subject of pain whose human right to a life "worth living" must be fully defended, has become central to Butler's work.[16] In this debate, Drucilla Cornell had her own version of Hegelian feminism, inspired by Derrida and psychoanalysis, which she developed into a brilliant theory of womanhood as the "imaginary domain" in subsequent works.[17] Nancy Fraser, whose illuminating early article on Foucault called "Empirical Insights and Normative Confusions" alerted us all to the pitfalls of Foucauldian thinking, was originally closer to Butler in that she defended a nonfoundationalist, pragmatist theory, and argued that feminism without foundations could well function as an emancipatory theory.[18]

There is a great deal more to be recounted about this moment in my intellectual trajectory but undoubtedly these conversations also reflected the shifting ground under our feet in an increasingly globalizing world. In 1989 the Berlin Wall had come down, and along with it, half a century of the division of Europe through competing world-historical ideologies and narratives of the two World Wars came to an end as well. The late Helmut Dubiel, a sociologist colleague whom I had met while I was a Humboldt student at the Max Planck Institute in Starnberg in the late 1980s, wrote an article in *Praxis International* (the predecessor of *Constellations*) about the fall of the Berlin Wall and the subsequent unification of Germany, "Beyond Mourning and Melancholy on the Left."[19] Mourning, according to Freud, is the healthy and necessary reaction of pain and sadness felt upon the loss of a loved one; melancholia sets in when the process of mourning is interrupted and is less than wholesome, leading to the memory of the love object haunting the present. Dubiel asked what it was about East Germany or even Eastern Europe that acted as an object of melancholia for the Western Left? What made one nostalgic about "really existing socialisms," with their police states, their permanently dysfunctional economies, and their charade of peoples' congresses?

Dubiel's questions were not new. Already Friedrich Pollock, a member of the Frankfurt School and a close ally of Max Horkheimer's, had visited the Soviet Union in 1927 and had come back with dire observations about what would later be termed "state capitalism" by the Frankfurt School. Far from being a workers' paradise, the command economy of the Soviet Union, whatever excuses you want to make for it, was not an abolition of capitalism but one in which capital was concentrated in state-run monopolies and cartels that were profiting their own party-elite, their *Nomenklatura*. The critique of really existing socialisms, along with the critique of bourgeois capitalist democracies as they were transitioning to fascism and the painful parallels between them, is at the heart of the critical theory of the Frankfurt School. It is thus no accident that a new generation of student activists would rediscover the writings of the Frankfurt School, this time not during the heated moment of student uprisings that confronted Adorno, and led Habermas to speak of "left Fascism" in 1969. Those of us who returned to the texts of the Frankfurt School in the 1980s were seeking for a deeper analysis of fascism, democracy, and capitalism.

I spent the years from 1979 to 1986 in Germany, and even after accepting a position as assistant professor of philosophy at Boston University in 1981, I commuted to Germany for half the year. My daughter, Laura Schaefer, was born in Frankfurt in 1986, and it was not until 1991 that we finally gave up our family apartment in that city.

Those years were decisive for my intellectual journey and they would leave their mark on my work in the years to come: the Yugoslav Civil War broke out in 1991; the ethnic carnage in the midst of Europe not only shocked everyone deeply, but for those of us gathered around the journal *Praxis International*, the Yugoslav War was a real catastrophe. I had become coeditor in chief of *Praxis International* in 1987 with Sveta Stojanovich. The honorable legacy of this journal extended to the summer meetings in Korcula, attended by Ernst Bloch, Karl Korsch, Herbert Marcuse, and younger representatives of the antiauthoritarian praxis group, led by Mihailo Markovíc. The journal *Praxis* grew out of these efforts and was edited jointly by Richard Bernstein and Markovíc from 1981 to 1987.

To reprise the traumatic effect of the Yugoslav Civil War on *Praxis* is difficult. Some of us decided that it was no longer possible to continue under the banner of *Praxis International*, and after a tense editorial board meeting in Frankfurt in 1992, we founded the journal *Constellations*, of which Andrew Arato and I became coeditors for the next five years until Nancy Fraser came on as coeditor after I stepped down.

An unexpected consequence of the Yugoslav Civil War was to bring me face to face with the refugee, statelessness, and migration crisis in Europe. Many have wondered why in the last twenty years my scholarly work has been so dominated by questions of citizenship, migrants, refugees, and statelessness. Well, one very brief answer is: "Spend ten years in Europe, and not just in Germany, as a Turkish Jew, and you will understand why." Living through those post-1989 years when, on the one hand, the process of European unification was accelerating and, on the other, Europe's cosmopolitan promise was being deeply compromised through the securitization of its borders, the treatment of refugees from the Yugoslav Civil War, and unending negotiations about Turkey's entry into the European Union, I was pushed to reflect on the constitutive violence inherent in moments of formation and foundation of new political unities. Who were the others? What were their rights?

Hannah Arendt proved my guide. I am indebted to Arendt for much more than the enduring legacy of the phrase "the right to have rights." Arendt, together with Hegel and Habermas, had been a star in my intellectual firmament since 1972 when I first read *The Origins of Totalitarianism* and then *The Human Condition*. In 1996, after nearly twenty years of contending with Arendt, I finally wrote my monograph, *The Reluctant Modernism of Hannah Arendt* (1996). This book was preceded by an essay, "Judgment and the Moral Foundations of Politics in Hannah Arendt's Thought," first delivered at a Hannah Arendt Colloquium at the New School for Social Research.[20]

In this essay I focused on Arendt's incomplete reflections on judgment, and in particular, her provocative claim that Kant's Third Critique was Kant's unwritten political philosophy. Arendt vividly reminded us of Kant's distinction between "determinative" and "reflective" judgments. I saw in Kant's doctrine of "reflective judgment" not only the kernel of Habermas's concept of communicative reason but also the key to mediating between the universal and the particular, between normative principles and concrete action, and between the generalized and the concrete other. Arendt's doctrine of judgment provided me with the key to the "concrete universal." This term does not signify an identity of the universal and the particular; quite to the contrary, it refers to a process of judging, acting, dialoging, and negotiating that is always also full of tension. It is an iterative process through which those who have never been given a voice or those whose voice has never been heard could now speak in the name of the universal itself. Here is Arendt:

> The power of judgment rests on a potential agreement with others, and the thinking process which is active in judging something is not, like the thought process of pure reasoning, a dialogue between me and myself, but finds itself always and primarily, even if I am quite alone in making up my mind, in an anticipated communication with others with whom I know I must finally come to an agreement.... And this *enlarged way of thinking*, which as judgment knows how to transcend its individual limitations, cannot function in strict solitude; it needs the presence of others "in whose place" it must think, whose perspective it must take into consideration and without whom it never has the opportunity to operate at all.[21]

It is hard to find a more beautiful invocation of the idea of a free public sphere and communicative reason. Already I hear many voices rising in objection: Are you serious that in the age of post-truth politics, in an age when facts have become fictions willfully perpetrated by the foes of democracy, are you serious that in such an age we can still believe in "an anticipated communication with others, in whose place we can think"? Aren't these the dangerous illusions of the Enlightenment that will only disarm progressives? Wasn't Lyotard right when he said, "to speak is to fight"?

As we face the global rise of autocracies tinged with neofascist elements of nativism, xenophobia, racism, sexism, the hatred of LGBTQ2+ people, and—not to forget—the burning rage against nature exercised by perpetrating deforestation and the killing of more and more species, don't Arendt's words sound more like a prayer for civility, an evocation of a more genteel society when an ideal of an "enlarged way of thinking" could have normative pull? Is it really relevant for our times? Why console ourselves with the illusions of constitutional democracies that have grown so weak the world over?

We have to listen to these voices and understand the justified anger and even hopelessness lying behind them. But they are wrong, and Hannah Arendt and Jürgen Habermas are right. To speak is not to fight; if we lose sight of the constitutive dimension of every speech-act, that even when we cannot reach agreement there is an imperative to communicate, if we forget that, then indeed force and violence will take the place of argument and reasoning. Isn't this precisely what autocrats threaten us with: from the vigilantes armed by Jair Bolsonaro in Brazil to Erdogan in Turkey to the ICE (Immigration and Customs Enforcement) and CBP (Customs Border Patrol) officers who threaten, intimidate, push, and shove refugees and asylum seekers across the U.S. border to Mexico? Doesn't the threat of violence always lurk in the shadows? The threat to stifle dissent and the free public sphere, the threat to step on the neck of the weak, and the vulnerable, as George Floyd's tragic death showed us, isn't this threat always there?

Yet this juxtaposition of violence and communication may be too stark; we need to look at the ambivalent cases. Just as there are modes of resistance, civil disobedience, and mass nonviolent protest movements, so too there are institutional constraints of discipline, imprisonment, and punishment through which more subtle forms of violence are exercised. So far Michel Foucault and Jim Scott are right. "Seeing like a state" is a constitutive dimension of liberal constitutional democratic politics.[22] Yet the power that emerges "from acting in concert" need not be weak or meek; nor is strategic thinking incompatible with the exercise of collective power—as long as, that is, one does not confuse philosophy with strategy and critical theory with a manual for subversion. The task of philosophy remains what it has been since Socrates: to reveal that reason and the search for justice and freedom are intrinsically linked. The task of political thinking that we exercise as citizens, residents, and others is judging how to mediate principle and action.

I am not at all sure that in the days ahead we will not be called upon to exercise civil disobedience and other forms of resistance to the global forces of autocratic subversion. We are not out of the danger yet and we will not be for some time to come since the causes that have weakened American democracy and have brought the oldest civilian democracy in the world to the brink of fascism are still at work.

I am so grateful to all of you—my friends, my students, my colleagues, and my family—who have thought together with me and who have taught me over the years. The life of the mind is a lonely vocation and good scholarship demands that one make no shortcuts. It is the friendship of a community of interlocutors that nourishes one; dialogue and dialectic have always been interlaced. I have witnessed the power of dialogue and dialectic as well as of friendship and the honor of being part of a community of inquiry through the essays collected in this volume.

NOTES

This text is a revised version of the lecture that I delivered at the end of the online conference dedicated to my work, "In Search of the Concrete Universal," which took place on December 11, 2020. It had been our intention to hold the conference at Yale University, but the start of the COVID-19 pandemic in the spring of 2020 made that impossible.

1. G. W. F. Hegel, *Hegel's Philosophy of Right*, trans with notes by T. M. Knox (1952; Oxford: Clarendon, 1971). Abbreviated in the text as PhR. All references in the text are to the Knox edition.
2. Isaiah Berlin, "The Hedgehog and the Fox: An Essay on Tolstoy's View of History," https://uniteyouthdublin.files.wordpress.com/2015/01/the_hedgehog_and_the_fox-copy.pdf.
3. Seyla Benhabib, *Critique, Norm and Utopia: On the Normative Foundations of Critical Theory* (New York: Columbia University Press, 1986).
4. Seyla Benhabib, "Habermas's New Phenomenology of Spirit: Two Centuries After Hegel," *Constellations* 28, no. 1 (March 2021): 33–44; Seyla Benhabib, "Hegel's Concept of the Person and International Human Rights," in *Debating Critical Theory: Engagements with Axel Honneth*, ed. Julia Christ, Kristina Leopold, Daniel Loick, and Titus Stahl (Lanham, MD: Rowman and Littlefield, 2021), 187–205.

5. Hannah Arendt, *The Origins of Totalitarianism*, 2nd ed. (New York: Meridian, 1958).
6. Benhabib, "Habermas's New Phenomenology of Spirit," 33–44.
7. Rainer Forst, "The Autonomy of Autonomy: On Jürgen *Habermas's Auch eine Geschichte der Philosophie*," *Constellations* 28, no. 1 (2021): 17–25.
8. Jürgen Habermas, *Auch eine Geschichte der Philosophie* (Frankfurt: Suhrkamp, 2019), 1:86.
9. Habermas, *Auch eine Geschichte der Philosophie*, 1:109.
10. Dipesh Chakrabarty, *Provincializing Europe: Postcolonial Thought and Historical Difference* (Princeton, NJ: Princeton University Press, 2000), 7.
11. Chakrabarty, 7.
12. Chakrabarty, 8.
13. Seyla Benhabib and Drucilla Cornell, eds., *Feminism as Critique: Essays on the Politics of Gender in Late-Capitalist Societies* (London: Polity; Minneapolis: University of Minnesota Press, 1987).
14. Seyla Benhabib, with Judith Butler, Nancy Fraser, Drucilla Cornell, *Der Streit um Differenz* (Frankfurt: Fischer, 1993); English translation (revised and expanded) as *Feminist Contentions: A Philosophical Exchange* (New York: Routledge, Kegan and Paul, 1996).
15. Seyla Benhabib, "Epistemologies of Postmodernism," in *Situating the Self: Gender, Community and Post-Modernism in Contemporary Ethics* (London: Polity; New York: Routledge, Kegan, Paul, 1992).
16. Judith Butler, *Precarious Life: The Powers of Mourning and Violence* (London: Verso, 2006); Judith Butler, *Frames of War: When Is Life Grievable?* (London: Verso, 2009).
17. Drucilla Cornell, *The Imaginary Domain: Abortion, Pornography, and Sexual Harassment* (New York: Routledge, 1995). See also my in memoriam for Drucilla Cornell in view of her untimely death in December 2022, "Re-Reading Drucilla Cornell: In Memoriam For a Dear Friend," *Philosophy and Global Affairs* 3, no. 2 (September 2023).
18. See Nancy Fraser, "False Antitheses," in *Feminist Contentions*, 59–75, and Fraser's collection of essays in *Justice Interruptus: Critical Reflections on the "Postsocialist" Condition* (New York: Routledge, 1997).
19. Helmut Dubiel, "Beyond Mourning and Melancholy on the Left," *Praxis International* 11, nos. 3 and 4 (1991): 241–49.
20. Seyla Benhabib, "Judgment and the Moral Foundations of Politics in Hannah Arendt's Thought," *Political Theory* 16, no. 1 (February 1988): 29–51; Seyla Benhabib, *The Reluctant Modernism of Hannah Arendt* (Thousand Oaks, CA: Sage, 1996). Reprinted with a new introduction and afterword by Rowman and Littlefield in 2003.
21. Hannah Arendt, "Crisis in Culture: Its Social and Its Political Significance," in *Between Past and Future: Eight Exercises in Political Thought* (1954; London: Penguin, 1968), 217.
22. James Scott, *Seeing Like a State: How Certain Schemes to Improve the Human Condition Have Failed* (New Haven, CT: Yale University Press, 1999).

22

Swimming

CAROLIN EMCKE

When I was asked to give the keynote at the conference, I was not just slightly worried. I was in full panic mode. It didn't help when Seyla said that nobody would expect a philosophical lecture, and that I could speak about her personally and be funny! Brilliant. Telling a German "don't worry, just be funny" is a losing campaign, and so I shall save the funny stories for another time. In all seriousness, there are few people to whom I owe so much, and I hope you will forgive me for searching for my own way to thank her. I want to weave together the personal and the political by taking on three themes like musical motifs, working them through, and thereby celebrating Seyla Benhabib.

LEARNING

In the Talmud, there is a passage that describes the duties of a father to his son. A father is obliged to "circumcise him, to redeem him (if he is the first-born son who must be redeemed by a payment to a priest), to teach him Torah, to marry him to a woman and to teach him a trade; and some say, also to teach him how to swim."[1]

At first, it seems surprising that instruction in the art of swimming should be part of this list of obligations. Why should training how to swim belong to the grave duties of a father? Certainly, if you live by the sea, your life may depend on it. But what else is it that a father relates to his son while swimming that is so important to be mentioned next to teaching Torah? Interestingly, it is not only the Talmud that considers learning how to swim so crucial. For Plato, too, swimming was indispensable knowledge. In *The Laws*, it says that ignorant are those "who do not know how to swim or read."[2]

What is key in learning how to swim is that you need another. You do not learn it by yourself. It requires a relationship and a process of showing, explaining, correcting, and supporting; it requires trying, failing, trying again; and finally, it requires a moment of letting go, of not-showing-anymore. It requires trust: trust to be held. Trust not to be let go before one is really able to swim all by oneself. And trust, ultimately, to swim alone, to swim into the open. Maybe that is how learning how to swim can be seen as related to learning how to read.

Maybe learning how to swim is also about the movement itself: to dive into a fluid material and not drown, to coordinate one's arms and legs and yet keep one's head above the water to be able to breathe, to move through the water easily. All that seems helpful for diving into other materials, too. You may only once learn how to read, but that does not restrict you to read in one language. Rather, with each new language you repeat this lesson of slowly deciphering letters and meaning until they make sense to you.

When honoring Seyla Benhabib, when thanking her for all she has given and offered, it is not just about her writing, her books, her inspiring contributions to critical theory, but it is about her teaching me how to swim.

Her lessons were demanding, and she would never make false promises or dishonest compliments, which is why I knew I could trust her. I also knew she would let me go eventually, maybe a little bit too early, maybe a little bit before I thought I could do it. But what is most remarkable is that I knew I would not have to swim into the same direction as her. I knew she wanted to teach me how to swim; she did not want to dictate where to or what for. There was no attempt to form the next generation of critical theorists as mimetic reproductions of oneself. One could be different and equal at the same time. It never occurred to Seyla that I could be somehow less relevant to her or to the tradition of critical theory just because I did not choose an academic career.

Seyla taught us how to read and reread, how to understand the architecture of a theory, to see the structures but also its weak points. She showed me how to take criticism, how to reflect on one's own writing and thinking, not just to repeat and defend it like so many others in this profession, but to *improve* it. Seyla Benhabib does not just pretend to listen to counterarguments; she does not just perform interest in critique because that is the social code at philosophical conferences. She is actually serious about critique: look at her texts. Her work is a permanent engagement with critique.

I did not just learn how to swim from Seyla, I learned—and maybe that is what the passage in the Talmud is all about—*I learned what it means to learn*. But there was also something even more existential in her approach, something prior to the process of learning, there was something about the relationship as the basis of learning. With Seyla, I never had the impression I had to "deserve" attention, I never felt I had to "gain" trust. There was no precondition of thinking together, no precondition of being seen or heard, no precondition of being included. This applies not only in that realm of thinking but also in her family. Before learning anything about cosmopolitanism and "contested universals," before being instructed in the art of swimming, I learned that *it didn't have to be* a firstborn son and a father, but that it could be *people like us* in that lesson. In retrospect, it may seem normal. But such assurances were not a given at the time, certainly not for me.

As with every tradition, to be truthful to it, it cannot be passed on without disruptions, without transformations, without dissidence. To learn with and from Seyla Benhabib—after studying in Frankfurt with Jürgen Habermas, Alfred Schmidt, Karl-Otto Apel, Iring Fetscher, Axel Honneth—contained this sense of reiteration, a different line of thinking or writing, one that was not blind to who one was (female, queer, multilingual), one that would be able to think with and for marginalized and excluded histories, experiences, bodies, desires, and voices.

In *Situating the Self* Benhabib writes: "The moral self is not a moral geometrician, but an embodied, finite, suffering and emotive being."[3] It is interesting that she uses "suffering" here, a term that does not appear often in the texts of Benhabib, but that nevertheless is, as I would argue, an underlying theme in her work. The suffering of an individual or a community is permanently there, in the background, like a haunting *basso continuo* that accompanies and colors the entire composition.

This is my second theme: suffering.

SUFFERING

In his memoir *Colored People*, Henry Louis Gates, Jr., writes, "Of course, the colored world was not so much a neighborhood as a condition of existence. And though our own world was seemingly self-contained, it impinged upon the white world ... in almost every direction."[4] The condition of existence of the migrant, of the refugee, as well as the fragility of exile and statelessness and how they impinge upon the world of the nation-state, is at the core of Benhabib's thinking and writing.

This is evident in the later works *The Rights of Others*, "Cosmopolitanism Without Illusions," and *Exile, Statelessness and Migration,* which address the questions of equality and difference, human rights beyond the nation-state, and the concept of hospitality.[5] All are written with the figure of the migrant or refugee as the central subject for whose condition *any* social theory, *any* universalist philosophy, *any* legal or political framework must find answers. The figure of the migrant is almost like a contrast agent, injected into the body of a society (or the body of a theory) and it will highlight what is wrong with it. That is how Hannah Arendt framed the question of "the right to have rights" in *The Origins of Totalitarianism.*

The figure of the migrant, their loneliness, their suffering, and the exclusion of the refugee were always central to Benhabib; even in her very early work, even when it was not the topic at hand, she evokes the migrant. There is a small but remarkable example of this in *Critique, Norm, and Utopia*. In the reworked German edition of 1992, in a passage in which she offers an epistemic-pragmatic reformulation of truth and rationality according to the principles of discourse ethics and the plausibility of communicative ethics as an adequate description of postconventional moral reflection, she writes: "To justify means to prove that we, when you and I discuss a certain moral judgment ('It was wrong not to help the refugees and let them die on the high sea'), could in principle come to a rational agreement."[6] It is no coincidence that in her definition of justification she comes up with the image of the refugee who dies on the high sea. This is what is the litmus test for discourse ethics: it has to justify that we could come to a rational agreement on the judgment that one must help a refugee.

I recommend reading the wider context of this passage: it is a rather dry and abstract argument here, no images, no examples, no stories in the scenery. Just Karl-Otto Apel, Jürgen Habermas, and Albrecht Wellmer on the presuppositions of ultimate justification in discourse ethics. So, the image of the refugee at sea is all the more shocking because, within this landscape of philosophical theory, it stands out, it is strange, an isolated sequence. What Benhabib does here is double the situation of the refugee itself in and with her text, and thereby resists the refugee's condition of existence, their exclusion.

The rightlessness of refugees, the negation and exclusion of refugees, is always both a condition of and a result of their invisibility. Benhabib makes sure that the refugee is visible, that prior to all moral judgments or legal reflections on the rights and status, the refugee is represented.

We have witnessed in the last decade the collective effort of the global north not only to mutilate the right of asylum and reduce it to a humanitarian gesture—something that can be *given* like an act of paternalistic generosity, but not a right that can be appealed to—but we have also witnessed the creation of an archipelago of camps and detention centers, often extraterritorialized, displaced, disconnected, out of sight, on the other side of a wall, or on the other side of the Mediterranean Sea.

What remains locally are the camps and detention centers at the periphery of our cities, or sometimes, as in Paris, the informal settlements of tents and shacks on abandoned rail tracks, underneath the highways, or on the hot water pipes underground. In rural areas it may be even in old army barracks. What remains always are guarded and fenced zones, policed by private security forces, which control and restrict access and movement.

Sometimes, nowadays, the fences around the camps are built not to prevent refugees from escaping, but to prevent fascists from attacking them. I remember one fence at a refugee accommodation in Eisenhüttenstadt in east Germany where the barbed wire was on the *outside* of the fence, not the inside, in order to protect against a racist violent mob.

We have seen during the Trump presidency not only intentional separation of children from their parents, the neglect of their most basic needs, the dehumanizing, cruel treatment by the Immigration and Customs Enforcement (ICE), but also the Kafkaesque dysfunctionality of a system that simulates legality but does not even care enough to have procedures to collect and archive the necessary information about which detained child belongs to which separated mother.

Adorno wrote, "Es gehört zum Mechanismus der Herrschaft, die Erkenntnis des Leidens, das sie produziert, zu verbieten" (It belongs to the mechanism of domination to prevent the knowledge of the suffering it produces).[7] That is the mechanism we need to deconstruct.

Seyla Benhabib's writing does not need autobiographical narration, and she rarely refers to her own family's history of migration. There might even be a certain discomfort about speaking with a subjective voice and saying "I" in a text. But she does not have to. Her sensitivity not just to the legal status of the migrant or the refugee but to their condition of existence, their pain and confusion, their displacement but also their dignity, their courage, their incredible achievements is striking. Her empathy with the suffering of refugees is like a watermark shining through every text.

For theorists socialized and trained in the Frankfurt School and discourse ethics, though, the suffering of refugees, of victims of violence, of traumatized survivors constitutes a philosophical problem. It is a problem that had an enormous impact on my life: What if a person is not able to present their point of view rationally? What if a person's account does not qualify as "intelligible"? What if discourse ethics' presuppositions for discourse-participants that deserve justifications are too exclusive or discriminatory? What if the experience of rape, of torture, of displacement has traumatized a person to the extent that she cannot or does not want to offer an account, cannot or does not want to express an interest, what if her account sounds absurd, disrupted, contradictory, circular, what if a person is speechless? Does that disqualify or exclude her as unreliable, irrelevant, irrational?

In *Critique, Norm and Utopia* Benhabib addresses this in taking up an argument by Thomas Scanlon. She writes, "Scanlon suggests that a being can be assigned morality if the idea of justification towards such a being makes sense."[8] Scanlon offers three necessary conditions for this: first, the being has a good that can be represented by a trustee; second, this good is similar to ours; and third, such a being marks a "point of view" in the world. Benhabib writes, "The capacity to feel pain fulfills all of these conditions. So even though it may not be possible to consider children, mentally ill or animals as discourse partners, we can, with a little imagination, know how they suffer."[9] Therefore, the *capacity to feel pain* is at the core, even if this pain cannot be translated into narration, even if the experience of pain or the sense of shame silences a person. Benhabib argues that we only need "a little imagination" to understand how they suffer.

This, I think, is what we both took upon ourselves as the horizon for our writing: to address the pain and its political, structural, social causes and to include those whose humanity or dignity is denied. We only work with different instruments or genres. In my case, it is the task of witnessing: to give words to those who don't trust them anymore, to develop a hermeneutic of understanding victims of violence, to translate their broken, shattered accounts into a narrative that would be heard and understood, potentially even when speaking at the Hague or a truth commission. In your case, Seyla, it is the task of creating an impressive political and legal theory that focuses on the dialectical relation of rights and identities, one that knows when to change tone or gear when necessary. To quote from *The Rights of Others*: "We need to decriminalize the worldwide movement of peoples, and treat each person, whatever his or her political citizenship status, in accordance with the dignity of the moral personhood—this implies acknowledging that crossing borders and seeking entry into different polities is not a criminal act but an expression of human freedom."[10] No matter how sensitive Benhabib is to the suffering of the refugee or the migrant, no matter how passionately she argues for their rights, she never mistakes an experience for an identity, she never essentializes suffering or injury, she never misconstrues the refugee or the migrant as merely a victim. She always sees the refugee and the migrant as an agent, someone who desires freedom and equality, someone who dares, someone who moves, someone who swims into the open.

In "On Earth We Were Briefly Gorgeous," Ocean Vuong writes: "The thing is, I don't want my sadness to be othered from me just as I don't want my happiness to be othered. They are both mine."[11] I think Seyla Benhabib would agree.

In her acceptance speech of the Dr. Leopold Lucas Preis in 2012 with the title "Equality and Difference," Benhabib quotes a passage from the German-Jewish writer Moritz Goldstein, who described the Jewish condition in Europe as that of the "eternal half-ones [*die Ewig-Halben*], the excluded and the homeless." For Benhabib, not only does the eternal half-one belong to the culture that tries to exclude him and fails, but "far from being a cultural aberration and a political misfit, this interpretation of the 'eternal half-one' projects a new identity that acknowledges this marginality to be a central source of creativity."[12] Therefore, it is the hybrid figures, those with multiple languages or perspectives, those who transgress borders or conventions, those who are in between, or—if I may say so—queer, that form the center of a democratic society. Benhabib writes, "All cultures are hybrid, it is only nationalist ideology that tries to freeze the living and self-contradictory flow that constitute cultures, by hierarchically organizing them into an 'official' center, leaving an unofficial, homeless marginality to the so-called 'others.'"[13] Therefore, to deprovincialize the postnational condition, the deessentialization of identities must be understood as constitutive of our ability to act together.

This brings me to my last theme: sharing.

SHARING

Seyla's ability to share is one of her most striking features. What surprised me most when I came to study with her was how generous she is. Generous with her time, with her affection, her care, and her incredible hospitality. Seyla immediately creates a space and an atmosphere where one feels at home. She creates with absolute certainty a sense of belonging. Since the first moment as a guest at your house, you have acted as if I belonged there, as if there was an invisible thread that had connected us all along. My suspicion was that it had to do with my Latin American background, or my speaking Spanish. From the beginning you did not just share your time and food with me, but also your friends, your concert tickets, and your car. Considering how unbelievably hierarchical and status-driven Harvard University was, this was simply mind-blowing. And I have kept some of your friends as my own lifelong friends.

It seemed absolutely natural to you that you would offer to me what was most precious to yourself. I remember, I think it was during my first month in Boston, that you just trusted me to take Laura by train to New York. You also shared your worries, but you could speak without the old shame women are brought up with and trained in, and you would not reproduce that tradition of silencing our bodies, our desires, our illnesses or fears. You were and are a feminist who is ready and able to share stories of our lives, our siblings, our parents, our lovers, our partners. What you write about democratic iterations in "Cosmopolitanism Without Illusions" is true of your personal life, too: everyone can always change or expand the agenda of our conversation.

I remember how we once went to the Opera in Berlin, the Komische Oper, for a production of Mozart's *The Abduction from the Seraglio* by Calixto Bieito. We had anticipated a certain wildness, but it was just *way* over the top, an orgiastic, obscene, crazy, silly production. I remember how I sat there next to you and wondered why on Earth I had chosen this opera, but you just laughed and laughed and when it was finally over we ended up discussing it late into the night.

Sharing for you is not just sharing what you personally own or think, but it is also going out into the public sphere, speaking and acting in concert. Sharing means, essentially, to believe that there is a world, a reality that we have in common. Something that has come under attack during the reign of a president who does not just undermine the difference between right and wrong, between facts and lies, but who questions reality as a common reference point.[14] Your sense of sharing is so powerful and moving because it is part of your engagement with the res publica. Your dedication to sharing is also a democratic, political virtue. You believe in public goods, in using political theory—and literature, and law, and music, and storytelling—to dismantle and deconstruct hierarchies, mechanisms of exclusion and stigmatization, and to reiterate, reinvent, re-create a more inclusive, more just, more heterogenous democratic society.

Now begins a new phase in your life, a transition, a passage. You will continue to think and write, but still, something will be different, it will be unknown waters. So, let me just say, if you need someone to swim with you, I will be at your side.

NOTES

This contribution was delivered as the keynote address at "In Search of the Concrete Universal: A Conference in Honor of Seyla Benhabib," December 11, 2020.

1. Kiddushin, 29a, 10.
2. Plato, *The Laws*, book 3.

3. Seyla Benhabib, *Situating the Self: Gender, Community and Postmodernism in Contemporary Ethics* (New York: Routledge, 1992), 50.
4. Henry Louis Gates, Jr., *Colored People: A Memoir* (New York: Knopf, 1994), 5.
5. Seyla Benhabib, "Defending a Cosmopolitanism Without Illusions: Reply to My Critics," *Critical Review of International Social and Political Philosophy* 17, no. 6 (2014): 697–715.
6. Seyla Benhabib, *Kritik, Norm und Utopie: Die normativen Grundlagen der Kritischen Theorie* (Frankfurt: Fischer, 2017), 208, translation mine.
7. Theodor W. Adorno, *Minimal Moralia* (Frankfurt: Suhrkamp, 1991), 75.
8. Translation mine.
9. Benhabib, *Kritik, Norm und Utopie*, 213.
10. Seyla Benhabib, *The Rights of Others: Aliens, Residents and Citizens* (Cambridge: Cambridge University Press, 2004), 177.
11. Ocean Vuong, *On Earth We're Briefly Gorgeous* (London: Penguin, 2019), 181.
12. Seyla Benhabib, *Gleichheit und Differenz: Die Würde des Menschen und die Souveränitätsansprüche der Völker im Spiegel der politischen Moderne* (Tübingen: Mohr Siebeck, 2013), 43.
13. Benhabib, *Gleichheit und Differenz*, 42.
14. Referring to Donald Trump.

Contributors

UMUR BASDAS is Assistant Professor of Political Theory at Koç University in Istanbul.

SEYLA BENHABIB is the Eugene Meyer Professor of Political Science and Philosophy Emerita at Yale University, and Senior Research Fellow at Columbia Law School. She is also a Senior Fellow at the Columbia Center for Contemporary Critical Thought.

ANGÉLICA MARÍA BERNAL is Associate Professor of Political Science at the University of Massachusetts, Amherst.

SONALI CHAKRAVARTI is Professor of Government at Wesleyan University.

THE LATE DRUCILLA CORNELL was Emerita Professor of Political Science, Women's and Gender Studies, and Comparative Literature at Rutgers University.

CARMEN LEA DEGE is Assistant Professor in the Department of Philosophical Ethics and Political Philosophy at Radboud University.

GAYE İLHAN DEMİRYOL is Assistant Professor of Political Theory at Bogaziçi University in Istanbul.

STEFAN EICH is Assistant Professor of Government at Georgetown University.

CAROLIN EMCKE is a writer based in Berlin.

RAINER FORST is Professor of Political Theory and Philosophy and Director of the Research Center Normative Orders at the Johann Wolfgang Goethe University in Frankfurt.

AYTEN GÜNDOĞDU is Associate Professor of Political Science at Barnard College-Columbia University.

BERNARD E. HARCOURT is the Isidor and Seville Sulzbacher Professor of Law and Professor of Political Science at Columbia University and a chaired professor (*directeur d'études*) at the Ecole des Hautes Etudes en Sciences Sociales in Paris, as well as the founding director of the Columbia Center for Contemporary Critical Thought.

ANNA JURKEVICS is Assistant Professor of Political Science at the University of British Columbia.

CRISTINA LAFONT is the Harold H. and Virginia Anderson Professor of Philosophy at Northwestern University.

PAUL LINDEN-RETEK is Associate Professor of Law and Co-director of the Buffalo Human Rights Center at the University at Buffalo School of Law, The State University of New York.

MATTHEW LONGO is Assistant Professor of Political Science at Leiden University.

PATCHEN MARKELL is Associate Professor of Government at Cornell University.

THOMAS MCCARTHY is Professor Emeritus of Philosophy at Northwestern University.

CONTRIBUTORS

EDUARDO MENDIETA is Professor of Philosophy in the Department of Philosophy at Penn State University.

NISHIN NATHWANI is a PhD candidate in Political Science at Yale University and the Senior Adviser at Rainbow Railroad.

MAX PENSKY is Professor of Philosophy and Codirector of the Institute for Genocide and Mass Atrocity Prevention (I-GMAP) at Binghamton University, SUNY.

WILLIAM E. SCHEUERMAN is the James H. Rudy Professor of Political Science at Indiana University, Bloomington.

NICA SIEGEL is Visiting Assistant Professor in Law, Jurisprudence, and Social Thought at Amherst College.

BRANDON M. TERRY is the John L. Loeb Associate Professor of the Social Sciences at Harvard University.

SHATEMA THREADCRAFT is Associate Professor of Philosophy, Gender and Sexuality Studies, and Political Science at Vanderbilt University.

PETER J. VEROVŠEK is Senior Assistant Professor in History and Theory of European Integration at the University of Groningen.

CHRISTIAN VOLK is Professor of Political Theory in the Department of Social Science at the Humboldt-Universität zu Berlin.

Index

Abduction from the Seraglio, The (Mozart and Bietus), 424
absolutism: Habermas's distancing from, 61; for Hegel, 61; in *Situating the Self*, 53
abstraction, universalism and, 2
acting-against-one-another, power and, 171
acting-for-one-another: power and, 169–71; republicanism of dissent and, 184
acting-with-one-another: power and, 169–71; republicanism of dissent and, 174, 184, 186–87
Act of Killing, The (documentary), 8–9, 128–34, 136–41, 143–46; in Indonesian historical record, 129; reenactment in, 138; Stangneth and, 129; Suharto in, 132. *See also* Congo, Anwar; Eichmann, Adolf
Adorno, Theodor W., 69, 421; *The Authoritarian Personality*, 130–31, 136; critical theory for, 84; *Dialectic of Enlightenment*, 6, 54, 130–31; Habermas influenced by, 199; on mimesis, 139; reason for, 131; utopia for, 81–83
aesthetic judgments, 69, 75; beauty and, 72–73; disinterest of, 70, 72–73; intellectual interest in nature, 70, 73–74; moral interest in nature and, 70; *sensus communis* and, 71; universalism of, 70
African American political charisma: democracy and, 369–70; scaffolding in, 369
African National Congress, in South Africa, 332
AIM. *See* American Indian Movement
algorithms, 296
alternative modernities, 33

American Indian Movement (AIM), 313
Améry, Jean, 146
amor mundi, 52, 58
"Analytic of the Beautiful" (Kant), 70–71, 76
Anaya, James, 312
androcentrism, 387
Another Cosmopolitanism (Benhabib), 3–4, 14, 253n39; democratic iteration theory in, 249–50; ethical particularism and, 329; moral universalism and, 329; the other in, 328–33; transnational decolonization in, 329–31
Antaki, Mark, 222–23
Anthropocene epoch, 64
anthropocentric universalism, 67
Apel, Karl-Otto, 268, 419–20
Arendt, Hannah: *amor mundi* concept, 52, 58; anti-Marxism of, 7; Benhabib influenced by, 3, 7–9, 264, 371, 413–14; Benjamin as influence on, 103; civic citizenship for, 119; on communicative cosmopolitanism, 194–98, 203–4, 208; on community of memory, 225; on consensus, 170; cosmopolitanism and, 310; *The Crises of the Republic*, 109; criticism of treatment of Eichmann, 134; as critic of the state, 188n7; critiques of, 189n36; on deception/self-deception, 117; on democratic iteration theory, 219–21; doctrine of judgment, 3, 413–14; on domination, 175–78; *Eichmann in Jerusalem*, 278, 284–85; feminist political theory and, 100–3; Frankfurt School and, 1, 7; on freedom, 407; on genocide,

Arendt, Hannah (*continued*)
277–78, 283–84, 286; Genocide Convention (1948) and, 12; on global federalism, 196–97; Heidegger and, 106*n*10; Holocaust and, 134; *The Human Condition,* 97, 100, 170, 194–95; Jaspers and, 16; *Jewish Writings,* 196; on jurisgenerativity, 11–12; on justification, 38; *Kant Notebook,* 260; *Lectures on Kant's Political Philosophy,* 260; on Lessing, 125*n*28; *The Life of the Mind,* 101; "Lying and Politics," 109–10, 118; modernism of, 106*n*10; Montesquieu and, 181; on networked council systems, 197–98; *On Violence,* 170; on phenomenology, 342–43; *Philosophical Notebooks,* 260; on philosophical truth, 48*n*1; *polis* for, 195, 225; political existentialism of, 52; on political opinion, 48*n*1; on postnational sovereignty, 225; on post-truth, 114; public response to Pentagon Papers, 109–10, 120; on public sphere, 109; Republicanism and, 166–73; on republicanism of dissent, 166–67, 173–82, 185–87, 190*n*36; on right to have rights, 86, 88, 254–55, 260–64, 407; "rise of the social" for, 204; on sovereignty, 220; as theorist of action, 109; as thinker of the *polis,* 195; totalitarianism in works of, 195; on truth, 108–22; "Truth and Politics," 109, 114, 116, 123*nn*6–7, 125*n*43; *Vita Activa,* 170; on Western political thought, 101. *See also Eichmann in Jerusalem*; *Origins of Totalitarianism, The*
Aristophanes, 97
Aristotle, 97–98
Ash, Timothy Garton, 379
Atatürk, Mustafa Kemal, 203
authoritarianism, in political theory, 37
authoritarian personality, for Eichmann, 130–31
Authoritarian Personality, The (Adorno), 131, 136; conventionalism in, 130; lack of introspection in, 130; mimetic engagement and, 130

Baker, Ella, 368–71, 382, 395*n*3, 396*n*23
Basdas, Umur, 6
Baudelaire, Charles, 215
beauty: imperial interest in, 72; intellectual interest in, 72
becoming savage. *See ensauvagement*
Benhabib, Seyla: academic career of, 19; on *amor mundi,* 52, 58; Arendt as influence on, 3, 7–9, 264, 371, 413–14; on communicative cosmopolitanism, 194, 203–8; on concrete other, 141; on concrete universal, 2, 5; on cosmopolitanism, 86–87; "Cosmopolitanism Reconsidered," 86–87; critical rationality for, 4; on critical theory, 2, 15; *Critique and Praxis,* 92*n*6; *Democracy and Difference,* 9; democratic iteration theory, 4, 9–11, 45, 289–91, 316–17; on development theory, 25; *Dignity in Adversity,* 295; dignity in adversity for, 2; on discursive cosmopolitanism, 206–7, 209; *Exile, Statelessness, and Migration,* 21, 58, 214, 277; on feminist political theory, 97–104; "Fragments of an Intellectual Biography," 2; Frankfurt School and, 1, 3, 69; Habermas and, 3, 19–34, 51–52, 406–7; Hegel and, 2; on home, 59; on human rights, 86, 89; intellectual autobiography for, 405–15; intellectual journey of, 87–90; on international law, 89; juridical theory for, 87–88, 268–69; on juridification, 252*n*30; jurisgenerativity for, 4, 11–13; Kantianism for, 89–90, 408; on learning, 417–19; philosophical influences on, 89, 97; on practical discourse, 27–30; rational agency theory, 2; *The Reluctant Modernism of Hannah Arendt,* 97, 100–4, 413; *The Rights of Others,* 3–4, 10, 264–65, 269, 316, 321; on right to have rights, 264–65, 270; on selfhood, 52; on sharing, 423–24; on social criticism, 42; on sovereignty, 88–89, 227; on suffering, 419–23; universalism for, 23–26, 91, 268–69; on utopia, 81–92; Weimar Syndrome and, 22–24. *See also Another Cosmopolitanism*; *Critique, Norm, and Utopia*; *Situating the Self*
"Benhabib and Habermas on Discourse and Development" (McCarthy), 5
Benjamin, Walter, 102; Arendt influenced by, 103; on democratic iterations, 218; on Republicanism, 168; on utopia, 82–83
Berlin, Isaiah, 183, 406
Bernal, Angélica María, 13–14
Bernstein, J. M., 262
Between Facts and Norms (Habermas), 154, 243–44, 249, 300
Beyond the Pleasure Principle (Freud), 133
Bieito, Calixto, 424
Big Data: algorithms, 296; during Black Lives Matter movement, 294–95, 300–1; data logic, 302; data mining, 296; definition of, 295–97;

democratic iterations and, 294–95; as discipline, 297–98; discrimination as result of, 303*n*2; Foucault and, 297–98; inequality through, 303*n*2; jurisgenerativity and, 294–303; predictive analytics and, 296; profiling and, 296; in public sphere, 299–302; in statecraft, 302

Binder, Guyora, 232

Birnbaum, Norman, 406

birthright citizenship, 254–55; constitutional citizenship and, 270–71

Black Lives Matter movement (#BLM), Big Data and, 294–95, 300–1

Black Power movement: M. L. King's critique of, 371–75; Malcolm X and, 373–74; paradox of, 377

Black Protest masculinity: deflation and, 375–76; dignity and, 387; M. L. King critique of, 371–75; nonviolence and, 374–75; violence and, 372, 375

Black Skin, White Mask (Fanon), 353

#BLM. *See* Black Lives Matter movement

Bloch, Ernst: *Natural Law and Human Dignity*, 85; *The Principle of Hope*, 83; utopia for, 82–84

body schemas, 348, 363*n*86

Bogdandy, Armin von, 235*n*47

Boire, Gary, 353

Bolsonaro, Jair, 414

border deaths, as forced disappearances: under colonial law, 353; colonial partitions and, 344–47; definition of, 339; under dictatorships, 336; Fanon on, 337–38, 347–52; hyperlegality and, 355; under international criminal law, 340–41; under international human rights law, 340–41; International Organization of Migration and, 335; language for, 340; law as site of, 352–56; legal analysis of, 341–47; in Libya, 342; phenomenology and, 337, 341–47; politics of immobilization and, 344–47; as racialized form of violence, 336; racial schemas as condition of, 347–52; rights allocation and, 339–41; in Spain, 336–37, 345–46; in sub-Saharan Africa, 346; Tarajal massacre, 336–37, 345–46, 355; territorial sovereignty and, 336; theoretical approaches to, 335–38

Branco, Juan, 340

Brandom, Robert, 268

Brecht, Bertolt, 119

Brexit, 203

Brown, Wendy, 372

Burke, Edmund, 261

Burks, Mary Fair, 383–85

Bush, George W., 114

Butler, Judith, 89–90, 410–11

Byrd, B. Sharon, 272*n*10

Callamard, Agnes, 340

Canovan, Margaret, 225

Catch-22 (Heller), 118

CELDF. *See* Community Environmental Legal Defense Fund

certainty, loss of, 52–56, 63–64

Chakrabarty, Dipesh, 409

Chakravarti, Sonali, 8

Char, René, 119

Charter of Fundamental Rights (EU), 227–28

Chenoweth, Erica, 379

Chinese Exclusion Act, U.S. (1882), 350 Cicero, 168

citizenship: birthright, 254–55, 270–71; civic, 119; constitutional, 270–71; democratic legitimacy and, 158, 160–61; *jus sanguinis* and, 255; *jus soli* and, 254–55, 271

Citizenship School movement, 366

citizenship through parental citizenship. *See jus sanguinis*

civic activism, Republicanism and, 168

civic citizenship, 119

civil rights movement. *See* Black Lives Matter movement; Black Power movement; Black Protest masculinity

civitas, 89

Clapham, Andrew, 341–42

Clark, Septima, 366, 395*n*1, 395*n*3

Clemenceau, Georges, 116

climate crisis, 311; Paris Agreement, 317

Cohen, Bob, 19

Cohen, Jean, 235*n*47

Cohen, Joshua, 300

collective remembrance, communicative cosmopolitanism and, 205

Collins-Dexter, Brandi, 300–1

colonialism: Fanon on, 337, 346; in *The Wretched of the Earth*, 330, 344–45

colonial law, 353

colonial partitions, 344–47

Colored People (Gates), 419

Colvin, Claudette, 383
Commonwealth Immigrants Act, UK (1962), 350
communicative action theory, 90
communicative cosmopolitanism: Arendt on, 194–98, 203–4, 208; Benhabib on, 194, 203–8; collective remembrance and, 205; concrete other and, 203–8; democratic iterations and, 206; discursive cosmopolitanism and, 206–7, 209; economic incentives and, 193; environmental imperatives and, 193; ethical commitments in, 193; in European Union, 198; generalized other and, 203–8; global norms and, 203; Habermas on, 194, 198–203, 208; in *The Human Condition*, 194–95; identity and, 205; international law and, 203, 205; legitimacy and, 205; migration of law, 207; nation-states and, 193; nonstate actors and, 207; postnational constellation in, 194, 198–203; in postwar political theory, 193; in public sphere, 206; responsibility to protect doctrine, 203; social movements and, 207–9; sovereignty and, 193, 205; state actors and, 207; in transnational public sphere, 194; Westphalian sovereignty and, 193
communicative ethics, 4; *The Communicative Ethics Controversy*, 19; concrete other in, 77–79; universalism and, 23–24
Communicative Ethics Controversy, The, 19
communicative freedom, right to have rights and, 266, 268
communitarian cosmopolitanism, genocide and, 283
communitarian self, 53, 55
Community Environmental Legal Defense Fund (CELDF), 326n36
community of memory, 225
CONAIE. *See* Confederation of Indigenous Nationalities of Ecuador
concept of the world, 175
concrete other: Benhabib on, 141; communicative cosmopolitanism and, 203–8; in communicative ethics, 77–79; in *Critique, Norm, and Utopia*, 4–5; in *Eichmann in Jerusalem*, 141–46; Kant on, 68–69, 75–78; nature as, 75–77
concrete universal: Benhabib on, 2, 5; democratic legitimacy and, 151; justification and, 38; mediation of, 2
Confederation of Indigenous Nationalities of Ecuador (CONAIE), 315–16

Congo, Anwar, 8, 132–34, 142; mimetic experience for, 143; Oppenheimer and, 143–44
Connor, Bull, 380
consensus, 170
Conservatism, 167
constitutional citizenship, 270–71
constitutional democracy, universalism of, 32
constitutionalism, digital, 255, 270
constitutional jurisgenerativity, 255, 270
constitutional theory, sovereignty and, 216
Constitution of Free Prior and Informed Consent (FPIC), 321
constructivism, 22
contestatory democracy, 184–85
conventionalism, 130
Cornell, Drucilla, 14, 89–90, 410–11
Correa, Rafael, 317–19
correctness theories, for democratic legitimacy, 156, 159
cosmopolitanism, 9, 11; Arendt and, 310; Benhabib on, 86–87; communicative, 193–209; communitarian, 12, 283; decolonial, 322–24; decolonial cosmos and, 310; democratic legitimacy and, 310–11; discursive, 206–7, 209; domination and, 206; globalization as factor in, 10; Indigenous peoples and, 316–24; Kant and, 89, 244, 310; universalism and, 279; utopia and, 81–82, 86–87, 90–92
"Cosmopolitanism Reconsidered" (Benhabib), 86–87
cosmopolitan rights, 257–58
Cover, Robert, 11, 231, 253n48; on democratic iteration theory, 219, 316; on International Court of Justice, 293n18; on jurispathic courts, 326n40, 326n42; *Nomos and Narrative*, 320; on sovereignty, 227. *See also* jurisgenerativity
Covey, William, 373
Crises of The Republic, The (Arendt), 109
crisis of justification, 47
"critical ransacking," in feminist political theory, 99, 102
critical rationality, 4
critical theory: Benhabib approach to, 2, 15; deprovincialization of, 13–15; for Frankfurt School, 3, 5–6, 92; Hegel on, 245–48; justification and, 45–46; of law, 244; political theory and, 45–46; utopia and, 81–85

Critique, Norm, and Utopia (Benhabib), 3, 6–7, 19, 21, 31–34, 422; "concrete other" in, 4–5; democratic iteration theory and, 245; developmental approach in, 26; Habermas in, 243; Hegel in, 20, 241–43; juridical theory in, 87–88; jurisgenerativity and, 245; Kant critiques in, 20; liberalism in, 22; practical discourse in, 27–30; sovereignty in, 88–89; universalism in, 23–26; utopia in, 81, 84–90

Critique and Praxis (Harcourt), 92n6

Critique of Judgment, The (Kant), 67, 69, 77–79, 260, 413

Critique of Power, The (Honneth), 84

Critique of Practical Reason (Kant), 222

Critique of Pure Reason (Kant), 222

cultural development theory, 25, 30

cultural genocide, 283, 291

cultural polyphony, 32

Dahl, Robert, 39–40

Daniel, Fred, 386

Darker Side of Modernity, The (Mignolo), 323

Darmanin, Gérald, 351

Darwin, Charles, 31

data logic, 302

data mining, 296

deception, 117

Declaration on the Rights of Indigenous Peoples, 309, 311, 313–14, 317–18

decolonial cosmopolitanism, 322–24

decolonial cosmos, cosmopolitanism and, 310

"Deduction of Pure Aesthetic Judgments" (Kant), 71–72

Dege, Carmen Lea, 5–6

Deleuze, Gilles, 84

deliberative democracy, 110; democratic legitimacy and, 164n2

Demiryol, Gaye İlhan, 8

democracy: constitutional, 32; contestatory, 184–85; crisis of, 108; definition of, 396n23; deliberative, 110, 164n2; democratic iteration theory, 4, 9–11, 45; domination and, 176–77; electoral, 184–85; justice and, 45; in political theory, 37–38; post-truth and, 109–10; radical, 185–86; universalism of, 32. *See also* democratic iteration theory; democratic legitimacy; majority rule

Democracy and Difference (Benhabib), 9

democratic iteration theory: in *Another Cosmopolitanism*, 249–60; Arendt on, 219–21; Benhabib on, 4, 9–11, 45, 289–91; Big Data and, 294–95; communicative cosmopolitanism and, 206; Cover on, 219, 316; in *Critique, Norm, and Utopia*, 245; definitions for, 316–17; democratic legitimacy and, 151–52, 161–64; Derrida on, 219, 249–50, 316; description practices in, 218–19; expectations of, 219; Indigenous peoples and, 316–22; judgment and, 222; jurisgenerativity and, 248–51; justification and, 38, 45; Michelman on, 316; postnational sovereignty and, 224; presentism and, 220; right to have rights and, 264–70; selection in, 218–19; semantic meanings and, 218–19; sovereignty and, 218–19, 227

democratic legitimacy: alternative evaluations of, 161–64; antidemocratic shortcuts and, 161–64; citizen agreement and, 158, 160–61; concrete universal and, 151; constitutional constraints and, 165n12; correctness theories of, 156, 159; cosmopolitanism and, 310–11; deliberative democracy and, 164n2; democratic iterations and, 151–52, 161–64; human rights and, 158–59, 163; inclusive elements of, 159–60, 162, 164; institutional approach to, 152–53, 156–61; instrumental approach to, 164n4; judicial review and, 162; majoritarian institutions and, 161–64, 165n12; majority rule and, 157–58; nonmajoritarian institutions and, 161–64; Orientalism and, 151; paradox of, 310–11; proceduralism and, 152–56, 163, 164n3; pure majoritarianism and, 155–56, 163; recursivity of legal contestation in, 160; self-government and, 162–63; substantive grounds for, 158–59, 162; transnational institutions and, 164

depoliticization, republicanism of dissent and, 177, 187

Deputy, The (Hochhuth), 125n42

Derrida, Jacques, 214, 411; on iterability, 219, 249–50, 316

desk murderer. *See Schreibtischtäter*

development, as theory: Benhabib on, 25; in *Critique, Norm, and Utopia*, 26; critique of, 30–31; cultural, 25, 30; cultural polyphony and, 32; functional, 31; for Habermas, 19–20, 26, 29; modern law and, 32; social, 25; sociohistorical heuristic of, 29

Dewey, John, 396n23
Dialectic of Enlightenment (Adorno and Horkheimer), 6, 54, 130; mimesis in, 131
Dick, Philip K., 296
dictatorships: border deaths under, 336; truth under, 113–14
Dietz, Mary, 103n5
digital constitutionalism, 255, 270
dignity: Black Protest masculinity and, 387; justification and, 44; Kant on, 44, 68–69, 77–78; norms for, 2
Dignity in Adversity (Benhabib), 4, 295
disaggregated sovereignty, 215
disagreement. *See* reasonable disagreement
Discipline and Punish (Foucault), 298
discourse-theoretical reconstruction of justification, 46; right to have rights and, 265–66
discrimination, Big Data and, 303n2
discursive cosmopolitanism, communicative cosmopolitanism and, 206–7, 209
Doctrine of Right (Kant), 272n10
domestic law, jurisgenerativity for, 289
domination: Arendt critique of, 175–78; cosmopolitanism and, 206; in democracies, 176–77; justification and, 44–45; of nature, 67; in Nazi Germany, 176; as politicization, 176, 179; power as, 41; republicanism of dissent and, 174–78; universalism and, 2
Douglass, Frederick, 373
Dubiel, Helmut, 411
Du Bois, W. E. B., 385
Dussel, Enrique, 322–23
dwelling concept, 58
Dworkin, Ronald, 250, 266

Ebony, 390–91
ECHR. *See* European Convention on Human Rights
ECSC. *See* European Coal and Steel Community
ECtHR. *See* European Court of Human Rights
Ecuador: Confederation of Indigenous Nationalities of Ecuador, 315–16; Constitution of Free Prior and Informed Consent, 321; hermeneutics of resistance in, 320; Indigenous peoples in, 309, 315–16; international law in, 315; jurispathic courts in, 326n40, 326n42; nature rights in, 318; Provincial Court in, 320. *See also* Correa, Rafael

Edwards, Erica, 369
Eichmann, Adolf: Arendt criticized for treatment of, 134; authoritarian personality for, 130–31; clichés evoked by, 128, 139; Final Solution for, 137–38; lack of empathy, 128; mimesis and, 139; as *schreibtischtäter*, 128, 135
Eichmann in Jerusalem (Arendt), 8, 109, 136; concrete other in, 141–46; Final Solution in, 137–38; genocide in, 278, 284–85; German Enlightenment and, 135; reenactment in, 142; right to have rights in, 255, 263; role reversal in, 141–46; *schreibtischtäter* term in, 128, 135; Stangneth and, 135, 137
Einstein, Albert, 111
electoral democracy, 184–85
emancipatory political action, 1
Emcke, Carolin, 10, 15
ensauvagement (becoming savage), 351
epidermal racial schema, 338, 349
epistemic proceduralism, 154
equality: justification and, 44; norms for, 2; relational, 179
Escobar, Arturo, 323, 326n36
Eslava, Luis, 333
essentialist universalism, 267
ethical-existential discussion, 27–28
ethical-political discussion, 27–28
ethics: communicative, 4, 19, 23–24, 77–79; in communicative cosmopolitanism, 193; Kant on, 20; truth in, 121; universalist, 20, 34
ethnonationalism, 199
EU. *See* European Union
Eurocentrism, universalism and, 2
European Coal and Steel Community (ECSC), 197
European Convention on Human Rights (ECHR), 229–30
European Court of Human Rights (ECtHR), 354
European Court of Justice, 227–31
European Union (EU): Charter of Fundamental Rights, 227–28; collective memories of, 200; communicative cosmopolitanism in, 198; global domestic policy in, 201; human rights in, 228; migration policies in, 351; Minority Treaties, 282; postnational sovereignty in, 223–24, 232; as project, 200; sovereignty in, 217; Treaty on the Functioning of the European Union, 231
EU Trust Fund for Africa, 351

INDEX   435

Exile, Statelessness, and Migration (Benhabib), 21, 58, 214, 277
existentialism: ethical-existential discussion, 27–28; of Heidegger, 55; of Nietzsche, 55; political, 52
existentialist self, 57

factual truth, 110–13, 122; during Second World War, 125*n*42
false consciousness, justification and, 46–47
falsehoods. *See* lies
family wage, 389–92, 395
Fanon, Frantz, 14, 331; *Black Skin, White Mask*, 353; on body schemas, 348, 363*n*86; on border deaths, 337–38, 347–52; colonialism for, 337, 346; on colonial law, 353; epidermal racial schema, 338, 349; historical-racial schema, 338, 349; on racialized bodies, 343–44; on racial schemas, 338, 347–52; on racism, 338, 347–52; on white gaze, 343; *The Wretched of the Earth*, 330, 344–45
fascism, 130, 412, 415
federalism, global, 196–97
Feminism as Critique, 19, 410
Feminist Contentions, 90, 94n39
feminist political theory, 97; Arendt and, 100–103; in canonical texts, 104*nn*2–3; "critical ransacking" in, 99, 102; M. L. King political philosophy and, 366–71; public-private distinction in, 98, 102; "thinking with and against" in, 99, 103–4, 106*n*14
Ferguson, Michaele, 99, 103*n*6
Fetscher, Iring, 419
Film Quarterly, 144
Final Solution, 137–38
Flathman, Richard E., 103*n*5
Flax, Jane, 94*n*39
Foner, Eric, 271
forced disappearances. *See* border deaths
formal international law, 201–2
Forst, Rainer, 5, 89, 244, 268, 408
Foucault, Michel, 84, 414; Big Data and, 297–98; *Discipline and Punish*, 298
Fourth World, The (Manuel), 315
FPIC. *See* Constitution of Free Prior and Informed Consent
fragmentary historiography, of Republicanism, 168
"Fragments of an Intellectual Biography" (Benhabib), 2, 55

framework of universal agreements. *See* universal agreements
Frank, Jill, 103
Frankfurt School, 19–20, 175, 242–43, 322, 406, 411–12; Arendt and, 1, 7; Benhabib and, 1, 3, 69; critical theory for, 3, 5–6, 92; Hegel and, 246; mimesis tradition in, 128; on nature, 67; second generation of, 13; utopia for, 81–83
Fransson case, 229
Franzius, Claudio, 235*n*47
Fraser, Nancy, 89, 244, 410
Frazier, E. Franklin, 389
freedom: Arendt on, 407; communicative, 266, 268; norms for, 2; as original right, 272*n*10; positive, 183; Republicanism and, 172–73
Freedom Charter, in South Africa, 334*n*14
Freedom's Right (Honneth), 245–46
Freud, Sigmund, 31, 133
functional development, 31

Gadamer, Hans-Georg, 84
GAI. *See* guaranteed annual income
Galilei, Galileo, 31, 111
Garner, Eric, 414
Gates, Henry Louis, Jr., 419
Gay Science, The (Nietzsche), 91
gender: justice and, 370–71, 387–94; labor divisions by, 368–69; segregation by, 399*n*64
genealogical reconstruction of justification, 46
generalized other: communicative cosmopolitanism and, 203–8; in *Situating the Self*, 328–29
genocide: Arendt on, 277–78, 283–84, 286; categories of, 279; communitarian cosmopolitanism and, 283; cultural, 283, 291; definitions of, 279–81; distinctiveness as crime, 283, 285; in *Eichmann in Jerusalem*, 278, 284–85; under Genocide Convention of 1948, 12, 278–84, 290; human pluralism and, 284–85; of Indigenous peoples, 282; in international criminal courts, 293*n*18; jurisgenesis and, 12, 277–92; legal meanings of, 287; Lemkin on, 277–78, 281–83, 286, 293; under Minority Treaties, 282; in *The Origins of Totalitarianism*, 278, 283–84; public appropriation of, 191; special intent requirement for, 280; of targeted groups, 191; theoretical approach to, 277–78; under Universal Declaration of Human Rights, 284. *See also* Holocaust

Genocide Convention of 1948, 12, 278–84, 290
German Enlightenment, 135
Germany: nationalism in, 200; Spartacist Uprising in, 196. *See also* Nazi Germany
Gilligan, Carol, 142, 328
global federalism. *See* federalism
globalization: cosmopolitanism and, 10; sovereignty and, 226–27
Global South, genocide in, 282
Goldstein, Moritz, 423
Gordon, Peter E., 59, 62–63, 130
Gray, Jesse Glenn, 119
Groundwork for the Metaphysics of Morals (Kant), 68, 260
guaranteed annual income (GAI), 392–93
Guartambel, Yaku Pérez, 321
Guenther, Lisa, 363n86
Gündoğdu, Ayten, 14

Habermas, Jürgen, 7, 249, 322, 419–20; on absolutism, 61; Adorno as influence on, 199; Benhabib and, 3, 19–34, 51–52, 406–7; *Between Facts and Norms*, 154, 243–44, 249, 300; communicative action theory, 90; on communicative cosmopolitanism, 194, 198–203, 208; communicative ethics for, 4; on constitutionalization of international law, 201–2; critical rationality for, 4; critical theory for, 84; in *Critique, Norm, and Utopia*, 243; critique of Marx, 26; development theory and, 19–20, 26, 29; ethical abstinence for, 247; on German nationalism, 200; on Heidegger, 99–100; history of philosophy, 61; on justification, 38; on left Fascism, 412; on motivational sources of modernity, 59–63; on nation-state formation, 199–200; in Nazi Germany, 198; postnational constellation and, 198–203; *pouvoir constituant mixte* and, 223–26; on power, 199; on practical discourse, 27–30; on proceduralism, 154; on Promethean self, 63; on public sphere, 305n30; on reason, 131; *Toward a Reconstruction of Historical Materialism*, 25–26; on religion, 60; in *Situating the Self*, 60; *The Theory of Communicative Action*, 25–26; *This Too a History of Philosophy*, 6, 24, 29, 51, 408; on United Nations, 202; on universalism, 24–25, 201, 268; utopia for, 81–82, 84
Harcourt, Bernard E., 6–7, 92n6

Hartmann, Heidi, 391
Hegel, Georg Wilhelm Friedrich, 322; absolutism of, 61; Benhabib and, 2; concept of person, 407; critical theory for, 84, 245–48; in *Critique, Norm, and Utopia*, 20, 241–43; critique of natural law, 242; Frankfurt School and, 246; immanent critique for, 242–43; on Kant, 242; on law, 245–48; metaphysics of, 2; on natural rights, 242; *Phenomenology of Spirit*, 29, 54, 408–9; *Philosophy of Right*, 2, 245; system of needs for, 204; "thinking with and against" procedure for, 100
Heidegger, Martin: Arendt and, 106n10; concept of the world for, 175; dwelling concept, 58; existentialism of, 55; Habermas on, 99–100; *Introduction to Metaphysics*, 99–100; search for authenticity for, 58
Heller, Joseph, 118
Helvétius, Claude-Adrien, 267
Herder, Johann Gottfried, 12, 282
hermeneutics of resistance, in Ecuador, 320
Hill, Lance, 374
historical change, macrosociological theories of, 34
historical-racial schema, 338, 349
Hitler, Adolf, 117
Hobbes, Thomas, 97, 242; mathematical truth for, 111; on sovereignty, 216, 234n11; on universalism, 267
Hochhuth, Rolf, 125n42
d'Holbach, Baron (Thiry, Paul-Henri), 267
Holocaust: Arendt as representation of survivors of, 134; creative appropriation of, 290–91; Final Solution in, 137–38
homelessness, 59
Honig, Bonnie, 253n43
Honneth, Axel, 7, 84, 90, 245, 252n30, 407, 419; on legalism, 246–47
hooks, bell, 366–67
Horkheimer, Max, 20, 69, 411; critical theory for, 84; *Dialectic of Enlightenment*, 6, 54, 130–31; mimesis and, 139; on reason, 131; "Traditional and Critical Theory," 84–85; utopia for, 81–83
Hruschka, Joachim, 272n10
Human Condition, The (Arendt), 97, 100, 170–71; communicative cosmopolitanism in, 194–95
human rights: Arendt on, 86, 88; Benhabib on, 86, 89; cosmopolitan rights, 257–58; democratic

legitimacy and, 158–59, 163; in EU, 228; in European Court of Human Rights, 354; freedom as original right, 272*n*10; under International Human Rights Law, 289; natural rights and, 242; principle of rights, 265; terrestrial anthropology and, 255–59; under Universal Declaration of Human Rights, 267, 284. *See also* international human rights; natural rights; right to have rights
Hume, David, 267
Hungarian Revolution, 196
Hussein, Saddam, 114
hyperlegality, 355
Hyvönen, Ari-Elmeri, 114

ICC. *See* International Criminal Court
idealism, Platonic, 37, 43–44
identity, communicative cosmopolitanism and, 205
Ideology and Utopia (Mannheim), 83
ILO. *See* International Labor Organization
immanent critique, 242–43
immigration policies, racism and, 350. *See also* migration policies
imperfect proceduralism, 154
In a Different Voice (Gilligan), 328
inclusion, democratic legitimacy and, 159–60, 162, 164
Indigenous peoples: American Indian Movement, 313; cosmopolitanism and, 316–24; decolonial cosmopolitanism and, 322–24; democratic iterations and, 316–22; in Ecuador, 309, 315–16; genocide of, 282; global approach to, 314; International Indian Treaty Council, 313; internationalism and, 311–14; International Labor Organization and, 313–14; national mobilization of, 315–16; Pachamama rights, 316–22; self-determination for, 312; under UN Declaration on the Rights of Indigenous Peoples, 309, 311, 313–14, 317–18; in UN Economic Security and Social Council, 313; Working Group on Indigenous Populations, 313; World Council of Indigenous Peoples, 312–13
Indigenous Peoples in International Law (Anaya), 312
inequality, Big Data and, 303*n*2
institutional approach, to democratic legitimacy, 152–53, 156–61

institutionalized power, 169
instrumental approach, to democratic legitimacy, 164*n*4
International Court of Justice, 293*n*18
International Criminal Court (ICC), 340
international criminal courts, 293*n*18; genocide in, 293*n*18
international criminal law, border deaths under, 340–41
international human rights: border deaths and, 340–41; EU Charter of Fundamental Rights, 227–28; European Convention on Human Rights, 229–30; under Kyoto Protocol, 317; under Paris Agreement, 317; rights of nature, 317–20; under Rio Declaration, 317; Universal Declaration of Human Rights, 267, 284
International Human Rights Law, 289
International Indian Treaty Council, 313
internationalism: Indigenous peoples and, 311–14; sovereignty and, 234*n*11
International Labor Organization (ILO), 313–14
international law: Benhabib on, 89; communicative cosmopolitanism and, 203, 205; constitutionalization of, 201–2; in Ecuador, 315; formal, 201–2; Habermas on, 201–2; International Human Rights Law, 289. *See also* human rights
international liberalism, 329
International Organization of Migration (IOM), 335, 359*n*27
Introduction to Metaphysics (Heidegger), 99–100
IOM. *See* International Organization of Migration
Irvin-Erickson, Douglas, 282
Isaac, Jeffrey, 103*n*5

Jaeggi, Rahel, 90, 173, 245; on law, 247
Jameson, Fredric, 268
Jaspers, Karl, 16, 197; framework of universal agreements, 196
Jefferson, Thomas, 196
Jewish Writings (Arendt), 196
judgment: democratic iteration theory and, 222; sovereignty and, 223, 226–27
judicial review: democratic legitimacy and, 162; republicanism of dissent and, 182
juridical theory: for Benhabib, 87–88, 268–69; in *Critique, Norm, and Utopia,* 87–88
juridification, 252*n*30

jurisgenerativity, jurisgenesis and, 4, 13; Arendt on, 11–12; Big Data and, 294–303; constitutional, 255, 270; Cover on, 11, 86, 88, 248–51, 279, 288–91, 331; *Critique, Norm, and Utopia* and, 245; definition of, 288; democratic iterations and, 248–51; for domestic law, 289; genocide and, 12, 277–92; as law in action, 288, 295; legal meanings in, 301; in nomic communities, 288, 292*n*14; paideiac, 288; right to have rights and, 267, 270; sovereignty and, 227

jurispathic courts, in Ecuador, 326*n*40, 326*n*42

Jurkevics, Anna, 274*n*38

jus sanguinis (citizenship through parental citizenship), 255

jus soli (birthright citizenship), 254–55, 271. *See also* birthright citizenship

justice: democracy and, 45; gendered, 370–71, 387–94; Kant on, 246

justification: Arendt on, 38; concrete universal and, 38; crisis of, 47; critical theory and, 45–46; critique of relations of, 46–47; democratic iterations theory and, 38, 45; dignity and, 44; discourse-theoretical reconstruction of, 46; domination and, 44–45; equality and, 44; fabrication of, 42; false consciousness and, 46–47; genealogical reconstruction of, 46; Habermas on, 38; liberty and, 44; as mediating term, 38; narratives of, 42; orders of, 41; Plato on, 38–39, 47; in politics, 38–47; power of, 39–41; rationalization of, 42; reality of, 39; right to, 44; structure of, 46

Kafka, Franz, 221

Kant, Immanuel: on aesthetic judgments, 69–75; "Analytic of the Beautiful," 71, 76; Benhabib and, 89–90, 408; on concrete other, 68–69, 75–78; constructivism for, 22; cosmopolitanism and, 89, 244, 310; *The Critique of Judgment*, 260; *Critique of Practical Reason*, 222; *Critique of Pure Reason*, 222; "Deduction of Pure Aesthetic Judgments," 71–72; on dignity of nature, 69–77; on dignity of persons, 44, 68–69, 77–78; *Doctrine of Right*, 272*n*10; *Groundwork*, 68; *Groundwork for the Metaphysics of Morals*, 260; Hegel on, 242; on imperial interest in beauty, 72; on intellectual interest in beauty, 72; on justice, 246; *Lectures and Drafts on Political Philosophy*, 258; on legalism, 246; liberalism of, 22; *Metaphysics of Morals*, 255–56, 258–60, 265; on morality, 69, 72, 75, 77–78; normative theories for, 21; *Toward Perpetual Peace*, 257–58; prefigurative critique for, 243; on price of things dichotomy, 68–69, 77; rational beings and, 256–57; *Religion and Rational Theology*, 272*n*8; on *sensus communis*, 67–75, 77; on sovereignty, 216; "Third Critique," 67, 69, 77–79, 413; "Towards Perpetual Peace," 201; on universalism, 68, 78, 268; universalist ethics for, 20, 34

Kant Notebook (Arendt), 260

Kelley, Robin D. G., 381, 384

Kelsen, Hans, 216

Kennedy, John F., 400*n*95

Khosravi, Shahram, 231–32

Kierkegaard, Søren, 408

King, Coretta Scott, 394, 398*n*40

King, Homay, 133–34

King, Martin Luther, Jr., political philosophy of: androcentrism and, 387; critique of Black Power movement, 371–75; deflation as dissociation and, 376–78; deflation as diversion, 375–76; on disintegration of Black families, 390–91; economic justice in, 387–94; on family wage, 389–92, 395; feminist approach to, 366–71; gendered division of labor and, 368–69; gendered justice in, 370–71, 387–94; on guaranteed annual income, 392–93; leadership style for, 396*n*25; National Welfare Rights Organization and, 393–94; nonviolence movement and, 374–75, 380–87; Poor People's Campaign, 393; on poverty, 388–89; sexist ideologies in, 387; Southern Christian Leadership Conference and, 366, 368, 370, 387, 393–94; theoretical approach to, 366–71; women in, 379–87

Kirchheimer, Otto, 243, 249, 253*n*48

Knowledge and Human Interests (Miller), 405

Kohn, Jerome, 118

Kolk, Bessel van der, 133

Kyoto Protocol, 317

Lafont, Cristina, 9

late sovereignty, 215

Lauterpacht, Hersch, 286

law: communicative cosmopolitanism and, 207; critical theory of, 244; domestic, 289; Hegel on, 245–48; Jaeggi on, 247; jurisgenerative potential of, 288, 295; Marxism and, 242; migration of, 207; rationality of, 182; Roman, 168; as site for border deaths, 352–56; universalism of, 32. *See also* international law
law as relationship, republicanism of dissent and, 174–75, 180–82
Lawrence, T. E., 119
Lawtoo, Nidesh, 139
learning, 417–19
Lectures and Drafts on Political Philosophy (Kant), 258
Lectures on Kant's Political Philosophy (Arendt), 260
left Fascism, 412
legalism: Honneth on, 246–47; Kant on, 246
legal patriarchy, 57
legitimacy, democratic, 151–64
Lemkin, Raphael: on genocide, 277–78, 281–83, 286, 293; Genocide Convention and, 12; Herder and, 12
Lessing, Doris, 125n28
Lhermitte, Jean, 348
liberalism, 167; in *Critique, Norm, and Utopia*, 22; international, 329; Kantian, 22; Rawls on, 22; in *Situating the Self*, 21
liberal nationalism, 329
liberty, justification and, 44
Libya, border deaths in, 342
lies, falsehoods and: as counterproductive, 117; cynicism as result of, 122; deception and, 117; in politics, 109, 113; self-deception and, 117
Life of the Mind, The (Arendt), 101
Linden, Markus, 179
Linden-Retek, Paul, 10–11
Ling, Peter J., 371–74
living power, 169
Locke, John, 97
Longo, Matthew, 12–13
Look of Silence, The, 144
"Loss of World" (Dege), 5–6
Louis, Joe, 374–75
Luban, David, 285–86
Lugones, María Cristina, 323
Luxemburg, Rosa, 196
"Lying and Politics" (Arendt), 109–10, 118
Lyotard, Jean-François, 2–3, 84, 410

Machiavelli, Niccolò, 168, 183
MacIntyre, Alasdair, 405
majoritarianism: democratic legitimacy and, 161–64, 165n12; modified, 156–57; pure, 154–56, 163
majority rule: democratic legitimacy and, 157–58; proceduralism and, 154
Mamdani, Mahmood, 86
Mannheim, Karl, 82–83
Manuel, George, 315
Marcuse, Herbert, 7, 69, 405; utopia for, 82–83
Margil, Mari, 326n36
Markell, Patchen, 7, 217–18
Marks, Susan, 341–42
Marx, Karl, 20, 97, 408; critical theory for, 84; Habermas critique of, 26; utopia for, 81
Marxism, 167; Arendt and, 7; reductionist views of law, 242
masculinity, poverty and, 389. *See also* Black Protest masculinity
mathematical truth, 111
Max Planck Institute for the Study of the Scientific-Technical World, 204, 411
Mbembe, Achille, 357
McCarthy, Thomas, 5, 367
McClure, Kirstie, 103n5
McGuire, Danielle, 381–83
McIntosh, Heather, 145
McNamara, Robert, 118
Mendieta, Eduardo, 12
Merleau-Ponty, Maurice, 343, 348
metaphysics, for Hegel, 2
Metaphysics of Morals (Kant), 255–56, 258–59; right to have rights in, 260, 265
Michelman, Frank, 266; on democratic iterations, 316; digital constitutionalism and, 255, 270
Mignolo, Walter, 323
Migrants in the Profane (Gordon), 59
migration policies: in European Union, 351; International Organization of Migration, 335, 359n27
Mill, John Stuart, 97
mimesis, 128; Adorno on, 139; *The Authoritarian Personality*, 130; for Congo, 143; definition of, 139; in *Dialectic of Enlightenment*, 131; Eichmann and, 139; Horkheimer on, 139; Lawtoo on, 139
Minority Treaties, in Europe, 282
Mitscherlich, Alexander, 406

mixed sovereignty, 215
modernism, 106n10. *See also* postmodernism
modernity: alternative, 33; motivational sources of, 59–63; multiple, 33; practical discourse on, 30; in *Situating the Self*, 56–57; universalism on, 33; for Weber, 63
Modern Review in Origins, 261–63
modified majoritarianism, 156–57
Mokgoro, Yvonne, 332
Montesquieu: Arendt and, 181; Republicanism and, 168
moral anthropology, 255–56
morality: Kant on, 69, 72, 75, 77–78; rules of, 80n14; universalism of, 32
Moreno, Lenin, 230
Moses, A. Dirk, 282
Moten, Fred, 92
motivation: modernity and, 59–63; in *Situating the Self*, 52–53
Mouffe, Chantal, 186
Moyn, Samuel, 86
Moynihan, Daniel, 388–89
"Moynihan Report," 388–89
Mozart, Wolfgang Amadeus, 424
multiculturalism, 58
multiple modernities, 33

NAACP. *See* National Association for the Advancement of Colored People
Nagel, Thomas, 86
NAM. *See* Non-Aligned Movement
National Association for the Advancement of Colored People (NAACP), 368
nationalism: in Germany, 200; liberal, 329
National Socialism, Nazi Germany and, 135, 137, 195
National Welfare Rights Organization (NWRO), 393–94
nation-states: Big Data and, 302; communicative cosmopolitanism and, 193; development of, 195–96; ethnic identities in, 196; ethnonationalism in, 199; formation of, 199; Habermas on, 199–200; in *The Origins of Totalitarianism*, 195–96
Natural Law and Human Dignity (Bloch), 85
Natural Right and History (Strauss), 405
natural rights: freedom as, 272n10; Hegel on, 242
nature: aesthetic judgments and, 70; as concrete other, 75–77; dignity of, 69–77; domination of, 67; Frankfurt School critique of, 67; as metaphor in *Situating the Self*, 54
nature rights: Community Environmental Legal Defense Fund and, 326n36; in Ecuador, 318; international human rights and, 317–20
Nazi Germany: domination in, 176; Final Solution and, 137–38; German Enlightenment, 135; Habermas in, 198; Holocaust and, 134, 137–38; National Socialism and, 195; Weimar Republic and, 195
Negro Family, The (Frazier), 389
Nesiah, Vasuki, 333
neocolonial extractivism, 311
neo-Roman Republicanism, neorepublicanism and, 166, 168, 183–85
networked council systems, 197–98
Neumann, Franz L., 242–43, 249, 251n13, 253n48
Nietzsche, Friedrich: existentialism of, 55; *The Gay Science*, 91
Nixon, E. D., 382
nomic communities, jurisgenerativity in, 288, 292n14
Nomos and Narrative (Cover), 320
Nomos of the Earth (Schmitt), 274n38
Non-Aligned Movement (NAM), 330
nonmajoritarian institutions, democratic legitimacy and, 161–64
nonstate actors, communicative cosmopolitanism and, 207
nonviolence movement: Black Protest masculinity and, 374–75; boycotts and, 381–83; gender segregation in, 380–87; M. L. King role in, 374–75, 380–87
"Normativity and Reality" (Forst), 5
NS and others case, 229
Nussbaum, Martha, 87
NWRO. *See* National Welfare Rights Organization

O'Hara, Grainne, 354
Okin, Susan Moller, 97, 367
One Dimensional Man (Marcuse), 405
On Violence (Arendt), 170
Oppenheimer, Joshua, 8–9, 128–34, 136–41, 145–46; Congo and, 143–44. *See also Act of Killing, The*
order, Republicanism and, 172–73
orders of justification, 41
Orientalism, 151

Origins of Totalitarianism, The (Arendt), 107*n*17, 120, 273*n*20, 407; genocide in, 278, 283–84; right to have rights in, 260, 263; state development in, 195–96
other. *See* concrete other; generalized other
Ovid, 219

Pachamama rights, 316–22
paideiac jurisgenesis, 288
Paris Agreement, 317
Paris Commune of 1789, 196
Parks, Rosa, 368, 381
Pateman, Carole, 97
patriarchy. *See* legal patriarchy; political patriarchy
Peirce, Charles Sanders, 408
Pełczyński, Zbigniew, 406
Pensky, Max, 12, 270
Pentagon Papers, 109–10, 120
Peter, Fabienne, 164*n*4
Pettit, Philip, 173, 183–88
phenomenology: Arendt on, 342–43; border deaths and, 337, 341–47; Merleau-Ponty on, 343
Phenomenology of Spirit (Hegel), 29, 54, 408–9
Philosophical Notebooks (Arendt), 260
philosophical truth, 111–12; Arendt on, 48*n*1
philosophy: Habermas on, 6, 24, 29, 51, 61; Hegel on, 2; sovereignty and, 215–16
Philosophy of Right (Hegel), 2, 245, 407
Pius XII (Pope), 125*n*42
Plato: on justification, 38–39, 47; political theory of, 36–37; Republic, 36, 37
Platonic idealism, 37, 43–44
Plato's Paradox, 36–37, 48*n*1
pleasure, *in sensus communis*, 71–72
pluralism: genocide and, 284–85; politicization and, 178; practical discourse and, 28; proceduralism and, 153–54; sovereignty and, 216–17, 221
polis, 89, 106*n*10; Arendt on, 195, 225; community of memory and, 225
political action: emancipatory, 1; Republicanism and, 169–71
political existentialism, of Arendt, 52
political patriarchy, 57
political power: Republicanism and, 169–71; republicanism of dissent and, 177–78
political science, 36–38; scope of, 44
politicization: definition of, 179; domination as, 176, 179; forces of, 179–80; plurality conditions and, 178; relational equality and, 179; republicanism of dissent and, 174–75, 178–80, 187. *See also* depoliticization
Politics (Aristotle), 97–98
politics, theory of: Arendt on, 48*n*1, 101; authoritarianism and, 37; communicative cosmopolitanism in, 193; critical theory and, 45–46; democratic future in, 37–38; justification in, 38–47; lies and falsehoods in, 109, 113; in multicultural systems, 37; narratives in, 41–42; normative view of, 43–45; for Plato, 36–37; Platonic idealism and, 37, 43–44; Plato's Paradox, 36–37, 48*n*1; political science, 36–38, 44; positivism in, 37–38; postwar, 193; power in, 41; propaganda in, 109; realism in, 37, 41–43; renunciation of, 173; in Republic, 36; republicanism of dissent, 186–87; rule of law in, 37; shared language in, 37–38; structured politics, 172; structures of, 41–42; truth and, 110; Western political thought, 101
Pollock, Friedrich, 411
pooled sovereignty, 215
Poor People's Campaign, 393
popular sovereignty, 198, 205
populism, Republicanism and, 166, 183
positive freedom, 183
positivism, in political theory, 37–38
postmodernism, 94*n*39
postmodern self, 56
postnational constellation: communicative cosmopolitanism and, 194, 198–203; Habermas and, 198–203
postnational sovereignty, 217; Arendt on, 225; democratic iterations and, 224; in EU, 223–24, 232; pouvoir constituant mixte and, 223–26; presentism and, 224; state actors and, 224–25; supranational actors in, 224–25
poststucturalism, 94*n*39
post-truth, 109–10; Arendt on, 114
postwar political theory, 193
pouvoir constituant mixte, 223–26
poverty: family wage and, 389–92, 395; guaranteed annual income and, 392–93; M. L. King on, 388–89; masculinity and, 389

power: acting-against-one-another and, 171; acting-for-one-another and, 169–71; acting-with-one-another and, 169–71; definition of, 39–40; domination and, 41; exercise of, 40; Habermas on, 199; institutionalized, 169; of justifications, 39–41; living, 169; noumenal nature of, 40; political, 169–71, 177–78; in politics, 41; rule as form of, 40; social, 177–78; of truth, 112; violence as, 41

practical discourse: Benhabib on, 27–30; ethical-existential discussion, 27–28; ethical-political discussion, 27–28; Habermas on, 27–30; idealized form of, 29; on modernity, 30; pluralism and, 28; reasonable disagreement and, 28, 31; as socialization process, 29

Praxis International, 412
predictive analytics, 296
prefigurative critique, 243
presentism, 220; postnational sovereignty and, 224
price of things dichotomy, Kant on, 68–69, 77
Principle of Hope, The (Bloch), 83
principle of rights, 265
proceduralism: democratic legitimacy and, 152–56, 163, 164n3; epistemic, 154; Habermas on, 154; imperfect, 154; majority rule and, 154; pluralism and, 153–54; pure, 154, 163; pure majoritarianism and, 154–56; Rawls on, 154
profiling, 296
Promethean self: Habermas on, 63; in *Situating the Self*, 53–55, 60
propaganda: in politics, 109; post-truth as, 109. *See also* lies
Protestantism. *See* Western European Protestantism
public-private distinction: Aristotle on, 97–98; in feminist political theory, 98, 102
public sphere: Arendt on, 109; Big Data in, 299–302; communicative cosmopolitanism in, 206; fragmentation of, 108, 110; Habermas on, 305n30; in *Situating the Self*, 55; transnational, 194
pure majoritarianism: democratic legitimacy and, 155–56, 163; proceduralism and, 154–56; rejection of, 163

pure proceduralism, 154, 163
Putnam, Hilary, 268

quasi-transcendental universalism, 23–26
Quijano, Aníbal, 322–23

R2P. *See* responsibility to protect doctrine
racialized bodies, 343–44
racial schemas: body schemas, 348, 363n86; border deaths and, 347–52; epidermal, 338, 349; historical, 338, 349
racism: in Australia, 350; *ensauvagement* and, 351; Fanon on, 338, 347–52; immigration policy and, 350; nationality and, 350; racialized forms of violence, 336; in United Kingdom, 350; in U.S., 350\
radical democracy, 185–86
Rancière, Jacques, 185–86
Ransby, Barbara, 368–70, 382
rational agency theory, 2
rational beings, Kant and, 256–57
rationality, critical, 4
rational truth, 110; categories of, 111–12
Rawls, John, 268; on constructivism, 22; on liberalism, 22; on proceduralism, 154; veil of ignorance, 141
realism, in political theory, 37, 41–43
reason, 131
reasonable disagreement, practical discourse and, 28, 31
reductionism, 27
reenactment: in *The Act of Killing*, 138; in *Eichmann in Jerusalem*, 142
relational equality, politicization and, 179
relationist school, of sovereignty, 216–17, 233n9
religion: Habermas on, 60; in *Situating the Self*, 64
Religion and Rational Theology (Kant), 272n8
Reluctant Modernism of Hannah Arendt, The (Benhabib), 97, 100–1, 413
Republic (Plato), 36, 137
Republicanism: Arendt and, 166–73; Benjamin on, 168; "break in tradition" and, 167–68; civic activism and, 168; fragmentary historiography and, 168; freedom and, 172–73; good life and, 168; Machiavelli and, 168; Montesquieu and, 168; neo-Roman, 166, 168, 183, 185; order and, 172–73; political action and, 169–71; political power and, 169–71; popular sovereignty and, 168; populist

approaches to, 166, 183; renunciation of politics and, 173; Roman law and, 168; Rousseau and, 168; statism and, 168; structured politics and, 172; virtues as element of, 168

republicanism of dissent: acting-for-one-another and, 184; acting-with-one-another and, 174, 184, 186–87; Arendt on, 166–67, 173–82, 185–87, 190n36; concept of the world and, 175; contestatory democracy and, 184–85; depoliticization and, 177, 187; domination and, 174–78; electoral democracy and, 184–85; judicial review and, 182; law as relationship and, 174–75, 180–82; with mixed constitutions, 181; neorepublicanism and, 183–85; political power and, 177–78; as political theory, 186–87; politicization and, 174–75, 178–80, 187; radical democracy and, 185–86; relevance of, 183–86; social power and, 177–78

Resnik, Judith, 207

responsibility to protect doctrine (R2P), failure of, 208

rights of nature. *See* nature rights

Rights of Others, The (Benhabib), 3–4, 10, 264–65, 269, 316, 321

right to have rights: Arendt on, 86, 88, 254–55, 260–64, 407; Benhabib on, 264–65, 270; Burke on, 261; communicative freedom and, 266, 268; democratic iterations and, 264–70; digital constitutionalism and, 255, 270; discourse-theoretic terms for, 265–66; Dworkin on, 250, 266; in *Eichmann in Jerusalem*, 255, 263; essentialist universalism and, 267; government protections and, 261; jurisgenerativity and, 267, 270; in *The Metaphysics of Morals*, 260, 265; in *Modern Review in Origins*, 261–63; in *The Origins of Totalitarianism*, 260, 263; principle of rights and, 265; relevance of, 262; in *The Right of Others*, 264–65; theoretical approach to, 254–55; Universal Declaration of Human Rights and, 267

Rio Declaration, 317

Ripstein, Arthur, 256

Robinson, Jackie, 374

Robinson, Jo Ann, 381–82, 384–86

Robinson, Joanne Hibson, 368

Roman law, Republicanism and, 168

Rorty, Richard, 84

Rosanvallon, Pierre, 179

Rousseau, Jean-Jacques, 97; paradox of founding and, 233n9; Republicanism and, 168; on universalism, 267–68

rule, as form of power, 40

rule of law: in political theory, 37; sovereignty as distinct from, 242

Rule of Law (Neumann), 251n13

Russian Revolution, 196

Sartre, Jean-Paul, 268

schemas. *See* body schemas; racial schemas

Scheuerman, William E., 11

Schmidt, Alfred, 419

Schmitt, Carl, 274n38; on sovereignty, 216, 233n9

Schreibtischtäter (desk murderer), 128, 135

scientific truth, 111

SCLC. *See* Southern Christian Leadership Conference

Scott, David, 310

Scott, James, 384, 414

Second World War (WWII): factual truth during, 125n42; Final Solution, 137–38. *See also* Holocaust; Nazi Germany

Segato, Rita Laura, 323

self-consciousness, in *Situating the Self*, 54–55, 60

self-deception, 117

self-government, democratic legitimacy and, 162–63

selfhood, 52; communitarian self, 53, 55; existentialist self in, 57; postmodern self, 56; Promethean self, 53–55, 60

semantic meanings, in democratic iteration theory, 218–19

sensus communis: aesthetic judgments and, 71; in "Analytic of the Beautiful," 71; in "Deduction of Pure Aesthetic Judgments," 71; definition of, 71; Kant on, 67–75, 77; pleasure in, 71–72

Serrano, Paul, 320–21

sexism, in Southern Christian Leadership Conference, 366

Shakur, Tupac, 374

Shanley, Mary, 97

sharing, 423–24

Shatz, Omer, 340

Sidibé, Abou Bakar, 355

Sierra Club v. Morton case, 317

Situating the Self (Benhabib), 3, 5–6, 19, 90; absolutism in, 53; academic study of, 51; communitarian self, 53, 55; cosmopolitan codependence in, 329; existentialist self in, 57; generalized other in, 328–29; Habermas in, 60; international liberalism in, 329; language structure in, 55–56; legal patriarchy in, 57; liberalism in, 21; liberal nationalism in, 329; loss of certainty in, 52–56, 63–64; modernity and, 56–57; motivation in, 52–53; nature metaphor in, 54; pessimism in, 56; political patriarchy in, 57; postmodern self in, 56; Promethean self, 53–55, 60; in public sphere, 55; religion in, 64; self-consciousness in, 54–55, 60; social criticism in, 56–59; *This Too a History of Philosophy* and, 51; tolerance in, 58; Western European Protestantism in, 60
Smith, Adam, 267
SNCC. *See* Student Non-Violent Coordinating Committee
social criticism, in *Situating the Self*, 56–59
social development theory, 25
social power, republicanism of dissent and, 177–78
Socrates, 121, 125n43, 415; on universalism, 23
Socratic dialogues, universalism and, 23
Sophocles, 97
South Africa: African National Congress, 332; Constitution in, 331, 334n15; Freedom Charter in, 334n14; Revolution in, 331; Ubuntu Project, 332, 334n15
Southern Christian Leadership Conference (SCLC), 368, 370, 387, 393–94; sexism in, 366
sovereignty: Arendt on, 220; Benhabib on, 227; communicative cosmopolitanism and, 193, 205; constitutional theory and, 216; Cover on, 227; in *Critique, Norm, and Utopia*, 88–89; democratic iterations and, 218–19, 227; disaggregated, 215; elasticity of, 215–16; in European Union, 217; forgiveness and, 221; globalization and, 226–27; Hobbes on, 216, 234n11; internationalism and, 234n11; judgment and, 223, 226–27; jurisgenerativity and, 227; Kant on, 216; Kelsen on, 216; late, 215; mixed, 215; modes of, 222; narrative agency and, 221; philosophical foundations of, 215–16; pluralism and, 216–17, 221; pooled, 215; popular, 205; postnational, 217, 223–26; relationist school of, 216–17, 233n9; Republicanism and, 168; revised character of,

221–22; rule of law as distinct from, 242; Schmitt on, 216, 233n9; territorial, 336; Westphalian, 198
Spain, border deaths in, 336–37, 345–46
Spartacist Uprising, 196
Spirit of Hope, The (Bloch), 83
Stalin, Joseph, 117
Stangneth, Bettina, 129, 135, 137
state actors: communicative cosmopolitanism and, 207; postnational sovereignty and, 224–25
statism: Arendt's critique of, 188n7; Republicanism and, 168. *See also* nation-states
Stephan, Maria, 379
Sternberger, Dolf, 195
Strauss, Leo, 405
Stride Toward Freedom (King, M. L.), 372
structured politics, 172
Student Non-Violent Coordinating Committee (SNCC), 368
suffering, 419–23
Suharto, 132
supranational actors, in postnational sovereignty, 224–25
"Swan, The" (Baudelaire), 215
system of needs, for Hegel, 204

Tarajal massacre, 336–37, 345–46, 355
Taylor, Charles, 33
Taylor, Recy, 382
terrestrial anthropology, human rights and, 255–59
territorial sovereignty, 336
Terry, Brandon M., 15
Theory of Communicative Action, The (Habermas), 25–26; utopia in, 84
"thinking with and against" procedure: in feminist political theory, 99, 103–4, 106n14; Hegel and, 100; holism of, 103–4
This Too a History of Philosophy (Habermas), 6, 24, 29, 408; *Situating the Self* and, 51
Threadcraft, Shatema, 15
totalitarianism: The Origins of Totalitarianism, 107n17, 120; truth under, 113–16
Toward a Reconstruction of Historical Materialism (Habermas), 25–26
"Toward Perpetual Peace" (Kant), 201, 257–58
"Traditional and Critical Theory" (Horkheimer), 84–85

INDEX   445

transnational institutions, 164
transnational public sphere, communicative cosmopolitanism in, 194
Treaty on the Functioning of the European Union, 231
Trotsky, Leon, 116–17
Trump, Donald, 8, 421
truth: Arendt on, 108–22; attacks on, 113–14; under dictatorships, 113–14; in ethics, 121; factual, 110–13, 122, 125n42; guardians of, 110–13; individual truth-tellers, 120–21; mathematical, 111; nature of, 110–13; philosophical, 48n1, 111–12; political regimes as influenced on, 113–16; politics and, 110; power of, 112; rational, 110–12; scientific, 111; in totalitarian regimes, 113–16; universities and, 118. *See also* lies; post-truth
"Truth and Politics" (Arendt), 109, 114, 116, 123nn6–7, 125n43
Turkey, 203

Ubuntu Project, in South Africa, 332, 334n15
UDHR. *See* Universal Declaration of Human Rights
UK. *See* United Kingdom
UN. *See* United Nations
UNDRIP. *See* United Nations
United Kingdom (UK): Brexit and, 203; Commonwealth Immigrants Act, 350; racism in, 350
United Nations (UN), 202; Declaration on the Rights of Indigenous Peoples, 309, 311, 313–14, 317–18; Economic Security and Social Council, 313
United States (U.S.): Chinese Exclusion Act, 350; constitutional amendments in, 271; crisis of democracy in, 108; Reconstruction Amendments in, 271
universal agreements, framework of, 196
Universal Declaration of Human Rights (UDHR), 267; genocide under, 284
universalism: abstraction and, 2; anthropocentric, 67; for Benhabib, 23–26, 91, 268–69; communicative ethics and, 23–24; concrete universal, 2–5, 38; of constitutional democracy, 32; cosmopolitanism and, 279; in *Critique, Norm, and Utopia*, 23–26; of discourse on modernity, 33; domination and, 2; essentialist, 267; Eurocentrism and, 2; Habermas and, 24–25, 201, 268; Hobbes on, 267; Kant on, 68, 78, 268; of law, 32; of morality, 32; quasi-transcendental, 23–26; Rousseau on, 267–68; Socratic dialogues and, 23; Weimar Syndrome and, 23–24
universalist ethics, 20, 34
U.S. *See* United States
utopia: for Adorno, 81–83; Benhabib on, 81–92; for Benjamin, 82–83; for Bloch, 82–84; cosmopolitanism and, 81–82, 86–87, 90–92; critical theory and, 81–85; in *Critique, Norm, and Utopia*, 81, 84–90; for Frankfurt School, 81–83; for Habermas, 81–82, 84; for Horkheimer, 81–83; for Mannheim, 82–83; for Marcuse, 82–83; for Marx, 81; meanings of, 81; in new social movements, 81; sociological theory of, 83

Valetta Summit, 351
Verdeja, Ernesto, 131
Verovšek, Peter, 10
Villa, Dana, 103n5
violence: Black Protest masculinity and, 372, 375; as form of power, 41
virtues, in Republicanism, 168
Vita Activa (Arendt), 170
Volk, Christian, 9, 195

Waldron, Jeremy, 103n5, 172
Walker, Ferdie, 381–82
Waller, James, 191
Walsh, Catherine, 323
Walzer, Michael, 86
Wartofsky, Marx W., 19
Weber, Max, 20, 63, 145
Weimar Republic, collapse of, 195
Weimar Syndrome, 22–24
Wellmer, Albrecht, 420
Western European Protestantism, 60
Westphalian sovereignty, 198
WGIP. *See* Working Group on Indigenous Populations
White, James Boyd, 230
"White Australia" policy, 350
White gaze, 343
Whitman, Walt, 58
Wilkins, Roy, 388
Williams, Bernard, 43
Williams, Robert F., 373

women, role in political philosophy of King, M. L., 379–87. *See also* gender
Working Group on Indigenous Populations (WGIP), 313
World Council of Indigenous Peoples, 312–13
Wretched of the Earth, The (Fanon), 330, 344–45
WWII. *See* Second World War
Wynter, Sylvia, 87, 91

X, Malcolm, 373–75, 379
X and X v. Belgium, 227

Yancy, George, 350, 367
Yeats, W. B., 119
Young, Iris Marion, 99
Young-Bruehl, Elisabeth, 118–19

Zerilli, Linda, 226, 375